REA: THE TEST PREP AP® TEACHERS RECOMMEND

AP® U.S. HISTORY ALL ACCESS®

Gregory Feldmeth, M.A.
Assistant Head of School
AP U.S. History Teacher
Polytechnic School
Pasadena, California

Christine Custred, M.Ed.
AP U.S. History Teacher
Edmond Memorial High School
Edmond, Oklahoma

Research & Education Association
Visit our website: www.rea.com

Research & Education Association
61 Ethel Road West
Piscataway, New Jersey 08854
E-mail: info@rea.com

AP® U.S. HISTORY ALL ACCESS®

Published 2017

Printed in the United States of America

Library of Congress Control Number 2014945574

ISBN-13: 978-0-7386-1172-3
ISBN-10: 0-7386-1172-7

Contents

Preface: The AP U.S. History Exam

In 2014–2015, the College Board rolled out a new AP U.S. History course and exam framework. Further revisions to the exam were made in 2016. REA's second edition of *AP U.S. History All Access* has been revised not just to align with the curriculum and exam changes, but also to give AP students the best possible shot at a high score.

In line with these changes, our comprehensive review material covers American history in nine periods, some of which overlap chronologically. Our practice test items in the multiple-choice, short-answer, long-essay, and document-based question sections all have been written based on the redesigned exam, which places increased emphasis on interpretation and historical thinking.

The AP U.S. History framework takes a thematic approach to issues and events, identifying key and supporting concepts in each. Students are expected to be proficient in identifying themes and mastering skills such as causation, periodization, and synthesis.

Today's APUSH exam requires students to focus on reasoning and analysis. Each multiple-choice question, for example, asks the student to evaluate a primary or secondary source. The former may be presented as a speech, letter, photograph or political cartoon. The latter may be a historian's or other informed observer's interpretation of an event.

In the short-answer section, test-takers are asked to demonstrate their grasp of events, trends, and movements in their historical context and explain them succinctly. The long essay asks examinees to explain and analyze significant issues in U.S. history. The document-based question requires students to interpret information found in historical documents.

While the current APUSH exam is designed to require less memorization of individual facts and dates, students earning high scores will have demonstrated a thorough knowledge of the key events, movements, and individuals contributing to American history. Although facts are the stuff of history and still need to be mastered, today's exam asks students to weave their knowledge of these facts into an analytical framework that shows connections over time.

AP U.S. History All Access provides the tools you need to be successful on the AP U.S. History exam.

Greg Feldmeth
Co-Chair, History Department
Polytechnic School
Pasadena, California

About Our Authors

Greg Feldmeth earned an A.B. degree from Occidental College and master's degrees from the University of California at Berkeley, California State University at Los Angeles, and Columbia University in New York City. He has taught U.S. history for over 40 years, while also offering courses in Contemporary Ethical Issues, Globalization and Human Rights, European History, and World History.

In addition to his teaching, Mr. Feldmeth has served in a number of administrative roles, including Dean of Students, Head of the Upper and Middle Schools, and Interim Head of School. He is currently History Department Co-Chair and Assistant Head of School at the Polytechnic School in Pasadena, California. He also teaches an online course, Genocide and Human Rights through the Global Online Academy. Mr. Feldmeth has written or edited twelve U.S. history review books for teachers and students.

Christine Custred teaches AP United States History and AP World History at Edmond Memorial High School, in Edmond, Oklahoma. She holds a master's degree in education administration (M.Ed.) and is a National Board Certified Teacher.

Ms. Custred has been a College Board consultant since 2000, presenting at numerous College Board institutes, including international institutes. She has been an AP Summer Institute consultant since 2003, presenting at more than 50 summer institutes. She is a contributing author to the AP World History multiple-choice questions on Learnerator.com, a website that provides students with comprehensive AP review materials. Ms. Custred has developed and team-taught a combination course that bridges AP U.S. History and AP English Language, and has co-presented at a Southwest Regional College Board conference. She has served as a reader for both the AP United States History and AP World History exams.

About REA

Founded in 1959, Research & Education Association (REA) is dedicated to publishing the finest and most effective educational materials—including study guides and test preps—for students of all ages.

Today, REA's wide-ranging catalog is a leading resource for students, teachers, and other professionals. Visit *www.rea.com* to see a complete listing of all our titles.

Authors' Acknowledgments

I would like to thank everyone who helped me in preparing this review book. At REA, Diane Goldschmidt and Larry Kling have been constant encouragers. At home, my wife, Patti, and my children Adam, Devon, and Gillian have patiently listened to my digressions on American history and have helped me keep the text simple, direct, and clear. My colleagues at Polytechnic School have acted as evaluators and critics and I appreciate their input. Particularly valuable were the insights and advice of the Communications Department, notably Leslie Carmell and Michelle Feynman. But my biggest thanks has to go to my students who for over 40 years have challenged me and worked with me to understand and explain the difference between the trivial and the really important parts of American history.—*Greg Feldmeth*

I would like to thank my husband, Steven, my daughters, Abby and Amelia, my parents, and the faculty and staff at Edmond Memorial High School for their ongoing support.—*Christine Custred*

Publisher Acknowledgments

REA would like to thank Larry B. Kling, Vice President, Editorial, for supervising development; Pam Weston, Publisher, for setting the quality standard for production integrity and managing the publication to completion; John Paul Cording, Vice President, Technology, for coordinating the design and development of the online REA Study Center; Diane Goldschmidt, Managing Editor, for coordinating development of this edition; Jody Berman for copyediting; Ellen Gong for proofreading; Terry Casey for indexing; Bernard Yanelli and Mitch Gross for technically reviewing the practice exams; and Transcend Creative Services for typesetting.

In addition, we would like to thank Jerome McDuffie, Ph.D., Gary Piggrem, Ph.D., and Steven E. Woodworth, Ph.D., for foundational content.

Chapter 1

Welcome to REA's All Access for AP U.S. History

REA's *AP U.S. History All Access* is organized to get you on track with a study plan so you can take the APUSH exam with confidence and earn a high score. The more you know about the AP U.S. History exam and how the questions will be presented, the better you'll do.

Here are some of the valuable features you'll find in *AP U.S. History All Access*:

- A complete course review, spanning pre-Columbian societies to the early 21st century, that's structured to help you apply the four skill types the College Board says you need: chronological reasoning, comparison and contextualization, crafting historical arguments from historical evidence, and historical interpretation and synthesis.
- Carefully constructed true-to-format practice tests—one in the book and one online—give you the look and feel of the actual exam.
- A recap of major figures in American history organized by the nine historical periods covered by the test.
- Quick-access summaries of major wars, important treaties, and the presidential elections.
- A glossary of must-know AP U.S. History terms.
- A detailed index to allow you to flip to any topic for quick review.

A Snapshot of the Exam

Let's take a look at the two sections of the APUSH exam.

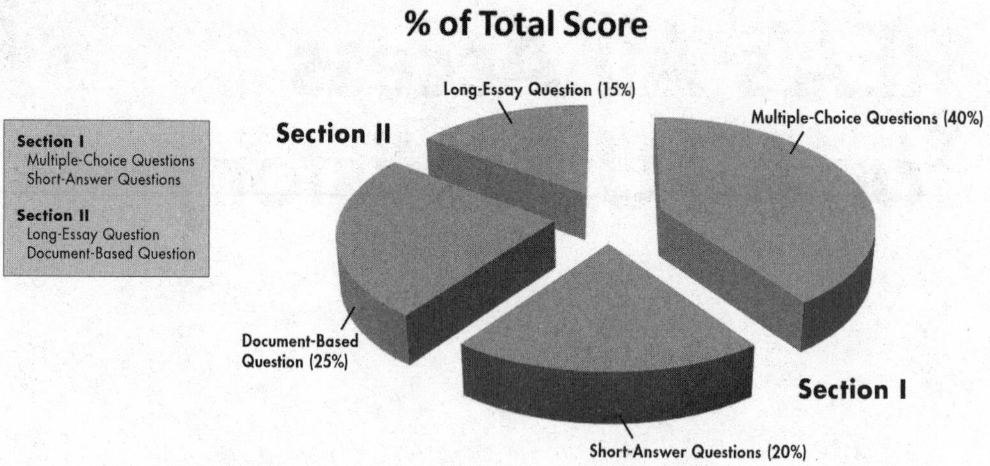

% of Total Score

Section I
Multiple-Choice Questions
Short-Answer Questions

Section II
Long-Essay Question
Document-Based Question

Section II
Long-Essay Question (15%)
Document-Based Question (25%)
Multiple-Choice Questions (40%)
Short-Answer Questions (20%)
Section I

(Source: College Board, AP United States History Course and Exam Description, Fall 2015)

Section I includes 55 multiple-choice questions, which you will see in Part A, and four short-answer questions, which will appear in Part B. You will be given 55 minutes for the multiple-choice part and 50 minutes for the short-answer part. The entire section accounts for 60% of your total score.

The APUSH exam begins with multiple-choice questions, which account for more of your score than any other part—40% of total available score points. You will be presented with a number of question sets, each with at least two questions. These questions are associated with stimulus material, which sets the tone for the exam's emphasis on critical thinking. The stimulus material can be primary or secondary sources, which may include texts, images (e.g., photographs or cartoons), graphs, or maps. Be prepared to compare and contrast historical periods by identifying underlying or prevailing themes.

The four short-answer questions are worth 20% of your score. You will be given 50 minutes to answer all of the questions. Each short-answer question consists of a prompt and three focused questions. The short-answer questions will require the test-taker to apply historical thinking skills.

Section II includes the document-based and long-essay questions. The exam has one of each. You are given 90 minutes to complete this section. The College Board recommends spending 15 minutes reading the material for the document-based question and 40 minutes writing your answer. They suggest using the remaining 35 minutes to write the long essay. This entire section accounts for 40% of your total exam score.

The document-based question, or DBQ as it's better known, is a mainstay of the exam that "measures students' ability to analyze and synthesize historical data and to assess verbal, quantitative, or visual materials as historical evidence," according to the College Board. Your key to success with the DBQ, which is worth 25% of your total available score points, is to use your outside knowledge to lend context to documents with which you're presented.

Then there's the long essay, which, while worth the least in terms of score value—15%—could be just the thing to help you earn a top score. Here you will have a choice between two comparable long-essay options. Pick the one you're more comfortable with, and show the AP readers the historical thinking skills you've honed with help from REA.

Now that you've got a good grasp of what's on the AP U.S. History exam, let's learn how this *All Access* prep package can help you study more effectively and score higher on the test.

How to Use REA's AP *All Access*

There are many different ways to prepare for an AP exam. What's best for you depends on how much time you have to study and how comfortable you are with the subject matter. To score your highest, you need a system that can be customized to fit you: your schedule, your learning style, and your current level of knowledge.

This book, and the online tools that come with it, will help you personalize your AP prep by testing your understanding, pinpointing your weaknesses, and delivering flashcard study materials unique to you.

The REA AP *All Access* system allows you to create a personalized study plan through three simple steps: targeted review of exam content, assessment of your knowledge, and focused study in the topics where you need the most help.

Here's how it works:

Review the Book	Study the topics tested on the AP exam and learn proven strategies that will help you tackle any question you may see on test day.
Test Yourself & Get Feedback	As you review the book, test yourself. Score reports from your online tests and quizzes give you a fast way to pinpoint what you really know and what you should spend more time studying.
Improve Your Score	Armed with your score reports, you can personalize your study plan. Review the parts of the book where you are weakest, and use the REA Study Center to create your own unique e-flashcards, adding to the 100 cards included with this book.

Finding Your Strengths and Weaknesses: The REA Study Center

The best way to personalize your study plan and truly focus on the topics where you need the most help is to get frequent feedback on what you know and what you don't. At the online REA Study Center, you can access three types of assessment: end-of-chapter quizzes, mini-tests, and a full-length practice test. Each of these tools delivers a detailed score report that follows the topics set by the College Board.

✓ 9 End-of-Chapter Quizzes

Short online quizzes are available throughout the review and are designed to test your immediate grasp of the topics just covered.

✓ 2 Mini-Tests (Just like your own midterm and final)

Available both in this book and online, two mini-tests cover what you've studied in each half of the book. These tests are like the actual AP exam, only shorter, and will help you evaluate your overall understanding of the subject.

✓ 2 Full-Length Practice Tests

After you've finished reviewing the book, take our full-length exams to practice under test-day conditions. Practice Test 1 is available in this book and Practice Test 2 is online at the REA Study Center (*www.rea.com/studycenter*). These practice tests give you the most complete picture of your strengths and weaknesses. We strongly recommend that you take the online version of the exam for the added benefits of timed testing, automatic scoring, and a detailed score report.

Improving Your Score: e-Flashcards

Once you get your score reports from the online quizzes and tests, you'll be able to see exactly which topics you need to review. Use this information to create your own flashcards for the areas where you still need additional practice. And, because you will create these flashcards through the online REA Study Center, you'll be able to access them from any computer or smartphone.

Not quite sure what to put on your flashcards? Start with the 100 cards that accompany this book.

Need More Review?

Pick up a copy of REA's *Crash Course*® for AP U.S. History, the fastest way to raise your score during the last few weeks before the exam. Use your *All Access*® score reports to focus on the topics where you still need extra review.

REA's Suggested 8-Week AP Study Plan

Depending on how much time you have until test day, you can expand or condense our eight-week study plan as you see fit. To score your highest, use our study plan and customize it to fit your schedule, targeting the areas where you need the most review.

	Review 1-2 hours	Quiz 15 minutes	e-Flashcards	Mini-Test 30 minutes	Full-length Practice Test 3 hours, 15 minutes
Week 1	Chapters 1 – 3	Quiz 1	Access your e-flashcards from your computer or smartphone whenever you have a few extra minutes to study.		
Week 2	Chapters 4 – 5	Quizzes 2 – 3			
Week 3	Chapter 6	Quiz 4		Mini-Test 1 (The Midterm)	
Week 4	Chapters 7 – 8	Quizzes 5 – 6			
Week 5	Chapter 9	Quiz 7			
Week 6	Chapters 10 – 11	Quizzes 8 – 9	Start with the 100 cards that accompany this book. Personalize your prep by creating your own cards for topics where you need extra study.	Mini-Test 2 (The Final)	
Week 7					Full-length Practice Exam 1 (Just like test day)
Week 8					Full-length Practice Exam 2 (available online at *www.rea.com/studycenter*)

Test-Day Checklist

- ❑ Get a good night's sleep. You perform better when you're not tired.
- ❑ Wake up early and eat a good breakfast.
- ❑ Dress comfortably. You'll be testing for hours, so wear something casual and layered.
- ❑ Bring these items to the test center:
  - Several sharpened No. 2 pencils
  - Admission ticket
  - Two pieces of ID (one with a recent photo and your signature)
  - A noiseless wristwatch to help pace yourself
- ❑ Arrive at the test center early. You will not be allowed in after the test has begun.

Remember: eating, drinking, smoking, cellphones, dictionaries, textbooks, notebooks, briefcases, and packages are all prohibited in the test center.

Chapter 2

Strategies for the Exam

What Will I See on the AP U.S. History Exam?

On a May morning, you will stroll confidently into a school classroom or library where you're scheduled to take the AP U.S. History exam. You know your stuff: you paid attention in class, followed your textbook, analyzed lots of primary sources, took plenty of notes, and reviewed your coursework by reading a special test prep guide. You can identify major technological advances, explain the characteristics of different eras of history, and describe the effects of different methods of war on broad economic and social changes. So how will you show your knowledge on the test?

The Multiple-Choice and Short-Answer Sections

First, you'll complete a multiple-choice section that tests your ability to apply your knowledge of U.S. history to interpret and analyze historical information. This section will require you to answer 55 multiple-choice questions in 55 minutes. Next you will answer four short-answer questions in 50 minutes. Here are the major time periods and the approximate percentages of questions found on the AP U.S. History exam relating to each period:

- Period 1, 1491–1607 (5%)
- Periods 2–5, 1607–1877 (45%)
- Periods 6–8, 1865–1980 (45%)
- Period 9, 1980–present (5%)

The College Board has identified nine thinking skills. Every question on the exam will ask students to apply one or more of these skills.

- Historical Causation—What are the causes and effects of events?
- Patterns of Continuity and Change over Time—How do attitudes and values continue and change over a period of time?
- Periodization—Identify the time period of an event or movement (chronological reasoning).
- Comparison—Compare or contrast multiple historical developments during a period or several periods.
- Contextualization—How does an event or movement fit into the larger picture of American history?
- Historical Argument—How does the evidence support a specific argument or position?
- Appropriate Use of Relevant Historical Evidence—questions will include written sources, but also graphical ones, including cartoons, political broadsides, art, artifacts, and statistical information.
- Interpretation—Historians often disagree as to the meaning or importance of an event or movement. Students will be asked to identify and evaluate historical perspectives.
- Synthesis—Historical evidence is sometimes contradictory or confusing. Students will be asked to synthesize information from a variety of sources or time periods to demonstrate an understanding of historical events.

The Essay Sections (Document-Based Question and Long Essay Question)

After time is called on the multiple-choice and short-answer sections, you'll get a short break before starting the free-response, or essay, section. This section requires you to produce two written responses in 90 minutes. Like the multiple-choice and short-answer sections, the free-response portion of the exam expects you to be able to *apply your own knowledge to analyze historical information,* in addition to being able to provide essential facts and definitions. One free-response question will require you to interpret several primary source documents to create a historical argument. This is known as the document-based question, or DBQ. The other free-response item, or long essay question, will ask you to use your historical knowledge to build a thesis-based essay.

What's the Score?

The scoring weights of the various parts of the redesigned AP exam are presented in the table below. The multiple-choice section accounts for 40 percent of your overall score and is generated by awarding one point toward your "raw score" for each question you answered correctly. There is no penalty for guessing. The short-answer section accounts for 20 percent of your total score. Within the essay section, the DBQ accounts for 25 percent of your overall score, and the long essay makes up 15 percent of your overall score. Trained graders read students' written responses and assign points according to grading rubrics. The number of points you accrue out of the total possible will form your score on the essay section.

Section	Question Type	Number of Questions	Timing	Percentage of Total Exam Score
I	Part A: Multiple-choice questions	55 questions	55 minutes	40%
	Part B: Short-answer questions	4 questions	50 minutes	20%
II	Part A: Document-based question	1 question	55 minutes	25%
	Part B: Long essay question	1 question (chosen from a pair)	35 minutes	15%

The College Board scores the AP exam on a scale of 1 to 5. Although individual colleges and universities determine what credit or advanced placement, if any, is awarded to students at each score level, these are the assessments typically associated with each numeric score:

5 Extremely well qualified

4 Well qualified

3 Qualified

2 Possibly qualified

1 No recommendation

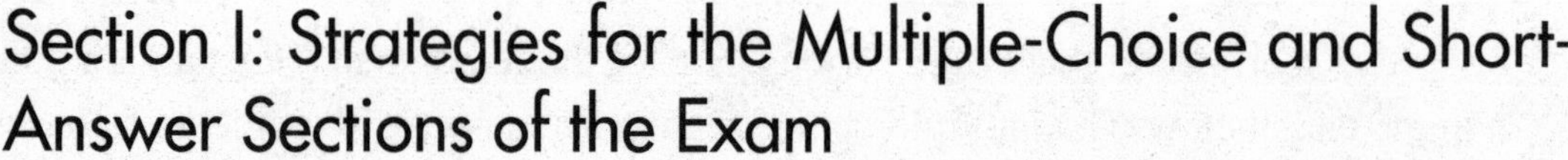

Section I: Strategies for the Multiple-Choice and Short-Answer Sections of the Exam

Because the AP exam is a standardized test, each version of the test from year to year must share many similarities to be fair. That means that you can always expect certain things to be true about your AP U.S. History exam.

Which of the following phrases accurately describes a multiple-choice question on the AP U.S. History exam?

(A) Always has four choices

(B) May rely on a cartoon, photo, or other visual stimulus

(C) May ask you to find a wrong idea or group related concepts

(D) All of the above*

Did you pick option "D"? Good job!

Historical Themes

You've already seen a list of the general content areas you'll encounter on the AP U.S. History exam. But what historical themes will be encountered? The College Board has developed a list of seven themes.

AP U.S History Themes

• Identity	*Formation of national identity.*
• Work, Exchange & Technology	*Economic progress from agriculture to industrialization.*
• Peopling	*Patterns of movement throughout the nation during its history.*
• Politics and Power	*Political parties, elections, and government at the local, state, and national level*

*On the actual AP exam you won't see any choices featuring "all of the above" or "none of the above."

• America in the World	*The global presence of the U.S. and how it has developed throughout its history.*
• Environment and Geography—Physical and Human	*How did the physical environment impact Americans in various regions of the U.S.? What impact did Americans have on their environment?*
• Ideas, Beliefs, and Culture	*Cultural aspects of American life, including art, ideas, literature, religion, and science.*

Throughout this book, you will find tips on the features and strategies you can use to answer different types of questions.

Achieving Multiple-Choice Success

It's true that you don't have a lot of time to finish this section of the AP exam. But it's also true that you don't need to get every question right to get a great score. Answering just two-thirds of the questions correctly—along with a good showing on the free-response section—can earn you a score of a 4 or 5. That means that not only do you not have to answer every question right, you don't even need to answer every question at all. By *working quickly and methodically,* however, you'll have all the time you'll need. Plan to spend about 60 seconds on each multiple-choice question.

If timing is hard for you, set a timer for fifteen minutes each time you take one of the 15-question online quizzes that accompany this book to help you practice working at speed. Let's look at some other strategies for answering multiple-choice items.

Process of Elimination

You've probably used this strategy, intentionally or unintentionally, throughout your entire test-taking career. The process of elimination requires you to read each answer choice and consider whether it is the best response to the question given. Because the AP exam typically asks you to find the *best* answer rather than the *only* answer, it's almost always advantageous to read each answer choice. More than one choice may have some grain of truth to it, but one answer—the right answer—will be the most correct. Let's examine a multiple-choice question and use the process-of-elimination approach:

> You come to us and tell us that the great cities are in favor of the gold standard. I tell you that the great cities rest upon these broad and fertile prairies. Burn down your cities and leave our farms, and your cities will spring up again as if by magic. But destroy our farms and the grass will grow in the streets of every city in the country.
>
> —William Jennings Bryan, 1896

Which of the following would be most receptive to Democrat William Jennings Bryan's speech in the presidential campaign of 1896?

(A) an Eastern banker

(B) a supporter of high protective tariffs

(C) a Midwestern farmer facing a large mortgage payment

(D) a Southern sharecropper

Two of these options are clearly wrong. Eastern bankers and supporters of high protective tariffs both would have favored the gold standard. So (A) and (B) are not good options and can be eliminated. But one could make a case for options (C) and (D). The correct answer is (C), as supporting the free coinage of silver and rejecting the gold standard would most help those who owed money, particularly farmers with large mortgages.

Predicting

Although using the process of elimination certainly helps you consider each answer choice thoroughly, testing each and every answer can be a slow process. To help answer the most questions in the limited time given AP test-takers, you may find it helpful to instead try predicting the right answer *before* you read the answer choices. For example, you know that the answer to the math problem 2 + 2 will always be 4. If you saw this multiple-choice item on a math test, you wouldn't need to systematically test each response. Instead you go straight to the right answer. You can apply a similar technique to even complex items on the AP exam. Brainstorm your own answer to the question before reading the answer choices. Then, pick the answer choice closest to the one you brainstormed. Let's look at how this technique could work on a common type of question on the AP U.S. History exam—one with a visual stimulus.

Cartoon by Joseph Ferdinand Kepler, Published February 1880. (U.S. Library of Congress).

In the cartoon shown, Ulysses Grant is presented as

(A) ~~adequately prepared for a third term.~~

(B) ~~honest and competent.~~

(C) caught up in several types of corruption.

(D) ~~weeding out corruption.~~

Consider each of the possible answer choices. Compare each choice to the prediction you have made. You probably predicted that the cartoonist showed Grant as tied to several other people who were pulling him down. You probably also noticed that the depiction of Grant in the cartoon was negative. Pick the answer choice that best fits with these two ideas. See how simple answering that tricky question was?

Political cartoons give opinions about events taking place at the time of their creation. Because of this, they may reference specific people or events with which you are unfamiliar.

When this cartoon was created, for example, its audience would have been able to easily identify all of the people depicted. However, you don't need to do this. Focusing on the broad historical themes and symbolism behind the cartoons will give you all the information you need to answer the question.

Read the question and look at the cartoon. Notice that it shows Ulysses Grant as an acrobat tethered to a group of men. The AP exam will ask you about major themes of Grant's administration, not minor events. Think about the events that defined Grant's term in office. Recall that many people linked to his administration were involved in corrupt activities. Make a prediction about what the correct answer will be. Has the cartoonist depicted Grant in a positive or negative way?

What should you do if you don't see your prediction among the answer choices? Your prediction should have helped you narrow down the choices. You may wish to apply the process of elimination to the remaining options to further home in on the right answer. Then, you can use your historical knowledge to make a good guess.

Learning to predict takes some practice. You're probably used to going right to the answer choices for a question. But in order to predict well, you should avoid doing this. Remember, the test maker doesn't want to make the correct answer too obvious, so the wrong answers are intended to sound appealing. You may find it helpful to physically cover the answer choices to a question as you practice predicting. This will ensure you don't sneak a premature peek at the choices.

Avoiding Common Errors

Answering questions *correctly* is always more important than answering every question. So work at a pace that allows you to avoid these common mistakes:

- Missing key words that change the meaning of a question, such as *not, except,* or *least.* You might want to circle these words in your test booklet so you're tuned into them when answering the question.
- Overthinking an item and spending too much time agonizing over the correct response.
- Changing your answer, but incompletely erasing your first choice.

Some More Advice

Let's review what you've learned about answering multiple-choice questions effectively on the AP exam. Using these techniques on practice tests will help you become comfortable with them before diving into the real exam, so be sure to apply these ideas as you work through this book.

- Big ideas are more important than minutiae. Focus on learning important historical concepts, causation, and connections instead of memorizing names and dates.

- You have just 60 seconds to complete each multiple-choice question. Pacing yourself during practice tests and exercises can help you get used to these time constraints.
- Because there is no guessing penalty, remember that making an educated guess is to your benefit. Remember to use the process of elimination to narrow your choices. You might just guess the correct answer and get another point!
- Instead of spending valuable time pondering narrow distinctions or questioning your first answer, trust yourself to make good guesses most of the time.
- Read the question and think of what your answer would be *before* reading the answer choices.
- Expect the unexpected. You will see questions that ask you to apply information in various ways, such as interpreting a map, a chart, or a photograph.

Achieving Success on the Short-Answer Questions

In the next section of the exam, you will have 50 minutes to complete four short-answer questions. Each short-answer question consists of three parts and each part can earn a score of 0 or 1. This means that the highest score you can earn on a question is 3 points. All four questions will be based on source material and be derived from a thematic learning objective. As with the multiple-choice questions, the source could be from primary or secondary sources or an historian's perspective on American history.

The following sample short-answer question is based on the following passage from Thomas Paine's *Common Sense* published in 1776:

> "But Britain is the parent country, say some. Then the more shame upon her conduct. Even brutes do not devour their young, nor savages make war upon their families. Wherefore, the assertion, if true, turns to her reproach. ... Europe, and not England, is the parent country of America. This new World hath been the asylum for the persecuted lovers of civil and religious liberty from every part of Europe. Hither have they fled, not from the tender embraces of the mother, but from the cruelty of the monster; and it is so far true of England, that the same tyranny which drove the first emigrants from home, pursues their descendants still."

Use the passage and your knowledge of colonial–British relations in the period leading up to the Revolutionary War to answer parts a, b, and c.

a. What conduct of Great Britain is Paine referring to in his complaint about the mistreatment of the colonies?

b. When Paine points to the "first emigrants from home," to which group is he referring?

c. Paine notes that "Europe, not England, is the parent country of America." Why does he make this distinction?

This question requires you to be familiar with the period between 1763 and 1776 when Britain's new imperial policies led to taxation and the imposition of duties that angered many colonists, particularly merchants. In addition, colonists felt that Parliament and King George III had exceeded their authority in their dealings with the American colonies. It also refers to the reasons the original colonists came to the colonies.

Part a requires you to recognize that Paine is referring to the new imperial policy that was put in place following the conclusion of the French and Indian War. A sample response to Part a would be:

When Thomas Paine complains about the shameful conduct of the British government toward her American colonies, he is referring to both the new taxes and duties being levied in the colonies as well as the policies that the British implemented following the French and Indian War. Beginning with the 1765 Stamp Act, the colonists were required to pay revenue-producing taxes that they had no voice in imposing.

Part b asks about "the first emigrants from home." Paine is noting that the search for freedom in the 1770s is the same as that of the 17th century Puritans and others, who came for religious and political freedom. Here is a sample response:

Paine's readers would be aware that the American colonies were founded by religious and political refugees, mainly the Puritans, who came to the New World to experience freedom they were being denied at home. By linking the current 18th century economic and political crisis faced by the colonists with the 17th century experiences of Colonial America's first settlers, he is building a case for an American identity that is separate from England.

Part c asks about Paine's reference to the parentage of the American colonies. Paine states that the true parent of America is Europe, not England. He wants his readers to know that they owe no loyalty to the English government which has treated them so tyrannically. Here is a sample response:

One of Paine's goals is to break down the assumption that the colonists needed to be loyal to England. He describes the British officials as being tyrannical and devouring their young. He contends that Europe, not England is the true parent of America, because a responsible parent would not behave as the British king and Parliament had behaved. He views America as an asylum for all of those who have been denied civil and religious liberties.

Section II: Strategies for the Free-Response Section of the Exam

The AP U.S. History exam contains two free-response questions in its second section. This section allows you 90 minutes to respond to these questions. The first question (the Document-Based question) requires you to interpret a series of primary source documents to make a historical argument. The second question (the Long Essay Question) follows a more traditional essay format. Let's examine these two kinds of free-response questions in turn.

Taking on the Document-Based Question

The document-based question, the DBQ, will present you with an essay prompt along with seven written or visual primary source documents. Before you begin writing, you are advised to spend 15 minutes reviewing the documents. You must refer to at least six of the seven documents in your response. You may take notes on the documents in your test booklet. DBQs rarely present you with documents with which you are already familiar. You will thus need to use what you know about the topic in order to interpret the documents. Let's take a look at a typical DBQ.

The U.S. war with Mexico has been labeled, both then and since, as an unprovoked and unjustifiable war of aggression and territorial aggrandizement. Using the following documents as well as your knowledge of the diplomatic history of the years from 1836 to 1846, evaluate this assertion.

- *Joint Congressional Resolution Offering Annexation to Texas (March 1, 1845)*
- *Letter from President James K. Polk to U.S. Senator William H. Haywood (August 1845)*
- *Memoirs of John Charles Frémont*

- *Diary of President James K. Polk (September–October 1845)*
- *Order from Secretary of War William L. Marcy to General Zachary Taylor, U.S. Army (January 13, 1846)*
- *Diary of James K. Polk (May 8, 1846)*
- *Polk's War Message to Congress (May 11, 1846)*

This list shows you the typical types of documents that you might see in a document-based question. An actual item would provide text passages or images on which you could base your analysis. Remember, you will have a 15-minute reading period at the beginning of the time allotted for the document-based question during which you are required to read and consider the documents. Use this time wisely by thoroughly examining the documents and taking good notes in your test booklet.

To score well, you must include information other than that given in the documents. For this item, you could describe U.S. expansion in the Southwest, for example, or describe the tense feelings that resulted from the annexation of Texas. However, your score will not depend on which position you choose to argue as DBQs usually support multiple viewpoints. Rather, your score will depend on how well you state a thesis and support it with both your own historical knowledge and the evidence provided.

Step One: Evaluating Primary Source Documents

Since the document-based question requires you to draw on the documents provided, you should first evaluate your sources in the context of the essay question given on the exam; in fact, the 15-minute reading period on the exam ensures that you have the chance to do just that. Remember, when interpreting primary sources, you should think about the author or creator of the work. Ask yourself, *What was the author's intention? What biases did the author have? Is the author reliable? What was the historical context in which this document was produced?* Keep in mind that even seemingly bland documents, such as law decrees, are products of their time and place. Jim Crow laws, for example, exist strongly in their historical context and should be considered just as critically as a diary entry.

Take notes and mark up the documents as you consider them. Circle key ideas or points that you may wish to include in your argument, and jot down ideas and historical connections in the margins of your booklet. This is a good time to brainstorm, but try to stay focused on the question presented in the essay prompt.

Step Two: Developing an Outline

The test maker recommends that students plan to spend 45 minutes beyond the reading period to plan and write the DBQ essay. Even though time is relatively short, you should dedicate 5 minutes to developing a simple outline to guide your writing. That's because creating a simple outline will allow you to organize your thoughts, brainstorm good examples, and reject ideas that don't really work once you think about them. Your outline should include a thesis statement and the main points you wish to include in your essay. To help organize your essay, you may want to divide your ideas up paragraph-by-paragraph, or list them in the order in which you plan to discuss them. In your outline, add references to the specific documents you wish to include in your argument to help you remember what you've read. Make your outline short, to the point, and complete. By following it, your response will naturally have the same qualities.

Your thesis statement is perhaps the most important part of your outline. Your thesis statement should be a clear and direct response to the question posed in the essay prompt. Including a relevant and well-supported thesis is the single most important step you can take to achieve a good score in this section. A well-written essay with no thesis will score much lower than an average-quality essay that accomplishes its goal of supporting a historical argument. To help you generate a suitable thesis, restate the question with your answer in a complete sentence. For example, a good thesis for the example question might be:

Claims that the United States waged an unprovoked and unjustified war on Mexico cannot be maintained because Mexico was guilty of belligerent, provocative actions against the United States.

Step Three: Writing a Response

Once you've written a good outline, stick to it! As you write your response, you'll find that most of the hard work is already done, and you can focus on *expressing your ideas clearly, concisely, and completely.* Remember, too, that the essay scorers know what information has been provided in the documents. Don't waste time and effort quoting the contents of the documents unless you are adding your own interpretation. Be sure to include all of the major ideas from your outline and stick to the topic. You'll have plenty of time to complete your essay if you don't get distracted.

As you're writing your response, keep in mind what the AP readers will see when they sit down to consider your answers weeks from now. Expressing your ideas clearly and succinctly will help them best understand your point and ensure that you get the best possible score. Using your clearest handwriting will also do wonders for your overall score; free-response graders are used to reading poor handwriting, but that doesn't mean they can decipher every scribble you might make. Printing your answers instead of writing them in cursive may make them easier to read, as will skipping lines between paragraphs.

Another good way to help AP readers through your arguments is to state your thesis clearly and succinctly in the opening sentence of your essay. This will highlight your main argument from the start and let scorers know what they're looking for throughout the rest of the essay. Restating your thesis and main points at the end of the essay is another good practice.

Step Four: Revising Your Response

Even the best writers make mistakes, especially when writing quickly: skipping or repeating words, misspelling names of people or places, neglecting to include an important point from an outline are all common errors when rushed. Reserving a few minutes at the end of your writing period will allow you to quickly review your response and make necessary corrections. Adding skipped words or including forgotten information are the two most important edits you can make to your writing, because these will clarify your ideas and help your score.

A Sample DBQ Response

After you've read, considered, outlined, planned, written, and revised, what do you have? A thoughtful written answer likely to earn you a good score, that's what. Review the sample response below to help you understand what a well-planned, thoughtful DBQ essay should contain.

Claims that the United States waged an unprovoked and unjustified war on Mexico cannot be maintained because Mexico was guilty of belligerent, provocative actions against the United States. In assessing guilt for the Mexican War, one must examine the factors that led to it, some of which, as President James K. Polk observed in his war message to Congress, predated it by 20 years. Chronic instability in Mexico had, in those years, resulted in a number of claims by U.S. citizens for reimbursement by the Mexican government for debts owed and damages suffered during the country's frequent upheavals. Mexico declined to pay these claims, which amounted to several million dollars, despite the ruling of an international arbitrator. This was the first U.S. grievance against Mexico.

Mexico also had grievances against the United States. Foremost of these were the well-known expansionist goals of Americans who wished to control increasing amounts of Mexican territory. U.S. Army expeditions had explored the territory of what was to become Mexico as early as the first decade of the nineteenth century, and more recently, "Pathfinder" John C. Frémont had traveled through Mexican lands on two trips. Americans were especially interested in California, which had assets that aroused hopes of U.S. annexation. This desire was no secret.

Mexicans had therefore been prepared to see the 1836 revolt of the largely American settlers of their northern province of Texas as a Yankee plot to grab more Mexican land, and they believed their suspicions were confirmed when, in 1845, Congress, by joint resolution, agreed to accept Texas's long-standing request to join the Union. Mexico, which had for 20 years threatened war in such an event, broke diplomatic relations with the United States and began making warlike preparations.

Newly inaugurated U.S. President James K. Polk had three resulting concerns: (1) As indicated by Frémont's memoirs and Polk's own diary, he and his Cabinet feared California, only weakly held by Mexico, would fall into the hands of Great Britain; (2) he wanted the legitimate claims of U.S. citizens against Mexico to be satisfied; and (3) he was concerned about the disputed southern boundary of Texas. Mexico claimed the land to the Nueces River, the old boundary of the province of Texas. This conflicted with what Congress had claimed in its resolution: "the territory belonging to the Republic of Texas," which had for a decade claimed and maintained the Rio Grande as its southern and western boundary. To deal with these concerns Polk dispatched (1) Frémont on another western expedition with orders to help take California should war break out; (2) General Zachary Taylor with a military force to protect Texas against possible Mexican invasion; and (3) John Slidell on a mission to Mexico City to deal with all matters of disagreement between the two countries. Polk's diary reveals that Slidell was authorized to purchase both California and New Mexico for a price of $10 million to $40 million.

Meanwhile, in Mexico, yet another military coup had toppled the government. Anxious to gain popularity at home by hostility toward the United States, the new president refused to receive Slidell, referring to his mission as "this new insult." On his return Slidell recommended to Polk that there was no alternative but to "take the redress of the wrongs and injuries which we have so long borne from Mexico into our own hands." Polk was inclined to agree, and when shortly thereafter news reached Washington of a clash between Taylor's troops and Mexicans in the disputed territory south of the Nueces, Polk presented Congress with his war message claiming that American blood had been shed on American soil.

A careful consideration of this evidence demonstrates that the allocation of guilt for the coming of the Mexican War is by no means as simple as those who complain of U.S. aggression would claim. Causes of the war can be traced to both sides—land-hunger on the U.S. side, belligerence and refusal to negotiate or pay legitimate claims on the Mexican side. For all the American guilt, equal or greater Mexican guilt can be found. Therefore, the assertion that the Mexican War was an unprovoked and unjustifiable war of aggression and territorial aggrandizement cannot be maintained.

Taking on the Long Essay

You've conquered the DBQ and now you're ready for the next part of the free-response section: the Long Essay. Like the DBQ, your success on this essay will hinge on your ability to make and support a thesis-based historical argument. The AP exam places an emphasis on analysis and interpretation in all of its questions, but it is especially important in the Long Essay, where you will not be provided with any documents to use.

The Long Essay differs from the DBQ in that there is no reading period and no primary sources to interpret. You will, however, have the opportunity to exercise some choice in this section of the AP exam. You must select and answer just one question out of two essay prompts. It will be worth a few minutes of your precious test time to preview the questions and choose the one that seems easiest for you. Your ability to use historical evidence in discussing and analyzing issues is the main focus of the grading of the Long Essay question. Let's examine a sample essay question:

> *Discuss the United States as it existed under the Articles of Confederation. What were the strengths and weaknesses of the Confederation government, and how did the Constitution attempt to correct those flaws?*

Notice that the essay prompt asks you to respond to a direct question using historical facts and interpretation. Because the most important thing that you must do to score well is to fully answer the question, you should begin by asking yourself what, exactly, the question wishes you to do. You may wish to rephrase the question in your own words. For example, this essay question could be rephrased as: *How did the Articles of Confederation help government do its job? What problems did the Articles of Confederation cause? What changes did the Constitution make to government in order to fix these problems?*

Step One: Developing an Outline

With no primary sources to evaluate, you can skip straight to outlining the Long Essay. If you spent the recommended 55 minutes outlining, writing, and revising your DBQ response—and you should have!—you'll have a total of 35 minutes remaining for the final Long Essay question. Again, you'll be scored on content, not length!

The Long Essay doesn't demand as extensive an answer as the DBQ. Plan to write a traditional five-paragraph essay in response to the prompt you choose. In this case, organize your outline by paragraph. Be sure to include your thesis statement in your first paragraph to make sure the AP reader gets your argument right off the bat. Then include one or two ideas or details in each of your three supporting paragraphs, depending on how much support your thesis needs. Write these main points in your outline so you don't forget them when it comes time to write. Your final paragraph should contain a conclusion that wraps up your ideas and restates your thesis.

Step Two: Writing a Response

All the same rules apply when writing answers to the Long Essay question. Stick to your outline, stick to the point, and stick to the topic to produce the best and most concise response possible. The AP exam isn't a term paper, so you're not being scored on spelling and grammar. However, don't forget to include transition words to help guide the AP reader through your argument and to follow the ideas you brainstormed in your outline.

Step Three: Revising Your Response

Remember that essay graders are not mind readers, so they will only grade what's on the page, not what you thought you were writing. At the same time, remember that essay graders do not deduct points for wrong information, so you don't need to spend time erasing errors. Just write a sentence at the end of your essay.

A Sample Response

How would you have answered the essay question given earlier in the chapter? Review this sample response to see what a good answer looks like. Remember, there's no one right answer to a given essay question, although high-scoring responses will always be based on accurate historical facts. You may choose to interpret those facts in a way that's out of the ordinary as long as you adequately support the ideas in your thesis.

The Articles of Confederation established a federal government consisting of one branch of government, Congress, and allowing the individual states to reign supreme. This system created numerous problems for the young nation, such as the absence of any national central power to administer treaties, collect taxes, or have a military, even as it eased the new United States into existence. After a relatively short time, the Constitution emerged with a federal system of checks and balances designed to allow the nation to function as a whole while still protecting the rights of the states.

Under the Articles, the states retained sovereignty and were granted all legal control over commerce and legislation within their boundaries, except those not "expressly delegated to the United States" government. The Articles granted very few powers expressly to that government, however. The federal government could not collect taxes to fund the government properly. Congress could request that states send funding, but it could not demand payment. Individual states could refuse to appropriate funds if they so desired. This alone made it difficult for the government to operate effectively. Since individual states could "veto" most federal mandates, the U.S. government found that it could not even enforce its international treaties! For example, the Treaty of Paris ending the American Revolution called for repayment of prewar debts owed to British merchants and return of lands confiscated from British loyalists during the war. Many states opposed these provisions and passed laws to prevent their enforcement. This revealed the inherent weaknesses in the Confederation government. Congress had no power to prevent individual states from blocking enforcement of the treaty provisions.

Shays's Rebellion also showed the weakness of the Confederation government in that it carried the basic beliefs about local sovereignty to their extreme. It raised the possibility of rebellions of a much greater scale unless a philosophy cementing the states together in a permanent union subservient to a strong federal government was established. In a country as geographically large as the United States, with priorities that varied so greatly from one section of the nation to the other, there was no hope of survival unless the sovereignty of the individual states was brought under a centrally controlled federal government.

Most people considered the strength of the Confederation to be its focus on local self-government. By limiting the federal government, people could rule themselves as they felt best at the state and local level. This removed the worry about some distant tyrant, ignorant of local needs, dictating over them. There was a real fear of a strong central government deteriorating into a European-style monarchy, and few wanted to renew that experience. While the Articles guaranteed there could be no autocracy in America, this very strength was the weakness that undid the Articles. For under the rule of the Articles, there could be no effective central government at all. States could do virtually whatever they wanted, resulting in no cohesive national policies on anything.

Under the Constitution, the sovereignty of the federal government replaced the sovereignty of the individual states. While states retained certain rights, state laws were subservient to federal laws. States could no longer refuse to enforce federal treaties and laws. Congress was given the power to raise taxes, and states could not *refuse to pay them. An executive branch was created with an elected president who controlled foreign policy. A federal judiciary was set up to resolve legal disputes regarding the Constitution and the actions of Congress, the executive branch, and the various states. While the Constitution protected many of the rights of states, it placed enough power in the hands of the federal government to ensure that it could carry out effective foreign policy, regulate interstate commerce, and collect taxes. The Constitution and the accompanying Bill of Rights struck a working balance that proved to be much more effective than the balance struck under the Articles.*

Scoring the Long Essay Question

The highest possible score you can earn on the Long Essay question is 6 points. The following elements will be scored:

- Thesis: 0-1 point
- Support for Argument: 0-2 points
- Application of Historical Thinking Skills: 0-2 points
- Synthesis: 0-1 point

Some More Advice About the DBQ and Long Essay Questions

What have you learned about the free-response section? Keep these ideas in mind as you prepare for the AP U.S. History exam. Becoming comfortable with these techniques will make you feel confident and prepared when you sit for the exam in May.

- Remember the DBQ and Long Essay questions require different yet similar approaches. You should be mentally prepared to address both of these essay types.
- Be sure to thoroughly read and evaluate all of the sources given with the DBQ. Make notes in your test booklet and think of additional information to further contextualize the provided sources. Remember you must refer to at least six of the seven documents provided to score well on the DBQ.
- Make a clear and concise outline before you begin writing. This will help you organize your thoughts and speed up the actual writing process.
- Stay on topic and answer the question! Addressing the question fully is the single most important way to earn points on this section.
- Handwriting is important and must be legible! If the AP reader can't read your writing, you'll get no points, even if your response is correct.

- Leave a few minutes to review and revise your answers. You don't need to check the spelling of every single word, but you do need to make sure that all of your ideas made it onto the page.

Two Final Words: Don't Panic!

The free-response questions can and probably will ask you about specific historical concepts and examples you haven't thought about in much detail before: The effects of the annexation of Texas on sectional disputes before the Civil War? The influence of popular music and television on public perception of the Vietnam War? The possibilities are practically endless. Remember that all free-response questions seek to test your knowledge of big-picture historical themes and concepts and not your ability to write a list of battles or recite the Declaration of Independence. Applying what you know about broad historical causation to these specific scenarios will help you get a great score, even if you've never thought much about the particular event presented in the question.

Chapter 3

Pre-Columbian America and Early European Contact (1491*–1607 C.E.)

DNA evidence shows a close relationship between Asian and American Indian populations. While historians disagree as to when the first Americans reached the Western Hemisphere, there is no disagreement as to where: the Bering Strait between Siberia and Alaska. Scholars place the arrival of the first group of Asians at about 30,000 years ago; it appears that the receding waters exposed enough of a land bridge over the 56 miles that separate North America and Asia for groups to migrate across. A second group moved south following the end of the Ice Age (probably 13,000 B.C.E.) along the eastern side of the Rocky Mountains. The Asian immigrants probably followed large game animals, such as mammoths, bison, and giant ground sloths. The small groups gradually spread across North and South America, and there is evidence that some reached the tip of South America by 9000 B.C.E.

DID YOU KNOW?

The Bering Strait between Russia and Alaska was once an ice-free grassland named Beringia. Although water now covers the area that was once the Bering Land Bridge, the region still connects people on two separate continents. The native peoples of northwestern Alaska and the Russian Far East share a language and other cultural traditions.

* The College Board's course framework is built around the study of central themes and key concepts across nine chronological periods. These periods span pre-Columbian contacts in North America (symbolized by the year 1491) to the present.

The history of pre-Columbian societies, of course, actually stretches back many thousands of years. This chapter briefly covers the aspects of those societies you most need to know about to do well in your course and on the redesigned AP U.S. History exam.

2,000 Separate Cultures

The most advanced civilizations of the more than 2,000 separate cultures that developed in the New World all developed south of what is now the United States. These were the Incas, the Mayas, and the Aztecs.

Around 1000 C.E., the Incas successfully conquered neighboring tribes and eventually controlled an area more than 2,500 miles in length. By 1500, the Incas were the largest and richest of the ancient empires of the Americas. The Incas built palaces surrounded by high walls in Peru and connected a series of mountain towns and villages with an elaborate network of roads. They developed a system of terraces to effectively farm on the steep hillsides and used canals and aqueducts to irrigate crops. The potato and the tomato were two of the Incan contributions to world diets. Despite the lack of a written language, the Incan governmental and trading system was well organized when Spanish conquistador Francisco Pizarro arrived in 1532 with fewer than 200 soldiers. Pizarro defeated the Incan army and executed their king, Atahualpa, who had allowed the Spaniards to enter the city because he did not sense a threat from their small force against his 80,000-member army. The Spaniards then captured the capital of Cuzco and looted its wealth of silver and gold.

On the Yucatan Peninsula the Mayas built temples and pyramids surrounding broad plazas in the mountains, deserts, and rain forests of what is now Guatemala, Belize, Honduras, and Mexico. The Mayas also constructed observatories, developed accurate calendars, knew of the mathematical concept of zero, and invented their own writing system, which used both syllables and single written characters known as glyphs. Most of the written record of the Mayas was destroyed by Spanish invaders. The first ceremonial buildings appear to have been constructed about 1000 B.C.E. The Mayas were sophisticated farmers and used raised fields to plant maize, the cereal grain that is the ancestor of modern corn. The Mayas went into a decline around 800 C.E. and were ruled as smaller city-states when the Spanish conquest began in the 1520s.

DID YOU KNOW?

The Spanish constructed European-style churches, palaces, and other buildings on the site of the Incan city of Cuzco. Today, Cuzco is a UNESCO World Heritage Centre because of its blend of Incan and colonial architecture.

Highly Organized Society

The Aztecs were the latest of the three advanced civilizations to develop, having arrived at what is now Mexico City (Tenochtitlán) in the thirteenth century C.E. The city featured elaborate temples and canals, boasted a population of over 100,000, and served as the center of a large empire. The Aztecs developed a highly organized society ruled by a king which included a class of priests and tax collectors, a warrior elite, and an active merchant class. The Aztecs were a warlike people, exacting tribute from other tribes and capturing prisoners for the human sacrifice that was central to their religion. The Aztecs were conquered shortly after the arrival of Spaniard Hernán Cortés in 1519, and their king, Moctezuma, was killed. The Spaniards' accounts say that Moctezuma attempted to address his subjects, who took a dim view of their leader's submission to Spanish forces, resulting in his being attacked with stones and arrows that inflicted fatal wounds. But the Aztecs' belief that their king had been murdered at the hands of the Spaniards caused Cortés's force heavy loss of life and treasure as it tried to leave the Aztec capital under cover of darkness.

By the time the Aztecs were conquered by the Spanish, the population of Mexico may have numbered 25 million people. Farther north, in what is now the United States and Canada, there were only about 1 million Indians. Most of the inhabitants were nomadic tribes subsisting as hunters or gatherers. Very few, mostly in the American Southwest, settled in one location as farmers.

The Anasazi built five-story pueblos in Chaco Canyon and cliff dwellings in what is now Arizona and New Mexico. They created a system of roads that reached villages 400 miles away. They watered their crops with a system of irrigation canals. But their canals, even combined with other techniques to counter lengthy dry seasons, were not enough to overcome the prolonged drought of the thirteenth century. This drought, the effects of which were compounded by attacks by neighboring tribes, contributed to their decline.

Pueblo peoples also used cliff dwellings (some survive to this day at Mesa Verde, Colorado) that were built during the fourteenth and fifteenth centuries. The Pueblos adopted architectural and religious practices from the Anasazi and, in addition, used plants that were more drought resistant.

Indian tribes living in the Mississippi River Valley found conditions that were less harsh and thus more favorable to continued settlement. The area provided rich soil and a network of rivers that allowed for fishing, hunting, and trade. Beginning in about 800 C.E., immigrants to the area, perhaps from the Yucatán Peninsula, planted new strains of maize (corn) and beans. The largest settlement, Cahokia, near present-day

St. Louis, may have included as many as 40,000 people in the thirteenth century. Even though, as for almost all other New World groups, no written records exist, huge earthen pyramids reveal a sophisticated religious system. Cahokia featured more than 100 of these temple mounds. The main pyramid at Cahokia covers over 15 acres and is over 35 feet high. Residents traded with groups throughout the eastern half of what is now the United States, including tribes on the Atlantic coastline. As with the Anasazi, the people of Cahokia disappeared for unknown reasons sometime in the fourteenth century, though it is thought that overpopulation, warfare, and urban diseases, such as tuberculosis, took huge tolls.

One group of Mississippi River Valley residents that survived well past the arrival of whites was the Natchez. Their ruler, known as the Great Sun, presided over a class-based society. Advisors to the Great Sun comprised the noble class and served as chiefs of villages. The mass of peasants, called Stinkards, cultivated the land. The Natchez were warlike and practiced torture and human sacrifice. Organized into confederacies of local farming villages, they proved unable to resist the diseases and conquests of the invading Europeans.

The Eastern Woodland Indians of North America occupied the lands east of the Mississippi River. They usually lived in small, self-governing clans of related families and were governed by clan elders. Unlike the Aztec or Mayan rulers, however, these kinship-based systems often used consensus, rather than coercion, to govern. The peoples of this region spoke a wide variety of languages belonging to a few language groups. Most of the Indians living between the St. Lawrence River and Chesapeake Bay (Pequots and Delaware, for example) spoke Algonquian languages. The area between the Hudson River and the Great Lakes was home to the Five Nations of the Iroquois (Seneca, Cayuga, Oneida, Onondaga, and Mohawk), who spoke Iroquoian languages. The tribes in the Southeast, such as the Choctaw and Creek, spoke Muskhogean language dialects.

Cahokia Mounds

Cahokia Mounds, the site of the largest pre-Columbian Indian city north of Mexico. This painting, by L. K. Townsend, shows central Cahokia circa 1150 to 1200 B.C.E. (Courtesy Cahokia Mounds Historic Site.)

Most Eastern Woodland tribes did not live in permanent settlements, though tribes did claim territorial lands as their own. Groups moved about seasonally, gathering berries and seeds, fishing and hunting, and settling in the summer on fertile lands. While men were responsible for hunting and fishing, women controlled agricultural production. In some tribes, such as the Iroquois, the eldest women selected the clan chief, and inheritance of goods was matrilineal, with rights to land and other property passing to daughters from mothers. The economic nature of Eastern Woodland life was primarily one of subsistence agriculture, and these groups never developed large urban centers that the Native Americans of Mexico inhabited.

The arrival of Europeans on the American continent greatly impacted Native American cultures and almost always negatively. The tribes along the Atlantic Coast were pressured almost immediately to adapt to the white settlers and traders. Some very early contact was peaceful. Trade seemed to be the main interest of many. Whites provided metal tools and weapons in exchange for beaver and other pelts, which were in abundant supply to the Indians.

Trading encounters often led to efforts of the Europeans to civilize the Indians, attempting to persuade them to live in permanent houses, learn to read and write, and, almost always, to accept Christianity. Jesuits and Franciscan priests and missionaries seeking to convert the Indians they encountered, accompanied Spanish explorers in the American Southwest, and French fur traders in what is now Canada.

TEST TIP

The AP U.S. History exam does not penalize test takers for incorrect responses to the multiple-choice questions. Entering a response for every question—even a wild guess—may help improve your score.

Some Native Tribes Rendered Nearly Extinct

While the interaction between the natives and the new immigrants was largely negative, at times it benefited Indians. Horses, which had first evolved in the New World, returned with the Spanish in the 1500s and became central to the lives of many peoples, particularly those who lived in the Great Plains. While nomadic before the horse's re-introduction to the continent, these tribes now could range much farther and develop new means of hunting and fighting other tribes. In total, however, the benefits of the contact with whites were drastically outweighed by the devastation caused by conquest and disease. Superior European weapons resulted in many decisive defeats for Indian groups throughout the Americas. In addition, illnesses such as measles, typhus, and smallpox ravaged Indian groups that had developed no immunities. Within 50 years of Columbus's arrival in the Caribbean, some native tribes on the islands were virtually extinct. On the island of Hispaniola, the population dropped from approximately 1 million to just *500* by 1600. In Peru the population dropped from 9 million in 1530 to 500,000 in 1630. Some historians estimate that in some regions as many as 95 percent of Indian peoples died of European diseases in the first century after contact.

In this Columbian exchange, whites fared much better than Indians. While sexually transmitted diseases were carried by sailors returning to Europe, other New World contributions were of great positive value. New agricultural techniques and new crops, such as tomatoes, potatoes, pumpkins, beans, and squash, enriched European diets. Maize, which Columbus brought back to Spain after his first voyage, became an important part of European diets, as did potatoes.

In sum, the contact with European civilizations proved disastrous for the Indian residents of the New World. They were devastated by conquering armies and by disease, and made to work as slaves. While vestiges of their cultures have survived to the present day, most of their traditions, cities, villages, and populations have been wiped out.

The Age of Exploration (1492–1607)

Excited by the gold Columbus had brought back from America (after Amerigo Vespucci, an Italian member of a Portuguese expedition to South America whose widely disseminated report suggested a new world had been found), Ferdinand and Isabella, joint monarchs of Spain, sought to obtain formal confirmation of their ownership of these new lands. At Spain's urging, fearing the interference of Portugal, which was at that time a powerful seafaring nation active in overseas exploration, the pope in 1493 drew a Line of Demarcation 100 leagues west of the Cape Verde Islands, dividing the heathen world into two equal parts—that east of the line for Portugal and that west of it for Spain.

Because this line tended to be largely favorable to Spain and because Portugal had the stronger navy, the two countries signed the Treaty of Tordesillas (1494), moving the line farther west. As a result, Brazil eventually became a Portuguese colony, while Spain maintained claims to the rest of the Americas. As other European nations joined the hunt for colonies, the Treaty of Tordesillas was mostly ignored.

The Spanish Conquistadores

To conquer the Americas, the Spanish monarchs used their powerful army, led by independent Spanish adventurers known as *conquistadores.* At first the conquistadores confined their attentions to the Caribbean islands, where the European diseases they unwittingly carried with them devastated the local Indian populations, who had no immunities against such diseases.

Juan Ponce de León. (Courtesy State Library and Archives of Florida.)

After about 1510, the conquistadores turned their attention to the American mainland. In 1513, Vasco Núñez de Balboa crossed the isthmus of Panama and became the first European to see the Pacific Ocean. The same year, Juan Ponce de León explored Florida in search of gold and a fabled fountain of youth. He found neither, but claimed Florida for Spain. In 1519, Hernando (Hernán) Cortés led his dramatic expedition against the Aztecs of Mexico. Aided by the fact that the Indians at first mistook him for a god, as well as by firearms, armor, horses, and (unbeknownst to him) smallpox germs, all previously unknown in America, Cortés destroyed the Aztec empire and won enormous riches. By the 1550s, other such fortune seekers had conquered much of South America.

In North America the Spaniards sought in vain for riches. In 1528, Pánfilo de Narváez led a disastrous expedition through the Gulf Coast region from which only four of the original 400

DID YOU KNOW?

Smallpox and other infectious diseases carried by Europeans devastated native peoples because they lacked the natural immunities built up from previous exposure. An estimated 95 percent of the native pre-Columbian population of the Americas died from European diseases by the end of the seventeenth century.

men returned. One of them, Cabeza de Vaca, brought with him a story of seven great cities full of gold (the "Seven Cities of Cibola") somewhere to the north. In response to this, two Spanish expeditions explored the interior of North America. Hernando de Soto led a 600-man expedition (1539–1541) through what is now the southeastern United States, penetrating as far west as Oklahoma and discovering the Mississippi River, on whose banks de Soto was buried. Francisco Vasquez de Coronado led an expedition (1540–1542) from Mexico, north across the Rio Grande and through New Mexico, Arizona, Texas, Oklahoma, and Kansas. Some of Coronado's men were the first Europeans to see the Grand Canyon. While neither expedition discovered rich Indian civilizations to plunder, both increased Europe's knowledge of the interior of North America and asserted Spain's territorial claims to the continent.

New Spain

Spain administered its new holdings as an autocratic, rigidly controlled empire in which everything was to benefit the parent country. Tight control of even mundane matters was carried out by a suffocating bureaucracy run directly from Madrid. Annual treasure fleets carried the riches of the New World to Spain for the furtherance of its military-political goals in Europe.

As population pressures were low in 16th-century Spain, only about 200,000 Spaniards came to America during that time. To deal with the consequent labor shortages—and as a reward to successful conquistadores—the Spaniards developed a system of large manors, or estates *(encomiendas),* with Indian slaves ruthlessly managed for the benefit of the conquistadores. The *encomienda* system was later replaced by the similar, but somewhat milder, *hacienda* system. As the Indian population died from overwork and European diseases, Spaniards began importing African slaves to supply their labor needs. Society in New Spain was rigidly stratified, with the highest level reserved for natives of Spain *(peninsulares)* and the next for those of Spanish parentage born in the New World *(creoles).* Those of mixed or Indian blood occupied lower levels.

English and French Beginnings

In 1497, the Italian John Cabot (Giovanni Caboto), sailing under the sponsorship of the king of England in search of a Northwest Passage (a water route to the Orient through or around the North American continent), became the first European since the Viking voyages more than four centuries earlier to reach the mainland of North America, which he claimed for England.

In 1524, the king of France authorized another Italian, Giovanni da Verrazzano, to undertake a mission similar to Cabot's. Endeavoring to duplicate the achievement of Portuguese Ferdinand Magellan, who had five years earlier found a way around the southern tip of South America, Verrazzano followed the American coast from present-day North Carolina to Maine.

Beginning in 1534, Jacques Cartier, also authorized by the king of France, mounted three expeditions to the area of the St. Lawrence River, which he believed might be the hoped-for Northwest Passage. He explored up the river as far as the site of Montreal, where—as he saw it—rapids prevented him from continuing to China. He claimed the area for France before abandoning his last expedition and returning to France in 1542. France made no further attempts to explore or colonize in America for sixty-five years.

England showed little interest in America as well during most of the 16th century. But when the English finally did begin colonization, commercial capitalism in England had advanced to the point that the English efforts were supported by private, rather than government funds, allowing the English colonists to enjoy a greater degree of freedom from government interference.

DID YOU KNOW?

The first permanent settlement in the New World was Santo Domingo in what is now the Dominican Republic. It was founded by Christopher Columbus's brother Bartholomew in 1496.

Partially as a result of the New World rivalries and partially through differences between Protestant and Catholic countries, the 16th century was a violent time both in Europe and in America. French Protestants, called Huguenots, who attempted to escape persecution in Catholic France by settling in the New World, were massacred by the Spaniards. One such incident led the Spaniards, nervous about any possible encroachment on what they considered to be their exclusive holdings in America, to build a fort that became the beginning of a settlement at St. Augustine, Florida, the first city in North America. Spanish priests ventured north from St. Augustine, but no permanent settlements were built in the interior.

French and especially English sea captains made great sport of—and considerable profit from—plundering the Spaniards of the wealth they had first plundered from the Indians. One of the most successful English captains, Francis Drake, sailed around South America and raided the Spanish settlements on the Pacific coast of Central America before continuing on to California, which he claimed for England and named Nova Albion. Drake then returned to England by sailing around the world. England's

Queen Elizabeth, sister and Protestant successor to Mary, had been quietly investing in Drake's highly profitable voyages. On Drake's return from his round-the-world voyage, Elizabeth openly showed her approval.

Angered by this, as well as by Elizabeth's support of the Protestant cause in Europe, Spain's King Philip II in 1588 dispatched a mighty fleet, the Spanish Armada, to conquer England. Instead, the Armada was defeated by the English navy and largely destroyed by storms in the North Sea. This victory established England as a great power and moved it a step closer to overseas colonization, although the war with Spain continued until 1604.

Gilbert, Raleigh, and the First English Attempts at Colonization

English nobleman Sir Humphrey Gilbert believed England should found colonies and find a Northwest Passage. In 1576, he sent English sea captain Martin Frobisher to look for such a passage. Frobisher scouted along the inhospitable northeastern coast of Canada and brought back large amounts of a yellow metal that turned out to be fool's gold. In 1578, Gilbert obtained a charter allowing him to found a colony with his own funds and guaranteeing the prospective colonists all the rights of those born and residing in England, thus setting an important precedent for future colonial charters. His attempts to found a colony in Newfoundland failed, and while pursuing these endeavors he was lost at sea.

With the queen's permission, Gilbert's work was taken up by his half-brother, Sir Walter Raleigh. Raleigh turned his attention to a more southerly portion of the North American coastline, which he named Virginia, in honor of England's unmarried queen. He selected as a site for the first settlement Roanoke Island just off the coast of present-day North Carolina.

After one abortive attempt, a group of 114 settlers—men, women, and children—landed in July 1587. Shortly thereafter, Virginia Dare became the first English child born in America. Later that year, the expedition's leader, John White, returned to England to secure additional supplies. Delayed by the war with Spain, he did not return until 1590, when he found the colony deserted. It is not known what became of the Roanoke settlers. After this failure, Raleigh was forced by financial constraints to abandon his attempts to colonize Virginia. Hampered by unrealistic expectations, inadequate financial resources, and the ongoing war with Spain, English interest in American colonization was submerged for fifteen years.

(Before taking the quiz noted below, please review the summary timeline for this chapter on the following page.)

Pre-Columbian America & Early European Contact (13,000 B.C.E.–1607 C.E.)

Historical Timeline (13,000 B.C.E.–1607 C.E.)

ca. 13,000 B.C.E.	Asians begin the first of several migrations over Bering Strait
5000 B.C.E.	Maize cultivation begins in southern Mexico
700 B.C.E.	Olmec people flourish along Gulf of Mexico
100 C.E.	Hopewell culture sets up massive trading network
300	Mayan city of Tikal features 20,000 residents and many temples
500	Teotihuacán's population reaches 100,000 at peak of culture
600	Hohokam civilization develops in present-day Arizona and New Mexico
800	Collapse of many Mayan cities
900	Anasazi build cliff villages in American Southwest
1000	Leif Ericson and Norsemen settle Vinland in current Newfoundland
1125	City of Cahokia (near present-day St. Louis) has 15,000 residents and 100 temple mounds
1325	Aztecs build Tenochtitlán on site of current Mexico City
1438	Incas begin conquest of Andean region of South America
1492	Columbus lands at San Salvador in Bahamas
1517	Martin Luther challenges Roman Catholic authority, beginning Protestant Reformation in Europe
1521	Cortés conquers Aztecs in Mexico Magellan circumnavigates the globe
1533	Pizarro captures Inca capital in Peru
1539	De Soto explores southeastern U.S.
1540	Coronado explores southwestern U.S.
1555	Elizabeth I takes throne in England
1585	Roanoke Island colony established off Virginia coast, then disappears
1607	Virginia Colony established

Chapter 4

The English Colonies (1607–1754)

Virginia

In the first decade of the 1600s, Englishmen, exhilarated by the recent victory over Spain and influenced by the writings of Richard Hakluyt (who urged American colonization as the way to national greatness and the spread of the gospel), once again undertook to plant colonies.

Two groups of merchants gained charters from James I, Queen Elizabeth's successor. One group of merchants was based in London and received a charter to North America between the Hudson and Cape Fear rivers. The other was based in Plymouth and was granted the right to colonize in North America from the Potomac to the northern border of present-day Maine. They were called the Virginia Company of London and the Virginia Company of Plymouth, respectively. These were joint-stock companies, which raised their capital by the sale of shares of stock. Companies of this sort had already been used to finance and carry on English trade with Russia, Africa, and the Middle East.

In 1607, the Virginia Company of Plymouth attempted to start a colony in Maine, but after one winter the colonists became discouraged and returned to Britain. Thereafter, the company folded.

In the same year, the Virginia Company of London sent out an expedition of three ships with 104 men to establish a colony some forty miles up the James River from Chesapeake Bay. Like the river on which it was located, the new settlement was named Jamestown in honor of England's king. It became the first permanent English settlement in North America, but for a time it appeared to be going the way of the earlier attempts. During the early years of Jamestown, the majority of the settlers died of starvation, various diseases, or hostile action by Indians.

There were several reasons for these difficulties. Since the company owned the entire colony and all members shared the profits regardless of how much or how little they worked, there was a lack of incentive. Many of the settlers were gentlemen who considered themselves too good to work at growing the food the colony needed to survive. Others were simply unambitious and little inclined to work in any case. Furthermore, the settlers had come with the expectation of finding gold or other quick and easy riches and wasted a great deal of time looking for these instead of providing for their survival.

For purposes of defense, the settlement had been sited on a peninsula formed by a bend in the river; but this low and swampy location proved to be a breeding ground for all sorts of diseases and, at high tide, even contaminated the settlers' drinking supply with seawater. To make matters worse, relations with Powhatan, the powerful local Indian chief, were at best uncertain and often openly hostile, with disastrous results for the colonists.

In 1608 and 1609, the dynamic and ruthless leadership of John Smith kept the colony from collapsing. Smith's simple rule was, "He who works not, eats not." After Smith returned to England in late 1609, the condition of the colony again became critical.

In 1612, a Virginia resident named John Rolfe discovered that a superior strain of tobacco, native to the West Indies, could be grown in Virginia. There was a large market for this tobacco in Europe, and Rolfe's discovery gave Jamestown a major cash crop. The cultivation of tobacco enabled the colony to survive.

To secure more settlers and boost Virginia's shrinking labor force, the company moved to make immigration possible for Britain's poor, who were without economic opportunity at home or financial means to procure transportation to America. This was achieved by means of the indenture system, by which a poor worker's passage to America was paid by an American planter (or the company itself), who in exchange was indentured to work for the planter (or the company) for a specified number of years. The system was open to abuse and often resulted in the mistreatment of the indentured servants.

To control the workers shipped to Virginia, as well as the often lazy and unruly colonists already present, the company gave its governors in America almost dictatorial powers. Governors such as Lord De La Warr, Sir Thomas Gates, and Sir Thomas Dale made use of such powers, imposing a harsh rule.

For such reasons, in addition to its well-known reputation as a death trap, Virginia continued to fail to attract an adequate numbers of immigrants. To solve this, a reform-minded faction within the company proposed a new approach, and under its leader, Edwin Sandys, made changes designed to attract more settlers. Colonists were promised the same rights they had in England. A representative assembly, the House of Burgesses, was founded in 1619—the first in America. Additionally, private ownership of land was instituted.

Despite these reforms, Virginia's unhealthy reputation kept many Englishmen away. Large numbers of indentured servants were brought in, especially young, single men. The first Africans were brought to Virginia in 1619 but were treated as indentured servants rather than slaves.

Virginia's Indian relations remained difficult. In 1622, an Indian massacre took the lives of 347 settlers. In 1644, the Indians struck again, massacring another 300 settlers. Shortly thereafter, the coastal Indians were subdued and no longer presented a serious threat.

Impressed by the potential profits from tobacco growing, King James I determined to have Virginia for himself. Using the high mortality and the 1622 massacre as a pretext, he revoked the London Company's charter in 1624 and made Virginia a royal colony. This pattern was followed throughout colonial history; both company colonies and proprietary colonies tended eventually to become royal colonies. Upon taking over Virginia, King James revoked all political rights and the representative assembly—he did not believe in such things—but fifteen years later his son, Charles I, was forced, by constant pressure from the Virginians and the continuing need to attract more settlers, to restore these rights.

TEST TIP

Be sure to carefully read the question stem of multiple-choice questions so that you understand exactly what the item is asking you. You may wish to rephrase questions in your own words. As you read each of the four possible answers, start by eliminating options that you know are incorrect.

New France

Shortly after England returned to the business of colonization, France renewed its interest in the areas previously visited by French explorers, such as Jacques Cartier. The French, with the cooperation of the Indians, started a lucrative trade in furs, plentiful in America and much sought after in Europe.

The St. Lawrence River was the French gateway to the interior of North America. In 1608, Samuel de Champlain established a trading post in Quebec, from which the rest of what became New France eventually spread.

Relatively small numbers of Frenchmen came to America, and, partially because of this, they were generally able to maintain good relations with the Indians. French Canadians were energetic in exploring and claiming new lands for France.

French exploration and settlement spread throughout the Great Lakes region and the valleys of both the Mississippi and Ohio rivers. In 1673, Jacques Marquette explored the Mississippi Valley, and in 1682 Sieur de la Salle followed the river to its mouth. French settlements in the Midwest were generally forts and trading posts serving the fur trade, rather than real towns.

Throughout its history, an inadequate population and a lack of support from the parent country handicapped New France. One of the main problems was the *seigneur et habitant* system in which French nobles owned the land and tenant farmers worked it. The chance for land ownership by the tenant farmers was slim, and there was little incentive for large-scale immigration to New France to take place.

New Netherlands

Other countries also took an interest in North America. In 1609, Holland sent Englishman Henry Hudson to search for a Northwest Passage. In this endeavor, Hudson discovered the river that bears his name.

Arrangements were made to trade with the Iroquois for furs, especially beaver pelts for the hats then popular in Europe. In 1624, Dutch trading outposts were established on Manhattan Island (New Amsterdam) and at the site of present-day Albany (Fort Orange). A profitable fur trade was carried on and became the main source of revenue for the Dutch West India Company, the joint-stock company that ran the colony.

To encourage enough farming to keep the colony supplied with food, the Dutch instituted the patroon system, by which large landed estates would be given to wealthy men who transported at least fifty families to New Netherlands. These families would then become tenant farmers on the estate of the patroon who had transported them. As Holland's home economy was healthy, few Dutch felt desperate enough to take up such unattractive terms.

Like New France, New Netherlands was internally weak and unstable. It was poorly governed by inept and lazy governors, and its population was a mixture of people from all over Europe as well as many African slaves, forming what historians have called an "unstable pluralism," in which societal differences are so deep that governance is virtually impossible.

The Pilgrims at Plymouth

The Protestant Reformation had a great impact on the early English colonies established in North America. Martin Luther introduced the concept of the priesthood of all believers, which led religious dissenters to form their own sects. In addition, Luther and his followers challenged the authority of the Roman Catholic Church, which before the Reformation had been a monolithic force. The desire to worship in one's own way led many English citizens to the New World. For the most part, these fell into two groups of Protestants: Puritans and Separatists. Though holding theological beliefs similar to those of the Puritans, the Separatists believed the corrupt Church of England was beyond saving and felt they must separate from it. They also accused the Church of England of being "popish," of following the forms of the Roman Catholic Church, which were considered unbiblical to the Puritans.

One group of Separatists, suffering government harassment, fled to Holland. Dissatisfied there, they decided to go to America and, thus, became the famous Pilgrims of Plymouth Colony.

Pilgrims Landing at Plymouth Rock
Saromy & Major, "The Landing of the Pilgrims on Plymouth Rock," Dec. 11, 1620.
(U.S. Library of Congress.)

Led by William Bradford, they departed in 1620, having obtained from the London Company a charter to settle just south of the Hudson River. Driven by storms, their ship, the *Mayflower,* made landfall at Cape Cod in Massachusetts. They decided it was God's will for them to settle in that area. This, however, put them outside the jurisdiction of any established government, and so, before going ashore, they drew up and signed the *Mayflower Compact,* establishing a foundation for orderly government based on the consent of the governed. After a difficult first winter that resulted in many deaths, the Pilgrims went on to establish a quiet and modestly prosperous colony. After a number of years of hard work, they were able to buy out the investors who had originally financed their voyage and thus gain greater autonomy.

The Massachusetts Bay Colony

The Puritans were far more numerous than the Separatists. Contrary to stereotype, they did not dress in drab clothes and were neither ignorant nor bigoted. They did, however, take the Bible and their religion seriously and felt the Anglican Church still retained too many unscriptural practices leftover from Roman Catholicism.

King James I had no use for the Puritans but, mindful of their growing political power, he refrained from bringing on a confrontation. His son, Charles I, decided in 1629 to persecute the Puritans aggressively and to rule without the Puritan-dominated Parliament. This course would lead eventually (ten years later) to civil war, but in the meantime some of the Puritans decided to set up a community in America.

To accomplish their purpose, they sought in 1629 to charter a joint-stock company to be called the Massachusetts Bay Company. Whether because Charles was glad to be rid of the Puritans or because he did not realize the special nature of this joint-stock company, the charter was granted. The charter, however, neglected to specify where the company's headquarters would be located. Taking advantage of this unusual omission, the Puritans determined to make their headquarters in the colony itself, 3,000 miles from meddlesome royal officials.

Under the leadership of John Winthrop, who taught that a new colony should provide the world with a model of what a Christian society ought to be, the Puritans carefully organized their venture and, upon arriving in Massachusetts in 1630, did not undergo the "starving time" that had often plagued other first-year colonies.

DIDYOUKNOW?

The modern U.S. holiday of Thanksgiving traces its roots to a feast held in Plymouth in 1621. Local Wampanoags and pilgrims gathered that fall to celebrate the colony's first successful harvest. Abraham Lincoln established Thanksgiving as an official U.S. holiday in 1863.

The government of Massachusetts evolved to include a governor and a representative assembly (called the General Court) selected by the "freemen"—adult male church members. As Massachusetts's population increased (20,000 Puritans had come by 1642 in what came to be called the Great Migration), new towns were chartered, with each town granted a large tract of land by the Massachusetts government. As in European villages, these towns consisted of a number of houses clustered around the church house and the village green. Farmland was located around the outside of the town. In each new town, the elect—those who testified of having experienced saving grace—covenanted together as a church.

Rhode Island, Connecticut, and New Hampshire

Puritans saw their colony as a place to serve God and build His kingdom. Winthrop spoke of Massachusetts Bay as being "a city upon a hill," demonstrating to the world what a godly community should be like. Dissidents would be tolerated only insofar as they did not interfere with the colony's mission.

One such dissident was Roger Williams, a Puritan preacher. Williams was received warmly in Massachusetts in 1631, but he had a talent for carrying things to their logical (or sometimes not so logical) extreme. When his activities became disruptive, he was asked to leave the colony. To avoid having to return to England—where he would have been even less welcome—he fled to the wilderness around Narragansett Bay, bought land from the Indians, and founded the settlement of Providence (1636), which was soon populated by his many followers.

Another dissident was Anne Hutchinson, who openly taught lessons contrary to Puritan doctrine and challenged the Puritan political and religious authorities. Called before the General Court to answer for her teachings and practices, such as teaching men, she claimed to have had special revelations from God superseding the Bible. This was unthinkable in Puritan theology and led to Hutchinson's banishment from the colony. She also migrated to the area around Narragansett Bay and with her followers founded Portsmouth (1638). She later migrated farther west and was killed by Indians.

In 1644, Roger Williams secured from Parliament a charter combining Providence, Portsmouth, and other settlements that had sprung up in the area to form the colony of Rhode Island. Through Williams' influence, the colony granted complete religious toleration. Thus, Rhode Island tended to be populated by exiles and troublemakers who were not welcome in the other colonies or in Europe. It suffered constant political turmoil.

Connecticut was founded by Puritans who had slight religious disagreements with the leadership of Massachusetts. In 1636, Thomas Hooker led a group of settlers westward to found Hartford. (Hooker, though a good friend of Massachusetts Governor John Winthrop, felt the governor was exercising somewhat more authority than was prudent.) Others also moved into Connecticut from Massachusetts. In 1639, the *Fundamental Orders of Connecticut,* the first written constitution in America, was drawn up, providing for representative government.

In 1637, a group of Puritans led by John Davenport founded the neighboring colony of New Haven. Davenport and his followers felt that Winthrop, far from being too strict, was not being strict enough. In 1662, a new charter combined both New Haven and Connecticut into an officially recognized colony of Connecticut.

New Hampshire's settlement did not involve any disagreement at all among the Puritans. It was simply settled as an overflow from Massachusetts. In 1677, King Charles II chartered the separate royal colony of New Hampshire. It remained economically dependent on Massachusetts.

Were the Puritans Puritanical?

Quaker Mary Dyer being led to the gallows, 1660 (Wikimedia Commons)

The word "puritan" today connotes narrow-minded, rigid, dour, judgmental. After all, they fined people for celebrating Christmas. Most would probably agree with Mencken's definition of Puritanism as "the haunting fear that someone, somewhere may be happy." But many of the stereotypes associated with Puritans are either exaggerated or just wrong. And many of the positive qualities that have defined Americans can be traced directly to the Puritans.

Historian Perry Miller described Puritans as "moral athletes." They had an intense desire to please God and lead godly lives, though they recognized that it was not human striving but God's choosing a person that determined salvation. Because salvation was an individual matter, a belief grounded in the Protestant Reformation doctrine of the priesthood of all believers, Puritans were fiercely independent in their thinking.

They valued education for both boys and girls, and literacy was higher in Puritan New England than in any other colonial region. Puritan leaders insisted that each village of at least fifty families hire a teacher paid by residents to teach their children. The main goal for instruction was to be able to read the Bible. The first education law in Massachusetts begins, "It being one chief project of that old deluder Satan to keep men from the knowledge of the Scriptures ..."

(Continued)

TEST TIP

Do you get especially nervous when taking tests? Test anxiety is a common concern, particularly for high-stakes exams like the AP exams. If you find yourself getting nervous during the exam, put down your pencil, close your eyes, empty your mind, and take a few deep breaths. A short mental break may help you refocus and save you time in the long run.

Maryland

By the 1630s, the English crown showed more interest in exercising control over the colonies, and therefore turned away from the practice of granting charters to joint-stock companies and toward granting such charters to single individuals or groups of individuals known as proprietors. The proprietors would actually own the colony and would be directly responsible for it to the king in an arrangement similar to the feudalism of medieval Europe. Though this was seen as providing more opportunity for royal control and less for autonomy on the part of the colonists, in practice, proprietary colonies turned out much like the company colonies because settlers insisted on self-government.

The first proprietary colony was Maryland, granted in 1632 to George Calvert, Lord Baltimore. It was to be located just north of the Potomac River and to be both a reward

Did they object to music and art? Yes, but only in churches, which they felt should be plain to avoid distractions. No organs were allowed in Puritan churches. It is also true that Puritans in England banned theatrical performances when they were in power in the 1650s, but historian Carl Degler asserts it was more "a matter of objection to their degenerate lewdness . . . than an objection to the drama as such."

It would, however, be a stretch to characterize Puritans as fun-lovers. They were serious folk. They saw themselves as part of the cosmic struggle between good and evil here on earth. "Convinced of the utter desirability of salvation on the one hand, and equally cognizant of the total depravity of man's nature on the other," Degler writes, "the Puritan was caught in an impossible dilemma which permitted him no rest short of the grave." Puritans believed strongly in both predestination and election and trusted Divine Providence to guide them in their daily lives.

Puritans also displayed degrees of self-righteousness, intolerance, and narrow-mindedness that led to banishing individuals such as Roger Williams and Anne Hutchinson, who dared express beliefs not conforming to the views of Puritan authorities. Quaker Mary Dyer was hanged for preaching that God communicated to individuals through an inner light and that men and women were equal in church life.

Puritans were ironic in several ways. They came to New England seeking religious freedom and denied it to others. They believed each person was directly accountable to God for his or her actions, yet punished those who dared defy the social order. They valued reason and distrusted emotion, yet allowed the hysteria of the Salem witch trials to define them as cruel and heartless.

One legacy of the Puritans was their work ethic, which impacted Americans of all religious beliefs. Perhaps the greatest contribution of the Puritans to American life was the concept of public support of education at the local level. Their system was a prototype for public education across the United States in the 19th century.

for Calvert's loyal service to the king and a refuge for English Catholics, of whom Calvert was one. George Calvert died before the colony could be planted, but the venture was carried forward by his son Cecilius.

From the start, more Protestants than Catholics came. To protect the Catholic minority, Calvert approved an Act of Religious Toleration (1649) guaranteeing political rights to Christians of all persuasions. Calvert also allowed a representative assembly. Economically and socially, Maryland developed as a virtual carbon copy of neighboring Virginia.

The Carolinas

In 1663, Charles II, having recently been restored to the throne after a twenty-year Puritan revolution that had seen his father beheaded, moved to reward eight of the noblemen who had helped him regain the crown by granting them a charter for all the lands lying south of Virginia and north of Spanish Florida.

The new colony was called Carolina, after the king. In hopes of attracting settlers, the proprietors came up with an elaborate plan for a hierarchical, almost feudal, society. Not surprisingly, this proved unworkable, and despite offers of generous land grants to settlers, the Carolinas grew slowly compared to other colonies.

The area of North Carolina developed as an overflow from Virginia with similar economic and cultural features. South Carolina was settled by English planters from the island of Barbados. The planters founded Charles Town (Charleston) in 1670 and brought with them their black slaves; thus, unlike the Chesapeake colonies of Virginia and Maryland, South Carolina had slavery as a fully developed institution from the outset.

New York and New Jersey

In addition to being immoral and dissolute, Charles II was also cunning and had an eye for increasing Britain's power. The Dutch colony of New Netherlands, lying between the Chesapeake and the New England colonies, caught his eye as a likely target for British expansion. In 1664, Charles gave his brother, James, Duke of York, title to all the Dutch lands in America, provided James conquered them first. To do this, James sent an invasion fleet under the command of Colonel Richard Nicols. New Amsterdam fell almost without a shot and became New York.

James was adamantly opposed to representative assemblies and ordered that there should be none in New York. To avoid unrest, Nicols shrewdly granted as many other civil and political rights as possible; but residents, particularly Puritans who had settled on Long Island, continued to agitate for self-government. Finally, in the 1680s, James relented, only to break his promise when he became king in 1685.

To add to the confusion in the newly renamed colony, James granted a part of his newly acquired domain to John Lord Berkeley and Sir George Carteret (two of the Carolina proprietors), who named their new proprietorship New Jersey. James neglected to tell Colonel Nicols of this, with the result that both Nicols, on the one hand, and Carteret and Berkeley, on the other, were granting title to the same land—to different settlers. Conflicting claims of land ownership plagued New Jersey for decades, being used by the crown in 1702 as a pretext to take over New Jersey as a royal colony.

The Colonial World

Life in the Colonies

New England grew not only from immigration but also from natural increase during the 17th century. The typical New England family had more children than the typical English or Chesapeake family, and more of those children survived to have families of their own. A New Englander could expect to live 15 to 20 years longer than his counterpart in the parent country and 25 to 30 years longer than his fellow colonist in the Chesapeake. Because of the continuity provided by these longer lifespans, because the Puritans had migrated as intact family units, and because of the homogeneous nature of the Puritan New England colonies, New England enjoyed a much more stable and well-ordered society than did the Chesapeake colonies.

Puritans placed great importance on the family, which in their society was highly patriarchal. Young people were generally subject to their parents' direction in the matter of when and whom they would marry. Few defied this system and illegitimate births were rare. Puritans also placed great importance on the ability to read, for they believed everyone should be able to read the Bible, God's word, himself. As a result, New England was ahead of the other colonies educationally and enjoyed widespread literacy.

Since New England's climate and rocky soil were unsuited to large-scale farming, the region developed a prosperous economy based on small farming, home industry, fishing, and a large shipbuilding industry. Boston became a major international port.

Life in the Chesapeake colonies was drastically different. The typical Chesapeake colonist lived a shorter, less healthy life than his New England counterpart and was survived by fewer children. As a result, the Chesapeake's population steadily declined despite a constant influx of new settlers. Nor was Chesapeake society as stable as that of New England. Most Chesapeake settlers came as indentured servants; and since planters desired primarily male servants for work in the tobacco fields, men largely outnumbered women in Virginia and Maryland. This hindered the development of family life. Life in the Chesapeake was hard and the death rate was high. The short lifespans also contributed to the region's unstable family life, as few children reached adulthood without experiencing the death of one or both parents. Remarriage resulted in households that contained children from several different marriages. While women in the Chesapeake had limited legal and political rights compared to today, they were allowed to own property and make some decisions allowed in very few other places in the world at that time.

The system of indentured servitude was open to serious abuse, with masters sometimes treating their servants brutally or contriving through some technicality to lengthen their terms of indenture. It was not uncommon for indentured servants to run away and break their contracts. In any case, 40 percent of the Chesapeake region's indentured servants failed to survive long enough to gain their freedom.

By the late 17th century, life in the Chesapeake was beginning to stabilize, with death rates declining and life expectancies rising as fewer died of diseases. As society stabilized, an elite group of wealthy families such as the Byrds, Carters, Fitzhughs, Lees, and Randolphs, among others, began to dominate the social and political life of the region. Aping the lifestyle of the English country gentry, they built lavish manor houses from which to rule their vast plantations. For every one of these, however, there were many small farmers who worked hard for a living, showed deference to the great planters, and hoped someday they, or their children, might reach that level.

On the bottom rung of Southern society were the black slaves. During the first half of the 17th century, blacks in the Chesapeake made up only a small percentage of the population and were treated more or less as indentured servants. In the decades between 1640 and 1670, this gradually changed, and blacks came to be seen and treated as lifelong chattel slaves whose status would be inherited by their children. Larger numbers of them began to be imported and with this came natural population growth. By 1750, slaves composed 30 to 40 percent of the Chesapeake population.

DID YOU KNOW?

By 1700, the English colonies had a population of about 275,000. Some 7,000 people lived in Boston, the largest colonial city.

While North Carolina tended to follow Virginia in its economic and social development (although with fewer great planters and more small farmers), South Carolina developed a society even more dominated by large plantations and chattel slavery. By the early decades of the 18th century, blacks had come to outnumber whites in that colony. South Carolina's economy remained dependent on the cultivation of its two staple crops, rice and, to a lesser extent, indigo.

Mercantilism and the Navigation Acts

Beginning around 1650, British authorities began to take more interest in regulating American trade for the benefit of the mother country. A key idea that underlay this policy was the concept of mercantilism. Mercantilists believed the world's wealth was sharply limited, and therefore one nation's gain was automatically another nation's loss. Each nation's goal was to export more than it imported (i.e., to have a "favorable balance of trade"). The difference would be made up in gold and silver, which, so the theory ran, would make the nation strong both economically and militarily. To achieve their goals, mercantilists believed the government should regulate economic activity. Colonies could fit into England's mercantilist scheme by providing staple crops, such as rice, tobacco, sugar, and indigo, and raw materials, such as timber, that England would otherwise have been forced to import from other countries.

To make the colonies serve this purpose, Parliament passed a series of Navigation Acts (1651, 1660, 1663, and 1673). These were the foundation of England's worldwide commercial system and some of the most important pieces of imperial legislation during the colonial period. They were also intended as weapons in England's ongoing struggle against its chief seventeenth-century maritime rival, Holland. The system created by the Navigation Acts stipulated that trade with the colonies was to be carried out only on ships made in Britain or America and with at least 75 percent British or American crews. Additionally, when certain "enumerated" goods were shipped from an American port, they were to go only to Britain or to another American port. Finally, almost nothing could be imported to the colonies without going through Britain first.

Mercantilism's results were mixed. Though ostensibly for the benefit of all subjects of the British Empire, its provisions benefited some at the expense of others. It boosted the prosperity of New Englanders, who engaged in large-scale shipbuilding (something Britain's mercantilist policy-makers chose to encourage), while it hurt the residents of the Chesapeake by driving down the price of tobacco (an enumerated item). On the whole, the Navigation Acts, as intended, transferred wealth from America to Britain by increasing the prices Americans had to pay for British goods and lowering the prices Americans received for the goods they produced. Mercantilism also helped bring on a series of three wars between England and Holland in the late 1600s.

Charles II and his advisors worked to tighten up the administration of colonies, particularly the enforcement of the Navigation Acts. In Virginia, tempers grew short as tobacco prices plunged. Virginians were also angry with Royal Governor Sir William Berkeley, whose high-handed, high-taxing ways they despised and whom they believed was running the colony for the benefit of himself and his circle of cronies.

In 1674, an impoverished nobleman with a shady past by the name of Nathaniel Bacon came to Virginia and failed to gain admittance to Berkeley's inner circle with its financial advantages. He began to oppose Berkeley at every turn and came to head a faction of like-minded persons. In 1676, disagreement over Indian policy brought the matter to the point of armed conflict. Bacon and his men burned Jamestown, but then the whole matter came to an anticlimactic ending when Bacon died of dysentery.

The British authorities, hearing of the matter, sent ships, troops, and an investigating commission. Berkeley, who had had twenty-three of the rebels hanged in reprisal, was removed. Thenceforth, Virginia's royal governors had strict instructions to run the colony for the benefit of the mother country. In response, Virginia's gentry, who had been divided over Bacon's Rebellion, united to face this new threat to their local autonomy. By political means they consistently obstructed the governors' efforts to increase royal control. Bacon's Rebellion was alarming to the gentry, as they saw the possibility of revolt from the poor whites and the large number of slaves in Virginia.

The Half-Way Covenant

By the latter half of the 17th century, many Puritans sensed that New England was drifting away from its religious purpose. The children and grandchildren of the first generation were clearly more concerned with making money than creating a godly society.

To deal with this, some clergymen in 1662 proposed the "Half-Way Covenant," providing a sort of half-way church membership for the children of members, even though those children, having reached adulthood, did not profess saving grace as was normally required for Puritan church membership. Those who embraced the Half-Way Covenant felt that in an increasingly materialistic society it would at least keep church membership rolls full and might preserve some of the church's influence in society.

Some communities rejected the Half-Way Covenant as an improper compromise, but in general the shift toward secular values continued, though slowly.

TEST TIP

Spelling not your strong point? Don't worry. Spelling errors will not affect your essay score as long as the graders can determine your intent. While style is important, the content of your answers is what the AP exam graders are looking at most closely.

King Philip's War

As New England's population grew, local Indian tribes felt threatened, and conflict sometimes resulted. Puritans endeavored to convert Indians to Christianity. The Bible was translated into Algonquian; four villages ("praying towns") were set up for converted Indians, who, by 1650, numbered over a thousand. Still, most Indians remained unconverted.

In 1675, a Wampanoag chief named King Philip (Metacomet) led a war to exterminate the whites. Some 2,000 settlers lost their lives before King Philip was killed and his tribe subdued. New England continued to experience Indian troubles from time to time, though not as severe as those suffered by Virginia.

The Dominion of New England

The trend toward increasing imperial control of the colonies continued. In 1684, the Massachusetts charter was revoked in retaliation for that colony's large-scale evasion of the restrictions of the Navigation Acts.

The following year Charles II died and was succeeded by his brother, James II. James was prepared to go even further in controlling the colonies, favoring the establishment of a unified government for all of New England, New York, and New Jersey. This was to be called the "Dominion of New England," and the fact that it would abolish representative assemblies and facilitate the imposition of the Church of England on Congregationalist (Puritan) New England made it still more appealing to James, though disturbing to New Englanders, whose parents had come from England to escape Anglican authority.

To head the Dominion, James sent the obnoxious and dictatorial Sir Edmond Andros. Arriving in Boston in 1686, Andros quickly alienated the New Englanders. When news reached America of England's 1688 Glorious Revolution, replacing the Catholic James with his Protestant daughter Mary and her husband, William of Orange, New Englanders cheerfully shipped Andros back to England.

Similar uprisings occurred in New York and Maryland. William and Mary's new government generally accepted these actions, though Jacob Leisler, leader of Leisler's

Rebellion in New York, was executed for hesitating to turn over power to the new royal governor. This unfortunate incident poisoned the political climate of New York for many years.

The charter of Massachusetts, now including Plymouth, was restored in 1691, this time as a royal colony, though it was not as tightly controlled as others.

The Salem Witch Trials

In 1692, Massachusetts was shaken by an unusual incident in which several young girls in Salem Village claimed to be tormented by the Satanic activities of certain neighbors of theirs. A witch-hunting hysteria led to many arrests and trials in which witnesses described visions and prosecutors introduced other spectral evidence. Before the resulting Salem witch trials could be stopped by the intervention of calmer Puritan ministers such as Cotton Mather, twenty men and women had been executed (nineteen by hanging and one crushed under a pile of rocks). The Salem hysteria and executions revealed the uneasy mindset of some Puritans, who lived in a state of fear of Satan, Indian attacks, and the possibility of losing their charter from the king. The presence of witchcraft was viewed as one more challenge to their existence.

Pennsylvania and Delaware

Pennsylvania was founded as a refuge for Quakers. One of a number of radical religious sects that had sprung up about the time of the English Civil War, the Quakers held many controversial beliefs. They believed all persons had an "inner light" that allowed them to commune directly with God. They believed human institutions were, for the most part, unnecessary and, since they believed they could receive revelation directly from God, placed much less importance on the Bible than other Protestants. They were also pacifists and declined to show customary deference to those who were considered to be their social superiors. This and their aggressiveness in denouncing established institutions brought them trouble in both Britain and America.

William Penn, a member of a prominent British family, converted to Quakerism as a young man. Desiring to found a colony as a refuge for Quakers, in 1681 he sought and received from Charles II a grant of land in America as payment of a large debt the king had owed Penn's late father.

Penn advertised his colony widely in Europe, offered generous terms on land, and guaranteed a representative assembly and full religious freedom. He personally went to America to set up his colony, laying out the city of Philadelphia. He succeeded in maintaining peaceful relations with the Indians.

In the years that followed, settlers flocked to Pennsylvania from all over Europe. The colony grew and prospered, and its fertile soil made it not only attractive to settlers, but also a large exporter of grain to Europe and the West Indies.

Delaware, at first part of Pennsylvania, was granted by Penn a separate legislature, but until the American Revolution, Pennsylvania's proprietary governors also governed Delaware.

TEST TIP

Remember the multiple-choice section of the AP U.S. History exam gives you 55 minutes to answer 55 questions. That's one minute per question. Learning to pace yourself will help ensure that you have enough time to comfortably respond to every item.

The 18th Century

Economy and Population

British authorities continued to regulate the colonial economy, though usually without going so far as to provoke unrest. An exception was the Molasses Act of 1733, which would have been disastrous for New England merchants. In this case, customs agents wisely declined to enforce the act stringently and averted trouble. However, to enact a law and then not enforce it set a precedent that would cause problems for Parliament in the future.

The constant drain of wealth from America to Britain, created by the mother country's mercantilistic policies, led to a corresponding drain in hard currency (gold and silver). The artificially low prices that this shortage of money created for American goods was even more advantageous to British buyers. When colonial legislatures responded by endeavoring to create paper money, British authorities blocked such moves. Despite these hindrances, the colonial American economy remained, for the most part, extremely prosperous and the tax rate in the colonies was much less than it was in England.

America's population continued to grow rapidly in the first half of the 18th century, both from natural increases due to prosperity and a healthy environment, and from large-scale immigration, not only of English, but also of such other groups as Scots-Irish and Germans.

The Germans were prompted to migrate because of frequent wars, poverty, and religious persecution in their homeland. They found Pennsylvania especially attractive and settled there fairly close to the frontier, where land was more readily available. They eventually came to be called the "Pennsylvania Dutch."

The Scots-Irish, Scottish Presbyterians who had been living in northern Ireland for several generations, left their homes because of high rent and economic depression. In America they settled even farther west than the Germans, on or beyond the frontier in the Appalachians in what became known as the backcountry. Backcountry residents were less dependent on England and tended to resent both political and religious authority.

The Early Wars of the Empire

Between 1689 and 1763, Britain and its American colonies fought a series of four wars with Spain, France, and France's Indian allies, in part to determine who would dominate North America.

The first, King William's War (1689–1697), was a limited conflict involving no major battles in America, though it did bring a number of bloody and terrifying border raids by Indians.

The second, Queen Anne's War (1702–1713), brought America twelve years of sporadic fighting against France and Spain. The war ended with the Treaty of Utrecht, the terms of which gave Britain major territorial gains and trade advantages.

In 1739, war once again broke out with France and Spain in King George's War. American troops played an active role, accompanying the British on several important expeditions and suffering thousands of casualties. In 1745, an all-New England army, led by William Pepperrell, captured the powerful French fortress of Louisbourg at the mouth of the St. Lawrence River. However, the 1748 Treaty of Aix-la-Chapelle gave Louisbourg back to France in exchange for lands in India, much to the disgust of American colonists.

Georgia

With this almost constant imperial warfare in mind, it was decided to found a colony as a buffer between South Carolina and Spanish-held Florida. A group of British philanthropists, led by General James Oglethorpe, obtained a charter for such a colony in 1732, to be located between the Savannah and Altamaha rivers and to be populated by inmates in debtors' prisons and others struggling economically.

The philanthropist trustees, who were to control the colony for twenty-one years before it reverted to royal authority, made elaborate and detailed rules to mold the new colony's society as they felt best. As a result, relatively few settlers came, and those who did complained endlessly. By 1752, Oglethorpe and his colleagues acknowledged that their efforts were a failure and Georgia became a royal colony.

Table 4.1 English Colonies in America

Colony	Year Founded	Region	Founder	Dominant Religion	Government	Original Purpose
Roanoke	1585	Southern	Sir Walter Raleigh			Establish English colony in New World
Virginia	1607	Southern	John Smith	Anglican	Royal	Trade and profits
Plymouth	1620	New England	William Bradford	Puritan	Corporate	Religious freedom for Separatists
New York	1626	Middle	Peter Minuit	None	Proprietary, then royal	Trade and profits
Massachusetts Bay	1630	New England	John Winthrop	Puritan	Corporate	Religious freedom for Puritans
New Hampshire	1630	New England	John Mason	Puritan	Corporate, then royal	Religious and economic freedom
Maryland	1634	Middle	George Calvert	None	Proprietary	Religious freedom for Catholics
Connecticut	1636	New England	Thomas Hooker	Puritan	Corporate	Religious and economic freedom
Rhode Island	1636	New England	Roger Williams	None	Corporate	Religious freedom
Delaware	1638	Middle	Peter Minuit	None	Proprietary	Trade and profits
North Carolina	1653	Southern	Group of proprietors	Anglican	Proprietary	Trade and profits
New Jersey	1660	Middle	Lord Berkeley	None	Proprietary	Trade and profits
South Carolina	1670	Southern	Group of proprietors	Anglican	Proprietary	Trade and profits
Pennsylvania	1682	Middle	William Penn	None	Proprietary	Religious freedom for Quakers
Georgia	1733	Southern	James Oglethorpe	Anglican	Proprietary, then royal	Debtor colony

The Enlightenment

As the eighteenth century progressed, Americans came to be influenced by European ways of thought, culture, and society. Some Americans embraced the European intellectual movement known as the "Enlightenment."

The key concept of the Enlightenment was rationalism—the belief that human reason was adequate to solve all of mankind's problems and, correspondingly, much less faith was needed in the central role of God as an active force in the universe.

A major English political philosopher of the Enlightenment was John Locke. Writing partially to justify England's 1688 Glorious Revolution, he strove to find in the social and political world the sort of natural laws Isaac Newton had recently discovered in the physical realm. He held that such natural laws included the rights of life, liberty, and property; that to secure these rights people submit to governments; and that governments which abuse these rights may justly be overthrown. His writings were enormously influential in America, though usually indirectly, by way of early eighteenth-century English political philosophers. Americans tended to equate Locke's law of nature with the universal law of God.

DID YOU KNOW?

Founded in 1636, Harvard is the nation's oldest college. It takes its name from John Harvard, a Charlestown, Massachusetts, minister who left the institution his library and half of his estate when he died in 1638. Harvard trained most of the educated clergy in New England in its first hundred years.

The most notable Enlightenment thinker in America was Benjamin Franklin. While Franklin never denied the existence of God, he focused his attention on human reason and what it could accomplish.

The Great Awakening

Of much greater impact on the lives of the common people in America was the movement known as the Great Awakening. It consisted of a series of religious revivals occurring throughout the colonies from the late 1720s to the 1740s. Preachers such as Dutch Reformed Theodore Frelinghuysen, Presbyterians William and Gilbert Tennent, and Congregationalist Jonathan Edwards—best known for his sermon "Sinners in the Hands of an Angry God"—proclaimed a message of God's sovereignty and personal repentance and faith in Jesus Christ for salvation from an otherwise certain eternity in hell. The most dynamic preacher of the Great Awakening was Englishman George Whitefield, who traveled through the colonies several times, speaking persuasively to crowds of up to 30,000.

The Great Awakening had several important results. America's religious community came to be divided between the "Old Lights," who rejected the great Awakening, and the "New Lights," who accepted it—and sometimes suffered persecution because of their fervor. A number of colleges were founded (many of them today's Ivy League schools) primarily for the purpose of training New Light ministers. The Great Awakening also fostered a greater readiness to challenge the claims of established authority (in this case, religious authority) alongside a fixed standard (in this case the Bible) and to reject any claims it found wanting. This tendency to resist religious authority would make resistance to political authority more acceptable in subsequent years. One result of the Great Awakening was the proliferation of Protestant denominations, as doctrinal differences often led to divisions in congregations.

(Before taking the quiz noted below, please review the summary timeline for this chapter on the following page.)

The English Colonies (1607–1754)

Historical Timeline (1607–1754)

1607	Jamestown colony founded
1608	Champlain founds Quebec
1611	First Virginia tobacco crop harvested
1619	First Africans arrive in Virginia
1620	Plymouth Colony founded House of Burgesses established in Virginia
1622	Powhatan Confederacy attacks Virginia settlers
1630	Massachusetts Bay Colony founded
1635	Roger Williams establishes Rhode Island after being expelled from Massachusetts Bay Colony
1636	Harvard College founded
1637	Anne Hutchinson expelled from Massachusetts Bay Colony
1642–1648	English Civil War brings Cromwell to power
1647	Massachusetts law requires a public school in every town
1649	King Charles I executed
1660	Charles II becomes king
1662	Half-Way Covenant established in New England
1676	Bacon's Rebellion in Virginia
1681	Pennsylvania established by William Penn
1688	Glorious Revolution in England William and Mary succeed James II
1692	Witchcraft trials begin in Salem
1714	George I takes throne, beginning Hanover dynasty
1734	Great Awakening begins
1739	Stono Rebellion in North Carolina George Whitefield begins preaching in America
1743	Benjamin Franklin sets up the American Philosophical Society
1754	French and Indian War begins Albany Plan of Union

Chapter 5

The New Nation (1754–1800)

England's American colonies enjoyed a period of salutary (benign) neglect through the first half of the 18th century. They provided huge profits, raw materials, and a growing market for English manufactured goods. Many of the laws regulating trade that had been passed over the previous century, such as the Navigation Acts and the Sugar Act, had not been strictly enforced and the colonies had prospered with the low level of interference in their internal affairs. A costly war with France was about to change this mutually beneficial situation. Even though England would end up winning the war, it would lose the American colonies in the aftermath.

The French and Indian War

The Treaty of Aix-la-Chapelle (1748), ending King George's War, provided little more than a breathing space before the next European and imperial war. England and France continued on a collision course as France determined to take complete control of the Ohio Valley and western Pennsylvania.

British authorities ordered colonial governors to resist this, and Virginia's Robert Dinwiddie, already involved in speculation on the Ohio Valley lands, was eager to comply. George Washington, a young major of the Virginia militia, was sent to western

Pennsylvania to request the French to leave. When the French declined, Washington was sent in 1754 with 200 Virginia militiamen to expel them. After success in a small skirmish, Washington was forced by superior numbers to fall back on his hastily built Fort Necessity and then to surrender.

The war these operations initiated spread to Europe two years later, where it was known as the Seven Years' War. In America, it later came to be known as the French and Indian War.

While Washington skirmished with the French in western Pennsylvania, delegates of seven colonies met in Albany, New York, to discuss common plans for defense. Delegate Benjamin Franklin proposed a plan for an intercolonial government. While the other colonies showed no support for the idea, it was an important precedent for the concept of uniting in the face of a common enemy, although Britain was uninterested in the concept.

To deal with the French threat, the British dispatched Major General Edward Braddock with several regiments of British regular troops. Braddock marched overland toward the French outpost of Fort Duquesne, at the place where the Monongahela and Allegheny rivers join to form the Ohio River. About eight miles short of his goal, a small force of French and Indians ambushed him. Two-thirds of the British regulars, including Braddock himself, were killed. However, Britain bounced back from this humiliating defeat and several others that followed, and under the leadership of its capable and energetic prime minister, William Pitt, had, by 1760, taken Quebec and Montreal and virtually liquidated the French empire in North America.

By the Treaty of Paris of 1763, which officially ended hostilities, Britain gained all of Canada and all of what is now the United States east of the Mississippi River. France lost all of its North American holdings. This was a huge territorial gain for the British, but it actually made it more difficult to govern the American colonies and increased tension between the colonies and the mother country, particularly Parliament.

Americans at the end of the French and Indian War were proud to be part of the victorious British Empire and proud of the important role they had played in making it so. Most felt affection for Great Britain, and thoughts of independence would not have crossed their minds. But the seeds of trouble were planted with the terms of the Treaty of Paris. Gaining an enormous amount of territory in the colonies required a commitment of troops, who were expensive to maintain. In addition, a large contingent of British soldiers remained in the American colonies following the war. This also was a drain on the British treasury. As Parliament sought sources for funding these troops as well as financing the debt acquired during the war, it looked toward the prosperous American colonies.

The Coming of the American Revolution

Writs of Assistance

While Americans' feelings toward Great Britain were predominantly pride and affection, many British officials felt contemptuous of Americans and were eager to increase imperial control over them beyond anything that had previously been attempted. This drive to gain new authority over the colonies and the increased taxes that accompanied it beginning in 1763 led directly and inexorably to American independence.

Even before that time, the writs of assistance cases had demonstrated that Americans would not resist restrictions of their freedom.

In 1761, a young Boston lawyer named James Otis argued before a Massachusetts court that writs of assistance (general search warrants issued to help royal officials stop evasion of Britain's mercantilist trade restrictions) were contrary to natural law. Although he lost his case, he made his point and others in the colonies joined in protesting against the writs.

Grenville and the Stamp Act

In 1763, the strongly anti-American George Grenville became prime minister and set out to solve some of the empire's more pressing problems. Chief among these was the large national debt incurred in the recent war.

Another concern was the cost of defending the American frontier, recently the scene of a bloody Indian uprising led by an Ottawa chief named Pontiac. Goaded by French traders, Pontiac had aimed to drive the entire white population into the sea. While failing in that endeavor, he had succeeded in killing a large number of settlers along the frontier.

Grenville created a comprehensive program to deal with these problems and moved energetically to put it into effect. He sent the Royal Navy to suppress American smuggling and vigorously enforce the Navigation Acts. He also issued the Proclamation of 1763, forbidding white settlement west of the crest of the Appalachians, in hopes of keeping the Indians happy and the settlers close to the coast and thus easier to control.

In 1764, Grenville pushed the Sugar Act (also known as the Revenue Act) through Parliament. Aimed at raising revenue by taxing goods imported by the Americans, the Sugar Act cut in half the duties imposed by the Molasses Act. However, unlike the

Molasses Act, it was stringently enforced, with accused violators facing trial in admiralty courts without benefit of jury or the normal protections of due process.

Grenville determined to maintain up to 10,000 British regulars in America to control both colonists and Indians and secure passage of the Quartering Act, requiring the colonies in which British troops were stationed to pay for their maintenance. Americans had never before been required to support a standing army in their midst.

Grenville also obtained passage of the Currency Act of 1764, which forbade once and for all any colonial attempts to issue currency not redeemable in gold or silver, making it more difficult for Americans to avoid the constant drain of money that Britain's mercantilist policies were designed to create in the colonies.

Most important, however, Grenville got Parliament to pass the Stamp Act (1765), imposing a direct tax on Americans for the first time. The Stamp Act required Americans to purchase revenue stamps on everything from newspapers to legal documents and would have created an impossible drain on hard currency in the colonies. Because it overlooked the advantage already provided by Britain's mercantilist exploitation of the colonies, Grenville's policy was shortsighted and foolish, yet few in Parliament were inclined to see this.

Americans reacted first with restrained and respectful petitions and pamphlets, in which they pointed out that "taxation without representation is tyranny." From there, resistance progressed to stronger and stronger protests that eventually became violent and involved intimidation of those Americans who had contracted to be the agents for distributing the stamps.

Resistance was particularly intense in Massachusetts, where it was led first by James Otis and then by Samuel Adams, who formed the organization known as the Sons of Liberty.

Other colonies copied Massachusetts's successful tactics while adding some of their own. In Virginia, a young burgess named Patrick Henry introduced seven resolutions denouncing the Stamp Act. Though only the four most moderate of them were passed by the House of Burgesses, newspapers picked up all seven and circulated them widely through the colonies, giving the impression all seven had been adopted. By their denial of Parliament's authority to tax the colonies, they encouraged other colonial legislatures to issue strongly worded statements.

In October 1765, delegates from nine colonies met as the Stamp Act Congress. Assembled by the Massachusetts legislature at the instigation of James Otis, the Stamp Act Congress passed moderate resolutions against the act, asserting that Americans could not be taxed without their consent, given by their representatives. They pointed out that Americans were not, and because of their location could not practically be, truly represented in Parliament and concluded by calling for the repeal of both the Stamp and Sugar Acts. Most important, however, the Stamp Act Congress provided an opportunity for representatives of the colonies to work together, giving political leaders in the various colonies a chance to become acquainted with each other.

Most effective in achieving repeal of the Stamp Act was colonial merchants' nonimportation (boycott) of British goods. Begun as an agreement among New York merchants, the boycott spread throughout the colonies and had a powerful effect on British merchants and manufacturers, who began calling for Parliament to repeal the act.

Meanwhile, the fickle King George III had dismissed Grenville over an unrelated disagreement and replaced him with a Cabinet headed by Charles Lord Rockingham. In March 1766, under the leadership of the new ministry, Parliament repealed the Stamp Act, which ended the boycotts and pacified British merchants. At the same time, however, it passed the Declaratory Act, claiming power to tax or make laws for the Americans "in all cases whatsoever."

Though the Declaratory Act denied exactly the principle Americans had just been at such pains to assert—that of no taxation without representation—the Americans generally ignored it in their exuberant celebration of the repeal of the Stamp Act. Americans continued to eagerly proclaim their loyalty to Great Britain.

DIDYOUKNOW?

The arguments of "no taxation without representation" that were expressed by a number of colonists before the Revolutionary War were partly based in the American tradition of local control. Beginning with the Virginia House of Burgesses in 1619, colonists taxed themselves. When the British Parliament began imposing internal taxes on the colonists, opponents questioned the constitutionality of that practice.

The Townshend Acts

The Rockingham ministry proved to be even shorter lived than Grenville's. It was replaced with a Cabinet dominated by Chancellor of the Exchequer Charles Townshend. Townshend had boasted that he could successfully tax the colonies, and in 1767 Parliament gave him his chance by passing the Townshend Acts, an extensive program of taxes on items imported into the colonies. These taxes came to be known as the Townshend duties. Townshend mistakenly believed the Americans would accept this method while rejecting the use of direct internal taxes. The Townshend Acts also included the use of admiralty courts to try those accused of violations, the use of writs of assistance, and the paying of customs officials out of the fines they levied. Townshend also had the New York legislature suspended for noncompliance with the Quartering Act.

American reaction was at first slow. Philadelphia lawyer John Dickinson wrote an anonymous pamphlet entitled "Letters from a Farmer in Pennsylvania," in which he pointed out in moderate terms that the Townshend Acts violated the principle of no taxation without representation and that if Parliament could suspend the New York legislature, it could do the same to others. At the same time he urged a restrained response on the part of his fellow Americans.

In February 1768, the Massachusetts legislature, at the urging of Samuel Adams, passed the Massachusetts Circular Letter, reiterating Dickinson's mild arguments and urging other colonial legislatures to pass petitions calling on Parliament to repeal the acts. Had the British government done nothing, the matter might have passed quietly.

Instead, British authorities acted decisively. They ordered that if the letter was not withdrawn, the Massachusetts legislature should be dissolved and new elections held. They forbade the other colonial legislatures from taking up the matter, and they also sent four regiments of troops to Boston to prevent intimidation of royal officials and intimidate the populace instead.

The last of these actions was in response to the repeated pleas of the Boston customs agents. Corrupt agents had used technicalities of the confusing and poorly written Sugar and Townshend Acts to entrap innocent merchants and line their own pockets. Mob violence had threatened when agents had seized the ship *Liberty,* belonging to Boston merchant John Hancock. Such incidents prompted the call for troops.

The sending of troops, along with the British authority's repressive response to the Massachusetts Circular Letter, aroused the Americans to resistance. Non-importation was again instituted, and soon British merchants were calling on Parliament to repeal the acts. In March 1770, Parliament, under the new prime minister, Frederick Lord North, repealed all of the taxes except that on tea, which was retained to prove Parliament had the right to tax the colonies if it so desired.

By the time of the repeal, however, friction between British soldiers and Boston citizens had led to an incident in 1770 in which five Bostonians were killed. Although the British soldiers had acted essentially in self-defense, Samuel Adams labeled the incident the "Boston Massacre" and publicized it widely. At their trial the British soldiers were defended by prominent Massachusetts lawyer John Adams and were acquitted on the charge of murder. But word of the killing of American colonists by British soldiers proved effective propaganda for those opposing restrictive British policies.

TEST TIP

On the day of the AP exam, leave your cell phone at home or in your car. When it rings during an AP U.S. History class, it might be embarrassing. If it rings during the AP U.S. History Exam administration, however, it may be a disaster! All electronic devices, including phones, are prohibited in the test room. The test proctor can make you leave the test immediately and cancel your score if he or she sees that you have any of these devices with you.

The Return of Relative Peace

Following the repeal of the Townshend duties, a period of relative peace set in. The tax on tea remained as a reminder of Parliament's claims, but it was easily avoided by widespread smuggling.

Much goodwill had been lost during the period since the new imperial policies began being enforced in 1763, and colonists remained suspicious of the British government. Many Americans believed the events of the previous decade to have been the work of a deliberate conspiracy to take their liberty.

Occasional incidents marred the relative peace. In 1772, a seagoing mob of Rhode Islanders disguised as Indians burned the *Gaspee,* a British customs schooner that had run aground offshore. The *Gaspee*'s captain and crew had alienated Rhode Islanders by their extreme zeal for catching smugglers as well as by their theft and vandalism when ashore.

In response to this incident, British authorities appointed a commission to find the guilty parties and bring them to England for trial. Though those responsible for the burning of the *Gaspee* were never found, this action on the part of the British prompted the colonial legislatures to form Committees of Correspondence to communicate with each other regarding possible threats from the British government.

The Tea Act

The Tea Act of 1773 brought the relative peace in the American colonies to an end.

In desperate financial condition—partially because the Americans were buying the smuggled Dutch tea rather than the taxed British product—the British East India Company sought and obtained from Parliament concessions allowing it to ship tea directly to the colonies rather than only by way of Britain. The result would be that East India Company tea, even with the tax, would be cheaper than smuggled Dutch tea. The colonists would thus, it was hoped, buy the tea, tax and all. The East India Company would be saved and the Americans would be tacitly accepting Parliament's right to tax them.

The Americans, however, proved resistant to this approach, and rather than appearing to admit Parliament's right to tax, they vigorously resisted the cheaper tea. Various methods, including tarring and feathering of tax collectors, were used to prevent the collection of the tax on tea. In most ports, Americans did not allow the tea to be unloaded at the docks.

In Boston, however, pro-British Governor Thomas Hutchinson forced a confrontation by ordering Royal Navy vessels to prevent the tea ships from leaving the harbor. After twenty days this would, by law, result in the cargoes being sold at auction and the tax paid. The night before the time was to expire, December 16, 1773, Bostonians thinly disguised as Indians boarded the ships and threw the tea into the harbor.

Many Americans felt this—the destruction of private property—was going too far, but the reaction of Lord North and Parliament quickly united Americans in support of Boston and in opposition to Britain.

DIDYOUKNOW?

The perhaps 100 participants in the Boston Tea Party choosing to disguise themselves as Mohawk warriors was not merely to avoid identification. It symbolized their identification as Americans, not as British subjects.

The Intolerable Acts

Parliament responded with four acts collectively titled the Coercive Acts (called the Intolerable Acts in the colonies). First, the Boston Port Act closed the port of Boston to all trade until local citizens would agree to pay for the lost tea (they would not). Second, the Massachusetts Government Act greatly increased the power of Massachusetts's royal governor at the expense of the legislature. Third, the Administration of Justice Act provided that royal officials accused of crimes in Massachusetts could be tried elsewhere, where chances of acquittal might be greater. Finally, a strengthened Quartering Act allowed the new governor, General Thomas Gage, to quarter his troops anywhere, including unoccupied private homes.

A further act of Parliament also angered and alarmed Americans. This was the Quebec Act, which extended the province of Quebec to the Ohio River, established Roman Catholicism as Quebec's official religion, and set up for Quebec a government without a representative assembly.

For Americans this was a denial of the hopes and expectations of westward expansion for which they had fought the French and Indian War. New Englanders especially saw it as a threat in that Parliament could establish both autocratic government and the hated Church of England in their colonies as well.

Americans lumped the Quebec Act together with the Coercive Acts and referred to them all as the Intolerable Acts.

In response to the Coercive Acts, the First Continental Congress was called and met in Philadelphia in September 1774. It once again petitioned Parliament for relief but also passed the Suffolk Resolves (so called because they were first passed in Suffolk County, Massachusetts), denouncing the Intolerable Acts and calling for strict non-importation (boycotts) and rigorous preparation of local militia companies in case the British resorted to military force.

The Congress then narrowly rejected a compromise plan, submitted by Joseph Galloway of Pennsylvania, calling for a union of the colonies within the empire and a re-arrangement of relations with Parliament. Most of the delegates felt matters had already gone too far for such a mild measure. Finally, before adjournment, it was agreed that there should be a Second Continental Congress to meet in May of the following year if the colonies' grievances had not been righted by then.

The War for Independence

Lexington and Concord

The British government ignored the First Continental Congress, having decided to teach the Americans a military lesson. More troops were sent to Massachusetts, which was officially declared to be in a state of rebellion. Orders were sent to General Gage to arrest the leaders of the resistance or, failing that, to provoke any sort of confrontation that would allow him to turn British military might loose on the Americans.

Gage decided on a reconnaissance-in-force to find and destroy a reported stockpile of colonial arms and ammunition at Concord, north of Boston. Seven hundred British troops set out on this mission on the night of April 18, 1775. Their movement was detected by American surveillance and news was spread throughout the countryside by dispatch riders Paul Revere and William Dawes.

At the neighboring village of Lexington, Captain John Parker and some seventy Minutemen (militiamen trained to respond at a moment's notice) awaited the British on the village green. As the British approached, a British officer shouted at the Minutemen to lay down their arms and disperse. The Minutemen did not lay down their arms, but did turn to file off the green. A shot was fired, and then the British opened fire and charged. Eight Americans were killed and several others wounded, most shot in the back.

DID YOU KNOW?

Paul Revere was the son of a French Huguenot and a prominent silversmith in Boston whose business was severely affected by British legislation such as the Stamp Act. He became active in the Sons of Liberty and served as an officer for colonial forces during the Revolutionary War.

The British continued to Concord only to find that nearly all of the military supplies they had expected to find had already been moved. Attacked by growing numbers of Minutemen, they began to retreat toward Boston. As the British retreated, Minutemen, swarming from every village for miles around, fired on the column from behind rocks, trees, and stone fences. Only a relief force of additional British troops saved the first column from destruction.

Open warfare had begun, and the myth of British invincibility was destroyed. Militia came in large numbers from all the New England colonies to join the force besieging Gage and his army in Boston.

Bunker Hill

In May 1775, three more British generals, William Howe, Henry Clinton, and John Burgoyne, arrived in Boston urging Gage to further aggressive action. The following month the Americans tightened the noose around Boston by fortifying Breed's Hill (a spur of Bunker Hill), from which they could, if necessary, bombard Boston.

The British determined to remove them by a frontal attack that would demonstrate the awesome power of British arms. Twice the British were thrown back and finally succeeded as the Americans ran out of ammunition. Over a thousand British soldiers were killed or wounded in what turned out to be the bloodiest battle of the war (June 17, 1775). Yet the British had gained very little and remained bottled up in Boston.

Meanwhile in May 1775, American forces under Ethan Allen and Benedict Arnold captured Fort Ticonderoga on Lake Champlain.

Congress, hoping Canada would join in resistance against Britain, authorized two expeditions into Quebec. One, under General Richard Montgomery, took Montreal and then turned toward the city of Quebec. It was met there by the second expedition under Benedict Arnold. The attack on Quebec (December 31, 1775) failed. Montgomery was killed, Arnold wounded, and American hopes for conquering Canada ended.

The Second Continental Congress

While these events were taking place in New England and Canada, the Second Continental Congress met in Philadelphia in May 1775. Congress was divided into two main factions. One was composed mostly of New Englanders and leaned toward declaring independence from Britain. The other, led by John Dickinson of Pennsylvania, drew its strength primarily from the Middle Colonies and was not yet ready to go that far.

Congress took action to deal with the difficult situation facing the colonies by adopting the New England army around Boston, calling on the other colonies to send troops and sending George Washington to command it, passing a "Declaration of the Causes and Necessity for Taking Up Arms" and adopting the "Olive Branch Petition," pleading with King George III to intercede with Parliament to restore peace.

This last overture was virtually ignored in Britain, where the king gave his approval to the Prohibitory Act, declaring the colonies in rebellion and no longer under his protection. Preparations were made for full-scale war against America.

Throughout 1775, most Americans remained deeply loyal to Britain and King George III, despite the king's proclamations declaring them to be in revolt. In Congress, moderates still resisted independence.

In January 1776, Thomas Paine published a pamphlet entitled *Common Sense,* calling for immediate independence. Its arguments were extreme and sometimes illogical and its language intemperate, but it sold widely and may have had much influence in favor of independence. Continued evidence of Britain's intention to carry on the war throughout the colonies also weakened the moderates' resistance to independence. The Prohibitory Act, with its virtual declaration of war against America, convinced many to support colonial independence.

On June 7, 1776, Richard Henry Lee of Virginia introduced a series of formal resolutions in Congress calling for independence and a national government. Accepting these ideas, Congress named two committees. One, headed by John Dickinson, was to work out a framework for a national government. The other was to draft a statement of the reasons for declaring independence. This statement, the Declaration of Independence, was primarily the work of Thomas Jefferson of Virginia. It was a restatement of political ideas by then commonplace in America, showing why the former colonists felt justified in separating from Great Britain. Jefferson included both philosophical and practical arguments in his eloquent phrasings. Congress formally adopted it on July 4, 1776.

TEST TIP

If you change your answer to a multiple-choice question, be sure to erase your original answer completely. Otherwise, the machines that grade these sections may record your response as a wrong answer.

Washington Takes Command

Britain, meanwhile, was preparing a massive effort to conquer the United States. Gage was removed for being too timid and top command went to Howe. To supplement the British army, large numbers of troops were hired from various German principalities. Since many of these Germans came from the state of Hesse-Kassel, Americans referred to all such troops as Hessians.

Although the London authorities desired a quick and smashing campaign, General Howe and his brother, British naval commander Richard Admiral Lord Howe, intended to move slowly, using their powerful force to cow the Americans into signing loyalty oaths.

In March 1776, Washington placed some of the large cannons that had been captured at Ticonderoga on Dorchester Heights, overlooking Boston, forcing the British to evacuate the city for the remainder of the fighting.

The British shipped their troops to Nova Scotia and then, together with large reinforcements from Britain, landed that summer at New York City. They hoped to find many loyalists there and make that city the key to their campaign to subdue America.

Washington anticipated the move and was waiting at New York, which Congress had ordered should be defended. However, the under-trained, under-equipped, and badly outnumbered American army was no match for the powerful forces under the Howes. Defeated at the Battle of Long Island (August 27, 1776), Washington narrowly avoided being trapped there (an escape partially due to the Howes' slowness). Defeated again at the Battle of Washington Heights (August 29–30, 1776) on Manhattan, Washington was forced to retreat across New Jersey with the aggressive British General Lord Cornwallis, a subordinate of General William Howe, in pursuit. By December, what was left of Washington's army had escaped into Pennsylvania.

With his victory almost complete, Howe decided to wait till spring to finish annihilating Washington's army. Scattering his troops in small detachments so as to hold all of New Jersey, he went into winter quarters.

Washington preparing to cross the Delaware. (Currier and Ives print.)

Washington, with his small army melting away as demoralized soldiers deserted, decided on a bold stroke. On Christmas night 1776, his army crossed the Delaware River and struck the Hessians at Trenton. The Hessians, still groggy from their hard-drinking Christmas party, were easily defeated. A few days later Washington defeated a British force at Princeton (January 3, 1777).

> **DID YOU KNOW?**
>
> During the American Revolution, about one-third of American colonists were loyalists who supported Great Britain. Perhaps the most famous loyalist was William Franklin, the illegitimate son of Benjamin Franklin. The famed statesman never forgave his son for his loyalist beliefs, essentially writing him out of his will with the comment, "The part he acted against me in the late war, which is of public notoriety, will account for my leaving him no more of an estate he endeavoured to deprive me of."

Howe was so shocked by these two unexpected defeats that he pulled his outposts back close to New York. Much of New Jersey was regained. Those who had signed British loyalty oaths in the presence of Howe's army were now at the mercy of their patriot neighbors, and Washington's army was saved from disintegration.

Early in the war France began making covert shipments of arms to the Americans. This it did, not because the French government loved freedom (it did not), but because it hated Britain and saw the war as a way to weaken Britain by depriving it of its colonies. Arms shipments from France were vital for the Americans.

Saratoga and Valley Forge

During the summer of 1777, the British home authorities adopted an elaborate campaign plan urged on them by General Burgoyne. According to the plan, Burgoyne himself would lead an army southward from Canada along the Lake Champlain corridor while another army under Howe moved up the Hudson River to join forces with Burgoyne at Albany. This, it was hoped, would cut off New England and allow the British to subdue that region, which they considered the hotbed of the "rebellion."

Howe had other ideas and shipped his army by sea to Chesapeake Bay, hoping to capture the American capital, Philadelphia, and destroy Washington's army at the same time. At Brandywine Creek (September 1, 1777), Washington tried but failed to stop Howe's advance. The American army, though badly beaten, remained intact. Howe occupied Philadelphia as the Congress fled westward to York, Pennsylvania.

In early October, Washington attempted to drive Howe out of Philadelphia. His attack at Germantown, though at first successful, failed, at least partially due to thick fog and the still imperfect level of training in the American army, both of which contributed to confusion among the troops. Thereafter, Howe settled down to comfortable winter quarters in Philadelphia, and Washington and his army to very uncomfortable ones at nearby Valley Forge. Far to the north, the British strategy that Howe had ignored was going badly awry.

Burgoyne's advance began well, but slowed as the Americans placed obstructions on the rough wilderness trails by which his army, including numerous cannon and much bulky baggage, had to advance. A diversionary force of British troops and Iroquois Indians under the command of Colonel Barry St. Leger swung east of Burgoyne's column, but although it defeated and killed American General Nicholas Herkimer at the Battle of Oriskany (August 6, 1777), it was finally forced to withdraw to Canada.

In mid-August, a detachment of Burgoyne's force was defeated by New England militia under General John Stark near Bennington in what is now Vermont. By autumn Burgoyne found his way blocked by an American army: continentals (American regular troops such as those that made up most of Washington's army, paid, in theory at least, by Congress); and New England militia, under General Horatio Gates, at Saratoga, about thirty miles north of Albany. Burgoyne's two attempts to break through (September 19 and October 7, 1777) were turned back by the Americans under the brilliant battlefield leadership of Benedict Arnold. On October 17, 1777, Burgoyne surrendered to Gates.

The American victory at Saratoga convinced the French to join openly in the war against England. Eventually, the Spanish (1779) and the Dutch (1780) joined as well, and England was faced with a world war.

The British Move South

The new circumstances brought a change in British strategy. With fewer troops available for service in America, the British would have to depend more on loyalists, and since they imagined that larger numbers of these existed in the South than elsewhere, it was there they turned their attention.

Howe was relieved and replaced by General Henry Clinton, who was ordered to abandon Philadelphia and march to New York. In doing so, he narrowly avoided defeat at the hands of Washington's army—much improved after a winter's drilling at Valley Forge under the direction of Prussian nobleman Baron von Steuben—at the Battle of Monmouth, New Jersey (June 28, 1778).

Clinton was thenceforth to maintain New York as Britain's main base in America while detaching troops to carry out the new Southern strategy. In November 1778, the British easily conquered Georgia. Late the following year Clinton moved on South Carolina with a land and naval force, and in May 1780, U.S. General Benjamin Lincoln surrendered Charleston. Clinton then returned to New York, leaving Cornwallis to continue the Southern campaign.

Congress, alarmed at the British successes, sent General Horatio Gates to lead the forces opposing Cornwallis. Gates blundered to a resounding defeat at the Battle of Camden in South Carolina (August 16, 1780).

The general outlook seemed bad for America at that point in the war. Washington's officers grumbled about their pay in arrears. The army was understrength and then suffered successive mutinies by the Pennsylvania and New Jersey troops. Benedict Arnold went over to the British as a traitor. In short, the British seemed to be winning the contest of endurance. This outlook was soon to change.

In the West, George Rogers Clark, acting under the auspices of the state of Virginia, led an expedition down the Ohio River and into the area of present-day Illinois and Indiana, defeating a British force at Vincennes, Indiana, and securing the area north of the Ohio River for the United States.

TEST TIP

In addition to the 55 multiple-choice questions, the redesigned AP U.S. History exam features new short-answer writing questions that focus on students' use of particular historical thinking skills.

In the South, Cornwallis began to move northward toward North Carolina, but on October 7, 1780, American frontiersmen at the Battle of Kings Mountain in South Carolina defeated a detachment of his force, under the leadership of Major Patrick Ferguson. To further increase the problems facing the British, Cornwallis had unwisely moved north without bothering to secure South Carolina first. The result was that the British would no sooner leave an area than American militia or guerilla bands, such as that under Francis Marion ("the Swamp Fox"), were once again in control and able to deal with those who had expressed loyalty to Britain in the presence of Cornwallis's army.

To command the continental forces in the South, Washington sent his most able subordinate, military genius Nathaniel Greene. Greene's brilliant strategy led to a crushing victory at Cowpens, South Carolina (January 17, 1781), by troops under Greene's subordinate, General Daniel Morgan of Virginia. It also led to a near victory by Greene's own force at Guilford Court House, North Carolina (March 15, 1781).

Yorktown

The frustrated and impetuous Cornwallis now abandoned the Southern strategy and moved north into Virginia. Clinton, disgusted at this departure from the plan, sent instructions for Cornwallis to take up a defensive position and wait for further orders. Against his better judgment Cornwallis did so, selecting Yorktown, Virginia, on a peninsula that reaches into Chesapeake Bay between the York and James rivers.

Washington now saw and seized the opportunity this presented. With the aid of a French fleet that took control of Chesapeake Bay and a French army that joined him in sealing off the land approaches to Yorktown, Washington succeeded in trapping Cornwallis. After three weeks of siege, Cornwallis surrendered on October 17, 1781.

The War at Sea

Britain had other problems as well during the war. U.S. Navy ships, as well as privateers (privately owned vessels outfitted with guns and authorized by a warring government to capture enemy merchant ships for profit), preyed on the British merchant marine. John Paul Jones, the most famous of American naval leaders, captured ships and carried out audacious raids along the coast of Britain itself. French and Spanish naval forces also struck against various outposts of the British Empire.

The Treaty of Paris of 1783

News of the debacle at Yorktown brought the collapse of Lord North's ministry, and the new Cabinet opened peace negotiations. The extremely able American negotiating team was composed of Benjamin Franklin, John Adams, and John Jay. The negotiations continued for some time, delayed by French and Spanish maneuvering. When it became apparent that France and Spain were planning to achieve an agreement unfavorable to the United States, the American envoys negotiated a separate treaty with Britain.

The final agreement became known as the Treaty of Paris, which was signed on September 3, 1783, and ratified by the Continental Congress on January 14, 1784. Its terms stipulated the following:

1. The United States was recognized as an independent nation by the major European powers, including Britain;
2. Its western boundary was set at the Mississippi River;
3. Its southern boundary was set at 31° north latitude (the northern boundary of Florida);
4. Britain retained Canada but had to surrender Florida to Spain;
5. Private British creditors would be free to collect any debts owed by U.S. citizens; and
6. Congress was to recommend that the states restore confiscated loyalist property.

The Creation of New Governments

The State Constitutions

After the collapse of British authority in 1775, it became necessary to form new state governments. By the end of 1777, ten new state constitutions had been created.

Connecticut and Rhode Island kept their colonial charters, which were republican in nature, simply deleting references to British sovereignty. Massachusetts waited until 1780 to complete the adoption of its new constitution. The constitutions ranged from such extremely democratic models as the virtually unworkable Pennsylvania constitution (soon abandoned), in which a unicameral legislature ruled with few checks or balances, to more reasonable frameworks such as those of Maryland and Virginia, which included more safeguards against popular excesses.

Massachusetts voters set an important precedent by insisting that a constitution should be made by a special convention rather than the legislature. This would make the constitution superior to the legislature and, it was hoped, ensure that the legislature would be subject to the constitution.

Most state constitutions included bills of rights—a list of things states were required to enforce to protect the rights of citizens.

The Articles of Confederation

In the summer of 1776, Congress appointed a committee to begin devising a framework for a national government. When completed, this document was known as the Articles of Confederation. John Dickinson, who had played a leading role in writing the Articles, believed a strong national government was needed; but by the time Congress finished revising them, the Articles went to the opposite extreme of preserving the sovereignty of the states and creating a very weak national government.

The Articles of Confederation provided for a unicameral Congress in which each state would have one vote, as had been the case in the Continental Congress. Executive authority under the Articles would be vested in a committee of thirteen, one member from each state. In order to amend the Articles, the unanimous consent of all the states was required.

The Articles of Confederation government was empowered to make war, make treaties, determine the number of troops and amount of money each state should contribute to the war effort, settle disputes between states, admit new states to the Union, and borrow money. It was, however, *not* empowered to levy taxes, raise troops, or regulate commerce.

Ratification of the Articles of Confederation was delayed by a disagreement over the future status of the lands that lay to the west of the original thirteen states. Some states, notably Virginia, held extensive claims to these lands based on their original colonial charters. Maryland, which had no such claim, withheld ratification until 1781 when Virginia agreed to surrender its western claims to the new national government.

DIDYOUKNOW?

Was John Hanson actually the first American president? Although George Washington is commonly identified as the first president of the United States, seven presidents actually served before him—under the Articles of Confederation. Some argue that Payton Randolph, who served as president of the Continental Congress but died before the Declaration of Independence was signed, was our first president. Others argue for Hanson, who governed from November 1781 to November 1782.

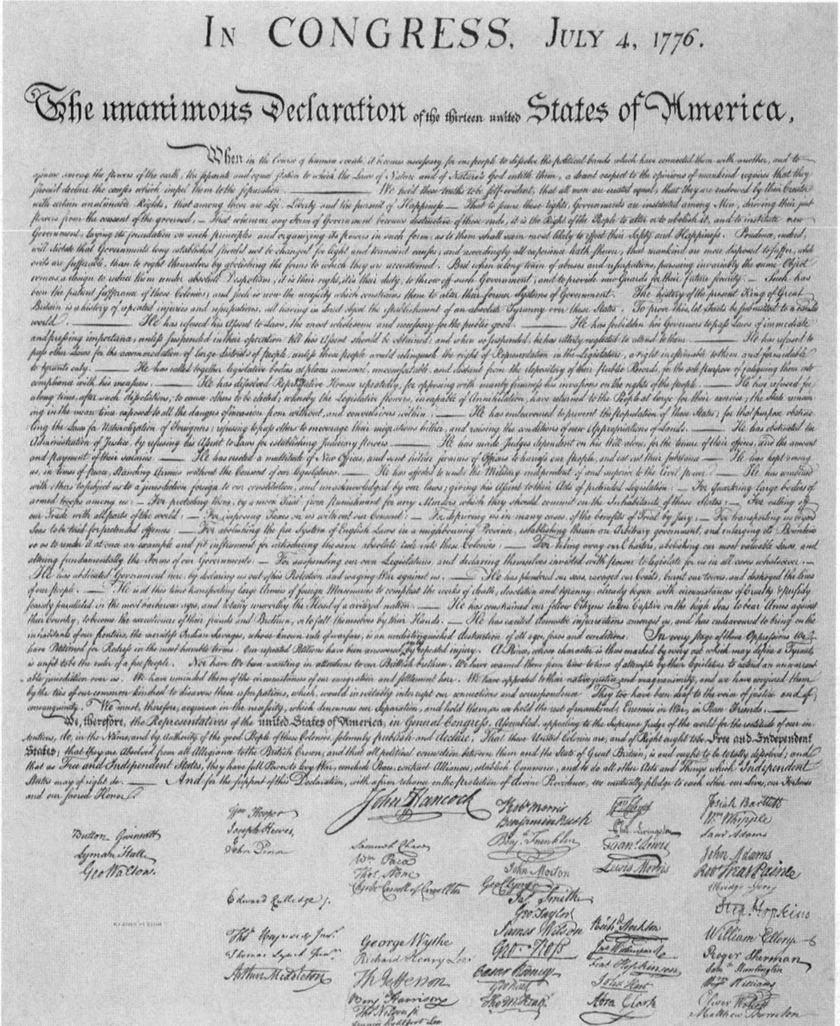

IN CONGRESS, JULY 4, 1776.

The unanimous Declaration of the thirteen united States of America,

Declaration of Independence. (Courtesy of the National Archives.)

Meanwhile, the country was on its way to deep financial trouble. Unable to do more than request taxes from the states, Congress resorted to printing large amounts of paper money to finance the war. These inflated "Continentals" were soon worthless. Other financial schemes fell through, and only grants and loans from France and the Netherlands staved off complete financial collapse. A plan to amend the Articles to give Congress power to tax was stopped by the lone opposition of Rhode Island. The army, whose pay was far in arrears, threatened mutiny. Some of those who favored a stronger national government welcomed this development and, in what became known as the Newburgh Conspiracy (1783), consulted with army second-in-command Horatio Gates as to the possibility of using the army to force the states to surrender more power to the national government. This movement was stopped by a moving personal appeal to the officers by George Washington.

TEST TIP

Essay questions ask you to respond to a direct question using historical facts and interpretation. Because the most important thing that you must do to score well on these questions is fully and directly answer the question, you should begin by asking yourself what, exactly, the question wants you to do. Try to rephrase the question in your own words.

The Trans-Appalachian West and the Northwest Ordinance

For many Americans, the enormous trans-Appalachian frontier represented an opportunity to escape the economic hard times that followed the end of the war.

In 1775, Daniel Boone opened the "Wilderness Road" through the Cumberland Gap and on to the "Bluegrass" region of Kentucky. Others scouted down the Ohio River from Pittsburgh. By 1790, over 100,000 had settled in Kentucky and Tennessee, despite the risk of violent death at the hands of Indians. This risk was made worse by the presence of the British in northwestern military posts that were supposed to have been evacuated at the end of the war. From these posts they supplied Indians with guns and encouraged them to use them on Americans. The Spaniards on the Florida frontier behaved in much the same way.

The settlement of Kentucky and Tennessee increased the pressure for the opening of the lands north of the Ohio River. To facilitate this, Congress passed two important land ordinances in 1785 and 1787.

The Land Ordinance of 1785 provided for the orderly surveying and distribution of land in townships six miles square, each composed of 36 one-square-mile (640-acre) sections, of which one should be set aside for the support of education.

The Northwest Ordinance of 1787 allowed for the entry of new states once 60,000 citizens settled there, provided a bill of rights for settlers, and forbade slavery north of the Ohio River. These new states would enter the Union as equals with the original thirteen states.

These ordinances were probably the most important legislation of the Articles of Confederation government.

DIDYOUKNOW?

Along with the designation of one section for the use of public schools in each township, the federal government reserved four sectors of each township for land bounties to veterans of the American Revolution under the Northwest Ordinance.

The Jay-Gardoqui Negotiations

Economic depression followed the end of the war as the United States remained locked into the disadvantageous commercial system of the British Empire, but without the trade advantages this system had provided.

One man who thought he saw a way out of the economic quagmire was Congress's secretary of foreign affairs, John Jay. In 1784, Jay began negotiating with Spanish minister Don Diego Gardoqui a treaty that would have granted lucrative commercial privileges—benefiting large East Coast merchants such as Jay—in exchange for U.S. acceptance of Spain's closure of the Mississippi River as an outlet for the agricultural goods of the rapidly growing settlements in Kentucky and Tennessee. This the Spanish desired because they feared that extensive settlement in what was then the western part of the United States might lead to American hunger for Spanish-held lands.

When Jay reported this to Congress in the summer of 1786, the West and South were outraged. Negotiations were broken off. Some, angered that Jay could show so little concern for the other sections of the country, talked of dissolving the Union. This helped spur to action those who desired not the dissolution of the Union, but the strengthening of it.

Shays's Rebellion

Nationalists were further stimulated to action by Shays's Rebellion (1786). Economic hard times coupled with high Massachusetts state taxes intended to pay off the state's war debt drove western Massachusetts farmers to desperation. Led by war veteran Daniel Shays, they shut down courts to prevent judges from seizing property or condemning people to debtors' prison for failing to pay their taxes.

The unrest created a disproportionate amount of panic in the rest of the state and the nation. The citizens of Boston subscribed money to raise an army to suppress the rebels. The success of this army, together with timely tax relief, caused the "rebellion" to fizzle out fairly quickly.

Amid the panic caused by the news of the uprising, many observers throughout the colonies came to feel that a stronger government was needed to control such violent public outbursts as those of the western Massachusetts farmers.

TEST TIP

Before you begin writing your response to either an essay or a document-based question on the AP exam, create an outline of your thoughts. Your outline should include a thesis statement and the main points you wish to include in your essay. To help organize your essay, you may wish to divide up your ideas paragraph by paragraph or list them in the order in which you plan to discuss them.

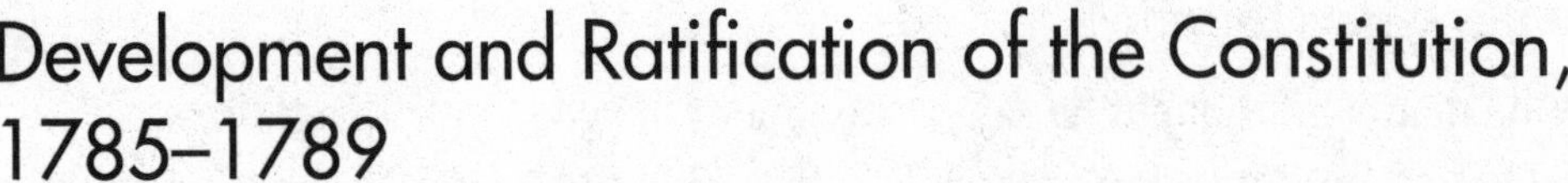

Development and Ratification of the Constitution, 1785–1789

As time went on, the inadequacy of the Articles of Confederation became increasingly apparent. Congress could not compel the states to comply with the terms of the Treaty of Paris of 1783 regarding debts and loyalists' property. The British used this as an excuse for not evacuating their northwestern posts, hoping to be on hand to make the most of the situation when, as they not unreasonably expected, the new government fell to pieces. In any case, Congress could do nothing to force them out of the posts, nor to solve any of the nation's other increasingly pressing problems.

In this seemingly dismal situation, some called for disunion, others for monarchy. Others felt that a republican government could still work if given a better constitution, and they made it their goal to achieve this.

In 1785, a meeting of representatives of Virginia, Maryland, Pennsylvania, and Delaware was held at George Washington's residence, Mount Vernon, for the purpose of discussing current problems of interstate commerce. At their suggestion, the Virginia legislature issued a call for a convention of all the states on the same subject, to meet the following summer in Annapolis, Maryland.

The Annapolis Convention met in September of 1786, but only five states were represented. Among those present, however, were such nationalists as Alexander Hamilton, John Dickinson, and James Madison. With so few states represented, it was decided instead to call for a convention of all the states to meet the following summer in Philadelphia for the purpose of revising the Articles of Confederation.

Table 5.1 Comparing the Articles of Confederation and the Constitution

Issue	Articles of Confederation	Constitution
Levying taxes	Congress could request states to pay taxes	Congress has right to levy taxes on individuals
Federal courts	No system of federal courts	Court system created to deal with issues between citizens, states
Regulation of trade	No provision to regulate interstate trade	Congress has right to regulate trade between states
Executive	No executive with power. President of U.S. merely presided over Congress	Executive branch headed by President who chooses Cabinet and has checks on power of judiciary and legislature

Table 5.1 *Continued*

Issue	Articles of Confederation	Constitution
Amending document	13/13 needed to amend Articles	2/3 of both houses of Congress plus 3/4 of state legislatures or national convention
Representation of states	Each state received 1 vote regardless of size	Upper house (Senate) with 2 votes; lower house (House of Representatives) based on population
Raising an army	Congress could not draft troops and was dependent on states to contribute forces	Congress can raise an army to deal with military situations
Interstate commerce	No control of trade between states	Interstate commerce controlled by Congress
Disputes between states	Complicated system of arbitration	Federal court system to handle disputes between states and residents of different states
Sovereignty	Sovereignty resides in states	Constitution was established as the supreme law of the land
Passing laws	9/13 states needed to approve legislation	50%+1 of both houses plus signature of President

The Constitutional Convention

The men who met in Philadelphia in 1787 were remarkably able, highly educated, and exceptionally accomplished. For the most part they were lawyers, merchants, and planters. Though representing individual states, most thought in national terms. Prominent among them were James Madison, Alexander Hamilton, Gouverneur Morris, Robert Morris, John Dickinson, and Benjamin Franklin. Even Thomas Jefferson, while leery of a strong central government, referred to the representatives from his position representing American interests in Paris as "an assembly of demigods*".

George Washington was unanimously elected to preside, and the enormous respect he commanded helped hold the convention together through difficult times (as it had the Continental Army) and make the product of the convention's work more attractive to the rest of the nation. Washington asked that the representatives not discuss proceedings with others during the Convention's meeting to avoid the distorting and confusing influence of the press and publicity. The delegates agreed.

The delegates shared a basic belief in the innate selfishness of man, which must somehow be kept from abusing the power of government. For this purpose the docu-

* literally half-gods

ment they finally produced contained many checks and balances, designed to prevent the government, or any one branch of the government, from gaining too much power.

Madison, who has been called the "father of the Constitution," devised a plan of national government and persuaded fellow Virginian Edmund Randolph, who was more skilled at public speaking, to introduce it. Known as the "Virginia Plan," it called for an executive branch and two houses of Congress, each based on population.

Smaller states, which would thus have seen their influence decreased, objected and countered with William Paterson's "New Jersey Plan," calling for the continuation of a unicameral legislature with equal representation for the states as well as sharply increased powers for the national government.

A temporary impasse developed that threatened to break up the convention. At this point, Benjamin Franklin played an important role in reconciling the often wrangling delegates, suggesting that the sessions of the convention henceforth begin with prayer (they did) and making various other suggestions that eventually helped the convention arrive at the "Great Compromise." The Great Compromise provided for a Presidency, a Senate with all states represented equally (by two senators each), and a House of Representatives with representation according to population.

Another crisis involved North-South disagreement over the issue of slavery. Here also a compromise was reached. Slavery was neither endorsed nor condemned by the Constitution. Each slave was to count as three-fifths of a person for purposes of apportioning representation and direct taxation on the states (the Three-Fifths Compromise). The federal government was prohibited from stopping the importation of slaves prior to 1808.

The third major area of compromise was the nature of the presidency. This was made easier by the virtual certainty that George Washington would be the first president and the universal trust that he would not abuse the powers of the office or set a bad example for his successors. The result was a strong presidency with control of foreign policy and the power to veto Congress's legislation. Should the president commit a crime, Congress would have the power to impeach him. Otherwise the president would serve for a term of four years and be re-electable without limit. As a check to the possible excesses of democracy, the president was to be elected by an Electoral College, in which each state would have the same number of electors as it did senators and representatives combined. The person with the second-highest total in the Electoral College would be vice president. If no one gained a majority in the Electoral College, the House of Representatives would choose the president.

The new Constitution was to take effect when nine states, through special state conventions, had ratified it.

The Struggle for Ratification

As the struggle over ratification got under way, those favoring the Constitution astutely took for themselves the name Federalists (i.e., advocates of centralized power) and labeled their opponents Antifederalists. The Federalists proved effective in explaining the convention and the document it had produced. *The Federalist Papers,* written as a series of eighty-five newspaper articles by Alexander Hamilton, James Madison, and John Jay, brilliantly expounded the Constitution and demonstrated how it was designed to prevent the abuse of power from any direction. These essays are considered to be the best commentary on the Constitution by those who helped write it.

DIDYOUKNOW?

As president of the Constitutional Convention, George Washington regularly sat in a chair that had been decorated with a painting of the sun. After the group finally agreed on the text of the Constitution, a pleased Benjamin Franklin famously remarked, "I have...often...looked at that [sun] behind the president without being able to tell whether it was rising or setting; but now at length I have the happiness to know that it is a rising and not a setting Sun." (John R. Vile, *The Constitutional Convention of 1787,* Volume 2.)

At first, ratification progressed smoothly, with five states approving it in quick succession. In Massachusetts, however, a tough fight developed. By skillful maneuvering, Federalists were able to win over to their side such popular opponents of the Constitution as Samuel Adams and John Hancock. Others were won over by the promise that a bill of rights would be added to the Constitution, limiting the federal government just as the state governments were limited by their bills of rights. With such promises, Massachusetts ratified it by a narrow margin.

By June 21, 1788, the required nine states had ratified, but the crucial states of New York and Virginia still held out. In Virginia, where George Mason and Patrick Henry opposed the Constitution, the influence of George Washington and the promise of a bill of rights finally prevailed and ratification was achieved there as well. In New York, where Alexander Hamilton led the fight for ratification, *The Federalist Papers,* the promise of a bill of rights, and the news of Virginia's ratification were enough to carry the day.

Only North Carolina and Rhode Island still held out, but they both ratified within the next fifteen months.

In March 1789, George Washington was inaugurated as the nation's first president.

Outline of the United States Constitution

Here is a summary of the U.S. Constitution, including the Preamble (which sets out the purpose of the Constitution), the seven Articles (which explain how the government is organized), and the 27 Amendments ratified by the states since the government of the United States of America began functioning under the Constitution on March 4, 1789 (the first elections under the Constitution took place late the previous year).

Preamble

"We the People of the United States, in order to form a more perfect Union, establish justice, insure domestic tranquility, provide for the common defense, promote the general welfare, and secure the blessings of liberty to ourselves and our posterity, do ordain and establish this Constitution for the United States of America."

Articles of the Constitution

Article I – Legislature

The legislature is divided into two parts—the House of Representatives (435 members currently; determined by proportional representation of the population) and the Senate (100 members currently; two from each state).

The House of Representatives may bring impeachment charges. All bills that concern money must originate in the House. Because of the size of the body, debate is limited except in special cases, where all representatives may meet as the Committee of the Whole. The Speaker of the House presides over the proceedings. Terms of representatives are two years, re-electable without limit, to persons who are at least 25 years of age.

The Senate, originally elected by state legislatures but now by direct election (17th Amendment), approves or rejects presidential nominations and treaties, and serves as the court and jury in impeachment proceedings. Debate within the Senate is unlimited. The President pro tempore usually presides, but the Vice President of the United States is the presiding officer, and may vote to break a tie. Senate terms are for six years, re-electable without limit, to persons who are at least 30 years of age.

Article II – Executive

The President of the United States is elected for a four-year term, originally electable without limit (the 22nd Amendment limits election to two terms), and must be at least 35 years old.

Responsibilities for the President as outlined in the Constitution include acting as the Chief of State, the Chief Executive, Commander-in-Chief of the Armed Forces, the Chief Diplomat, and Chief Legislature.

Article III – Judiciary

While the Constitution describes the Supreme Court in Article III, the actual construction of the court system was accomplished by the Judiciary Act of 1789. The Supreme Court has jurisdiction for federal courts and appellate cases on appeal from lower courts.

Article IV – Interstate Relations

This article guarantees that court decisions and other legal actions (marriage, incorporation, etc.) valid in one state are valid in another. Extradition of criminals (and, originally, runaway slaves) and the exchange of citizenship benefits are likewise guaranteed. Article IV also provides for the admission of new states and guarantees federal protection against invasion and violence for each state. States admitted maintain the same status as the original states. All states are guaranteed a republican form of government.

Article V – Amendment Process

Amendments are proposed by a two-thirds vote of each house of Congress or by a special convention called by Congress upon the request of two-thirds of the state legislatures. Amendments are ratified by three-fourths of the state legislatures or state conventions.

Article VI – Supremacy Clause

Article VI sets up the hierarchy of laws in the United States. The Constitution is the "supreme law of the land" and supersedes treaties. Treaties supersede federal laws, federal laws (later to include federal regulatory agency directives) supersede state constitutions, state laws and local laws, respectively. All federal and state officials, including judges, must take an oath to support and defend the Constitution.

Article VII – Ratification

This article specified the ratification process necessary for the Constitution to take effect. Nine of the original thirteen states had to ratify the Constitution before it became operative.

Amendments to the Constitution

The Amendments to the Constitution guarantee certain individual rights and amend original dictates of the Constitution. The first ten amendments are known as the Bill of Rights, for which Thomas Jefferson provided the impetus.

First Amendment: protects the freedom of religion, speech, press, assembly, as well as the right to petition the government for the redress of grievances (1791)

Second Amendment: protects the right to bear arms[1] (1791)

Third Amendment: ensures that troops will not be housed in private citizens' homes (1791)

Fourth Amendment: protects against unreasonable search and seizure (need for search warrant) (1791)

Fifth Amendment: protects the rights of the accused, including required indictments, double jeopardy, self-incrimination, due process, and just compensation (1791)

Sixth Amendment: guarantees a speedy and public trial, the confrontation by witnesses, and the right to call witnesses on one's own behalf (1791)

Seventh Amendment: guarantees a jury trial (1791)

Eighth Amendment: protects against excessive bail and cruel and unusual punishment (1791)

Ninth Amendment: says that all rights not enumerated are nonetheless retained by the people (1791)

Tenth Amendment: declares that all powers not specifically delegated to the federal government are retained by the states (1791)

Eleventh Amendment: states may not be sued by individuals (1798)

Twelfth Amendment: dictates that electors will cast separate ballots for President and Vice President; in the event of no clear winner, the House will select the President and the Senate the Vice President (1804)

Thirteenth Amendment: abolished slavery (1865)

Fourteenth Amendment: extends citizenship to all persons; made Confederate debt void and Confederate leaders ineligible for public office; states that denied voting rights to qualified citizens (blacks) would have their representation in Congress reduced; conferred "dual" citizenship (both of the United States and of a specific state) on all citizens (1868)

Fifteenth Amendment: extends voting rights to blacks (1870)

Sixteenth Amendment: legalized the income tax (1913)

Seventeenth Amendment: provides for the direct election of senators (1913)

1 In the 2008 decision, *District of Columbia v. Heller*, the Supreme Court struck down the sweeping ban on handguns in Washington, D.C., thus breathing new life into the Second Amendment. The high court had only examined the Second Amendment once before, in 1939, since the Amendment's certification, as part of the Bill of Rights, in 1791.

Eighteenth Amendment: prohibited the general manufacture, sale, and use of alcoholic beverages (1919)

Nineteenth Amendment: extends voting rights to women (1920)

Twentieth Amendment: changed the presidential inauguration date from March 4 to January 20; eliminated the "lame duck" session of Congress (after the November elections) (1933)

Twenty-first Amendment: repealed the 18th Amendment (1933)

Twenty-second Amendment: limits presidents to two terms (1951)

Twenty-third Amendment: gives presidential electoral votes to the District of Columbia (1961)

Twenty-fourth Amendment: prohibits poll taxes (1964)

Twenty-fifth Amendment: changed the order of the presidential line of succession and provides guidelines for presidential disability (1967)

Twenty-sixth Amendment: extends voting rights to eighteen-year-olds (1971)

Twenty-seventh Amendment: restricts the practice of congressional salary adjustment (1992)

TEST TIP

The revised AP exam places an emphasis on historical argumentations. Proficient students should be able to do the following: analyze commonly accepted historical arguments and explain how an argument has been constructed from historical evidence; construct convincing interpretations through analysis of disparate, relevant historical evidence; and evaluate and synthesize conflicting historical evidence to construct persuasive historical arguments.

Separation and Limitation of Powers

Powers Reserved for the Federal Government Only

- Regulate foreign commerce regulation
- Regulate interstate commerce regulation
- Mint money
- Create and establish post offices and post roads

- Regulate naturalization and immigration
- Grant copyrights and patents
- Declare and wage war; declare peace
- Admit new states
- Fix standards for weights and measures
- Raise and maintain an army and a navy
- Govern the federal city (Washington, D.C.)
- Conduct relations with foreign powers
- Universalize bankruptcy laws

Powers Reserved for the State Governments Only

- Conduct and monitor elections
- Establish voter qualifications
- Provide for local governments
- Ratify proposed amendments to the Constitution
- Regulate contracts and wills
- Regulate intrastate commerce
- Provide education for its citizens
- Levy direct taxes (the 16th Amendment permits the federal government to levy direct taxes as well)
- Maintain police power over public health and safety
- Maintain integrity of state borders

Powers Shared by Federal and State Governments

- Taxing, borrowing, and spending money
- Controlling the militia

Restrictions on the Federal Government

- No ex post facto laws
- No bills of attainder
- Two-year limit on appropriation for the military
- No suspension of habeas corpus (except in a crisis)
- One port may not be favored over another
- All guarantees as stated in the Bill of Rights

Restrictions on State Governments

- Treaties, alliances, or confederations may not be entered into
- Letters of marque and reprisal may not be granted
- Contracts may not be impaired
- Money may not be printed or bills of credit emitted
- No import or export taxes
- May not wage war (unless invaded)

Required Percentages of Voting

Actions that require a simple majority include raising taxes, requesting appropriations, declaring war, increasing the national debt, instituting a draft, and introducing impeachment charges (House).

Actions that require a two-thirds majority include overriding a presidential veto, proposing amendments to the Constitution, expelling a member of Congress (in the individual chamber only), ratifying treaties (Senate), acting as a jury for impeachment (Senate), ratifying presidential appointments (Senate).

The action that requires a three-fourths majority is approving a proposed constitutional amendment (states).

The Federalist Era, 1789–1800

The results of the first elections held under the new Constitution made it clear that the fledgling government was going to be controlled by those who had drawn up the document and by their supporters. Few Antifederalists were elected to Congress, and many of the new legislators had served as delegates to the Philadelphia Convention two years before. This Federalist majority immediately set about to draft legislation that would fill in the gaps left by the convention and to erect the structure of a strong central government.

The New Executive

There had never been any doubt who would be the first president. George Washington received virtually all the votes of the presidential electors, and John Adams received the next highest number, thus becoming the vice president. After a triumphal journey from Mount Vernon, Washington was inaugurated in New York City, the temporary seat of government, on April 30, 1789.

TEST TIP

Remember that 90 percent of the AP U.S. History exam focuses on events that took place after 1607 and before 1980.

Congress Builds the New Governmental Structure

The new national legislature immediately acted to honor the Federalist pledge of a bill of rights made to those voters who had hesitated to ratify the new Constitution. Twelve amendments were drafted that embodied the guarantees of personal liberties, most of which had been traditionally enjoyed by English citizens. Ten of these were ratified by the states by the end of 1791, and they became America's Bill of Rights. The first nine spelled out specific guarantees of personal freedoms, such as religion, speech, press, assembly, petition, and a speedy trial by one's peers, and the 10th Amendment reserved to the states all those powers not specifically withheld or granted to the federal government. This last was a concession to those who feared the potential of the central government to usurp the sovereignty of the individual states.

The Establishment of the Federal Court System

The Judiciary Act of 1789 provided for a Supreme Court, with six justices, and invested it with the power to rule on the constitutional validity of state laws. It was to be the interpreter of the "supreme law of the land." A system of district courts was established to serve as courts of original jurisdiction, and three courts of appeal were also provided for.

The Establishment of the Executive Departments

The Constitution had not specified the names or number of the departments of the executive branch. Congress established three—state, treasury, and war—and also the offices of attorney general and postmaster general. President Washington immediately appointed Thomas Jefferson, Alexander Hamilton, and Henry Knox, respectively, to fill the executive posts, and Edmund Randolph became attorney general. These four men were called upon regularly by the president for advice, and they later formed the nucleus of what became known as the Cabinet, although no provision for such was made in the Constitution.

Washington's Administration, 1789–1797

Hamilton's Financial Program

Treasury Secretary Alexander Hamilton, in his "Report on the Public Credit," proposed the funding of the national debt at face value, federal assumption of state debts, and the establishment of a national bank. In his "Report on Manufactures," Hamilton proposed an extensive program for federal stimulation of industrial development, through subsidies and tax incentives. The money needed to fund these programs, proposed Hamilton, would come from an excise tax on distillers and from tariffs on imports.

Opposition to Hamilton's Program

Jefferson and others objected to the funding proposal because it obviously would benefit speculators who had bought up state and confederation obligations at depressed prices, and who would thus profit handsomely by their redemption at face value. The original purchasers, they claimed, should at least share in the windfall. They opposed the tax program because the burden would fall primarily on the small farmers. They saw Hamilton's entire program as enriching a small elite group at the expense of the more worthy common citizen.

The Appearance of Political Parties

Political parties had been considered a detrimental force by the founding fathers because they were seen as contributing to the rise of "factions." Thus, the word "party" does not appear in the Constitution. But differences in philosophy very quickly began to drive the leaders of government into opposing camps—the Federalists and the Democrat-Republicans.

Alexander Hamilton and the Federalists

Hamilton, the theorist of the group who favored a strong central government, interpreted the Constitution as having vested extensive powers in the federal government. This "implied powers" stance claimed that the government was given all powers that were not expressly denied to it. This is the "broad" interpretation.

Thomas Jefferson and the Democrat-Republicans

Jefferson and Madison held the view that any action not specifically permitted in the Constitution was thereby prohibited. This is the "strict" interpretation, and the Republicans opposed the establishment of Hamilton's national bank on this view of government. The Jeffersonian supporters, primarily under the guidance of James Madison, began to organize political groups in opposition to the Federalist program, and called themselves Democrat-Republicans.

Sources of Partisan Support

The Federalists received their strongest support from the business and financial groups in the commercial centers of the Northeast and in the port cities of the South. The strength of the Democrat-Republicans lay primarily in the rural and frontier areas of the South and West.

Table 5.2 Comparing Federalists and Democrat-Republicans

Issue	Federalists	Democrat-Republicans	Notes
National vs. state governments	Favored a strong central government with the power to control commerce, tax, declare war, and make treaties	Sought to limit the role of the national government, favoring local control	This issue, not settled until the Civil War, was the basic philosophical point of contention between the two parties.
French Revolution	Opposed the Revolution and opposed American support for the anti-monarchy group	Supported the popular forces in the French Revolution and favored American assistance	The debt of America to France for its assistance during the American Revolution was seen as due and unpaid by the Democrat-Republicans.
Jay Treaty	Supported as an effort to build better relations with Britain	Opposed. More positive relations with France are favored.	The Jay Treaty was seen by the Democrat-Republicans as an attempt to dump cheap British imports in the American market.
Alien and Sedition Acts	Supported as necessary to prevent growth of Democrat-Republicans and to limit criticism of Federalist officials	Opposed, along with the enlarged army, as a threat to citizens' individual liberties.	Criticized by Jefferson and Madison in the Kentucky and Virginia Resolutions, where the doctrine of nullification was first explained.
Area of support	New England	South and West	Mid-Atlantic states moved from the Federalist to the Democrat-Republicans column, particularly after 1798.
Hamilton's economic plans	Supported enthusiastically	Opposed. Hamilton's plans were seen as aiding his cronies, helping Northern states that had not yet paid off their debts; and generally weakening the power of the states.	The proposal to establish the national bank became the point of greatest contention and provided the first open break between Jefferson and Hamilton.

Foreign and Frontier Affairs

The French Revolution

When revolutionary France went to war with the European powers in 1792, Washington's response was a Proclamation of Neutrality. Most Democrat-Republicans felt sympathy for the French as they saw direct parallels between the French and American Revolutions. Federalists, on the other hand, identified more with the monarchical British. French representative Citizen Genet tried to encourage popular support and funds in this country for the French government. His campaign embarrassed Washington. American merchants traded with both sides, though the most lucrative business was carried on with the French West Indies. This brought retaliation by the British, who began to seize American merchant ships and force their crews into service with the British navy.

Jay Treaty with Britain (1794)

John Jay negotiated a treaty with the British attempting to settle the conflict at sea, as well as to curtail English agitation of their Indian allies on the western borders. The agreement actually settled few of the issues and merely bought time for the new nation in the worsening international conflict. Jay was severely criticized for his efforts, and was even hanged in effigy, but the Senate accepted the treaty as the best possible resolution under the circumstances.

Pinckney Treaty with Spain (1795)

Thomas Pinckney was invited to the Spanish court to strengthen what Madrid perceived to be its deteriorating position on the American frontier. The result was the Pinckney Treaty, ratified by the Senate in 1796, in which the Spanish opened the Mississippi River to American traffic, including the right of deposit in the port city of New Orleans, and recognized the 31st parallel as the northern boundary of Florida.

Frontier Problems

Indian tribes on the northwest and southwest borders were increasingly resisting the encroachment on their lands by American settlers. British authorities in Canada were encouraging the Indians in their depredations against frontier settlements.

In 1794, General Anthony Wayne decisively defeated the Indians at the Battle of Fallen Timbers, and the resulting Treaty of Greenville cleared the Ohio territory of Indian tribes.

Internal Problems

The Whiskey Rebellion (1794)

Western farmers refused to pay the excise tax on whiskey that formed the backbone of Hamilton's revenue program. When a group of Pennsylvania farmers terrorized the tax collectors, President Washington sent out a federalized militia force of some 15,000 men, and the rebellion evaporated, thus strengthening the credibility of the young government.

Land Policy

As the original thirteen states ceded their Western land claims to the new federal government, new states were organized and admitted to the Union, thus strengthening the ties of the Western farmers to the central government (Vermont, 1791; Kentucky, 1792; and Tennessee, 1796).

John Adams' Administration, 1797–1801

The Election of 1796

In the 1796 presidential campaign John Adams was the Federalist candidate and Thomas Jefferson ran under the opposition banner of the Democrat-Republicans. John Adams was elected president. Since Jefferson received the second-highest number of electoral votes, he became vice president. Thus, a Federalist president and a Democrat-Republican vice president served together, an obviously awkward arrangement. Adams was a brilliant lawyer and statesman, but too dogmatic and uncompromising to be an effective politician, and he endured a very frustrating and unproductive term in office.

The XYZ Affair

A three-man delegation was sent to France in 1798 to persuade the French to stop harassing American shipping. When they were solicited for a bribe by three subordinates of the French Minister Talleyrand, they indignantly refused, and their report of this insult produced outrage at home. Adams stood firm in the crisis. The cry "millions for defense, but not one cent for tribute" was raised, and public feelings against the French ran high. Since Talleyrand's officials were unnamed in the dispatches, the incident became known as the "XYZ Affair."

Quasi-War, 1798–1799

This uproar moved Adams to suspend all trade with the French, and American ship captains were authorized to attack and capture armed French vessels. Congress created the Department of the Navy, and war seemed imminent. In 1800, the new French government, now under Napoleon, signed a new treaty, and the peace was restored. Adams believed avoiding war with France was the greatest accomplishment of his presidency.

Repression and Protest

The Alien and Sedition Acts

The elections in 1798 had increased the Federalist majorities in both houses of Congress and they used their "mandate" to enact legislation to stifle foreign influences. The Alien Act raised new hurdles in the path of immigrants trying to obtain citizenship, and the Sedition Act widened the powers of the Adams administration to muzzle its newspaper critics. Both bills were aimed at actual or potential Democrat-Republican opposition, and a number of editors were actually jailed for printing critical editorials.

The Kentucky and Virginia Resolutions

Democrat-Republican leaders were convinced that the Alien and Sedition Acts were unconstitutional, but the process of deciding on the constitutionality of federal laws was as yet undefined. Jefferson and Madison decided that the state legislatures should have that power, and they drew up a series of resolutions that they presented to the Kentucky and Virginia legislatures, respectively. They proposed that John Locke's "compact theory" be applied, which would empower the state bodies to "nullify" federal laws within those states. These resolutions were adopted, but only in these two states, and so the issue died. A principle, however, had now been set forth that would later bear fruit in the nullification controversy of the 1830s and ultimately in the secession crisis of 1860–1861.

The Revolution of 1800

The Election

Thomas Jefferson and Aaron Burr ran on the Democrat-Republican ticket, though not together, against John Adams and Charles Pinckney for the Federalists. All ran for the presidency; the candidate winning the second-highest number of votes would become vice president. Jefferson and Burr received the same number of electoral votes, so the selection went to the House of Representatives. After a lengthy deadlock, Alexander Hamilton threw his support to Jefferson, and Burr had to accept the vice presidency, the result obviously intended by the electorate. This increased the ill will between Hamilton and Burr and helped set the stage for their famous duel in 1804. The 12th Amendment to the Constitution was ratified in 1804 to prevent this from reoccurring.

DIDYOUKNOW?

The Election of 1800 was one of the most bitter presidential campaigns in U.S. history. Federalists accused Thomas Jefferson of being an atheist, a political fanatic, and even a drunkard. One Federalist newspaper even proclaimed that in the event of a Jefferson victory, "Murder, robbery, rape, adultery, and incest will be openly taught and practiced." Democrat-Republican supporters, for their part, accused Adams of secretly wishing to return the United States to British rule and of sending a U.S. general to England to bring back four women to serve as mistresses.

(Before taking the quiz noted below, please review the summary timeline for this chapter on the following pages.)

The New Nation (1754–1800)

Historical Timeline (1754–1800)

1754	French and Indian War
1759	British victorious at Battle of Quebec
1760	British defeat French at Montreal in final battle of the war
1763	Treaty of Paris Proclamation of 1763
1765	Stamp Act Stamp Act Congress
1767	Townshend duties passed
1770	Boston Massacre
1772	Burning of the *Gaspee*
1773	Boston Tea Party
1774	Intolerable Acts First Continental Congress
1775	Lexington and Concord Battle of Bunker Hill
1776	*Common Sense* published by Thomas Paine Declaration of Independence Battle of New York City Battle of Trenton
1777	British surrender 5,800 men at Saratoga American army winters at Valley Forge
1778	French-American alliance established British begin Southern strategy and capture Savannah
1780	British capture Charleston French army lands in Connecticut
1781	Articles of Confederation approved Gen. Cornwallis surrenders at Yorktown
1783	Treaty of Paris ends war, grants American independence Newburgh Conspiracy of American army officers
1785	Land Ordinance provides for orderly development of territories Spain closes the Mississippi River to American shipping
1786	Annapolis Convention Virginia adopts Jefferson's "Statute of Religious Freedom" Shays's Rebellion

Historical Timeline (1754–1800)

1787	Northwest Ordinance prohibits slavery in new territories Constitutional Convention meets in Philadelphia
1788	*Federalist Papers* published New Hampshire is ninth state to ratify Constitution, making it the law of the land
1789	Washington elected and inaugurated as president French Revolution begins as Bastille is stormed French National Assembly issues "Declaration of Rights of Man" Judiciary Act sets up federal court system
1791	Bill of Rights approved First Bank of United States chartered
1793	Washington issues Proclamation of Neutrality Louis XVI executed in France Cotton gin patented by Eli Whitney
1794	Whiskey Rebellion
1795	Jay Treaty Pinckney Treaty Treaty of Greenville
1796	Adams defeats Jefferson for presidency
1798	XYZ Affair Alien and Sedition Acts Virginia and Kentucky Resolutions
1800	Jefferson defeats Adams for presidency Prosser's Rebellion

Chapter 6

Democracy, Economic Growth, and Social Reform (1800–1848)

With the victory of Thomas Jefferson and the Democrat-Republican Party over John Adams and the Federalists in the 1800 presidential election, the United States experienced its first transition of political power. While some predicted popular unrest and even anarchy, the changeover was peaceful, though the Federalists attempted to retain power. The Federalist Congress passed a new Judiciary Act early in 1801 and President Adams filled the newly created vacancies with party supporters, many of them with last-minute commissions. John Marshall was appointed Chief Justice of the U.S. Supreme Court, thus guaranteeing continuation of Federalist policies from the bench of the high court.

The Jeffersonian Era

Thomas Jefferson and his Republican followers envisioned a society in vivid contrast to that of Hamilton and the Federalists. They dreamed of a nation of independent small farmers, living under a central government that exercised a minimum of control over their lives and served mainly to protect the individual liberties guaranteed by the Constitution. This agrarian paradise would be free from the industrial smoke and urban blight of Europe, and would serve as a beacon of Enlightenment rationalism to a world searching for direction. That vision was to prove a mirage, and Jefferson was to preside over a nation that was growing more industrialized and urban, and one that seemed to need an ever-stronger hand at the presidential tiller.

The New Federal City

The city of Washington had been designed by Pierre L'Enfant and was briefly occupied by the Adams administration. When Jefferson moved in, it was a provincial town, with muddy streets and muggy summers. Most of its inhabitants moved out when Congress was not in session.

Jefferson the President

The new president projected an image of democratic simplicity, walking to his boarding-house for lunch following his inauguration and sometimes appearing so casually dressed as to appear slovenly. But he was a brilliant thinker and a shrewd politician. He appointed men to his Cabinet who agreed with his political philosophy: James Madison as Secretary of State and Albert Gallatin as Secretary to the Treasury.

Lewis and Clark and the Corps of Discovery

Napoleon's decision to sell the massive Louisiana Purchase to the United States in 1803 provided President Thomas Jefferson with a major challenge: how to determine exactly what was in this vast, largely unexplored region of North America between the Mississippi River and the headwaters of the Missouri River. A British explorer, Alexander Mackenzie, had ventured across Canada and reached the Pacific Coast in 1793, but no European-American had made the trek up the Missouri River, over the Rockies, and then down the Columbia River to the Pacific Ocean.

Soon after the purchase, Jefferson asked Congress for $2,500 "to send intelligent officers with ten or twelve men, to explore even to the western ocean." While commissioned to study and map the terrain, make contact with the Indian tribes living there, and collect scientific specimens, Jefferson was most interested in the possibility of a Northwest Passage by water to the Pacific. The expedition was also an attempt to gain information about the activities of British and French fur trappers, who had been in the area for years.

Jefferson chose Captain Meriwether Lewis as the leader of this Corps of Discovery. Lewis immediately asked an old friend, William Clark, to be his co-commander. While officially still a second lieutenant, Lewis from the start treated Clark as an equal and referred to him as "Captain" with the men of the Corps, which consisted of 33 members. The Corps left from Camp River Dubois, near present-day Hartford, Illinois, on May 14, 1804. They traveled up the Missouri and passed the last white settlement at La Charrette. On August 20, 1804, the Corps of Discovery lost one member, Sergeant Charles Floyd, who apparently died from acute appendicitis. That was the only fatality of the nearly three-year journey. The group spent the winter of 1804–1805 at Fort Mandan, in present-day North Dakota. They hired a French Canadian, Toussaint Charbonneau, as a guide. Charbonneau's Shoshone wife, Sacagawea, also accompanied the Corps and proved to be an invaluable guide and source of information. She had a son, Jean Baptiste (or Pomp, as he was called by Clark), who was born just before the expedition left the Mandans. Because the Corps

(Continued)

Conflict with the Judges

Marbury vs. Madison

William Marbury, one of Adams' "midnight appointments," sued Secretary of State Madison to force delivery of his commission as a justice of the peace in the federal district. Supreme Court Justice John Marshall refused to rule on the request, claiming that the law which gave the Supreme Court jurisdiction over such matters had exceeded the constitutional grant of powers and thus was unconstitutional. Marshall thus asserted the power of judicial review over federal legislation. This power, though not specified in the Constitution, has become the foundation of the Supreme Court's check on the other two branches of government.

The Impeachment Episodes

Jefferson began a campaign to remove Federalist judges by impeachment. One district judge was removed, and proceedings were begun to impeach Supreme Court Justice

traveled with a woman and a child, the Indian tribes they encountered recognized that this strange group of whites (and one African American, York, Clark's slave) was not a war party and mostly aided the voyage.

The journey up the Missouri River was difficult because of heat, injuries, mosquitoes, and the river itself, which was difficult to navigate. The Corps employed a keelboat and two smaller boats, called pirogues, on the voyage and averaged 15 miles per day. The expedition followed the Missouri through what are now the states of Missouri, Nebraska, North Dakota, and Montana, where they discovered the Missouri's headwaters. They then crossed the Rocky Mountains and reached the West Coast of North America by paddling down the Clearwater River, the Snake River, and the Columbia River through what is now Oregon until they reached the Pacific Ocean in December 1805. The trip ran into several huge obstacles, such as the need for horses to cross the Rockies, but the expedition was aided in that quest by the chance encounter of Sacagawea with her brother, Kamahweit, and his tribe of Shoshones, from whom she had been kidnapped as a girl years earlier. It was from the Shoshones that the expedition was able to purchase the horses it needed. When the Corps reached the Pacific, they camped on the south side of the Columbia River and built Fort Clatsop near the modern town of Astoria, Oregon. When a hoped-for European ship never showed up during their rain-soaked wait, they started a return trip across the continent on March 23, 1806, and arrived back in St. Louis on September 23.

The Corps of Discovery traveled over 8,000 miles, lost only one member of their party, and cost the government the small sum of $40,000. The Lewis and Clark expedition made a major contribution in mapping a vastly unexplored segment of the North American continent. The journals of Lewis and Clark documented valuable information about the natural history of the area and the Native Americans living there. Hundreds of new plant and animal species were identified. Perhaps most importantly, they focused the attention of the nation on the West and paved the way for the many emigrants who would follow on the Oregon Trail to the Pacific Northwest.

Samuel Chase. According to the Constitution, judges could be removed from office for "high crimes or misdemeanors." That effort failed, but the threat had encouraged the judiciary to be less blatantly political.

Domestic Affairs

Enforcement of the Federalist-sponsored Alien and Sedition Acts was immediately suspended, and the men convicted under those laws were released.

Jefferson supported the concept of a limited federal government as a protection against tyranny. The federal bureaucracy was reduced and expenses were drastically cut. The size of the army was reduced and the expansion program of the Navy was cancelled.

Excise taxes passed during the Federalist Era were repealed and federal income was limited to land sale proceeds and customs duties. Federal land sale policy was liberalized, smaller parcels were authorized, and less cash was required—policies that benefited small farmers and reduced the level of speculation that had become prevalent during the 1790s.

The 12th Amendment, adopted and ratified in 1804, ensured that a tie vote between candidates of the same party could not again cause the confusion of the Jefferson-Burr affair.

Following the constitutional mandate, the importation of slaves was stopped by law in 1808. The issue of slavery, however, would not go away with the end of imported slaves. The invention of the cotton gin allowed Southern farmers to process ever-increasing amounts of cotton, creating a constant demand for more workers.

The Louisiana Purchase

Napoleon, in an effort to regain some of France's New World empire, obtained the old French trans-Mississippi territory from Spain through political pressure. Jefferson sent a delegation to Paris in an attempt to buy New Orleans, fearful that the new French officials might close it to American traffic. Napoleon's defeat in Santo Domingo persuaded him that Louisiana could not be exploited, and indeed was now subject to potential American incursions. So he offered to sell the entire territory to the United States for

$15 million. The American delegation accepted the offer in April 1803, even though they had no authority to buy more than the city of New Orleans.

DIDYOUKNOW?

The territory included in the Louisiana Purchase was so vast that it included all of the land that is now the states of Louisiana, Missouri, Arkansas, Iowa, North Dakota, South Dakota, Nebraska, and Oklahoma, along with much of the land that is now Kansas, Colorado, Wyoming, Montana, and Minnesota.

The Constitutional Dilemma

Jefferson's stand on the strict interpretation of the Constitution would not permit him to purchase land without Congressional approval. But he accepted his advisors' counsel that his treaty-making powers included the authority to buy the land. Congress concurred, after the fact, and the purchase price was appropriated, thus doubling the territory of the nation overnight. Jefferson's political philosophy came into conflict with the reality of the opportunity of expanding both the territory of the United States and the strength of the Democrat-Republicans. In this case, reality won out.

Exploring the West

Even before Napoleon's offer, Jefferson had authorized an expedition to explore the Western territory to the Pacific. The Lewis and Clark Corps of Discovery, with 33 men, left St. Louis in 1804, and returned two years later with a wealth of scientific and anthropological information, having strengthened the United States' claim to the Oregon territory. At the same time, Zebulon Pike and others had been traversing the middle parts of Louisiana and mapping the land.

The Essex Junto (1804)

Some New England Federalists saw the Western expansion as a threat to their position in the Union, and they tried to organize a secessionist movement. They courted Aaron Burr's support by offering to back him in a bid for the governorship of New York. Hamilton led the opposition to that campaign and when Burr lost the election, he challenged Hamilton to a duel, which resulted in Hamilton's death.

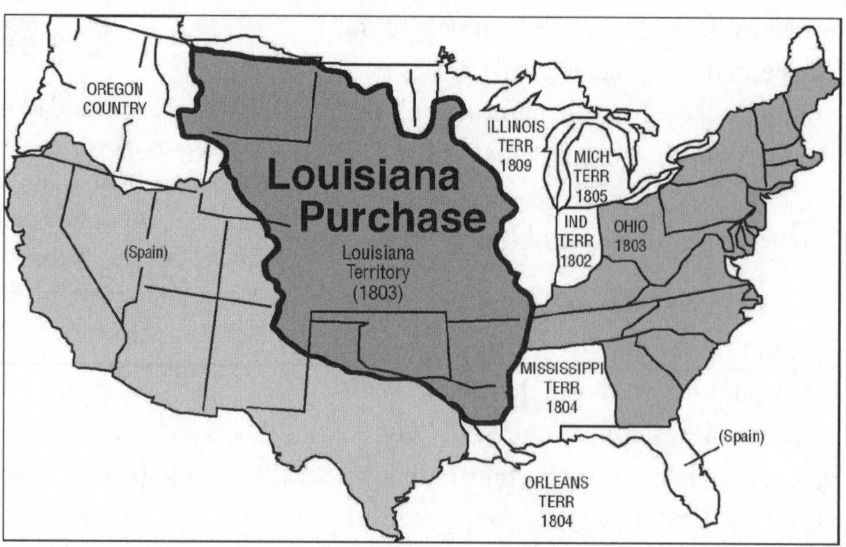

The Louisiana Purchase, completed in 1803, doubled the size of the United States.

The Burr Conspiracy

Aaron Burr was now a fugitive, without a political future. He became involved in a bizarre scheme to take Mexico from Spain and establish a new nation in the West.

In the fall of 1806, he led a group of armed men down the Mississippi River system toward New Orleans. He was arrested in Natchez and tried for treason in Richmond, Virginia. Justice John Marshall's decision for acquittal helped to narrow the legal definition of treason. Jefferson's attempts to influence and prejudice the trial were justified by his claims of "executive privilege," but they were fruitless.

John Randolph and the Yazoo Claims

Jefferson's Republican opponents, under the leadership of his cousin John Randolph of Roanoke, called themselves the "Quids." They accused the president of complicity in the Yazoo Land controversy that had followed Georgia's cession of Western lands to the federal government. This created serious strife within the Democrat-Republican Party and weakened Jefferson's effectiveness in his second term.

TEST TIP

On the AP Exam, a question using a painting or photograph will never ask you to simply identify what person, place, or event the image shows. Instead, you will be asked to apply your knowledge about the contents of the painting or photograph to a broader historical situation or theme.

International Involvement

The Barbary (or Tripolitan) Wars

In 1801, Jefferson sent a naval force to the Mediterranean to break the practice of North African Muslim rulers using pirates to exact tribute from Western merchant ships in a blackmail operation. The intermittent undeclared war dragged on until 1805, with no decisive settlement.

The Napoleonic Wars

War continued in Europe between France under Napoleon and the European powers led by Britain. Both sides tried to prevent trade with their enemies by neutral powers, especially the United States. Napoleon's "Continental System" was answered by Britain's "Orders in Council." American ships were seized by both sides and American sailors were impressed into the British navy. The relatively small and ineffective U.S. Navy was unable to prevent most of the impressment incidents.

The Chesapeake-Leopard Affair (1807)

The British ship H.M.S. *Leopard* stopped the U.S.S. *Chesapeake* off the coast of Virginia, and four alleged British deserters were taken off. Public outcry for war followed, and Jefferson was hard-pressed to remain neutral.

The Embargo of 1807

Jefferson's response to the cry for war was to draft a law prohibiting American ships from leaving port for any foreign destination, thus avoiding contact with vessels of either belligerent. The result was economic depression, particularly in the heavily commercial Northeast. This proved to be his most unpopular policy of both terms in office. Although it hurt trade, it spurred "industrial" growth in the United States.

Madison's Administration, 1809–1817

The Election of 1808

Republican James Madison won the 1808 presidential election over Federalist Charles Pinckney, but the Federalists gained seats in both houses of the Congress. The embargo-induced depression was obviously a heavy political liability left over from the Jefferson administration, and Madison was to face growing pressures to deal with the international crisis. He was a brilliant man but had few social or political skills. His greatest asset was probably his wife, the vivacious and energetic Dolley.

The War of 1812

Congress had passed a modified embargo just before Madison's inauguration. Known as the Non-Intercourse Act, it opened trade to all nations except France and Britain. When it expired in 1810, it was replaced by Macon's Bill No. 2, which gave the president power to prohibit trade with any nation that violated U.S. neutrality.

The Indian tribes of the Northwest and the Mississippi Valley were resentful of the government's policy of pressured removal to the West, and the British authorities in Canada exploited their discontent by encouraging border raids against the American settlements.

The Shawnee chief Tecumseh set out to unite the Mississippi Valley tribes and re-establish Indian dominance in the Old Northwest. With the help of his brother, the Prophet, and the timely New Madrid earthquake, he persuaded a sizable force of warriors to join him. On November 11, 1811, General William Henry Harrison destroyed Tecumseh's village on Tippecanoe Creek and dashed his hopes for an Indian confederacy.

Southern frontiersmen coveted Spanish Florida, which included the southern ranges of Alabama, Mississippi and Louisiana. They resented Spanish support of Indian depredations against the borderlands, and since Spain was Britain's ally, they saw Britain as the background cause of their problems.

The Congress in 1811 contained a strong pro-war group called the War Hawks, led by Henry Clay and John C. Calhoun. They gained control of both houses and began agitating for war with the British. On June 1, 1812, President Madison asked for a declaration of war, and Congress readily complied.

A three-pronged invasion of Canada met with disaster on all three fronts, and the Americans fell back to their own borders. At sea, American privateers and frigates, including "Old Ironsides," scored early victories over British warships, but were soon driven back into their home ports and blockaded by the powerful British ships-of-the-line.

Admiral Oliver Hazard Perry constructed a fleet of ships on Lake Erie and on September 10, 1813, defeated a British force at Put-in-Bay, establishing control of the lake. His flagship flew the banner, "Don't Give Up the Ship." This victory opened the way for William Henry Harrison to invade Canada in October and defeat a combination British and Indian force at the Battle of the Thames.

The War in the Southwest

Andrew Jackson led a force of frontier militia into Alabama in pursuit of Creek Indians who had massacred the white inhabitants of Fort Mims. On March 27, 1814, he crushed the Indians at Horseshoe Bend and then seized the Spanish garrison at Pensacola.

British Strategy Changes, 1814

A British force came down Lake Champlain and met defeat at Plattsburgh, New York, in September. A British armada sailed up the Chesapeake Bay and sacked and burned Washington, D.C., including the White House. It then proceeded toward Baltimore, which was guarded by Fort McHenry. That fort held firm through the British bombardment, inspiring Francis Scott Key's "Star Spangled Banner."

DID YOU KNOW?

Francis Scott Key set "The Star-Spangled Banner" to the tune of a popular English song of the time called "To Anacreon in Heaven." The original song was the theme of a London music club known as the Anacreontic Society, named for the ancient Greek poet Anacreon.

The Battle of New Orleans

The most serious British threat came at the port of New Orleans. A powerful invasion force was sent there to close the mouth of the Mississippi River, but Andrew Jackson decisively defeated it with a polyglot army of frontiersmen, blacks, Creoles, and pirates. The battle was fought on January 8, 1815, two weeks after a peace treaty had been signed at the city of Ghent, in Belgium.

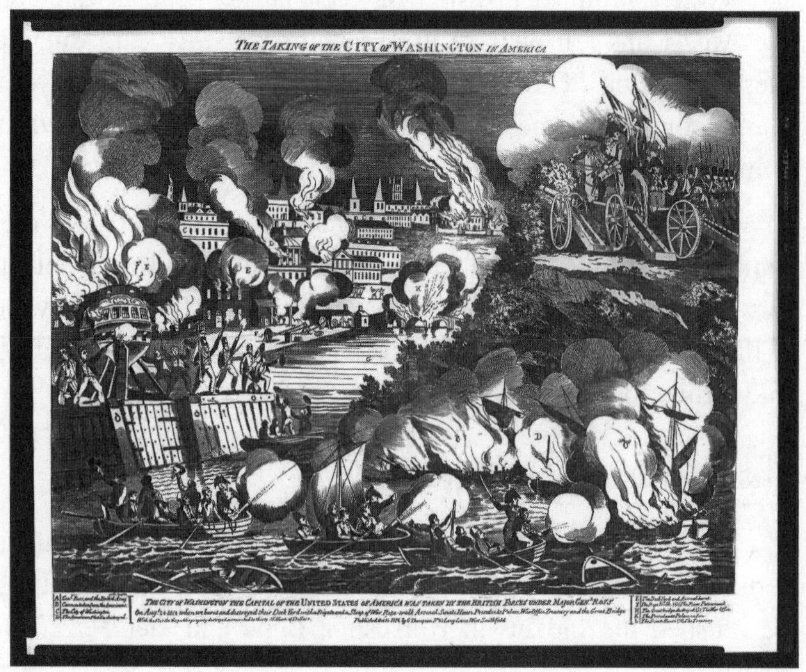

The War of 1812 forced the President and the Congress to flee from Washington as the British set public buildings ablaze. (From Reginald Horsman, *The War of 1812*, 1969, London, Eyre & Spottiswoode Ltd.)

The Treaty of Ghent, Christmas Eve, 1814

With the European wars ended, the major causes for the dispute with Britain had ceased to be important, so both sides were eager for peace. The treaty provided for the acceptance of the status quo at the beginning of hostilities; therefore, both sides restored their wartime conquests to the other.

The Hartford Convention, December 1814

The Federalists had become increasingly a minority party. They vehemently opposed the war, with Daniel Webster and other New England congressmen consistently blocking the Madison administration's efforts to prosecute the war effort. They resented the influence of the War Hawks, particularly in their antagonism toward Great Britain. On December 15, 1814, delegates from the New England states met in Hartford, Connecticut, and drafted a set of resolutions suggesting nullification—and even secession—if their interests were not protected against the growing influence of the South and the West.

Soon after the convention adjourned, the news of the victory at New Orleans was announced and their actions were discredited. The Federalist Party ceased to be a political force following the Hartford Convention.

Postwar Developments

Protective Tariff (1816)

The first protective tariff in the nation's history was passed in 1816 to slow the flood of cheap British manufactures into the country. Tariffs were to be an increasingly important economic tool for the government in raising revenue. They favored the industrial Northeast over the agricultural South and West and thus became unpopular, particularly in those areas dependent on imported manufactured goods.

Rush-Bagot Treaty (1817)

An agreement was reached in 1817 between Britain and the United States to stop maintaining armed fleets on the Great Lakes. This first "disarmament" agreement, known as the Rush-Bagot Treaty, is still in effect.

Jackson's Florida Invasion (1817)

Indian troubles in the newly acquired areas of western Florida prompted General Andrew Jackson, acting under dubious authority, to invade Spanish East Florida and to hang two British subjects whom he suspected of selling guns and supplies to the Indians. He then reoccupied Pensacola and raised the American flag, a clear violation of international law. Only popular support, based on Jackson's war hero status, prevented his arrest and prosecution by the government.

Indian Policy

The government began to systematically pressure all the Indian tribes remaining in the East to cede their lands and accept new homes west of the Mississippi, a policy that met with disappointing results. Most declined the offer.

The Barbary Wars (1815)

In response to continued piracy and extortion in the Mediterranean, Congress declared war on the Muslim state of Algiers in 1815, dispatching a naval force to the area under Stephen Decatur. He quickly defeated the North African pirates and forced them to pay indemnities for past tribute they had exacted from American ship captains. This action finally gained the United States free access to the Mediterranean basin and a measure of respect internationally.

The Adams-Onis Treaty (1819)

Spain had decided to sell the remainder of the Florida territory to the Americans before they took it anyway. Under the Adams-Onis Treaty, the Spanish surrendered all their claims to the territory and drew the boundary of Mexico all the way to the Pacific. The United States in exchange agreed to assume $5 million in debts owed to American merchants.

The Monroe Doctrine

Around 1810, national revolutions had begun in Latin America, so the colonial populations refused to accept the rule of the new Napoleonic governments in Europe. Leaders such as Argentina's José de San Martin and Venezuela's Simón Bolívar had declared independence for their countries and, after Napoleon's fall in 1814, were defying the restored Hapsburg and Bourbon rulers of Europe.

British and American leaders feared that the new European governments would try to restore the former New World colonies to their former royal owners.

In December 1823, President Monroe included in his annual message to Congress a statement "that the American continents...are henceforth not to be considered as subjects for future colonization by any European powers." Known now as the Monroe Doctrine and written by his Secretary of State, John Quincy Adams, this statement of policy exerted influence over American attitudes toward the Western Hemisphere well into the 20th century.* Monroe's speech also inaugurated a thirty-year period of freedom from serious foreign involvement for the United States.

TEST TIP

It's okay to skip an item that you're unsure about or that you would like to come back to later. Be careful to also skip that line on your answer sheet, however, so that you continue to bubble in your answers on the correct line. Mark the test question in your booklet so that you can remember to come back to it later.

*Even 139 years later, the doctrine was invoked symbolically during the Cuban Missile Crisis in 1962, after the Soviet Union was discovered to be building nuclear missile sites on the island of Cuba.

Internal Development, 1820–1830

The years following the War of 1812 were marked by rapid economic and social development—too rapid, in fact, setting the stage for a severe depression in 1819. But this slump was temporary, and it became obvious that the country was galloping from its agrarian origins toward an industrial, urban future. Westward expansion accelerated, and the mood of the people became very positive. In fact, these years are often referred to as the "Era of Good Feelings."

The Monroe Presidency, 1817–1825

James Monroe, the last of the "Virginia Dynasty," had been hand-picked by the retiring Madison, and he was elected with only one electoral vote opposed: a symbol of national unity.

Postwar Boom

The years following the war were also characterized by a high foreign demand for American cotton, grain, and tobacco. Commerce flourished. The Second National Bank, through its overly liberal credit policies, proved to be an inflationary influence, and the price level rose rapidly.

The Depression of 1819

Inventories of British manufactured goods had built up during the war, and English merchants began to dump their products on the American market at cut-rate prices. American manufacturers suffered from this influx of imports. The U.S. Bank tried to slow the inflationary spiral by tightening credit, and a sharp business slump resulted.

This depression was most severe in the newly expanding West, partly because of its economic dependency and partly because of heavy speculation in Western lands.

The Marshall Court

John Marshall delivered the majority opinions in a number of critical decisions in these formative years, all of which served to strengthen the power of the federal government and restrict the powers of state governments. Following is a summary of cases decided by the Marshall Court:

Marbury v. Madison (1803)

This case established the Supreme Court's power of judicial review over federal legislation. This positioned the judicial branch in an important independent position that would allow it to challenge acts of Congress.

Fletcher v. Peck (1810)

The Georgia legislature had issued extensive land grants in a shady deal with the Yazoo Land Company. A subsequent legislative session repealed that action because of the corruption that had attended the original grant. The Court decided that the original action by the Georgia Assembly had constituted a valid contract that could not be broken regardless of the corruption that followed. This was the first time a state law was voided on the grounds that it violated a principle of the U.S. Constitution.

Dartmouth College v. Woodward (1819)

The quarrel between the president and the trustees of New Hampshire's Dartmouth College became a political issue when the Republicans backed the president and the Federalists supported the trustees. The president tried to change Dartmouth from a private to a public institution by having its charter revoked. The Court ruled that the charter, though issued by King George III during colonial days, still constituted a contract and thus could not be arbitrarily changed or revoked without the consent of both parties. The result of this decision was to severely limit the power of state governments to control the corporation, which was the emerging form of business organization.

McCulloch v. Maryland (1819)

The state of Maryland had tried to levy a tax on the Baltimore branch of the Bank of the United States, to protect the competitive position of its own state banks. Marshall's ruling declared that no state has the right to control an agency of the federal government. Since "the power to tax is the power to destroy," such state action violated Congress's "implied powers" to establish and operate a national bank.

Gibbons v. Ogden (1824)

The State of New York had granted a monopoly to Ogden to operate a steamboat between New York and New Jersey. Gibbons obtained a Congressional permit to operate a steamboat line in the same waters. When Ogden sued to maintain his monopoly, the New York courts ruled in his favor. Gibbons's appeal went to the Supreme Court.

Marshall ruled that commerce included navigation, and that only Congress has the right to regulate commerce among states. Thus, the state-granted monopoly was void.

TEST TIP

On the AP exam, you'll never be asked to recall specific dates. However, you'll need to understand sequence and cause-and-effect relationships among events in order to answer questions effectively. The inclusion of a date in a question can often provide a clue to its answer.

Statehood: A Balancing Act

The Missouri Compromise (1820)

The Missouri Territory, the first to be organized from the Louisiana Purchase, applied for statehood in 1819. Since the Senate membership was evenly divided between slave-holding and free states at that time, the admission of a new state was obviously going to give the voting advantage either to the North or to the South. Slavery was already well established in the new territory, so the Southern states were confident in their advantage, until Representative Tallmadge of New York proposed an amendment to the bill that would prohibit slavery in Missouri.

The Southern outcry was immediate, and the ensuing debate grew hot. The Senate was deadlocked.

Henry Clay's Compromise Solution

As the debate dragged on, the northern territory of Massachusetts applied for admission as the state of Maine. This offered a way out of the dilemma, and House Speaker Henry Clay formulated a package that both sides could accept. The two admission bills were combined, with Maine coming in as a free state and Missouri as a slave state. To make the package palatable for the House, a provision was added to prohibit slavery in the remainder of the Louisiana Territory, north of the southern boundary of Missouri (latitude 36°30′). Clay guided this bill through the House and it became law, thus maintaining the number of free and slave states in the Senate.

The debates in Congress had reminded everyone of the deep division between the sections, and some saw it as evidence of trouble to come. Thomas Jefferson, in retirement at Monticello, remarked that the news from Washington was like a "fire bell in the night." The failure of politicians to directly address the issue of slavery and instead rely on patchwork compromises would mean that slavery, particularly in the new territories of the West, would continue to be a divisive issue for the nation.

The Expanding Economy

The Growing Population

The U.S. population continued to double about every 25 years. The migration of people to the West increased in volume and by 1840 over one-third of all Americans lived west of the Alleghenies. Immigration from abroad was not significant until 1820; then it began to increase rapidly, mostly from the British Isles. There were no immigration laws, and the United States began to be seen as a land of opportunity, particularly for the landless poor.

The Farming Sector

The growth of markets for farm products in the expanding cities, coupled with liberal land-sale policies by the federal government, made the growing of staple agricultural crops increasingly profitable. More and more land was put into cultivation, and the prevailing system of clearing and planting became more wasteful of timber as well as compromising the fertility of the land.

The Cotton Kingdom

The new lands in the Southwest, then constituting Alabama, Mississippi, Louisiana, and Texas, proved ideal for the production of short-staple cotton. Eli Whitney's invention of the cotton gin solved the problem of separating the seeds from the fibers, and the cotton boom was under way.

The growing market for food and work animals in the South provided the opportunity for the new Western farmers to specialize in those items and further stimulated the westward movement.

TEST TIP

A key change in the AP exam is in the multiple-choice section. Multiple-choice questions will now ask students to apply their content knowledge to understanding historical evidence. You will still need to know the events and facts of U.S. history, but multiple-choice questions will ask you to apply your knowledge to interpret their importance.

Fishing

New England and Chesapeake fishing proved very profitable. Deep-sea whaling became a significant enterprise, particularly from the Massachusetts/Rhode Island ports.

Lumbering

The expanding population created a need for building materials, and timber remained a profitable export item. Shipbuilding thrived in a number of Eastern Seaboard and Gulf Coast ports.

Fur Trade

John Jacob Astor established the American Fur Company. He and others opened up business all the way to the Northwest coast. "Mountain men" probed deeper and deeper into the Rocky Mountain ranges in search of the beaver.

Trade with the Spanish

The Santa Fe Trail, which ran from New Mexico northeast to Independence, Missouri, became an active trading corridor, opening up the Spanish territories to American migration and influence, and also providing the basis for future territorial claims.

The Transportation Revolution

The first half of the 19th century witnessed an extraordinary sequence of inventions and innovations, producing a true revolution in transport and communications.

River Traffic

The steamboats built by Robert Fulton, the *Clermont* in 1807 and the *New Orleans* in 1811, transformed river transport. As shipment times and freight rates both dropped tremendously, regular steam service was established on all the major river systems.

Road Building

By 1818, the National Road, built with federal funds, had been completed from Cumberland, Maryland, to Wheeling, Virginia, linking the Potomac with the Ohio River. A network of privately owned toll roads (turnpikes) began to reach out from every sizable city. They were usually built for only a few miles out, and they never accounted for a significant share of the total freight tonnage moved, but they formed the nucleus of a growing road system in the new nation.

The Canal Era

The Erie Canal, linking the Hudson River at Albany, New York, with Lake Erie, was completed in 1825 and became the first and most successful example of an artificial waterway. It was followed by a rash of construction until canals linked every major waterway system east of the Mississippi River.

Canals were the first development projects to receive large amounts of public funding. They ran east-west and so tied the new West to the old East, with later implications for sectional divisions. Because the South had a number of navigable rivers leading to ports on both the Atlantic and Gulf coasts, canals were not a significant factor in that region.

Lockport on the Erie Canal by W.H. Bartlett, 1839. (Wikimedia Commons)

The Rise of New York City

Its location as a transport hub, coupled with innovations in business practices, boosted New York City into a primary trade center, and made it America's largest city by 1830. One such innovation was the packet boats, which operated on a guaranteed schedule and helped to rationalize commerce, both internal and international.

New York soon dominated the domestic market for cotton, a situation that progressively reduced the South to the status of an economic colony.

TEST TIP

When writing your essays, be sure to use neat, legible handwriting. Printing may be a better choice than writing in cursive if your handwriting tends to be messy. Essay readers cannot grade what they cannot read!

Industrialization

The Rise of the Factory System

Samuel Slater had migrated from Britain in 1789, having served as an apprentice under inventor Richard Arkwright and then as a mill manager. He used his knowledge to build the first successful cotton-spinning mill in this country. The first cotton manufacturing plant in the world to include all the elements of manufacturing under one roof was then built in Boston in 1813.

Eli Whitney's development and application of the principle of interchangeable parts, first used in his firearms factories, helped to speed the growth of mass-production operations. Though Whitney made little profit selling rifles, his methods became a staple in American industry.

The expansion of markets in Latin America and the Far East, as well as domestic markets, both resulted from and helped to develop the factory system.

Manufacturers and industrialists found it necessary to organize banks, insurance companies, and real estate firms to meet the needs of their growing business organizations.

The Corporation

The corporate form, with its limited liability and its potential for raising and utilizing large amounts of capital, became the typical type of business organization. By the 1830s, most states had enacted general laws for incorporating.

The Labor Supply

In the early days, the "Lowell System" became a popular method of staffing the New England textile factories. Young women were hired from the surrounding countryside, brought to town and housed in dormitories in the mill towns. They were paid low wages for hard work under poor conditions; but they were only working for a short time, to earn a dowry or help out with the family income, so they soon went back home. This "rotating labor supply" was ideal for the owners, since the mill girls—some as young as 10 or 11 years old—were not motivated to agitate for better wages and conditions.

Labor was always in short supply in this country, so the system depended on technology to increase production. This situation always placed a premium on innovation in machinery and technique.

The Growth of Unions

The factory system separated the owners from the workers, often depersonalizing the workplace. It also made the skilled artisan less important, since the repetitive processes of the mill could be performed by relatively unskilled laborers.

Although the first organized strike took place in 1828, in Paterson, New Jersey, by child workers, periodic economic downturns helped keep workers relatively dependent and passive until the 1850s.

A major goal of early unions was the ten-hour day, and this effort sparked a period of growth in organized labor that was later effectively quenched by the depression of 1837.

Educational Development

The Growth of Public Schools

Before 1815, there were no public schools to speak of in the United States. Some states had endorsed the idea of free schools for the people, but they shrank from the task of financing such a system. Jefferson, a true educational visionary and the founder of the University of Virginia, had outlined such a plan for Virginia, but it came to nothing.

Schools were primarily sponsored by private institutions—corporate academies in the Northeast and religious institutions in the South and mid-Atlantic states. Most were aristocratic in orientation, training the nation's leaders, and few had any interest in schooling the children of the poor.

Women were likewise considered unfit for academic training, and the female schools that existed concentrated on homemaking skills and the fine arts, which would make "ornaments" of the young ladies enrolled.

The New York Free School, one of those rare examples of a school for the poor, experimented for a time with the Lancastrian system, in which older students tutored the younger ones, thus stretching scarce budget dollars.

Higher Education

Although the numbers of institutions of higher learning increased sharply in the early years of the nineteenth century, none was truly public. All relied upon high tuition rates for survival, so less than one in ten young men—and no women—ever attended a college or university until Oberlin College admitted women beginning in 1837.

The training these schools provided was very limited as well. The only professional training was in theology, and only a smattering of colleges offered brief courses of study in law or medicine. The University of Pennsylvania, for example, offered one year of medical schooling, after which a person could obtain a license to practice the healing arts. Medical practices were quite primitive.

The Growth of Cultural Nationalism

Jeffersonian Americans tried to demonstrate their newly won independence by championing a strong sense of cultural nationalism, a feeling that their young republic represented the "final stage" of civilization, the "last great hope of mankind."

Literary Nationalism

Although most Americans had access to one or more newspapers, the market for native authors was quite limited. Publishers preferred to print works from British authors or to import books from Europe. A few Americans who were willing to pay the costs of publishing their own works, however, found a growing number of readers.

Significant American Authors

Washington Irving was by far the best-known native writer in America. He excelled in the telling of folktales and local color stories, and is best remembered for his portraits of Hudson River characters.

Mercy Otis Warren, the revolutionary pamphleteer, published a multi-volume *History of the Revolution* in 1805.

"Parson" Mason Weems wrote the best-seller *Life of Washington* in 1806, which was short on historical accuracy but long on nationalistic hero worship.

Educational Literature

Early schoolbooks, like Noah Webster's *Blue Backed Speller,* as well as his dictionary of the "American" language, reflected the intense desire to promote patriotism and a feeling of national identity.

DIDYOUKNOW?

Noah Webster introduced many Americanized spellings of words that are widely used today, including the dropped "u" from words such as "color" and "humor" and respellings of words like "jail" and "draft." However, not all of his new spellings caught on, including "wimmen" (women), "tung" (tongue), and "sley" (sleigh).

Developments in Religious Life

The Post-Revolution Years

The Revolutionary War weakened the position of the traditional, established churches. The doctrines of the Enlightenment became very popular, and its religious expression—deism—gained a considerable following among the educated classes. Rationalism, Unitarianism, and Universalism all saw a period of popularity. Thomas Paine's exposition of the rationalist posture, *The Age of Reason,* attacked the traditional Christian values and was read widely.

Lithograph of a religious revival meeting in a Western forest. Lippincott, Grambo & Co., 1854. (U.S. Library of Congress)

The Second Great Awakening

The reaction to the trend toward rationalism, the decline in church membership, and the lack of piety, was a renewal of personal, heart-felt evangelicalism. A second Great Awakening began in 1801 at Cane Ridge, Kentucky, in the first "camp meeting."

As the revival spread, its characteristics became more uniform—an emphasis on personal salvation, an emotional response to God's grace, and an individualistic faith. Women took a major part in the movement. Blacks were also heavily involved, and the emphasis on individual salvation created unrest among their ranks, particularly in the slave-holding South.

The revival produced strong nationalistic overtones, and the Protestant ideas of a "called nation" were to flourish later in some of the Manifest Destiny doctrines of expansionism. The social overtones of this religious renewal were to spark the great reform movements of the 1830s and 1840s.

Jacksonian Democracy, 1829–1841

While the "Age of Jackson" did not bring perfect political, social, or economic equality to all Americans, it did mark a transformation in the political life of the nation that attracted the notice of European travelers and observers. Frenchman Alexis de Tocqueville observed an "equality of condition" in America that existed nowhere else in the world, and an egalitarian spirit among the people that was unique. Certainly the electorate had become broadened so that all white males had access to the polls, even if blacks and women were still outside the system. It was, in that sense, the "age of the common man."

The Election of 1824

The Expansion of the Electorate

Most states had already eliminated property ownership qualifications for voting before the campaigns for the 1824 election began. The new Massachusetts state constitution of 1820 had led the way in this liberalization of the franchise, and most Northern states followed soon after, usually with some conservative opposition, but not violent reactions. In Rhode Island, Thomas Dorr led a bloodless "rebellion" in an effort to expand the franchise in that state, and though he was briefly imprisoned for his efforts, the incident led the conservative legislature to relent and grant the vote to non-property owners. The movement for reform was much slower in the Southern states.

Free blacks were excluded from the polls across the South and in most of the Northern states. In those areas where they had held the franchise, they were gradually excluded from the social and economic mainstream—as well as from the political arena—in the early years of this period.

National elections had never attracted much enthusiasm until 1824. Legislative caucuses had made the presidential nominations and kept the ruling cliques in power by excluding the voters from the process. But this year the system failed, and the caucuses were bypassed. Another change came in the selection of the Electoral College members, who were now being almost universally elected by the people, rather than by the state legislatures as in the early days.

The Candidates

Secretary of the Treasury William H. Crawford of Georgia was the pick of the Congressional caucus. Secretary of State John Quincy Adams held the job, which traditionally had been the stepping-stone to the executive office. Speaker of the House Henry Clay presented the only coherent program to the voters, the "American System," which provided a high tariff on imports to finance an extensive internal improvement package. Andrew Jackson of Tennessee presented himself as a war hero from the 1812 conflict. All four candidates claimed to be Democrat-Republicans.

The Election

Jackson won 43 percent of the popular vote, but the four-way split meant that he received only 38 percent of the electoral votes. Under the provisions of the 12th Amendment, the House of Representatives voted on the top three candidates. This left Henry Clay out of the running, and he threw his support to Adams. The votes had no sooner been counted when the new president, Adams, appointed Henry Clay his Secretary of State.

Andrew Jackson and his supporters immediately cried "foul!" and accused Clay of making a deal for his vote. The rallying cry of "corrupt bargain" became the impetus for their immediate initiation of the campaign for the 1828 election.

The Adams Administration

The new president pushed for an active federal government in areas like internal improvements and Native American affairs. These policies proved unpopular in an age of increasing sectional jealousies and conflicts over states' rights. Like his father, John, John Quincy Adams was an ineffective president.

Adams was frustrated at every turn by his Jacksonian opposition, and his unwillingness, or inability, to compromise further antagonized his political enemies. His refusal to endorse the Creek Native Americans' land cession to the state of Georgia was negated by their recession of their lands under pressure from Georgia's Jacksonian government.

John C. Calhoun and Nullification

In 1828, Congress passed a new tariff bill that had originally been supported by Southern congressmen in order to embarrass the administration. The finished bill, however, included higher import duties for many goods bought by Southern planters, so they bitterly denounced the law as the "Tariff of Abominations."

John C. Calhoun was serving as Adams's vice president, so to protest the tariff and still protect his position, he anonymously published the "South Carolina Exposition and Protest," which outlined his theory of the "concurrent majority": that a federal law deemed harmful to the interests of an individual state could be declared null and void within that state by a convention of the people. Thus, a state holding a minority position could ignore a law enacted by the majority, an idea first espoused by Jefferson and Madison in the Kentucky and Virginia Resolutions.

The Election of 1828

Adams's supporters now called themselves the National Republicans, and Jackson's party ran in the 1828 election as the Democratic Republicans (or Democrats). Andrew Jackson had aggressively campaigned since his defeat in the House in 1825.

It was a dirty campaign. Adams's supporters accused Jackson of adultery and of the murder of several militiamen who had been executed for desertion during the War of 1812. His wife was accused of bigamy. Jackson's followers in turn defamed Adams and his programs and accused him of extravagance with public funds.

When the votes were counted, Jackson had won 56 percent of the popular vote and swept 178 of the 261 electoral votes. John C. Calhoun was elected vice president.

Andrew Jackson as President

Jackson was popular with the common man. He seemed to be the prototype of the self-made Westerner: rough-hewn, violent, vindictive, with few ideas but strong convictions. He ignored his appointed Cabinet officers and relied instead on the counsel of his "Kitchen Cabinet," a group of partisan supporters who had the ear and the confidence of the president.

Andrew Jackson's Inauguration, March 4, 1829. (U.S. Library of Congress)

Jackson expressed the conviction that government operations could be performed by untrained common folk, and he threatened the dismissal of large numbers of government employees, to replace them with his supporters. Actually, he talked more about this "spoils system" than he acted on it.

DIDYOUKNOW?

Andrew Jackson lived during a time of great industrial advances. As such, he was the first president to enjoy a system of running water in the White House.

He exercised his veto power more than any other president before him. A famous example was the Maysville Road, a project in Kentucky that required a federal subsidy. Jackson opposed it because it would exist only within the boundaries of a single state and thus did not qualify for federal funding.

Jacksonian Indian Policy

Jackson supported the removal of all Indian tribes to west of the Mississippi River. The Indian Removal Act in 1830 provided for federal enforcement of that process.

The portion of the Cherokee Nation that occupied northern Georgia claimed to be a sovereign political entity within the boundaries of that state. The Supreme Court supported that claim in its decision in *Worcester v. Georgia* (1832), but President Jackson refused to enforce the Court's decision.

The result of this policy was the Trail of Tears, the forced march under U.S. Army escort of thousands of Cherokees to the West. A quarter or more of the Indians, mostly women and children, perished on the journey.

The Webster-Hayne Debate, 1830

Federal Land Policy

The method of disposing of government land raised sectional differences. Westerners wanted cheap land made available to the masses. Northeasterners opposed this policy because it would lure away their labor supply and drive up wages. Southerners supported the West, hoping to weaken the ties between East and West.

The Senate Confrontation

Senator Robert Hayne of South Carolina made a speech in support of cheap land and he used Calhoun's anti-tariff arguments to support his position. In his remarks, he referred to the possibility of nullification, of a state defying a national law.

Daniel Webster's famous replies to this argument moved the debate from the issue of land policy to the nature of the Union and states' rights within it. Webster argued for the Union as indissoluble and sovereign over the individual states. His concluding statements have become a part of our rhetorical heritage: "It is, Sir, the people's Constitution, the people's government, made for the people, made by the people, and answerable to the people. . . . Liberty and Union, now and forever, one and inseparable!"

The Nullification Crisis

The final split between Andrew Jackson and his vice president, John C. Calhoun, came over the new Tariff of 1832, and over Mrs. Calhoun's snub of Peggy Eaton, the wife of Secretary of War John Eaton.

Mrs. Eaton was a commoner, and the aristocratic Mrs. Calhoun refused to include her on the guest lists for the Washington parties. Jackson, no doubt remembering the slights to his own beloved wife, Rachel, defended his friends Peggy and John and demanded that they be included in the social life of the capital.

Jackson was a defender of states' rights, but within the context of a dominant Union. When he supported the higher rates of the new tariff, Calhoun resigned his office in a huff and went home to South Carolina. There he composed an Ordinance of Nullification, which was duly approved by a special state convention, and the customs officials were ordered to stop collecting the duties at the port of Charleston.

Jackson's response was immediate and decisive. He obtained a Force Bill from Congress (1833), which empowered him to use federal troops to enforce the collection of the taxes. And he suggested the possibility of hanging Calhoun. At the same time, he offered a gradual reduction in the levels of the duties. Calhoun backed down, both sides claimed victory, and a crisis was averted.

Political cartoon during Nullification Crisis showing the manufacturing North profiting from high tariffs while the South suffered. (U.S. Library of Congress)

The War on the Bank

The Controversy

The Bank of the United States had operated under the direction of Nicholas Biddle since 1823. He was a cautious man, and his conservative economic policy enforced conservatism among the state and private banks—which many bankers resented. Many of the Bank's enemies opposed it simply because the Bank was big and powerful. Many still disputed its constitutionality.

The Election of 1832

Andrew Jackson freely voiced his antagonism toward the Bank and his intention to destroy it. During the campaign for the presidency in 1832, Henry Clay and Daniel Webster promoted a bill to re-charter the Bank, even though its charter did not expire until 1836. They feared that Jackson would gain support over time and could kill the Bank as a parting shot as he retired. Congress passed the re-charter bill, but Jackson vetoed it. This left that institution a lame duck agency.

Jackson soundly defeated Henry Clay in the presidential race and he considered his victory a mandate from the people to destroy the Bank. His first move was to remove the federal government's deposits from Biddle's vaults and distribute the funds to various state and local banks, called by his critics the "pet banks." Biddle responded by tightening up on credit and calling in loans, hoping to embarrass the government and force a withdrawal by Jackson. Jackson stood firm and the result was a financial recession.

The Panic of 1837

When Biddle was forced to relent through pressure from business interests, the economy immediately rebounded. With credit policies relaxed, inflation began to pick up. The government contributed to this expansion by offering millions of acres of Western land for sale to settlers at low prices.

In 1836, Jackson ordered a distribution of surplus funds and thus helped to further fuel the inflationary rise in prices. Finally, even Jackson recognized the danger and tried to slow the spiral by issuing the Specie Circular, which required payment for public land in hard money; no more paper or credit. Depression quickly followed this move.

The business recession lasted well into the 1840s. The national economy was by this time so tied in with international business and finance that the downturn affected the entire Atlantic community and was in turn worsened by the global impact. But most Americans blamed everyone in power, including Jackson, as well as private institutions and business practices. This disillusionment helped to initiate and intensify the reform movement, which so occupied this nation in the 19th century's second quarter.

The Election of 1836

In the campaign for the 1836 election, Jackson had handpicked his Democratic successor, Martin Van Buren of New York. The Whigs ran three regional candidates in hopes of upsetting the Jacksonians. The Whig Party had emerged from the ruins of the National Republicans and other groups who opposed Jackson's policies. The name was taken from the British Whig tradition, which simply refers to the "opposition."

Van Buren's Presidency

Van Buren, known as Old Kinderhook (O.K.), inherited all the problems and resentments generated by his mentor. He spent most of his term in office dealing with the financial chaos left by the death of the Second Bank. The best he could do was to eventually persuade Congress to establish an Independent Treasury to handle government funds. It began functioning in 1840.

TEST TIP

Let's face it: cramming doesn't work. A 2008 study by University of California–San Diego psychologists found that if you review material relatively close to when you first learn it, you will remember it better (www.popsci.com). So if you have a history lesson on Monday and a quiz on the following Monday, the best time to study for the quiz would be Wednesday.

The Election of 1840

The Candidates

In the campaign for the presidential election of 1840 the Whigs nominated William Henry Harrison, "Old Tippecanoe," a Western Indian fighter. Their choice for vice president was John Tyler, a former Democrat from Virginia. The Democrats put up Van Buren again, but they could not agree on a vice presidential candidate, so they ran no one.

Record Election Day Turnout

The 1840 election saw the largest voter turnout in the nation's history up to that point. The campaign was dramatic. The Whigs stressed the depression and the opulent lifestyle of the incumbent in contrast to the simple "log cabin" origins of their candidate.

Harrison won a narrow popular victory but swept 80 percent of the electoral vote. Unfortunately for the Whigs, President Harrison died only a month after the inauguration, having served the shortest term in presidential history.

The Significance of Jacksonian Politics

The Party System

The Age of Jackson was the beginning of the modern party system. Popular politics, based on emotional appeal, became the accepted style. The practice of meeting in mass conventions to nominate national candidates for office was established during the Jackson years.

The Strong Executive

Jackson, more than any president before him, used his office to dominate his party and the government to such an extent that his critics called him "King Andrew."

The Changing Emphasis Toward States' Rights

Andrew Jackson supported the authority of the states against the national government, but he drew the line at the concept of nullification. He advocated a strong union made up of sovereign states, and this created some dissonance in his political thinking.

The Supreme Court reflected this shift in thinking in its decision on the *Charles River Bridge* case in 1837, delivered by Jackson's new Chief Justice, Roger Taney. He ruled that a state could abrogate a grant of monopoly if that original grant had ceased to be in the best interests of the community. This was clearly a reversal of the *Dartmouth College* principle of the sanctity of contracts, in a case where the general welfare was perceived as being involved.

Party Philosophies

The Democrats opposed big government and the requirements of modernization: urbanization and industrialization. Their support came from the working classes, small merchants, and small farmers.

The Whigs promoted government participation in commercial and industrial development, the encouragement of banking and corporations, and a cautious approach to westward expansion. Their support came largely from Northern business and manufacturing interests, and from large Southern planters. Calhoun, Clay, and Webster dominated the Whig party during these early decades of the nineteenth century.

Tocqueville's *Democracy in America*

Alexis de Tocqueville, a French civil servant, traveled to the U.S. in the early 1830s to study the American prison system, which was one of the more innovative systems in the world. His book, *Democracy in America,* published in 1835, was the result of his observations, and it reflected a broad interest in the entire spectrum of the American democratic process and the society in which it had developed. His insightful commentary on the American way of life has proven to be almost prophetic in many respects, and provides the modern reader with an outsider's objective view of what this country was like in the Age of Jackson.

The Flowering of Literature

Northern Writers and Themes

James Fenimore Cooper's *Leatherstocking Tales* emphasized the independence of the individual and also the importance of a stable social order.

Walt Whitman's *Leaves of Grass* likewise celebrated the importance of individualism.

Henry Wadsworth Longfellow's epic poems *Evangeline* and *Hiawatha* spoke of the value of tradition and the impact of the past on the present.

Herman Melville's classic stories—*Typee, Billy Budd* and *Moby-Dick*—all lashed out at the popular optimism of his day. He believed in the Puritan doctrine of original sin and his characters spoke of the mystery of life.

Historian and nationalist Francis Parkman vividly portrayed the struggle for empire between France and Britain in his *Montcalm and Wolfe. The Oregon Trail* described the new frontier of the Rocky Mountains and beyond.

James Russell Lowell, poet and editor, wrote the *Bigelow Papers* and the *Commemoration Ode,* honoring Civil War casualties of Harvard.

A writer of romances and tales, Nathaniel Hawthorne is best remembered for his criticism of Puritan bigotry in *The Scarlet Letter.*

Southern Writers and Themes

Author of *The Raven, Tamerlane,* and many tales of terror and darkness, Edgar Allan Poe explored the world of the spirit and the emotions.

South Carolina poet William Gilmore Simms changed from a staunch nationalist to a defender of the slave system and the uniqueness of the Southern way of life.

A Georgia storyteller, Augustus Longstreet used vulgar, earthy language and themes to paint the common folk of the South.

TEST TIP

Short-answer questions are a new addition to the AP exam. This type of question asks students to respond to historical source material and problems. The questions measure students' ability to use specific historical thinking skills rather than to develop a thesis.

The Fine Arts

Artists and Themes

The Hudson River School was a group of landscape painters who portrayed the awesomeness of nature in America. George Catlin painted the American Indian, whom he saw as a vanishing race. John James Audubon painted the wide array of American birds and animals.

Music and the Theatre

The theatre was popular, but generally condemned by the church and conservatives as a "vagabond profession." Few towns had local theatre companies, though traveling troupes sometimes performed plays, often those of William Shakespeare. The only original American contribution was the blackface minstrel show.

The Transcendentalists

Major Themes

The transcendental movement had its origins in Concord, Massachusetts. The basic objective of these thinkers was to transcend the bounds of the intellect and to strive for emotional understanding and to attain unity with God without the help of the institutional church, which they saw as reactionary and stifling to self-expression.

Major Writers

Ralph Waldo Emerson, essayist and lecturer, authored "Nature" and "Self-Reliance." Henry David Thoreau, best known for his *Walden,* repudiated the repression of society and preached civil disobedience to protest unjust laws.

The Utopians

Their Purpose

A variety of secular and religious cooperative communities attempted to improve the life of the common man in the face of increasing impersonal industrialism. Their motives, beliefs, and methods differed, yet all sought to withdraw from the larger society to form their own communities.

The Utopian Communities

Brook Farm, in Massachusetts, was the earliest commune in America, and it was short-lived. Nathaniel Hawthorne was a short-term resident, and his *Blithedale Romance* was drawn from that experience. This work and *The Scarlet Letter* were both condemnations of the life of social isolation.

Robert Owen, of the New Lanark experiment in Wales, founded New Harmony, Indiana, but it failed after two years. He attacked religion, marriage, and the institution of private property, so he encountered resistance from neighboring communities.

Nashoba was in the environs of Memphis, Tennessee, established by the free-thinking Englishwoman Frances Wright as a communal haven for freed slaves. Needless to say, her community experiment encountered fierce opposition from her slaveholding neighbors and it survived only briefly.

Oneida Community in New York was based on free love and open marriages.

The Shakers were directed by Mother Ann Lee. The communities were socialistic experiments that practiced celibacy, sexual equality, and social discipline. The name was given to them by onlookers at their community dancing sessions.

Amana Community, in Iowa, was another socialist experiment, with a rigidly ordered society.

The Mormons

The Origins of the Religion

Joseph Smith claimed that he was visited by an angel and received sacred writings in New York State in 1830, and organized the Church of Jesus Christ of Latter-Day

Saints. They were unpopular with their neighbors because of their unorthodox beliefs, and were forced to move about, first to Missouri, then to Nauvoo, Illinois, where they established one of the larger cities in the state. There Smith was killed by a mob, and in 1847 the community was led to the valley of the Great Salt Lake by their new leader, Brigham Young, in one of the great epic migrations to the West.

The Church

The Mormons established a highly organized, centrally controlled system, which provided security and order for the faithful, while practicing polygamy, a practice considered immoral by their non-Mormon neighbors. They held a strong belief in human perfectability and so were among the American religious utopian groups. In their new church home in Utah, the Mormons created a self-sufficient, thriving community.

Educating the Public

This was the golden age of oratory. Speechmaking drew huge and patient crowds, and four-hour-long orations were not uncommon, especially at public events like Fourth of July celebrations.

Newspapers and magazines multiplied and were available to everyone.

Women more and more became the market for magazines oriented to their interests. Periodicals like *Godey's Ladies Book* reached mass circulation figures.

Colleges sprang up everywhere, the products of religious sectarianism as well as local pride, which produced "booster colleges" in every new community as population moved west. Many of these were poorly funded and managed, and thus did not survive.

Diverging Societies—Life in the North

Although the United States was a political entity, with all of the institutions of government and society shared among the people of the various states, there had always been a wide diversity of cultural and economic goals among the various states of the union. As the nineteenth century progressed, that diversity seemed to grow more pronounced, and the collection of states seemed to polarize more into the two sections—the North and the South—with the expanding West becoming ever more identified with the North.

Increase in Median Age

Birth rates began to drop after 1800, more rapidly in the cities than in the rural areas. Families who had averaged six children in 1800 only had five in 1860. Some of the reasons were economic: children were becoming liabilities rather than assets. The new "cult of domesticity" reflected a shift in family responsibilities. The father was typically out of the home working, so the burden of child rearing fell more upon the mother. Primitive birth control methods were used, and abortion was becoming common enough that several states passed laws restricting it. One result of all this was an aging population, with the median age rising from 16 to 20 years.

Immigration

The influx of immigrants had slowed during the conflicts with France and England, but the flow increased between 1815 and 1837, when the economic downturn again sharply reduced their numbers. Thus, the overall rise in population during these years was due more to incoming foreigners than to natural increase. Most of the newcomers were from Britain, Germany, and southern Ireland. The Germans usually fared best, since they brought more money and more skills. Discrimination was common in the job market, primarily directed against the Catholics. "Irish Need Not Apply" signs were common. However, the persistent labor shortage prevented the natives from totally excluding the foreign elements. These newcomers huddled in ethnic neighborhoods in the cities, or those who could moved west to try their hand at farming.

Growth of the Cities

In 1790, five percent of the U.S. population lived in cities of 2,500 or more. By 1860, that figure had risen to 25 percent. This rapid urbanization created an array of problems.

Problems of Urbanization

The rapid growth in urban areas was not matched by the growth of services. Clean water, trash removal, housing, and public transportation all lagged behind, and the wealthy got them first. Bad water and poor sanitation produced poor health, and epidemics of typhoid fever, typhus, and cholera were common. Police and fire protection were usually inadequate, and the development of professional forces was resisted because of the cost and the potential for political patronage and corruption.

Social Unrest

Rapid growth helped to produce a wave of violence in the cities. In New York City in 1834, the Democrats fought the Whigs with such vigor that the state militia had to be called in. New York and Philadelphia witnessed race riots in the mid-1830s, and a New York mob sacked a Catholic convent in 1834. In the 1830s, 115 major incidents of mob violence were recorded. Street crime was common in all the major cities.

The Role of Women and Minorities

Women

Women were treated as minors before the law. In most states, a woman's property became her husband's with marriage. Political activity was limited to the formation of associations in support of various pious causes, such as abolition and religious and benevolent activity. Professional employment was largely limited to school teaching and that occupation became dominated by women. The women's rights movement focused on social and legal discrimination, and women like Lucretia Mott and Sojourner Truth became well-known figures on the speakers' circuit.

Blacks

By 1848, approximately 200,000 free blacks lived in the North and West. Their lives were restricted everywhere by prejudice, and "Jim Crow" laws separated the races. Black citizens organized separate churches and fraternal orders. The African Methodist Episcopal Church, for example, had been organized in 1794 in Philadelphia, and flourished in the major Northern cities. Black Masonic and Odd Fellows lodges were likewise established. The economic security of the free blacks was constantly threatened by the newly arrived immigrants, who were willing to work at the least desirable jobs for less wages. Racial violence was a daily threat.

DIDYOUKNOW?

In 1850, the United States had an African American population of 1,811,258, or 15.3% of a total population of 11,837,660 (U.S. Census).

The Northeast Leads the Way

The Growth of Industry

By the end of the 1840s, the value of industrial output had surpassed that of agricultural production. The Northeastern states led the way in this movement. Over one-half of the manufacturing establishments were located there, and most of the larger enterprises. Seventy percent of the workers who were employed in manufacturing lived in New England and the middle states, and the Northeast produced more than two-thirds of the manufactured goods for the country.

Inventions and Technology

The level of technology used in American manufacturing already exceeded that of European industry. Eli Whitney's applications of interchangable parts were being introduced into a wide variety of manufacturing processes. Coal was replacing water as the major source of industrial power. Machine tools were reaching a high level of sophistication. Much of this progress was due to the contributions of America's inventors. Between 1830 and 1850 the number of patents issued for industrial inventions almost doubled. Charles Goodyear's process of vulcanizing rubber was put to 500 different uses and formed the basis for an entire new industry. Elias Howe's sewing machine was to revolutionize the clothing industry. The mass production of iron, with its new techniques and uses, created an array of businesses, of which the burgeoning railroad industry was the largest consumer. Samuel B. Morse's new electric telegraph was first used in 1840 to transmit business news and information.

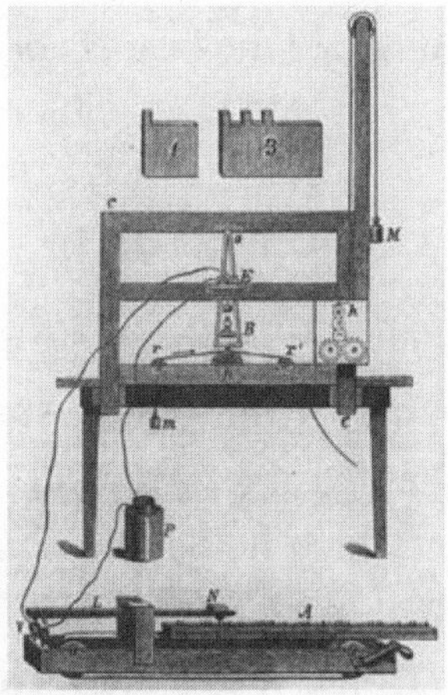

Samuel Morse's telegraph helped unite the country. (Wikimedia Commons)

The Rise of Unions

The growth of the factory system was accompanied by the growth of the corporate form of business ownership, which further separated the owners from the workers. One result was the organization of worker groups to fight for benefits, an early example of which was the 10-hour day. In 1835, Boston construction craftsmen struck for seven months to win a 10-hour workday, and Paterson, New Jersey, textile workers became the first factory workers to strike for shorter hours. The federal government's introduction of the 10-hour day for federal projects, in 1840, helped to speed the acceptance of this goal. The influx of immigrants who were willing to work for low wages helped to spur the drive for unions, and in turn their numbers helped to weaken the bargaining position of union members.

The Revolution in Agriculture

Farm and industry reinforced each other and developed simultaneously. As more urban workers became dependent on food grown by others, the potential profits of farming increased. Many of the technological developments and inventions were applied to farm machinery, which enabled farmers to produce more food more cheaply for the urban workers. As in industry, specialization and mechanization became the rule in agriculture, particularly on the newly opening Western prairies of Illinois, Iowa, and Kansas.

Inventions and Technology

Large-scale farming on the prairies spurred critical inventions. McCormick's mechanical reaper, patented in 1834, enabled a crew of six men to harvest in one day as much wheat as 15 men could using older methods. John Deere's steel plow, patented in 1837, provided a more durable tool to break the heavy prairie sod. Jerome Case's threshing machine multiplied the bushels of grain that could be separated from the stalk in a day's time.

The New Market Economy

These developments not only made large-scale production possible—they also shifted the major emphasis from corn to small-grain production and made farming for the international market feasible, which in turn made the Western farmer dependent on economic forces over which he had no control. This dependence produced the rising demand for government provision of free land and the agricultural colleges that later were provided by the Homestead and Morrill bills during the Civil War.

In the East, the trend was toward truck farming for the nearby burgeoning urban areas, and the production of milk, fruits, and berries. In both the East and the West, there was much interest in innovative practices that could increase production efficiency and profits.

The Revolution in Commerce

Before the coming of the railroad, coastal sailing ships practically monopolized domestic trade. The canal construction boom of the 1830s had taken commercial traffic from the river systems, but by 1840 the railroad had begun to emerge as the carrier of the future. Pennsylvania and New York State contained most of the 3,328 miles of track, but the rail system was rapidly expanding across the northern tier of states, tying the industrializing East to the expanding, agricultural West.

Everyday Life in the North

In the first half of the 19th century, the purchasing power of the average worker doubled. The household labor system was breaking down, and the number of wage earners exceeded for the first time the numbers of independent, self-employed Americans. Even so, everyday living was still quite primitive. Most people bathed only infrequently, and washed clothes and dishes even less. Housing was primitive for most, consisting of one- or two-room cabins heated by open fireplaces, with water carried in from springs or public faucets. For the working man, rural or urban, life was hard.

TEST TIP

Don't forget to break up your essay responses into several paragraphs to help make your argument clearer and easier to understand. Introduce just one main idea at the beginning of each paragraph, and use the remainder of that paragraph to support your main idea with relevant historical evidence.

Diverging Societies—Life in the South

The Southern states experienced dramatic growth in the second quarter of the nineteenth century. The economy grew more productive and more prosperous, but still the section called the South was basically agrarian, with few important cities and scattered industry. The plantation system, with its cash-crop production driven by the use of slave labor, remained the dominant institution. In the words of one historian, "The South grew, but it did not develop." The South grew more unlike the North, and it became more defensive of its distinctive way of life.

The Cotton Kingdom

The most important economic phenomenon of the early decades of the nineteenth century was the shift in population and production from the old "upper South" of Virginia and the Carolinas to the "lower South" of the newly opened Gulf States of Alabama, Mississippi, and Louisiana. This shift was the direct result of the increasing importance of cotton. In the older Atlantic states, tobacco retained its importance, but had shifted westward to the Piedmont and was replaced in the East by food grains. The southern Atlantic coast continued to produce rice, and southern Louisiana and east Texas retained their emphasis on sugarcane. But the rich black soil of the new Gulf states proved ideal for the production of short-staple cotton, especially after the invention of the gin, and cotton became the center of the Southern economy. Nearly three million bales were being produced annually by 1850.

Classes in the South

Although the large plantation with its white-columned mansion and its aristocratic owners is frequently seen as typical of Southern life, the truth is quite different.

The Planter Class

Owners of large farms who also owned 50 or more slaves actually formed a small minority of the Southern population. Three-fourths of Southern whites owned no slaves at all, almost half of slave-owning families owned fewer than six, and 12 percent owned 20 or more. But this minority of large slave owners exercised political and economic power far beyond what their numbers would indicate. They became a class to which all others paid deference, and they dominated the political and social life of their region.

The Yeoman Farmers

The largest group of Southern whites was the independent small farmers who worked their land with their family, sometimes side-by-side with one or two slaves, to produce their own food, with sometimes enough surplus to sell for a little extra cash. These simple folk predominated in the upland South and constituted a sizable element even in the lower cotton-producing states. Their major crop was corn, and indeed the South's corn crop was more valuable than its cotton. The corn was used at home for dinner tables and for animal feed, however, and so ranked behind cotton as an item of export. These people were generally poorer than their Northern counterparts.

The Poor Whites

Perhaps half a million white Southerners lived on the edge of the agrarian economy, in varying degrees of poverty. These "crackers," or "sandhillers," occupied the barren soils of the red hills or sandy bottoms, and they lived in squalor worse than the slaves. They formed a true underclass.

The Institution of Slavery

As the necessary concomitant of this expanding plantation system, the "Peculiar Institution" of black slavery fastened itself upon the Southern people, even as it isolated them from the rest of the world.

Slavery as a Labor System

The utilization of slave labor varied according to the region and the size of the growing unit. The large plantations growing cotton, sugar, or tobacco used the gang system, in which white overseers directed black drivers, who supervised large groups of workers in the fields, all performing the same operation. In the culture of rice, and on the smaller farms, slaves were assigned specific tasks, and when those tasks were finished, the worker had the remainder of the day to himself.

House servants usually were considered the most favored since they were spared the hardest physical labor and enjoyed the most intimate relationship with the owner's family. This could be considered a drawback, because they were frequently deprived of the social communion of the other slaves, enjoyed less privacy, and were more likely to suffer the direct wrath of a dissatisfied master or mistress.

It is still debated as to whether the living conditions of the Southern plantation slaves were better or worse than the Northern wage laborers. Some Northerners argued that the lack of the demeaning and family-splitting phenomenon of slave auctions in the North was evidence that wage labor was better than slavery. Certainly the lot of American slaves was better than virtually all their counterparts in South America and the Caribbean.

Urban Slavery in the Southern City

A sizable number of black slaves worked in the towns, serving as factory hands, domestics, artisans, and construction workers. They lived fairly independent lives and indeed a good number purchased their freedom with their savings, or quietly crossed the color line and disappeared into the general population. As the 19th century progressed, these people were increasingly seen as a bad model and a threat to the institution, and so urban slavery practically disappeared.

The Slave Trade

The most significant demographic shift in the first half of the 19th century was the movement of blacks from the Old South to the new Southwest. Traders shipped servants by the thousands to the newly opened cotton lands of the Gulf States. A prime field hand fetched an average price of $800 and as high as $1,500 in peak years. Families were frequently split apart by this miserable traffic. Planters freely engaged in this trade but assigned very low status to the traders who carried it out.

Although Congress had outlawed the importation of slaves from abroad since 1808, they continued to be smuggled in until the 1850s. The import ban kept the price up and encouraged the continuation of the internal trade.

Slaves' Reaction to Slavery

Blacks in bondage suffered varying degrees of repression and deprivation. The harsh slave codes were comprehensive in their restrictions on individual freedom, but they were unevenly applied, and so there was considerable variation in the severity of life. The typical slave probably received a rough, but adequate, diet and enjoyed crude but sufficient housing and clothing.

But the loss of freedom and the injustice of the system produced a variety of responses. Many "soldiered" on the job, and refused to work hard, or they found ways to sabotage the machinery or the crops. There was an underground system of ridicule toward the masters that was nurtured, as reflected in such oral literature as the "Br'er Rabbit" tales.

Violent reaction to repression was not uncommon. Gabriel Prosser in Richmond (1800), Denmark Vesey in Charleston (1822), and Nat Turner in coastal Virginia (1831) all plotted or led uprisings of blacks against their white masters. Fear of such uprisings kept whites in a state of constant apprehension.

The ultimate rebellion was to simply leave, and many tried to run away, some successfully. Especially from the states bordering the North, an ever-increasing number of slaves fled to freedom, many with the aid of the "underground railroad" and smugglers such as Harriet Tubman, who led over 300 of her family and friends to freedom after she herself had escaped.

"Inspection and Sale of a Negro," an 1854 engraving by Whitney, Jocelyn & Annin, depicts an African man being inspected for sale into slavery. (U.S. Library of Congress)

Most of those in bondage, however, were forced simply to adapt, and they did. A rich culture was developed within the confines of the system, and included distinctive patterns of language, music, and religion.

Commerce and Industry

The lack of manufacturing and business development has frequently been blamed for the South's losing its bid for independence in 1861–1865. Actually, the South was highly industrialized for its day, and compared favorably with most European nations in the development of manufacturing capacity. Obviously, it trailed far behind the North, so much so that when war erupted in 1861, the Northern states owned 81 percent of the factory capacity in the United States.

Manufacturing

The Southern states saw considerable development in the 1820s and 1830s in textiles and iron production and in flour milling. Richmond's Tredegar Iron Works compared favorably with the best in the North. Montgomery Bell's forges in Tennessee produced a good proportion of the ironware used in the upper South. Even so, most of the goods manufactured in these plants were for plantation consumption rather than for export, and they never exceeded two percent of the value of the cotton crop.

Commercial Activity

The businessmen of the South worked primarily with the needs and products of the plantation and the merchants of New Orleans and Charleston had to serve as bankers and insurance brokers as well as the agents for the planters. An organized network of commerce never developed in the South, even though the planters themselves were recognized as businessmen, since they operated large, complex staple-producing units.

Voices for Change

There were those who saw their native South sinking ever more into the position of dependency upon Northern bankers and businessmen, and they cried out for reform. James B. D. DeBow's *Review* advocated commercial development and agricultural diversification, but his cries fell largely on deaf ears.

Why were Southerners so wedded to the plantation system in the face of much evidence that it was retarding development? Certainly one reason is that cotton was profitable. Over the long run, capital return on plantation agriculture was at least as good as on Northern industrial capital. Even though skilled slaves abounded and could have manned factories, they were more profitable in the field.

Since most of the planter's capital was tied up in land and slaves, there was little left to invest in commerce or manufacturing. Most important, perhaps, was the value system of the Southern people, who put great store in traditional rural ideals: chivalry, leisure, and genteel elegance. Even the yeoman farmer held these values and hoped someday to attain the planters' position.

TEST TIP

The document-based question (DBQ) of the AP U.S. History exam will present you with an essay prompt along with several written or visual primary source documents. Before you begin writing, you should spend 15 minutes reviewing the documents. You may take notes on the documents in your DBQ booklet. DBQs often present you with documents that you're unfamiliar with, so you will need to use what you know about the topic in order to interpret the documents. Your score will not depend on which position you choose to argue; DBQs usually support multiple viewpoints. Rather, your score depends on how well you state a thesis and support it with both your historical knowledge and the evidence provided.

Life in the Southern States

The Role of Women

The position of the Southern woman was similar in many ways to her Northern counterpart, but also very different. She had fewer opportunities for anything but home life. The middle-class wife was heavily involved in the operation of the farm, and served as supervisor and nurse for the servants, as well as manager of the household, while the upper-class women served merely as ornaments. Education was rare and centered on the "domestic arts." High birth and death rates took their toll on childbearing women, and many men outlived several wives. The half-breed slave children were constant reminders of the planters' dalliances and produced constant tension and frustration among plantation wives.

Education

Schooling beyond literacy training was available only to the sons of the well-to-do. Academics and colleges abounded, but not for the working classes, and the few public schools were usually inferior and ill-supported.

Daily Life in the South

The accounts of travelers in the Southern states provide us with vivid pictures of living conditions on the average homestead. Housing was primitive—one- or two-room cabins being the rule. Corn, sweet potatoes, and pork formed the staples of the Southern diet, and health problems reflected the resulting vitamin deficiencies. Rickets and pellagra were common ailments.

Although the prevalence of violence has probably been overstated, it certainly existed, and the duel remained an accepted avenue for settling differences well into the nineteenth century.

Southern Response to the Anti-Slavery Movement

As the crusade for abolition intensified in the North, the South assumed an ever more defensive position. Biblical texts were used to justify the enslavement of an "inferior race." Scientific arguments were advanced to prove the inherent inferiority of the black African. Southern postal authorities refused to deliver any mail that contained information antagonistic to the slave system. Any kind of dissent was brutally suppressed, and the South became more and more a closed society. Literature and scholarship shriveled, and creative writers like Edgar Allan Poe and William Gilmore Simms became the rare exception.

The last serious Southern debate over the institution of slavery took place in the Virginia legislature in 1832, in the aftermath of Nat Turner's revolt. That discussion squelched any move toward emancipation. In 1836, Southern members of the U.S. House of Representatives pushed through the infamous "gag rule," which forbade any discussion on the question of slavery on the floor of the House. That rule remained in effect until 1844.

The most elaborate product of this ferment was John C. Calhoun's theory of the "concurrent majority," in which a dual presidency would ensure a South independent of Northern dominance and would forever keep majority rule at bay.

Beginning in 1837, regular conventions were held across the South to discuss ways to escape Northern economic and political hegemony.

As the decade of the 1840s opened, the two sections were becoming more and more estranged, and the channels of compromise were becoming more and more poisoned by the emotional responses to black slavery. The development that contributed most to keeping the sore festering was westward expansion.

Westward Movement

The rising sense of nationalism, which followed the War of 1812, was fed by the rapidly expanding population, the reform impulse of the 1830s, and the desire to acquire new markets and resources for the burgeoning economy of "Young America." Americans increasingly began looking to the West as an area for economic development and expansion.

Louisiana and the Far West Fur Trade

The Lewis and Clark expedition had scarcely filed its reports before a variety of adventurous entrepreneurs began to penetrate the newly acquired territory and the lands beyond. "Mountain men" like Jim Bridges trapped the Rocky Mountain streams and the headwaters of the Missouri River system for greatly prized beaver pelts. Explorers like Jedediah Smith mapped the vast territory that stretched from the Rockies to the Sierra Nevada range and on into California. John Jacob Astor established a fur post at the mouth of the Columbia River, which he named Astoria, and challenged the British claim to the Northwest. Though he was forced to sell out his establishment to the British, he lobbied

Congress to pass trade restrictions against British furs, and eventually became the first American millionaire from the profits of the American Fur Company. The growing trade with the Orient in furs and other specialty goods was sharpening the desire of many businessmen for American ports on the Pacific Coast.

"Fur Traders Descending the Missouri," 1845, a painting by George Caleb Bingham. This image characterized the impact of the opening of new territory following the Lewis and Clark expedition. (Metropolitan Museum of Art)

The Oregon Country

The Adams-Onis Treaty of 1819 had set the northern boundary of Spanish possessions near the present northern border of California. The territory north of that line and west of the vague boundaries of the Louisiana Territory had been claimed over the years by Spain, England, Russia, France, and the United States. By the 1820s, all these claims had been yielded to Britain and the United States. The Hudson's Bay Company had established a fur trading station at Fort Vancouver and claimed control south to the Columbia. The United States claimed all the way north to the 54°40′ parallel. Unable to settle the dispute, they had agreed on a joint occupation of the disputed land.

In the 1830s American missionaries followed the traders and trappers to the Oregon country, and began to publicize the richness and beauty of the land, sending back official reports on their work, which were published in the new, inexpensive "penny press" papers. Everyone read these reports, and the result was the "Oregon Fever" of the 1840s, as thousands of settlers trekked across the Great Plains and the Rocky Mountains to settle the new Shangri-La.

The Texas Question: 1836–1845

Texas had been a state in the Republic of Mexico since 1822, following the Mexican revolution against Spanish control. The United States had offered to buy the territory at the time, as it had renounced its claim to the area in the Adams-Onis agreement of 1819. The new Mexican government indignantly refused to sell, but immediately began to invite immigration from the north by offering land grants to Stephen Austin and other Americans. They needed to increase the population of the area and to produce revenue for the infant government. The Americans responded in great numbers, and by 1835 approximately 35,000 "gringos" were homesteading on Texas land.

The Mexican officials saw their power base eroding as the foreigners flooded in, and so they moved to tighten control through restrictions on new immigration and tax increases. The Texans responded in 1836 by proclaiming independence and establishing a new republic. The ensuing war was short-lived. The Mexican dictator Antonio López de Santa Anna advanced north and annihilated the Texan garrisons at the Alamo and at Goliad. On April 23, 1836, Sam Houston defeated him at San Jacinto, and the Mexicans were forced to let Texas go its way.

Houston immediately asked the American government for recognition and annexation, but President Andrew Jackson feared the revival of the slavery issue since the new state would come in on the slave-holding side of the political balance, and he also feared war with Mexico, so he did nothing. When Van Buren followed suit, the new republic sought foreign recognition and support, which the European nations eagerly provided, hoping thereby to create a counterbalance to rising American power and influence in the Southwest. France and England both quickly concluded trade agreements with the Texans.

DID YOU KNOW?

When the United States annexed Texas in 1845, it agreed to allow up to four additional states be formed from the territory contained in the Republic of Texas.

New Mexico and California

The district of New Mexico had, like Texas, encouraged American immigration, and for the same reasons. Soon that state was more American than Mexican. The Santa Fe Trail—from Independence, Missouri, to the town of Santa Fe—created a prosperous trade in mules, gold, silver, and furs that moved north in exchange for manufactured goods which went south. American settlements sprung up all along the route.

Though the Mexican officials in California had not encouraged it, American immigration nevertheless had been substantial. First traders and whaling crews, then merchants, arrived to set up stores and developed a brisk trade. As the decade of the 1830s passed, the number of newcomers increased. Since the Missouri Compromise had established the northern limits for slavery at the 36°30′ parallel, most of this Mexican territory lay in the potential slave-holding domain, and many of the settlers had carried their bondsmen with them.

Manifest Destiny and Sectional Stress

The question of expansion was universally discussed. Although the strongest sentiment was found in the North and West, the South had its own ambitions, and they usually involved the extension of their "peculiar institution."

The Democrats generally favored the use of force, if necessary, to extend American borders. The Whigs favored more peaceful means, through diplomacy. Some Whigs, like Henry Clay, feared expansion under any circumstances, because of its potential for aggravating the slavery issue.

Clay was closest to the truth. As the decade of the 1840s opened, the questions of Texas, California, and the New Mexican territory were increasingly prominent, and the sectional tension was destined to light the fires of civil war.

Tyler, Polk, and Continued Westward Expansion

Tyler and the Whigs

When William Henry Harrison became president, he immediately began to rely on Whig leader Henry Clay for advice and direction, just as Clay had planned and expected he would. He appointed to his Cabinet those whom Clay suggested, and at Clay's behest he called a special session of Congress to vote the Whig legislative program into action. To the Whigs' dismay, Harrison died of pneumonia just one month into his term, to be replaced by Vice President John Tyler.

A states' rights Southerner and a strict constitutionalist who had been placed on the Whig ticket to draw Southern votes, Tyler rejected the entire Whig program of a national bank, high protective tariffs, and federally funded internal improvements (roads, canals, etc.). Clay stubbornly determined to push the program through anyway. In the resulting legislative confrontations, Tyler vetoed a number of Whig-sponsored bills.

The Whigs were furious. Every Cabinet member but one resigned in protest. Tyler was officially expelled from the party and made the target of the first serious impeachment attempt. (It failed.) In opposition to Tyler over the next few years, the Whigs, under the leadership of Clay, transformed themselves from a loose grouping of diverse factions to a coherent political party with an elaborate organization.

One piece of important legislation that did get passed during Tyler's administration was the Preemption Act (1841), allowing settlers who had squatted on unsurveyed federal lands first chance to buy the land (up to 160 acres at low prices) once it was put on the market.

The Webster-Ashburton Treaty

The member of Tyler's Cabinet who did not immediately resign in protest was Secretary of State Daniel Webster. He stayed on to negotiate the Webster-Ashburton Treaty with Great Britain.

There were now several causes of tension between the U.S. and Great Britain, including:

1. The Canada-Maine boundary in the area of the Aroostook Valley was disputed. British efforts to build a military road through the disputed area led to reaction by Maine militia in a bloodless confrontation known as the "Aroostook War" (1838).

2. The Caroline Affair (1837) involved an American ship, the *Caroline*, that had been carrying supplies to Canadian rebels. It was burned by Canadian loyalists who crossed the U.S. border in order to do so.

3. In the *Creole* Incident, Britain declined to return escaped slaves who had taken over a U.S. merchant ship, the *Creole*, and sailed to the British-owned Bahamas.

4. British naval vessels, patrolling the African coast to suppress slave smuggling, sometimes stopped and searched American ships.

The Webster-Ashburton Treaty (1842) dealt with these problems in a spirit of mutual concession and forbearance:

1. Conflicting claims along the Canada-Maine boundary were compromised.

2. The British expressed regret for the destruction of the *Caroline.*

3. The British promised to avoid "officious interference" in freeing slaves in cases like that of the *Creole*.

4. Both countries agreed to cooperate in patrolling the African coast to prevent slave smuggling.

The Webster-Ashburton Treaty was also important in that it helped create an atmosphere of compromise and forbearance in U.S.-British relations.

After negotiating the treaty, Webster too resigned from Tyler's Cabinet.

TEST TIP

Be sure you eat a good breakfast the day of the exam. It's a long morning. Although you cannot eat or drink anything during the test, you may bring along a snack or a bottle of water for your break time.

The Texas Issue

Rejected by the Whigs and without ties to the Democrats, Tyler was a politician without a party, but not without ambitions. Hoping to gather a political following of his own, he sought an issue with powerful appeal and believed he had found it in the question of Texas annexation.

The Republic of Texas had gained its independence from Mexico in 1836 and, since most of its settlers had come from the U.S., immediately sought admission as a state. It was rejected because anti-slavery forces in Congress resented the presence of slavery in Texas and because Mexico threatened war should the U.S. annex Texas.

To excite American jealousy and thus hasten annexation, Texas President Sam Houston made much show of negotiating for closer relations with Great Britain. Southerners feared that Britain, which opposed slavery, might bring about its abolition in Texas and then use Texas as a base from which to undermine slavery in the American South. Other Americans were disturbed at the possibility of a British presence in Texas because of the obstacle it would present to what many Americans were coming to believe—and what New York journalist John L. O'Sullivan would soon express—as America's "manifest destiny to overspread the continent."

Tyler's new secretary of state, John C. Calhoun, negotiated an annexation treaty with Texas. Calhoun's identification with extreme pro-slavery forces and his insertion in the treaty of pro-slavery statements brought the treaty's rejection by the Senate (1844). Nevertheless, the Texas issue had been injected into national politics and could not be made to go away.

An Age of Social Reform

The American people in 1840 found themselves living in an era of transition and instability. The society was changing and traditional values were being challenged. The responses to this uncertainty were two-fold: a movement toward reform and a rising desire for order and control.

We have a fairly vivid picture of what Americans were like during this period, from accounts by hundreds of foreign visitors who came to this country to observe our society-in-the-making. These observers noted a restless population, always on the move, compulsive joiners of associations, committed to progress, working hard and playing hard, driven relentlessly by a desire for wealth. They believed in and talked about equality, but the reality was that the system was increasingly creating a class society. Americans seemed to lean toward violence, and mob incidents were common.

Dorothea Dix: America's Mental Health Pioneer

National Library of Medicine

"In a world where there is so much to be done, I felt strongly impressed that there must be something for me to do."

—Dorothea Dix

At a time when most American women could not vote, attend college, or in many states even own property, Dorothea Dix was a young woman who overcame an unhappy childhood and serious depression to become one of America's important early social reformers of the 19th century. In her quest to establish insane asylums throughout the United States, Dix became the first woman to speak before the U.S. Congress. During the Civil War, she became Superintendent of Female Nurses for the Union Army and convinced the Army that women could take on tasks normally handled by male nurses.

Dix began her career as a teacher and writer. Entering a period of severe illness (either depression or tuberculosis) in the mid-1830s, she was sent in 1836 by friends to England to recover on the family estate of the Rathbones, wealthy Quaker reformers. She spent a year in England, emerged from her depression, and noticed the humane and effective programs Quakers had developed in institutions for the mentally ill. She studied these asylums, such as York Retreat, and noted the family-type setting that rehabilitated the mentally ill.

Upon returning to America in 1841, she began teaching a Sunday school class to women in a Boston jail where—in addition to criminals—drunkards, prostitutes, and the retarded, mentally ill, and insane were often sent by their families. She asked to see how the mentally ill were treated and was shown their quarters, which amounted to a cold, damp, smelly room with straw on the floor. The patients, half-clothed, were huddled together for warmth. Dix began visiting jails and almshouses throughout Massachusetts, observing conditions and taking extensive notes. It was assumed at the time that mental illness was incurable and that money spent trying to improve institutional conditions was wasted. Dix

(Continued)

The Reform Impulse: Major Sources of Reform

Romanticism held a belief in the innate goodness of man, and thus in his improvability. This movement had its roots in turn-of-the-century Europe, and it emphasized the emotions and feelings over rationality. It appeared as a reaction against the excesses of the Enlightenment, which had stressed reason to the exclusion of feelings.

There was also a growing need perceived for a stable social order and control over the forces that were threatening the traditional values.

One theme of the Second Great Awakening was the imminent return of Jesus in what is known as the Second Coming. Evangelicals felt an urgency to reform society to hasten the Second Coming.

Each of these major streams of reform activity was centered in the Northeast, especially in New England.

argued that, in fact, improving conditions would provide an opportunity for the mentally ill to get better and be productive. She assembled a report, which she then delivered to the Massachusetts legislature. After a long debate, the state legislature approved financing for institutions for the mentally ill.

Following this initial success in Massachusetts, Dix visited every state east of the Mississippi, observing conditions, lobbying state legislatures, and raising awareness about mental illness. She traveled over 80,000 miles, visiting more than 9,000 mentally ill individuals in a wide variety of facilities. In Rhode Island in 1843, she reported to the state legislature about a patient in a poorhouse named Abram Simmons. Simmons, though ill and covered with sores, was confined in a cage for 30 years. Her report shocked the Rhode Island legislators into action. Dix went on to found 32 hospitals, a number of schools for the mentally retarded, and a number of nursing training facilities. Despite her own poor health, she tirelessly advocated for the mentally ill and insane. In 1848 she submitted a request to the U.S. Congress for five million acres to be set aside to take care of the mentally ill and addressed Congress herself, the first woman to do so. Despite its passage by both houses, the bill was vetoed by President Franklin Pierce in 1854.

Exhausted and discouraged, Dix returned to Europe to investigate conditions and recommend improvement for the treatment of the mentally ill there. She visited Russia, Denmark, Sweden, Holland, England, France, Scotland, Germany, and Belgium. Dix's efforts resulted in improvements in many nations.

At the start of the Civil War she volunteered to be Superintendent of Union Army Nurses. While she was not as successful in this effort, her efforts did convince the Army that women nurses could effectively serve in field hospitals.

In the years following the Civil War, Dix returned to her mental health reform work, though her work by now was mainly confined to letter writing. Unfortunately the family-type care that she advocated in asylums became increasingly rare as the mental hospitals grew into overcrowded, impersonal establishments.

Dix was one of the most effective advocates for the mentally ill in the nineteenth century, yet she was incredibly humble, refusing to put her names on many publications and insisting that hospitals she helped found not be named after her. She spent her last six years in a New Jersey hospital and died at the age of 85 in 1887. Her life work is best summarized by her own words: "If I am cold, they are cold; if I am weary, they are distressed; if I am alone, they are abandoned."

Remaking Society: Organized Reform

Protestant Revivalism was a powerful force for the improvement of both individuals and society. Preachers at Second Great Awakening revivals stressed that to achieve salvation, individuals needed to work for the moral perfection of society in addition to repenting personal sins. Evangelist Charles G. Finney, who served as president of Oberlin College, strongly opposed slavery as being in conflict with the spirit of Christianity and encouraged women to pray in public meetings, a new practice for American churches. A strong sectarian spirit split the Protestant movement into many denominations.

Abolitionism

The early anti-slavery movement was relatively benign, advocating only the purchase and transportation of slaves to free states in Africa. The American Colonization Society was organized in 1817 and established the colony of Liberia in 1830. Returning slaves to Africa continued to be supported by many as an answer to American slavery, though more radical thinkers called for the abolition of slavery.

In 1831, William Lloyd Garrison started his paper, *The Liberator,* and began to advocate total and immediate emancipation, thus giving new life to the movement. He founded the New England Anti-Slavery Society in 1832 and the American Anti-Slavery Society in 1833. Theodore Weld pursued the same goals, but advocated more gradual means.

Frederick Douglass, having escaped from his Maryland owner, became a fiery orator for the movement, and published his own newspaper, the *North Star.*

There were frequent outbursts of anti-abolition violence in the 1830s against the fanaticism of the radicals. Abolitionist editor Elijah Lovejoy was killed by a mob in Illinois.

The movement split into two wings: Garrison's radical followers, and the moderates who favored "moral suasion" and petitions to Congress. In 1840, the Liberty Party, the first national anti-slavery party, fielded a presidential candidate on the platform of "free soil," nonexpansion of slavery into the new Western territories.

The literary crusade continued with Harriet Beecher Stowe's *Uncle Tom's Cabin* being the most influential among the many books that presented the abolitionist message.

Temperance

Concern about alcoholism led to the creation of the American Society for Promotion of Temperance in 1826. It was strongly supported by Protestants and just as strongly opposed by new Catholic immigrants.

Public Education

The motivations for the free school crusade were mixed. Some wanted to provide opportunity for all children to learn the skills for self-fulfillment and success in a republic. Others wanted to use schools as agencies for social control—to Americanize the new immigrant children as well as to promote Protestant values to Catholics and to defuse the growing problems of urbanization. The stated purpose of the public schools was to instill social values: thrift, order, discipline, and democracy.

Public apathy and even opposition met the early reformers: Horace Mann, the first secretary of the Massachusetts Board of Education, and Henry Barnard, his counterpart in Connecticut and Rhode Island.

The movement picked up momentum in the 1830s, but progress was very spotty. Few public schools were available in the West, fewer still for Southern whites, and none at all for Southern blacks.

Higher Education

In 1839, the first state-supported school for women, Troy Female Seminary, was founded in Troy, New York. Oberlin College in Ohio was the nation's first coeducational college. The Perkins School for the Blind in Boston was the first of its kind in the United States.

Asylums for the Mentally Ill

Dorothea Dix (see sidebar) led the fight for reforming institutions for the mentally ill, advocating more humane treatment.

Prison Reform

The purpose of the new penitentiaries was not to just punish, but to rehabilitate. The first was built in Auburn, New York, in 1821.

Feminism

The Seneca Falls, New York, meeting in 1848 and its "Declaration of Sentiments and Resolutions" marked the beginning of the modern feminist movement. The goals of early women's rights reformers for equality were clearly presented. "All men and women are created equal," the declaration stated, as it rewrote the Declaration of Independence with men in the role of the tyrant instead of King George III. The Grimké sisters, Elizabeth Cady Stanton, and Harriet Beecher Stowe were active in these early days. The movement was linked with that of the abolitionists, as many saw that both blacks and women were denied rights guaranteed to white men.

Table 6.1 Reforms and Reformers in Antebellum America

Issue	Reform Target	Key Reformers/ Organizations	Methods
Abolitionism	Enslavement of 4,000,000 blacks	William Lloyd Garrison, Theodore Weld, American Anti-Slavery Society	Petitions, newspapers, mail campaigns
Institutional improvement	Treatment of criminals, delinquents, insane	Dorothea Dix, Auburn System	Lobbying of state legislatures, separate asylums for the mentally ill, efforts to rehabilitate, discipline prisoners
Temperance	Alcoholism (7.1 gallons of pure alcohol consumed annually per person over the age of 14 in 1830)	Lyman Beecher, American Temperance Society, churches	Sermons, tracts, rallies, abstinence pledges, prohibition laws, *result* in consumption dropping to 2 gallons per person by 1845
Women's rights	Legal subordination of women	Lucretia Mott, Elizabeth Cady Stanton, Susan B. Anthony, Seneca Falls Convention	Lobbying, petitions, speaking tours
School reform	Low literacy, school attendance rates	Horace Mann, state school boards	Lobbying, rewarding good behavior rather than using corporal punishment, hiring women as teachers; by 1850, 50% of white children were enrolled in schools—highest in the world
Moral improvement	Breakdown in social order seen with the growth of cities, industrialization, and westward migration	Charles G. Finney, American Bible Society, Sabbatarian movement	Growth in Sunday schools, literature, speaking tours, laws against work on Sunday, petitions

(Before taking the quiz noted below, please review the summary timeline for this chapter on the following pages.)

Democracy, Economic Growth, and Social Reform (1800–1848)

Historical Timeline (1800–1848)

1801	John Marshall becomes Chief Justice Midnight judges appointed by Adams
1803	*Marbury v. Madison* decision Louisiana Purchase
1804	Lewis and Clark expedition
1807	*Chesapeake-Leopard* incident Embargo Act Robert Fulton builds *Clermont*, first steamboat
1811	Battle of Tippecanoe
1812	Congress declares war on Britain
1814	British burn Washington, D.C. Treaty of Ghent ends War of 1812 Hartford Convention
1815	Jackson defeats British at New Orleans
1819	First section of Erie Canal is opened Panic of 1819 *McCullough v. Maryland* decision
1820	Missouri Compromise
1823	Monroe Doctrine
1824	Congress sets protective tariffs *Gibbons v. Ogden* decision promotes interstate trade
1825	John Quincy Adams wins Corrupt Bargain presidential election
1828	Tariff of Abominations Jackson wins presidency
1830	Jackson vetoes Maysville Road extension Baltimore & Ohio becomes first railroad company Joseph Smith publishes *Book of Mormon*
1831	*Cherokee Nation v. Georgia* denies Indian claim of nationhood Nat Turner's Rebellion
1832	Jackson vetoes U.S. Bank re-charter Nullification crisis in South Carolina

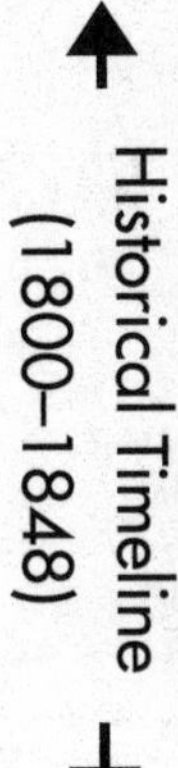

1834	Women workers at Lowell, Massachusetts, stage first strike
1836	Texas independence fight Gag rule prevents discussion of slavery in Congress
1837	Panic of 1837 caused by Jackson's economic policy
1838	Cherokees moved west on Trail of Tears
1842	*Commonwealth v. Hunt* legalizes unions
1848	Seneca Falls Convention urges equal treatment for women

AP U.S. History

Mini-Test 1 (covers chapters 3-6)

This mini-test is also available online at the REA Study Center with the additional benefits of timed testing, automatic scoring, and a detailed topic-level score report (www.rea.com/studycenter).

TIME: 20 minutes
20 multiple-choice questions

Directions: Each of the questions or incomplete statements below is followed by four suggested answers or completions. Select the best answer for each question.

Questions 1 and 2 refer to the following excerpt:

"But you do not do this, and maliciously make delay in it, I certify to you that, with the help of God, we shall powerfully enter into your country and shall make war against you in all ways and manners that we can and shall subject you to the yoke and obedience of the Church and of their Highnesses; we shall take you and your wives and your children, and shall make slaves of them, and as such shall sell and dispose of them as their Highnesses may command; and we shall take away your goods, and shall do you all the mischief and damage that we can, as to vassals who do not obey and refuse to receive their lord and resist and contradict him; and we protest that the deaths and losses which shall accrue from this are your fault, and not that of their Highnesses, or ours, nor of these cavaliers who come with us."

—Palacio Robles, Council of Castille, "El Requerimiento," 1510

(*The Requerimiento was to be read to indigenous peoples encountered by Spanish conquistadors*)

1. What was the long-term cause of the statement made by Palacio Robles?

(A) The native populations in North America developed a wide variety of economic structures.

(B) the *encomienda* system used to support plantation-based agriculture

(C) European expansion into the Western hemisphere

(D) French and Dutch rivalry for control of the new world

2. Robles' views best reflect the ideology of which of the following developments in the 1500s?

   (A) the spread of Enlightenment ideas

   (B) the growth of an Atlantic economy

   (C) the belief in white superiority

   (D) native peoples striving to maintain their cultural autonomy

Questions 3 and 4 refer to the following excerpt:

> Resolved, That it is true as a general principle, and is also expressly declared by one of the amendments to the Constitutions, that "the powers not delegated to the United States by the Constitution, our prohibited by it to the States, are reserved to the States respectively, or to the people"; and that no power over the freedom of religion, freedom of speech, or freedom of the press being delegated to the United States by the Constitution, nor prohibited by it to the States, all lawful powers respecting the same did of right remain, and were reserved to the States or the people: that thus was manifested their determination to retain to themselves the right of judging how far the licentiousness of speech and of the press may be abridged without lessening their useful freedom, and how far those abuses which cannot be separated from their use should be tolerated, rather than the use be destroyed.
>
> —Thomas Jefferson, "Virginia Resolution," 1798

3. This resolution was an example of which of the following?

   (A) the debate that centered on the relationship between the national government and the states

   (B) the debate that centered on the conduct of foreign affairs

   (C) the compromises made to form a constitution for a new national government

   (D) the debate that centered on early American economic policy

4. Which of the following was a long-term effect of the conflict Jefferson is describing in the Virginia Resolution?

   (A) the Spanish American War

   (B) the Civil War

   (C) the ratification of the Bill of Rights

   (D) the 1820 Missouri Compromise

Questions 5 and 6 are based on the following excerpt:

We maintain that no compensation should be given to the planters emancipating their slaves:

- Because it would be a surrender of the great fundamental principle, that man cannot hold property in man;
- Because slavery is a crime, and therefore is not an article to be sold;
- Because the holders of slaves are not the just proprietors of what they claim; freeing the slave is not depriving them of property, but restoring it to its rightful owner; it is not wronging the master, but righting the slave—restoring him to himself;
- Because, if compensation is to be given at all, it should be given to the outraged and guiltless slaves, and not to those who have plundered and abused them.

We regard as delusive, cruel and dangerous, any scheme of expatriation which pretends to aid, either directly or indirectly, in the emancipation of the slaves, or to be a substitute for the immediate and total abolition of slavery.

—Declaration of Sentiments of the American Anti-Slavery Convention, December 1833

5. The language used in this excerpt most directly reflects the influence of which of the following?

(A) states rights
(B) the Second Great Awakening
(C) nativism
(D) regional economic specialization

6. This excerpt is most clearly an example of which of the following developments in the mid-19th century?

(A) the outlawing of the international slave trade
(B) the resistance to an initiative for a stonger democracy
(C) abolitionists mounting a highly visible campaign against slavery
(D) racial stereotyping that provided the foundation for the Southern defense of slavery as a positive good

Questions 7 and 8 refer to the following excerpt from a letter:

If I was in any doubt, as to the right which the Parliament of Great Britain had to tax us without our consent, I should most heartily coincide with you in opinion, that to petition, and petition only, is the proper method to apply for relief; because we should then be asking a favor, and not claiming a right, which, by the law of nature and our constitution, we are, in my opinion, indubitably entitled to. I should even think it criminal to go farther than this, under such an idea; but none such I have. I think the Parliament of Great Britain hath no more right to put their hands into my pockets, without my consent, than I have to put my hands into yours for money; and this being already urged to them in a firm, but decent manner, by all the colonies, what reason is there to expect any thing from their justice?

—George Washington, letter to Bryan Fairfax (July 20, 1774)

7. The long term cause of Washington's complaints was which of the following?

   (A) loyalist opposition

   (B) desire for independence by colonial elites

   (C) the French Revolution's spread throughout Europe

   (D) the Seven Years' War

8. Which of the following was one of the effects of the sentiments expressed by Washington?

   (A) growing independence movement led by colonial elites

   (B) the Seven Years' War

   (C) imperial control over North America

   (D) George Washington's Farewell Address

Questions 9 and 10 refer to the following act of Congress:

An act to provide for an exchange of lands with the Indians residing in any of the states or territories, and for their removal west of the river Mississippi: That it shall and may be lawful for the President of the United States to cause so much of any territory belonging to the United States, west of the river Mississippi, not included in any state or organized territory, and to which the Indian title has been extinguished [revoked], as he [the president] may judge necessary, to be divided into a suitable number of districts, for the reception of such tribes or nations of Indians as may choose to exchange the lands where they now reside, and remove there; and to cause each of said districts to be so described by natural or artificial marks, as to be easily distinguished from every other...

— Indian Removal Act of 1830

9. Jackson's policy in removing Indians from their lands led to which of the following?

(A) the increased settlement in areas forcibly taken from American Indians

(B) U.S. interest in expanding trade

(C) territorial boundaries of the U.S. expanding overseas

(D) a renewed commitment to nullification by Southerners

10. The excerpt reflects which of the following ideologies?

(A) Manifest Destiny

(B) Nativism

(C) American cultural superiority

(D) a stronger governmental role in the American economic system

Questions 11 and 12 refer to the following excerpt from a letter from Thomas Jefferson:

This momentous question, like a fire bell in the night, awakened and filled me with terror. I considered it, at once as the [death] knell of the Union. It is hushed, indeed, for the moment. But this is a reprieve only, not a final sentence. A geographical line, coinciding with a marked principle, moral and political, once conceived and held up to the angry passions of men, will never be obliterated; and every new irritation will mark it deeper and deeper.

—Thomas Jefferson to John Randolph, April 22, 1820

11. Which of the following events is Jefferson referencing in this excerpt?

(A) the Louisiana Purchase

(B) the tariffs

(C) the Market Revolution

(D) the Missouri Compromise

12. The issue described by Jefferson is most similar to an issue that arose in which of the following decades?

    (A) 1830s

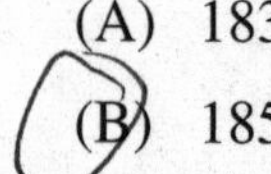

    (B) 1850s

    (C) 1870s

    (D) 1880s

Questions 13 and 14 refer to the following excerpt:

> "The hysteria began with two young girls, both of whom suffered fits, screaming and rolling on the floor…A special court was set up to get to the bottom of the matter—in sorcery cases it was now judged that the ordinary law would not suffice. The proceedings were as outrageous as the accusations. Those who confessed to doing the "Devil's work" were released; ironically those who refused to plead to crimes they had not committed were judge guilty…By early autumn [of1692], fourteen women and five men were hanged. Giles Corey was, of course, uniquely pressed to death with heavy stones. Even two dogs were slaughtered. Meanwhile, another 150 people awaited trial in damp, stinking, overcrowded jails; some died there."
>
> —Jay Winik, *The Great Upheaval: America and the Birth of the Modern World 1788–1800*

13. Which of the following was the cause of the events described in the excerpt?

    (A) Africans resisting the dehumanizing aspects of slavery

    (B) the Chesapeake colonies reliance on tobacco

    (C) New England Puritans establishing a community of like-minded religious believers

    (D) English settlers dissatisfied with territorial settlements

14. A similar decade of an increasingly homogeneous culture was which of the following?

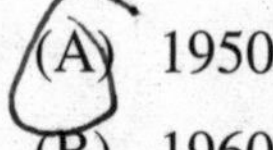

    (A) 1950s

    (B) 1960s

    (C) 1970s

    (D) 1980s

Questions 15 and 16 refer to the following excerpts from speeches at the Constitutional Convention:

"In a government consisting of enumerated powers, such as is proposed for the United States, a bill of rights would not only be unnecessary, but, in my humble judgment, highly imprudent. In all societies, there are many powers and rights, which cannot be particularly enumerated. A bill of rights annexed to a constitution, is an enumeration of the powers reserved. If we attempt an enumeration, every thing that is not enumerated, is presumed to be given. The consequence is, that an imperfect enumeration would throw all implied power into the scale of the government, and the rights of the people would be rendered incomplete…[A]n enumeration of the powers of government...is neither so dangerous nor important as an omission in the enumeration of the rights of the people."

—James Wilson, speech to Constitutional Convention, November 1787

"If, indeed, the constitution itself so well defined the powers of the government that no mistake could arise, and we were well assured that our governors would always act right, then we might be satisfied without an explicit reservation of those rights with which the people ought not, and mean not to part. But…we know that it is the nature of power to seek its own augmentation and thus the loss of liberty is the necessary consequence of a loose or extravagant delegation of authority. National freedom has been, and will be the sacrifice of ambition and power, and it is our duty to employ the present opportunity in stipulating such restrictions as are best calculated to protect us from oppression and slavery."

—Robert Whitehill, speech to the Constitutional Convention, November 1787

15. The basic disagreement between Wilson and Whitehill at the Constitutional Convention concerns

    (A) the separation of powers

    (B) the need for the inclusion of a bill of rights in the Constitution

    (C) the freedoms of press, speech, and religion

    (D) political parties

16. Which of the following led to the arguments made by Wilson and Whitehill?

    (A) the Bill of Rights

    (B) the French withdrawal from North America

    (C) the seizure of Indian lands

    (D) the Articles of Confederation

Questions 17 and 18 refer to the following excerpt:

"Englishman Nicholas Cresswell dryly observed that [colonial] America was a paradise for women because the chances for marriage were so good. Though on the frontier women undoubtedly worked as hard or harder than most urban women in Europe, the poorer women in America were usually better off than their counterparts in the old country....From the beginning, the social freedom of young women, which is still in marked contrast with custom in some European countries today, was evident in America. ...The wife and mother in the rude settlement on or near the frontier was more than a housekeeper; she was an indispensable part of the apparatus of survival. [Historians] found that husbands usually gave over the administration and distribution of their estates to their wives, something that seems not to have been common in England."

—Carl Degler, *Out of Our Past* (Harper & Row, 1984)

17. Which of the following groups would disagree with Degler's assessment of American women?

    (A) female progressive reformers

    (B) plantation owners

    (C) radical republicans

    (D) federalist leaders

18. Which of the following movements best represents a desire to expand on the social phenomena described by Degler?

    (A) the populist movement

    (B) the conservationists

    (C) the nativist movement

    (D) the Second Great Awakening

Questions 19 and 20 refer to the following excerpt:

I HEARTILY ACCEPT the motto, — "That government is best which governs least"; and I should like to see it acted up to more rapidly and systematically. Carried out, it finally amounts to this, which also I believe, — "That government is best which governs not at all"; and when men are prepared for it, that will be the kind of government which they will have. Government is at best but an expedient; but most governments are usually, and all governments are sometimes, inexpedient...Witness the present Mexican war, the work of comparatively a few individuals using the standing government as their tool; for, in the outset, the people would not have consented to this measure... Unjust laws exist; shall we be content to obey them, or shall we endeavor to amend them, and obey them until we have succeeded, or shall we transgress them at once? Men generally, under such a government as this, think that they ought to wait until they have persuaded the majority to alter them. They think that, if they should resist, the remedy would be worse than the evil. But it is the fault of the government itself that the remedy *is* worse than the evil. *It* makes it worse. Why is it not more apt to anticipate and provide for reform? Why does it not cherish its wise minority? Why does it cry and resist before it is hurt? Why does it not encourage its citizens to be on the alert to point out its faults, and *do* better than it would have them?

—Henry David Thoreau, *Civil Disobedience* (1849)

19. In this statement by Thoreau, his resistance to the government is triggered by

    (A) the Fugitive Slave Act

    (B) the annexation of Texas

    (C) the Mexican-American War

    (D) tariffs

20. Which of the following groups would have most supported Thoreau's ideas as articulated in just the first three sentences of this excerpt?

    (A) Supporters of the Great Society

    (B) progressive reformers

    (C) Republicans in the 1980s

    (D) African American civil rights activists

Answer Key
Mini-Test 1

1. (C)
2. (C)
3. (A)
4. (B)
5. (B)
6. (C)
7. (D)
8. (A)
9. (A)
10. (B)
11. (D)
12. (B)
13. (C)
14. (A)
15. (B)
16. (D)
17. (A)
18. (D)
19. (C)
20. (C)

Answer Explanations
Mini Test 1

1. (C)

European exploration into the new world was driven by a desire for riches, increased glory, and to spread the gospel (Gold, Glory, and Gospel).

2. (C)

The "Requerimiento" reflects the racism that many Europeans used to justify their treatment of the Native Americans as well as African Slaves.

3. (A)

During John Adams' presidency, the Alien and Sedition Acts were passed which limited the power of the Democrat-Republicans. Thomas Jefferson and James Madison authored the Virginia and Kentucky Resolutions, which argued in favor of nullifying the unconstitutional Sedition Act. This was one of the first of many disputes that centered on the power of the national government.

4. (B)

Jefferson continually worried about the growth in power of the federal government as he believed this would result in a decrease in influence for state and local governments. This conflict over states', rights with regard to the issue of slavery would eventually lead to disunion and the Civil War.

5. (B)

The American Anti-Slavery Convention was not interested in any plan of compensation to slave owners. As abolitionists, they wanted an immediate end to slavery; the belief in human perfectibility led to the rise of numerous abolition groups and was a part of the Second Great Awakening, which took place in the early to mid-19th century.

6. (C)

While it would represent a huge outlay of money to purchase all slaves from their masters, the Convention focused on the moral and legal opposition to slavery in making their case against compensation. Many abolitionists became very vocal, calling attention to the issues by holding conventions and publishing abolitionist newspapers (i.e., *The Liberator* by William Lloyd Garrison).

7. (D)

Washington echoes what many colonial leaders such as Patrick Henry and Sam Adams had been stating since the Stamp Act—that taxation without representation was tyranny. The long-term cause of the taxes that Washington is complaining about was the Seven Years' War, which left Great Britain in massive debt.

8. (A)

The independence movement was driven by the wealthy and educated colonial elites. They often invoked Enlightenment ideals to strengthen support for independence.

9. (A)

While the Cherokee Trail of Tears is the most famous, the Indian Removal Act resulted in several different tribes being forced to move to new territory. The result of the movement of the Five Civilized Tribes to Oklahoma territory was the increased movement of white Americans into land previously controlled by American Indians.

10. (B)

Jackson, while recognizing the political value of removing the Indians from the Southeast, genuinely thought his actions were humane because he believed they would prevent further violence against the Indians by white citizens, but his actions clearly reflect the racist ideology that accompanied U.S. expansionism.

11. (D)

In 1820, Henry Clay crafted a compromise that would temporarily settle the issue of whether slavery should expand into western states or territories. The compromise divided the nation into Northern free states and Southern slave states. Jefferson does not raise any constitutional issues in his concerns about the Missouri Compromise. His main worries were that it would lead to the emancipation of slaves and eventually to war.

12. (B)

Jefferson's "fire bell in the night" reference indicated his fear that the Missouri Compromise would eventually lead to the dissolution of the Union over the issue of slavery. After the Mexican-American War in the 1840s, the United States was once again faced with the issue of expanding the institution of slavery into newly acquired territories. The Compromise of 1850, again crafted by Henry Clay, was a temporary plan to settle the issue. According to the Compromise of 1850, California would be admitted to the Union as a free state and the South would get a strict fugitive slave act.

13. (C)

The Puritans who settled in Massachusetts wanted to create a utopian religious society that would become a beacon of religious piety for the entire world. As the colony became more secular, there were more problems and eventually these problems manifested into the Salem Witchcraft Trials.

14. (A)

The 1950s is often known as the Age of Conformity. The cold war and the affluence that followed World War II created the desire for a homogeneous society. In the early 1950s, the Second Red Scare occurred, which was a witch hunt for suspected communists within the United States.

15. (B)

Both Wilson and Whitehill view the main issue to be whether a bill of rights should be included in the proposed Constitution. Wilson argues that to list some, but not all, rights would be worse than not including a list at all, while Whitehill worries that the nature of governments is to accrue more, not less, power and that this will mean a loss of liberty for citizens.

16. (D)

The Articles of Confederation was the first form of government for the new nation. They provided for a very weak federal government while the state governments remained largely sovereign. The failure of the Articles of Confederation led to the Constitutional Convention and the ensuing debate over the power of the federal government.

17. (A)

Women in the American colonies, while certainly not equal to their husbands in many ways, did enjoy more social freedoms than European women. By the early 20th century, female progressive reformers were demanding more democracy and social justice. Women were fighting for suffrage.

18. (D)

The reformers during the Second Great Awakening included women who fought for abolition as well as expanding democracy for women. In 1848, women met at Seneca Falls to demand voting rights.

19. (C)

Thoreau saw the Mexican-American War as an unjust means of extending the power of the slaveholding states. He refused to pay his taxes and encouraged others to disobey the government in this way.

20. (C)

In the first three sentences of the excerpt, Thoreau makes an argument for less government. The Republicans of the 1980s, led by Ronald Reagan, also denounced "big government."

Chapter 7

Expansion, Divisions, Civil War, and Reconstruction (1844–1877)

The issues that would dominate American political discussions in the 1840s were sectionalism, territorial expansion, and slavery. Southerners in Congress increasingly found themselves in disagreement with their Northern colleagues on a number of questions, including tariffs, the presence of slavery in newly acquired territories, and federal funding of internal improvements such as roads and canals. Slavery was the most divisive issue, leading Congress to pass a "gag rule" in 1836 to prevent any discussion of the topic in either the House of Representatives or the Senate. Preventing its discussion in Congress did not reduce the impact of slavery or resolve the problems it created for the United States. The 1850s witnessed the hardening of both sides in their attitudes toward slavery and states' rights. It finally took the Civil War and a huge loss of life to bring an end to slavery. Following the war, the nation stumbled through a period of Reconstruction as the South re-entered the Union politically, if not entirely culturally.

The Election of 1844

Democratic front-runner Martin Van Buren and Whig front-runner Henry Clay agreed privately that neither would endorse Texas annexation and that it would not become a campaign issue in the 1844 presidential election, but expansionists at the Democratic convention succeeded in dumping Van Buren in favor of James K. Polk.

Polk, called "Young Hickory" by his supporters, was a staunch Jacksonian who opposed protective tariffs and a national bank but, most important, favored territorial expansion, including not only annexation of Texas but also occupation of all the Oregon country (up to latitude 54°40′) hitherto jointly occupied by the U.S. and Britain. The latter claim was expressed in his campaign slogan, "Fifty-four forty or fight."

Tyler, despite his incumbency and the introduction of the issue that was to decide that year's presidential campaign, was unable to build a party of his own and withdrew from the race.

The Whigs nominated Clay, probably the most experienced politician in the United States. He continued to oppose Texas annexation but, sensing the mood of the country was against him, began to equivocate. His wavering cost him votes among those Northerners who were extremely sensitive to the issue of slavery and believed that the settlement, independence, and proposed annexation of Texas was a gigantic plot to add slave states to the Union. Some of these voters shifted to the Liberty Party.

The anti-slavery Liberty Party nominated James G. Birney. Apparently because of Clay's wavering on the Texas issue, Birney was able to take enough votes away from Clay in New York to give that state, and thus the election, to Polk.

Tyler, as a lame-duck president, made one more attempt to achieve Texas annexation before leaving office. By means of a joint resolution, which unlike a treaty required only a simple majority rather than a two-thirds vote, he was successful in getting the measure through Congress. Texas was finally admitted to the Union in 1845.

Polk as President

Though a relatively unknown "dark horse" at the time of his nomination for the presidency, Polk had considerable political experience within his home state of Tennessee and was an adept politician. He turned out to be a skillful and effective president.

As a good Jacksonian, Polk favored a low revenue-only tariff rather than a high protective tariff. This he obtained in the Walker Tariff (1846). He also opposed a national debt and a national bank and re-established Van Buren's Independent Sub-Treasury system, which remained in effect until 1920.

The Settlement of Oregon

A major issue in the election campaign of 1844, Oregon comprised all the land bounded on the east by the Rockies, the west by the Pacific, the south by latitude 42°, and the north by the boundary of Russian-held Alaska at 54°40′. Oregon had been visited by Lewis and Clark and in later years by American fur traders and especially missionaries, such as Jason Lee and Marcus Whitman. Their reports sparked interest in Oregon's favorable soil and climate. During the first half of the 1840s, some 6,000 Americans had taken the 2,000-mile, six-month journey on the Oregon Trail, from Independence, Missouri, across the plains along the Platte River, through the Rockies at South Pass, and down the Snake River to their new homesteads. Most of them settled in the Willamette Valley, south of the Columbia River.

The area had been under the joint occupation of the U.S. and Great Britain since 1818, but Democrats in the election of 1844 had called for U.S. ownership of all of Oregon. Though this stand had helped him win the election, Polk had little desire to fight the British for land he considered unsuitable for agriculture and unavailable for slavery, which he favored. This was all the more so since trouble seemed to be brewing with Mexico over territory Polk considered far more desirable.

The British, for their part, hoped to obtain the area north of the Columbia River, including the natural harbor of Puget Sound (one of only three on the Pacific Coast), with its adjoining Strait of Juan de Fuca.

By the terms of the Oregon Treaty (1846), a compromise solution was reached. The existing U.S.-Canada boundary east of the Rockies (49°) was extended westward to the Pacific, thus securing Puget Sound and shared use of the Strait of Juan de Fuca for the U.S. Some northern Democrats were angered and felt betrayed by Polk's failure to insist on all of Oregon, but the Senate readily accepted the treaty.

The Mormon Migration

In addition to the thousands of Americans who streamed west on the Oregon Trail during the early 1840s and those who migrated to what was then Mexican-held California, another large group of Americans moved west, but to a different destination and for different reasons. These were the Mormons.

Mormonism is a religion founded in 1832 by Joseph Smith at Palmyra, New York. Mormons were often in trouble with their neighbors because of both their unorthodox beliefs and practices, and had been forced to migrate to Kirtland, Ohio, then Clay County, Missouri, and finally Nauvoo, Illinois.

There, on the banks of the Mississippi River, they built the largest city in the state, had their own militia, and were a political force to be reckoned with.

In 1844, Mormon dissidents published a newspaper critical of church leader Smith and his newly announced doctrine of polygamy. Smith had their printing press destroyed. Arrested by Illinois authorities, Smith and his brother were confined to a jail in Carthage, Illinois, but later killed by a crowd of hostile non-Mormons who forced their way into the jail.

The Mormons then decided to migrate to the far West, preferably someplace outside U.S. jurisdiction. Their decision to leave was hastened by pressure from their non-Mormon neighbors, among whom anti-Mormon feelings ran high as a response to polygamy and the Mormons' monolithic social and political structure.

Under the leadership of new church leader Brigham Young, some 85,000 Mormons trekked overland in 1846 to settle in the valley of the Great Salt Lake in what is now Utah (but was then owned by Mexico). Young founded the Mormon republic of Deseret and openly preached (and practiced) polygamy. Young was alleged to have as many as 56 wives.

After Deseret's annexation by the U.S. as part of the Mexican Cession, Young was made territorial governor of Utah. Nevertheless, friction developed with the federal government. By 1857, public outrage over polygamy prompted then-President James Buchanan to replace Young with a non-Mormon governor. Threats of Mormon defiance led Buchanan to send 2,500 army troops to compel Mormon obedience to federal law. Young responded by calling out the Mormon militia and blocking the passes through which the army would have to advance. This standoff, known as the "Mormon War," was resolved in 1858, with the Mormons accepting the new governor and Buchanan issuing a general pardon.

DID YOU KNOW?

Mormonism, a truly American religious tradition, is one of the fastest growing religions in the world. Mormons hold seats in both the Senate and the House of Representatives, and the Republican candidate for president in 2012, Mitt Romney, is a devout Mormon. As of 2010, Mormons made up an estimated 60 percent of Utah's population. Some analysts believe that the proportion of Mormons in the state will drop below 50 percent by 2030 as people move to Utah from other parts of the country and the non-Mormon population grows.

The Coming of War with Mexico

For some time, American interest had been growing in the far western lands then held by Mexico.

Since the 1820s, Americans had been trading with Santa Fe and other Mexican settlements along the Rio Grande by means of the Santa Fe Trail. Though not extensive enough to be of economic importance, the trade aroused further American interest in the area.

Also, since the 1820s, American mountain men, trappers who sought beaver pelts in the streams of the Rockies, had explored the mountains of the far West, opening new trails and discovering fertile lands. They later served as guides for settlers moving West.

At the same time whaling ships and other American vessels had carried on a thriving trade with the Mexican settlements on the coast of California.

Beginning in 1841, American settlers came overland to California by means of the California Trail, a branch from the Oregon Trail that turned southwest in the Rockies and crossed Nevada along the Humboldt River. By 1846, several hundred Americans lived in California.

The steady flow of American pioneers into Mexican-held areas of the far West led to conflicting territorial desires and was thus an underlying cause of the Mexican-American War. However, several more immediate causes existed:

- Mexico's ineffective government was unable to protect the lives and property of American citizens in Mexico during the country's frequent and recurring revolutions and repeatedly declined to pay American claims for damages even when such claims were supported by the findings of mutually agreed-upon arbitration.
- Mexico had not reconciled itself to the loss of Texas and considered its 1845 annexation by the U.S. a hostile act.
- The southern boundary of Texas was disputed. Whereas first the independent Republic of Texas and now the U.S. claimed the Rio Grande as the boundary, Mexico claimed the Nueces River, 130 miles farther north, because it had been the boundary of the province of Texas when it had been part of Mexico.
- Mexican suspicions had been aroused regarding U.S. designs on California when, in 1842, a U.S. naval force under Commodore Thomas Catsby Jones had seized the province in the mistaken belief that war had broken out between the U.S. and

Mexico. When the mistake was discovered, the province was returned and apologies made.

- Mexican politicians had so inflamed the Mexican people against the U.S. that no Mexican leader could afford to take the risk of appearing to make concessions to the U.S. for fear of being overthrown.

Though Mexico broke diplomatic relations with the U.S. immediately upon Texas's admission to the Union, there still seemed to be some hope of a peaceful settlement.

In the fall of 1845, Polk sent John Slidell to Mexico City with a proposal for a peaceful settlement of the differences between the two countries. Slidell was empowered to cancel the damage claims and pay $5 million for the disputed land in southern Texas. He was also authorized to offer $25 million for California and $5 million for other Mexican territory in the far West. Polk was especially eager to obtain California because he feared the British would snatch it from Mexico's extremely weak grasp.

Nothing came of these attempts at negotiation. Racked by coup and countercoup, the Mexican government refused even to receive Slidell.

Polk responded by sending U.S. troops into the disputed territory in southern Texas. A force under General Zachary Taylor (who was nicknamed "Old Rough and Ready") took up a position just north of the Rio Grande. Eight days later, on April 5, 1846, Mexican troops attacked an American patrol. When news of the clash reached Washington, Polk sought and received from Congress a declaration of war against Mexico, on May 13, 1846.

The Mexican-American War

Americans were sharply divided about the war. Some favored it because they felt Mexico had provoked the war or because they felt it was the destiny of America to spread the blessings of freedom to oppressed peoples. Others opposed the war. Some, primarily Polk's political enemies the Whigs, accused the president of having provoked it. Others, generally Northern abolitionists, saw in the war the work of a vast conspiracy of Southern slaveholders greedy for more slave territory.

In planning military strategy, Polk showed genuine skill. American strategy consisted originally of a three-pronged attack—land movement westward through New Mexico into California, a sea movement against California, and a land movement southward into Mexico.

The first prong of this three-pronged strategy, the advance through New Mexico and into California, was led by Colonel Stephen W. Kearny. Kearny's force easily secured New Mexico, entering Santa Fe on August 16, 1846, before continuing west to California. There, American settlers, aided by an Army exploring party under John C. Fremont in northern California, had already revolted against Mexico's weak rule in what was called the Bear Flag Revolt.

As part of the second prong of U.S. strategy, naval forces under Commodore John D. Sloat had seized Monterey and declared California to be part of the United States. Forces put ashore by Commodore Robert Stockton joined with Kearny's troops to defeat the Mexicans at the Battle of San Gabriel near Los Angeles in January 1847 and complete the conquest of California.

The third prong of the American strategy, an advance southward into Mexico, was itself divided into two parties:

1. Troops under Colonel Alexander W. Doniphan defeated Mexicans at El Brazito (December 25–28, 1846) to take El Paso, and then proceeded southward, winning the Battle of Sacramento (February 28, 1847) to take the city of Chihuahua, capital of the Mexican province of that name.

2. The main southward thrust, however, was made by a much larger American army under General Zachary Taylor. After soundly defeating larger Mexican forces at the battles of Palo Alto (May 7, 1846) and Resaca de la Palma (May 8, 1846), Taylor advanced into Mexico and overwhelmed an even larger Mexican force at the Battle of Monterey (September 20–24, 1846). Then, after substantial numbers of his troops had been transferred to other sectors of the war, he successfully withstood, though his forces were badly outnumbered, an attack by a Mexican army of 20,000 under Antonia Lopez de Santa Anna at the Battle of Buena Vista, February 22–23, 1847.

DID YOU KNOW?

Like the Louisiana Purchase, the Mexican Cession added a vast amount of territory to the United States for a relatively small monetary payment. The Mexican Cession included all of what is now California, Nevada, and Utah, along with parts of what is now Arizona, Colorado, New Mexico, and Wyoming.

Despite the success of all three parts of the American strategy, the Mexicans refused to negotiate. Polk, therefore, ordered U.S. forces under General Winfield Scott to land on the east coast of Mexico, march inland, and take Mexico City.

Scott landed at Veracruz March 9, 1847, and by March 27 had captured the city with the loss of only twenty American lives. He advanced from there, being careful to maintain good discipline and avoid atrocities in the countryside. At Cerro Cord (April 18, 1847), in what has been called "the most important single battle of the war," Scott outflanked and soundly defeated a superior enemy force in a seemingly impregnable position. After beating another Mexican army at Churubusco (August 19–20, 1847), Scott paused outside Mexico City to offer the Mexicans another chance to negotiate. When they declined, U.S. forces stormed the fortress of Chapultepec (September 13, 1847) and the next day entered Mexico City. Still, Mexico refused to negotiate a peace and instead carried on guerilla warfare.

Negotiated peace finally came about when the State Department clerk Nicholas Trist, though his authority had been revoked and he had been ordered back to Washington two months earlier, negotiated and signed the Treaty of Guadalupe Hidalgo (February 2, 1848), ending the Mexican War. Under the terms of the treaty, Mexico ceded to the U.S. the territory Polk had originally sought to buy, this time in exchange for a payment of $15 million and the assumption of $3.25 million in American citizens' claims against the Mexican government. This territory, the Mexican Cession, included the natural harbors at San Francisco and San Diego, thus giving the U.S. all three of the major West Coast natural harbors.

Despite the appropriation of vast territories, many observers, including Polk, believed the treaty was far too generous. There had been talk of annexing all of Mexico or of forcing Mexico to pay an indemnity for the cost of the war. Still, Polk felt compelled to accept the treaty as it was, and the Senate subsequently ratified it.

On the home front, many Americans supported the war enthusiastically and flocked to volunteer. Some criticized the war, among them Henry David Thoreau, who, to display his protest, refused to pay his taxes. Jailed for this, he wrote *Civil Disobedience*, an important treatise on natural law that became a foundation for 20th century reformers, including Mahatma Gandhi and Martin Luther King, Jr.

Although the Mexican-American War increased the nation's territory by one-third, it also brought to the surface serious political issues that threatened to divide the country, particularly the question of slavery in the new territories.

Table 7.1 Key Events in the Mexican-American War

Event	Date	Location	Significance
Mexico snubs Slidell	November 1845	Mexico City	Pres. Polk instructs John Slidell to offer up to $25 million for New Mexico and California. Insulted Mexicans refuse to see Slidell.
Polk orders troops to southern Texas	January 1846	Rio Grande River	Zachary Taylor and 4000 men are sent to disputed territory, expecting attack. Conflict with Mexican troops results in 16 American casualties.
Congress declares war on Mexico	May 1846	Washington, D.C.	Polk asks for war with Mexico. Northern Whigs fear victory would add more slave states to U.S. Declaration passes 40–2 in Senate, 174–14 in House.
Bear Flag Republic established	June 1846	Northern California	John C. Fremont and volunteers capture town of Sonoma and hoist Bear flag.
Americans capture Monterey	July 1846	Monterey, California	250 sailors capture Mexico's California capital without a shot.
Kearny takes Santa Fe	August 1846	New Mexico	Marching from Kansas to California, Stephen Kearny's 1,700 men take Santa Fe, a key Mexican trading post.
Battle of San Pascual	December 1846	San Diego, California	In fierce fighting, Kearny's forces barely survive attack of Mexican lancers.
Battle of San Gabriel	January 1847	San Gabriel, California	California forces retreat as American forces cross San Gabriel River and take Los Angeles.
Battle of Buena Vista	February 1847	Central Mexico	With a much larger army (20,000 to Taylor's 5,000), Santa Anna is unable to defeat Taylor's American forces.
Veracruz	March 1847	East coast of Mexico	Winfield Scott and 14,000 men capture port and begin following Cortes's route to Mexico City.
Rep. Lincoln issues "spot resolution"	December 1847	Washington, D.C.	First-term Congressman Abraham Lincoln of Illinois, who opposed Polk's conduct of the war, questions its validity by asking about the spot of American soil on which American blood was spilt. For a time, he earned the derisive nickname "Spotty Lincoln" for his resolution, which was never passed by the House.
Mexico City	September 1847	Central Mexico	U.S. captures the city. Santa Anna loses 4,000 of his 25,000-man army, while Scott loses 900 of his 10,000.
Treaty of Guadalupe-Hidalgo	February 2, 1848	Central Mexico	Mexico gives up all claim to Texas. The U.S. pays Mexico $15 million and agrees to assume American citizens' claims ($3,250,000) against Mexico. Expansionists call for "All Mexico." Senate passes the treaty 38–14.

The Crisis of 1850 and America at Mid-Century

The Wilmot Proviso

The Mexican War had no sooner started when, on August 8, 1846, freshman Democratic Congressman David Wilmot of Pennsylvania introduced his Wilmot Proviso as a proposed amendment to a war appropriations bill. It stipulated that "neither slavery nor involuntary servitude shall ever exist" in any territory to be acquired from Mexico. It was passed by the House, and though rejected by the Senate, it was reintroduced again and again amid increasingly acrimonious debate.

The Wilmot Proviso aroused intense sectional feelings. Southerners, who had supported the war enthusiastically, felt they were being treated unfairly. Northerners, some of whom had been inclined to see the war as a slaveholders' plot to extend slavery, felt they saw their worst suspicions confirmed by the Southerners' furious opposition to the Wilmot Proviso. There came to be four views regarding the status of slavery in the newly acquired territories.

1. **The Southern Position**. Expressed by John C. Calhoun, now serving as senator from South Carolina, it argued that the territories were the property not of the U.S. federal government but of all the states together, and therefore Congress, had no right to prohibit in any territory any type of "property" (by which he meant slaves) that was legal in any of the states.

2. **Anti-slavery Northern Position**. Pointing to the Northwest Ordinance of 1787 and the Missouri Compromise of 1820 as precedents, this group argued that Congress had the right to make what laws it saw fit for the territories, including, if it so chose, laws prohibiting slavery.

3. **Moderate Southern Compromise Position**. A compromise proposal favored by President Polk and many moderate Southerners called for the extension of the 36°30′ line of the Missouri Compromise westward through the Mexican Cession to the Pacific, with territory north of the line to be closed to slavery and territory south of it open to slavery.

4. **Northern Democrat Compromise Position.** Another compromise solution, favored by Northern Democrats such as Lewis Cass of Michigan and Stephen A. Douglas of Illinois, was known as "squatter sovereignty" and later as "popular sovereignty." It held that the residents of each territory should be permitted to decide

for themselves whether or not to allow slavery, but it did not indicate when they might exercise that right.

The Election of 1848

Both parties sought to avoid as much as possible the hot issue of slavery in the territories as they prepared for the 1848 presidential election campaign.

The Democrats nominated Lewis Cass, and their platform endorsed his middle-of-the-road popular sovereignty position with regard to slavery in the territories.

The Whigs dodged the issue even more effectively by nominating General Zachary Taylor, whose fame in the Mexican War made him a strong candidate. Taylor knew nothing of the current political issues, had never voted, and liked to think of himself as above politics. He took no position at all with respect to slavery in the territories.

Some anti-slavery Northern Whigs and Democrats, disgusted with their parties' failure to take a clear stand against the spread of slavery, deserted the party ranks to form another antislavery third party. They were known as "Conscience" Whigs (because they voted their conscience) and "Barnburner" Democrats (because they were willing to burn down the whole Democratic "barn" to get rid of the pro-slavery "rats"). Their party was called the Free Soil Party, since it stood for keeping the soil of new Western territories free of slavery. Its candidate was Martin Van Buren.

The election excited relatively little public interest. Taylor won a narrow victory, apparently because Van Buren took enough votes from Cass in New York and Pennsylvania to throw those states into Taylor's column.

Gold in California

The question of slavery's status in the Western territories was made more immediate when, on January 24, 1848, gold was discovered at Sutter's Mill, not far from Sacramento, California. In the next year, gold seekers from the eastern U.S. and from many foreign countries swelled California's population from 14,000 to 100,000.

Once in the gold fields these "forty-niners" proved to contain some rough characters, and that fact, along with the

DID YOU KNOW?

Gold and other mineral discoveries drew thousands of people to places, creating boomtowns across the West. The town of Bodie, California, grew to include some 8,500 residents and 2,000 buildings within two decades of the discovery of gold there in 1859. As resources were exhausted, however, populations of these boomtowns plummeted. By 1886, Bodie's population dropped to just 1,500, and it eventually became a ghost town, which can be visited today.

presence, or at least the expectation, of quick and easy riches, made California a wild and lawless place. No territorial government had been organized since the U.S. had received the land as part of the Mexican Cession, and all that existed was an inadequate military government. In September 1849, having more than the requisite population and being much in need of better government, California petitioned for admission to the Union as a state.

Since few slaveholders had chosen to risk their valuable investments in human property in the turbulent atmosphere of California, the people of the area not surprisingly sought admission as a free state, touching off a serious sectional crisis back East.

The Compromise of 1850

President Zachary Taylor, though himself a Louisiana slaveholder, actually opposed the further spread of slavery. Hoping to sidestep the dangerously divisive issue of slavery in the territories, he encouraged California as well as the rest of the Mexican Cession to organize and seek admission directly as states, thus completely bypassing the territorial stage.

Southerners were furious. They saw admission of a free-state California as a back-door implementation of the hated Wilmot Proviso they had fought so hard to turn back in Congress. They were also growing increasingly alarmed at what was becoming the minority status of their section within the country. Long outnumbered in the House of Representatives, the South would now find itself, should California be admitted as a free state, also outvoted in the Senate.

Other matters created friction between the North and the South. A large tract of land was disputed between Texas, a slave state, and the as-yet-unorganized New Mexico Territory, where slavery's future was at best uncertain. Southerners were angered by the small-scale but much-talked-of efforts of Northern abolitionists' "underground railroad" to aid escaped slaves in reaching permanent freedom in Canada. Northerners were disgusted by the presence of slave pens and slave markets in the nation's capital. Radical Southerners talked of secession and scheduled an all-Southern convention to meet in Nashville in June 1850 to propose ways of protecting Southern interests, inside or outside the Union.

At this point the aged Henry Clay attempted to craft a compromise over the various matters of contention between North and South. He proposed an eight-part package deal that he hoped would appeal to both sides.

For the North, the package contained these aspects: California would be admitted as a free state; the land in dispute between Texas and New Mexico would go to New Mexico; New Mexico and Utah Territories (all of the Mexican Cession outside of California) would not be specifically reserved for slavery, but its status there would be decided by popular sovereignty; and slave trade would be abolished in the District of Columbia.

For the South, the package offered the following: A tougher Fugitive Slave Law would be enacted; the federal government would pay Texas's $10 million pre-annexation debt; Congress would declare that it did not have jurisdiction over the interstate slave trade; and Congress would promise not to abolish slavery itself in the District of Columbia.

What followed the introduction of Clay's compromise proposal was eight months of heated debate, during which Clay, Calhoun, and Daniel Webster, the three great figures of Congress during the first half of the 19th century—none of them with more than two years to live—made some of their greatest speeches. Clay called for compromise and "mutual forbearance." Calhoun gravely warned that the only way to save the Union was for the North to grant all the South's demands and keep quiet on the issue of slavery. Webster abandoned his previous strong opposition to the spread of slavery (as well as sacrificing most of his popularity back in his home state of Massachusetts) to support the compromise in an eloquent speech.

The opponents of the compromise were many and powerful and ranged from President Taylor, who demanded admission of California without reference to slavery, to Northern extremists such as Senator William Seward of New York, who spoke of a "higher law" than the Constitution, forbidding the spread of slavery, to Southern extremists such as Calhoun or Senator Jefferson Davis of Mississippi. By mid summer all seemed lost for the compromise, and Clay left Washington exhausted and discouraged.

Then the situation changed dramatically. President Taylor died (apparently of gastroenteritis) July 9, 1850, and was succeeded by Vice President Millard Fillmore, a quiet but efficient politician and a strong supporter of compromise. In Congress the fight for the Compromise was taken up by Senator Stephen A. Douglas of Illinois. Called the "Little Giant" for his small stature and large political skills, Douglas broke Clay's proposal into its component parts so that he could use varying coalitions to push each part through Congress. This method proved successful, and the compromise was adopted.

The Compromise of 1850 was received with joy and relief by most of the nation. Sectional harmony returned, for the most part, and the issue of slavery in the territories seemed to have been permanently settled. That this was only an illusion became apparent within a few years.

The Election of 1852

The 1852 Democratic convention deadlocked between Cass and Douglas, and so instead settled on dark horse Franklin Pierce of New Hampshire. The Whigs, true to form, chose General Winfield Scott, a war hero of no political background.

The result was an easy victory for Pierce in the 1852 election largely because the Whig Party, badly divided along North-South lines as a result of the battle over the Compromise of 1850, was beginning to come apart. The Free Soil Party's candidate, John P. Hale of New Hampshire, fared poorly, demonstrating the electorate's weariness of the slavery issue.

Pierce and "Young America"

Americans eagerly turned their attention to railroads, cotton, clipper ships, and commerce. The world seemed to be opening up to American trade and influence.

President Pierce expressed the nation's hope that a new era of sectional peace was beginning. To assure this, he sought to distract the nation's attention from the slavery issue to focus on an aggressive program of foreign economic and territorial expansion known as "Young America."

In 1853, Commodore Matthew Perry led a U.S. naval force into Tokyo Bay on a mission to open Japan—previously closed to the outside world—to American diplomacy and commerce.

By means of the Reciprocity Treaty (1854), Pierce succeeded in opening Canada to greater U.S. trade. He also sought to annex Hawaii, increase U.S. interest in Central America, and acquire territories from Mexico and Spain.

From Mexico he acquired in 1853 the Gadsden Purchase, a strip of land in what is now southern New Mexico and Arizona along the Gila River. The purpose of this purchase was to provide a good route for a transcontinental railroad across the southern part of the country, though that particular route never was funded.

Pierce sought to buy Cuba from Spain. When Spain declined, three of Pierce's diplomats, meeting in Ostend, Belgium, sent him the Ostend Manifesto urging military seizure of Cuba should Spain remain intransigent.

Pierce was the first "doughface" president—"a northern man with

DIDYOUKNOW?

Commodore Matthew Perry's journey to Japan had significant effects for both nations. Despite attempts to keep out Western influences, increased foreign trade destabilized the Japanese economy, and in time the ruling Tokugawa shogunate there fell in favor of a centralized government under a Japanese emperor.

southern principles"—and his expansionist goals, situated as they were in the South, aroused suspicion and hostility in anti-slavery northerners. Pierce's administration appeared to be dominated by southerners, such as Secretary of War Jefferson Davis, and whether in seeking a southern route for a transcontinental railroad or seeking to annex potential slave territory such as Cuba, it seemed to be working for the good of the South.

Economic Growth

The chief factor in the economic transformation of America during the 1840s and 1850s was the dynamic rise of the railroads. In 1840, America had less than 3,000 miles of railroad track. By 1860, that number had risen to over 30,000 miles. Railroads pioneered big-business techniques, and by improving transportation helped create a nationwide market. They also helped create new cities such as Chicago and linked the Midwest to the Northeast rather than the South, as would have been the case had only water transportation been available.

Water transportation during the 1850s saw the heyday of the steamboat on inland rivers and the clipper ship on the high seas. The period also saw rapid and sustained industrial growth. The factory system began in the textile industry, where Elias Howe's invention of the sewing machine (1846) and Isaac Singer's improved model (1851) aided the process of mechanization, which quickly spread to other industries.

Agriculture varied according to region. In the South, large plantations and small farms existed side by side for the most part, and both prospered enormously during the 1850s from the production of cotton. Southern leaders referred to the fiber as "King Cotton," an economic power that no one would dare fight against. By the end of the 1850s, seven-eighths of all of the world's cotton was produced in the American South.

In the North, the main centers of agricultural production shifted from the Middle Atlantic states to the more fertile lands of the Midwest. The main unit of agriculture was the family farm, and the main products were grain and livestock. Unlike the South, where 3.5 million slaves provided abundant cheap (actually free) labor, the North faced incentives to introduce labor-saving machines. Cyrus McCormick's mechanical reaper came into wide use,

DID YOU KNOW?

Steam power fueled the expansion of the railroad system during the mid-nineteenth century. The first steam-powered locomotive in the United States was the Tom Thumb, which reached an unheard-of speed of 30 miles per hour during an early journey in 1830. From the time of Alexander the Great until Andrew Jackson, men and women could travel no faster than a horse could run. Railroads revolutionized transportation.

and by 1860 over 100,000 were in operation on Midwestern farms. Mechanical threshers also came into increasing use.

Decline of the Two-Party System

Meanwhile, ominous developments were taking place in politics. America's second two-party system, which had developed during the 1830s, was in the process of breaking down. The Whig Party, whose dismal performance in the election of 1852 had signaled its weakness, was now in the process of complete disintegration. Partially this was the result of the issue of slavery, which tended to divide the party along North-South lines. Partially, though, it may have been the result of the nativist movement opposing the growing presence of immigrants.

The nativist movement and its political party, the American, or the Know-Nothing Party, grew out of alarm on the part of native-born Americans at the rising tide of German and Irish immigration during the late 1840s and early 1850s. The Know-Nothing Party, so called because its members were told to answer "I know nothing" when asked about its secret proceedings, was anti-foreign and, since many of the foreigners were Catholic, also anti-Catholic. It surged briefly to become the country's second-largest party by 1855 but faded even more quickly due to the ineptness of its leaders and the growing urgency of the slavery question, which, though ignored by the Know-Nothing Party, was rapidly coming to overshadow all other issues. To some extent the Know-Nothing movement may simply have benefited from the already progressing disintegration of the Whig Party, but it may also have helped to complete that disintegration.

All of this proved fateful because the collapse of a viable nationwide two-party system made it much more difficult for the nation's political process to contain the explosive issue of slavery.

The Return of Sectional Conflict

Continuing Sources of Tension

While Americans hailed the apparent sectional harmony created by the Compromise of 1850 and enjoyed the rapid economic growth of the decade that followed, two items that continued to create tension centered on the issue of slavery.

The Strengthened Fugitive Slave Law

The more important of these was a part of the compromise itself, the strengthened federal Fugitive Slave Law. The law enraged Northerners, many of whom believed it to be little better than a legalization of kidnapping. Under its provisions blacks living in the North and claimed by slave catchers were denied trial by jury and many of the other protections of due process. Even more distasteful to anti-slavery Northerners was the provision that required all U.S. citizens to aid, when called upon, in the capture and return of alleged fugitives or be found in violation of a federal law. So violent was Northern feeling against the law that several riots erupted as a result of attempts to enforce it. Some Northern states passed personal liberty laws in an attempt to prevent the working of the Fugitive Slave Law.

The effect of all this was to polarize the country even further. Many Northerners who had not previously taken an interest in the slavery issue now became opponents of slavery as a result of having its injustices forcibly brought home to them by the Fugitive Slave Law. Southerners saw in Northern resistance to the law further proof that the North was determined to tamper with the institution of slavery.

Uncle Tom's Cabin

One Northerner who was outraged by the Fugitive Slave Act was Harriet Beecher Stowe. In response, she wrote *Uncle Tom's Cabin,* a fictional book depicting what she perceived as the evils of slavery. Furiously denounced in the South, the book became an overnight best-seller around the world and in the North, where it turned many toward active opposition to slavery. This, too, was a note of harsh discord among the seemingly harmonious sectional relations of the early 1850s.

TEST TIP

Eliminating answer choices one by one can be slow. One technique to help you work more quickly would be for you to come up with your own answer to the question before reading the answer choices. Then, select the choice that seems to most closely match the answer you have suggested.

The Kansas-Nebraska Act

All illusion of sectional peace ended abruptly when in 1854 Senator Stephen A. Douglas of Illinois introduced a bill in Congress to organize the area west of Missouri and Iowa as the territories of Kansas and Nebraska. Douglas, a calculating politician who had no moral convictions on slavery one way or the other, hoped organizing the territories would facilitate the building of a transcontinental railroad on a central route, something that would benefit him and his Illinois constituents.

Though he sought to avoid directly addressing the touchy issue of slavery, Douglas was compelled by pressure from Southern senators such as David Atchison of Missouri to include in the bill an explicit repeal of the Missouri Compromise (which banned slavery in the areas in question) and a provision that the status of slavery in the newly organized territories be decided by popular sovereignty.

The bill was opposed by most Northern Democrats and a majority of the remaining Whigs, but with the support of the Southern-dominated Pierce administration it was passed and signed into law.

The Republican Party

The Kansas-Nebraska Act aroused a storm of outrage in the North, where the repeal of the Missouri Compromise was seen as the breaking of a solemn agreement. It hastened the disintegration of the Whig Party and divided the Democratic Party along North-South lines.

In the North, many Democrats left the party and were joined by former Whigs and Know-Nothings in the newly created Republican Party, which was formally organized in 1854. Springing to life almost overnight as a result of Northern fury at the Kansas-Nebraska Act, the Republican Party included diverse elements whose sole unifying principle was the firm belief that slavery should be banned from all the nation's territories, confined to the states where it already existed, and allowed to spread no further.

Though its popularity was confined entirely to the North, the Republican Party quickly became a major power in national politics.

Bleeding Kansas

With the status of Kansas (Nebraska was never in much doubt) to be decided by the voters there, North and South began competing to see which could send the greatest number. Northerners formed the New England Emigrant Aid Company to promote the settling of anti-slavery men in Kansas, and Southerners responded in kind. Despite these efforts the majority of Kansas settlers were Midwesterners who were generally opposed to the spread of slavery but were more concerned with finding good farmland than deciding the national debate over slavery in the territories.

Despite this large anti-slavery majority, large-scale election fraud, especially on the part of heavily armed Missouri "border ruffians" who crossed into Kansas on election day to vote their pro-slavery principles early and often, led to the creation of a virulently pro-slavery territorial government. When the presidentially appointed territorial governor protested this gross fraud, Pierce removed him from office.

Free-soil Kansans responded by denouncing the pro-slavery government as illegitimate and forming their own free-soil government in an election boycotted by the pro-slavery faction. Kansas now had two rival governments, each claiming to be the only lawful one.

Both sides began arming themselves and soon the territory was being referred to in the Northern press as "Bleeding Kansas" as full-scale guerilla war erupted. In May 1856, Missouri border ruffians sacked the free-soil town of Lawrence, killing two and destroying homes, businesses, and printing presses. Two days later a small band of anti-slavery zealots under the leadership of fanatical abolitionist John Brown retaliated by killing and mutilating five unarmed men and boys at a pro-slavery settlement on Pottawatomie Creek. In all, some 200 died in the months of guerilla fighting that followed.

Meanwhile, violence had spread even to Congress itself. In the same month as the Sack of Lawrence and the Pottawatomie Massacre, Senator Charles Sumner of Massachusetts made a two-day speech entitled "The Crime Against Kansas," in which he not only denounced slavery but also made degrading personal references to aged South Carolina Senator Andrew Butler. Two days later Butler's nephew, Congressman Preston Brooks, also of South Carolina, entered the Senate chamber and, approaching Sumner from behind, beat him about the head and shoulders with a cane, leaving him bloody and unconscious.

Once again the North was outraged, while in the South, Brooks was hailed as a hero. New canes were sent to him to replace the one he had broken over Sumner's head. Denounced by Northerners, he resigned his seat and was overwhelmingly re-elected. Northerners were further incensed and bought thousands of copies of Sumner's inflammatory speech.

TEST TIP

When answering the document-based question, don't take up your valuable writing time or your energy using long quotes or creating extensive descriptions of the documents provided in your document-based question response. The essay graders are familiar with the documents on the exam, and repeating their contents will not help you gain any points. Do not start paragraphs with "Document A says ..." Instead, weave the documents in a logical and persuasive way into your analysis in order to support your arguments.

The Election of 1856

The election of 1856 was a three-way contest that pitted Democrats, Know-Nothings, and Republicans against each other.

The Democrats dropped Pierce and passed over Douglas to nominate James Buchanan of Pennsylvania. Though a veteran of forty years of politics, Buchanan was a weak and vacillating man whose chief qualification for the nomination was that during the slavery squabbles of the past few years he had been out of the country as American minister to Great Britain and, therefore, had not been forced to take public positions on the controversial issues.

The Know-Nothings, including the remnant of the Whigs, nominated Millard Fillmore. However, the choice of a Southerner for the nomination of vice president so alienated Northern Know-Nothings that many shifted their support to the Republican candidate.

The Republicans nominated John C. Frémont of California. A former officer in the army's Corps of Topographical Engineers and a hero to many, Frémont was known as "the Pathfinder" for his explorations in the Rockies and the far West. The Republican platform called for high tariffs, free Western homesteads (160 acres) for settlers, and, most important, no further spread of slavery. Their slogan was "Free Soil, Free Men, and Frémont." Southerners denounced the Republican Party as an abolitionist organization and threatened secession should it win the election.

Against divided opposition, Buchanan won with apparent ease. However, his victory was largely based on the support of the South, since Frémont carried most of the Northern states. Had the Republicans won Pennsylvania and either Illinois or Indiana, Frémont would have been elected. In the election the Republicans demonstrated surprising strength for a political party only two years old and made clear that they, and not the Know-Nothings, would replace the moribund Whigs as the other major party along with the Democrats.

The *Dred Scott* Case

Meanwhile, there had been, rising through the court system, a case that would give the Supreme Court a chance to state its opinion on the question of slavery in the territories. The case was *Dred Scott v. Sandford,* which involved a Missouri slave, Dred Scott, who had been encouraged by abolitionists to sue for his freedom on the basis that his owner, an Army doctor, had taken him for a stay of several years in a free state, Illinois, and then in a free territory, Wisconsin. By 1856 the case had made its way to the Supreme Court, and by March of the following year the Court was ready to render its decision.

The justices were at first inclined to rule simply that Scott, as a slave, was not a citizen and could not sue in court. Buchanan, however, shortly before his inauguration, urged the justices to go further and attempt to settle the whole slavery issue once and for all, thus removing it from the realm of politics where it might prove embarrassing to the president.

The Court obliged. Under the domination of aging pro-Southern Chief Justice Roger B. Taney of Maryland, it attempted to read the extreme Southern position on slavery into the Constitution, ruling not only that Scott had no standing to sue in federal court, but also that temporary residence in a free state, even for several years, did not make a slave free, and that the Missouri Compromise (already a dead letter by that time) had been unconstitutional all along because Congress did not have the authority to exclude slavery from any territory whatsoever. Nor did territorial governments, which were considered to receive their power from Congress, have the right to prohibit slavery.

Far from settling the sectional controversy, the *Dred Scott* case only made it worse. Southerners were encouraged to take an extreme position and refuse compromise, while anti-slavery Northerners became more convinced than ever that there was a pro-slavery conspiracy controlling all branches of government, and expressed an unwillingness to accept the Court's dictate as final. Positions on slavery's expansion into the territories and even its existence in the South were becoming hardened on both sides.

TEST TIP

Even though you have limited time to construct your essay on the free-response question, take a few minutes to create a brief outline of the ideas and evidence you wish to include. Doing this will make your response more organized and concise, and help ensure that you don't forget any important points you want to make. Readers look for specific information, so avoid generalities.

Buchanan and Kansas

Later in 1857, the pro-slavery government in Kansas, through largely fraudulent means, arranged for a heavily pro-slavery constitutional convention to meet at the town of Lecompton. The result was a state constitution that allowed slavery. To obtain a pretense of popular approval for this constitution, the convention provided for a referendum in which the voters were to be given a choice only to prohibit the entry of additional slaves into the state.

Disgusted free-soilers boycotted the referendum, and the result was a constitution that put no restrictions at all on slavery. Touting this Lecompton Constitution, the pro-slavery territorial government petitioned Congress for admission to the Union as a slave state. Meanwhile, the free-soilers drafted a constitution of their own and submitted it to Congress as the legitimate one for the prospective state of Kansas.

Eager to appease the South, which had started talking of secession again, and equally eager to suppress anti-slavery agitation in the North, Buchanan vigorously backed the Lecompton Constitution. Douglas, appalled at this travesty of his position, popular sovereignty, broke with the administration to oppose it. He and Buchanan became bitter political enemies, with the president determined to use all the power of the Democratic organization to crush Douglas politically.

After extremely bitter and acrimonious debate, the Senate approved the Lecompton Constitution, but the House insisted that Kansans be given a chance to vote on the entire document. Southern congressmen did succeed in managing to apply pressure to the Kansas voters by adding the stipulation that, should the Lecompton Constitution be approved, Kansas would receive a generous grant of federal land, but should it be voted down, Kansas would remain a territory.

Nevertheless, Kansas voters, when given a chance to express themselves in a fair election, turned down the Lecompton Constitution by an overwhelming margin, choosing to remain a territory rather than become a slave state. Kansas was finally admitted as a free state in 1861.

The Panic of 1857

In 1857, the country was struck by a short but severe depression. There were three basic causes for this "Panic of 1857":

1. Several years of overspeculation in railroads and lands;
2. Faulty banking practices; and
3. An interruption in the flow of European capital into American investments as a result of the Crimean War. The North blamed the Panic on low tariffs, while the South, which had suffered much less than the industrial North, saw the Panic as proof of the superiority of the Southern economy in general and slavery in particular.

The Lincoln-Douglas Debates

The 1858 Illinois senatorial campaign produced a series of debates that got to the heart of the issues that were threatening to divide the nation. In that race, incumbent Democratic Senator and front-runner for the 1860 presidential nomination Stephen A. Douglas was opposed by a Springfield lawyer, little known outside the state, by the name of Abraham Lincoln.

Though Douglas had been hailed in some free-soil circles for his opposition to the Lecompton Constitution, Lincoln, in a series of seven debates that the candidates agreed to hold during the course of the campaign, stressed that Douglas's doctrine of popular sovereignty failed to recognize slavery for the moral wrong it was. Again and again Lincoln hammered home the theme that Douglas was a secret defender of slavery because he did not take a moral stand against it.

Douglas, for his part, maintained that his guiding principle was democracy, not any moral standard of right or wrong with respect to slavery. The people could, as far as he was concerned, "vote it up or vote it down." At the same time he strove to depict Lincoln as a radical and an abolitionist who believed in racial equality and race mixing.

At the debate held in Freeport, Illinois, Lincoln pressed Douglas to reconcile the principle of popular sovereignty with the Supreme Court's decision in the *Dred Scott* case. How could the people "vote it up or vote it down" if, as the Supreme Court said, no territorial government could prohibit slavery? Douglas, in what came to be called his "Freeport Doctrine," replied that the people of any territory could exclude slavery simply by declining to pass any of the special laws that slave jurisdictions usually passed for their protection.

Douglas's answer was good enough to win him re-election to the Senate, although by the narrowest of margins, but hurt him in the coming presidential campaign. The Lecompton fight had already destroyed Douglas's hopes of uniting the Democratic Party and defusing the slave issue. It had also damaged his 1860 presidential hopes by alienating the South. Now his Freeport Doctrine hardened the opposition of Southerners already angered by his anti-Lecompton stand.

DID YOU KNOW?

Abraham Lincoln made one of his most famous speeches at the beginning of his failed 1858 run for the U.S. Senate, stating in part, " 'A house divided against itself cannot stand.' I believe this government cannot endure, permanently, half slave and half free. I do not expect the Union to be dissolved; I do not expect the house to fall; but I do expect it will cease to be divided. It will become all one thing, or all the other."

For Lincoln, despite the failure to win the Senate seat, the debates were a major success, propelling him into the national spotlight and strengthening the backbone of the Republican Party to resist compromise on the free-soil issue.

The Coming of the Civil War

John Brown's Raid

On the night of October 16, 1859, John Brown, the Pottawatomie Creek murderer, led eighteen followers in seizing the federal arsenal at Harpers Ferry, Virginia (now West Virginia), taking hostages, and endeavoring to incite a slave uprising. Brown, supported and bankrolled by several prominent Northern abolitionists (later referred to as "the Secret Six"), planned to arm local slaves and then spread his uprising across the South. His scheme was ill-conceived and had little chance of success. Several slaves in town refused to join. Quickly cornered by Virginia militia, he was eventually captured by a force of U.S. Marines under the command of Army Colonel Robert E. Lee. Ten of Brown's eighteen men were killed in the fight, and Brown himself was wounded.

Abolitionist John Brown

From a daguerreotype; Levin C. Handy, photographer. (U.S. Library of Congress.)

Charged under Virginia law with treason and various other crimes, Brown was quickly tried, convicted, sentenced, and, on December 2, 1859, hanged. Throughout his trial and at his execution he conducted himself with fanatical resolution, making eloquent statements that convinced many Northerners that he should be seen as a martyr rather than a criminal. His death was marked in the North by signs of public mourning.

Though responsible Northerners, such as Lincoln, denounced Brown's raid as a criminal act that deserved to be punished by death, many Southerners became convinced that the entire Northern public approved of Brown's action and that the only safety for the South lay in a separate Southern confederacy. This was all the more so because Brown, in threatening to create a slave revolt, had touched on the foremost fear of white Southerners. For both the North and the South, John Brown, though his raid was a complete failure, became a symbolic figure of great importance.

DID YOU KNOW?

At the time of John Brown's raid on Harpers Ferry, just 217 African Americans lived in the community.

Hinton Rowan Helper's Book

The second greatest fear of Southern slaveholders was that Southern whites who did not own slaves, by far the majority of the Southern population, would come to see the continuation of slavery as not being in their best interest. This fear was touched on by a book, *The Impending Crisis in the South,* by a North Carolinian named Hinton Rowan Helper. In it Helper argued that slavery was economically harmful to the South and that it enriched the large planter at the expense of the yeoman farmer.

Southerners were enraged, and more so when the Republicans reissued a condensed version of the book as campaign literature. When the new House of Representatives met in December 1859 for the first time since the 1858 elections, angry Southerners determined that no Republican who had endorsed the book should be elected speaker.

The Republicans were the most numerous party in the House, although they did not hold a majority. Their candidate for speaker, John Sherman of Ohio, had endorsed Helper's book. A rancorous two-month battle ensued in which the House was unable even to organize itself, let alone transact any business. Secession of Southern states was talked of openly by many Southerners, and as tensions rose congressmen came to the sessions carrying revolvers and Bowie knives. The matter was finally resolved by the withdrawal of Sherman and the election of a moderate Republican as speaker. Tensions remained fairly high.

The Election of 1860

In this mood the country approached the election of 1860, a campaign that eventually became a four-man contest.

The Democrats met in Charleston, South Carolina. Douglas had a majority of the delegates, but at that time a party rule required a two-thirds vote for the nomination. Douglas, faced with the bitter opposition of the Southerners and the Buchanan faction, could not gain this majority. Finally, the convention split up when Southern "fire-eaters" led by William L. Yancey walked out in protest of the convention's refusal to include in the platform a plank demanding federal protection of slavery in all the territories.

A second Democratic convention several weeks later in Baltimore also failed to reach a consensus, and the split halves of the party nominated separate candidates. The Southern wing of the party nominated Buchanan's vice president, John C. Breckinridge of Kentucky, on a platform calling for a federal slave code in all the territories. What was left of the national Democratic Party nominated Douglas on a platform of popular sovereignty.

A third presidential candidate was added by the Constitutional Union Party, a collection of aging former Whigs and Know-Nothings from the Southern and border states as well as a handful of moderate Southern Democrats. It nominated John Bell of Tennessee on a platform that sidestepped the issues and called simply for the Constitution, the Union, and the enforcement of the laws.

The Republicans met in Chicago, confident of victory and determined to do nothing to jeopardize their favorable position. Accordingly, they rejected as too radical front-running New York Senator William H. Seward in favor of Illinois' favorite son, Abraham Lincoln. The platform was designed to have something for all Northerners, including the provisions of the 1856 Republican platform as well as a call for federal support of a transcontinental railroad. Once again, its centerpiece was a call for the containment of slavery.

Douglas, believing only his victory could reconcile North and South, became the first U.S. presidential candidate to make a vigorous nationwide speaking tour, a tradition followed by every subsequent presidential candidate. In his speeches he urged support for the Union and opposition to any extremist candidates that might endanger its survival, by which he meant Lincoln and Breckinridge.

On election day the voting went along strictly sectional lines. Breckinridge carried the Deep South; Bell, the border states; and Lincoln, the North. Douglas, although second in popular votes, carried only a single state and part of another. Lincoln's name was not even printed in several Southern states. He led in popular votes, and though he only won 40 percent of the votes cast, he did have the needed majority in electoral votes and was elected.

The Secession Crisis

Lincoln had declared he had no intention of disturbing slavery where it already existed, but many Southerners thought otherwise. They also feared further raids of the sort John Brown had attempted and felt their pride injured by the election of a president for whom no Southerner had voted.

On December 20, 1860, South Carolina, by vote of a special convention made up of delegates elected by the people of the state, declared itself out of the Union. By February 1, 1861, six more states (Alabama, Georgia, Florida, Mississippi, Louisiana, and Texas) had followed suit.

Representatives of the seven seceded states met in Montgomery, Alabama, in February 1861 and declared themselves to be the Confederate States of America. They elected former Secretary of War and U.S. Senator Jefferson Davis of Mississippi as president and Alexander Stephens of Georgia as vice president. They also adopted a constitution for the Confederate States that, while similar to the U.S. Constitution in many ways, contained several important differences:

1. Slavery was specifically recognized, and the right to move slaves from one state to another was guaranteed.
2. Protective tariffs were prohibited.
3. The president was to serve for a single nonrenewable six-year term.
4. The president was given the right to veto individual items within an appropriations bill.
5. State sovereignty was specifically recognized.

In the North, reaction was mixed. Some, such as prominent Republican Horace Greeley of the *New York Tribune,* counseled, "Let erring sisters go in peace." President Buchanan, now a lame duck, seemed to be of this mind, since he declared secession to be unconstitutional but at the same time stated his belief that it was unconstitutional for the federal government to do anything to stop states from seceding. Taking his own advice, he did nothing.

Others, led by Senator John J. Crittenden of Kentucky, strove for a compromise that would preserve the Union. Throughout the period of several weeks as the Southern states one by one declared their secession, Crittenden worked desperately with a congressional compromise committee in hopes of working out some form of agreement.

The compromise proposals centered on the passage of a constitutional amendment forever prohibiting federal meddling with slavery in the states where it existed as well as the extension of the Missouri Compromise line (36°30′) to the Pacific, with slavery specifically protected in all the territories south of it.

Some Congressional Republicans were inclined to accept this compromise, but President-elect Lincoln urged them to stand firm for no further spread of slavery. Southerners would consider no compromise that did not provide for the spread of slavery, and talks broke down.

The Civil War and Reconstruction, 1860–1877

Hostilities Begin—Fort Sumter Falls

Lincoln did his best to avoid angering the slave states that had not yet seceded. In his inaugural address he urged Southerners to reconsider their actions but warned that the Union was perpetual, that states could not secede, and that he would therefore hold the federal forts and installations in the South.

Of these, only two remained in federal hands: Fort Pickens, off Pensacola, Florida; and Fort Sumter, in the harbor of Charleston, South Carolina. Lincoln soon received word from Major Robert Anderson, commanding the small garrison at Sumter, that supplies were running low. Desiring to send in the needed supplies, Lincoln informed the governor of South Carolina of his intention but promised that no attempt would be made to send arms, ammunition, or reinforcements unless Southerners initiated hostilities.

Not satisfied, Southerners determined to take the fort. Confederate General P. G. T. Beauregard, acting on orders from President Davis, demanded Anderson's surrender. Anderson said he would if not resupplied. Knowing supplies were on the way, the Confederates opened fire at 4:30 a.m. on April 12, 1861. The next day the fort surrendered. Lincoln had succeeded in getting the Southern rebels to fire the first shots of the Civil War.

The day following Sumter's surrender Lincoln declared the existence of an insurrection and called for the states to provide 75,000 volunteers to put it down. In response to this, Virginia, Tennessee, North Carolina, and Arkansas declared their secession.

The remaining slave states, Delaware, Kentucky, Maryland, and Missouri, wavered to varying degrees but stayed in the Union. Delaware, which had few slaves, gave little serious consideration to the idea of secession. Kentucky declared itself neutral and then sided with the North when the South failed to respect this neutrality. Maryland's incipient secession movement was crushed by Lincoln's timely imposition of martial law. Missouri was saved for the Union by the quick and decisive use of federal troops as well as the sizable population of pro-Union, anti-slavery German immigrants living in St. Louis.

Relative Strengths at the Outset

An assessment of available assets at the beginning of the war did not look favorable for the South.

The North enjoyed at least five major advantages over the South.

1. **Economic Wealth**. It had overwhelming preponderance in wealth and thus was better able to finance the enormous expense of the war.

2. **Industrial Production**. The North was also vastly superior in industry and thus capable of producing the needed war materials; the South, as a primarily agricultural society, often had to improvise or do without.

3. **Population**. The North furthermore had an advantage of almost three-to-one in manpower, and over one-third of the South's population was composed of slaves, whom Southerners would not use as soldiers. Unlike the South, the North received large numbers of immigrants during the war.

4. **Naval Strength**. The North retained control of the U.S. Navy and thus would command the sea and be able, by blockading, to cut the South off from outside sources of supply.

5. **Railroads**. Finally, the North enjoyed a far superior system of railroads, while the South's relatively sparse railroad net was composed of a number of smaller railroads, often not interconnected and with varying gauges of track. They were more useful for carrying cotton from the interior to port cities than for moving large amounts of war supplies or troops around the country.

The South did, however, have several advantages of its own.

1. **Size**. It was vast in size, and this would make it difficult to conquer; it did not need to conquer the North, but only resist being conquered itself.

2. **Home Territory**. Its troops would also be fighting on their own ground, a fact that would give them the advantage of familiarity with the terrain, as well as the added motivation of defending their homes and families. Its armies would often have the opportunity of fighting on the defensive, a major advantage in the warfare of that day.

3. **Experienced Military Leaders**. At the outset of the war the South drew a number of highly qualified senior officers, such as Robert E. Lee, Joseph E. Johnston, and Albert Sidney Johnston, from the U.S. Army. By contrast, the Union command structure was already set when the war began, with the aged Winfield Scott, of Mexican War fame, at the top. It took young and talented officers, such as Ulysses S. Grant and William T. Sherman, time to work up to high rank. Meanwhile, Union armies were often led by inferior commanders, as Lincoln experimented while in search of good generals.

At first glance, the South might also have seemed to have an advantage in its president. Jefferson Davis had extensive military and political experience and was acquainted with the nation's top military men and, presumably, with their relative abilities. On the other hand, Lincoln had been, up until his election to the presidency, less successful politically and had virtually no military experience. In fact, Lincoln was much superior to Davis as a war leader, showing firmness, flexibility, mental toughness, great political skill, and, eventually, an excellent grasp of strategy.

Opposing Strategies

Both sides were full of enthusiasm for the war. In the North, the battle cry was "On to Richmond," the new Confederate capital established after the secession of Virginia. In the South, the battle cry was "On to Washington." Yielding to popular demand, Lincoln ordered General Irvin McDowell to advance on Richmond with his army. At a creek called Bull Run near the town of Manassas Junction, Virginia, just southwest of Washington, D.C., they met a Confederate force under generals P. G. T. Beauregard and Joseph E. Johnston on July 21, 1861. In the First Battle of Bull Run (called the First Battle of Manassas in the South), the Union army was forced to retreat in confusion back to Washington.

Bull Run demonstrated the unpreparedness and inexperience of both sides. It also demonstrated that the war would be long and hard, and, particularly in the North, that greater efforts would be required. Lincoln would need an overall strategy. To supply this, Winfield Scott suggested the Anaconda Plan to squeeze the life out of the Confederacy. This plan included a naval blockade to shut out supplies from Europe, a campaign to take the Mississippi River, thereby splitting the South in two, and the taking of several strategic points, then waiting for pro-Union sentiment in the South to overthrow the secessionists. Lincoln liked the first two points of Scott's strategy, but considered the third point unrealistic.

DIDYOUKNOW?

The First Battle of Bull Run had an unexpected audience—average citizens. Hundreds of area residents, along with politicians, diplomats, and their wives from Washington, D.C., packed picnic baskets and settled near Bull Run Creek to watch the battle, a sign of how quickly and bloodlessly people expected the Civil War to end.

Lincoln ordered a naval blockade, an overwhelming task considering the South's long coastline. Under Secretary of the Navy Gideon Welles, the Navy was expanded enormously and the blockade, derided in the early days as a "paper blockade," became increasingly effective.

Lincoln also ordered a campaign to take the Mississippi River. A major step in this direction was taken when naval forces under Captain David G. Farragut captured New Orleans in April 1862.

Rather than waiting for pro-Unionists in the South to gain control, Lincoln hoped to raise huge armies and apply overwhelming pressure from all sides at once until the Confederacy collapsed. The strategy was good; the problem was finding good generals to carry it out.

The Union Preserved

Lincoln Tries McClellan

To replace the discredited McDowell, Lincoln chose General George B. McClellan. McClellan was a good trainer and organizer and was loved by the troops, but was unable to effectively use the powerful army (now named the Army of the Potomac) he had built. Despite much prodding from Lincoln, McClellan hesitated to advance, badly overestimating his enemy's numbers.

Finally, in the spring of 1862, he took the Army of the Potomac by water down Chesapeake Bay to land between the York and James rivers in Virginia. His plan was to advance up the peninsula formed by these rivers directly to Richmond.

The operations that followed were known as the Peninsula Campaign. McClellan advanced slowly and cautiously toward Richmond, while his equally cautious Confederate opponent, General Joseph E. Johnston, drew back to the outskirts of the city before turning to fight at the Battle of Seven Pines, May 31–June 1, 1862. In this inconclusive battle, Johnston was wounded. To replace him Jefferson Davis appointed his military advisor, General Robert E. Lee.

Lee summoned General Thomas J. "Stonewall" Jackson and his army from the Shenandoah Valley (where Jackson had just finished defeating several superior federal forces, causing consternation in Washington) and the combined forces attacked McClellan.

After two days of bloody but inconclusive fighting, McClellan lost his nerve and began to retreat. In the remainder of what came to be called the Battle of the Seven Days, Lee continued to attack McClellan, forcing him back to his base, though at great cost in lives. McClellan's army was loaded back onto its ships and taken back to Washington.

Before McClellan's army could reach Washington and be completely deployed in northern Virginia, Lee saw and took an opportunity to thrash Union General John Pope, who was operating in northern Virginia with another Northern army, at the Second Battle of Bull Run.

Union Victories in the West

In the western area of the war's operations (essentially everything west of the Appalachian Mountains), matters were proceeding in a much different fashion. The Northern commanders there, Henry W. Halleck and Don Carlos Buell, were no more enterprising than McClellan, but Halleck's subordinate, Ulysses S. Grant, definitely was.

Seeking and obtaining permission from Halleck, Grant mounted a combined operation—army troops and navy gunboats—against two vital Confederate strongholds, Forts Henry and Donelson, which guarded the Tennessee and Cumberland rivers in northern Tennessee, and which were the weak point of the thinly-stretched Confederate line under General Albert Sidney Johnston. When Grant captured the forts in February 1862, Johnston was forced to retreat to Corinth in northern Mississippi.

TEST TIP

Some questions on the AP U.S. History exam ask you to interpret a political cartoon. Political cartoons give opinions about events taking place at the time of their creation. Because of this, the cartoons may reference specific people or events with which you are unfamiliar. However, you don't need to focus on identifying the individuals in the cartoon. Focus instead on the broader historical themes and symbolism behind the cartoon, which should provide you all the information you need to answer the question.

Grant pursued but was ordered by Halleck to wait until all was in readiness before proceeding. He halted his troops at Pittsburg Landing on the Tennessee River, twenty-five miles north of Corinth. On April 6, 1862, Johnston, who had received reinforcements and been joined by General P. G. T. Beauregard, surprised Grant there, but in the two-day battle that followed (Shiloh) failed to defeat him. Johnston himself was among the many killed in what was, up to this point, the bloodiest battle in American history.

Grant was severely criticized in the North for having been taken by surprise. Yet with other Union victories and Farragut's capture of New Orleans, the North had taken all of the Mississippi River except for a 110-mile stretch between the Confederate fortresses of Vicksburg, Mississippi, and Port Hudson, Louisiana.

The Success of Northern Diplomacy

Many Southerners believed Britain and France would rejoice in seeing a divided and weakened America. The two countries would likewise be driven by the need of their factories for cotton and thus intervene on the Confederacy's behalf. So strongly was this view held that, during the early days of the war, when the Union blockade was still too weak to be very effective, the Confederate government itself prohibited the export of cotton in order to hasten British and French intervention.

This view proved mistaken for several reasons. Britain already had large stocks of cotton on hand from the bumper crops of the years immediately prior to the war. During the war, the British had been somewhat successful in finding alternative sources of cotton, importing the fiber from India and Egypt. British leaders may also have weighed their country's need to import wheat from the northern United States against its desire for cotton from the Southern states. Finally, British public opinion opposed slavery.

Skillful Northern diplomacy had a great impact. In this, Lincoln had the extremely able assistance of Secretary of State William Seward, who took a hard line in warning Europeans not to interfere, and of Ambassador to Great Britain Charles Francis Adams. Britain therefore remained neutral and other European countries, France in particular, followed its lead.

One incident nevertheless came close to fulfilling Southern hopes for British intervention. In November 1861, Captain Charles Wilkes of the U.S.S. *San Jacinto* stopped the British mail and passenger ship *Trent* and forcibly removed Confederate emissaries James M. Mason and John Slidell. News of Wilkes's action brought great rejoicing in the North, but outrage in Great Britain, where it was viewed as an act of piracy and a violation of Britain's rights on the high seas. Lincoln and Seward, faced with British threats of war at a time when the North could ill afford it, wisely chose to release the envoys and smooth things over with Britain.

The Confederacy was able to obtain some loans and to purchase small amounts of arms, ammunition, and even commerce-raiding ships such as the highly successful C.S.S. *Alabama.* However, Union naval superiority kept such supplies to a minimum.

The War at Sea

The Confederacy's major bid to challenge the Union's naval superiority was based on the employment of a technological innovation, the ironclad ship. The first and most successful of the Confederate ironclads was the C.S.S. *Virginia.* Built on the hull of the abandoned Union frigate *Merrimac,* the *Virginia* was protected from cannon fire by iron plates bolted over her sloping wooden sides. In May 1862 she destroyed two wooden warships of the Union naval force at Hampton Roads, Virginia, and was seriously threatening to destroy the rest of the squadron before being met and fought to a standstill by the Union ironclad U.S.S. *Monitor.*

The Domestic Front

The war on the home front dealt with the problems of maintaining public morale, supplying the armies, and resolving constitutional questions regarding authority and the ability of the respective governments to deal with crises.

For the general purpose of maintaining public morale but also as items many Republicans had advocated even before the war, Congress in 1862 passed two highly important acts dealing with domestic affairs in the North:

- The Homestead Act granted 160 acres of government land free of charge to any person who would farm it for at least five years. Much of the West was eventually settled under the provisions of this act.
- The Morrill Land Grant Act offered large amounts of the federal government's land to states that would establish "agricultural and mechanical" colleges. Many of the nation's large state universities were founded in later years under the provisions of this act.

Keeping the people relatively satisfied was made more difficult by the necessity, apparent by 1863, of imposing conscription (a draft of citizens into the army) in order to obtain adequate manpower for the huge force that would be needed to crush the South. Especially hated by many working-

DID YOU KNOW?

With so many men fighting in the war, a large number of Southern women faced new challenges. They ran plantations, managed businesses, stretched limited supplies, and helped nurse the wounded and ill soldiers at rudimentary field hospitals.

class Northerners was the provision of the conscription act that allowed a drafted individual to avoid service by hiring a substitute or paying $300. Resistance to the draft led to riots in New York City in which hundreds were killed.

The Confederacy, with its much smaller manpower pool to draw from, had instituted conscription itself in 1862. Here, too, it did not always meet with cooperation. Some Southern governors objected to it on states' rights grounds, doing all they could to obstruct its operation. A provision of the Southern conscription act allowing one man to stay home as overseer for every twenty slaves led the non-slaveholding whites who made up most of the Southern population to grumble that it was a "rich man's war and a poor man's fight." Draft dodging and desertion became epidemic in the South by the latter part of the war.

Scarcity of food and other consumer goods in the South, as well as high prices, led to further desertion as soldiers left the ranks to care for their starving families. Discontent also manifested itself in the form of a "bread riot" in Richmond.

Supplying the war placed an enormous strain on both societies, but the North, with its diversified economy, was better able to bear it.

To finance the Northern side of the war, high tariffs and the nation's first income tax were resorted to, yet even more money was needed. The Treasury Department, under Secretary of the Treasury Salmon P. Chase, issued "greenbacks," an unbacked currency that nevertheless fared better than the Southern paper money because of greater confidence in a Northern victory. To facilitate the financing of the war through credit expansion, the National Banking Act was passed in 1863.

The South, with its scant financial resources, found it all but impossible to cope with the expenses of war. Excise and income taxes were levied and some small loans were obtained in Europe, yet the Southern Congress still felt compelled to issue paper money in such quantities that it became virtually worthless. That, and the scarcity of almost everything created by the war and its disruption of the economy, led to skyrocketing prices.

The Confederate government responded to the inflation it created by imposing taxes-in-kind and impressment, the seizing of produce, livestock, etc., by Confederate agents in return for payment according to an artificially set schedule of prices. Since payment was in worthless inflated currency, this amounted to confiscation and soon resulted in goods of all sorts becoming even scarcer when a Confederate impressment agent was known to be in the neighborhood.

Questions of constitutional authority to deal with crises plagued both presidents.

To deal with the emergency of secession, Lincoln stretched the presidential powers to beyond the limit of the Constitution. To quell the threat of secession in Maryland, Lincoln suspended the writ of *habeas corpus* and imprisoned numerous suspected secessionists without charges or trial, ignoring the insistence of pro-Southern Chief Justice Roger B. Taney in *ex parte Merryman* (1861) that such action was unconstitutional.

"Copperheads"—Northerners such as Clement L. Vallandigham of Ohio who opposed the war—denounced Lincoln as a tyrant and would-be dictator, but remained a minority. Though occasionally subject to arrest and/or deportation for their activities, they were generally allowed a considerable degree of latitude.

Davis encountered obstructionism from various state governors, the Confederate Congress, and even his own vice president, who denounced him as a tyrant for assuming too much power and failing to respect states' rights. Hampered by such attitudes, the Confederate government proved less effective than it might have been.

The Emancipation Proclamation

By mid-1862, Lincoln was under pressure from radical elements of his own party and hoping to create a favorable impression on foreign public opinion. He determined to issue the Emancipation Proclamation, declaring free, as of January 1, 1863, all slaves in areas still in rebellion. In order that this not appear an act of panic and desperation in view of the string of defeats the North had recently suffered on the battlefields of Virginia, Lincoln, at Seward's recommendation, waited to announce the proclamation until the North should win some measure of victory. This was provided by the Battle of Antietam on September 17, 1862, which wasn't a clear-cut victory, but also wasn't a defeat.

Though the Radical Republicans, pre-war abolitionists for the most part, had for some time been urging Lincoln to take such a step, Northern public opinion as a whole was less enthusiastic, as the Republicans suffered major losses in the November 1862 congressional elections.

TEST TIP

Worried about needing to remember the difference between various weapons or interpret battlefield maps? Don't sweat it. The AP U.S. History exam does not ask questions about specific battles or military technology. Instead, it will focus on the social, political, and diplomatic aspects and effects of conflicts.

The Turning Point in the East

After his victory at the Second Battle of Bull Run, August 27–30, 1862, Colonel Lee moved north and crossed into Maryland, where he hoped to win a decisive victory that would force the North to recognize Southern independence.

He was confronted by the Army of the Potomac, once again under the command of General George B. McClellan. Through a stroke of good fortune early in the campaign, detailed plans for Lee's entire audacious operation fell into McClellan's hands, but the Northern general, by extreme caution and slowness, threw away this incomparable chance to annihilate Lee and win—or at least shorten—the war.

The armies finally met along Antietam Creek, just east of the town of Sharpsburg in western Maryland. In a bloody but inconclusive daylong battle, known as Antietam in the North and as Sharpsburg in the South, McClellan's timidity led him to miss another excellent chance to destroy Lee's cornered and badly outnumbered army. After the battle, Lee retreated to Virginia, and Lincoln, besides issuing the Emancipation Proclamation, removed McClellan from command.

To replace him, Lincoln chose General Ambrose E. Burnside, who promptly demonstrated his unfitness for command by blundering into a lopsided defeat at Fredericksburg, Virginia, on December 13, 1862.

Lincoln then replaced Burnside with General Joseph "Fighting Joe" Hooker. Handsome and hard-drinking, Hooker had bragged of what he would do to "Bobby Lee" when he got at him; but when he took his army south, "Fighting Joe" quickly lost his nerve. He was out-generaled and soundly beaten at the Battle of Chancellorsville, May 5–6, 1863. At this battle the brilliant Southern General "Stonewall" Jackson was accidentally shot by his own men and died several days later.

Lee, anxious to shift the scene of the fighting out of his beloved Virginia, sought and received permission from President Davis to invade Pennsylvania. He was pursued by the Army of the Potomac, now under the command of General George G. Meade, whom Lincoln had selected to replace the discredited Hooker. They met at Gettysburg, and in a three-day battle (July 1–3, 1863) that was the bloodiest in the history of the Western Hemisphere, Lee, who sorely missed the services of Jackson and whose cavalry leader, the normally reliable J. E. B. Stuart, failed to provide him with timely reconnaissance, was defeated. However, he was allowed by the victorious Meade to retreat to Virginia with his army intact if battered, much to Lincoln's disgust. Still, Lee would never again have the strength to mount such an invasion.

New York City Draft Riots

While Lee was suffering the turning-point defeat of the war at Gettysburg, draft riots broke out in New York City to protest conscription. Mobs of men, many Irish immigrants who were being drafted to fill enlistment quotas, stormed through the city, beating African Americans, burning buildings, and actually killing many innocent victims. Lincoln was forced to dispatch troops to New York to quell the rioting.

Lincoln Finds Grant

Meanwhile, Grant undertook to take Vicksburg, one of the two last Confederate bastions on the Mississippi River. In a brilliant campaign, he bottled up the Confederate forces of General John C. Pemberton inside the city and placed them under siege. After six weeks of siege, the defenders surrendered on July 4, 1863. Five days later, Port Hudson surrendered as well, giving the Union complete control of the Mississippi.

After Union forces under General William Rosecrans suffered an embarrassing defeat at the Battle of Chickamauga in northwestern Georgia, September 19–20, 1863, Lincoln named Grant overall commander of Union forces in the West.

Grant then went to Chattanooga, Tennessee, where Confederate forces under General Braxton Bragg were virtually besieging Rosecrans, and immediately took control of the situation. Gathering Union forces from other portions of the western theater and combining them with reinforcements from the east, Grant won a resounding victory at the Battle of Chattanooga (November 23–25, 1863), in which federal forces stormed seemingly impregnable Confederate positions on Lookout Mountain and Missionary Ridge. This victory put Union forces in position for a drive into Georgia, which began the following spring.

Early in 1864, Lincoln made Grant commander of all Union armies. Grant devised a coordinated plan for constant pressure on the Confederacy. General William T. Sherman would lead a drive toward Atlanta, Georgia, with the goal of destroying the Confederate army under General Joseph E. Johnston (who had replaced Bragg). Grant himself would accompany Meade and the Army of the Potomac in advancing toward Richmond with the goal of destroying Lee's Confederate army.

In a series of bloody battles (the Wilderness, Spotsylvania, Cold Harbor) in May and June of 1864, Grant drove Lee to the outskirts of Richmond. Still unable to take the city or get Lee at a disadvantage, Grant circled around to try to take both by way of the back door, attacking Petersburg, Virginia, an important railroad junction just south of Richmond and the key to that city's—and Lee's—supply lines. Once again turned back by entrenched Confederate troops, Grant settled in to besiege Petersburg and Richmond in a stalemate that lasted nine months.

Sherman had been advancing simultaneously in Georgia. He maneuvered Johnston back to the outskirts of Atlanta with relatively little fighting. At that point Confederate President Davis lost patience with Johnston and replaced him with the aggressive General John B. Hood. Hood and Sherman fought three fierce but inconclusive battles around Atlanta in late July, then settled in to a siege of their own during the month of August.

TEST TIP

Remember to leave your AP U.S. History textbook and review materials at home or in your locker during the exam. You are not allowed to refer to any potential sources of information during the break period between test sections.

The Election of 1864 and Northern Victory

In the North, discontentment grew with the long casualty lists and seeming lack of results. Yet the South could withstand the grinding war even less. By late 1864, Jefferson Davis had reached the point of calling for the use of blacks in the Confederate armies, though the war ended before black troops could see action for the Confederacy. The South's best hope was that Northern war-weariness would bring the defeat of Lincoln and the victory of a peace candidate in the election of 1864.

Lincoln ran on the ticket of the National Union Party, essentially the Republican Party with loyal or "War" Democrats. His vice-presidential candidate was Andrew Johnson, a loyal Democrat from Tennessee.

The Democratic Party's presidential candidate was General George B. McClellan, who, with some misgivings, ran on a platform labeling the war a failure and calling for a negotiated peace settlement even if that meant Southern independence.

The outlook was bleak for a time, and even Lincoln himself believed that he would be defeated. Then in September 1864 came word that Sherman had taken Atlanta.

The capture of this vital Southern rail and manufacturing center brought an enormous boost to Northern morale. Along with other Northern victories that summer and fall, it ensured a resounding election victory for Lincoln and the continuation of the war to complete victory for the North.

To speed that victory, Sherman marched through Georgia from Atlanta to the sea, arriving at Savannah in December 1864 and turning north into the Carolinas, leaving behind a 60-mile-wide swath of destruction. His goal was to impress on Southerners that continuation of the war could mean only ruin for all of them. He and Grant planned that his army should press on through the Carolinas and into Virginia to join Grant in finishing off Lee.

Before Sherman's troops could arrive, Lee abandoned Richmond (April 3, 1865) and attempted to escape with what was left of his army. Pursued by Grant, he was cornered and forced to surrender at Appomattox, Virginia, on April 9, 1865. Other Confederate armies still holding out in various parts of the South surrendered over the next few weeks.

As the industrial and political capital of the Confederacy, Richmond, Virginia, found itself caught in the bloody crossfire between two mighty American armies. Here, the Petersburg Railway Depot lies in ruins in 1865. (AP/Wide World Photo)

Lincoln did not live to receive news of the final surrenders. On April 14, 1865, he was shot in the back of the head while watching a play at Ford's Theatre in Washington. His assassin, pro-Southern actor John Wilkes Booth, broke his leg in jumping to the stage while making his escape. Hunted down by Union cavalry several days later in northern Virginia, he died of a gunshot wound. Several other individuals were tried, convicted, and hanged by a military tribunal for participating with Booth in a conspiracy to assassinate not only Lincoln, but also Vice President Johnson and Secretary of State Seward.

Table 7.2 Key Events and Battles of the Civil War

Event	Date	Location	Significance
Lincoln elected president	November 1860	U.S.	Though winning in the Electoral College, Lincoln's lack of a popular majority (1.9 million out of 4.7 million votes cast) is an indication of the problems he would face with a divided nation.
South Carolina secedes	December 1860	South Carolina	On news of Lincoln's election, South Carolina (site of nullification fight in 1830s) secedes.
Confederacy formed	February 1861	Montgomery, Alabama	Seven states form Confederacy, write their own constitution, and plan for an independent nation.
Lincoln inaugurated	March 1861	Washington, D.C.	Lincoln enters Washington, D.C., in disguise because of unrest. Southerners begin seizing federal posts.
Ft. Sumter attacked	April 1861	Charleston, South Carolina	Lincoln decides to supply Fort. Sumter, but wants the South to fire the first shot.
Bull Run (Manassas), first battle	July 21, 1861	Northern Virginia	Gen. McDowell leads 30,000 men against Gen. Johnston's 22,000 Southern troops in an attempt to crush the rebels and go "On to Richmond." South scores victory as Union troops flee back to Washington in disarray. McDowell is replaced by Gen. McClellan.
Ft. Henry & Ft. Donelson	February 1862	Tennessee rivers	Gen. Grant captures 2 forts on the Tennessee and Cumberland Rivers. Confederates are forced out of Kentucky and yield much of Tennessee.
Monitor vs. *Merrimac*	March 1862	Off Hampton Roads, Virginia	First ironclad battle in history ends in a draw as the *Merrimac* withdraws after daylong exchange of fire. Union blockade of South is maintained.
Shiloh (Pittsburgh Landing)	April 1862	Tennessee	Grant overcomes Southern forces with heavy losses for each side: 13,000 Union casualties, 11,000 for South.
New Orleans	April 1862	Louisiana	Farragut seizes New Orleans for Union after boldly attacking Southern position; 11 Southern ships sunk.
Peninsular Campaign (Yorktown, Seven Days' Battle, Fair Oaks)	March–July 1862	Southern Virginia	After continual prodding by Lincoln, McClellan decides to attack Richmond via the South. He moves his large army down the Potomac, marches on Richmond, and then assumes a defensive position rather than pushing for victory. Gen. Lee takes command of Southern troops.
Bull Run (Manassas) second battle	August 1862	Northern Virginia	McClellan replaced by Gen. Pope. Lee and Gen. Stonewall Jackson defeat Union troops again at Manassas and Pope is replaced by McClellan.
Antietam	September 1862	Maryland	Heavily outnumbered, Lee's troops face McClellan in bloody fighting. Over 23,000 casualties (more than all previous American wars combined). Lee retreats to Virginia.

Table 7.2 *Continued*

Event	Date	Location	Significance
Emancipation Proclamation	Proclaimed September 23, 1862 Effective January 1, 1863	Washington, D.C.	With victory at Antietam, Lincoln announces that on 1/1/63, all slaves in the rebelling states would be free. The proclamation does not affect border states. Forces European nations to recognize that choosing sides in the Civil War is to take a stand on slavery.
Fredericksburg	December 1862	Central Virginia	General Burnside attacks Lee's fortified position and suffers 10,000 casualties (to Lee's 5000).
Chancellorsville	May 1863	Northern Virginia	General Hooker defeated by Lee, but Jackson is mistakenly shot and killed by his own men.
Vicksburg	July 1863	Mississippi	After a long siege, Vicksburg surrenders to Grant. All of the Mississippi River is now in Union control.
Gettysburg	July 1863	Pennsylvania	Over 165,000 soldiers participate in the largest battle in the Western Hemisphere. After three days of fighting, Lee retreats, leaving 4,000 dead Confederates. Total casualties: 23,000 Union, 28,000 Confederates.
Chattanooga	November 1863	Tennessee	Reinforced with troops from the East, Grant is able to push Southern troops back and prepare for assault on Atlanta and the heart of the Confederacy.
Grant promoted to Lt. General and given command of all Union troops	March 1864	Washington, D.C.	Grant prepares for assault on Richmond. When Lincoln's Cabinet complains that Grant is a drunk and seeks to interfere with his command, Lincoln gives him unconditional support and asks not to be notified of his plans.
Wilderness and Spotsylvania	May 1864	Central Virginia	Lee stops Union troops at the Wilderness, but Grant resumes march to Richmond. Though suffering huge losses (55,000 men to South's 31,000), Grant states "I propose to fight on this line if it takes all summer."
Petersburg	June 1864–April 1865	South of Richmond, Virginia	Grant focuses on important railroad junction and communication outside Richmond. Long siege of Petersburg begins with troops living in trenches that stretched for 50 miles.
Atlanta to Savannah	September–December 1864	Georgia	General Sherman destroys Atlanta and then sends troops on a 300-mile destructive march to the sea. Railroads are torn up, buildings destroyed, and crops burned in an attempt to break the will of the South.
Lee surrenders	April 9, 1865	Appomattox Court House, Virginia	Lee, refusing to see his troops suffer any further, surrenders to Grant. Southern troops given generous terms of surrender.

The Ordeal of Reconstruction

Lincoln's Plan of Reconstruction

Reconstruction began well before the fighting of the Civil War came to an end. It brought a time of difficult adjustments in the South.

Among those who faced such adjustments were the recently freed slaves, who flocked into Union lines, followed advancing Union armies, or whose plantations were part of the growing area of the South that came under Union military control. Some slaves had left their plantations, and thus their only means of livelihood, to obtain freedom within Union lines. Many felt they had to leave their plantations to be truly free, and some sought to find relatives separated during the days of slavery. Some former slaves also seemed to misunderstand the meaning of freedom, thinking they need never work again.

To ease the adjustment for these recently freed slaves, Congress in 1865 created the Freedmen's Bureau, to provide food, clothing, homes, and education, and generally look after the interests of former slaves.

Even before the need to deal with this problem had forced itself on the Northern government's awareness, steps had been taken to deal with another major adjustment of Reconstruction, the restoration of loyal governments to the seceded states. By 1863, substantial portions of several Southern states had come under Northern military control, and Lincoln had set forth a policy for re-establishing governments in those states.

Lincoln's policy, known as the Ten Percent Plan, stipulated that Southerners, except for high-ranking rebel officials, could take an oath promising future loyalty to the Union and acceptance of the end of slavery. When the number of those who had taken this oath within any one state reached ten percent of the population who had been registered to vote in that state in 1860, a loyal state government could be formed. Only those who had taken the oath could vote or participate in the new government.

Tennessee, Arkansas, and Louisiana met the requirements right away and formed loyal governments but were refused recognition by Congress, which was dominated by Radical Republicans.

The Radical Republicans, such as Thaddeus Stevens of Pennsylvania, believed Lincoln's plan did not adequately punish the South, restructure Southern society, and boost the political prospects of the Republican Party. The loyal Southern states were denied representation in Congress and electoral votes in the election of 1864.

Instead, the Radicals in Congress drew up the Wade-Davis Bill. Under its stringent terms, a majority of the number who had been alive and registered to vote in 1860 would have to swear an "ironclad" oath stating that they were now loyal and had never been disloyal. This was obviously impossible in any former Confederate state unless blacks were given the vote, something Radical Republicans desired but virtually all Southern whites definitely did not. Unless the requisite number swore the "ironclad" oath, Congress would not allow the state to have a government.

DIDYOUKNOW?

The pocket veto reflects a different era in U.S. government, when Congress typically met for one marathon session before adjourning for several months. Then, Congress gathered again for a shorter second session. Improvements in transportation and a change in the congressional meeting calendar have ended these long intersession breaks, but presidents still have the power of the pocket veto.

Lincoln killed the Wade-Davis bill with a "pocket veto," and the Radicals were furious. When Lincoln was assassinated the Radicals rejoiced, believing Vice President Andrew Johnson would be less generous to the South or at least easier to control.

Johnson's Attempt at Reconstruction

To the dismay of the Radicals, Johnson followed Lincoln's policies very closely, making them only slightly more stringent by requiring ratification of the 13th Amendment (officially abolishing slavery), repudiation of Confederate debts, and renunciation of secession. He also recommended the vote be given to blacks.

Southern states proved reluctant to accept these conditions, some declining to repudiate Confederate debts or ratify the 13th Amendment (it nevertheless received the ratification of the necessary number of states and was declared part of the Constitution in December 1865). No Southern state extended the vote to blacks (at this time no Northern state did, either). Instead, the Southern states promulgated black codes, which, like the slave codes, imposed various restrictions on the freedom of the former slaves.

Foreign Policy Under Johnson

On coming into office Johnson had inherited a foreign policy problem involving Mexico and France. The French Emperor, Napoleon III, had made Mexico the target of one of his many grandiose foreign adventures. In 1862, while the U.S. was occupied with the Civil War and therefore unable to prevent this violation of the Monroe Doctrine, Napoleon III had Archduke Maximilian of Austria installed as a puppet emperor of Mexico, supported by French troops. The U.S. had protested, but for the time could do nothing.

With the war over, Johnson and Secretary of State Seward were able to take more vigorous steps. General Philip Sheridan was sent to the Rio Grande with a military force. At the same time Mexican revolutionary leader Benito Juarez was given the tacit recognition of the U.S. government. Johnson and Seward continued to invoke the Monroe Doctrine and to place quiet pressure on Napoleon III to withdraw his troops. In May 1866, facing difficulties of his own in Europe, the French emperor did so, leaving the unfortunate Maximilian to face a Mexican firing squad.

Johnson's and Seward's course of action in preventing the extension of the French Empire into the Western Hemisphere strengthened America's commitment to, and the rest of the world's respect for, the Monroe Doctrine.

In 1866, the Russian minister approached Seward with an offer to sell Alaska to the U.S. The Russians wished to sell Alaska because its fur resources had been largely exhausted and because they feared that in a possible war with Great Britain (something that seemed likely at the time), they would lose Alaska anyway.

Seward, who was an ardent expansionist, pushed hard for the purchase of Alaska, known as "Seward's Folly" by its critics, and it was largely through his efforts that it was pushed through Congress. It was argued that purchasing Alaska would reward the Russians for their friendly stance toward the U.S. government during the Civil War, at a time when Britain and France had seemed to favor the Confederacy.

In 1867, the sale went through and Alaska was purchased for $7.2 million.

DIDYOUKNOW?

Alaska leads the nation in many geographic respects. It is the largest U.S. state by land area, has a coastline longer than all other U.S. states combined, and is home to the nation's highest point, Mount McKinley.

Congressional Reconstruction

Southern intransigence in the face of Johnson's relatively mild plan of Reconstruction manifested itself in the refusal of some states to repudiate the Confederate debt and ratify the 13th Amendment. The refusal to give the vote to blacks, the passage of black codes, and the election of many former high-ranking Confederates to Congress and other top positions in the Southern states played into the hands of the Radicals, who were anxious to impose harsh rule on the South. They could now assert that the South was refusing to accept the verdict of the war.

Once again Congress excluded the representatives of the Southern states. Determined to reconstruct the South as it saw fit, Congress passed a Civil Rights Act and extended the authority of the Freedmen's Bureau, giving it both quasi-judicial and quasi-executive powers.

Johnson vetoed both bills, claiming they were unconstitutional; but Congress overrode the vetoes. Fearing that the Supreme Court would agree with Johnson and overturn the laws, Congress approved and sent on to the states for ratification (June 1866) the 14th Amendment, making constitutional the laws Congress had just passed. The 14th Amendment defined citizenship and forbade states to deny various rights to citizens, reduced the representation in Congress of states that did not allow blacks to vote, forbade the paying of the Confederate debt, and made former Confederates ineligible to hold public office.

A brilliant orator and writer, Frederick Douglass, shown ca. 1879, became one of the leading human-rights champions of the nineteenth century. (Photograph by George K. Warren.)

With only one Southern state, Tennessee, ratifying, the amendment failed to receive the necessary approval of three-fourths of the states. But the Radicals in Congress were not finished. Strengthened by victory in the 1866 elections, they passed, over Johnson's veto, the Military Reconstruction Act, dividing the South into five military districts to be ruled by military governors with almost dictatorial powers. Tennessee, having ratified the 14th Amendment, was spared the wrath of the Radicals. The rest of the Southern states were ordered to produce constitutions giving the vote to blacks and to ratify the 14th Amendment before they could be "readmitted." In this manner the 14th Amendment was ratified.

Realizing the unprecedented nature of these actions, Congress moved to prevent any check or balance from the other two branches of government. Steps were taken toward limiting the jurisdiction of the Supreme Court so that it could not review cases pertaining to congressional Reconstruction policies. This proved unnecessary as the Court, now headed by Chief Justice Salmon P. Chase in place of the deceased Taney, readily acquiesced and declined to overturn the Reconstruction acts.

To control the president, Congress passed the Army Act, reducing the president's control over the Army. In obtaining the cooperation of the Army, the Radicals had the aid of General Grant, who already had his eye on the 1868 Republican presidential nomination. Congress also passed the Tenure of Office Act, forbidding Johnson to dismiss Cabinet members without the Senate's permission. In passing the latter act, Congress was especially thinking of Radical Secretary of War Edwin M. Stanton, a Lincoln holdover whom Johnson desired to dismiss.

Johnson obeyed the letter but not the spirit of the Reconstruction acts, and Congress, angry at his refusal to cooperate, sought in vain for grounds to impeach him until, in August 1867, Johnson violated the Tenure of Office Act (by dismissing Stanton) in order to test its constitutionality. The matter was not tested in the courts, however, but instead in Congress, where Johnson was impeached by the House of Representatives and came within one vote of being removed by the Senate. For the remaining months of his term, he offered little further resistance to the Radicals.

The Election of 1868 and the 15th Amendment

In 1868, the Republican convention, dominated by the Radicals, drew up a platform endorsing Radical Reconstruction. For president, the Republicans nominated Ulysses S. Grant, who had no political record and whose views—if any—on national issues were unknown. The vice-presidential nominee was Schuyler Colfax.

Though the Democratic nomination was sought by Andrew Johnson, the party knew he could not win and instead nominated former Governor Horatio Seymour of New York for president and Francis P. Blair, Jr., of Missouri for vice president. Both had been Union generals during the war. The Democratic platform mildly criticized the excesses of Radical Reconstruction and called for continued payment of the war debt in greenbacks, although Seymour himself was a hard-money man.

Grant, despite his enormous popularity as a war hero, won by only a narrow margin, drawing only 300,000 more popular votes than Seymour. Some 700,000 blacks had voted in the Southern states under the auspices of Army occupation, and since all of these had almost certainly voted for Grant, it was clear he had not received a majority of the white vote.

The narrow victory of even such a strong candidate as Grant prompted Republican leaders to decide that it would be politically expedient to give the vote to all blacks, North as well as South. For this purpose the 15th Amendment was drawn up and submitted to the states. Ironically, the idea was so unpopular in the North that it won the necessary three-fourths approval only with its ratification by Southern states required to do so by Congress.

TEST TIP

Creating graphic organizers as you study can help you better understand the connections among events. Several educational websites offer free organizers that you can print or construct online.

Postwar Life in the South

Reconstruction was a difficult time in the South. During the war approximately one in ten Southern men had been killed. Many more were maimed for life. Those who returned from the war found destruction and poverty. The federal government confiscated property of the Confederate government, and dishonest Treasury agents confiscated private property as well. Capital invested in slaves or in Confederate war bonds was lost. Property values fell to one-tenth of their pre-war level. The economic results of the war stayed with the South for decades.

The political results were less long-lived, but more immediately disturbing to Southerners. Southerners complained of widespread corruption in governments sustained by federal troops and composed of "carpetbaggers" (Northerners who came to the South to participate in Reconstruction governments), "scalawags" (Southerners who supported the Reconstruction regimes), and recently freed blacks.

Under the Reconstruction governments, social programs were greatly expanded, leading to higher taxes and growing state debts. Some of the financial problems were due to corruption, a problem in both the North and the South in this era when political machines, such as William Marcy "Boss" Tweed's Tammany Hall machine in New York, dominated many Northern city governments and grew rich.

Southern whites sometimes responded to Reconstruction governments with violence, carried out by groups such as the Ku Klux Klan, aimed at intimidating blacks and white Republicans out of voting. The activities of these organizations were sometimes a response to those of the Union League, an organization used by Southern Republicans to control the black vote. The goal of Southerners not allied with the Reconstruction governments, whether members of the Ku Klux Klan or not, was "redemption" (i.e., the end of the Reconstruction governments).

By 1876, Southern whites had been successful, by legal means or otherwise, in "redeeming" all but three Southern states.

Reconstruction ended primarily because the North lost interest. Corruption in government, economic hard times brought on by the Panic of 1873, and general weariness on the part of Northern voters with the effort to remake Southern society all sapped the will to continue. Diehard Radicals such as Thaddeus Stevens and Charles Sumner were dead.

Corruption Under Grant

Having arrived in the presidency with no firm political positions, Grant found that the only principle he had to guide his actions was his instinctive loyalty to his old friends and the politicians who had propelled him into office. This principle did not serve him well as president. Though personally of unquestioned integrity, he naïvely placed his faith in a number of thoroughly dishonest men. His administration was rocked by one scandalous revelation of government corruption after another. Not every scandal involved members of the executive branch, but together they tended to taint the entire period of Grant's administration as one of unparalleled corruption.

"Man with the (Carpet) Bags," Thomas Nast, 1872. This caricature of Carl Schurz appeared in *Harper's Weekly*. (U.S. Library of Congress)

The "Black Friday" Scandal

In the "Black Friday" scandal, two unscrupulous businessmen, Jim Fiske and Jay Gould, schemed to corner the gold market. To further their designs, they got Grant's brother-in-law to persuade the president that stopping government gold sales would be good for farmers. Grant naïvely complied, and many businessmen were ruined as the price of gold was bid up furiously on "Black Friday." By the time Grant realized what was happening, much damage had already been done.

The Credit Mobilier Scandal

In the Credit Mobilier scandal, officials of the Union Pacific Railroad used a dummy construction company called Credit Mobilier to skim off millions of dollars of the subsidies the government was paying Union Pacific to build a transcontinental railroad. To ensure that Congress would take a benevolent attitude toward all this, the officials bribed many of its members lavishly. Though much of this took place before Grant came into office, its revelation in an 1872 congressional investigation created a general scandal.

TEST TIP

Even though you will complete the multiple-choice portion of the exam using a pencil, bring a couple of pens with black or blue ink to write your essays. Pens write more quickly and don't require sharpening.

The Salary Grab Act

In the Salary Grab Act of 1873, Congress voted a 100 percent pay raise for the president and a 50 percent increase for itself and made both retroactive two years. Public outrage led to a Democratic victory in the next congressional election and the law was repealed.

The Sanborn Contract Fraud

In the Sanborn Contract fraud, a politician named Sanborn was given a contract to collect $427,000 in unpaid taxes for a 50 percent commission. The commission found its way into Republican campaign funds.

The Whiskey Ring Fraud

In the Whiskey Ring fraud, distillers and treasury officials conspired to defraud the government of large amounts of money from the excise tax on whiskey. President Grant's personal secretary was in on the plot, and Grant himself guilessly accepted gifts of a questionable nature. When the matter came under investigation, Grant endeavored to shield his secretary.

The Bribing of Belknap

Grant's Secretary of War, W.W. Belknap, accepted bribes from corrupt agents involved in his department's administration of Indian affairs. When the matter came out, he resigned to escape impeachment.

The Liberal Republicans

Discontentment within Republican ranks with regard to some of the earlier scandals as well as with the Radicals' vindictive Reconstruction policies led a faction of the party to separate and constitute itself as the Liberal Republicans. Besides opposing corruption and favoring sectional harmony, the Liberal Republicans favored hard money and a laissez-faire approach to economic issues. For the election of 1872 they nominated *New York Tribune* editor Horace Greeley for president. Eccentric, controversial, and ineffective as a campaigner, Greeley proved a poor choice. Though nominated by the Democrats as well as the Liberal Republicans, Grant, who was again the nominee of the Radicals, easily defeated him.

Economic Issues Under Grant

Many of the economic difficulties the country faced during Grant's administration were caused by the necessary readjustments from a wartime footing to a peacetime economy.

The central economic question was deflation versus inflation or, more specifically, whether to retire the unbacked paper money, greenbacks, printed to meet the wartime emergency, or to print more.

Most economic conservatives, creditors, and business interests favored retirement of the greenbacks and an early return to the gold standard.

Debtors, who had looked forward to paying off their obligations in depreciated paper money worth less than the gold-backed money they had borrowed, favored a continuation of currency inflation through the use of more greenbacks. The deflation that would come through the retirement of existing greenbacks would make debts contracted during or immediately after the war much harder to pay.

Indian prisoners, from Black Kettle's camp, captured by General Custer, traveling through snow. Illustrated by Theodore R. Davis, *Harper's Weekly,* v. 12, 1868. p. 825. (U.S. Library of Congress)

Generally, Grant's policy was to let the greenbacks float until they were on par with gold and could then be retired without economic dislocation.

Early in Grant's second term the country was hit by an economic depression known as the Panic of 1873. Brought on by the overexpansive tendencies of railroad builders and businessmen during the immediate postwar boom, the Panic was triggered by economic downturns in Europe and, more immediately, by the failure of Jay Cooke and Company, a major American financial firm.

The financial hardship brought on by the Panic led to renewed clamor for the printing of more greenbacks. In 1874, Congress authorized a small new issue of greenbacks, but it was vetoed by Grant. Pro-inflation forces were further enraged when Congress, in 1873, demonetized silver, going to a straight gold standard. Silver was becoming more plentiful due to Western mining and was seen by some as a potential source of inflation. Pro-inflation forces referred to the demonetization of silver as the "Crime of '73."

In 1875, Congress took a further step toward retirement of the greenbacks and the return to a working gold standard when, under the leadership of John Sherman, it passed the Specie Resumption Act, calling for the resumption of specie payments (i.e., the redeemability of the nation's paper money in gold) by January 1, 1879.

Disgruntled proponents of inflation formed the Greenback Party and nominated Peter Cooper for president in 1876. However, they gained only an insignificant number of votes.

The Disputed Election of 1876

In the election of 1876, the Democrats campaigned against corruption and nominated New York Governor Samuel J. Tilden, who had broken the Tweed political machine of New York City.

The Republicans passed over Grant, who was interested in another term and had the backing of the remaining hardcore Radicals, and turned instead to Governor Rutherford B. Hayes of Ohio. Like Tilden, Hayes was decent, honest, in favor of hard money and civil service reform, and opposed to government regulation of the economy. In their campaigning, the Republicans resorted to a tactic known as "waving the bloody shirt." Successfully used in the last two presidential elections, this meant basically playing on wartime animosities, urging Northerners to vote the way they had shot, and suggesting that a Democratic victory and a Confederate victory would be about the same thing.

DID YOU KNOW?

Eight U.S. presidents, including Ulysses S. Grant and Rutherford B. Hayes, have hailed from Ohio, making that state home to the most presidents.

This time the tactic was less successful. Tilden won the popular vote and led in the electoral vote 184 to 165. However, 185 electoral votes were needed for election, and 20 votes from the three Southern states still occupied by Federal troops and run by Republican governments were disputed.

Though there had been extensive fraud on both sides, Tilden undoubtedly deserved at least the one vote he needed to win. Congress created a special commission to decide the matter. It was to be composed of five members each from the Senate, the House, and the Supreme Court. Of these, seven were to be Republicans, seven Democrats, and one an independent. The Republicans arranged, however, for the independent justice's state legislature to elect him to the Senate. When the justice resigned to take his Senate seat, it left all the remaining Supreme Court justices Republican. One of them was chosen, and in a series of eight-to-seven votes along straight party lines, the commission voted to give all 20 disputed votes—and the election—to Hayes.

When outraged congressional Democrats threatened to reject these obviously fraudulent results, a compromise was worked out. In the Compromise of 1877, Hayes promised to show consideration for Southern interests, end Reconstruction, and withdraw the remaining Federal troops from the South in exchange for Democratic acquiescence in his election.

Reconstruction would probably have ended anyway, since the North had already lost interest in it.

(Before taking the quiz noted below, please review the summary timeline for this chapter on the following pages.)

Expansion, Divisions, Civil War & Reconstruction (1844–1877)

Historical Timeline (1844–1877)

1844	Polk elected president on the promise of expanding the U.S. in the West
1845	Annexation of Texas
1846	U.S. declares war on Mexico Oregon Treaty
1847	Winfield Scott captures Mexico City
1848	Gold discovered in northern California Treaty of Guadalupe Hidalgo
1849	California gold rush
1850	Compromise of 1850 Fugitive Slave Law passed
1852	*Uncle Tom's Cabin* published
1854	Ostend Manifesto Kansas-Nebraska Act Republican Party formed
1856	"Bleeding Kansas"
1857	*Dred Scott* decision Lecompton Constitution in Kansas
1858	Lincoln-Douglas debates
1859	John Brown's raid
1860	Lincoln elected president Crittenden Compromise proposed South Carolina secedes
1861	Confederacy formed Firing on Ft. Sumter First Battle of Bull Run
1862	Shiloh Antietam Homestead Act Emancipation Proclamation announced

Historical Timeline (1844–1877)

1863	Vicksburg Gettysburg New York City draft riots
1864	Grant takes command of all Union armies Sherman captures Atlanta
1865	Lee surrenders at Appomattox Lincoln assassinated 13th Amendment ends slavery Freedmen's Bureau established
1867	Alaska purchased from Russia Grange founded
1868	President Johnson impeached 14th Amendment passed Grant elected president
1869	Transcontinental railroad completed Knights of Labor formed
1873	Slaughterhouse Cases Panic of 1873
1875	Dwight L. Moody begins urban revivalism movement
1876	Custer defeated by Sioux at Little Big Horn
1877	Compromise of 1877 Reconstruction ends

Chapter 8

Industrialism and the Gilded Age (1865–1898)

The period between the end of the Civil War and the beginning of the 20th century is known as the Gilded Age. Mark Twain first used the term "Gilded Age" to describe the years after the Civil War. He saw rampant greed, materialism, and corruption dominating American political and social life and viewed the outward appearance of prosperity and gaiety as being nothing more than a thin coating of gold on a fundamentally flawed society.

Politics of the Period, 1877–1882

The presidencies of Abraham Lincoln (1861–1865) and Theodore Roosevelt (1901–1909) mark the boundaries of half a century of relatively weak executive leadership, and legislative domination by Congress and the Republican Party.

The Compromise of 1877

With Southern Democratic acceptance of Rutherford B. Hayes's Republican presidency, the last remaining Union troops were withdrawn from the Old Confederacy (South Carolina, Florida, Louisiana), and the country was at last reunified as a modern nation-state led by corporate and industrial interests. The Hayes election arrangement also marked the government's abandonment of its earlier vague commitment to African American equality.

Republican Factions

"Stalwarts" led by New York Senator Roscoe Conkling favored the old spoils system of political patronage. "Half-Breeds" headed by Maine Senator James G. Blaine pushed for civil service reform and merit appointments to government posts.

Election of 1880

In the 1880 presidential election, James A. Garfield of Ohio, a Half-Breed, and his vice presidential running mate, Chester A. Arthur of New York, a Stalwart, defeated the Democratic candidate, General Winfield S. Hancock of Pennsylvania and former Indiana congressman William English. Tragically, the Garfield administration was brief, as the president was assassinated in 1881 by a disturbed office-seeker, Charles Guiteau. Though lacking much executive experience, the stalwart Arthur had the courage to endorse reform of the political spoils system by supporting passage of the Pendleton Act (1883), which established open competitive examinations for civil service positions.

The Greenback-Labor Party

In the mid-term election of 1878, the new Greenback-Labor Party movement, which had been formed only four years earlier, polled over one million votes lofting 14 members to Congress. The party, especially popular in the Midwest, worked to promote the inflation of farm prices and the cooperative marketing of agricultural produce. In 1880, the party's presidential candidate, James Weaver of Iowa, who polled only 3.4% of the popular vote (306,867), advocated public control and regulation of private enterprises such as railroads in the common interest of more equitable competition. Weaver theorized that because railroads were so essential, they should be treated as a public utility.

The Economy, 1877–1882

Industrial expansion and technology assumed major proportions in this period. Between 1860 and 1894 the United States moved from being the fourth-largest manufacturing nation to the world's leader through capital accumulation, natural resources (especially iron, oil, and coal), an abundance of labor helped by massive immigration, railway transportation and communications (the telephone was introduced by Alexander Graham Bell in 1876), and major technical innovations, such as the development of the modern steel industry by Andrew Carnegie and electrical energy by Thomas Edison. In the petroleum industry, John D. Rockefeller controlled 95 percent of U.S. oil refineries by 1877.

The New South

By 1880, Northern capital erected the modern textile industry in the New South by bringing factories to the cotton fields. Birmingham, Alabama, emerged as the South's leading steel producer, and the introduction of machine-made cigarettes propelled the Duke family to prominence as tobacco producers.

Social Darwinism

The theory of Social Darwinism, which asserted that survival of the fittest applied in society as well as nature, gained popularity in the Gilded Age. Many industrial leaders used the doctrines associated with the "Gospel of Wealth" to justify the unequal distribution of national wealth. Self-justification by the wealthy was based on the notion that God had granted wealth to a select few. These few, according to William Graham Sumner, relied heavily on the teachings of Charles Darwin.

Labor Unrest

When capital overexpansion and overspeculation led to the economic panic of 1873, massive labor disorders spread through the country leading to the paralyzing railroad strike of 1877. Unemployment and salary reductions caused major labor conflicts. President Hayes used federal troops to restore order after dozens of workers were killed. Immigrant workers began fighting among themselves in California where Irish and Chinese laborers fought for economic survival.

Labor Unions

The depression of the 1870s weakened national labor organizations. The National Labor Union (1866) had a membership of 600,000, but failed to withstand the impact of economic adversity. The Knights of Labor (1869) managed to open its membership to immigrants, women, and African Americans, in addition to white native American workers. Although they claimed one million members, they too could not endure the hard times of the 1870s, and eventually went under in 1886 in the wake of the bloody Haymarket Riot in Chicago.

Agricultural Militancy

Agrarian discontent, expressed through the activities of the National Grange and the Farmers' Alliances in the West and South, showed greater lasting power. During the Civil War, many farmers had overexpanded their operations, purchased more land

and machinery, and gone heavily into debt. When relatively high wartime agricultural prices collapsed in the decades following the Civil War, farmers worked collectively to promote currency inflation, higher farm prices, the unlimited coinage of silver, debt relief, cooperative farm marketing ventures, and regulation of monopolies and railroads by the federal and state governments. Although not extremely successful as a political force in the 1870s, farmer militancy continued to be a powerful political and economic force in the decades of the 1880s and 1890s.

Social and Cultural Developments, 1877–1882

Urbanization was one of the primary social and cultural phenomena of the period. Internal migration and the arrival of many new immigrants contributed to an industrial urban nation that grew from 40 million people in 1870 to almost 80 million in 1900. New York, Chicago, and Philadelphia emerged as cities with populations topping 1 million.

Skyscrapers and Immigrants

Cities grew both up and out as the skyscraper made its appearance after the introduction of the mechanical elevator by Elisha Otis. The city also grew outward into a large, impersonal metropolis divided into various business, industrial, and residential sectors, usually segregated by ethnic group, social class, and race. Slums and tenements often sprang up within walking distance of upscale department stores and townhouses. Two million immigrants from northern Europe poured into the U.S. during the 1870s. In the 1880s, another 5 million entered the country, but by this time they were coming from southern and eastern Europe.

DIDYOUKNOW?

Ellis Island was the busiest immigration station in the eastern United States. Over 12 million people entered the United States through Ellis Island between 1892 and 1954 (www.nps.gov). On the West Coast, Angel Island served as the main point of entry for many immigrants from China and other Asian nations. The Chinese Exclusion Act of 1883 effectively ended Chinese immigration, which had been encouraged earlier to help construct the transcontinental railroad.

Lack of Effective Government Policy

There were few programs to deal with the vast influx of humanity other than the housing of the criminal and the insane. City governments soon developed the primary responsibility for immigrants—often trading employment, housing, and social services for political support. Corruption in city government was rampant, as political machines exerted control over politics and city services.

Social Gospel

In time, advocates of the social gospel such as Walter Rauschenbusch, Jane Addams, and Washington Gladden urged the application of the teachings of Jesus to the problems of modern society. The creation of settlement houses and better health and education services provided support for the new urban immigrants. New religions also appeared, including the Salvation Army and Mary Baker Eddy's Church of Christian Science in 1879.

Education

Public education continued to expand, especially on the secondary level. Private Catholic parochial schools and teaching colleges grew in number as well. Adult education and English instruction became important functions of both public and private schooling. In higher education, President Charles Eliot of Harvard introduced electives and a seminar approach to replace the large lectures and memorization featured in most university settings.

Black Leaders

Booker T. Washington emerged in 1881 as the president of Tuskegee Institute in Alabama, a school devoted to teaching and vocational education for blacks with a mission to encourage self-respect and economic equality of the races. In the Atlanta Compromise speech of 1895, he suggested that blacks should focus on gradual economic progress and manual labor rather than push for political or social equality. It was at Tuskegee that George Washington Carver emerged in subsequent years as an agricultural chemist who did much to find industrial applications for agricultural products. Ida Wells, a journalist and early civil rights leader, investigated lynchings in the South and helped organize a black boycott of the 1893 World Exposition in Chicago.

Feminism

The new urban environment encouraged feminist activism. Millions of women worked outside the home and continued to demand voting rights. Women could vote in a number of Western states. Many women became active in social reform movements such as the prohibitionist Women's Christian Temperance Movement, anti-prostitution crusades, and equal rights for all, regardless of gender, race, or class.

Literature

Important books appeared such as Henry George's *Progress and Poverty* (1879), a three-million-copy seller that advocated one single tax on land as the means to redistribute wealth for greater social and economic justice. In fiction, Lew Wallace's *Ben*

Hur (1880), and the many Horatio Alger stories promoting values such as hard work, honesty, and a touch of good fortune sold many millions of copies. Other famous works of the era included Mark Twain's *The Gilded Age* (1873) and *The Adventures of Tom Sawyer* (1876), Bret Harte's stories of the Old West, William Dean Howell's social commentaries, and Henry James's *Daisy Miller* (1879) and *Portrait of a Lady* (1881).

The Reaction to Corporate Industrialism, 1882–1887

The rise of big business and monopoly capitalism—especially in banking, railroads, mining, and the oil and steel industries—generated a reaction on the part of working-class Americans in the form of new labor organizations and collective political action. Most Americans, however, were not opposed to free enterprise economics, but simply wanted an opportunity to share in the profits.

Politics of the Period, 1882–1888

The only Democrat elected president in the half century after the Civil War was Grover Cleveland, who has been the only president to serve two nonconsecutive terms.

Election of 1884

In the 1884 presidential campaign, the Republicans nominated James G. Blaine (Maine) for president and John Logan (Illinois) for vice president. The Democrats chose New York governor Grover Cleveland and Thomas A. Hendricks (Indiana). The defection of Independent Republicans (such as E.L. Godkin and Carl Schurz) supporting civil service reforms, known as "Mugwumps," to the Cleveland camp cost, Blaine, the former Speaker of the House, the election. The Democrats held control of the House and the Republicans controlled the Senate.

Presidential Succession Act of 1886

The death of Vice President Hendricks in 1885 led to a decision to change the line of succession (established in 1792) from the president *pro tempore* of the Senate to the Cabinet officers in order of creation of their departments to maintain party leadership. This system lasted until 1947, when the Speaker of the House was declared third in line.

Election of 1888

In the presidential election of 1888, although the Democrat Grover Cleveland won the popular vote by about 100,000 over the Republican Benjamin Harrison, Harrison carried the Electoral College 233 to 168, and was declared president after waging a vigorous campaign to protect American industrial interests with a high protective tariff. In Congress, Republicans won control of both the House and Senate.

The Economy, 1882–1887

The American corporation generally prospered in the Gilded Age. Captains of industry, or robber barons, such as John D. Rockefeller in oil, J. P Morgan in banking, Gustavus Swift in meat processing, Andrew Carnegie in steel, and E. H. Harriman in railroads, assembled major industrial empires with virtually no interference or regulation from the federal government.

Big Business

The concentration of wealth and power in the hands of a relatively small number of large firms in many industries led to monopoly capitalism that minimized competition. This process, in turn, led to a demand by small businessmen, farmers, and laborers for government regulation of the economy in order to promote capital competition for the salvation of free enterprise economics. In vertical organization, corporations sought to control an item or industry at each step of production. In horizontal organization, each distributor or business at one level of a product's creation was controlled by one large corporation. If a corporation exerted both vertical and horizontal control, it had a monopoly.

The Interstate Commerce Act (1887)

Popular resentment of railroad policy abuses, such as price-fixing, kickbacks, and discriminatory freight rates frequently created demands for state regulation of the railway industry. When the Supreme Court ruled individual state laws unconstitutional (*Wabash* case, 1886) because only Congress had the right to control interstate commerce, the Interstate Commerce Act was passed. It provided that a commission be established to oversee fair and just railway rates, prohibit rebates, end discriminatory practices, and require annual reports and financial statements. The Supreme Court, however, remained a friend of special interests, and often undermined the work of the Interstate Commerce Commission.

Expanding Cultivation

Agrarians and ranchers continued their westward expansion. The amount of land under cultivation between 1870 and 1890 more than doubled from 408 to 840 million acres. Transcontinental railroads, modern farm machinery, and soil conservation practices contributed to national prosperity.

Low Farm Prices

Despite success, many farmers were concerned about capital indebtedness, low farm prices resulting from surplus production, railroad rate discrimination, and the lack of sufficient silver currency to promote price inflation. Agrarian groups, such as the National Grange and the Farmers' Alliances, called for economic controls to redress their grievances. To a certain extent, however, many of these problems were determined by participation of American agriculture in global markets. Farmers did not completely understand all the risks in an international free market economy.

American Federation of Labor, 1886

Confronted by big business, Samuel Gompers and Adolph Strasser put together a combination of national craft unions to represent the material interests of labor in the matter of wages, hours, and safety conditions. The American Federation of Labor philosophy was pragmatic and not directly influenced by the dogmatic Marxism of some European labor movements. Although militant in its use of the strike and its demand for collective bargaining in labor contracts with large corporations, such as those in railroads, mining, and manufacturing, the American Federation of Labor did not intend violent revolution or political radicalism.

Scientific Management

Frederick W. Taylor, an engineer credited as the father of scientific management, introduced modern concepts of industrial engineering, plant management, and time and motion studies. This gave rise to efficiency experts and a separate class of managers in industrial manufacturing.

TEST TIP

Remember you may only work on the multiple-choice and short-answer sections during the stated time period. You may not look ahead to the essays during this period. Correspondingly, you will not be able to go back to the multiple-choice and short-answer sections after you have begun the essay section.

Indians in the American West, 1865–1890

The conclusion of the Civil War and the completion of the transcontinental railroad brought more settlers west. U.S. military actions, the destruction of the buffalo, the confinement of American Indians to reservations, and attempts to reduce tribal loyalty and assimilate Indians into American culture took a huge toll on their numbers and their culture.

The conclusion of the Civil War allowed the federal government to direct its military efforts to the American West.

Battle of Little Bighorn

Conflicts between Indians and newly arriving ranchers, miners, and farmers escalated as settlement increased. Miners encroaching on Indian lands in the Dakota Territory led to raids and reprisals. In 1876, when a cavalry unit led by General George Armstrong Custer tried to pursue a large group of Sioux Indians, it was wiped out at the Battle of Little Bighorn and resulted in the deaths of 268 soldiers.

Dawes Severalty Act (1887)

In an attempt to speed the assimilation of Indians into the white American culture, Congress passed the Dawes Act, which granted reservation land and American citizenship to Indians who renounced their tribal affiliations. Unscrupulous speculators soon acquired much of the Indian land, which was then sold to the increasing number of settlers heading west.

Advertisement by the U.S. Department of Interior offering surplus Indian lands for sale, 1910–1911. (U.S. Library of Congress)

Battle of Wounded Knee (1890)

As bison herds were decimated by hunters and Plains Indians were forced onto reservations, a group of Lakota Sioux in what is now South Dakota began following a religious leader, Wovoka, who taught them a Ghost Dance, which he said would protect them from the bullets of the U.S. Army. Army officials became concerned with the practice and decided to disarm them. A gunfight broke out and more than 150 Indians, mostly unarmed, were killed.

Social and Cultural Developments, 1882–1887

The continued growth of urban America contributed to the dissemination of knowledge and information in many fields.

Newspapers and Magazines

The linotype machine (1886) invented by Otto Mergenthaler cut printing costs dramatically. Press associations flourished and publishing became big business. In 1884, Joseph Pulitzer, a Hungarian-born immigrant, was the first publisher to reach a mass audience, selling 100,000 copies of the *New York World.* New magazines such as *Forum* appeared in 1886 with a hard-hitting editorial style that emphasized investigative journalism and controversial subjects.

Women's Colleges

Bryn Mawr (1885) was established and soon found a place among such schools as Vassar, Wellesley, and Mount Holyoke in advancing education for women.

Natural Science

Albert Michelson at the University of Chicago, working on measuring the speed of light, contributed in the 1880s to theories that helped pave the way for Einstein's Theory of Relativity. In 1907, Michelson was the first American to win a Nobel Prize.

The New Social Science

Richard T. Ely studied the ethical implications of economic problems. Henry C. Adams and Simon Patten put forth theories to justify government regulation and planning in the economy. In sociology, Lester Frank Ward's *Dynamic Sociology* (1883) stressed intelligent planning and decision making over genetic determinism as promoted by Social Darwinists such as William Graham Sumner. Woodrow Wilson's *Congressional Government* was a critique of the committee system in Congress which called for a better working relationship between the executive and legislative branches of government. After winning the presidency in 1912, Wilson would be in a position to put his ideas into practice.

Literary Realism

Romanticism declined in favor of a more realistic approach to literature. Novelists explored social problems such as crime and political corruption, urban ghetto life, class conflict, evolution, and the environment. Mark Twain's masterpiece *Huckleberry Finn* appeared in 1884. In 1885, William Dean Howell's *The Rise of Silas Lapham* presented the theme of business ethics in a competitive society. *The Bostonians* (1886) by Henry

James attempted a complex psychological study of female behavior. Stephen Crane's cynical poem "War Is Kind" was published in 1899.

Art

Realism could also be seen in the artistic works of Thomas Eakins, Mary Cassatt, Winslow Homer, and James Whistler. Museums and art schools expanded. Wealthy patrons spent fortunes on personal art collections.

TEST TIP

Not sure where to start in a free-response essay? Construct a straightforward, one-sentence response that directly answers the question posed. This sentence can now act as your thesis statement.

The Economy, 1887–1892

Anti-monopoly measures, protective tariffs and reciprocal trade, and a billion dollar budget became the order of the day.

Sherman Anti-Trust Act, 1890

Corporate monopolies (trusts) that controlled whole industries were subject to federal prosecution if they were found to be combinations or conspiracies in restraint of trade. Although supported by smaller businesses, labor unions, and farm associations, the Sherman Anti-Trust Act was in time interpreted by the Supreme Court to apply to labor unions and farmers' cooperatives as much as to large corporate combinations.

Sherman Silver Purchase Act, 1890

Pro-silver interests passed legislation authorizing Congress to buy 4.5 million ounces of silver each month at market prices, and issue Treasury notes redeemable in gold and silver. This act created inflation and lowered gold reserves.

McKinley Tariff, 1890

This compromise protective tariff promised by the Republicans in 1888 and introduced by William McKinley of Ohio, was passed and extended to industrial and agricultural goods. The act also included reciprocal trade provisions that allowed the president to retaliate against nations that discriminated against U.S. products, and reward states that opened their markets to American goods. Subsequent price increases led to a popular backlash and a Democratic House victory in the 1890 congressional elections.

Social and Cultural Developments, 1887–1892

Entertainment for the masses became increasingly differentiated.

Popular Amusements

In addition to the legitimate stage, vaudeville shows presenting variety acts became immensely popular. The circus expanded when Barnum and Bailey formed a partnership to present "the greatest show on earth." Distinctively American Wild West shows toured North America and Europe. To record these activities, George Eastman's newly invented roll-film camera became popular with spectators.

Sports

In 1888, professional baseball sent an all-star team to tour the world. Boxing adopted leather gloves in 1892. Croquet and bicycle racing were new crazes. James Naismith, a Massachusetts YMCA instructor, invented basketball in 1891. Organized inter-collegiate sports such as football, basketball, and baseball created intense rivalries between colleges that attracted mass spectator interest.

Religion

Many churches took issue with the growing emphasis on materialism in American society. Dwight L. Moody introduced urban revivalism comparable to earlier rural movements among Protestant denominations and conducted crusades across the United States. In addition, the new immigrants generated significant growth for Roman Catholicism and Judaism. By 1890, there were about 150 religious denominations in the U.S.

TEST TIP

Making notes or crossing out answer choices in your test booklet can help you keep track of your thoughts. However, be sure not to make any extra marks on your answer sheet to avoid having it incorrectly scored.

Economic Depression and Social Crisis, 1892–1897

The economic depression that began in 1893 brought about a collective response from organized labor, militant agriculture, and the business community. Each group called for economic safeguards and a more humane free-enterprise system that would expand economic opportunities in an equitable manner.

Election of 1892

In 1892, Democrat Grover Cleveland (New York) and his vice presidential running mate, Adlai E. Stevenson (Illinois), regained the White House by defeating the Republican President Benjamin Harrison (Indiana) and Vice President Whitelaw Reid (New York). Voters generally reacted against the inflationary McKinley Tariff. Cleveland's conservative economic stand in favor of the gold standard brought him the support of various business interests. The Democrats won control of both houses of Congress.

Populist Party

The People's Party (Populist) nominated James Weaver (Iowa) for president and James Field (Virginia) for vice president in 1892. The party platform put together by such Populist leaders as Ignatius Donnally (Minnesota), Thomas Watson (Georgia), Mary Lease (Kansas), and "Sockless" Jerry Simpson (Kansas) called for the enactment of a program espoused by agrarians, but also for a coalition with urban workers and the middle class. Specific goals were the coinage of silver to gold at a ratio of 16 to 1; federal loans to farmers; a graduated income tax; postal savings banks; public ownership of railroads, telephone and telegraph systems; prohibition of alien land ownership; immigration restriction; a ban on private armies used by corporations to break up strikes; an eight-hour working day; a single six-year term for president and direct election of senators; and the right of initiative and referendum; and the use of the secret ballot.

Although the Populists were considered radical by some, they actually wanted to reform the system from within and allow for a fairer distribution of wealth. In a society with vast differences in income and wealth, the Populists were able to garner about one million votes (out of 11 million votes cast) and 22 electoral votes. By 1894, Populists had elected four senators, four congressmen, 21 state executive officials, 150 state senators, and 315 state representatives, primarily in the West and South. After the 1893 depression, the Populists planned a serious bid for national power in the 1896 election.

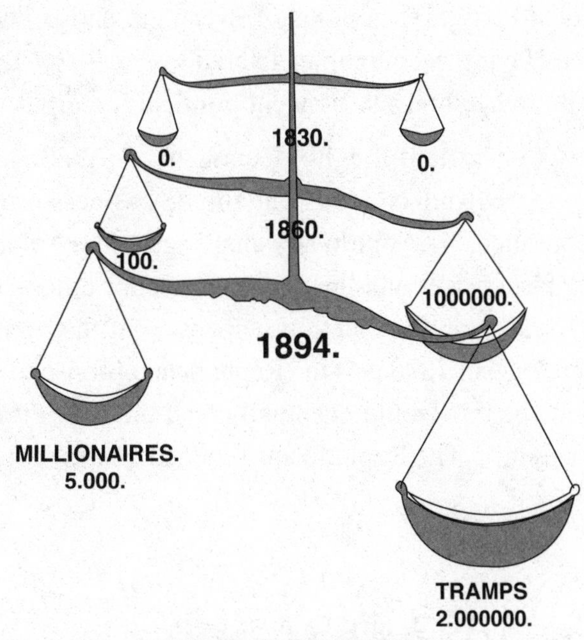

Reproduction of Populist Party cartoon, 1894. (*Anthony Weekly Bulletin*, Anthony, Kansas)

Repeal of Sherman Silver Purchase Act (1893)

After the economic panic of 1893, Cleveland tried to limit the outflow of gold reserves by asking Congress to repeal the Sherman Silver Act, which had provided for notes redemptive in either gold or silver. Congress did repeal the act, but the Democratic Party split over the issue.

Election of 1896

In the 1896 election campaign, the Republicans nominated William McKinley (Ohio) for president and Garrett Hobart (New Jersey) for vice president on a platform calling for maintaining the gold standard and protective tariffs. The Democratic Party repudiated Cleveland's conservative economics and nominated William Jennings Bryan (Nebraska) and Arthur Sewell (Maine) for president and vice president on a platform similar to the Populists: (1) coinage of silver at a ratio of 16 to 1; (2) condemnation of monopolies, protective tariffs, and anti-union court injunctions; and (3) criticism of the Supreme Court's removal of a graduated income tax from the Wilson-Gorman tariff bill (1894). Bryan delivered one of the most famous speeches in American history when he declared that the people must not be "crucified upon a cross of gold."

The Populist Party also nominated Bryan but chose Thomas Watson (Georgia) for vice president. Having been outmaneuvered by the Silver Democrats, the Populists lost the opportunity to become a permanent political force.

McKinley won a hard-fought election by only about one-half million votes as Republicans succeeded in creating fear among business groups and middle class voters that Bryan represented a revolutionary challenge to the American system. The manipulation of higher farm prices and the warning to labor unions that they would face unemployment if Bryan won the election helped to tilt the vote in favor of McKinley. An often forgotten issue in 1896 was the Republican promise to stabilize the ongoing Cuban revolution. This pledge would eventually lead the U.S. into war with Spain (1898) for Cuban independence. The Republicans retained control over Congress, which they had gained in 1894.

The Economy, 1892–1897

The 1890s was a period of economic depression and labor agitation.

Homestead Strike, 1892

Iron and steel workers went on strike in Pennsylvania against the Carnegie Steel Company to protest salary reductions. Carnegie employed strike-breaking Pinkerton security guards. Management-labor warfare led to a number of deaths on both sides.

Depression of 1893

The primary causes for the depression of 1893 were the dramatic growth of the federal deficit; withdrawal of British investments from the American market and the outward transfer of gold; and loss of business confidence. The bankruptcy of the National Cordage Company was the first among thousands of U.S. corporations that closed banks and businesses. As a consequence, 20 percent of the workforce was eventually unemployed. The depression would last four years. Recovery would be helped by war preparation.

Coxey's Army (1894)

The Populist businessman Jacob Coxey led a march on Washington of hundreds of unemployed workers asking for a government work-relief program. The government met the marchers with force and arrested their leaders.

Pullman Strike (1894)

In 1894, Eugene V. Debs's American Railway Union struck the Pullman Palace Car Company in Chicago over wage cuts and job losses. President Cleveland broke the violent strike with federal troops. Popular opinion deplored violence and militant labor tactics.

Social and Cultural Developments, 1892–1897

Economic depression and urban problems dominated thought and literature in the decade of the 1890s.

Literature

Lester Frank Ward of Brown University presented a critique of excessive competition in favor of social planning in *The Psychic Factors of Civilization,* (1893). William Dean Howells's *A Hazard of New Fortunes* (1890), was a broad attack on urban living conditions in industrial America and on the callous treatment of workers by wealthy tycoons. Stephen Crane wrote about society's abuse of women in *Maggie, A Girl of the Streets* (1892), and the pain of war in *The Red Badge of Courage* (1895). Edward Bellamy's *Looking Backward* (1888) presented a science fiction look into a prosperous but regimented future.

Thorstein Veblen's *Theory of the Leisure Class* (1899) attacked the "predatory wealth" and "conspicuous consumption" of the new rich in the Gilded Age. Veblen added evidence and argument to a critique begun by Jacob Riis in *How the Other Half Lives* (1890), documenting the gnawing poverty, illness, crime, and despair of New York's slums. Frank Norris's *McTeague* (1899) chronicled a man's regression to brutish animal behavior in the dog-eat-dog world of unbridled and unregulated capitalist competition. His novel *The Octopus* (1901) condemned monopolies.

Prohibition of Alcohol

The Anti-Saloon League was formed in 1893. Women were especially concerned about the increase of drunkenness during the depression.

Settlement Houses

Jane Addams's Hull House in Chicago continued to function as a means of settling poor immigrants from Greece, Germany, Italy, Poland, Russia and elsewhere into American society. Lillian Wald's Henry Street Settlement in New York and Robert Wood's

South End House in Boston performed similar functions. Such institutions also lobbied against sweatshop labor conditions, and for bans on child labor.

Chicago World's Fair (1893)

Beautifying the cities was the fair's main theme. One lasting development was the expansion of urban public parks. A huge steam dynamo generating electricity attracted a great deal of attention as the potential of electric lights became a reality. Over 26 million people visited the fair.

One of the most celebrated examples of early skyscrapers, the 21-story Flatiron Building rose in New York in 1902. (AP/Wide World Photo)

(Before taking the quiz noted below, please review the summary timeline for this chapter on the following page.)

Industrialism and the Gilded Age (1865–1898)

Historical Timeline (1865–1898)

1877	Compromise of 1877 ends Reconstruction San Francisco anti-Chinese riots
1878	Bland-Allison Act
1879	Edison invents the lightbulb
1881	President Garfield assassinated Helen Hunt Jackson writes *A Century of Dishonor*
1882	Standard Oil Trust formed Chinese Exclusion Act
1883	Pendleton Civil Service Act
1885	First skyscraper built in Chicago
1886	Haymarket Square bombing in Chicago American Federation of Labor formed
1887	Dawes Act
1889	Jane Addams founds Hull House in Chicago
1890	Sioux massacred at Wounded Knee Sherman Antitrust Act Sherman Silver Purchase Act U.S. Census declares frontier's end Alfred Mahan writes *The Influence of Sea Power upon History*
1891	Populist Party formed
1892	Homestead Steel Strike
1893	Panic of 1893 Great Northern Railroad completed
1894	Pullman strike Coxey's Army
1895	Booker T. Washington's Atlanta Compromise speech
1896	Plessy v. Ferguson upholds "separate but equal" McKinley defeats Bryan for president

Chapter 9

Global and Domestic Challenges (1890–1945)

International Relations, 1890–1897

Theoretical Works

In 1890, naval captain Alfred Thayer Mahan published *The Influence of Sea Power upon History*, which argued that control of the seas was the means to world power. Josiah Strong's *Our Country* presented the thesis that Americans had a mission to fulfill by exporting the word of God around the world, especially to non-white populations. Frederick Jackson Turner's "Frontier Thesis" (1893) justified overseas economic expansion as a way to secure political power and prosperity. In *The Law of Civilization and Decay* (1895), Brooks Adams postulated that a nation must expand or face inevitable decline.

In addition to the economic depression, international events in 1895 that propelled the United States foreign policy were the desire to annex Hawaii, the Cuban war for independence against Spain, and Britain's boundary dispute with Venezuela.

Hawaii

In 1891, Queen Lydia Kamekeha Liliuokalani resisted American attempts to promote a protectorate over Hawaii. By 1893, pro-American sugar planters overthrew the native Hawaiian government and established a new government friendly to the United States. The United States intervened in the Hawaiian revolution (1893) to overthrow the anti-American government of Queen Liliuokalani. President Cleveland rejected American annexation of Hawaii in 1894, but President McKinley agreed to annex it in 1898.

Cuba and Spain

The Cuban revolt against Spain in 1895 impacted the U.S. in that Americans had about $50 million invested in the Cuban economy and did an annual business of over $100 million in Cuba. During the election of 1896, McKinley promised to stabilize the situation and work for an end to hostilities. Sensational "yellow" journalism and nationalistic statements from officials such as Assistant Secretary of the Navy Theodore Roosevelt encouraged popular support for direct American military intervention on behalf of Cuban independence. President McKinley, however, proceeded cautiously through 1897.

Britain and Venezuela (1895)

The dispute over the border of Britain's colony of Guiana threatened war with Venezuela, especially after gold was discovered in the area. Although initially at odds with Britain, the United States eventually came to support British claims against Venezuela when Britain agreed to recognize the Monroe Doctrine in Latin America. Britain also sought U.S. cooperation in its dispute with Germany in South Africa. This rivalry would in time lead to the Boer War. The realignment of the United States and Britain would play a significant role during World War I.

War and the Americanization of the World, 1897–1902

In 1900 an Englishman named William T. Stead authored a book entitled *The Americanization of the World* in which he predicted that American productivity and economic strength would propel the United States to the forefront of world leadership in the twentieth century. The Spanish-American War and the events following it indicated that the U.S. would be a force in the global balance of power for years to come. Few, however, would have predicted that as early as 1920 the U.S. would achieve the pinnacle of world power as a result of the debilitating policies pursued by European political leaders during World War I (1914–1919). One question remained: Would the American people be prepared to accept the responsibility of world leadership?

Yellow Journalism's Role in Stoking Calls for War

Joseph Pulitzer's *New York World* and William Randolph Hearst's *New York Journal* competed fiercely to increase circulation through exaggeration of Spanish atrocities in Cuba. Such stories whipped up popular resentment of Spain and helped to create a climate of opinion receptive to war.

De Lôme Letter and Sinking of the *Maine*

On February 9, 1898, the newspapers published a private letter written by the Spanish minister in Washington, Enrique Depuy de Lôme. The note, which had been intercepted and leaked by Cuban revolutionaries, criticized President McKinley for being wishy-washy. Just days later, on February 15, the Battleship U.S.S. *Maine* blew up in Havana harbor with a loss of 250 Americans. The popular demand for war with Spain grew significantly even though it was likely that the *Maine* exploded by accident when spontaneous combustion in a coal bunker caused a powder magazine to explode.

U.S.S. *Maine* on February 16, 1898, the day after an explosion sank the battleship in Havana Harbor, killing 266 crew members. (AP/Wide World Photo/Key West Art/Historical Society)

U.S. Military Response

Facing its first war since the Civil War, the U.S. Army was not prepared for a full-scale effort in 1898. Although 245,000 men served in the war (with over 5,000 deaths), the Army at the outset consisted of only 28,000 troops. The volunteers who signed up in the early stages were surprised to be issued winter uniforms to train in the tropics for war in Cuba. Cans of food stockpiled since the Civil War were reissued. After getting past these early problems, the War Department settled into a more effective organizational procedure. Sadly, more deaths resulted from disease and food poisoning than from battlefield casualties. The U.S. Navy (26,000 men) was far better prepared for war as a result of past years of modernization.

The War's Price Tag

The financial cost of the Spanish-American War was $250 million. Eastern and midwestern industrial cities tended to favor war and benefit from it. Northeastern financial centers were more cautious until March 1898, questioning the financial gains of wartime production at the expense of peacetime expansion and product and market development.

Colonel Theodore Roosevelt and his Rough Riders in July 1898. (U.S. Library of Congress)

Territories

After the United States had defeated Spain, it was faced with the issue of what to do with such captured territories as the Philippines, Puerto Rico, and Guam. A major public debate ensued with critics of land acquisition forming the Anti-Imperialist League with the support of Mark Twain, William James, William Jennings Bryan, Grover Cleveland, Charles Francis Adams, Carl Schurz, Charles W. Eliot, David Starr Jordan, Andrew Carnegie, and Samuel Gompers, among others. Supporters of colonialism included Theodore Roosevelt, Mark Hanna, Alfred Thayer Mahan, Henry Cabot Lodge, Albert Beveridge, President McKinley, and many others. Ironically, many individuals in both camps favored U.S. economic expansion but had difficulty with the idea that a democracy would actually accept colonies and overseas armies of occupations.

Election of 1900

The unexpected death of Vice President Garrett Hobart led the Republican Party to choose the war hero and reform governor of New York, Theodore Roosevelt, as President William McKinley's vice presidential running mate. Riding the crest of victory against Spain, the GOP platform called for upholding the gold standard for full economic recovery, promoting economic expansion and power in the Caribbean and the Pacific, and building a canal in Central America. The Democrats once again nominated William Jennings Bryan and Adlai Stevenson on a platform condemning imperialism and the gold standard. McKinley easily won re-election by about 1 million votes (7.2 million to 6.3 million), and the Republicans retained control of both houses of Congress.

McKinley Assassination (1901)

While attending the Pan American Exposition in Buffalo, New York, President McKinley was shot on September 6 by Leon Czolgosz, an anarchist sworn to destroy all governments. The president died on September 14 after many officials had said they thought he would recover. Theodore Roosevelt became the nation's twenty-fifth president and—at age 42—its youngest to that time.

Foreign Policy, 1897–1902

The summer war with Spain and the expansion of American interests in Asia and the Caribbean were dominant factors in U.S. foreign policy. While many European nations possessed overseas colonies, the U.S. had not previously held possessions in other regions of the world. The U.S. became an imperialist power in the 1890s.

Decision for War (1898)

Loss of markets, threats to Americans in Cuba, and the inability of both Spain and Cuba to resolve the Cuban revolution either by force or diplomacy led to McKinley's request of Congress for a declaration of war. The sinking of the *Maine* in February 1898 and the return of Vermont Senator Redfield Proctor from a fact-finding mission on March 17, 1898, revealed how poor the situation was in Cuba.

McKinley's Ultimatum

On March 27, President McKinley asked Spain to call an armistice, accept American mediation to end the war, and end the use of concentration camps in Cuba. When Spain refused to comply, McKinley requested Congress to declare war. On April 21, Congress declared war on Spain with the objective of establishing Cuban independence (Teller Amendment).

Cuba

After the first U.S. forces landed in Cuba on June 22, 1898, the United States proceeded to victories at El Caney and San Juan Hill. By July 17, Admiral Sampson's North Atlantic Squadron destroyed the Spanish fleet, Santiago surrendered, and American troops quickly went on to capture Puerto Rico.

The Philippines

As early as December 1897, Commodore Perry's Asiatic Squadron was alerted to possible war with Spain. On May 1, 1898, the Spanish fleet in the Philippines was destroyed and Manila surrendered on August 13. Spain agreed to a peace conference to be held in Paris in October 1898.

Treaty of Paris

Secretary of State William Day led the American negotiating team, which secured Cuban independence, the ceding of the Philippines, Puerto Rico, and Guam to the U.S., and the payment of $20 million to Spain for the Philippines. The Treaty of Paris was ratified by the Senate on February 6, 1900.

Philippines Insurrection

Filipino nationalists under Emilio Aguinaldo rebelled against the United States (February 1899) when they learned the Philippines would not be given independence. The United States used 70,000 men to suppress the revolutionaries by June 1902. A special U.S. commission recommended eventual self-government for the Philippines.

China

Fearing the break-up of China into separate spheres of influence, Secretary of State John Hay called for acceptance of the Open Door Notes by all nations trading in the China market to guarantee equal opportunity of trade (1899) and the sovereignty of the Manchu government of China (1900).

Boxer Rebellion (1900)

Chinese nationalists ("Boxers") struck at foreign settlements in China, and at the Ch'ing dynasty government in Beijing for allowing foreign industrial nations—such as Britain, Japan, Russia, France, Germany, Italy, Portugal, Belgium, the Netherlands, and the United States—large concessions within Chinese borders. An international army helped to put down the rebellion and aided the Chinese government to remain in power.

Platt Amendment (1901)

Although Cuba received independence, the Platt Amendment provided that Cuba become a virtual protectorate of the United States. Cuba could not (1) make a treaty with a foreign state impairing its independence, or (2) contract an excessive public debt. Cuba was required to (1) allow the U.S. to preserve order on the island, and (2) lease a naval base for 99 years to the U.S. at Guantanamo Bay.

Hay-Pauncefote Treaty (1901)

This treaty between the U.S. and Britain abrogated an earlier agreement (1850, Clayton-Bulwer Treaty) to build jointly an isthmian canal. The United States was free unilaterally to construct, fortify, and maintain a canal that would be open to all ships.

Theodore Roosevelt and Progressive Reforms, 1902–1907

As a Republican progressive reformer committed to honest and efficient government designed to serve all social classes in America, Theodore Roosevelt restored the presidency to the high eminence it had held through the Civil War era and restored an executive-legislative balance of power with old-guard leaders in Congress.

Roosevelt's Anti-Trust Policy, 1902

The president pledged strict enforcement of the Sherman Anti-Trust Act (1890) to break up illegal monopolies and regulate large corporations for the public good through honest federal government administration.

Progressive Reform in the States

Progressives sought to use government at all levels to help create a just society. Taking their cue from Washington, many states enacted laws creating honest and efficient political and economic regulatory standards. Political reforms included enacting laws establishing primary elections (Mississippi, Wisconsin), initiative and referendum (South Dakota, Oregon), and the rooting out of political bosses at the state and municipal levels (especially in New York, Ohio, Michigan, and California).

DIDYOUKNOW?

Under the leadership of Progressives like Governor Robert La Follette, Wisconsin became one of the leading places of Progressive reform. Initiatives such as the formation of the first significant U.S. workers' compensation program, creation of a state income tax, limitations on working hours for women and children, and regulations on factory conditions helped earn the state the nickname of "the laboratory of democracy."

Election of 1904

Having assured Republican Party leaders that he wished to reform corporate monopolies and railroads, but not interfere with monetary policy or tariffs, Roosevelt was nominated for president along with Charles Fairbanks (Indiana) for vice president in the 1904 campaign. The Democratic Party nominated New York judge Alton B. Parker for president and Henry G. Davis (West Virginia) for vice president on a platform that endorsed Roosevelt's "trust busting," which called for even greater power for such regulatory agencies as the Interstate Commerce Commission, and accepted the conservative gold standard as the basis for monetary policy. Roosevelt easily defeated Parker by about two million votes, and the Republicans retained control of both houses of Congress.

Hepburn Act, 1906

Membership of the Interstate Commerce Commission was increased from five to seven. The I.C.C. could set its own fair freight rates, had its regulatory power extended over pipelines, bridges, and express companies, and was empowered to require a uniform system of accounting by regulated transportation companies. The Hepburn Act and the Elkins Act (which reiterated the illegality of railroad rebates) gave teeth to the original Interstate Commerce Act of 1887.

Pure Food and Drug Act (1906)

The Pure Food and Drug Act, signed into law in 1906, prohibited the manufacture, sale, and transportation of adulterated or fraudulently labeled foods and drugs in accordance with consumer demands to which Theodore Roosevelt was especially sensitive.

Conservation Laws

From 1902 to 1908 a series of laws and executive actions were enacted to create federal irrigation projects, national parks and forests, develop water power (Internal Waterways Commission), and establish the National Conservation Commission to oversee the nation's resources.

The Economy, 1902–1907

Anti-trust policy and government regulation of the economy gave way to a more lenient enforcement of federal laws after the Panic of 1907. Recognition of the rights of labor unions was enhanced.

Anti-Trust Policy (1902)

In order to restore free competition, President Roosevelt ordered the Justice Department to prosecute corporations pursuing monopolistic practices. Attorney General P.C. Knox first brought suit against the Northern Securities Company, a railroad holding corporation put together by J.P. Morgan; then he moved against Rockefeller's Standard

Oil Company. By the time he left office in 1909, Roosevelt had brought indictments against 25 monopolies.

Coal Strike (1902)

Roosevelt interceded with government mediation to bring about negotiations between the United Mine Workers union and the anthracite mine owners after a bitter strike in 1902 over wages, safety conditions, and union recognition. This was the first time that the government intervened in a labor dispute without automatically siding with management.

Panic of 1907

A brief economic recession and panic occurred in 1907 as a result, in part, of questionable bank speculations, a lack of flexible monetary and credit policies, and a conservative gold standard. This event called attention to the need for banking reform, which would lead to the establishment of the Federal Reserve System in 1913. Although Roosevelt temporarily eased the pressure on anti-trust activity, he made it clear that reform of the economic system to promote free-enterprise capitalism would continue.

Social and Cultural Developments, 1902–1907

Debate and discussion over the expanding role of the federal government commanded the attention of the nation.

Progressive Reforms

Progressivism was not a unified, well-organized movement but rather a series of reform causes designed to address specific social, economic, and political problems. Middle-class men and women were especially active in attempting to correct the excessive powers of giant corporations and the radical extremes of Marxist revolutionaries and radicals among intellectuals and labor activists. However, mainstream business and labor leaders were moderate in their desire to preserve economic opportunities and the free enterprise system.

Varieties of Reform

Progressive reform goals included honest government, economic regulation, environmental conservation, labor recognition, and new political structures. Reformers also called for gender equality for men and women in the workforce (Oregon Ten-Hour Law), an end to racial segregation (National Association for the Advancement of Colored People), child labor laws, prison reform, regulation of the stock market, direct election of senators, and a more efficient foreign service, among other reform activities.

A Chicago stockyard around the time of Upton Sinclair's muckraking book, *The Jungle* (1906), which exposed in vivid detail the sordid conditions of the meatpacking industry. (Photo courtesy of Dover Publications, Inc.)

Muckrakers

Muckrakers (a term coined by Roosevelt) were investigative journalists and authors who often spurred reforms. Popular magazines included *McClure's, Collier's, Cosmopolitan,* and *Everybody's.* Famous articles that led to reforms included "The Shame of the Cities" by Lincoln Steffens, "History of Standard Oil Company" by Ida Tarbell, and "The Treason of the Senate" by David Phillips.

Foreign Relations, 1902–1907

Theodore Roosevelt's "Big Stick" diplomacy and economic foreign policy were characteristics of the administration.

Panama Canal

Roosevelt used executive power to engineer both the separation of Panama from Colombia and the recognition of Panama as an independent country. The Hay-Bunau-Varilla Treaty of 1903 granted the United States control of the Canal Zone in Panama for $10 million and an annual fee of $250,000 beginning nine years after ratification of the treaty by both parties. Construction of the canal began in 1904 and was completed in 1914.

Roosevelt Corollary to the Monroe Doctrine

The U.S. reserved the right to intervene in the internal affairs of Latin American nations to keep European powers from using military force to collect debts in the Western Hemisphere. The U.S. eventually intervened in the affairs of Venezuela, Haiti, the Dominican Republic, Nicaragua, and Cuba by 1905 as an international policeman brandishing the "big stick" against Europeans and Latin Americans.

Russo-Japanese War (1904–1905)

With American encouragement and financial loans, Japan pursued and won a war against tsarist Russia. Roosevelt negotiated the Treaty of Portsmouth, which ended the war, and for which the president received the Nobel Peace Prize in 1906. Japan, however, was disappointed at not receiving more territory and financial compensation from Russia and blamed the United States.

The Later Progressive Era, 1907–1912

The progressive presidencies of Roosevelt and Taft brought the concept of big government to fruition. A complex corporate society needed rules and regulations as well as powerful agencies to enforce those measures necessary to maintain and enhance democratic free enterprise competition. The search for political, social, and economic standards designed to preserve order in American society while still guaranteeing political, social, and economic freedom was a difficult, but necessary task. The nation increasingly looked to Washington to protect the less powerful segments of the republic from the special interests that had grown up in the late 19th century. A persistent problem for the federal government was how best to preserve order and standards in a complex technological society while not interfering with the basic liberties Americans came to cherish in the Constitution and throughout their history.

Politics of the Period, 1907–1912

The continuation of progressive reforms by both Republican and Democratic leaders helped to form a consensus for the establishment of regulatory standards.

Election of 1908

Deciding not to run for re-election in 1908, Theodore Roosevelt opened the way for William H. Taft (Ohio) and James S. Sherman (New York) to run on a Republican platform calling for a continuation of anti-trust enforcement, environmental conservation, and a lower tariff policy to promote international trade. The Democrats nominated William Jennings Bryan for a third time, with John Kern (Indiana) for vice president on an anti-monopoly and low tariff platform. The Socialists once again nominated Eugene V. Debs. Taft easily won by over a million votes, and the Republicans retained control of both houses of Congress. For the first time, the American Federation of Labor entered national politics officially with an endorsement of Bryan. This decision began a long alliance between organized labor and the Democratic Party that would extend long into the 20th century.

Taft's Objectives

The president had two primary political goals in 1909. One was the continuation of Roosevelt's trust-busting policies, and the other was the reconciliation of the old-guard conservatives and young progressive reformers in the Republican Party.

Anti-Trust Policy

In pursuing anti-monopoly law enforcement, Taft chose as his Attorney General George Wickersham, who brought 44 indictments in anti-trust suits.

Political Rift

Taft was less successful in healing the Republican split between conservatives and progressives over such issues as tariff reform, conservation, and the almost dictatorial power held by the reactionary Republican Speaker of the House, Joseph Cannon (Illinois). Taft's inability to bring both wings of the party together led to the hardened division that would bring about a complete Democratic victory in the 1912 elections.

Ballinger-Pinchot Dispute (1909–1910)

Progressives backed Gifford Pinchot, chief of the U.S. Forest Service, in his charge that the conservative Secretary of the Interior, Richard Ballinger, was giving away the nation's natural resources to private corporate interests. A congressional investigatory committee found that Ballinger had done nothing illegal, but did act in a manner contrary to the government's environmental policies. Taft had supported Ballinger through the controversy, but negative public opinion forced Ballinger to resign in 1911. Taft's political standing with progressive Republicans was hurt going into the election of 1912.

The Sixteenth Amendment

In 1909 Congress passed a graduated income tax amendment to the Constitution. It was ratified in 1913.

Election of 1912

The election of 1912 was one of the most dramatic in American history. President Taft's inability to maintain party harmony led Theodore Roosevelt to return to national politics. When denied the Republican nomination, Roosevelt and his supporters formed the Progressive Party (Bull Moose) and nominated Roosevelt for president and Hiram Johnson (California) for vice president on a political platform nicknamed "The New Nationalism." It called for stricter regulation on large corporations, creation of a tariff commission, women's suffrage, minimum wages and benefits, direct election of senators, initiative, referendum and recall, presidential primaries, and prohibition of child labor. Roosevelt also called for a Federal Trade Commission to regulate the broader economy, a stronger executive, and more government planning. Theo-

DIDYOUKNOW?

The nickname "Bull Moose Party" came from Theodore Roosevelt's own description of himself as strong and vigorous as a bull moose when asked if he was fit to be president.

dore Roosevelt did not see big business as evil, but rather as needing regulation in a modern economy.

The Republicans

President Taft and Vice President Sherman retained control of the Republican Party after challenges by Roosevelt and Robert La Follette, and were nominated on a platform of "Quiet Confidence" calling for a continuation of progressive programs pursued by Taft over the past four years.

The Democrats

After 45 ballots without a nomination, the Democratic convention finally worked out a compromise whereby William Jennings Bryan gave his support to New Jersey Governor Woodrow Wilson on the forty-sixth ballot. Thomas Marshall (Indiana) was chosen as the vice presidential candidate. Wilson called his campaign the "New Freedom" based on progressive programs similar to those in the Progressive and Republican parties. Wilson, however, did not agree with Roosevelt on the issue of big business, which Wilson saw as morally evil. Therefore, Wilson called for breaking up large corporations rather than just regulating them. He differed from the other two party candidates by favoring independence for the Philippines and the exemption from prosecution of labor unions under the Sherman Anti-Trust Act. Wilson also supported such measures as lower tariffs, a graduated income tax, banking reform, and direct election of senators. Philosophically, Wilson was skeptical of big business and big government. In some respects, he hoped to return to an earlier and simpler concept of a free enterprise republic. After his selection, however, he would modify his views to conform more with those of Theodore Roosevelt.

Election Results

The Republican split clearly paved the way for Wilson's victory. Wilson received 6.2 million votes, Roosevelt 4.1 million, Taft 3.5 million, and the Socialist Debs 900,000 votes. In the Electoral College, Wilson received 435 votes, Roosevelt 88, and Taft 8. Although a minority president, Wilson garnered the largest electoral majority in American history to that time. Democrats won control of both houses of Congress.

The Economy, 1907–1912

The short-lived Panic of 1907 revealed economic weaknesses in U.S. banking and currency policy addressed by Presidents Roosevelt, Taft, and Wilson, and by Congress. Fortunately, the American economy was strengthened just in time to meet the challenges of World War I.

Anti-Trust Proceedings

Although a friend to the business community, President Taft ordered 90 legal proceedings against monopolies, and 44 anti-trust suits, including the one that broke up the American Tobacco Trust (1911). It was also under Taft that the government succeeded with its earlier suit against Standard Oil.

Social and Cultural Developments, 1907–1912

Progressive reform and government activism were important themes in American society.

Social Programs

States led the way with programs such as public aid to mothers of dependent children (Illinois, 1911) and the first minimum wage law (Massachusetts, 1912).

Race and Ethnic Attitudes

Despite the creation of the NAACP in 1909, many progressive reformers tended to be Anglo-Saxon elitists critical of the lack of accomplishments of Native American Indians, African Americans, and Asian, Southern and Eastern European immigrants. In 1905, the African American intellectual militant W. E. B. DuBois founded the Niagara Movement, which took square aim at Booker T. Washington's accommodationist stance and would provide ideological moorings for the NAACP. DuBois called for federal legislation to protect racial equality and the full rights of citizenship.

Radical Labor

Although moderate labor unions as represented by the American Federation of Labor functioned within the American system, a radical labor organization called the

Industrial Workers of the World (I.W.W., whose members were known as the Wobblies, 1905–1924) was active in promoting violence and revolution. Led by colorful figures such as Carlo Tresca, Elizabeth Gurley Flynn (the "Red Flame"), Daniel DeLeon, "Mother" Mary Harris Jones, the maverick priest Father Thomas Hagerty, and "Big Bill" Haywood, among others, the I.W.W. organized effective strikes in the textile industry in 1912 and among a few Western miners' groups, but generally had little appeal to the average American worker. After the Red Scare of 1919, the government worked to smash the I.W.W. and deported many of its immigrant leaders and members.

White Slave Trade

In 1910, Congress made interstate prostitution a federal crime with passage of the White Slave Trade Act, also known as the Mann Act.

Motion Pictures

By 1912, Hollywood had replaced New York and New Jersey as the center for silent-film production. There were 13,000 movie houses in the United States, and Paramount Pictures had just been formed as a large studio resembling other large corporations. Serials, epic features, and Mack Sennett slapstick comedies were in production. All these developments contributed to the "star system" in American film entertainment.

DID YOU KNOW?

Silent films became the first of many explosively popular forms of mass entertainment during the early twentieth century. The first successful nickelodeon theater—so named because admission cost a nickel—opened in Pittsburgh in 1905. Within five years, over 10,000 nickelodeons had sprung up across the nation.

Foreign Relations, 1907–1912

The expansion of American international interests through Taft's "dollar diplomacy" and world tensions foreshadowing the First World War were dominant themes.

Dollar Diplomacy

President Taft sought to avoid military intervention, especially in Latin America, by replacing "big stick" policies with "dollar diplomacy" in the expectation that American financial investments would encourage economic, social, and political stability. This idea proved an illusion, as investments never really filtered through all levels of Latin American societies, nor did such investments generate democratic reforms.

Mexican Revolution (1910–1920)

In Mexico, revolution began in 1910 that ultimately toppled a dictatorship that had lasted three decades. Francisco I. Madero overthrew the dictator Porfirio Diaz (1911), declaring himself a progressive revolutionary akin to reformers in the United States. American and European corporate interests (especially oil and mining) feared national interference with their investments in Mexico. President Taft recognized Madero's government but stationed 10,000 troops on the Texas border (1912) to protect Americans from the continuing fighting. In 1913, Madero was assassinated by General Victoriano Huerta. Wilson urged Huerta to hold democratic elections and adopt a constitutional government. When Huerta refused his advice, Wilson invaded Mexico with troops at Vera Cruz in 1914. A second U.S. invasion came in northern Mexico in 1916. War between the U.S. and Mexico might have occurred had not World War I intervened.

Root-Takahira Agreement (1908)

This agreement reiterated the status quo in Asia established by the United States and Japan by the Taft-Katsura Memo (1905).

Chinese Revolution, 1911

Chinese nationalists overthrew the Manchu dynasty and the last emperor of China, Henry Pu Yi. Although the military warlord Yuan Shih-Kai seized control, decades of factionalism, revolution, and civil war destabilized China and its market potential for American and other foreign investors.

The Wilson Years, 1913–1921

The Wilson Presidency

The Wilson administration brought together many of the policies and initiatives of the previous Republican administrations and reform efforts in Congress by both parties. Before the outbreak of World War I in 1914, President Wilson, working with cooperative majorities in both houses of Congress, achieved much of the remaining progressive agenda including lower tariff reform (Underwood-Simmons Act, 1913), the 16th Amendment (graduated income tax, 1913), the 17th Amendment (direct election of senators, 1913), the Federal Reserve System (which provided regulation and flexibility to monetary policy, 1913), the Federal Trade Commission (to investigate unfair business practices, 1914), and the Clayton Antitrust Act (improving the old Sherman Act and protecting labor unions and farm cooperatives from prosecution, 1914).

Other goals such as the protection of children in the workforce (Keating-Owen Act, 1916), credit reform for agriculture (Federal Farm Loan Act, 1916), and an independent tariff commission (1916) came later. By the end of Wilson's presidency, the New Freedom and the New Nationalism merged into one government philosophy of regulation, order, and standardization in the interest of an increasingly diverse and pluralistic American nation.

The New President

Woodrow Wilson was only the second Democrat (Cleveland was the first) elected president since the Civil War. He was born in Virginia in 1856, the son of a Presbyterian minister, and was reared and educated in the South. After earning a doctorate at Johns Hopkins University, he taught history and political science at Princeton, and in 1902 became president of that university. In 1910, he was elected governor of New Jersey as a reform, or progressive, Democrat.

The Cabinet

Wilson's key appointments were William Jennings Bryan as secretary of state and William Gibbs McAdoo as Secretary of the Treasury.

The Inaugural Address

Wilson called the Congress, now controlled by Democrats, into a special session beginning April 7, 1913, to consider three topics: reduction of the tariff, reform of the national banking and currency laws, and improvements in the antitrust laws. On April 8 he appeared before Congress, the first president since John Adams to do so, to promote his program.

Woodrow Wilson is the only U.S. president to have earned a Ph.D.

The Underwood-Simmons Tariff Act of 1913

Average rates were reduced to about 29 percent as compared with 37 to 40 percent under the previous Payne-Aldrich Tariff. A graduated income tax was included in the law to compensate for lost tariff revenue. It ranged from a tax of one percent on personal and corporate incomes over $4,000, a figure well above the annual income of the average worker, to seven percent on incomes over $500,000. The 16th Amendment to the Constitution, ratified in February 1913, authorized the income tax.

The Federal Reserve Act of 1913

Following the Panic of 1907, it was generally agreed that there was a need for more stability in the banking industry and for a currency supply, which would expand and contract to meet business needs.

Three points of view on the subject developed. Most Republicans backed the proposal of a commission headed by Senator Nelson W. Aldrich for a large central bank controlled by private banks. Bryanite Democrats, pointing to the Wall Street influence exposed by the 1913 Pujo Committee investigation of the money trust, wanted a reserve system and currency owned and controlled by the government. Conservative Democrats favored a decentralized system, privately owned and controlled, but free from Wall Street control.

The bill, which finally passed in December 1913, was a compromise measure. The law divided the nation into twelve regions with a Federal Reserve Bank in each region. Commercial banks in the region owned the Federal Reserve Bank by purchasing stock equal to six percent of their capital and surplus, and elected the directors of the bank. National banks were required to join the system, and state banks were invited to join. The Federal Reserve Banks held the gold reserves of their members. Federal Reserve Banks loaned money to member banks by rediscounting their commercial and agricultural paper; that is, the money was loaned at interest less than the public paid to the member banks, and the notes of indebtedness of businesses and farmers to the member banks were held as collateral. This allowed the Federal Reserve to control interest rates by raising or lowering the discount rate.

The money loaned to the member banks was in the form of a new currency, Federal Reserve Notes, which were backed by commercial paper (60 percent) and by gold (40 percent). This currency was designed to expand and contract with the volume of business activity and borrowing. Checks on member banks were cleared through the Federal Reserve System.

The Federal Reserve System serviced the financial needs of the federal government. The system was supervised and policy was set by a national Federal Reserve Board composed of the secretary of the Treasury, the comptroller of the currency, and five other members appointed by the president of the United States.

The Clayton Antitrust Act of 1914

The Clayton Antitrust Act of 1914 supplemented and interpreted the Sherman Antitrust Act of 1890. Under its provisions, stock ownership by a corporation in a competing corporation was prohibited. Interlocking directorates of competing corporations were prohibited; that is, the same persons could not manage competing corporations. Price discrimination (charging less in some regions than in others to undercut the competition) and exclusive contracts that reduced competition were prohibited. Officers of corporations could be held personally responsible for violations of antitrust laws. Lastly, labor unions and agricultural organizations were not to be considered "combinations or conspiracies in restraint of trade" as defined by the Sherman Antitrust Act.

The Federal Trade Commission Act of 1914

The Federal Trade Commission Act of 1914 prohibited all unfair trade practices without defining them and created a commission of five members appointed by the president. The commission was empowered to issue cease and desist orders to corporations to stop actions considered to be in restraint of trade, and to bring suit in the courts if the orders were not obeyed. Firms could also contest the orders in court. Under previous antitrust legislation, the government could act against corporations only by bringing suit.

Evaluation

The Underwood-Simmons Tariff, the Federal Reserve Act, and the Clayton Act were clearly in accord with the principles of the New Freedom, but the Federal Trade Commission reflected a move toward the kind of government regulation advocated by Roosevelt in his New Nationalism. Nonetheless, in 1914 and 1915, Wilson continued to oppose federal government action in such matters as loans to farmers, child labor regulation, and women's suffrage.

New Nationalism

Political Background

The Progressive Party dissolved rapidly after the election of 1912. The Republicans made major gains in Congress and in the state governments in the 1914 elections, and their victory in 1916 seemed probable. Early in 1916, Wilson and the Democrats abandoned most of their limited government and states' rights positions in favor of a legislative program of broad economic and social reforms designed to win the support of the former Progressives for the Democratic Party in the election of 1916. The urgency of their concern was heightened by Theodore Roosevelt's intention to seek the Republican nomination in 1916.

TEST TIP

As tempting as it may be to talk about the test with your friends, don't do it! Posting information on a social media website or blog about a certain AP exam test item that gave you trouble may seem harmless, but doing so will result in the cancellation of your score if it's found by the AP program. You could also face legal sanctions.

The Brandeis Appointment

Wilson's first action marking the adoption of the new program was the appointment on January 28, 1916, of Louis D. Brandeis, considered by many to be the principal advocate of social justice in the nation, as an associate justice of the Supreme Court.

The Child Labor Act of 1916

The Child Labor Act of 1916, earlier opposed by Wilson, forbade shipment in interstate commerce of products whose production had involved the labor of children under fourteen or sixteen, depending on the products. The legislation was especially significant because it was the first time that Congress regulated labor within a state using the interstate commerce power. The law was declared unconstitutional by the Supreme Court in 1918 on the grounds that it interfered with the powers of the states.

The Adamson Act of 1916

The Adamson Act of 1916 mandated an eight-hour day for workers on interstate railroads with time and a half for overtime and a maximum of sixteen hours in a shift. Its passage was a major victory for railroad unions and averted a railroad strike in September 1916.

The Election of 1916

The Democrats

The minority party nationally in terms of voter registration, the Democrats nominated Wilson in the 1916 campaign and adopted his platform calling for continued progressive reforms and neutrality in the European war. "He kept us out of war" became the principal campaign slogan of Democratic politicians.

The Republicans

The convention bypassed Theodore Roosevelt, who had decided not to run as a Progressive and had sought the Republican nomination. On the first ballot it chose Charles Evans Hughes, an associate justice of the Supreme Court and formerly a progressive Republican governor of New York. Hughes, an ineffective campaigner, avoided the neutrality issue because of divisions among the Republicans, and found it difficult to attack the progressive reforms of the Democrats. He emphasized what he considered the inefficiency of the Democrats, and failed to find a popular issue.

President Wilson throws out the first pitch on Opening Day, 1916. (U.S. Library of Congress)

The Election

Wilson won the 1916 election with 277 electoral votes and 9,129,000 popular votes, almost three million more than he received in 1912. Hughes received 254 electoral votes and 8,538,221 popular votes. The Democrats controlled Congress by a narrow margin. While Wilson's victory seemed close, the fact that he had increased his popular vote by almost 50 percent over four years previous was remarkable. It appears that most of his additional votes came from people who had voted for the Progressive or Socialist tickets in 1912.

Social Issues in the First Wilson Administration

Blacks

In 1913, Treasury Secretary William G. McAdoo and Postmaster General Albert S. Burleson segregated workers in some parts of their departments with no objection from Wilson. Many Northern blacks and whites protested, especially black leader W.E.B. DuBois, who had supported Wilson in 1912. William Monroe Trotter, a vocal champion of racial equality who was editor of the *Boston Guardian*, led a protest delegation to Washington and clashed verbally with the president. No further segregation in government agencies was initiated, but Wilson had gained a reputation for being inimical to civil rights.

Women

The movement for woman suffrage, led by the National American Woman Suffrage Association, was increasing in momentum at the time Wilson became president, and several states had granted the vote to women. Wilson opposed a federal woman suffrage amendment, maintaining that the franchise should be controlled by the states. When the U.S. entered World War I in 1917, he changed his view and supported the 19th Amendment.

DIDYOUKNOW?

The Wyoming territory became the first state to allow women to vote when it joined the Union in 1890. Over the next decade, Utah, Colorado, and Idaho also joined in allowing women's suffrage.

Wilson's Foreign Policy and the Road to War

Wilson's Basic Premise: New Freedom Policy

Wilson promised a more moral foreign policy than that of his predecessors, denouncing imperialism and dollar diplomacy, and advocating the advancement of democratic capitalist governments throughout the world.

Conciliation Treaties

Secretary Bryan negotiated treaties with 29 nations under which they agreed to submit disputes to international commissions for conciliation, not arbitration. The treaties also included provisions for a cooling-off period—usually one year—before the nations would resort to war. While the treaties probably had no practical effect, they illustrated the idealism of the administration.

Dollar Diplomacy

Wilson signaled his repudiation of Taft's dollar diplomacy by withdrawing American involvement from the six-power loan consortium of China.

The Caribbean

Like his predecessors, Wilson sought to protect the Panama Canal, which opened in 1914, by maintaining stability in the area. He also wanted to encourage diplomacy and economic growth in the underdeveloped nations of the region. In applying his policy, he became an interventionist, as Roosevelt and Taft had been.

In 1912, American marines had landed in Nicaragua to maintain order, and an American financial expert had taken control of the customs service. The Wilson administration kept the marines in Nicaragua and negotiated the Bryan-Chamorro Treaty of 1914, which gave the United States an option to build a canal through the country. In effect, Nicaragua became an American protectorate, although the Senate did not ratify treaty provisions authorizing such action.

Claiming that political anarchy existed in Haiti, Wilson sent marines in 1915 and imposed a treaty making the country a protectorate, with American control of its finances and constabulary. The marines remained until 1934.

In 1916, Wilson sent marines to the Dominican Republic to stop a civil war and established a military government under an American naval commander.

Wilson feared in 1915 that Germany might annex Denmark and its Caribbean possession, the Danish West Indies (known today as the Virgin Islands). After extended negotiations, the United States purchased the islands from Denmark by treaty on August 4, 1916, for $25 million, and took possession of them on March 31, 1917.

In 1913, Wilson refused to recognize the government of Mexican military dictator Victoriano Huerta, and offered unsuccessfully to mediate between Huerta and his Constitutionalist opponent, Venustiano Carranza. When the Huerta government arrested several American seamen in Tampico in April 1914, American forces occupied the port of Veracruz, an action condemned by both Mexican political factions. In July 1914, Huerta abdicated his power to Carranza, who was soon opposed by his former general, Francisco "Pancho" Villa. Seeking to draw in the United States as a means of undermining Carranza, Villa shot 16 Americans on a train in northern Mexico in January 1916, and burned the border town of Columbus, New Mexico, in March 1916, killing 19 people. Carranza reluctantly consented to Wilson's request that the United States be allowed to pursue and capture Villa in Mexico, but did not expect the force of about 6,000 Army troops under the command of General John J. Pershing who crossed the Rio Grande on March 18. The force advanced over 300 miles into Mexico, failed to capture Villa, and became, in effect, an army of occupation. The Carranza government demanded an American withdrawal, and several clashes with Mexican troops occurred. War threatened, but Wilson removed the American forces in January 1917.

Pan American Mediation, 1914

John Barrett, head of the Pan American Union (formerly Blaine's International Bureau of American Republics) called for multilateral mediation to bring about a solution to Mexico's internal problems and extract the United States from its military presence in Mexico. Although Wilson initially refused, Argentina, Brazil, and Chile did mediate among the Mexican factions and Wilson withdrew American troops. Barrett hoped to replace the unilateral Monroe Doctrine with a multilateral Pan American policy to promote collective responses and mediation to difficult hemispheric problems. Wilson, however, refused to share power with Latin America.

The Road to War in Europe

American Neutrality

When World War I broke out in Europe, Wilson issued a proclamation of American neutrality on August 4, 1914. Despite that action, the United States drifted toward closer ties with the Allies, especially Britain and France. While many Americans were sympathetic to the Central Powers, the majority, including Wilson, hoped for an Allied victory. Although British naval power effectively prevented American trade with the Central Powers and European neutrals, often in violation of international law, the United States limited itself to formal diplomatic protests. The value of American trade with the Central Powers fell from $169 million in 1914 to almost nothing in 1916, but trade with the Allies rose from $825 million to $3.2 billion during the same period. In addition, the British and French had borrowed about $3.25 billion from American sources by 1917. The United States had become a major supplier of Allied munitions, food, and raw materials.

The Submarine Crisis of 1915

The Germans began using submarines in 1915, announcing a submarine blockade of the Allies on February 4. They began to attack unarmed British passenger ships in the Atlantic. Wilson insisted to the Germans that Americans had a right as neutrals to travel safely on such ships, and that international law required a warship to arrange for the safe removal of passengers before attacking such a ship. The sinking of the British liner *Lusitania* off the coast of Ireland on May 7, 1915, with the loss of 1,198 lives, including 128 Americans, brought strong protests from Wilson. Secretary of State Bryan, who believed Americans should stay off belligerent ships, resigned rather than insist on questionable neutral rights, and was replaced by Robert Lansing. Following the sinking of another liner, the *Arabic*, on August 19, the Germans gave the "Arabic pledge" to stop attacks on unarmed passenger vessels.

DIDYOUKNOW?

Although the British sailed the *Lusitania* as a passenger vessel, the ship was carrying nearly 175 tons of war munitions in its cargo hold. German leaders, who had previously warned that the ship would be sunk, believed that their attack on the *Lusitania* was justified as a measure of war.

The *Sussex* Pledge

When the unarmed French channel steamer *Sussex* was torpedoed but not sunk on March 24, 1916, with seven Americans injured, Wilson threatened to sever relations unless Germany ceased all surprise submarine attacks on all shipping, whether belligerent or neutral, armed or unarmed. Germany acceded with the "*Sussex* pledge" at the beginning of May but threatened to resume submarine warfare if the British did not stop their violations of international law.

Preparedness

In November 1915, Wilson proposed a major increase in the Army and the abolition of the National Guard as a preparedness measure. Americans divided on the issue, with organizations like the National Security League proposing stronger military forces and others like the League to Enforce Peace opposing. After opposition by Southern and Western anti-preparedness Democrats, Congress passed a modified National Defense Act in June 1916, which increased Army strength from about 90,000 to 220,000, and enlarged the National Guard under federal control. In August, over $500 million was appropriated for naval construction. The additional costs were met by increased taxes on the wealthy.

Wilson's Final Peace Efforts, 1916–1917

On December 12, 1916, the Germans, confident of their strong position, proposed a peace conference, a step which Wilson previously had advocated. When Wilson asked both sides to state their expectations, the British seemed agreeable to reasonable negotiations, but the Germans were evasive and stated that they did not want Wilson at the conference. In an address to Congress on January 22, 1917, Wilson made his last offer to serve as a neutral mediator. He proposed a "peace without victory," based not on a "balance of power" but on a "community of power," alluding to his proposal of May 1916 for an "association of nations."

Unlimited Submarine Warfare

Germany announced on January 31, 1917, that it would sink all ships, belligerent or neutral, without warning in a large war zone off the coasts of the Allied nations in the eastern Atlantic and the Mediterranean. The Germans realized that the United States might declare war, but they believed that, after cutting the flow of supplies to the Allies, they could win the war before the Americans could send any sizable force to Europe. Wilson broke diplomatic relations with Germany on February 3. During February and March, several American merchant ships were sunk by submarines.

TEST TIP

Remember you will choose one of two long essay questions to answer during the free-response section of the AP U.S. History exam. Take a few moments to carefully read and consider the questions. Respond to whichever question you can answer most completely. Be specific and assertive in your response.

The Zimmermann Telegram

The British intercepted a secret message from the German foreign secretary, Arthur Zimmermann, to the German minister in Mexico, and turned it over to the United States on February 24, 1917. The Germans proposed that, in the event of a war between the United States and Germany, Mexico would attack the United States. After the war, the "lost territories" of Texas, New Mexico, and Arizona would be returned to Mexico. In addition, Japan would be invited to join the alliance against the United States. When the telegram was released to the press on March 1, many Americans became convinced that war with Germany was necessary.

The Declaration of War

On March 2, 1917, Wilson called Congress to a special session beginning April 2. When Congress convened, he requested a declaration of war against Germany. The declaration was passed by the Senate on April 4 by a vote of 82 to 6, by the House on April 6 by a vote of 373 to 50, and signed by Wilson on the same day.

Wilson's Reasons

Wilson's decision to ask for a declaration of war seems to have been based primarily on four considerations. He believed that the Zimmermann Telegram showed that the Germans were not trustworthy and would eventually go to war against the United States. He also believed that armed neutrality could not adequately protect American shipping. The democratic government established in Russia after the revolution in March 1917 also proved more acceptable as an ally than the tsarist government. Finally, he was convinced that the United States could hasten the end of the war and ensure for itself a major role in designing a lasting peace.

World War I: The Military Campaign

Raising an Army

Despite the enlistment of many volunteers, it was apparent that a military draft would be necessary. So the Selective Service Act was passed on May 18, 1917, after bitter opposition in the House led by Speaker Champ Clark. Only a compromise outlawing the sale of liquor in or near military camps secured passage. Originally including all males 21 to 30, the limits were later extended to 17 and 46. The first drawing of 500,000 names was made on July 20, 1917. By the end of the war 24,231,021 men had been registered and 2,810,296 had been inducted. In addition, about two million men and women volunteered.

Women and Minorities in the Military

Some women served as clerks in the Navy or in the Signal Corps of the Army. Originally, nurses were part of the Red Cross, but eventually some were taken into the Army. About 400,000 black men were drafted or enlisted, despite the objections of southern political leaders. They were kept in segregated units, usually with white officers, which were used as labor battalions or for other support activities. Some black units did see combat, and a few blacks became officers, but did not command white troops.

The War at Sea

In 1917, German submarines sank 6.5 million tons of Allied and American shipping, while only 2.7 million tons were built. German hopes for victory were based on the destruction of Allied supply lines. The U.S. Navy furnished destroyers to fight the submarines, and, after overcoming great resistance from the British navy, finally began the use of the convoy system in July 1917. Shipping losses fell from almost 900,000 tons in April 1917 to about 400,000 tons in December 1917, and remained below 200,000 tons per month after April 1918. The U.S. Navy transported over 900,000 American soldiers to France, while British transports carried over 1 million. Only two of the well-guarded troop transports were sunk. The Navy had over 2,000 ships and over half a million men by the end of the war.

The American Expeditionary Force

The soldiers and marines sent to France under the command of Major General John J. Pershing were called the American Expeditionary Force, or the AEF. From a small initial force that arrived in France in June 1917, the AEF increased to over two million by November 1918. Pershing resisted efforts by European commanders to amalgamate the Americans with the French and British armies, insisting that he maintain a separate command. American casualties included 112,432 dead, about half of whom died of disease, and 230,024 wounded.

Major Military Engagements

The American force of about 14,500 troops had arrived in France by September 1917 and was assigned a quiet section of the line near Verdun. As numbers increased, the American role became more significant. When the Germans mounted a major drive toward Paris in the spring of 1918, the Americans experienced their first important engagements. In June, they prevented the Germans from crossing the Marne at Chateau-Thierry and cleared the area of Belleau Woods. In July, eight American divisions aided French troops in attacking the German line between Reims and Soissons. The American First Army with over half a million men under Pershing's immediate command was assembled in August 1918, and began a major offensive at Saint-Mihiel on the southern part of the front on September 12. Following the successful operation, Pershing began a drive against the German defenses between Verdun and Sedan, an action called the

Meuse-Argonne offensive, and reached Sedan on November 7. During the same period, the English in the north and the French along the central front also broke through the German lines. The fighting ended with the armistice on November 11, 1918.

Mobilizing the Home Front

Industry

The Council of National Defense, comprised of six cabinet members and a seven-member advisory commission of business and labor leaders, was established in 1916 before American entry into the war to coordinate industrial mobilization, but it had little authority. In July 1917, the council created the War Industries Board to control raw materials, production, prices, and labor relations. The military forces refused to cooperate with the civilian agency in purchasing their supplies, and the domestic war effort seemed on the point of collapse in December 1917 when a Congressional investigation began. In 1918, Wilson took stronger action under his emergency war powers, which were bolstered by the Overman Act. In March 1918, Wilson appointed Wall Street broker Bernard M. Baruch to head the WIB, assisted by an advisory committee of 100 businessmen. The WIB allocated raw materials, standardized manufactured products, instituted strict production and purchasing controls, and paid high prices to businesses for their products. Even so, American industry was just beginning to produce heavy armaments when the war ended. Most heavy equipment and munitions used by the American troops in France were produced in Britain or France.

DIDYOUKNOW?

Because so many white men were needed to fight in World War I, factory owners facing labor shortages went South to recruit African American workers. The massive movement of African Americans north to work in factories began what is now known as the Great Migration.

Food

The United States had to supply not only its own food needs, but also those of Britain, France, and some of the other Allies as well. The problem was compounded by bad weather in 1916 and 1917, which crimped farm output. The Lever Act of 1917 gave the President broad control over the production, price, and distribution of food and fuel. Herbert Hoover was appointed by Wilson to head a newly created Food Administration. Hoover fixed high prices to encourage the production of wheat, pork, and other products, and encouraged the conservation of food through such voluntary programs as "Meatless Mondays" and "Wheatless Wednesdays." Despite the bad harvests in 1916 and 1917, food exports by 1919 were almost triple those of the pre-war years, and real farm income was up almost 30 percent.

Fuel

The Fuel Administration under Harry A. Garfield was established in August 1917. It was concerned primarily with coal production and conservation because coal was the predominant fuel of the time and was in short supply during the severe winter of 1917–1918. Also instituted were "Fuelless Mondays" in nonessential industries to conserve coal and "Gasless Sundays" for automobile owners to save gasoline. Coal production increased about 35 percent from 1914 to 1918.

Railroad

The American railroad system, which provided most of the inter-city transportation in the country, seemed near collapse in December 1917 because of the wartime demands and heavy snows that slowed service. Wilson created the United States Railroad Administration under William G. McAdoo, the secretary of the Treasury, to take over and operate all the railroads in the nation as one system. The government paid the owners rent for the use of their lines, spent over $500 million on improved tracks and equipment, and achieved its objective of an efficient railroad system.

Maritime Shipping

The United States Shipping Board was authorized by Congress in September 1916, and in April 1917 it created a subsidiary, the Emergency Fleet Corporation, to buy, build, lease, and operate merchant ships for the war effort. Edward N. Hurley became the director in July 1917, and the corporation constructed several large shipyards which were just beginning to produce vessels when the war ended. By seizing German and Dutch ships, and by the purchase and requisition of private vessels, the board had accumulated a large fleet by September 1918.

Labor

To prevent strikes and work stoppages in war industries, the War Labor Board was created in April 1918 under the joint chairmanship of former president William Howard Taft and attorney Frank P. Walsh with members from both industry and labor. In hearing labor disputes, the WLB in effect prohibited strikes, but it also encouraged higher wages, the eight-hour workday, and unionization. Union membership doubled during the war, from about 2.5 million to about 5 million.

War Finance and Taxation

The war is estimated to have cost about $33.5 billion by 1920, excluding such future costs as veterans' benefits and debt service. Of that amount at least $7 billion was loaned to the Allies, with most of the money actually spent in the United States for supplies. The government raised about $10.5 billion in taxes and borrowed the remaining $23 billion. Taxes were raised substantially in 1917, and again in 1918. The Revenue Act of 1918, which did not take effect until 1919, imposed a personal income tax of six percent on incomes up to $4,000, and 12 percent on incomes above that amount. In addition, a graduated surtax went to a maximum of 65 percent on large incomes, for a total of 77 percent. Corporations paid an excess profits tax of 65 percent, and excise taxes were levied on luxury items. Much public, peer, and employer pressure was exerted on citizens to buy Liberty Bonds, which covered a major part of the borrowing. Inflation surged during the war years, contributing substantially to the cost of the war.*

The Committee on Public Information

The Committee on Public Information, headed by journalist George Creel, was formed by Wilson in April 1917. Creel established a successful system of voluntary censorship of the press, and organized about 150,000 paid and volunteer writers, lecturers, artists, and other professionals in a propaganda campaign to build support for the American cause as an idealistic crusade, while portraying the Germans as barbaric and beastial Huns. The committee set up volunteer Liberty Leagues in every community, and urged their members, and citizens at large, to spy on their neighbors, especially those with foreign names, and to report any suspicious words or actions to the Justice Department.

War Hysteria

A number of volunteer organizations sprang up around the country to search for draft dodgers, enforce the sale of bonds, and report any opinion or conversation considered suspicious. Perhaps the largest such organization was the American Protective League with about 250,000 members, which claimed to have the approval of the Justice Department. Such groups publicly humiliated people accused of not buying war bonds

* Coincidentally, U.S. inflation had only begun to be measured and tracked in 1913, when the Federal Reserve was established. As the war machine began to impact the American economy, inflation surged as high as 17.8% in 1917, according to data from the Federal Reserve Bank of Minneapolis.

and persecuted, beat, and sometimes killed people of German descent. As a result of the activities of the Committee on Public Information and the vigilante groups, German language instruction and German music were banned in many areas, German measles became "liberty measles," pretzels were prohibited in some cities, and the like. The anti-German and anti-subversive war hysteria in the United States far exceeded similar public moods in Britain and France during the war.

The Espionage and Sedition Acts

The Espionage Act of 1917 provided for fines and imprisonment for persons who made false statements that aided the enemy, incited rebellion in the military, or obstructed recruitment or the draft. Printed matter advocating treason or insurrection could be excluded from the mails. The Sedition Act of May 1918 forbade any criticism of the government, flag, or uniform, even if there were not detrimental consequences, and expanded the mail exclusion. The laws sounded reasonable, but they were applied in ways that trampled on civil liberties. Eugene V. Debs, the perennial Socialist candidate for president, was given a ten-year prison sentence for a speech at his party's convention in which he was critical of American policy in entering the war and warned of the dangers of militarism. Movie producer Robert Goldstein released the movie *The Spirit of '76* about the Revolutionary War which, of course, showed the British fighting the Americans. Goldstein was fined $10,000 and sentenced to ten years in prison because the film depicted the British, who were now fighting on the same side as the United States, in an unfavorable light.

The Espionage Act was upheld by the Supreme Court in the case of *Schenck v. United States* in 1919. The opinion, written by Justice Oliver Wendell Holmes, Jr., stated that Congress could limit free speech when the words represented a "clear and present danger" and that, in effect, a person cannot cry "fire" in a crowded theater. The Sedition Act was similarly upheld in *Abrams v. United States* a few months later. Ultimately, 2,168 persons were prosecuted under the laws, and 1,055 were convicted, of whom only ten were charged with actual sabotage.

TEST TIP

Keep an eye on the clock as you work on your responses. Setting your watch to 12:00 at the beginning of each section can help you quickly see how much time you have used without having to remember your actual start time.

Wartime Social Trends

Women

With approximately 16 percent of the normal labor force in uniform and demand for goods at a peak, large numbers of mostly white women were hired by factories and other enterprises in jobs never before open to them. They were often resented and ridiculed by male workers. When the war ended, almost all returned to traditional "women's jobs" or to homemaking. Returning veterans replaced them in the labor market. Women continued to campaign for woman suffrage. In 1917, six states, including the large and influential states of New York, Ohio, Indiana, and Michigan, gave the vote to women. Wilson changed his position in 1918 to advocate woman suffrage as a war measure. In January 1918, the House of Representatives adopted a suffrage amendment to the Constitution, which was defeated later in the year by Southern forces in the Senate. The way was paved for the victory of the suffragists after the war.

Racial Minorities

The labor shortage opened industrial jobs to Mexican Americans and to blacks. W. E. B. DuBois, among the most prominent black leaders of the time, supported the war effort in the hope that a war to make the world safe for democracy would bring a better life for blacks in the United States. About half a million rural Southern blacks migrated to cities, mainly in the North and Midwest, to obtain employment in war and other industries, especially in steel and meatpacking. Some white Southerners, fearing the loss of labor when cotton prices were high, tried forcibly to prevent their departure. Some white Northerners, fearing job competition and encroachment on white neighborhoods, resented their arrival. In 1917, there were race riots in 26 cities in the North and South, with the worst in East St. Louis, Illinois. Despite the opposition and their concentration in entry-level positions, there is evidence that the blacks who migrated generally improved themselves economically.

Prohibition

Proponents of prohibition stressed the need for military personnel to be sober and the need to conserve grain for food, and depicted the hated Germans as disgusting beer drinkers. In December 1917, a constitutional amendment to prohibit the manufacture and sale of alcoholic beverages in the United States was passed by Congress and submitted to the states for ratification. While alcohol consumption was being attacked, annual cigarette consumption climbed from 26 billion in 1916 to 48 billion in 1918.

Peacemaking and Domestic Problems, 1918–1920

The Fourteen Points

From the time of the American entry into the war, Wilson had maintained that the war would make the world safe for democracy. He insisted that there should be peace without victory, meaning that the victors would not be vindictive toward the losers so that a fair and stable international situation in the postwar world would insure lasting peace. In an address to Congress on January 8, 1918, he presented his specific peace plan in the form of the Fourteen Points. The first five points called for open rather than secret peace treaties, freedom of the seas, free trade, arms reduction, and a fair adjustment of colonial claims. The next eight points were concerned with the national aspirations of various European peoples and the adjustment of boundaries, as, for example, in the creation of an independent Poland. The fourteenth point, which he considered the most important and had espoused as early as 1916, called for a "general association of nations" to preserve the peace. In Europe, the reception to the Fourteen Points was mixed, as there was a great desire to punish Germany. In the United States, many people opposed a peace plan that risked American involvement in another European war.

The Armistice

The German Chancellor, Prince Max of Baden, on October 3, 1918, asked Wilson to begin peace negotiations based on his concepts of a just peace and the Fourteen Points. Wilson insisted that the Germans must evacuate Belgium and France and form a civilian government. By early November, the Allied and American armies were advancing rapidly and Germany was on the verge of collapse. The German Emperor fled to the Netherlands and abdicated. Representatives of the new German republic signed the armistice on November 11, 1918, to be effective at 11:00 a.m. that day, and agreed to withdraw German forces to the Rhine and to surrender military equipment, including 150 submarines.

The Versailles Peace Conference, 1919

Wilson decided that he would lead the American delegation to the peace conference, which opened in Paris on January 12, 1919. In doing so, he became the first president to leave the country during his term of office. The other members of the delegation were Secretary of State Robert Lansing, General Tasker Bliss, Colonel Edward M. House, and attorney Henry White. Wilson made a serious strategic mistake in not appointing any leading Republicans to the commission and in not consulting the Republican leadership in the Senate about the negotiations. In Paris, Wilson joined Prime Minister David Lloyd George of Great Britain, Premier Georges Clemenceau of France, and Prime Minister Vittorio Orlando of Italy to form the "Big Four," which dominated the conference. In the negotiations, which continued until May 1919, Wilson found it necessary to make many compromises in forging the text of the treaty.

The Soviet Influence

Russia was the only major participant in the war that was not represented at the peace conference. Following the Communist Revolution of 1917, Russia had made a separate peace with Germany in March 1918. Wilson had resisted Allied plans to send major military forces to Russia to oust the Communists and bring Russia back into the war. An American force of about 5,000 was sent to Murmansk in the summer of 1918, in association with British and French troops, to prevent the Germans from taking military supplies, and was soon active in assisting Russian anti-Bolsheviks. It remained in the area until June 1919. In July 1918, Wilson also sent about 10,000 soldiers to Siberia where they took over the operation of the railroads to assist a Czech army that was escaping from the Germans by crossing Russia. They were also a counterbalance to a larger Japanese force in the area, and remained until April 1920. Wilson believed that the spread of communism was the greatest threat to peace and international order. His concern made him reluctant to dispute too much with the other leaders at the Versailles Conference, and more agreeable to compromise, because he believed it imperative that the democracies remain united in the face of the communist threat.

Important Provisions of the Versailles Treaty

In drafting the Versailles Treaty, Wilson achieved some of the goals in the Fourteen Points and compromised on others. He failed to secure freedom of the seas, free trade, reduction of armaments, or the return of Russia to the society of free nations. Some major decisions were as follows:

1. The League of Nations was formed, implementing the point that Wilson considered the most important. Article X of the Covenant, or charter, of the League called on all members to protect the "territorial integrity" and "political independence" of all other members.

2. Germany was held responsible for causing the war and was required to agree to pay the Allies for all civilian damage and veterans' costs, which eventually were calculated at $33 billion; the German army and navy were limited to tiny defensive

forces; and the west bank of the Rhine was declared a military-free zone forever and occupied by the French for 15 years. These decisions were clearly contrary to the idea of peace without victory.

3. New nations of Yugoslavia, Austria, Hungary, Czechoslovakia, Poland, Lithuania, Latvia, Estonia, and Finland partially fulfilled the idea of self-determination for all nationalities, but the boundaries drawn at the conference left many people under the control of other nationalities.

4. German colonies were made mandates of the League of Nations and given in trusteeship to France, Japan, and Britain and its dominions.

Germany and the Signing of the Treaty

The German delegates were allowed to come to Versailles in May 1919 after the completion of the treaty document. They expected to negotiate on the basis of the draft, but were told to sign it "or else," probably meaning a threat of an economic boycott of Germany. They protested but signed the Versailles Treaty on June 28, 1919.

The Senate and the Treaty

Following a protest by 39 senators in February 1919, Wilson obtained some changes in the League structure to exempt the Monroe Doctrine and domestic matters from League jurisdiction. Then, on July 26, 1919, he presented the treaty with the League within it to the Senate for ratification. Almost all of the 47 Democrats supported Wilson and the treaty, but the 49 Republicans were divided. About a dozen were "irreconcilables" who thought that the United States should not be a member of the League under any circumstances. The remainder included 25 "strong" and 12 "mild" reservationists who would accept the treaty with some changes. The main objection centered on Article X of the League covenant, where the reservationists wanted it understood that the United States would not go to war to defend a League member without the approval of Congress. The leader of the reservationists was Henry Cabot Lodge of Massachusetts, the chairman of the Foreign Relations Committee. More senators than the two-thirds necessary for ratification favored the treaty either as written or with reservations.

Wilson and the Senate

On September 3, 1919, Wilson set out on a national speaking tour to appeal to the people to support the treaty and the League, and to influence their senators. He collapsed after a speech in Pueblo, Colorado, on September 25, and returned to Washington where he suffered a severe stroke on October 2 that paralyzed his left side. He was seriously ill for several months and never fully recovered. In a letter to the Senate Democrats on November 18, Wilson urged them to oppose the treaty with the Lodge reservations. In votes the next day, the treaty failed to get a two-thirds majority either with or without the reservations.

DIDYOUKNOW?

As a result of Wilson's stroke, his wife Edith handled many of the administrative duties of the White House. Critics argued that she served as a de facto president—and not a very good one—but there is little historical evidence to support this claim.

The Final Vote

Many people, including British and French leaders, urged Wilson to compromise with Lodge on the reservations, including the issue of Article X. Instead, Wilson wrote an open letter to Democrats on January 8, 1920, urging them to make the election of a Democratic president in 1920 a "great and solemn referendum" on the treaty as written. Such partisanship only exacerbated the situation. Many historians believe Wilson's ill health impaired his judgment, and that he would have worked out a compromise had he not had the stroke. The Senate took up the treaty again in February 1920, and on March 19 it was again defeated both with and without the reservations. The United States officially ended the war with Germany by a resolution of Congress signed on July 2, 1921, and a separate peace treaty was ratified on July 25. The United States did not join the League.

Consequences of War

The impact of the war was far-reaching in the twentieth century. The United States emerged as the economic and political leader of the world—even if the American people were not prepared to accept the responsibility. The Russian Revolution overthrew the tsar and inaugurated a communist dictatorship. Britain, France, Austria, and Turkey went into various states of decline. Germany was devastated at the Versailles Peace Conference. Revenge and bitterness would contribute to the rise of Adolf Hitler and the Nazi movement. The European industrial nations would never recover from the cost of the war. Lingering economic problems would contribute to the Crash of 1929 and the Great Depression of the 1930s. The seeds of World War II had been planted.

Domestic Problems and the End of the Wilson Administration

Demobilization

The American Expeditionary Forces (AEF) were brought home as quickly as possible in early 1919, and members of the armed forces were rapidly discharged. Congress provided for wounded veterans through a system of veterans hospitals under the Veterans Bureau and funded relief, especially food supplies, for war-torn Europe. The wartime agencies for the control of the economy, such as the War Industries Board, were soon disbanded. During 1919, Congress considered various plans to nationalize the railroads or continue their public operation, but then passed the Esch-Cummings Transportation Act of 1920, which returned them to private ownership and operation. It did extend Interstate Commerce Commission control over their rates and financial affairs, and allowed supervised pooling. The fleet of ships accumulated by the Shipping Board during the war was sold to private owners at attractive prices.

Final Reforms of the Progressive Era

In January 1919, the 18th Amendment to the Constitution prohibiting the manufacture, sale, transportation, or importation of intoxicating liquors was ratified by the states, and it became effective in January 1920. The 19th Amendment providing for woman suffrage, which had been defeated in the Senate in 1918, was approved by Congress in 1919. It was ratified by the states in time for the election of 1920.

The Postwar Economy

Despite fear of unemployment with the return of veterans to the labor force and the end of war purchases, the American economy boomed during 1919 and the first half of 1920. Consumers had money from high wages during the war, and the European demand for American food and manufactured products continued for some months after the war. The demand for goods resulted in a rapid inflation. Prices in 1919 were 77 percent above the pre-war level, and in 1920 they were 105 percent above that level.

Strikes

The great increase in prices prompted 2,655 strikes in 1919 involving about four million workers, or 20 percent of the labor force. Unions were encouraged by the gains they had made during the war and thought they had the support of public opinion. However, the Communist Revolution in Russia in 1917 soon inspired in many Americans, including government officials, a fear of violence and revolution by workers. While most of the strikes in early 1919 were successful, the tide of opinion gradually shifted against the workers.

Four major strikes received particular attention. In January 1919, all unions in Seattle declared a general strike in support of a strike for higher pay by shipyard workers. The action was widely condemned, the federal government sent marines, and the strike was soon abandoned.

In September 1919, Boston police struck for the right to unionize. Governor Calvin Coolidge called out the National Guard and stated that there was "no right to strike against the public safety by anybody, anywhere, anytime." The police were fired and a new force was recruited.

The American Federation of Labor attempted to organize the steel industry in 1919. When Judge Elbert H. Gary, the head of U.S. Steel, refused to negotiate, the workers struck in September. After much violence and the use of federal and state troops, the strike was broken by January 1920.

The United Mine Workers of America under John L. Lewis struck for shorter hours and higher wages on November 1, 1919. Attorney General A. Mitchell Palmer obtained injunctions and the union called off the strike. An arbitration board later awarded the miners a wage increase.

The Red Scare

Americans feared the spread of the Russian Communist Revolution to the United States, and many interpreted the widespread strikes of 1919 as communist-inspired and the beginning of the revolution. Bombs sent through the mail to prominent government and business leaders in April 1919 seemed to confirm their fears, although the origin of the bombs has never been determined. The membership of the two communist parties founded in the United States in 1919 was less than 100,000, but many Americans worried that many workers, foreign-born persons, radicals, and members of the

DID YOU KNOW?

The Wobblies often used song to spread their labor messages, once proclaiming in a leaflet: "Sing and fight! Right was the tyrant king who said: 'Beware of a movement that sings.'" Some Wobbly songs include "Hallelujah, I'm a Bum," "The Rebel Girl," and "Solidarity Forever."

International Workers of the World (also known as "Wobblies"), a radical union in the Western states, were communists. The anti-German hysteria of the war years was transformed into the anti-communist and anti-foreign hysteria of 1919 and 1920, and continued in various forms through the twenties.

The Palmer Raids

Attorney General A. Mitchell Palmer was one of the targets of the anonymous bombers in the spring of 1919. He was also an aspirant for the Democratic nomination for president in 1920, and he realized that many Americans saw the threat of a communist revolution as a grave danger. In August 1919, he named J. Edgar Hoover to head a new Intelligence Division in the Justice Department to collect information about radicals. In November 1919, Palmer's agents arrested almost 700 persons, mostly anarchists, and deported 43 of them as undesirable aliens. On January 2, 1920, Justice Department agents, local police, and vigilantes in 33 cities arrested about 4,000 people accused of being communists. It appears that many people caught in the sweep were neither communists nor aliens. Eventually, 556 were shown to be communists and aliens and were deported. Palmer then announced that huge communist riots were planned for major cities on May Day, May 1, 1920. Police and troops were alerted, but the day passed with no radical activity. Palmer was discredited and the Red Scare subsided.

The Race Riots of 1919

During the war about half a million blacks had migrated from the South to industrial cities, mostly in the North and Midwest, to find employment. After the war, white hostility based on competition for lower-paid jobs and black encroachment into neighborhoods led to race riots in 25 cities with hundreds killed or wounded and millions of dollars in property damage. Beginning in Longview, Texas, the riots spread, among other places, to Washington, D.C., and Chicago. The Chicago riot in July was the worst, lasting 13 days and leaving 38 dead, 520 wounded, and 1,000 families homeless. Fear and resentment of returning black veterans in the South led to an increase of lynchings from 34 in 1917 to 60 in 1918 and 70 in 1919. Some of the victims were veterans still in uniform.

The Roaring Twenties and Economic Collapse (1920–1929)

The Election of 1920

It seemed to many political observers in 1920 that the Republicans had an excellent chance of victory in that year's presidential election. The Wilson administration was blamed by many for the wartime civil liberties abuses, the League of Nations controversy, and the strikes and inflation of the postwar period.

The Republican Convention

The principal GOP contenders for the nomination were General Leonard Wood, who had the support of the followers of the deceased Theodore Roosevelt, and Governor Frank O. Lowden of Illinois, the pick of many of the party bosses. When the convention seemed to deadlock, Henry Cabot Lodge, the convention chairman, and several other leaders arranged for the name of Senator Warren G. Harding of Ohio to be introduced as a dark-horse candidate. Harding was nominated on the tenth ballot, and Governor Calvin Coolidge of Massachusetts was chosen as the vice presidential nominee. The platform opposed the League, and promised low taxes, high tariffs, immigration restriction, and aid to farmers.

DIDYOUKNOW?

The results of the 1920 presidential election were the first to be broadcast on the radio as part of the nation's first-ever commercial radio programming on Pittsburgh's KDKA.

The Democratic Convention

For the Democrats, the front-runners were William Gibbs McAdoo, the secretary of the Treasury and Wilson's son-in-law, and Attorney General A. Mitchell Palmer. Governor James Cox of Ohio was entered as a favorite son. Wilson expected the convention to deadlock, at which point his name would be introduced and he would be nominated for a third term by acclamation. His plan never materialized. McAdoo and Palmer contended for 37 ballots with neither receiving the two-thirds necessary for nomination. Palmer then released his delegates, most of whom turned to Cox. Cox was nominated on the forty-fourth ballot, and Franklin D. Roosevelt, an assistant secretary of the Navy and distant cousin of Theodore, was selected as his running mate. The platform endorsed the League but left the door open for reservations.

The Campaign

Harding's managers decided that he should speak as little as possible, but he did address visiting delegations from his front porch in Marion, Ohio. It was impossible to tell where he stood on the League issue, but he struck a responsive chord in many people when he urged that the nation should abandon heroics, nostrums, and experiments, and return to what he called normalcy. Cox and Roosevelt traveled extensively, speaking mostly in support of the League. Many found neither presidential candidate impressive.

The Election

Harding received 16,152,200 popular votes, 61 percent of the total, for 404 electoral votes. Cox received 9,147,353 popular votes for 127 electoral votes. Socialist candidate Eugene V. Debs, in federal prison in Atlanta for an Espionage Act conviction, received 919,799 votes. The Democrats carried only states in the Solid South, and even there lost Tennessee. It appears that people voted Republican more as a repudiation of Wilson's domestic policies than as a referendum on the League. Wilson had alienated German Americans, Irish Americans, antiwar progressives, civil libertarians, and midwestern farmers, all groups that had given the Democrats considerable support in 1916.

The Twenties: Economic Advances and Social Tensions

The Recession of 1920–1921

The United States experienced a severe recession from mid-1920 until the end of 1921. Europe returned to normal and reduced its purchases in America, and domestic demand for goods not available in wartime was filled. Prices fell and unemployment exceeded 12 percent in 1921.

Prosperity and Industrial Productivity

Though overall the economy was strong between 1922 and 1929, certain sectors—notably agriculture—did not share in the nation's general prosperity. Improved industrial efficiency, which resulted in lower prices for goods, was primarily responsible. Manufacturing output increased about 65 percent, and productivity, or output per hour of work, increased about 40 percent. The number of industrial workers actually decreased from 9 million to 8.8 million during the decade. The increased productivity resulted from improved machinery, which in turn came about for several reasons. Industry changed from steam to electric power, allowing the design of more intricate machines that replaced the work of human hands. By 1929, 70 percent of industrial power came from electricity. The moving assembly line, first introduced by Henry Ford in the automobile industry in 1913 and 1914, was widely adopted. Scientific management, exemplified by the time and motion studies pioneered by Frederick W. Taylor before the war, led to more efficient use of workers and lower labor costs. Larger firms began, for the first time, to fund major research and development activities to find new and improved products, reduce production costs, and utilize by-products.

TEST TIP

Typically, one group of free-response questions will allow you to choose between two questions relating to the Age of Exploration to just before the Civil War, and the other between two questions relating to the Civil War onward. Expect to discuss two completely separate periods of U.S. history in your two essay responses.

The Automobile

The principal driving force of the economy of the 1920s was the automobile. There were 8,131,522 motor vehicles registered in the United States in 1920, and 26,704,825 in 1929. Annual output of automobiles reached 3.6 million in 1923 and remained at about that level throughout the decade. By 1925 the price of a Ford Model T had been reduced to $290, less than three months' pay for an average worker. Ford plants produced 9,000 Model Ts per day, and Henry Ford cleared about $25,000 a day throughout the decade. Just as information technology has been credited with enhancing, and even driving, innovation and productivity growth in the economy of early twenty-first-century America, Henry Ford's use of electric motors to power automobile assembly lines led to the revamping of a major production process. In turn, automobile manufacturing stimulated supporting industries such as steel, rubber, and glass, as well as gasoline refining and highway construction. It was during the 1920s that the United States became a nation of paved roads. Mileage of paved roads increased from 387,000 miles in 1921, most of which was in urban areas, to 662,000 in 1929. Highway construction costs averaged over $1 billion a year in the late 1920s, in part due to the Federal Highway Act of 1916, which started the federal highway system and gave matching funds to the states for construction. One estimate stated that the automobile industry directly or indirectly employed 3.7 million people in 1929.

Other Leading Industries

The electrical industry also expanded rapidly during the 1920s. The demand for power for industrial machinery as well as for business and lighting increased dramatically, and a host of electrical appliances such as stoves, vacuum cleaners, refrigerators, toasters, and radios became available. About two-thirds of American homes had electricity by 1929, leaving only those in rural areas without it. Home and business construction also experienced a boom from 1922 until 1928. Other large industries that grew rapidly were chemicals and printing. The movie industry expanded rapidly, especially after the introduction of sound films, or "talkies," and employed about 325,000 people by 1930. New industries that began in the period were radio and commercial aviation.

Consumer Credit and Advertising

Unlike earlier boom periods which had involved large expenditures for capital investments such as railroads and factories, the prosperity of the 1920s hinged on the sale of consumer products. Purchases of "big ticket" items such as automobiles, refrigerators, and furniture were made possible by installment, or time payment, credit. The idea was not new, but the availability of consumer credit expanded tremendously during the 1920s. Consumer interest and demand was spurred by a great increase in professional advertising using newspapers, magazines, radio, billboards, and other media. By 1929, advertising expenditures reached $3.4 billion, more than was spent on education at all levels that year.

The Dominance of Big Business

There was a trend toward corporate consolidation during the 1920s. By 1929, the 200 largest corporations held 49 percent of the corporate wealth and received 43 percent of corporate income. The top 5 percent of the corporations in the nation received about 85 percent of the corporate income. Corporate profits and dividends increased about 65 percent during the decade. In most fields, an oligopoly of two to four firms dominated, exemplified by the automobile industry, where Ford, General Motors, and Chrysler produced 83 percent of the nation's vehicles in 1929. Firms in many fields formed trade associations that represented their interests to the public and the government, and which claimed to stabilize each industry. Government regulatory agencies, such as the Federal Trade Commission and the Interstate Commerce Commission, were passive and generally controlled by persons from the business world. The public generally accepted the situation and viewed businesspeople with respect. Illustrating the attitudes of the time, *The Man Nobody Knows,* a book by advertising executive Bruce Barton, published in

1925, became a best-seller. It described Jesus as the founder of modern business and his apostles as an exemplary business management team.

Banking and Finance

As with other industries, banking saw a trend toward consolidation. Bank assets increased about 66 percent from 1919 to 1929. There was growth in branch banking, and in 1929, 3.2 percent of the banks with branch operations controlled 46 percent of the banking resources. Because corporations were raising much of their money through the sale of stocks and bonds, the demand for business loans declined. Commercial banks then put more of their funds into real estate loans, loans to brokers against stocks and bonds, and the purchase of stocks and bonds themselves. By doing so they made themselves vulnerable to economic disaster when the Depression began in late 1929. Even during the prosperous 1920s, 5,714 banks failed, most of them in rural areas or in Florida. Banks in operation in 1929 numbered 25,568.

Labor

The National Association of Manufacturers and its state affiliates began a drive in 1920 to restore the "open shop," or nonunion, workplace. As an alternative, firms sought to provide job satisfaction so that the workers would not want a union. Company-sponsored pension and insurance plans, stock purchase plans, efforts to ensure worker safety and comfort, social and sporting events, and company magazines were undertaken. Company unions, designed to give workers some voice with management under company control, were organized by 317 firms. The American Federation of Labor and other unions, which had prospered during World War I, found themselves on the defensive. Leaders, especially William Green, president of the American Federation of Labor after 1924, were conservative and nonaggressive. Union membership dropped about 20 percent, from five million to about four million, during the decade. The most violent labor confrontations occurred in the mining and Southern textile industries. The United Mine Workers of America, headed by John L. Lewis, was involved in bitter strikes in Pennsylvania, West Virginia, Kentucky, and Illinois, but by 1929 had lost most of its power. The United Textile Workers failed to organize southern textile workers in a campaign from 1927 to 1929, but violent strikes occurred in Tennessee, North Carolina, and Virginia.

The Farm Problem

Farmers did not share in the prosperity of the twenties. Farm prices had been high during World War I because of European demand and government price fixing. By 1920,

European demand had dropped considerably, and farm prices were determined by a free market. Farm income dropped from $10 billion annually in 1919 to about $4 billion in 1921, and then leveled off at about $7 billion a year from 1923 through 1929. During the same period, farm expenses rose with the cost of more sophisticated machinery and a greater use of chemical fertilizers.

American Society in the 1920s

Population

During the 1920s, the population of the U.S. increased by 16.1 percent, from 105,710,620 in 1920 to 122,775,046 in 1930, a lower rate of growth than in previous decades. The birthrate was also lower than in former times, dropping from 27.7 per 100,000 in 1920 to 21.3 per 100,000 in 1930. About 88 percent of the people were white.

Urbanization

In 1920, for the first time a majority of Americans—51 percent—lived in an urban place with a population of 2,500 or more. By 1930 the figure had increased to 56 percent. In terms of Standard Metropolitan Areas (SMA), which the Census Bureau defined as areas with central cities and a population of at least 50,000, 44 percent of the people lived in an SMA in 1920, and 50 percent in 1930. Farm residents dropped from 26 percent of the total population in 1920 to 21 percent in 1930. A new phenomenon of the 1920s was the tremendous growth of suburbs and satellite cities, which grew more rapidly than the central cities. Streetcars, commuter railroads, and automobiles contributed to the process, as well as the easy availability of financing for home construction. The suburbs had once been the domain of the wealthy, but the technology of the twenties opened them to working-class families.

The Standard of Living

Improved technology and urbanization led to a sharp rise in the standard of living. Urban living improved access to electricity, natural gas, telephones, and piped water. Two-thirds of American homes had electricity by 1929. The use of indoor plumbing, hot water, and central heating increased dramatically. Conveniences such as electric stoves, vacuum cleaners, refrigerators, washing machines, toasters, and irons made life less burdensome. Improved machinery produced better-fitting and more comfortable ready-made clothing and shoes. Diet improved as the consumption of fresh vegetables increased 45 percent and canned vegetables 35 percent. Sales of citrus fruit and canned fruit were also up. Correspondingly, per capita consumption of wheat, corn, and potatoes fell. Automobiles, radios, phonographs, and commercial entertainment added to the enjoyment of life. Yet enjoyment of the new standard of living was uneven. The one-third of the households which still did not have electricity in 1929 lacked access to many of the new products. For those who had access, the new standard of living required more money than had been necessary in former times. Despite heavy sales of appliances, by 1929 only 25 percent of American families had vacuum cleaners, and only 20 percent had electric toasters. The real income of workers increased about 11 percent during the decade, but the benefits of prosperity were not spread evenly across the nation. It is estimated that the bottom 93 percent of the population actually saw a 4 percent drop in real disposable per capita income from 1923 to 1929. In 1929, about 12 million families, or 43 percent of the total, had annual incomes under $1,500, which was considered by many to be the poverty line. About 20 million families, or 72 percent, had incomes under $2,500, the family income deemed necessary for a decent standard of living with reasonable comforts.

The Sexual Revolution

Traditional American moral standards regarding premarital sex and marital fidelity were widely questioned for the first time during the 1920s. There was a popular misunderstanding by people who had not read his works that Sigmund Freud had advocated sexual promiscuity. Movies, novels, and magazine stories were more sexually explicit and sensational. The "flaming youth" of the "Jazz Age" emphasized sexual promiscuity and drinking, as well as new forms of dancing considered erotic by the older generation. The automobile, by giving people mobility and privacy, was generally considered to have contributed to sexual license. Journalists wrote about "flappers," young women who were independent, assertive, and promiscuous. Birth control, though illegal, was promoted by Margaret Sanger and others, and was widely accepted. The sexual revolution occurred mostly among some urban dwellers, middle class people, and students, who were an economically select group at the time. Still, many continued to adhere to the old ways.

The flapper, a young woman of the 1920s, became a symbol of a decade of freedom for American women. (U.S. Library of Congress)

Women

Many feminists believed that the passage of the 19th Amendment in 1920 providing for woman suffrage would solve all problems for women. When it became apparent that woman did not vote as a block, political leaders gave little additional attention to the special concerns of women. The sexual revolution brought some emancipation. Woman adopted less bulky clothing, with short skirts and bare arms and necks. They could smoke and socialize with men in public more freely than before. Birth control was more acceptable. Divorce laws were liberalized in many states at the insistence of women. In 1920, there was one divorce for every 7.5 marriages. By 1929, the ratio had narrowed to 1 in 6. The number of employed women rose from 8.4 million in 1920 to 10.6 million in 1929, but the total workforce increased in about the same proportion. Black and foreign-born women comprised 57 percent of the female workforce, and domestic service was the largest job category. Most other women workers were in traditional female occupations such as secretarial and clerical work, retail sales, teaching, and nursing.

Rates of pay were below those for men. Most women still pursued the traditional role of housewife and mother, and society still accepted that as the norm.

Blacks

The migration of southern rural blacks to the cities continued, with about 1.5 million moving during the 1920s. By 1930 about 20 percent of blacks lived in the North, with the largest concentrations in New York, Chicago, and Philadelphia. While they were generally better off economically in the cities than they had been as tenant farmers, they tended to hold low-paying jobs and were confined to segregated areas of the cities. The Harlem section of New York City, with a black population of 73,000 in 1920 and 165,000 in 1930, was the largest black urban community and became the center for black writers, musicians, and intellectuals. Blacks throughout the country developed jazz and blues as music forms that enjoyed widespread popularity. This cultural movement came to be known as the Harlem Renaisssance and is usually described as lasting from 1919 to the 1930s. W. E. B. DuBois, the editor of *The Crisis,* continued to call for integration and to attack segregation despite his disappointment with the lack of progress after World War I. The National Association for the Advancement of Colored People was a conservative yet active voice for civil rights, and the National Urban League concentrated on employment and economic advancement. Lynchings continued in the South, and the often violent anti-black activities of the Ku Klux Klan are mentioned under the section on Social Conflicts later in this chapter.

Marcus Garvey

A native of Jamaica, Marcus Garvey founded the Universal Negro Improvement Association there in 1914, and moved to New York in 1916. He advocated black racial pride and separatism rather than integration, and a return of blacks to Africa. Some of his ideas soon alienated the older black organizations. He developed a large following, especially among Southern blacks, but his claim of six million members in 1923 may be inflated. An advocate of black economic self-sufficiency, he urged his followers to buy only from blacks, and founded a chain of businesses, including grocery stores, restaurants, and laundries. In 1921, he proclaimed himself the provisional president of an African empire and sold stock in the Black Star Steamship Line, which would take migrants to Africa. The line went bankrupt in 1923, Garvey was convicted and imprisoned for mail fraud in the sale of the line's stock, and then deported. His legacy was an emphasis on black pride and self-respect.

Mexicans and Puerto Ricans

Mexicans had long migrated to the southwestern part of the United States as agricultural laborers, but in the 1920s they began to settle in cities such as Los Angeles, San Antonio, and Denver. Like other immigrants, they held low-paying jobs and lived in poor neighborhoods, that they called "barrios." The 1920s also saw the first large migration of Puerto Ricans to the mainland, mostly to New York City. There they were employed in manufacturing, in service industries such as restaurants, and in domestic work. They lived in barrios in Brooklyn and Manhattan.

TEST TIP

You have the option to cancel your score on any AP exam, meaning that the score is permanently removed from your score report and thus not provided to any colleges or universities. You may even request that the test never be scored by submitting the cancellation form within 30 days of the test date. However, consider doing this only if an illness or some other unexpected mishap prevents you from completing your exam. You'll probably have done better than you think!

Education

Free elementary education was available to most students in 1920, except for many black children. Growth of elementary schools in the 1920s reflected population growth and the addition of kindergartens. High school education became more available, and the number of public secondary schools doubled, from 2.2 million in 1920 to 4.4 million in 1930. High school instruction shifted from an emphasis on college preparation to include vocational education, which was funded in part by the Smith-Hughes Act of 1917; this act provided federal funding for agricultural and technical studies, including home economics. There was also a substantial growth in enrollment in higher education, from 600,000 in 1920 to 1.1 million in 1930.

Religion

Church and synagogue membership increased more rapidly than the population during the 1920s, despite much religious tension and conflict. Most Protestants had been divided North and South since before the Civil War. By the 1920s, there was another major division between the modernists who accommodated their thinking with modern biblical criticism and evolution, and fundamentalists who stressed the literal truth of the Bible and creationism. There was also division on social issues such as support of labor. The only issue that united most Protestants, except Lutherans, was prohibition. The

Roman Catholic Church and Jewish congregations were assimilating the large number of immigrants who had arrived prior to 1922. They also found themselves under attack from the Ku Klux Klan and immigration restrictions.

Popular Culture

The trend whereby entertainment shifted from the home and small social groups to commercial profit-making activities had begun in the late nineteenth century and reached maturity in the 1920s. Spending for entertainment in 1929 was $4.3 billion. The movies attracted the most consumer interest and generated the most money. Movie attendance averaged 40 million a week in 1922 and 90 million a week in 1929. Introduction of sound with *The Jazz Singer* in 1927 generated even more interest. Stars like Douglas Fairbanks, Gloria Swanson, Rudolph Valentino, Clara Bow, and Charlie Chaplin were tremendously popular. Americans spent ten times more on movies than on all sports, the next attraction in popularity. It was considered the golden age of major-league baseball, with an attendance increase of over 50 percent during the decade. Millions followed the exploits of George Herman "Babe" Ruth and other stars. Boxing was popular and made Jack Dempsey and others famous. College football began to attract attention with Knute Rockne coaching at Notre Dame and Harold "Red" Grange playing for the University of Illinois. When Grange signed with the Chicago Bears in 1926, professional football began to grow in popularity. Commercial radio began when station KDKA in Pittsburgh broadcasted the election results in November 1920. By 1929, over 10 million families, more than one-third of all families, had radios. National network broadcasting began when the National Broadcasting Company was organized in 1926, followed by the Columbia Broadcasting System in 1927. Radio was free entertainment and paid for by advertising. Despite the many new diversions, Americans continued to read, and millions of popular magazines were sold each week. Popular books of the period included the Tarzan series and Zane Grey's stories of the Western frontier, as well as literary works, some of which are mentioned under Literary Trends below.

Literary Trends

Many talented writers of the 1920s were disgusted with the hypocrisy and materialism of contemporary American society, and expressed their concern in their works. Often called the "Lost Generation," many of them, such as novelists Ernest Hemingway and F. Scott Fitzgerald and poets Ezra Pound and T.S. Eliot, moved to Europe. Authors and the works that typified the period include Hemingway's *The Sun Also Rises* (1926) and *A Farewell to Arms* (1929); Sinclair Lewis's *Babbitt* (1922), *Arrowsmith* (1925), and *Elmer Gantry* (1927); F. Scott Fitzgerald's *The Great Gatsby* (1925) and *Tender Is the Night* (1929); John Dos Passos's *Three Soldiers* (1921); and Thomas Wolfe's *Look*

Homeward, Angel (1929). H. L. Mencken, a journalist who began publication of the *American Mercury* magazine in 1922, ceaselessly attacked the "booboisie," as he called middle-class America, but his literary talent did not match the leading literary lights of the period.

Social Conflicts

A Conflict of Values

The rapid technological changes represented by the automobile, the revolution in morals, and the rapid urbanization with many immigrants and blacks inhabiting the growing cities brought a strong reaction from white Protestant Americans of older stock who saw their traditional values gravely threatened. In many ways, their concerns continued the emotions of wartime hysteria and the Red Scare. The traditionalists were largely residents of rural areas and small towns, and the clash of farm values with those of an industrial society of urban workers was evident. The traditionalist backlash against modern urban industrial society expressed itself primarily through intolerance.

The Ku Klux Klan

On Thanksgiving Day in 1915, William J. Simmons founded the Knights of the Ku Klux Klan, modeled on the organization of the same name in the 1860s and 1870s, near Atlanta. Its purpose was mainly to intimidate blacks, who were experiencing an apparent rise in status during World War I. The Klan remained small until 1920 when two advertising experts, Edward Y. Clark and Elizabeth Tyler, were hired by the leadership. Clark and Tyler used modern advertising to recruit members, charged a $10 initiation fee of which they received $2.50, and made additional money from the sale of regalia and emblems. By 1923, the Klan had about five million members throughout the nation. The largest concentrations of members were in the South, the Southwest, the Midwest, California, and Oregon. The use of white hoods, masks, and robes, and secret rituals and jargon, seemed to appeal mostly to lower-middle-class men in towns and small cities. The Klan stood for "100 percent pure Americanism" to preserve "native, white, Protestant supremacy."

DIDYOUKNOW?

Released in 1915, D.W. Griffith's overtly racist silent film *The Birth of a Nation* helped relaunch the Ku Klux Klan. The combination of the film's controversial subject matter and numerous technical innovations made it one of the most talked-about movies of its era.

It opposed blacks and Catholics primarily. In addition, Jews and the foreign-born were often its targets. It also attacked bootleggers, drunkards, gamblers, and adulterers for violating moral standards. The Klan's methods of repression included cross burnings, tar and featherings, kidnappings, lynchings, and burnings. The Klan was not a political party, but it endorsed and opposed candidates, and exerted considerable control over elections and politicians in at least nine states. The Klan began to decline after 1925 when it was hit by scandals, especially the murder conviction of Indiana Grand Dragon David Stephenson. The main reason for its decline was the staunch opposition of courageous editors, politicians, and other public figures who exposed its lawlessness and terrorism in the face of great personal danger. Many historians see the Klan as the American expression of fascism, which was making headway in Italy, Germany, and other European nations during the twenties.

Immigration Restriction

There had been calls for immigration restriction since the late nineteenth century. Labor leaders believed that immigrants depressed wages and impeded unionization. Some progressives believed that they created social problems. In June 1917, Congress, over Wilson's veto, had imposed a literacy test for immigrants and excluded many Asian nationalities. During World War I and the Red Scare, almost all immigrants were considered radicals and communists, and the tradition was quickly picked up by the Klan. With bad economic conditions in postwar Europe, over 1.3 million immigrants came to the United States during 1919 through 1921. As in the period before the war, they were mostly from southern and eastern Europe and mostly Catholics and Jews, the groups most despised by nativist Americans. In 1921, Congress quickly passed the Emergency Quota Act, which limited immigration by nation to three percent of the number of foreign-born persons from that nation who resided in the United States in 1910. In practice, the law admitted about as many as wanted to come from such nations as Britain, Ireland, and Germany, while severely restricting Italians, Greeks, Poles, and eastern European Jews. It became effective in 1922 and reduced the number of immigrants annually to about 40 percent of the 1921 total. Congress then passed the National Origins Act of 1924 which set the quotas at two percent of the number of foreign-born persons of that nationality in the United States in 1890, excluded all Asians, and imposed an annual maximum of 164,000.

Immigration from Western Hemisphere nations, including Canada and Mexico, was not limited. The law further reduced the number of southern and eastern Europeans, and cut the annual immigration to 20 percent of the 1921 figure. In 1927, the annual maximum was reduced to 150,000. The quotas were not fully calculated and implemented until 1929. Objections to the law were not aimed at the idea of restriction but at the designation of certain nationalities and religious groups as undesirable. The law was resented by such groups as Italian- and Polish-Americans.

With the passage of the 18th Amendment, law enforcement efforts focused on destroying illegal alcohol. In most urban areas, the efforts failed. (Wikimedia Commons)

Prohibition

The 18th Amendment, which prohibited the manufacture, sale, or transportation of intoxicating liquors, took effect in January 1920. It was implemented by the Volstead Act, which was signed into law in October 1919. It defined intoxicating beverages as containing one-half of 1 percent alcohol by volume and imposed criminal penalties for violations. Many states had authorized the sale of light beer, believing that it was not covered by the amendment, but Anti-Saloon League lobbyists pushed through the Volstead Act. Many historians believe that prohibition of hard liquor might have been successful if light wine and beer had been allowed. As things turned out, the inexpensive light beverages were less available, and expensive illegal hard liquor was readily available.

Enforcement of prohibition was reasonably effective in some rural southern and midwestern states that had been dry before the amendment. In urban areas where both foreign-born and native citizens often believed that their liberty had been infringed upon, neither the public nor their elected officials were interested in enforcement. Speakeasies, supposedly secret bars operated by bootleggers, replaced the saloons. Smuggled liquor flowed across the boundaries and coastlines of the nation, and thousands undertook the manufacture of "bathtub gin" and similar beverages. Organized crime, which previously had been involved mainly with prostitution and gambling, grew tremendously to meet the demand. Al Capone of Chicago was perhaps the most famous of the bootlegging gangsters. The automobile was used both to transport liquor and to take customers to speakeasies. Women, who had not gone to saloons in the pre-prohibition period, frequented speakeasies and began to drink in public. By the mid-1920s, the nation was badly divided on the prohibition issue. Support continued from rural areas and almost all Republican office-holders. The Democrats were divided between the urban northerners who advocated repeal, and rural, especially Southern, Democrats who supported prohibition. Some people who originally favored prohibition changed their views because of the public hypocrisy and criminal activity it caused.

TEST TIP

Although there is no minimum number of words for the free-choice essay response, your answer needs to be long and detailed enough to fully answer the question. Consider writing a standard five-paragraph essay—one intro paragraph giving your thesis, three paragraphs of supporting information and examples, and one concluding paragraph summarizing your ideas and restating your thesis—to make sure that you provide enough information in your response.

Creationism and the Scopes Trial

Fundamentalist Protestants, under the leadership of William Jennings Bryan, began a campaign in 1921 to prohibit the teaching of evolution in the schools and thus protect the belief in the literal biblical account of creation. The idea was especially well received in the South. In 1925, the Tennessee legislature passed a law that forbade any teacher in the state's schools or colleges to teach evolution. The American Civil Liberties Union found a young high school biology teacher, John Thomas Scopes, who was willing to bring about a test case by deliberately breaking the law. Scopes was tried in Dayton, Tennessee, in July 1925. Bryan came to assist the prosecution, and Chicago trial lawyer Clarence Darrow defended Scopes. The trial attracted national attention through newspaper and radio coverage. The judge refused to allow expert testimony, so the trial was a duel of words between Darrow and Bryan. As was expected, Scopes was convicted and fined $100. Bryan died of exhaustion a few days after the trial. Both sides claimed a moral victory. The anti-evolution crusaders continued their efforts, and secured enactment of a statute in Mississippi in 1926. They failed after a bitter fight in North Carolina in 1927 and in several other states until Arkansas in 1928 passed an anti-evolution law by use of the initiative.

Clarence Darrow and William Jennings Bryan, 1925. (AP/Wide World Photo)

The Scopes "Monkey" Trial

One of the most famous trials of the 20th century took place in the tiny rural town of Dayton, Tennessee, in the summer of 1925. The trial of John Scopes pitted two of America's leading lawyers in a test of the Butler Act, which forbade the teaching of "any theory that denies the story of the Divine Creation of man as taught in the Bible, and to teach instead that man has descended from a lower order of animals." William Jennings Bryan, a three-time losing candidate for President and former U.S. Secretary of State led the prosecution of Scopes, while Clarence Darrow, perhaps the most famous defense attorney of his time, provided the defense.

When the Tennessee state legislature passed the Butler Act in March 1925, it was seen by most as more of a statement of support for religious fundamentalism rather than a practical educational law that would be enforced. The fine for breaking the law was to be no more than $500. The American Civil Liberties Union, however, decided to test the law and sought a teacher to challenge it. They found him in John T. Scopes, a 24-year-old football coach in Dayton, who also sometimes taught biology, using Hunter's *Civic Biology* as his textbook. Scopes agreed to test the case, was arrested for violating the Butler Act, and the battle began.

Dayton, with a population of 1,800 residents, mostly farmers, became the focus of the nation that summer. Besides Bryan and Darrow, H. L. Mencken, a reporter for *The Baltimore Sun* and a leading cultural critic, covered the trial, as did more than 100 newspapers. Many saw the entire spectacle as a publicity stunt. Mencken referred to the residents of Dayton as "yokels" and "morons." This was the first trial ever broadcast on radio, with station WGN of Chicago providing coverage.

Bryan, however, took the issues of the Scopes trial very seriously. He was perhaps the leading spokesman for fundamentalism, which accepted a literal interpretation of the Bible. This included the account of creation in the book of Genesis, which describes all of the universe as having been created in six days. Bryan viewed the teaching of Charles Darwin—who in his landmark book *Origin of Species* proposed that all plant and animal life, including humans, evolved over time—as an attack on the Bible and God.

(Continued on next page)

Sacco and Vanzetti

On April 15, 1920, two unidentified gunmen robbed a shoe factory and killed two men in South Braintree, Massachusetts. Nicola Sacco and Bartolomeo Vanzetti, Italian immigrants and admitted anarchists, were tried for murder. Judge Webster Thayer clearly favored the prosecution, which based its case on the political radicalism of the defendants. After they were convicted and sentenced to death in July 1921, there was much protest in the United States and in Europe that they had not received a fair trial. After six years of delays, they were executed on August 23, 1927. A debate on their innocence and the possible perversion of American justice continued long afterward. Massachusetts Governor Michael Dukakis ultimately vindicated the men in 1977.

Opposing Bryan was a team that included Darrow, a towering figure of the 20th century. An open agnostic, Darrow responded to an appeal by the American Civil Liberties Union to assist in Scopes' defense. The verdict was never in question: Scopes would be found guilty. After all, all but one of the jurors were church members. The town was firmly in opposition to Scopes, Darrow, and Darwin. Darrow's early strategy was to minimize the difference between evolution and the creation account in Genesis, using the written testimony of evolution experts.

As the trial progressed, however, the focus turned to Bryan. Defense counsel Darrow asked to cross-examine prosecution counsel Bryan, a very unorthodox procedure. Darrow's purpose was to suggest that belief in the historical accuracy and the miracles of the Bible was unreasonable in an age of modern science. Darrow questioned the story of Jonah and the whale, Joshua causing the earth to stand still, and Bishop James Ussher's contention that creation occurred in 4004 B.C.E. Darrow accused Bryan of insulting "every man of science and learning in the world because he does not believe in your fool religion." Bryan shot back that the purpose of the defense attack was "to cast ridicule on anyone who believed in the Bible." The questioning of Bryan by Darrow lasted for two hours on the trial's seventh day. The next morning the judge ruled the entire examination of Bryan irrelevant to the case and that it would be removed from the trial's records. Darrow then changed Scopes's plea to guilty, thus preventing Bryan from delivering a closing statement, which would amount to a speech opposing evolution. Scopes was found guilty after nine minutes of jury deliberation and fined $100. The defense team appealed the decision and the Tennessee Supreme Court overturned the conviction on a technicality, though it supported the constitutionality of the Butler Act, which remained on the books in Tennessee until 1967.

The Scopes trial was the first legal challenge to the teaching of evolution in public schools. Despite the Butler Act, evolution continued to be taught in biology classes in Tennessee. Scopes abandoned teaching after the trial and studied geology at the University of Chicago. While the Scopes trial was a 1925 Tennessee event, the evolution versus creation argument still rages across the nation. In 1968, the U.S. Supreme Court ruled in *Epperson v. Arkansas* that evolution can be taught in public schools because it is a science, but creationism cannot be taught, because it constitutes religious teaching. Bryan and Darrow provided the first major confrontation in a debate that continues today.

Government and Politics in the 1920s: The Harding Administration

Warren G. Harding

Harding was a handsome and amiable man of limited intellectual and organizational abilities. He had spent much of his life as the publisher of a newspaper in the small city of Marion, Ohio. He recognized his limitations but hoped to be a much-loved president. He showed compassion by pardoning socialist Eugene V. Debs for his conviction under the Espionage Act and inviting him to dinner at the White House. He also persuaded U.S. Steel to give workers the eight-hour day. A convivial man, he liked to drink and play poker with his friends, and kept the White House stocked with bootleg liquor despite prohibition. He was accused of keeping a mistress, Nan Britton. His economic philosophy was conservative.

Tax Reduction

Former banker and influential Secretary of the Treasury Andrew Mellon believed in low taxes and government economy to free the rich from "oppressive" taxes and thus encourage investment. The farm bloc of Midwestern Republicans and Southern Democrats in Congress prevented cuts in the higher tax brackets as great as Mellon recommended. The Revenue Acts of 1921 and 1924 cut the maximum tax rates to 50 percent and then to 40 percent. Taxes in lower brackets were also reduced, but inheritance and corporate income taxes were retained. Despite the cuts, Mellon was able to reduce the federal debt by an average of $500 million a year.

The Fordney-McCumber Tariff

Mellon sought substantial increases in the tariffs, but again there was a compromise with the farm bloc. The Fordney-McCumber Tariff of September 1922 imposed high rates on farm products and protected such infant industries as rayon, china, toys, and chemicals. Most other items received moderate protection, and a few items, including farm equipment, were duty-free. The president could raise or lower rates to a limit of 50 percent on recommendation of the Tariff Commission. The average rate was about 33 percent, compared with about 26 percent under the previous tariff.

The Harding Scandals

Harding apparently was completely honest, but several of his friends whom he appointed to office became involved in major financial scandals. Most of the information about the scandals did not become public knowledge until after Harding's death.

The Teapot Dome scandal began when Secretary of the Interior Albert B. Fall in 1921 secured the transfer of several naval oil reserves to his jurisdiction. In 1922, he secretly leased reserves at Teapot Dome in Wyoming to Harry F. Sinclair of Monmouth Oil and at Elk Hills in California to Edward Doheny of Pan-American Petroleum. A Senate investigation later revealed that Sinclair had given Fall $305,000 in cash and bonds and a herd of cattle, while Doheny had given him a $100,000 unsecured loan. Sinclair and Doheny were acquitted of charges of defrauding the government, but Fall was convicted, fined, and imprisoned for bribery.

Scandal also tainted Attorney General Harry M. Daugherty who, through his intimate friend Jesse Smith, took bribes from bootleggers, income tax evaders, and others in return for protection from prosecution. When the scandal began to come to light, Smith committed suicide in Daugherty's Washington apartment in May 1923. There was also evidence that Daugherty received money for using his influence in returning the American Metal Company, seized by the government during the war, to its German owners.

DIDYOUKNOW?

Scholars routinely rank Warren G. Harding as one of the nation's very worst presidents, alongside such dismal leaders as James Buchanan—widely considered the president who failed to prevent the Civil War—and Andrew Johnson, the first of only two presidents to undergo the impeachment process.

Harding's Death

Depressed by the first news of the scandals, Harding left in June 1923 for an extended trip that included a tour of Alaska. On his return to California, he died of an apparent heart attack on August 2, 1923. Rumors of foul play or suicide persisted for years.

Coolidge Becomes President

Vice President Calvin Coolidge became president to complete Harding's term. As the scandals of the deceased president's administration came to light, Coolidge was able to avoid responsibility for them. He had a reputation for honesty, although he did not remove Daugherty from the Cabinet until March 1924.

The Election of 1924

The Republicans

In the 1924 presidential campaign, Progressive insurgents failed to capture the Republican convention. Calvin Coolidge was nominated on the first ballot with Charles G. Dawes as his running mate. The platform endorsed business development, low taxes, and rigid economy in government. The party stood on its record of economic growth and prosperity since 1922.

The Democrats

The party had an opportunity to draw farmers and labor into a new progressive coalition. An attractive Democratic candidate would have had a good chance against the bland Coolidge and the Harding scandals. Instead, two wings of the party battled to exhaustion at the convention. The Eastern wing, led by Governor Alfred E. Smith of New York, wanted the platform to favor repeal of prohibition and to condemn the Ku Klux Klan. Southern and Western delegates, led by William G. McAdoo and William Jennings Bryan, narrowly defeated both proposals. Smith and McAdoo contested for 103 ballots with neither receiving the two-thirds necessary for nomination. John W. Davis, a conservative Wall Street lawyer, was finally chosen as a dark horse, with Charles W. Bryan, brother of William Jennings, as the vice presidential candidate. The platform favored a lower tariff but otherwise was similar to the Republican document.

The Progressives

Robert M. La Follette, after failing in a bid for the Republican nomination, formed a new Progressive Party with support from midwestern farm groups, socialists, and the American Federation of Labor. The platform attacked monopolies and called for the nationalization of railroads, the direct election of the president, and other reforms.

The Campaign

Neither Coolidge nor Davis were active or effective campaigners. Republican publicity concentrated on attacking La Follette as a communist. La Follette campaigned vigorously, but he lacked money and was disliked by many for his 1917 opposition to entrance into World War I.

The Election

Coolidge received 15,725,016 votes and 382 electoral votes, more than his two opponents combined. Davis received 8,385,586 votes and 136 electoral votes, while La Follette had 4,822,856 votes and 13 electoral votes from his home state of Wisconsin.

The Coolidge Administration

Calvin Coolidge

Coolidge was a dour and taciturn man. Born in Vermont, his adult life and political career were spent in Massachusetts. "The business of the United States is business," he proclaimed, and "the man who builds a factory builds a temple." His philosophy of life was stated in the remark that "four-fifths of all our troubles in this world would disappear if only we would sit down and keep still." Liberal political commentator Walter Lippmann wrote that "Mr. Coolidge's genius for inactivity is developed to a very high point." He intentionally provided no presidential leadership.

DIDYOUKNOW?

Coolidge's preference for brevity earned him the nickname "Silent Cal." Nevertheless, over the years he has become known for a certain dry wit. When asked about the burdens of the presidency, he once famously replied, "Oh, I don't know. There are only so many hours in the day, and one can do the best he can in the time he's got. When I was mayor of Northampton I was pretty busy most of the time, and I don't seem to be much busier here."

The McNary-Haugen Bill

In 1921, farm machinery manufacturers George Peek and Hugh S. Johnson developed a plan to raise prices for basic farm products. The government would buy and resell in the domestic market a commodity such as wheat at the world price plus the tariff. The surplus would be sold abroad at the world price, and the difference made up by an equalization fee on all farmers in proportion to the amount of the commodity they had sold. When farm conditions did not improve, the idea was incorporated in the McNary-Haugen Bill, which passed Congress in 1927 and 1928, but was vetoed by Coolidge both times. The plan was a forerunner of the agricultural programs of the 1930s.

Veterans' Bonus

Legislation to give veterans of World War I 20-year endowment policies with values based on their length of service was passed over Coolidge's veto in 1924. This decision, which meant veterans could not collect their bonuses until 1945, came to haunt the Republicans in 1932 when the Bonus Army marched on Washington demanding their due as they faced the Great Depression.

The Election of 1928

The Republicans

Coolidge did not seek another term, and the convention quickly nominated Herbert Hoover, the secretary of commerce, for president, with Charles Curtis as his running mate. The platform endorsed the policies of the Harding and Coolidge administrations.

The Democrats

Governor Alfred E. Smith of New York, a Catholic and an anti-prohibitionist, controlled most of the non-southern delegations. Southerners supported his nomination with the understanding that the platform would not advocate repeal of prohibition. Senator Joseph T. Robinson of Arkansas, a Protestant and a prohibitionist, was the vice presidential candidate. The platform differed little from that of the Republicans, except in advocating lower tariffs.

The Campaign

Hoover asserted that Republican policies would end poverty in the country. Smith was also economically conservative, but he attacked prohibition and bigotry. He was met in the South by a massive campaign headed by Bishop James Cannon, Jr., of the Methodist Episcopal Church South, attacking him as a Catholic and a wet.

The Election

Hoover received 21,392,190 votes and 444 electoral votes, carrying all of the North except Massachusetts and Rhode Island, and seven states in the Solid South. Smith had 15,016,443 votes and 87 electoral votes in eight states.

Foreign Policy in the Twenties

The Washington Conference

At the invitation of Secretary of State Charles Evans Hughes, representatives of the United States, Great Britain, France, Japan, Italy, China, the Netherlands, Belgium, and Portugal met in Washington in August 1921 to discuss naval limitations and Asian affairs. Three treaties resulted from the conference.

The Five-Power Treaty, signed in February 1922, committed the United States, Britain, Japan, France, and Italy to end new construction of capital naval vessels, to scrap some ships, and to maintain a ratio of 5:5:3:1.67:1.67 for tonnage of capital or major ships in order of the nations listed. Hughes did not realize that the treaty gave Japan naval supremacy in the Pacific.

The Nine-Power Treaty was signed by all of the participants at the conference. It upheld the Open Door in China by binding the nations to respect the sovereignty, independence, and integrity of China.

The Four-Power Treaty bound the United States, Great Britain, Japan, and France to respect each other's possessions in the Pacific, and to confer in the event of disputes or aggression in the area.

War Debts, Reparations, and International Finance

The United States had lent the Allies about $7 billion during World War I and about $3.25 billion in the postwar period, and insisted on full payment of the debts. Meanwhile, Germany was to pay reparations to the Allies, but, by 1923, Germany was bankrupt. The Dawes Plan, proposed by American banker Charles G. Dawes, was accepted in 1924. Under it, American banks made loans of $2.5 billion to Germany by 1930. Germany paid reparations of over $2 billion to the Allies during the same period, and the Allies paid about $2.6 billion to the United States on their war debts. The whole cycle was based on loans from American banks.

The Kellogg-Briand Pact

A group of American citizens campaigned during the 1920s for a treaty that would outlaw war. In 1927, the French foreign minister, Aristide Briand, proposed such a treaty with the United States. Frank B. Kellogg, Coolidge's secretary of state, countered by proposing that other nations be invited to sign. At Paris, in August 1928, almost all major nations signed the treaty, which renounced war as an instrument of national policy. It outlawed only aggression, not self-defense, and had no enforcement provisions.

Latin America

American investment in Latin America almost doubled during the 1920s to $5.4 billion, and relations with most nations in the region improved. Coolidge removed the Marines from Nicaragua in 1925, but a revolution erupted and the Marines were returned. Revolutionary General Augusto Sandino fought against the marines until they were replaced by an American-trained national guard under Anastasio Somoza. The Somoza family would rule Nicaragua until 1979, when revolutionaries known as the Sandinistas overthrew them.

The Great Depression: The 1929 Crash

Hoover Becomes President

Herbert Hoover, an Iowa farm boy and an orphan, graduated from Stanford University with a degree in mining engineering. He became a multimillionaire from mining and other investments around the world. After serving as the director of the Food Administration under Wilson, he became secretary of commerce under Harding and Coolidge. He believed that an associative economic system with voluntary cooperation of business and government would enable the United States to abolish poverty through continued economic growth.

DID YOU KNOW?

Much of the meteoric rise of the stock market during the 1920s was fueled by intense stock speculation that was possible because of margin-buying policies. When the stock market crashed, even famed movie star Groucho Marx was wiped out because of these risky investing practices.

The Stock Market Boom

Stock prices increased throughout the decade. The boom in prices and volume of sales was especially active after 1925, and was intensive during 1928–29. The Dow Jones Industrial Average finished the year 1924 at 120; for the month of September 1929 it rose to 381; and for the year 1932 it dropped to 41. Stocks were selling for more than 16 times earnings in 1929.

The Stock Market Crash

Careful investors, realizing that stocks were overpriced, began to sell to take their profits. During October 1929 prices declined as more stock was sold. On "Black Thursday," October 24, 1929, almost 13 million shares were traded, a large number for that time, and prices fell precipitously. Investment banks tried to boost the market by buying, but on October 29, "Black Tuesday," the market fell about 40 points, with 16.5 million shares traded. A long decline followed until early 1933, and with it came a deep depression.

Reasons for the Depression

A stock market crash does not mean that a depression must follow. A similar crash in October 1987, for example, did not lead to depression. In 1929, a complex interaction of many factors caused the decline of the economy.

Many people had bought stock on a margin of ten percent, meaning that they had borrowed 90 percent of the purchase through a broker's loan, and put up the stock as collateral. Brokers' loans totaled $8.5 billion in 1929, compared with $3.5 billion in 1926. When the price of a stock fell more than ten percent, the lender sold the stock for whatever it would bring and thus further depressed prices. The forced sales brought great losses to the banks and businesses that had financed the brokers' loans, as well as to the investors.

There were already signs of recession before the market crash in 1929. Because the gathering and processing of statistics was not as advanced as it is now, some factors were not so obvious to people at the time. The farm economy, which involved almost 25 percent of the population, had been depressed throughout the decade. Coal, railroads, and New England textiles had not been prosperous. After 1927 new construction declined and auto sales began to sag. Many workers had been laid off before the crash of 1929.

Many scholars believe that there was a problem of underconsumption, meaning that ordinary workers and farmers, after using their consumer credit, did not have enough money to keep buying the products that were being produced. One estimate says that the income of the top one percent of the population increased at least 75 percent during the decade, while that of the bottom 93 percent increased only 6 percent. The process continued after the Depression began. After the stock market crash, people were conservative and saved their money, thus reducing the demand for goods. As demand decreased, workers were laid off or had wage reductions, further reducing their purchasing power and bringing another decrease in demand.

With the decline in the economy, Americans had less money for foreign loans and bought fewer imported products. That meant that foreign governments and individuals were not able to pay their debts in the United States. The whole reparations and war debts structure collapsed. American exports dropped, further hurting the domestic economy. The Depression eventually spread throughout the world.

Economic Effects of the Depression

During the early months of the Depression most people thought it was just an adjustment in the business cycle that would soon be over. In fact, President Hoover repeatedly assured the public that prosperity was just around the corner. As time went on, the worst depression in American history set in, reaching its bottom point in early 1932. The gross national product fell from $104.6 billion in 1929 to $56.1 billion in 1933. Unemployment reached about 13 million in 1933, or about 25 percent of the labor force excluding farmers. National income dropped 54 percent, from $87.8 billion to $40.2 billion. Labor income fell about 41 percent, while farm income dropped 55 percent, from $11.9 billion to $5.3 billion. Industrial production dropped about 51 percent. The banking system suffered as 5,761 banks, over 22 percent of the total, failed by the end of 1932.

The Human Dimension of the Depression

As the Depression grew worse, more and more people lost their jobs or had their wages reduced. Many were unable to continue credit payments on homes, automobiles, and other possessions, and lost them. Families doubled up in houses and apartments. Both the marriage rate and the birth rate declined as people put off family formation. Hundreds of thousands became homeless and lived in groups of makeshift shacks called Hoovervilles in empty spaces around cities. Others traveled the country by foot and boxcar seeking food and work. State and local government agencies and private charities were overwhelmed in their attempts to care for those in need, although public and private soup kitchens and soup

DID YOU KNOW?

During the Depression, the wandering unemployed men known as hobos developed their own unique subculture. This included a system of simple glyphs representing concepts ranging from helpful directions, to safe places to sleep, to tips on how to get a homeowner to give out food, to warnings about potential dangers.

lines were set up throughout the nation. Malnutrition was widespread but few died of starvation, perhaps because malnourished people are susceptible to many fatal diseases.

Hoover's Depression Policies

The Hawley-Smoot Tariff

The Hawley-Smoot Tariff, passed in June 1930, raised duties on both agricultural and manufactured imports. It did nothing of significance to improve the economy, and historians argue over whether or not it contributed to the spread of the international Depression.

Voluntarism

Hoover believed that voluntary cooperation would enable the country to weather the Depression. He held meetings with business leaders at which he urged them to avoid lay-offs of workers and wage cuts, and he secured no-strike pledges from labor leaders. He urged all citizens to contribute to charities to help alleviate the suffering. While people were generous, private charity could not begin to meet the needs.

Public Works

In 1930, Congress appropriated $750 million for public buildings, river and harbor improvements, and highway construction in an effort to stimulate employment.

The Reconstruction Finance Corporation

Chartered by Congress in 1932, the Reconstruction Finance Corporation had an appropriation of $500 million and authority to borrow $1.5 billion for loans to railroads, banks, and other financial institutions. It prevented the failure of basic firms on which many other elements of the economy depended, but was criticized by some as relief for the rich.

The Federal Home Loan Bank Act

The Federal Home Loan Bank Act, passed in July 1932, injected $125 million of capital into newly created home loan banks so that loans could be made to building and loan associations, savings banks, and insurance companies to help them avoid foreclosures on homes.

A shantytown, or "Hooverville," in Seattle, Wash., March 20, 1933. (AP/Wide World Photo)

Relief

Hoover staunchly opposed the use of federal funds for relief for the needy. In July 1932, he vetoed the Garner-Wagner Bill, which would have appropriated funds for relief. He did compromise by approving legislation authorizing the Reconstruction Finance Corporation to lend $300 million to the states for relief, and to make loans to states and cities for self-liquidating public works.

The Bonus Army

The Bonus Army called the Bonus Expeditionary Force, took its name from the American Expeditionary Force of World War I. The group of about 14,000 unemployed veterans went to Washington in the summer of 1932 to lobby Congress for immediate payment of the bonus, which had been approved in 1926 for payment in 1945. At Hoover's insistence, the Senate did not pass the bonus bill, and about half of the BEF accepted a congressional offer of transportation home. The remaining 6,000, many with wives and children, continued to live in shanties along the Anacostia River and to lobby for their cause. After two veterans were killed in a clash with the police, Hoover, calling them insurrectionists and communists, ordered the Army to remove them. On July 28,

1932, General Douglas MacArthur, the Army chief of staff, assisted by Majors Dwight D. Eisenhower and George S. Patton, personally commanded the removal operation. With machine guns, tanks, cavalry, infantry with fixed bayonets, and tear gas, MacArthur drove the veterans from Washington and burned their camp. Although some contend MacArthur disobeyed orders by destroying the Bonus Army camp, Hoover was blamed by many for the Army action.

The Election of 1932

The Republicans

At the 1932 Republican convention in Chicago, Hoover was nominated on the first ballot. The platform called for a continuation of his Depression policies.

The Democrats

Franklin D. Roosevelt, the popular governor of New York, gained the support of many Southern and Western delegates through the efforts of his managers, Louis Howe and James Farley. When the Democratic convention opened in Chicago, he had a majority of delegates, but not the necessary two-thirds for nomination. House Speaker John Nance Garner, a favorite son candidate from Texas, threw support to Roosevelt, who was nominated on the fourth ballot. Garner then became the vice presidential candidate. Roosevelt took the unprecedented step of flying to the convention to accept the nomination in person, declaring that he pledged a "new deal" for the American people. The platform called for the repeal of prohibition, government aid for the unemployed, and a 25 percent cut in government spending.

The Campaign

Hoover declared that he would lead the nation to prosperity with higher tariffs and the maintenance of the gold standard. He warned that the election of Roosevelt would lead to grass growing in the streets of the cities and towns of America. Roosevelt called for "bold, persistent experimentation" and expressed his concern for the "forgotten man" at the bottom of the economic heap, but he did not give a clear picture of what he intended to do. Roosevelt had a broad smile and amiable disposition which attracted many people, while Hoover was aloof and cold in his personal style.

The Election

Roosevelt received 22,809,638 votes for 57.3 percent of the total and 472 electoral votes, carrying all but six northeastern states. Hoover had 15,758,901 votes and 59 electoral votes. Despite the hard times, Norman Thomas, the Socialist candidate, received only 881,951 votes. The Democrats also captured the Senate and increased their majority in the House.

The First New Deal

Franklin D. Roosevelt

The heir of a wealthy family and a fifth cousin of Theodore Roosevelt, Franklin was born in 1882 on the family estate at Hyde Park, New York. He graduated from Harvard University and Columbia Law School, married his distant cousin Anna Eleanor Roosevelt in 1905, and practiced law in New York City. He entered state politics, then served as assistant secretary of the Navy under Wilson, and was the Democratic vice presidential candidate in 1920. In 1921, he suffered an attack of polio that left him paralyzed for several years and on crutches or in a wheelchair for the rest of his life. In 1928, he was elected governor of New York to succeed Al Smith, and was re-elected in 1930. As governor, his Depression programs for the unemployed, public works, aid to farmers, and conservation attracted national attention.

DIDYOUKNOW?

Although most Americans were not aware of FDR's disability, the president worked diligently in support of polio research. He helped found the March of Dimes to seek a cure for polio, and the institution put millions of dollars into research by the time a vaccine was developed in the mid-1950s. FDR's contributions forever tied him to the dime in a unique way: his portrait now appears on that U.S. coin.

The Brain Trust

Roosevelt's inner circle of unofficial advisors, first assembled during the campaign, was more influential than the Cabinet. Prominent in it were agricultural economist Rexford G. Tugwell, political scientist Raymond Moley, lawyer Adolph A. Berle, Jr., the originators of the McNary-Haugen Farm Bill—Hugh S. Johnson and George Peek—and Roosevelt's personal political advisor, Louis Howe.

The New Deal Program

Roosevelt did not have a developed plan of action when he took office. He intended to experiment and to find that which worked. As a result, many programs overlapped or contradicted others, and were changed or dropped if they did not work.

Repeal of Prohibition

In February 1933, before Roosevelt took office, Congress passed the 21st Amendment to repeal prohibition, and sent it to the states. In March, the new Congress legalized light (lower alcohol content) beer. The amendment was ratified by the states and took effect in December 1933.

The Banking Crisis

In February 1933, as the inauguration approached, a severe banking crisis developed. Banks could not collect their loans or meet the demands of their depositors for withdrawals, and runs occurred on many banks. Eventually banks in 38 states were closed by the state governments, and the remainder were open for only limited operations. An additional 5,190 banks failed in 1933, bringing the Depression total to 10,951.

The Inaugural Address

By the time Roosevelt was inaugurated on March 4, 1933, the American economic system seemed to be on the verge of collapse. Roosevelt assured the nation that "the only thing we have to fear is fear itself," called for a special session of Congress to convene on March 9, and asked for "broad executive powers to wage war against the emergency." Two days later, he closed all banks, and forbade the export of gold or the redemption of currency in gold.

Legislation of the First New Deal

The Hundred Days and the First New Deal

The special session of Congress, from March 9 to June 16, 1933, passed a great body of legislation that has left a lasting mark on the nation, and the period has been referred to ever since as the "Hundred Days." Over the next two years, legislation was added, but the basic recovery plan of the Hundred Days remained in operation. Hence, the period from 1933 to 1935 is called the First New Deal. A new wave of programs beginning in 1935 is called the Second New Deal. The distinction was not known at the time, but is a device of historians to differentiate between two stages in Roosevelt's administration.

DIDYOUKNOW?

The Works Progress Administration (WPA) served as an important avenue for the preservation of U.S. history. Among other tasks, WPA employees collected oral histories about life under slavery from some 2,000 former slaves in 17 states.

Economic Legislation of the Hundred Days

The banking crisis was the most immediate problem facing Roosevelt and the Congress. A series of laws were passed to deal with the crisis and to reform the American economic system. While not consistent in his economic policies, Roosevelt generally followed the principles of Keynesian economics, which considered governmental monetary action to be more important than relying on the private sector.

The Emergency Banking Relief Act was passed on March 9, the first day of the special session. The law provided additional funds for banks from the Reconstruction Finance Corporation and the Federal Reserve, allowed the Treasury to open sound banks after ten days and to merge or liquidate unsound ones, and forbade the hoarding or export of gold. Roosevelt on March 12 assured the public of the soundness of the banks in the first of many "fireside chats," or radio addresses. People believed him and most banks were soon open with more deposits than withdrawals.

The Banking Act of 1933, or the Glass-Steagall Act, established the Federal Deposit Insurance Corporation (FDIC) to insure individual deposits in commercial banks, and separated commercial banking from the more speculative activity of investment banking.

The Truth-in-Securities Act required that full information about stocks and bonds be provided by brokers and others to potential purchasers.

The Home Owners Loan Corporation had authority to borrow money to refinance home mortgages and thus prevent foreclosures. Eventually, it lent over $3 billion to over 1 million homeowners.

Gold was taken out of circulation following the president's order of March 6, and the nation went off the gold standard. Eventually, on January 31, 1934, the value of the dollar was set at $35 per ounce of gold, 59 percent of its former value. The object of the devaluation was to raise prices and help American exports.

Later Economic Legislation of the First New Deal

The Securities and Exchange Commission was created in 1934 to supervise stock exchanges and to punish fraud in securities trading.

Congress created the Federal Housing Administration (FHA) in 1934 to insure long-term, low-interest mortgages for home construction and repair.

Relief and Employment Programs of the Hundred Days

Roosevelt's relief and employment programs were intended to provide temporary relief for people in need, and to be disbanded when the economy improved.

The Federal Emergency Relief Act appropriated $500 million for aid to the poor to be distributed by state and local governments. Half of the funds were to be distributed on a one to three matching basis with the states. It also established the Federal Emergency Relief Administration under Harry Hopkins. Additional appropriations were made many times later.

The Civilian Conservation Corps enlisted 250,000 young men ages 18 to 24 from families on relief to go to camps where they worked on flood control, soil conservation, and forest projects under the direction of the War Department. A small monthly payment was made to the family of each member. By the end of the decade, 2.75 million young men had served in the corps.

The Public Works Administration, under Secretary of the Interior Harold Ickes, had $3.3 billion to distribute to state and local governments for building projects such as schools, highways, and hospitals. The object was to "prime the pump" of the economy by creating construction jobs. Additional money was appropriated later.

Later Relief Efforts

After the Hundred Days, in November 1933, Roosevelt established the Civil Works Administration under Harry Hopkins with $400 million from the Public Works Administration to hire four million unemployed workers. The temporary and makeshift nature of the jobs, such as sweeping streets, brought much criticism, and the experiment was terminated in April 1934.

Agricultural Programs of the Hundred Days

The Agricultural Adjustment Act of 1933 created the Agricultural Adjustment Administration. It sought to return farm prices to parity with those of the 1909 to 1914 period. Farmers agreed to reduce production of principal farm commodities and were paid a subsidy in return. The money came from a tax on the processing of the commodities. Farm prices increased, but tenants and sharecroppers were hurt when owners took land out of cultivation. The law was declared unconstitutional in January 1936 on the grounds that the processing tax was not constitutional.

The Federal Farm Loan Act consolidated all farm credit programs into the Farm Credit Administration to make low-interest loans for farm mortgages and other agricultural purposes.

The National Industrial Recovery Act

The National Industrial Recovery Act, which passed on June 16, 1933, the last day of the Hundred Days, was viewed as the cornerstone of the recovery program. It sought to stabilize the economy by preventing extreme competition, labor-management conflicts, and overproduction. A board composed of industrial and labor leaders in each industry or business drew up a code for that industry which set minimum prices, minimum wages, maximum work hours, production limits, and quotas. The antitrust laws were temporarily suspended. The approach was based on the idea of many economists at the time; because a mature industrial economy produced more goods than could be consumed, it would be necessary to create a relative shortage of goods in order to raise prices and restore prosperity. The idea was proved wrong by the expansion of consumer goods after World War II. Section 7a of the law also provided that workers had the right to join unions and to bargain collectively. The National Recovery Administration (NRA) was created under the leadership of Hugh S. Johnson to enforce the law and generate public enthusiasm for it. In May 1935, the law was declared unconstitutional in the case of *Schechter v. United States* on the grounds that Congress had delegated legislative authority to the code-makers, and that Schechter, who slaughtered chickens in New York, was not engaged in interstate commerce. It was argued later that the NRA had unintentionally aided big firms to the detriment of smaller ones because the representatives of the larger firms tended to dominate the code-making process. It was generally unsuccessful in stabilizing small businesses such as retail stores, and was on the point of collapse when it was declared unconstitutional.

Businesses were encouraged to display the National Recovery Administration Blue Eagle as an indication of their support for fair wages and prices.

The Tennessee Valley Authority

Different from the other legislation of the Hundred Days that addressed immediate problems of the Depression, the Tennessee Valley Authority, a public corporation under a three-member board, was proposed by Roosevelt as the first major experiment in regional public planning. Starting from the nucleus of the government's Muscle Shoals property on the Tennessee River, the TVA built 20 dams in an area of 40,000 square miles to stop flooding and soil erosion, improve navigation, and generate hydroelectric power. It also manufactured nitrates for fertilizer, conducted demonstration projects for farmers, engaged in reforestation, and attempted to rehabilitate the whole area. It was fought unsuccessfully in the courts by private power companies. Roosevelt believed that it would serve as a yardstick to measure the true cost of providing electric power.

Effects of the First New Deal

The economy improved but remained far from recovered between 1933 and 1935. The gross national product rose from $74.2 billion in 1933 to $91.4 billion in 1935. Manufacturing salaries and wages increased from $6.24 billion in 1933 to over $9.5 billion in 1935, with average weekly earnings going from $16.73 to $20.13. Farm income rose from $1.9 billion in 1933 to $4.6 billion in 1935. The money supply, as currency and demand deposits, grew from $19.2 billion to $25.2 billion. Unemployment dropped from about 25 percent of nonfarm workers in 1933 to about 20.1 percent, or 10.6 million, in 1935. While the figure had improved, it was a long way from the 3.2 percent of pre-Depression 1929, and suffering as a result of unemployment was still a major problem.

TEST TIP

When writing responses to the document-based question or free-response question, be sure that you stay on topic and answer the question asked. Including facts and ideas, particularly if they are not in the chronological boundaries of the questions and don't directly relate to your argument, will take up time and will not help your score.

The Second New Deal: Opposition from the Right and Left

FDR Weathers Criticism

The partial economic recovery brought about by the First New Deal provoked criticism from the right for doing too much, and from the left for doing too little. Conservatives and businesspeople criticized the deficit financing, which accounted for about half of the federal budget, federal spending for relief, and government regulation of business. They frequently charged that the New Deal was socialist or communist in form, and some conservative writers labeled the wealthy Roosevelt "a traitor to his class." People on the lower end of the economic scale thought that the New Deal, especially the NRA, was too favorable to big business. Small-business people and union members complained that the NRA codes gave control of industry to the big firms, while farmers complained that the NRA set prices too high. The elderly thought that nothing had been done to help them. Several million people who were or had been tenant farmers or sharecroppers were badly hurt. When the agricultural adjustment administration paid farmers to take land out of production, the landowners took the money while the tenants and sharecroppers lost their livelihood. Several opposition organizations and persons were particularly active in opposing Roosevelt's policies.

The American Liberty League was formed in 1934 by conservatives to defend business interests and promote the open shop. While many of its members were Republicans and the Du Pont family primarily financed it, it also attracted conservative Democrats like Alfred E. Smith and John W. Davis. It supported conservative congressional candidates of both parties in the election of 1934 with little success.

Dr. Francis E. Townsend, a retired California physician, advanced the Old Age Revolving Pension Plan. The plan proposed that every retired person over 60 receive a pension of $200 a month, about double the average worker's salary, with the requirement that the money be spent within the month. The plan would be funded by a national gross sales tax. Townsend claimed that it would end the Depression by putting money into circulation, but economists thought it fiscally impossible. Some three to five million older Americans joined Townsend Clubs.

Senator Huey "The Kingfish" Long of Louisiana founded the Share Our Wealth Society in 1934. Long was a populist demagogue who was elected governor of Louisiana in 1928, established a practical dictatorship over the state, and moved to the United States Senate in 1930. He supported Roosevelt in 1932, but then broke with him, calling him a tool of Wall Street for not doing more to combat the Depression. Long called for the confiscation of all fortunes over $5 million and a tax of 100 percent on annual incomes over $1 million. With the money, the government would provide subsidies so that every family would have a "homestead" of house, car, and furnishings worth at least $5,000, a minimum annual income of $2,000, and free college education for those who wanted it. His slogan was "Every Man a King." Long talked of running for president in 1936, and published a book entitled *My First Days* in the White House. His society had over five million members when he was assassinated on the steps of the Louisiana Capitol on September 8, 1935. The Reverend Gerald L.K. Smith appointed himself Long's successor as head of the society, but he lacked Long's ability.

The National Union for Social Justice was headed by Father Charles E. Coughlin, a Catholic priest in Royal Oak, Michigan, who had a weekly radio program. Beginning as a religious broadcast in 1926, Coughlin turned to politics and finance and attracted an audience of millions of many faiths. He supported Roosevelt in 1932, but then turned against him. He advocated an inflationary currency and was anti-Semitic, but beyond that his fascist-like program was not clearly defined.

The Second New Deal Begins

Roosevelt's Position

With millions of Democratic voters under the sway of Townsend, Long, and Coughlin, with the destruction of the NRA by the Supreme Court imminent, and with the election of 1936 approaching the next year, Roosevelt began to push through a series of new programs in the spring of 1935. Much of the legislation was passed during the summer of 1935, a period sometimes called the Second Hundred Days.

Legislation and Programs of the Second New Deal

The Works Progress Administration (WPA) was started in May 1935 following the passage of the Emergency Relief Appropriations Act of April 1935. Headed by Harry Hopkins, the WPA employed people from the relief rolls for 30 hours of work a week at pay double the relief payment but less than private employment. There was not enough money to hire all of the unemployed, and the numbers varied over time, but an average of 2.1 million people per month were employed. By the end of the program in 1941, 8.5 million people had worked at some point for the WPA at a total cost of $11.4 billion. Most of the projects undertaken were in construction. The WPA built hundreds of thousands of miles of streets and roads, and thousands of schools, hospitals, parks, airports, playgrounds, and other facilities. Hand work was emphasized so that the money would go for pay rather than equipment, provoking much criticism for inefficiency. Unemployed artists painted murals in public buildings; actors, musicians, and dancers performed in poor neighborhoods; and writers compiled guidebooks and local histories.

The National Youth Administration was established as part of the WPA in June 1935 to provide part-time jobs for high school and college students to enable them to stay in school, and to help young adults not in school to find jobs.

The Rural Electrification Administration was created in May 1935 to provide loans and WPA labor to electric cooperatives to build lines into rural areas not served by private companies.

The Resettlement Administration was created in the Agriculture Department in May 1935 under Rexford Tugwell. It relocated destitute families from seemingly hopeless situations to new rural homestead communities or to suburban greenbelt towns.

The National Labor Relations Act, also known as the Wagner Act, was passed in May 1935 to replace the provisions of Section 7a of the NIRA. It reaffirmed labor's right to unionize, prohibited unfair labor practices, and created the National Labor Relations Board (NLRB) to oversee and insure fairness in labor-management relations.

The landmark Social Security Act was passed in August 1935. It established a retirement plan for persons over age 65 funded by a tax on wages paid equally by employee and employer. The first benefits, ranging from $10 to $85 per month, were paid in 1942. Another provision of the act had the effect of forcing the states to initiate unemployment insurance programs. It imposed an employer payroll tax that went to the state if it had an insurance program, and to the federal government if it did not. The act also provided matching funds to the states for aid to the blind, handicapped, and dependent children, and for public health services. The American Social Security system was limited compared with those of other industrialized nations, and millions of workers were not covered by it. Nonetheless, it marked a major change in American policy.

The Election of 1936

The Democrats

At the convention in Philadelphia in June, Roosevelt and Garner were renominated by acclamation on the first ballot. The convention also ended the requirement for a two-thirds vote for nomination. The platform promised an expanded farm program, labor legislation, more rural electrification and public housing, and enforcement of the antitrust laws. In his acceptance speech, Roosevelt declared that "this generation of Americans has a rendezvous with destiny." He further proclaimed that he and the American people were fighting for democracy and capitalism against the "economic royalists," business people he charged with seeking only their own power and wealth, and opposing the New Deal.

This iconic Dorothea Lange photo of 32-year-old migrant mother in California captured the pain of the Great Depression. (U.S. Library of Congress)

The Republicans

Governor Alfred M. Landon of Kansas, a former progressive supporter of Theodore Roosevelt, was nominated on the first ballot at the convention in Cleveland in June. Frank Knox, a Chicago newspaper publisher, was chosen as his running mate. The platform criticized the New Deal for operating under unconstitutional laws and called for a balanced budget, higher tariffs, and lower corporate taxes. It did not call for the repeal of all New Deal legislation, and promised better and less expensive relief, farm, and labor programs. In effect, Landon and the Republicans were saying that they would do about the same thing, but do it better.

The Union Party

Dr. Francis Townsend, Father Charles Coughlin, and the Reverend Gerald L.K. Smith, Long's successor in the Share Our Wealth Society, organized the Union Party to oppose Roosevelt. Their nominee was Congressman William Lemke of North Dakota, an advocate of radical farm legislation, but a bland campaigner. Vicious attacks by Smith and Coughlin on Roosevelt brought a backlash against them, and American Catholic leaders denounced Coughlin.

The Election

Roosevelt carried all of the states except Maine and Vermont, with 27,757,333 votes, or 60.8 percent of the total, and 523 electoral votes. Landon received 16,684,231 votes and 8 electoral votes. Lemke had 891,858 votes for 1.9 percent of the total. Norman Thomas, the Socialist candidate, received 187,000 votes, only 21 percent of the 881,951 votes he received in 1932.

The New Deal Coalition

Roosevelt had put together a coalition of followers who made the Democratic Party the majority party in the nation for the first time since the Civil War. While retaining the Democratic base in the Solid South and among white ethnics in the big cities, Roosevelt also received strong support from Midwestern farmers. Two groups which made a dramatic shift into the Democratic ranks were union workers and blacks. Unions took an active political role for the first time since 1924, providing both campaign funds and votes. Blacks had traditionally been Republican since emancipation, but by 1936 about three-fourths of the black voters, who lived mainly in the northern cities, had shifted into the Democratic Party.

The Last Years of the New Deal

Court-Packing Plan

Frustrated by a conservative Supreme Court that had overturned much of his New Deal legislation, Roosevelt, after receiving his overwhelming mandate in the election of 1936, decided to curb the power of the court. In doing so, he overestimated his own political power and underestimated the force of tradition. In February 1937, he proposed to Congress the Judicial Reorganization Bill, which would allow the president to name a new federal judge for each judge who did not retire by the age of 70 1/2. The appointments would be limited to a maximum of 50, with no more than six added to the Supreme Court. At the time, six justices were over the proposed age limit. Roosevelt cited a slowing of the judicial process due to the infirmity of the incumbents and the need for a modern outlook. The president was astonished by the wave of opposition from Democrats and Republicans alike, and uncharacteristically refused to compromise. In doing so, he not only lost the bill, but he lost control of the Democratic Congress which he had dominated since 1933. Nonetheless, the Court changed its position as Chief Justice Charles Evans Hughes and Justice Owen Roberts began to vote with the more liberal members. The National Labor Relations Act was upheld in March 1937 and the Social Security Act in April. In June, a conservative justice retired, and Roosevelt had the opportunity to make an appointment.

The Recession of 1937–1938

Most economic indicators rose sharply between 1935 and 1937. The gross national product had recovered to the 1930 level, and unemployment, if WPA workers were considered employed, had fallen to 9.2 percent. Average yearly earnings of the employed had risen from $1,195 in 1935 to $1,341 in 1937, and average hourly manufacturing earnings from 55 cents to 62 cents. During the same period there were huge federal deficits. In fiscal 1936, for example, there was a deficit of $4.4 billion in a budget of $8.5 billion. Roosevelt decided that the recovery was sufficient to warrant a reduction in relief programs and a move toward a balanced budget. The budget for fiscal 1938, from July 1937 to June 1938, was reduced to $6.8 billion, with the WPA experiencing the largest cut. During the winter of 1937–1938, the economy slipped rapidly and unemployment rose to 12.5 percent. In April 1938, Roosevelt requested and received from Congress an emergency appropriation of about $3 billion for the WPA, as well as increases for public works and other programs. In July 1938, the economy began to recover, and it regained the 1937 levels in 1939.

Legislation of the Late New Deal

With the threat of adverse Supreme Court rulings removed, Roosevelt rounded out his program during the late 1930s.

The National Housing, or Wagner-Steagall Act, passed in September 1937, established the United States Housing Authority, which could borrow money to lend to local agencies for public housing projects. By 1941, it had loaned $750 million for 511 projects.

The Second Agricultural Adjustment Act of February 1938 appropriated funds for soil conservation payments to farmers who would remove land from production. The law also empowered the Agriculture Department to impose market quotas to prevent surpluses in cotton, wheat, corn, tobacco, and rice if two-thirds of the farmers producing that commodity agreed.

The Fair Labor Standards Act, popularly called the minimum wage law, was passed in June 1938. It provided for a minimum wage of 25 cents an hour that would gradually rise to 40 cents, and a gradual reduction to a work week of 40 hours, with time and a half for overtime. Workers in small businesses and in public and nonprofit employment were not covered. The law also prohibited the shipment in interstate commerce of manufactured goods on which children under 16 worked.

TEST TIP

Instead of just highlighting sections as you study, you might try reading important pieces of information aloud to yourself or taking notes in your own words. The actions of speaking or writing may help you process the information more effectively and remember it better.

Social Dimensions of the New Deal Era

Blacks and the New Deal

Blacks suffered more than other people from the Depression. Unemployment rates were much higher for them than for the general population, and before 1933 they were often excluded from state and local relief efforts. Blacks did benefit from many New Deal relief programs, but about 40 percent of black workers were sharecroppers or tenant farmers who suffered from the provisions of the first Agricultural Adjustment Act. Roosevelt seems to have given little thought to the special problems of black people, and he was afraid to endorse legislation such as an antilynching bill for fear of alienating the southern wing of the Democratic Party. Eleanor Roosevelt and Harold Ickes strongly supported civil rights, and a "Black Cabinet" of advisors was assembled in the Interior Department. More blacks were appointed to government positions by Roosevelt than ever before, but the number was still small. When government military contracts began to flow in 1941, A. Philip Randolph, the president of the Brotherhood of Sleeping Car Porters, proposed a black march on Washington to demand equal access to defense jobs. To forestall such an action, Roosevelt issued an executive order on June 25, 1941, establishing the Fair Employment Practices Committee to ensure consideration for minorities in defense employment.

Native Americans and the New Deal

John Collier, the commissioner of the Bureau of Indian Affairs, persuaded Congress to repeal the Dawes Act of 1887 by passing the Indian Reorganization Act of 1934. The law restored tribal ownership of lands, recognized tribal constitutions and governments, and provided loans to tribes for economic development. Collier also secured the creation of the Indian Emergency Conservation Program, a Native American civilian conservation corps for projects on the reservations. In addition, he helped Native Americans secure entry into the WPA, the National youth administration, and other programs.

Mexican Americans and the New Deal

Mexican Americans benefitted the least from the New Deal, for few programs covered them. Farm owners turned against them as farm workers after they attempted to form a union between 1933 and 1936. By 1940, most had been replaced by whites dispossessed by the Depression. Many returned to Mexico, and the Mexican American population dropped almost 40 percent between 1930 and 1940.

Women During the New Deal

The burden of the Depression fell on women as much or more as it did on men. Wives and mothers found themselves responsible for stretching meager budgets by preparing inexpensive meals, patching old clothing, and the like. "Making do" became a slogan of the period. In addition, more women had to supplement or provide the family income by going to work. In 1930, there were 10.5 million working women comprising 29 percent of the workforce. By 1940, the figures had grown to over 13 million and 35 percent. There was much criticism of working women based on the idea that they deprived men of jobs. Male job losses were greatest in heavy industry such as factories and mills, while areas of female employment such as retail sales were not hit as hard. Unemployed men seldom sought jobs in the traditional women's fields.

Labor Unions

Unions During the First New Deal

Labor unions had lost members and influence during the twenties and slipped further during the economic decline of 1929 to 1933. The National Industrial Recovery Act gave them new hope when Section 7a guaranteed the right to unionize, and during 1933 about 1.5 million new members joined unions. It soon became clear that enforcement of the industrial codes by the NRA was ineffective, and labor leaders began to call it the "National Run Around." As a result, in 1934, there were many strikes, sometimes violent, including a general strike in San Francisco involving about 125,000 workers.

Craft Versus Industrial Unions

The passage of the National Labor Relations, or Wagner, Act in 1935 resulted in a massive growth of union membership, but only at the expense of bitter conflict within the labor movement. The American Federation of Labor (AFL) was made up primarily of craft unions. Some leaders, especially John L. Lewis, the dynamic president of the United Mine Workers, wanted to unionize the mass production industries, such as automobiles and rubber, with industrial unions. In 1934, the AFL convention authorized such unions, but the older unions continued to try to organize workers in those industries by crafts. In November 1935, Lewis and others established the Committee for Industrial Organization (CIO) to unionize basic industries, presumably within the AFL. President William Green of the AFL ordered the CIO to disband in January 1936. When the rebels refused, they were expelled by the AFL executive council in March 1937. The insurgents then reorganized the CIO as the independent Congress of Industrial Organizations to be composed of industrial unions.

The Growth of the CIO

During its organizational period, the CIO sought to initiate several industrial unions, particularly in the steel, auto, rubber, and radio industries. In late 1936 and early 1937, it used a tactic called the sit-down strike, with the strikers occupying the workplace to prevent any production. There were 477 sit-down strikes involving about 400,000 workers. The largest was in the General Motors plant in Flint, Michigan, as the union sought recognition by that firm. In February 1937, General Motors recognized the United Auto Workers as the bargaining agent for its 400,000 workers. When the CIO established its independence in March 1937, it already had 1.8 million members, and it reached a membership of 3.75 million six months later. The AFL had about 3.4 million members at that time. By the end of 1941, the CIO had about 5 million members, the AFL about 4.6 million, and other unions about one million. Union members made up about 11.5 percent of the workforce in 1933, and 28.2 percent in 1941.

Cultural Trends of the 1930s

Literary Developments

The writers and intellectuals who had expressed disdain for the middle-class materialism of the 1920s found it even more difficult to deal with the meaning of the crushing poverty in America and the rise of fascism in Europe during the 1930s. Some turned to communism, including the 53 writers who signed an open letter endorsing the Communist presidential candidate in 1932. Some turned to proletarian novels, such as Jack Conroy in *The Disinherited* (1933) and Robert Cantwell in *The Land of Plenty* (1934). Ernest Hemingway seemed to have lost his direction in *Winner Take All* (1933) and *The Green Hills of Africa* (1935), but in *To Have and Have Not* (1937), a strike novel, he turned to social realism, and *For Whom the Bell Tolls* (1941) expressed his concern about fascism. Sinclair Lewis also dealt with fascism in *It Can't Happen Here* (1935). John Dos Passos depicted what he saw as the disintegration of American life from 1900 to 1929 in his U.S.A. trilogy (1930–1936). William Faulkner sought values in southern life in *Light in August* (1932), *Absalom, Absalom!* (1936), and *The Unvanquished* (1938). The endurance of the human spirit and personal survival were depicted in James T. Farrell's trilogy *Studs Lonigan* (1936) about the struggles of lower-middle-class Irish Catholics in Chicago, while Erskine Caldwell's *Tobacco Road* (1932) dealt with impoverished Georgia sharecroppers, and John Steinbeck's *The Grapes of Wrath* (1939) depicted "Okies" migrating from the Oklahoma dust bowl to California in the midst of the Depression.

New Deal-era poster shows a man with a WPA shovel attacking a wolf called Rumor.

The Depression greatly reduced the amount of money available for recreation and entertainment. There was an increase in games and sports among family groups and friends. The WPA and the CCC constructed thousands of playgrounds, playing fields, picnic areas, and the like for public use. Roosevelt and Harry Hopkins, the director of the WPA, hoped to develop a mass appreciation of culture through the WPA murals in public buildings, with traveling plays, concerts, and exhibits, and with community arts centers. Beyond some revival of handicrafts, it is doubtful that the program had much effect. There were, however, several popular forms of entertainment.

Radio was the favorite form of daily entertainment during the Depression because, after the initial cost of the instrument, it was free. There were about forty million radios in the United States by 1938. It provided comedy and mystery shows, music, sports and news. A study at the time indicated that radio tended to make Americans more uniform in their attitudes, taste, speech, and humor.

While radio was the form of entertainment most used, the movies were the most popular. By 1939 about 65 percent of the people went to the movies at least once a week. The movie industry was one of the few that grew financially during the Depression. Movies provided a means of escape from the pressures of the Depression by transporting people to a make-believe world of beauty, mystery, or excitement. Spectacular musicals with dozens of dancers and singers, such as *Broadway Melody of 1936,* were popular. The dance team of Fred Astaire and Ginger Rogers thrilled millions in *Flying Down to Rio* and *Shall We Dance?* Shirley Temple charmed the public as their favorite child star. Judy Garland rose to stardom in *The Wizard of Oz,* while animated films like *Snow White* appealed to children of all ages. People enjoyed the triumph of justice and decency in *Mr. Smith Goes to Washington* and *You Can't Take It with You* with Jimmy Stewart. Dozens of light comedies starred such favorites as Cary Grant, Katharine Hepburn, Clark Gable, and Rosalind Russell, while Errol Flynn played larger-than-life roles such as Robin Hood. A different kind of escape was found in gangster movies with Edward G. Robinson, James Cagney, or George Raft. Near the end of the decade *Gone with the Wind,* released in 1939 and starring Clark Gable, captured the attention of American moviegoers with its depiction of an idealized and romantic American South in the Civil War era.

DIDYOUKNOW?

Among the most popular radio programs of the 1930s were the ongoing serial dramas known as "soap operas," so called because they were usually sponsored by household cleaning products. By 1940, soap operas made up as much as 90 percent of daytime sponsored radio programming.

The popular music of the decade was swing, and the big bands of Duke Ellington, Benny Goodman, Glenn Miller, Tommy Dorsey, and Harry James vied for public favor. The leading popular singer was Bing Crosby. City-based African Americans refined the country blues to city blues, and interracial audiences enjoyed both city blues and jazz. African American musicians were increasingly accepted by white audiences.

Comic strips existed before the thirties, but they became a standard newspaper feature as well as a source of comic books during the decade. "Dick Tracy" began his war on crime in 1931, and was assisted by "Superman" after 1938. "Tarzan" began to swing through the cartoon jungles in 1929, and "Buck Rogers" began the exploration of space in 1930.

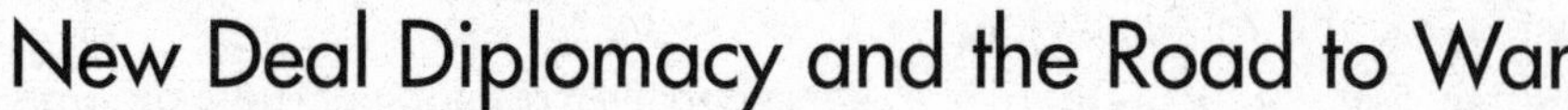

New Deal Diplomacy and the Road to War

The Good Neighbor Policy

Roosevelt and Secretary of State Cordell Hull continued the policies of their predecessors in endeavoring to improve relations with Latin American nations, and formalized their position by calling it the Good Neighbor Policy.

Nonintervention

At the Montevideo Conference of American Nations in December 1933, the United States renounced the right of intervention in the internal affairs of Latin American countries. In 1936, in the Buenos Aires Convention, the United States further agreed to submit all American disputes to arbitration. Accordingly, the marines were removed from Haiti, Nicaragua, and the Dominican Republic by 1934. The Haitian protectorate treaty was allowed to expire in 1936, the right of intervention in Panama was ended by treaty in 1936, and the receivership of the finances of the Dominican Republic ended in 1941.

Cuba

The United States did not intervene in the Cuban revolution in the spring of 1933, but it did back a coup by Fulgencio Batista to overthrow the liberal regime of Ramon Grau San Martin in 1934. Batista was given a favorable sugar import status for Cuba in return for establishing a conservative administration. In May 1934, the United States abrogated its Platt Amendment rights in Cuba except for control of the Guantanamo Bay Naval Base.

Mexico

The Mexican government of Lazaro Cardenas began to expropriate American property, including oil holdings, in 1934. Despite calls for intervention, Roosevelt insisted only on compensation. A joint commission worked out a settlement that was formally concluded on November 19, 1941.

The London Economic Conference

An international conference in London in June 1933 tried to obtain tariff reduction and currency stabilization for the industrialized nations. Roosevelt would not agree to peg the value of the dollar to other currencies because he feared that it might impede his recovery efforts. The conference failed for lack of American cooperation.

Recognition of Russia

The United States had not had diplomatic relations with the Union of Soviet Socialist Republics since it was established after the 1917 revolution. In an effort to open trade with Russia, mutual recognition was negotiated in November 1933. The financial results were disappointing.

United States Neutrality Legislation

Isolationism

The belief that the United States should stay out of foreign wars and problems began in the 1920s and grew in the 1930s. It was fed by House and Senate investigations of arms traffic and the munitions industry in 1933 and 1934, especially an examination of profiteering by bankers and munitions makers in drawing the United States into World War I by Senator Gerald Nye of North Dakota. Books of revisionist history, which asserted that Germany had not been responsible for World War I and that the United States had been misled, were also influential during the 1930s. A Gallup poll in April 1937 showed that almost two-thirds of those responding thought that American entry into World War I had been a mistake. Such feelings were strongest in the Midwest and among Republicans, but were found in all areas and across the political spectrum. Leading isolationists included Congressman Hamilton Fish of New York, Senator William Borah of Idaho, and Senator George Norris of Nebraska, all Republicans. Pacifist movements, such as the Fellowship of Christian Reconciliation, were influential among college and high school students and the clergy. Despite the aggressive postures of Adolf Hitler in Germany and Benito Mussolini in Italy, most Americans wanted to avoid being lured once again into a European war and felt neutrality was the best course.

The Johnson Act of 1934

When European nations stopped payment on World War I debts to the United States, the Johnson Act of 1934 prohibited any nation in default from selling securities to any American citizen or corporation.

The Neutrality Acts of 1935

Isolationist sentiment prompted Senator Key Pittman, a Nevada Democrat, to propose these laws. Roosevelt would have preferred more presidential flexibility, but Congress wanted to avoid flexibility and the mistakes of World War I. The laws provided that, on outbreak of war between foreign nations, all exports of American arms and munitions to them would be embargoed for six months. In addition, American ships were prohibited from carrying arms to any belligerent, and the president was to warn American citizens not to travel on belligerent ships.

The Neutrality Acts of 1936

The Neutrality Acts of 1936 gave the president authority to determine when a state of war existed, and prohibited any loans or credits to belligerents.

The Neutrality Acts of 1937

The Neutrality Acts of 1937 gave the president authority to determine if a civil war was a threat to world peace and covered by the Neutrality Acts, prohibited all arms sales to belligerents, and allowed the cash-and-carry sale of nonmilitary goods to belligerents.

TEST TIP

Try to leave a few minutes at the end of the time allotted for each essay to reread your work. This will help you ensure that you didn't accidentally skip an important word or idea as you were writing.

Threats to World Order

The Manchurian Crisis

In September 1931, the Japanese army invaded and seized the Chinese province of Manchuria. The action violated the Nine Power Pact and the Kellogg-Briand Pact. When the League of Nations sought consideration of some action against Japan, Hoover refused to consider either economic or military sanctions. The only American action was to refuse recognition of the action or the puppet state of Manchukuo that the Japanese created.

Ethiopia

Following a border skirmish between Italian and Ethiopian troops, the Italian army of Fascist dictator Benito Mussolini invaded Ethiopia from neighboring Italian colonies in October 1935. The League of Nations failed to take effective action, the United States looked on, and Ethiopia fell in May 1936.

Occupation of the Rhineland

In defiance of the Versailles Treaty, Nazi dictator Adolf Hitler sent his German army into the demilitarized Rhineland in March 1936.

The Rome-Berlin Axis

Germany and Italy, under Hitler and Mussolini, formed an alliance called the Rome-Berlin Axis on October 25, 1936.

The Sino-Japanese War

The Japanese launched a full-scale invasion of China in July 1937. When Japanese planes sank the American Gunboat *Panay* and three Standard Oil tankers on the Yangtze River in December 1937, the United States accepted a Japanese apology and damage payments, but the American public called for the withdrawal of all American forces from China.

The "Quarantine the Aggressor" Speech

In a speech in Chicago in October 1937, Roosevelt proposed that the democracies unite to quarantine the aggressor nations. When public opinion did not pick up on the idea, he did not press the issue.

German Expansion

Hitler brought about a union of Germany and Austria in March 1938, took the German-speaking Sudetenland from Czechoslovakia in September 1938, and occupied the rest of Czechoslovakia in March 1939.

The Invasion of Poland and the Beginning of World War II

On August 24, 1939, Germany signed a nonaggression pact with Russia that contained a secret provision to divide Poland between them. German forces then invaded Poland on September 1, 1939. Britain and France declared war on Germany on

September 3 because of their treaties with Poland. By the end of September, Poland had been dismembered by Germany and Russia, but the war continued in the west along the French-German border.

The American Response to the War in Europe

Preparedness

Even before the outbreak of World War II, Roosevelt began a preparedness program to improve American defenses. In May 1938, he requested and received a naval construction appropriation of about $1 billion. In October, Congress provided an additional $300 million for defense, and in January 1939 a regular defense appropriation of $1.3 billion with an added $525 million for equipment, especially airplanes. Defense spending increased after the outbreak of war. In August 1939 Roosevelt created the War Resources Board to develop a plan for industrial mobilization in the event of war. The next month he established the Office of Emergency Management in the White House to centralize mobilization activities.

The Neutrality Act of 1939

Roosevelt officially proclaimed the neutrality of the United States on September 5, 1939. He then called Congress into special session on September 21 and urged it to allow the cash-and-carry sale of arms. Despite opposition from isolationists, the Democratic Congress, in a vote that followed party lines, passed a new Neutrality Act in November. It allowed the cash-and-carry sale of arms and short-term loans to belligerents, but forbade American ships to trade with belligerents or Americans to travel on belligerent ships. The new law was helpful to the Allies because they controlled the Atlantic.

Changing American Attitudes

Hitler's armies invaded and quickly conquered Denmark and Norway in April 1940. In May, German forces swept through the Netherlands, Belgium, Luxembourg, and France. The British were driven from the continent, and France surrendered on June 22. Almost all Americans recognized Germany as a threat. They divided on whether to aid Britain or to concentrate on the defense of America. The Committee to Defend America by Aiding the Allies was formed in May 1940, and the America First Committee, which opposed involvement, was incorporated in September 1940.

Greenland

In April 1940, Roosevelt declared that Greenland, a possession of conquered Denmark, was covered by the Monroe Doctrine, and he supplied military assistance to set up a coastal patrol there.

Defense Mobilization

In May 1940, Roosevelt appointed a Council of National Defense chaired by William S. Knudson, the president of General Motors, to direct defense production and especially to build 50,000 planes. The Council was soon awarding defense contracts at the rate of $1.5 billion a month. The Office of Production Management was created to allocate scarce materials, and the Office of Price Administration was established to prevent inflation and protect consumers. In June, Roosevelt made Republicans Henry L. Stimson and Frank Knox secretaries of war and the navy, respectively, partly as an attempt to secure bipartisan support.

Selective Service

Congress approved the nation's first peacetime draft, the Selective Service and Training Act, in September 1940. Men ages 21 to 35 were registered, and many were called for one year of military training.

Destroyers-for-Bases Deal

Roosevelt had determined that to aid Britain in every way possible was the best way to avoid war with Germany. He ordered the army and navy to turn over all available weapons and munitions to private dealers for resale to Britain. In September 1940, he signed an agreement to give Britain 50 American destroyers in return for a 99-year lease on air and naval bases in British territories in Newfoundland, Bermuda, and the Caribbean.

The Election of 1940

The Republicans

As the election of 1940 approached, the Republicans passed over their isolationist front-runners, Senator Robert A. Taft of Ohio and New York attorney Thomas E. Dewey, to nominate Wendell L. Willkie of Indiana, a dark-horse candidate. Willkie was a liberal

Republican who had been a Democrat most of his life, and the head of an electric utility holding company that had fought against the TVA. The platform supported a strong defense program, but severely criticized the New Deal domestic policies.

The Democrats

Roosevelt did not reveal his intentions regarding a third term, but he neither endorsed another candidate nor discouraged his supporters. When the convention came in July, he sent a message to the Democratic National Committee implying that he would accept the nomination for a third time if it were offered. He was then nominated on the first ballot, breaking a tradition that had existed since the time of Washington. Only with difficulty did Roosevelt's managers persuade the delegates to accept his choice of vice president, Secretary of Agriculture Henry A. Wallace, to succeed Garner. The platform endorsed the foreign and domestic policies of the administration.

The Campaign

Willkie's basic agreement with Roosevelt's foreign policy made it difficult for him to campaign. Willkie had a folksy approach which appealed to many voters, but he first attacked Roosevelt for the slowness of the defense program, and then, late in the campaign, called him a warmonger. Roosevelt, who lost the support of many Democrats, including his adviser James Farley, over the third-term issue, campaigned very little. When Willkie began to gain on the warmongering issue, Roosevelt declared on October 30 that "your boys are not going to be sent into any foreign wars."

The Election

Roosevelt won by a much narrower margin than in 1936, with 27,243,466 votes, 54.7 percent, and 449 electoral votes. Willkie received 22,304,755 votes and 82 electoral votes. Socialist Norman Thomas had 100,264 votes, and Communist Earl Browder received 48,579.

DID YOU KNOW?

FDR is the only U.S. president to be elected to more than two terms in office, but he is not the only U.S. president to have won the popular vote more than twice. Both Andrew Jackson and Grover Cleveland carried the popular vote three times, but each failed to generate the necessary Electoral College votes to win office.

American Involvement with the European War

The Lend-Lease Act

The British were rapidly exhausting their cash reserves with which to buy American goods. In January 1941, Roosevelt proposed that the United States provide supplies to be paid for in goods and services after the war. The Lend-Lease Act was passed by Congress and signed on March 11, 1941, and the first appropriation of $7 billion was provided. In effect, the law changed the United States from a neutral to a nonbelligerent on the Allied side.

The Patrol of the Western Atlantic

The Germans stepped up their submarine warfare in the Atlantic to prevent the flow of American supplies to Britain. In April 1941 Roosevelt started the American Neutrality Patrol. The U.S. Navy would search out but not attack German submarines in the western half of the Atlantic, and warn British vessels of their location.

Greenland

In April 1941, United States forces occupied Greenland and in May the president declared a state of unlimited national emergency.

Occupation of Iceland

American Marines occupied Iceland, a Danish possession, in July 1941 to protect it from seizure by Germany. The U.S. Navy began to convoy American and Icelandic ships between the United States and Iceland.

The Atlantic Charter

On August 9, 1941, Roosevelt and Winston Churchill, the British prime minister, met for the first time on a British battleship off Newfoundland. They issued the Atlantic Charter, which described a postwar world based on self-determination for all nations. It also endorsed the principles of freedom of speech and religion and freedom from want and fear, which Roosevelt had proposed as the Four Freedoms earlier that year.

Aid to Russia

Germany invaded Russia in June 1941, and in November the United States extended lend-lease assistance to the Russians.

The Shoot-on-Sight Order

The American destroyer *Greer* was attacked by a German submarine near Iceland on September 4, 1941. Roosevelt ordered the American military forces to shoot on sight at any German or Italian vessel in the patrol zone. An undeclared naval war had begun. The American destroyer *Kearny* was attacked by a submarine on October 16, and the destroyer *Reuben James* was sunk on October 30, with 115 lives lost. In November, Congress authorized the arming of merchant ships.

The Road to Pearl Harbor

A Japanese Empire

Following their invasion of China in 1937, the Japanese began to speak of the Greater East Asia Co-Prosperity Sphere, a Japanese empire of undefined boundaries in east Asia and the western Pacific. Accordingly, they forced out American and other business interests from occupied China, declaring that the Open Door policy had ended. Roosevelt responded by lending money to China and requesting American aircraft manufacturers not to sell to Japan.

The Embargo of 1940

Following the fall of France, a new and more militant Japanese government in July 1940 obtained from the German-controlled Vichy French government the right to build air bases and to station troops in northern French Indochina. The United States, fearing that the step would lead to further expansion, responded in late July by placing an embargo on the export of aviation gasoline, lubricants, and scrap iron and steel to Japan, and by granting an additional loan to China. In December the embargo was extended to include iron ore and pig iron, some chemicals, machine tools, and other products.

The Tripartite Pact

Japan joined with Germany and Italy to form the Rome-Berlin-Tokyo Axis on September 27, 1940, when it signed the Tripartite Pact, or Triple Alliance, with the other Axis powers.

The Embargo of 1941

In July 1941, Japan extracted a new concession from Vichy France by obtaining military control of southern Indochina. Roosevelt reacted by freezing Japanese funds in the United States, closing the Panama Canal to Japan, activating the Philippine militia, and placing an embargo on the export of oil and other vital products to Japan.

Japanese-American Negotiations

Negotiations to end the impasse between the United States and Japan were conducted in Washington between Secretary Hull and Japanese Ambassador Kichisaburo Nomura. Hull demanded that Japan withdraw from Indochina and China, promise not to attack any other area in the western Pacific, and withdraw from the Tripartite Pact in return for the reopening of American trade. The Japanese offered to withdraw from Indochina when the Chinese war was satisfactorily settled, to promise no further expansion, and to agree to ignore any obligation under the Tripartite Pact to go to war if the United States entered a defensive war with Germany. Hull refused to compromise.

TEST TIP

No peeking! Wait until the test proctor tells you to begin work on your AP exam before opening your test booklet. Starting too soon can cause the proctor to disqualify you to take the exam.

A Summit Conference Proposed

The Japanese proposed in August 1941 that Roosevelt meet personally with the Japanese prime minister, Prince Konoye, in an effort to resolve their differences. Such an action might have strengthened the position of Japanese moderates, but Roosevelt replied in September that he would do so only if Japan agreed to leave China. No meeting was held.

Final Negotiations

In October 1941, a new military cabinet headed by General Hideki Tojo took control of Japan. The Japanese secretly decided to make a final effort to negotiate and to go to war if no solution was found by November 25. A new round of talks followed in Washington, but neither side would make a substantive change in its position, and on November 26, Hull repeated the American demand that the Japanese remove all their forces from China and Indochina immediately. The Japanese gave final approval on December 1 for an attack on the United States.

Japanese Attack Plans

The Japanese planned a major offensive to take the Dutch East Indies, Malaya, and the Philippines in order to obtain the oil, metals, and other raw materials that they needed. At the same time they would attack Pearl Harbor in Hawaii to destroy the American Pacific fleet to keep it from interfering with their plans.

American Awareness of Japanese Plans

The United States had broken the Japanese diplomatic codes and knew that trouble was imminent. Between December 1 and December 6, 1941, it became clear to administration leaders that Japanese task forces were being ordered into battle. American commanders in the Pacific were warned of possible aggressive action there, but not forcefully. Apparently, most American leaders thought that Japan would attack the Dutch East Indies and Malaya, but would avoid American territory so as not to provoke action by the United States. Some argue that Roosevelt wanted to let the Japanese attack so that the American people would be squarely behind the war.

The Pearl Harbor Attack

At 7:55 a.m. on Sunday December 7, 1941, the first wave of Japanese carrier-based planes attacked the American fleet in Pearl Harbor. A second wave followed at 8:50 a.m. American defensive action was almost nil, but by the second wave a few anti-aircraft batteries were operating and a few Army planes from another base in Hawaii engaged the enemy. The United States suffered the loss of two battleships sunk, six damaged and out of action, three cruisers and three destroyers sunk or damaged, and a number of lesser vessels destroyed or damaged. All of the 150 aircraft at Pearl Harbor were destroyed on the ground. Worst of all, 2,323 American servicemen were killed and about 1,100 wounded. The Japanese lost 29 planes, five midget submarines, and one fleet submarine.

The attack on Pearl Harbor by the Japanese pushed the United States into World War II. (U.S. Naval Historical Center Photo)

The Declaration of War

On December 8, 1941, Roosevelt told a joint session of Congress that the day before had been a "date that would live in infamy." Congress declared war on Japan with one dissenting vote. On December 11, Germany and Italy declared war on the United States.

Declaration of the United Nations

On January 1, 1942, representatives of 26 nations met in Washington, D.C., and signed the Declaration of the United Nations, pledging themselves to the principles of the Atlantic Charter and promising not to make a separate peace with their common enemies.

The Home Front

War Production Board

The War Production Board was established in 1942 by President Franklin D. Roosevelt for the purpose of regulating the use of raw materials.

DIDYOUKNOW?

Rationed goods ranged from sugar and meat to fabric and chicken wire. Even clothing styles were affected by rationing, with government regulations barring cuffs on women's dress sleeves and limiting the size of hems and belts.

Wage and Price Controls

In April 1942 the General Maximum Price Regulation Act froze prices and extended rationing. In April 1943 prices, wages, and salaries were all frozen.

Lula Barber, Meta Kres, and Meda Brendall (from left) outside welding shop at the Bethlehem-Fairfield Shipyards, 1942, Baltimore, Maryland. Women made a major contribution to the war effort without even leaving the States. Photo courtesy of Veterans History Project, American Folklife Center, (U.S. Library of Congress)

Social Changes

Rural areas lost population while coastal areas increased rapidly. Women entered the workforce in increasing numbers. Blacks moved from the rural South to northern and western cities with racial tensions often resulting, most notably in the June 1943 racial riot in Detroit.

Korematsu v. United States

In 1944, the Supreme Court upheld President Roosevelt's 1942 order that Issei (Japanese Americans who had emigrated from Japan) and Nisei (native-born Japanese Americans) be relocated to internment camps. The camps were closed in March 1946.

DIDYOUKNOW?

In 1988, the U.S. government issued a formal apology to Japanese Americans who were interned during World War II. Along with the apology, the government compensated former internees or their families and established an education fund to make sure people learned about this aspect of U.S. history.

Presidential Election of 1944

President Franklin D. Roosevelt, together with new vice presidential candidate Harry S. Truman of Missouri, defeated his Republican opponent, Governor Thomas Dewey of New York.

Death of Roosevelt

Roosevelt died on April 12, 1945, at Warm Springs, Georgia. Harry S. Truman became president.

The North African and European Theatres

Nearly 400 ships were lost in American waters of the Atlantic to German submarines between January and June 1942.

The United States joined in the bombing of the European continent in July 1942. Bombing increased during 1943 and 1944 and lasted to the end of the war.

The Allied army under Dwight D. Eisenhower attacked French North Africa in November 1942. The French surrendered.

In the Battle of Kassarine Pass in February 1943, North Africa, the Allied army met General Erwin Rommel's Africa Korps. Although the battle is variously interpreted as a standoff or a defeat for the U.S., Rommel's forces were soon trapped by the British moving in from Egypt. In May 1943, Rommel's Africa Korps surrendered.

Allied armies under George S. Patton invaded Sicily from Africa in July 1943 and gained control by mid-August. Moving from Sicily, the Allied armies invaded the Italian mainland in September. Benito Mussolini had already fallen from power and his successor, Marshal Pietro Badoglio, surrendered. The Germans, however, put up a stiff resistance with the result that Rome did not fall until June 1944.

In March 1944, the Soviet Union began pushing into eastern Europe.

On "D-Day," June 6, 1944, Allied armies under Dwight D. Eisenhower, now commander in chief of Supreme Headquarters, Allied Expeditionary Forces, began an invasion of Normandy, France. Allied armies under General Omar Bradley took the transportation hub of Saint-Lô, France in July.

Allied armies liberated Paris in August. By mid-September they had arrived at the Rhine, on the edge of Germany.

Beginning December 16, 1944, at the Battle of the Bulge, the Germans counterattacked, driving the Allies back about 50 miles into Belgium. By January, the Allies were once more advancing toward Germany.

The Allies crossed the Rhine in March 1945. In the last week of April, Eisenhower's forces met the Soviet army at the Elbe.

On May 7, 1945, Germany surrendered.

The Pacific Theatre

By the end of December 1941, Guam, Wake Island, the Gilbert Islands, and Hong Kong had fallen to the Japanese. In January 1942, Raboul, New Britain fell, followed in February by Singapore and Java and in March by Rangoon, Burma.

The U.S. air raids on Tokyo in April 1942 were militarily inconsequential, but they raised Allied morale.

U.S. forces surrendered at Corregidor, Philippines, on May 6, 1942.

In the Battle of the Coral Sea, May 7–8, 1942 (northeast of Australia, south of New Guinea and the Solomon Islands), planes from the American carriers *Lexington* and *Yorktown* forced Japanese troop transports to turn back from attacking Port Moresby. The battle stopped the Japanese advance on Australia.

Unable to obtain a Japanese surrender and fearing a Japanese invasion that advisors said could take half a million American lives, President Truman authorized the dropping of two atomic bombs in August 1945 over Hiroshima, shown, and Nagasaki. Truman's decision remains the subject of great scholarly debate. (AP/Wide World Photo)

At the Battle of Midway, June 4–7, 1942, American air power destroyed four Japanese carriers and about 300 planes while the U.S. lost the carrier *Yorktown* and one destroyer. The battle proved to be the turning point in the Pacific.

A series of land, sea, and air battles took place around Guadalcanal in the Solomon Islands from August 1942 to February 1943, stopping the Japanese.

The Allied strategy of island hopping, begun in 1943, sought to neutralize Japanese strongholds with air and sea power and then move on. General Douglas MacArthur commanded the land forces moving from New Guinea toward the Philippines, while Admiral Chester W. Nimitz directed the naval attack on important Japanese islands in the central Pacific.

U.S. forces advanced into the Gilberts (November 1943), the Marshalls (January 1944), and the Marianas (June 1944).

In the Battle of the Philippine Sea, June 19–20, 1944, the Japanese lost three carriers, two submarines, and over 300 planes while the Americans lost 17 planes. After the American capture of the Marianas, General Tojo resigned as premier of Japan.

The Battle of Leyte Gulf, October 25, 1944, involved three major engagements that resulted in Japan's loss of most of its remaining naval power. It also brought the first use of the Japanese kamikaze, or suicide, attacks by Japanese pilots who crashed into American carriers.

Forces under General Douglas MacArthur liberated Manila in March 1945.

Between April and June 1945, in the battle for Okinawa, nearly 50,000 American casualties resulted from the fierce fighting that virtually destroyed Japan's remaining defenses.

The Atomic Bomb

The Manhattan Engineering District was established by the Army engineers in August 1942 for the purpose of developing an atomic bomb. The mission eventually became known as the Manhattan Project. J. Robert Oppenheimer directed the design and construction of a transportable atomic bomb at Los Alamos, New Mexico.

On December 2, 1942, Enrico Fermi and his colleagues at the University of Chicago produced the first atomic chain reaction.

On July 16, 1945, the first atomic bomb was exploded at Alamogordo, New Mexico.

The *Enola Gay* dropped an atomic bomb on Hiroshima, Japan, on August 6, 1945, killing about 78,000 people and injuring 100,000 more. On August 9, a second bomb was dropped on Nagasaki, Japan. Some 40,000 people were killed in the explosion. Thousands more died later from burns, injuries, and radiation exposure.

On August 8, 1945, the Soviet Union entered the war against Japan.

Japan surrendered on August 15, 1945. The formal surrender was signed on September 2.

DID YOU KNOW?

First published in *The New Yorker* in 1946, John Hersey's *Hiroshima* recounted first-hand experiences of the dropping of the atomic bomb. The story was so popular that the magazine sold out within hours of reaching newsstands, and people sold copies for multiple times their face value. *Hiroshima* helped change many Americans' minds about the use of the nuclear bomb, and caused many to see the Japanese in a different way.

Diplomacy and Wartime Conferences

Casablanca Conference

On January 14–25, 1943, Franklin D. Roosevelt and Winston Churchill, prime minister of Great Britain, declared a policy of unconditional surrender for "all enemies."

Moscow Conference

In October 1943, Secretary of State Cordell Hull obtained Soviet agreement to enter the war against Japan after Germany was defeated and to participate in a world organization after the war was over.

Declaration of Cairo

Issued on December 1, 1943, after Roosevelt met with General Chiang Kai-shek in Cairo from November 22 to 26, the Declaration of Cairo called for Japan's unconditional surrender and stated that all Chinese territories occupied by Japan would be returned to China and that Korea would be free and independent.

Teheran Conference

The first "Big Three" (Roosevelt, Churchill, and Stalin) conference met at Teheran from November 28 to December 1, 1943. Stalin reaffirmed the Soviet commitment to enter the war against Japan and discussed coordination of the Soviet offensive with the Allied invasion of France.

Yalta Conference

On February 4–11, 1945 the "Big Three" met to discuss postwar Europe. Stalin said that the Soviet Union would enter the Pacific war within three months after Germany surrendered and agreed to the "Declaration of Liberated Europe," which called for free elections. They called for a conference on world organization, to meet in the U.S. beginning on April 25, 1945, and agreed that the Soviets would have three votes in the General Assembly and that the U.S., Great Britain, the Soviet Union, France, and China would be permanent members of the Security Council. Germany was divided into occupation zones, and a coalition government of communists and non-communists was agreed to for Poland. Roosevelt accepted Soviet control of Outer Mongolia, the Kurile

Islands, the southern half of Sakhalin Island, Port Arthur (Darien), and participation in the operation of the Manchurian railroads.

At the Yalta Conference in 1945, Churchill, Roosevelt, and Stalin planned for Nazi Germany's final defeat and occupation. (Photo by ITAR-Tass/Sovfoto)

Potsdam Conference

From July 17 to August 2, 1945, Truman, Stalin, and Clement Atlee (who during the conference replaced Churchill as prime minister of Great Britain) met at Potsdam. During the conference, Truman ordered the dropping of the atomic bomb on Japan. The conference disagreed on most major issues, but did establish a Council of Foreign Ministers to draft peace treaties for the Balkans. Approval was also given to the concept of war-crimes trials and the demilitarization and denazification of Germany.

(Before taking the quiz noted below, please review the summary timeline for this chapter on the following pages.)

Global and Domestic Challenges (1890–1945)

Historical Timeline (1890–1945)

1890	Alfred Mahan writes *The Influence of Sea Power Upon History*
1898	U.S.S. *Maine* sinks in Havana Harbor Spanish-American War Dewey captures Philippines U.S. annexes Hawaii
1899	Aguinaldo leads Filipinos against U.S. troops Treaty of Paris settles the Spanish-American War Open Door Policy in China
1900	Boxer Rebellion in China
1902	Platt Amendment President Roosevelt settles anthracite coal strike
1903	U.S. recognizes Panama's independence
1906	Upton Sinclair writes *The Jungle* Pure Food and Drug Act Hepburn Act
1909	NAACP formed
1911	Triangle Shirtwaist Factory Fire
1912	Wilson elected president as Roosevelt's third-party effort fails
1913	Underwood Tariff Federal Reserve Act 16th Amendment (income tax) ratified 17th Amendment (direct senator election) ratified
1914	Clayton Antitrust Act Panama Canal opens World War I begins
1915	Germans sink *Lusitania*
1916	Margaret Sanger organizes New York Birth Control League Gen. Pershing pursues Pancho Villa in Mexico
1917	Germany resumes unrestricted submarine warfare U.S. declares war on Germany War Industries Board established Espionage Act passed Russian Revolution Committee on Public Information established
1918	Wilson proposes Fourteen Points Armistice ends war U.S. troops intervene in Russia

Historical Timeline (1890–1945)

1919	Treaty of Versailles Red Scare and Palmer raids Senate rejects U.S. role in League of Nations 18th Amendment (prohibition) ratified Over 20 percent of U.S. labor force goes on strike *Schenck v. United States* Race riots and lynchings throughout U.S.
1920	19th Amendment (women's suffrage) ratified
1921	Washington Naval Conference Emergency Quota Act restricts immigration
1923	Teapot Dome scandal Marcus Garvey claims 6 million followers Ku Klux Klan claims 5 million members
1924	National Origins Act sets 2 percent quotas for immigration
1925	Scopes Tennessee evolution trial Model T Ford drops to cost of $290 (three months' wages)
1927	Lindbergh's solo flight across the Atlantic Sacco and Vanzetti executed Babe Ruth hits 60 home runs for the Yankees Al Jolson stars in *The Jazz Singer*, the first talking film
1928	Hoover elected president Fifty-two nations sign Kellogg-Briand Pact renouncing war
1929	Stock market crashes in October
1930	Hawley-Smoot Tariff raises duties on farm products and manufactured goods
1931	Japan invades Manchuria
1932	Reconstruction Finance Corporation attempts to support industry Bonus Expeditionary Force marches on Washington, D.C. Franklin Roosevelt wins presidency
1933	Prohibition repealed Hundred Days of legislation follows FDR's inauguration Banks closed after over 6,000 fail FDIC established by Glass-Steagall Act Agricultural Adjustment Act passed National Industrial Recovery Act passed Tennessee Valley Authority established Civilian Conservation Corps enrolls 250,000 young men Hitler becomes chancellor of Germany
1934	Securities and Exchange Commission established Huey Long begins Share Our Wealth clubs Dr. Francis Townsend promotes Old Age Revolving Pension Plan Nye Committee probes World War I profiteering by American industrialists

Historical Timeline (1890–1945)

1935	*Schecter v. United States* rules NIRA unconstitutional Works Progress Administration established National Labor Relations (Wagner) Act protects workers' rights Social Security Act passed Congress passes first of annual Neutrality Acts
1936	FDR defeats Republican Landon and third-party (Union Party) for president General Motors sitdown strike Germany occupies the Rhineland Spanish Civil War begins Ethiopia falls to Italy
1937	FDR proposes court-packing plan, which fails Japan invades China U.S. gunship *Panay* sunk by Japanese in Yangtze River
1938	Appeasement at Munich by England's Chamberlain as Germany takes Sudetenland
1939	Czechoslovakia falls to Germany Austria votes to be annexed by Germany Germany invades Poland Neutrality Act allows cash-and-carry for military purchases Germany and Soviet Union sign nonaggression pact
1940	Germany conquers Denmark, Norway, the Netherlands, Belgium, and France Congress approves first peace-time draft U.S. and Great Britain sign destroyers for bases deal America First Committee established, urging U.S. neutrality Italy, Germany, and Japan form the Rome-Berlin-Tokyo Axis FDR wins unprecedented third term for president
1941	Lend-Lease Act allows U.S. to financially assist Allied nations FDR and Churchill sign Atlantic Charter, pledging self-determination for all nations Germany invades Soviet Union Japan attacks Pearl Harbor, Hawaii, on December 7, killing 2,323 U.S. servicemen U.S. declares war on Japan on December 8
1942	Japan captures Philippine Islands as Bataan and Corregidor fall War Production Board established U.S. begins interning Japanese American citizens Germany sinks 400 American ships Battle of Coral Sea Battle of Midway U.S. attacks Vichy forces and Germans in North Africa Manhattan Project begins
1943	Casablanca Conference Americans seize Guadalcanal Island Soviets defeat Germans at Stalingrad Allies invade Italy Teheran Conference

Historical Timeline (1890–1945)

1944	Allies invade France at Normandy (D-Day) on June 6 Battle of Leyte Gulf Roosevelt elected president for fourth term Island-hopping campaign retakes Guam Island Battle of the Bulge
1945	Yalta Conference U.S. bombing raids destroy 250,000 buildings in Tokyo 50 nations approve United Nations Charter in San Francisco Conference Hitler commits suicide in Berlin bunker V-E Day Americans recapture the Philippine Islands Potsdam Conference Bomb dropped on Hiroshima Soviets declare war on Japan Bomb dropped on Nagasaki V-J Day

Chapter 10

Domestic Prosperity and International Responsibilities (1945–1980)

The Emergence of the Cold War and Containment

Failure of U.S.–Soviet Cooperation

By the end of 1945, the Soviet Union controlled most of Eastern Europe, Outer Mongolia, parts of Manchuria, northern Korea, the Kurile Islands, and Sakhalin Island. In 1946–47 it took over Poland, Hungary, Rumania, and Bulgaria. This growing sphere of influence alarmed U.S. officials.

Iron Curtain

In a speech in Fulton, Missouri, in 1946, Winston Churchill stated that an Iron Curtain had been spread across Europe separating the democratic from the authoritarian communist states.

Containment

In 1946, career diplomat and Soviet expert George F. Kennan warned that the Soviet Union had no intention of living peacefully with the United States. The next year, in July 1947, he wrote an anonymous article for *Foreign Affairs* in which he called for a counterforce to Soviet pressures for the purpose of "containing" communism. This approach dominated American policy throughout the Cold War.

Truman Doctrine

In February 1947, Great Britain notified the United States that it could no longer aid the Greek government in its war against communist insurgents. President Harry S. Truman asked Congress for $400 million in military and economic aid for Greece and Turkey. He argued, as part of what became known as the "Truman Doctrine," that the United States must support free peoples who were resisting communist domination.

Marshall Plan

Secretary of State George C. Marshall proposed in June 1947 that the United States provide economic aid to help rebuild Europe. Meeting in July, representatives of the European nations agreed on a recovery program jointly financed by the United States and the European countries. The following March, Congress passed the European Recovery Program, popularly known as the Marshall Plan, providing more than $12 billion in aid.

Berlin Crisis

After the United States, France, and Great Britain announced plans to create a West German Republic out of their German zones, the Soviet Union in June 1948 blocked surface access to Berlin, which was located in their zone. The U.S. then instituted an airlift to transport supplies to the city until the Soviets lifted their blockade in May 1949.

The Berlin Airlift, 1948, became a powerful symbol of the Allies' interest in stemming further Soviet expansion in Europe. (AP/Wide World Photo)

NATO

In April 1949, the North Atlantic Treaty Organization was established by the United States, Great Britain, France, Italy, Belgium, the Netherlands, Luxembourg, Denmark, Norway, Portugal, Iceland, and Canada. The signatories pledged that an attack against one would be considered an attack against all. Greece and Turkey joined the alliance in 1952 and West Germany in 1954. The Soviets formed the Warsaw Treaty Organization in 1955 to counteract NATO.

Atomic Bomb

The Soviet Union exploded an atomic device in September 1949.

United Nations

From April to June 1945, representatives from 50 countries met in San Francisco to establish the United Nations. The UN charter created a General Assembly composed of all member nations that would act as the ultimate policy-making body. A Security Council, made up of 11 members, including the United States, Great Britain, France, the Soviet Union, and China as permanent members and six additional nations elected by the General Assembly for two-year terms, would be responsible for settling disputes among UN member nations. Each of the permanent members of the Security Council was granted a veto over UN actions, which resulted in few interventions in international crises.

Containment in Asia

China

Between 1945 and 1948, the United States gave over $2 billion in aid to the Nationalist Chinese under Chiang Kai-shek and sent George C. Marshall to settle the conflict between Chiang's Nationalists and Mao Tse-tung's Communists. In 1949, however, Mao defeated Chiang and forced the Nationalists to flee to Formosa (Taiwan). Mao established the People's Republic of China on the mainland.

Korean War

On June 25, 1950, North Korea invaded South Korea. President Truman committed U.S. forces commanded by General MacArthur but under United Nations auspices. By October, the UN forces (mostly American) had driven north of the 38th parallel that divided North and South Korea. Chinese troops attacked MacArthur's forces on November 26, pushing them south of the 38th parallel, but by spring 1951, UN forces had recovered their offensive posture. MacArthur called for a naval blockade of China and bombing north of the Yalu River, criticizing the president for fighting a limited war. In April 1951, Truman removed MacArthur from command.

DID YOU KNOW?

The Korean War was the setting for one of the most popular U.S. television shows of all time: *M*A*S*H.* The program ran for 11 seasons, and its final episode in 1983 drew nearly 106 million viewers—a record-setting figure unbroken until the 2010 Super Bowl.

Armistice

Armistice talks began with North Korea in the summer of 1951. In June 1953, an armistice was signed leaving Korea divided along virtually the same boundary that had existed prior to the war.

Eisenhower-Dulles Foreign Policy

John Foster Dulles

Dwight D. Eisenhower, elected president in 1952, chose John Foster Dulles as secretary of state. Dulles talked of a more aggressive foreign policy, calling for "massive retaliation" and "liberation" rather than containment. He wished to emphasize nuclear deterrents rather than conventional armed forces. Dulles served as secretary of state until ill health forced him to resign in April 1959. Christian A. Herter took his place.

Hydrogen Bomb

The U.S. exploded its first hydrogen bomb in November 1952. The Soviets followed with theirs in August 1953.

Soviet Change of Power

Josef Stalin died in March 1953. After an internal power struggle that lasted until 1955, Nikita Khrushchev emerged as the Soviet leader. He talked of both "burying" capitalism and "peaceful coexistence."

Asia

In 1954, the French asked the U.S. to commit air forces to rescue French forces at Dien Bien Phu, Vietnam, as they were besieged by the nationalist forces led by Ho Chi Minh, but Eisenhower refused. In May 1954, Dien Bien Phu surrendered.

Geneva Accords Divide Vietnam

France, Great Britain, the Soviet Union, and China signed the Geneva Accords in July 1954, dividing Vietnam along the 17th parallel. The North would be under Ho Chi Minh and the South under Emperor Bao Dai. Elections were scheduled for 1956 to unify the country, but Ngo Dinh Diem overthrew Bao Dai and prevented the elections from taking place. The United States supplied economic aid to South Vietnam.

Southeast Asia Treaty Organization

Dulles attempted to establish a Southeast Asia Treaty Organization parallel to NATO, but was able to obtain only the Philippine Republic, Thailand, and Pakistan as signatories in September 1954.

Quemoy and Matsu

The small islands of Quemoy and Matsu off the coast of China were occupied by the Nationalist Chinese under Chiang Kai-shek, but claimed by the People's Republic of China. In 1955, after the mainland Chinese began shelling these islands, Eisenhower obtained authorization from Congress to defend Formosa (Taiwan) and related areas.

Middle East—The Suez Canal Crisis

The United States agreed to lend money to Egypt, under the leadership of Colonel Gamal Abdul Nasser, to build the Aswan Dam but refused to give arms. Nasser then drifted toward the Soviet Union and in 1956 established diplomatic relations with the People's Republic of China. In July 1956, the U.S. withdrew its loan to Egypt. In response, Nasser nationalized the Suez Canal. France, Great Britain, and Israel then attacked Egypt, but Eisenhower demanded that they pull out. On November 6, a cease-fire was announced.

Eisenhower Doctrine

President Eisenhower announced in January 1957 that the U.S. was prepared to use armed force in the Middle East against communist aggression. Under this doctrine, U.S. marines entered Beirut, Lebanon, in July 1958 to promote political stability during a change of governments. The Marines left in October.

Soviet-American Visitations

Vice President Richard M. Nixon visited the Soviet Union and Soviet Vice Premier Anastas I. Mikoyan came to the United States in the summer of 1959. In September, Premier Khrushchev toured the United States and agreed to another summit meeting.

U-2 Incident

On May 1, 1960, an American U-2 spy plane was shot down over the Soviet Union and pilot Francis Gary Powers was captured. While at first denying this was a U.S. spy mission, Eisenhower ultimately took responsibility for the plane, and Khrushchev angrily called off the Paris summit conference that was to take place in a few days.

Latin America

The U.S. supported the overthrow of President Jacobo Árbenz Guzmán of Guatemala in 1954 because he began accepting arms from the Soviet Union.

Vice President Nixon had to call off an eight-nation goodwill tour of Latin America after meeting hostile mobs in Venezuela and Peru in 1958.

In January 1959, Fidel Castro overthrew Fulgencio Batista, dictator of Cuba. Castro soon began criticizing the United States and moved closer to the Soviet Union, signing a trade agreement with the Soviets in February 1960. The United States prohibited the importation of Cuban sugar in October 1960 and broke off diplomatic relations in January 1961. Strained diplomatic and trade relations continue between the U.S. and Cuba to this day.

TEST TIP

Wondering whether your essay responses are scored fairly? AP exam essay graders are experienced college professors and high school teachers who are specially trained for the question they're scoring. Scores are checked to ensure that different graders score essays in a consistent, fair manner.

The Politics of Affluence: Demobilization and Domestic Policy

Truman Becomes President

Harry S. Truman, formerly a senator from Missouri and vice president of the United States, became president on April 12, 1945. In September 1945, he proposed a liberal legislative program, the Fair Deal, which included expansion of unemployment insurance, extension of the Employment Service, a higher minimum wage, a permanent Fair Employment Practices Commission, slum clearance, low-rent housing, regional TVA-type programs, and a public works program. Truman was unable to get it through Congress.

Atomic Energy

Congress created the Atomic Energy Commission in 1946, establishing civilian control over nuclear development and giving the president sole authority over the use of atomic weapons in warfare.

Price Controls

Truman vetoed a weak price control bill passed by Congress, thereby ending the wartime price control program. When prices quickly increased about six percent, Congress passed another bill in July 1946. Although Truman signed this bill, he used its powers inconsistently, especially when—bowing to pressure—he ended price controls on beef. In late 1946, he lifted controls on all items except rents, sugar, and rice.

Labor

In early 1946, the United Auto Workers, under Walter Reuther, struck General Motors, and steelworkers, under Philip Murray, struck U.S. Steel, demanding wage increases. Truman suggested an 18-cent-per-hour wage increase and in February allowed U.S. Steel to raise prices to cover the increase. This formula became the basis for settlements in other industries. After John L. Lewis's United Mine Workers struck in April 1946, Truman ordered the government to take over the mines and then accepted the union's demands, which included safety and health and welfare benefits. In addition, the president averted a railway strike by seizing the railroads and threatening to draft strikers into the Army.

Demobilization

By 1947, the total armed forces had been cut to 1.5 million. The Army fell to 600,000 from a World War II peak of 8 million. The Serviceman's Readjustment Act (G.I. Bill of Rights) of 1944 provided $13 billion in aid, ranging from education to housing.

Taft-Hartley Act

The Republicans, who had gained control of Congress as a result of the 1946 elections, sought to control the power of the unions through the Taft-Hartley Act, passed in 1947. Truman vetoed the bill, but Congress passed it over his veto. This act made the "closed-shop" illegal; labor unions could no longer force employers to hire only union members, although it allowed the "union shop" in which newly hired employees were required to join the union. It established an 80-day cooling-off period for strikers in key industries; ended the practice of employers collecting dues for unions; forbade such actions as secondary boycotts, jurisdictional strikes, featherbedding, and contributing to political campaigns; and required an anti-communist oath of union officials. The act slowed down efforts to unionize the South, and by 1954, 15 states had passed "right to work" laws, forbidding the "union shop."

Civil Rights

During World War II, black leaders had promoted a Double V Campaign: victory over fascism abroad and victory over discrimination at home. In 1946, Truman appointed the Presidents Committee on Civil Rights, which a year later produced its report, *To Secure These Rights.* The report called for the elimination of all aspects of segregation. In 1948, the president banned racial discrimination in federal hiring practices and ordered desegregation of the armed forces.

Presidential Succession

The Presidential Succession Act of 1947 placed the Speaker of the House and the president pro tempore of the Senate ahead of the secretary of state and after the vice president in the line of succession. The 22nd Amendment to the Constitution, ratified in 1951, limited the president to two terms.

Election of 1948

Truman was the Democratic nominee, but the Democrats were split by the States' Rights Democratic Party (Dixiecrats), which nominated Governor Strom Thurmond of South Carolina, and the Progressive Party, which nominated former Vice President Henry Wallace. The Republicans nominated Governor Thomas E. Dewey of New York. After traveling widely and attacking the "do-nothing Congress," Truman won a surprise victory.

Truman's Domestic Programs—The Fair Deal

The Fair Deal Program

Truman sought to enlarge and extend the New Deal. He proposed increasing the minimum wage, extending Social Security to more people, maintaining rent controls, clearing slums and building public housing, and providing more money to the TVA, rural electrification, and farm housing. He also introduced bills dealing with civil rights, national health insurance, federal aid to education, and repeal of the Taft-Hartley Act. A coalition of Republicans and southern Democrats prevented little more than the maintenance of existing programs.

Farm Policy

Because of improvements in agriculture, overproduction continued to be a problem. Secretary of agriculture Charles F. Brennan proposed a program of continued price supports for storable crops and guaranteed minimum incomes to farmers of perishable crops. It was defeated in Congress and surpluses continued to pile up.

Anticommunism

Smith Act

The Smith Act of 1940, which made it illegal to advocate the overthrow of the government by force or to belong to an organization advocating such a position, was used by the Truman administration to jail leaders of the American Communist Party.

Loyalty Review Board

In response to criticism, particularly from the House Committee on Un-American Activities, that his administration was "soft on communism," Truman established the Loyalty Review Board in 1947 to review government employees.

The Hiss Case

In 1948, Whittaker Chambers, formerly a communist and then an editor of *Time*, charged Alger Hiss, a former State Department official and then president of the Carnegie Endowment for International Peace, with having been a communist who supplied classified American documents to the Soviet Union. In 1950, Hiss was convicted of perjury, the statute of limitations on his alleged spying having run out.

McCarran Internal Security Act

Passed in 1950, this act required communist-front organizations to register with the attorney general and prevented their members from defense work and travel abroad. It was passed over Truman's veto.

Rosenberg Case

In 1950, Julius and Ethel Rosenberg, as well as Harry Gold, were charged with giving atomic secrets to the Soviet Union. The Rosenbergs were convicted and executed in 1953.

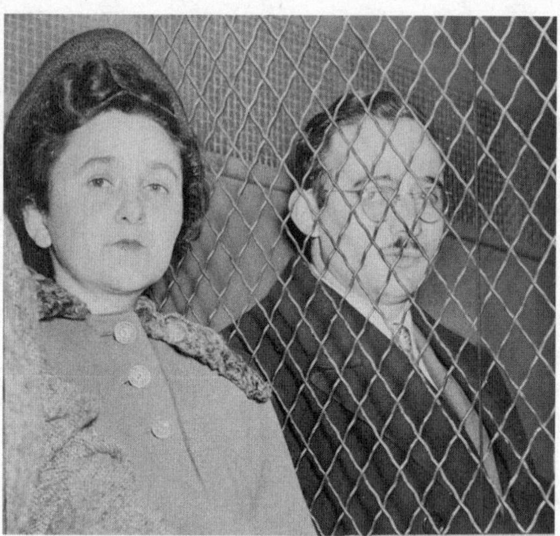

Julius and Ethel Rosenberg were executed in 1953 for espionage. (U.S. Library of Congress)

Joseph McCarthy

On February 9, 1950, Senator Joseph R. McCarthy of Wisconsin stated that he had a list of known communists who were working in the State Department. He later expanded his attacks to diplomats and scholars and contributed to the electoral defeat of two senators. After making charges against the army, he was censured and discredited by the Senate in 1954 (following landmark reporting by CBS News) and died in 1957.

TEST TIP

Always remember to make sure your free-response, DBQ, and short-answer responses directly answer the question asked. With both the free-response and DBQ, be sure to clearly state your thesis to ensure that your writing adequately conveys that you have responded to the question asked. With your short-answer responses, be economical with words, but specific in your examples.

Eisenhower's Dynamic Conservatism

1952 Election

In the 1952 presidential campaign, the Republicans nominated Dwight D. Eisenhower, most recently NATO commander, for the presidency and Richard M. Nixon, a senator from California, for the vice presidency The Democrats nominated Governor Adlai E. Stevenson of Illinois for president. Eisenhower won by a landslide and, for the first time since Reconstruction, the Republicans won some Southern states.

Conservatism

Eisenhower sought to balance the budget and lower taxes, but did not attempt to roll back existing social and economic legislation. Eisenhower first described his policy as "dynamic conservatism" and then as "progressive moderation." The administration abolished the Reconstruction Finance Corporation, ended wage and price controls, and reduced farm price supports. It cut the budget and in 1954 lowered tax rates for corporations and individuals with high incomes; an economic slump, however, made balancing the budget difficult.

Public Power

Opposed to the expansion of the TVA, the Eisenhower administration supported a plan to have a privately-owned power plant (called Dixon-Yates) built to supply electricity to Memphis, Tennessee. After two years of controversy and discovery that the government consultant would financially benefit from Dixon-Yates, the administration turned to a municipally-owned power plant. The Idaho Power Company won the right to build three small dams on the Snake River rather than the federal government establishing a single large dam at Hell's Canyon. The Atomic Energy Act of 1954 allowed the construction of private nuclear power plants under the Atomic Energy Commission's license and oversight.

Public Works

In 1954, Eisenhower obtained congressional approval for joint Canadian-U.S. construction of the St. Lawrence Seaway, giving ocean-going vessels access to the Great Lakes. In 1956, Congress authorized construction of the Interstate Highway System, with the federal government covering 90 percent of the cost and the states 10 percent. The program further undermined the American railroad system.

Supreme Court

Eisenhower appointed Earl Warren, formerly governor of California, chief justice of the Supreme Court in 1953. That same year he appointed William J. Brennan associate justice. Although originally perceived as conservatives, both justices used the court as an agency of social and political change.

Election of 1956

The 1956 election once again pitted Eisenhower against Stevenson. The president won easily, carrying all but seven states.

Space and Technology

The launching of the Soviet space satellite *Sputnik* on October 4, 1957, created fear that America was falling behind technologically. Although the U.S. launched *Explorer I* on January 31, 1958, the concern continued. In 1958, Congress established the National Aeronautics and Space Administration (NASA) to coordinate research and development of vehicles and activities for space exploration. Congress also passed the National Defense Education Act to provide grants and loans for education.

Sherman Adams Scandal

In 1958, the White House chief of staff, Sherman Adams, resigned after it was revealed that he had received a fur coat and an oriental rug in return for helping a Boston industrialist deal with the federal bureaucracy. This became known as the Sherman Adams Scandal.

Civil Rights

Initial Eisenhower Actions

Eisenhower completed the formal integration of the armed forces, desegregated public services in Washington, D.C., naval yards, and veteran's hospitals, and appointed a Civil Rights Commission.

Legal Background to *Brown*

In *Ada Lois Sipuel v. Board of Regents* (1948) and *Sweatt v. Painter* (1950), the Supreme Court ruled that African Americans must be allowed to attend integrated law schools in Oklahoma and Texas.

Brown v. Board of Education of Topeka

In *Brown v. Board of Education of Topeka,* a 1954 case, NAACP lawyer Thurgood Marshall challenged the doctrine of "separate but equal" *(Plessy v. Ferguson,* 1896). The Court declared that separate educational facilities were inherently unequal. In 1955, the Court ordered states to integrate "with all deliberate speed."

Southern Reaction

Although at first the South reacted cautiously, by 1955 there were calls for "massive resistance" and White Citizens, Councils emerged to spearhead the resistance. State legislatures used a number of tactics to get around *Brown*. By the end of 1956, desegregation of the schools had advanced very little.

Federal troops escort black students to Little Rock Central High School, 1957. (Wikimedia Commons)

Little Rock

Although he did not personally support the Supreme Court decision, Eisenhower sent 10,000 National Guardsmen and 1,000 paratroopers to Little Rock, Arkansas, to control mobs and enable blacks to enroll at Central High in September 1957, when Arkansas Governor Orval Faubus refused to implement the desegregation policy. A small force of soldiers remained stationed at the school throughout the year. The impact of foreign opinion influenced Eisenhower's decision to support desegregation, as he was concerned that charges of hypocrisy would be made by critics, particularly in the Soviet Union, were the government to remain silent on this issue of equality.

Montgomery Bus Boycott

On December 1, 1955, in Montgomery, Alabama, Rosa Parks, a black woman, refused to give up her seat on a city bus to a white passenger and was arrested. Under the leadership of Martin Luther King, Jr., a black pastor, blacks of Montgomery organized a bus boycott that lasted for a year, until in December 1956 the Supreme Court refused to review a lower court ruling that stated that "separate but equal" was no longer legal. King's actions were nonviolent but effective in changing segregationist policies and helped set the stage for further civil rights progress throughout the 1950s and 1960s.

Civil Rights Acts

Eisenhower proposed the Civil Rights Act of 1957, which established a permanent Civil Rights Commission and a Civil Rights Division of the Justice Department that was empowered to prevent interference with the right to vote. The Civil Rights Act of 1960 gave the federal courts power to register African American voters.

Sit-Ins

In February 1960, four black students who had been denied service at a segregated Woolworth lunch counter in Greensboro, North Carolina, staged a sit-in. This inspired sit-ins elsewhere in the South and led to the formation of the Student Nonviolent Coordinating Committee (SNCC). SNCC's primary aims included ending segregation in public accommodations and winning voting rights.

The Election of 1960

The Nominations

Vice President Richard M. Nixon won the Republican presidential nomination while the Democrats nominated Senator John F. Kennedy for the presidency with Lyndon B. Johnson, majority leader of the Senate, as his running mate.

Catholicism

Kennedy's Catholicism was a major issue until he told a gathering of Protestant ministers in Dallas, Texas, that he accepted the separation of church and state and that he would not allow Catholic leaders to tell him how to act as president.

Debates

A series of televised debates between Kennedy and Nixon helped create a positive image for Kennedy and may have been a turning point in the election. Most television viewers felt Kennedy had won the debates, while radio listeners declared Nixon the winner.

Kennedy's Victory

Kennedy won the election by slightly over 100,000 popular votes and 94 electoral votes, based on majorities in New England, the Middle Atlantic, and the South.

Society and Culture

Gross National Product

The GNP almost doubled between 1945 and 1960, growing at an annual rate of 3.2 percent from 1950 to 1960. Inflation meanwhile remained under two percent annually throughout the 1950s. Defense spending was the most important stimulant, and military-related research helped create or expand the new industries of chemicals, electronics, and aviation. The U.S. had a virtual monopoly over international trade because of the devastation of the World War. Technological innovations contributed to productivity, which jumped 35 percent between 1945 and 1955. After depression and war, Americans had a pent-up desire to consume. Between 1945 and 1960 the American population grew by nearly 30 percent, which contributed greatly to consumer demand.

Consumption Patterns

Home ownership grew by 50 percent between 1945 and 1960. These new homes required appliances, such as refrigerators and washing machines, but the most popular product was the television set—there were 7,000 sets in use in 1946 and 50 million sets in use by 1960. *TV Guide* became the fastest-growing magazine and advertising found the TV medium especially powerful. Consumer credit increased 800 percent between 1945 and 1957, while the rate of savings dropped to about 5 percent of income. The number of shopping centers rose from 8 in 1945 to 3,840 in 1960. Teenagers became an increasingly important consumer group, making—among other things—a major industry of rock 'n' roll music, with Elvis Presley as its first star, by the mid-1950s.

DIDYOUKNOW?

Elvis Presley is one of the best-selling music artists of all time. During his career, Presley released 40 top ten songs and starred in over 30 movies, including 1957's *Jailhouse Rock.*

Demographic Trends

Population Growth

In the 1950s, the U.S. population grew by over 28 million, 97 percent of which was in urban and suburban areas. This surge in population was known as the Baby Boom. The average life expectancy increased from 66 in 1955 to 71 in 1970. Dr. Benjamin Spock's *The Commonsense Book of Baby and Child Care* sold an average of 1 million copies a year between 1946 and 1960.

The Sun Belt

Aided by use of air conditioning, Florida, the Southwest, and California grew rapidly, with California becoming the most populous state by 1963. The Northeast, however, remained the most densely populated area.

Suburbs

The suburbs grew six times faster than the cities in the 1950s. William Levitt pioneered the mass-produced housing development when he built 10,600 houses (Levittown) on Long Island in 1947, a pattern followed elsewhere in the country. The Federal Housing Administration helped builders by insuring up to 95 percent of a loan and buyers by insuring their mortgages. Thanks in part to the development of the interstate highway system during the Eisenhower Administration, auto production increased from 2 million in 1946 to 8 million in 1955, which further encouraged the development of suburbia. As increasing numbers of blacks moved into the Northern and Midwestern cities, whites moved to the suburbs, a process dubbed "white flight." About 20 percent of the population moved their residence each year.

DID YOU KNOW?

In 1950, the average U.S. home was 983 square feet and was valued at $7,354.

Levittown, N.Y., a planned suburban community, 1959. (Wikimedia Commons)

Conformity and Security

Corporate Employment

Employees tended to work for larger organizations. By 1960, 38 percent of the workforce was employed by organizations with over 500 employees. Such environments encouraged the managerial personality and corporate cooperation rather than individualism.

Homogeneity

Observers found the expansion of the middle class an explanation for emphasis on conformity. David Riesman argued in *The Lonely Crowd* (1950) that Americans were moving from an inner-directed to an outer-directed orientation. William Whyte's *The Organization Man* (1956) saw corporate culture as emphasizing the group rather than the individual. Sloan Wilson's *The Man in the Grey Flannel Suit* (1955) expressed similar concerns in fictional form.

Leisure

The standard workweek shrank from six to five days. Television became the dominant cultural medium, with over 530 broadcast stations by 1961. Sales of books, especially paperbacks and comic books, increased annually.

Women

A cult of feminine domesticity re-emerged after World War II. Marynia Farnham and Ferdinand Lundberg published *Modern Woman: The Lost Sex* in 1947; Farnham suggested that science supported the idea that women could find fulfillment only in domesticity. Countless magazine articles also promoted the notion that a woman's place was in the home.

Religion

From 1940, when less than half the population belonged to a church, membership rose to more than 65 percent by 1960. Catholic Bishop Fulton J. Sheen had a popular weekly television show, "Life Worth Living," while Baptist evangelist Billy Graham held huge crusades. Norman Vincent Peale best represented the tendency of religion to emphasize reassurance with his best-seller *The Power of Positive Thinking* (1952). Critics noted the shallowness of this religion. Reinhold Niebuhr, the leading neo-orthodox theologian, criticized the self-centeredness of popular religion and its failure to recognize the reality of sin.

Seeds of Rebellion

Intellectuals

Intellectuals became increasingly critical of American life. John Kenneth Galbraith in *The Affluent Society* (1958) argued that the public sector was underfunded. John Keats's *The Crack in the Picture Window* (1956) criticized the homogeneity of suburban life in the new mass-produced communities. The adequacy of American education was questioned by James B. Conant in *The American High School Today* (1959).

Theatre and Fiction

Arthur Miller's *Death of a Salesman* (1949) explored the theme of the loneliness of the other-directed person. Novels also took up the conflict between the individual and mass society. Notable works included J.D. Salinger's *The Catcher in the Rye* (1951), James Jones's *From Here to Eternity* (1951), Joseph Heller's *Catch-22* (1955), Saul Bellow's *The Adventures of Augie March* (1953), and John Updike's *Rabbit, Run* (1960).

Art

Painter Edward Hopper portrayed isolated, anonymous individuals. Jackson Pollock, Robert Motherwell, Willem de Kooning, Arshile Gorky, and Mark Rothko were among the leaders in abstract expressionism, in which they attempted spontaneous expression of their subjectivity.

The Beats

The Beats were a group of young men alienated by twentieth-century life. Their movement began in Greenwich Village, New York, with the friendship of Allen Ginsburg, Jack Kerouac, William Burroughs, and Neal Cassady. The Beat movement broke with conventional, or "square," society, by seeking enhanced sensory awareness through alcohol, drugs, sex, jazz, Zen Buddhism, and a restless vagabond life, all of which were vehicles for their countercultural aspirations. Ginsberg's long poem *Howl* (1956) and Kerouac's novel *On the Road* (1957) were among the more important literary works to emerge from the Beat movement.

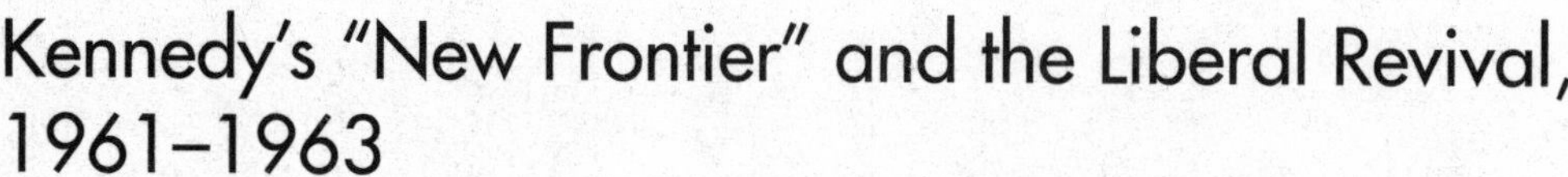

Kennedy's "New Frontier" and the Liberal Revival, 1961–1963

Legislative Failures

Kennedy was unable to get many of his programs through Congress because of an alliance of Republicans and southern Democrats that stood against him. He proposed plans for federal aid to education, urban renewal, medical care for the aged, reductions in personal and corporate income taxes, and the creation of a Department of Urban Affairs. None of these proposals passed.

Kennedy did, however, gain congressional approval for raising the minimum wage from $1.00 to $1.25 an hour and extending it to 3 million more workers.

Civil Rights

Freedom Riders

In May 1961, blacks and whites, sponsored by the Congress on Racial Equality, boarded buses in Washington, D.C., and traveled across the South to New Orleans to test federal enforcement of regulations prohibiting discrimination. They met violence in Alabama, but continued to New Orleans. Others came into the South to test the segregation laws.

Justice Department

The Justice Department, under Attorney General Robert F. Kennedy, the president's brother, began to push for civil rights, including desegregation of interstate transportation in the South, integration of schools, and supervision of elections.

Mississippi

In the fall of 1962, President Kennedy called the Mississippi National Guard to federal duty to enable an African American, James Meredith, to enroll at the University of Mississippi.

Dr. Martin Luther King, Jr., foreground, and Rev. Ralph Abernathy leave Birmingham, Alabama, prison on April 19, 1963, after having been arrested eight days earlier during a Good Friday pilgrimage to City Hall. (AP/Wide World Photo)

March on Washington

Kennedy presented a comprehensive civil rights bill to Congress in 1963. It banned racial discrimination in public accommodations, gave the attorney general power to bring suits on behalf of individuals for school integration, and withheld federal funds from state-administered programs that practiced discrimination. While the bill was held up in Congress, 200,000 people marched on August 28, 1963, in Washington, D.C. During their demonstration, Martin Luther King, Jr., gave his seminal "I Have a Dream" speech.

The Cold War Continues

Bay of Pigs

Under Eisenhower, the Central Intelligence Agency had begun training some 2,000 men for an invasion of Cuba to overthrow Fidel Castro, the left-leaning revolutionary who had taken power in 1959. On April 19, 1961, this force invaded at the Bay of Pigs, but was pinned down and forced to surrender. Some 1,200 men were captured.

Berlin Wall

After a confrontation between Kennedy and Khrushchev in Berlin, Kennedy called up reserve and National Guard units and asked for an increase in defense funds. In August 1961, Khrushchev responded by closing the border between East and West Berlin and ordering the erection of the Berlin Wall.

Nuclear Testing

The Soviet Union began the testing of nuclear weapons in September 1961. Kennedy then authorized resumption of underground testing by the United States.

Cuban Missile Crisis

On October 14, 1962, a U-2 reconnaissance plane brought photographic evidence that missile sites were being built in Cuba. Kennedy, on October 22, announced a blockade of Cuba and called on Khrushchev to dismantle the missile bases and remove from Cuba all weapons capable of attacking the United States. Six days later, Khrushchev backed down, withdrew the missiles, and Kennedy lifted the blockade. The United States promised not to invade Cuba and removed missiles from bases in Turkey, claiming they had planned to do so anyway.

Afterwards, a "hot line" telephone connection was established between the White House and the Kremlin to effect quick communication in threatening situations.

U-2 spy photo, taken in October 1962, depicted Soviet missiles under construction in Cuba. (National Archives and Records Administration)

Nuclear Test Ban

In July 1963, a treaty banning the atmospheric testing of nuclear weapons was signed by all the major powers except France and China.

Alliance for Progress

In 1961, Kennedy announced the Alliance for Progress, which would provide $20 million in aid to Latin America.

Peace Corps

The Peace Corps, established in 1961, sent young volunteers to third-world countries to contribute their skills in locally sponsored projects. The Peace Corps was seen as an important Cold War tool of American foreign policy, as volunteers were often sent to poor nations susceptible to Soviet influence.

DIDYOUKNOW?

Since 1961, the Peace Corps has placed over 200,000 volunteers to work in 137 countries.

Johnson and the Great Society, 1963–1969

Kennedy Assassination

On November 22, 1963, Kennedy was assassinated by Lee Harvey Oswald in Dallas, Texas. Jack Ruby, a nightclub owner, killed Oswald two days later. Conspiracy theories emerged. Chief Justice Earl Warren led an investigation of the murder and concluded that Oswald had acted alone, but questions remain.

Lyndon Johnson

Succeeding Kennedy, Johnson had extensive experience in both the House and Senate, and as a Texan, was the first Southerner to serve as president since Woodrow Wilson. He pushed hard for Kennedy's programs, which were languishing in Congress.

Civil Rights Act

The 1964 Civil Rights Act outlawed racial discrimination by employers and unions, created the Equal Employment Opportunity Commission to enforce the law, and eliminated the remaining restrictions on African American voting.

Following President Kennedy's assassination, Lyndon Johnson takes the oath of office aboard Air Force One at Love Field, Dallas, Texas. Photo by Cecil Stoughton, New York World-Telegram and the Sun Newspaper Photograph Collection. (U.S. Library of Congress)

Election of 1964

In 1964, Lyndon Johnson was nominated for president by the Democrats, with Senator Hubert H. Humphrey of Minnesota for vice president. The Republicans nominated Senator Barry Goldwater, a conservative from Arizona. Johnson won more than 61 percent of the popular vote and could now launch his own "Great Society" program.

Health Care

The Medicare Act of 1965 combined hospital insurance for retired people with a voluntary plan to cover physician's bills. Medicaid provided grants to states to help the poor below retirement age.

Education

In 1965, the Elementary and Secondary Education Act provided $1.5 billion to school districts to improve the education of poor people. Head Start prepared educationally disadvantaged children for elementary school.

Cities

The 1965 Housing and Urban Development Act provided 240,000 housing units and $2.9 billion for urban renewal. The Department of Housing and Urban Affairs was established in 1966, and rent supplements for low-income families also became available.

Emergence of Black Power

Voting Rights

In 1965, Martin Luther King, Jr., announced a voter registration drive. With help from the federal courts, he dramatized his effort by leading a march from Selma to Montgomery, Alabama, between March 21 and 25. The Voting Rights Act of 1965 authorized the attorney general to appoint officials to register voters.

Racial Riots

Seventy percent of blacks lived in city ghettos across the country. It did not appear that the nonviolent tactics used in the South would help them. Frustration built up. In August 1965, Watts, an area of Los Angeles, erupted in riot. More than 15,000 National Guardsmen were brought in; 34 people were killed, 850 wounded, and 3,100 arrested. Property damage reached nearly $200 million. In 1966, New York and Chicago experienced riots, and the following year there were riots in Newark and Detroit. The Kerner Commission, appointed to investigate the riots, concluded that they were directed at a social system that prevented blacks from getting good jobs and crowded them into ghettos.

Black Power

Stokely Carmichael, chairman of the Student Nonviolent Coordinating Committee (SNCC), was by 1964 unwilling to work with white civil-rights activists. In 1966, he called for the civil rights movements to be "black staffed, black controlled, and black financed." Later, he moved on to the Black Panthers, self-styled urban revolutionaries based in Oakland, California. Other leaders such as H. Rap Brown also called for Black Power. Another influential Black Power advocate was Malcolm X, a leader of the Black Muslims, who advocated black separatism. He was assassinated in 1965.

DIDYOUKNOW?

Although the Black Panthers are widely remembered for their militant actions, the Panthers also initiated a number of community service programs. These programs included free breakfast for school children, free medical clinics in black neighborhoods, and free afterschool classes teaching black history

King Assassination

On April 4, 1968, Martin Luther King, Jr., was assassinated in Memphis. James Earl Ray pleaded guilty and was convicted of the murder. Riots in more than 100 cities followed. Ray died in prison in 1998.

Civil rights march from Selma to Montgomery, Alabama, March 23, 1965. (AP/Wide World Photo)

Ethnic Activism

United Farm Workers

Cesar Chavez founded the United Farm Workers' Organizing Committee to unionize Mexican American farm laborers. He turned a grape pickers strike in Delano, California, into a national campaign by attacking the structure of the migrant labor system through a boycott of grapes.

Native Americans

The American Indian Movement (AIM) was founded in 1968. At first it staged sit-ins to bring attention to Native American demands. By the early 1970s, it was turning to the courts for relief.

The New Left

Demographic Origins

By the mid-1960s, the majority of Americans were under age 30. College enrollments increased fourfold between 1945 and 1970.

Students for a Democratic Society

Students for a Democratic Society (SDS) was organized by Tom Hayden and Al Haber of the University of Michigan in 1960. Hayden's Port Huron Statement (1962) called for "participatory democracy." The SDS drew much of its ideology from the writings of C. Wright Mills, Paul Goodman, and Herbert Marcuse.

Free-Speech Movement

Students at the University of California, Berkeley, staged sit-ins in 1964 to protest the prohibition of political canvassing on campus. Led by Mario Savio, the movement changed from emphasizing student rights to criticizing the bureaucracy of American society. In December, police broke up a sit-in; protests spread to other campuses around the nation.

1968 Demonstrations

More than 200 large campus demonstrations took place in the spring, culminating in the occupation of buildings at Columbia University to protest the university's involvement in military research and its poor relations with minority groups. Police wielding clubs eventually broke up the demonstration. In August, thousands gathered in Chicago to protest the war during the Democratic convention. Although police violence against the demonstrators aroused anger, the antiwar movement began to split between those favoring violence and those opposed to it.

The Counterculture

Origins

Like the New Left, the founders of the counterculture were alienated by bureaucracy, materialism, and the Vietnam War, but they turned away from politics in favor of an alternative society. In many respects, they were heirs of the Beats.

DID YOU KNOW?

In 1969, over 500,000 young people gathered in upstate New York to attend what became one of the most famous music festivals of all time—Woodstock. Performers included Jimi Hendrix, Janis Joplin, the Who, and Jefferson Airplane.

Counterculture Expression

Many young people formed communes in such places as San Francisco's Haight-Ashbury district or in rural areas. "Hippies," as they were called, experimented with Eastern religions, drugs, and sex, but most were unable to establish a self-sustaining lifestyle. Leading spokesmen included Timothy Leary, Theodore Roszak, and Charles Reich.

Women's Liberation

Betty Friedan

In *The Feminine Mystique* (1963), Betty Friedan argued that middle-class society stifled women and did not allow them to use their individual talents. She attacked the cult of domesticity.

National Organization for Women

Friedan and other feminists founded the National Organization for Women (NOW) in 1966, calling for equal employment opportunities and equal pay.

Problems

The women's movement was largely limited to the middle class. The Equal Rights Amendment, first proposed in the 1920s and introduced into Congress numerous times, failed to pass. Abortion rights stirred up a counter "right-to-life" movement.

DID YOU KNOW?

The number of U.S. women in the civilian labor force climbed from 11,970,000 in 1940 to 25,952,000 in 1965 (U.S. Census Bureau).

Vietnam

Background

After the French defeat in 1954, the United States sent military advisors to South Vietnam to aid the government of Ngo Dinh Diem. The pro-Communist Vietcong forces gradually grew in strength, partly because Diem failed to follow through on promised reforms. They received support from North Vietnam, the Soviet Union, and China. The U.S. government supported a successful military coup against Diem in the fall of 1963.

Escalation

In August 1964—after claiming that North Vietnamese gunboats had fired on American destroyers in the Gulf of Tonkin—President Johnson pushed the Gulf of Tonkin Resolution through Congress, authorizing him to use military force in Vietnam. After a February 1965 attack by the Vietcong on Pleiku, Johnson ordered operation "Rolling Thunder," the first sustained bombing of North Vietnam. Johnson then sent combat troops to South Vietnam. Under the leadership of General William C. Westmoreland, they conducted search and destroy operations. The number of troops increased to 184,000 in 1965, 385,000 in 1966, 485,000 in 1967, and 538,000 in 1968. Many of the soldiers were drafted into service.

Defense of American Policy

"Hawks" defended the president's policy and, drawing on containment theory, said that the nation had the responsibility to resist aggression. Secretary of State Dean Rusk became a major spokesman for the domino theory, which justified government policy by referencing England and France's appeasement of Hitler prior to 1939. If Vietnam should fall, it was said, all Southeast Asia would eventually go. The administration stressed its willingness to negotiate the withdrawal of all "foreign" forces from the war.

Student Protest

Student protests began focusing on the Vietnam War. In the spring of 1967, 500,000 gathered in Central Park in New York City to protest the war, many burning their draft cards. SDS became more militant and willing to use violence. It turned to Lenin for its ideology.

Tet Offensive

On January 31, 1968, the first day of the Vietnamese New Year (Tet), the Vietcong attacked numerous cities and towns, American bases, and even Saigon. Although they suffered large losses, the Vietcong won a psychological victory, as American opinion began turning against the war.

TEST TIP

Remember you need to sign up for the AP exam at least several weeks before the test date, so be sure to talk to your U.S. history teacher or your school's AP coordinator about taking the exam well before the scheduled exam time. If you are homeschooled or if your school does not offer AP programs, you can still take the exam. However, you will need to contact the College Board directly to learn how to register. You need to do this by the beginning of March to take the exam in mid-May.

Election of 1968

New Hampshire Democratic Primary

In February 1968, Senator Eugene McCarthy of Minnesota won 42 percent of the Democratic vote in the New Hampshire primary, compared with President Johnson's 48 percent. To make a strong showing against a sitting president in a primary was considered a major upset. Robert F. Kennedy then announced his candidacy for the Democratic presidential nomination.

Johnson's Withdrawal

Because of his lackluster New Hampshire primary showing and increasing criticism of his Vietnam War policies, Lyndon Johnson announced a cessation of bombing of North Vietnam and withdrew his candidacy on March 31, 1968.

Kennedy Assassination

After winning the California primary over McCarthy in June, Robert Kennedy was assassinated by Sirhan Sirhan, a young Palestinian who greatly resented American support for Israel during the 1967 Six-Day War. This event virtually assured Vice President Hubert Humphrey's nomination after a contentious Democratic Convention in Chicago. Protestors outside the convention and police engaged in violent encounters.

The Nominees

The Republicans nominated Richard M. Nixon, who chose Spiro T. Agnew, governor of Maryland, as his running mate in order to appeal to Southern voters. Governor George C. Wallace of Alabama ran for the presidency under the banner of the American Independent Party, appealing to fears generated by left-wing protestors and big government.

Nixon's Victory

None of the three candidates opposed the Vietnam War. Johnson suspended air attacks on North Vietnam shortly before the election. Nonetheless, Nixon, who emphasized stability and order, defeated Humphrey by a margin of one percent. Wallace's 13.5 percent was the best showing by a third-party candidate since 1924.

DID YOU KNOW?

Nixon's 1968 campaign strove to appeal to conservative white voters in the South who were unhappy with the recent changes wrought by the civil rights movement and Johnson's Great Society. This "Southern strategy" helped change the South from a reliably Democratic region to a firmly Republican stronghold, reshaping U.S. politics for decades to come.

The Nixon Conservative Reaction

Civil Rights

The Nixon administration sought to block renewal of the Voting Rights Act and delay implementation of court-ordered school desegregation in Mississippi. After the Supreme Court ordered busing of students in 1971 to achieve school desegregation, the administration proposed an antibusing bill, which was blocked in Congress.

Supreme Court

In 1969, Nixon appointed Warren E. Burger, a conservative, as chief justice, but ran into opposition with the nomination of southerners Clement F. Haynesworth, Jr., and G. Harrold Carswell. After these nominations were defeated, he nominated Harry A. Blackmun, who received Senate approval. He later appointed Lewis F. Powell, Jr., and William Rehnquist as associate justices. Although more conservative than the Warren court, the Burger court did declare the death penalty, as used at the time, unconstitutional in 1972, and struck down state anti-abortion legislation in 1973.

Congressional Legislation

Congress passed bills giving 18-year-olds the right to vote (1970), increasing Social Security benefits and funding for food stamps (1970), as well as establishing the Occupational Safety and Health Act (1970), the Clean Air Act (1970), laws to control water pollution (1970, 1972), and the Federal Election Campaign Act (1972). None was supported by the Nixon administration.

Space

Fulfilling a goal established by President Kennedy, Neil Armstrong and Edwin "Buzz" Aldrin became the first people to walk on the moon on July 20, 1969.

Fulfilling JFK's pledge eight years earlier to send an American to the moon before the end of the decade, Apollo 11's Buzz Aldrin walks on the lunar surface on July 20, 1969. Aldrin followed Neil Armstrong in setting foot on the moon. (Photo by Neil Armstrong, NASA)

Economic Problems and Policy

Unemployment climbed to six percent in 1970, real gross national product declined in 1970, and in 1971 the United States experienced a trade deficit. Inflation reached 12 percent by 1974. These problems resulted from federal deficits in the 1960s, growing international competition, and rising energy costs.

In 1969, Nixon cut spending and raised taxes. He encouraged the Federal Reserve Board to raise interest rates. The economy worsened. In 1970, Congress gave the president the power to regulate prices and wages. Nixon used this power in August 1971 by declaring a 90-day price and wage freeze and taking the United States off the gold standard.

Roe v. Wade

In what became a landmark decision of the Supreme Court, justices ruled 7-2 that the right to privacy under the due process clause of the 14th Amendment extended to a woman's decision to have an abortion (1973). The High Court ruled, however, that states still had responsibilities to protect prenatal life, so a trimester approach was applied to determine when abortions were legal.

Vietnamization

Nixon proposed that all non-South Vietnamese troops be withdrawn in phases and that an internationally supervised election be held in South Vietnam. The North Vietnamese rejected this plan.

The president then turned to "Vietnamization," the effort to build up South Vietnamese forces while withdrawing American troops. In 1969, Nixon reduced American troop strength by 60,000, but at the same time ordered the bombing of Cambodia, a neutral country, in the interests of flushing out Vietcong.

Protests

Two Moratorium Days in 1969 brought out several hundred thousand protesters, and reports of an American massacre of Vietnamese at My Lai reignited controversy over the nature of the war, but Nixon continued to defend his policy. Troop withdrawals continued, and a lottery system was instituted in 1970 to make the draft more equitable. In 1973, Nixon abolished the draft and established an all-volunteer army.

Cambodia

In April 1970, Nixon announced that Vietnamization was succeeding and that another 150,000 American troops would be out of Vietnam by the end of the year. A few days later, he announced that troops had been sent into Cambodia to clear out Vietcong sanctuaries and resumed bombing of North Vietnam.

Kent State University Deaths

Protests against escalation of the war were especially strong on college campuses. During a May 1970 demonstration at Kent State University in Ohio, National Guardsmen opened fire on protestors, killing four students. Soon after, two black students were killed by a Mississippi state policeman at Jackson State University. Several hundred colleges were soon closed down by student strikes, as moderates joined the radicals. Congress repealed the Gulf of Tonkin Resolution.

TEST TIP

Don't worry about including everything you ever learned about a particular topic in your essays. Scorers look for a strong thesis supported by a clear, logical argument and relevant evidence, not a list of names, dates, and facts.

Pentagon Papers

The publication in 1971 of the "Pentagon Papers," classified Defense Department documents that were leaked to the press, revealed that the government had misled the Congress and the American people about its intentions in Vietnam during the mid-1960s.

End of U.S. Involvement

In the summer of 1972, negotiations between the United States and North Vietnam began in Paris. By October, a draft agreement was developed which included provisions for a cease-fire, the return of American prisoners of war, and the withdrawal of U.S. forces from Vietnam. A few days before the 1972 presidential election, Henry Kissinger, the president's national security advisor, declared peace was at hand.

Resumption of Bombing

Nixon resumed bombing of North Vietnam in December 1972, claiming that the North Vietnamese were not bargaining in good faith. In January 1973, the opponents reached a settlement in which the North Vietnamese retained control over large areas of the South and agreed to release American prisoners of war within 60 days. After the prisoners were released, the United States would withdraw its remaining troops. On March 29, 1973, the last American combat troops left South Vietnam. More than 54,000 Americans had been killed and 300,000 more were wounded; the war's financial cost to the United States was $109 billion.

Nixon's Foreign Policy

China

With his national security advisor, Henry Kissinger, Nixon took some bold diplomatic initiatives. Kissinger traveled to China and the Soviet Union for secret sessions to plan summit meetings with the Communists. In February 1972, Nixon and Kissinger went to

China to meet with Mao Tse-tung and his associates. The United States agreed to support China's admission to the United Nations and to pursue economic and cultural exchanges.

Soviet Union

At a May 1972 meeting with the Soviets, the Strategic Arms Limitation Treaty (SALT) was signed. The signatories agreed to stop making nuclear ballistic missiles and to reduce the number of antiballistic missiles to 200 for each power.

Middle East

Following the Arab-Israeli (Yom Kippur) war of 1973, Arab states staged an oil boycott to push the Western nations into forcing Israel to withdraw from lands controlled since the Six-Day War of 1967. Kissinger, now secretary of state, negotiated the withdrawal of Israel from some of the lands and the Arabs lifted their boycott. The five-member Organization of Petroleum Exporting Countries (OPEC)—composed of Venezuela, Saudi Arabia, Kuwait, Iraq, and Iran—then raised the price of oil from about $3.00 to $11.65 a barrel. U.S. gas prices doubled and inflation shot above 10 percent.

DIDYOUKNOW?

Richard Nixon, who built his early political career as a staunch anti-communist, was the first U.S. president to attempt to normalize relations with communist countries such as the Soviet Union and China. This policy is known as *détente*.

Election of 1972

George McGovern

In the 1972 presidential campaign, the Democrats nominated South Dakota Senator George McGovern, who opposed American policy in Vietnam, for president and Senator Thomas Eagleton for vice president. After the press revealed that Eagleton had been treated for psychological problems, McGovern eventually forced him off the ticket, replacing him with Sargent Shriver.

George Wallace

George Wallace, a longtime segregationist, ran once again as the American Independent party candidate. While campaigning at a Maryland shopping center on May 15, 1972, he became the victim of an assassination attempt that left him paralyzed below the waist. Arthur Bremer, 21, was sentenced to 63 years for shooting Wallace and three others.

Richard M. Nixon

Richard M. Nixon and Spiro T. Agnew, who had been renominated by the Republicans, won a landslide victory, receiving 521 electoral votes to McGovern's 17.

The Watergate Scandal

The Break-In

What became known as the Watergate crisis began during the 1972 presidential campaign. Early on the morning of June 17, James McCord, a security officer for the Committee for the Re-Election of the President, and four other men broke into Democratic headquarters at the Watergate apartment complex in Washington, D.C., and were caught while going through files and installing electronic eavesdropping devices. On June 22, Nixon announced that the administration was in no way involved in the burglary attempt.

James McCord

The trial of the burglars began in early 1973, with all but McCord (who was convicted) pleading guilty. Before sentencing, McCord wrote a letter to U.S. District Court Judge John J. Sirica arguing that high Republican officials had known in advance about the burglary and that perjury had been committed at the trial.

Further Revelations

Soon Jeb Stuart Magruder, head of the Nixon re-election committee, and John W. Dean, Nixon's attorney, revealed that they had been involved. Dean testified before a Senate Watergate committee that Nixon had been involved in covering up the incident. Over the next several months, extensive involvement of the White House administration, including payment of "hush" money to the burglars, destruction of FBI records, forgery of documents, and wiretapping, was revealed. Dean was fired;

DIDYOUKNOW?

Watergate has inspired Hollywood more than once, from the Oscar-winning 1976 drama *All the President's Men* to the 1999 spoof *Dick*, which cast the scandal as an accident caused by two bumbling teenage girls.

H.R. Haldeman and John Ehrlichman, the duo who headed the White House staff, and Attorney General Richard Kleindienst, resigned. Nixon claimed he had not personally been involved in the cover-up but refused, on the grounds of executive privilege, to allow investigation of White House documents.

White House Tapes

Under considerable pressure, Nixon agreed to the appointment of a special prosecutor, Archibald Cox of Harvard Law School. When Cox obtained a subpoena for tape recordings of White House conversations (whose existence had been revealed in testimony during the Senate hearings)—and the administration lost an appeal in the appellate court—Nixon ordered Elliot Richardson, the attorney general, to fire Cox. Both Richardson and his subordinate, William Ruckelshaus, resigned, leaving Robert Bork, the solicitor general, to carry out the order. This "Saturday Night Massacre," which took place on October 20, 1973, caused a storm of controversy. The House Judiciary Committee, headed by Peter Rodino of New Jersey, began looking into the possibility of impeachment. Nixon agreed to turn the tapes over to Judge Sirica and named Leon Jaworski as the new special prosecutor. It soon became known that some of the tapes were missing and that a portion of another had been erased.

The Vice Presidency

Vice President Spiro Agnew was accused of income tax fraud and having accepted bribes while a local official in Maryland. He resigned the vice presidency in October 1973 and was replaced by Congressman Gerald R. Ford of Michigan under provisions of the new 25th Amendment.

Nixon's Taxes

Nixon was accused of paying almost no income taxes between 1969 and 1972, and of using public funds for improvements to his private residences in California and Florida. The IRS reviewed the president's tax return and assessed him nearly $500,000 in back taxes and interest.

Indictments

In March 1974, a grand jury indicted Haldeman, Ehrlichman, former Attorney General John Mitchell, and four other White House aides, and named Nixon as an unindicted co-conspirator.

Calls for Resignation

In April, Nixon released edited transcripts of the White House tapes, the contents of which led to further calls for his resignation. Jaworski subpoenaed 64 additional tapes, which Nixon refused to turn over, and the case went to the Supreme Court.

President Nixon departing from the White House following his resignation on August 9, 1974. (Richard Nixon Presidential Materials Project)

Impeachment Debate

Meanwhile, the House Judiciary Committee televised its debate over impeachment, adopting three articles of impeachment. It charged the president with obstructing justice, misusing presidential power, and failing to obey the committee's subpoenas.

Resignation

Before the House began to debate impeachment, the Supreme Court ordered the president to release the subpoenaed tapes to the special prosecutor. On August 5, Nixon, under pressure from his advisors, made public the tape of June 23, 1972. This tape, recorded less than a week after the break-in, revealed that Nixon had used the CIA to keep the FBI from investigating the case. After Congressional Republicans encouraged Nixon to resign for the good of the party, he announced his resignation on August 8, 1974, to take effect at noon the following day. Vice President Gerald Ford then became president.

Legislative Response

Congress responded to the Vietnam War and Watergate by enacting legislation intended to prevent such situations. In 1974, Congress limited the amount of contributions and expenditures in presidential campaigns. It also strengthened the 1966 Freedom of Information Act by requiring the government to act promptly when asked for information and to prove its case for classification when attempting to withhold information on grounds of national security.

The Ford Presidency

Gerald Ford

Gerald Ford was in many respects the opposite of Nixon. Although a partisan Republican, he was well liked and free from any hint of scandal. Ford almost immediately encountered controversy when, in September 1974, he offered to pardon Nixon. Nixon accepted the offer, although he admitted no wrongdoing and had not yet been charged with a crime.

The Economy

Ford also faced major economic problems, which he approached somewhat inconsistently. Saying that inflation was the major problem, he called for voluntary restraints and asked citizens to wear "Whip Inflation Now," or WIN, buttons. The economy went into decline. Ford asked for tax cuts to stimulate business and argued against spending for social programs.

When New York City teetered on the verge of bankruptcy in 1975, Ford at first opposed federal aid but changed his mind when the Senate and House Banking Committees guaranteed the loans.

Vietnam

As North Vietnamese forces pushed back the South Vietnamese, Ford asked Congress to provide more arms for the South. Congress rejected the request, and in April 1975, Saigon fell to the North Vietnamese.

Election of 1976

In the 1976 presidential campaign, Ronald Reagan, formerly a movie actor and governor of California, opposed Ford for the Republican nomination, but Ford won by a slim margin. The Democrats nominated James Earl Carter, formerly governor of Georgia, who ran on the basis of his integrity and lack of Washington connections. Carter, with Senator Walter Mondale of Minnesota as his vice presidential candidate, narrowly defeated Ford.

TEST TIP

Multiple-choice questions on the AP U.S. History exam do not appear in chronological order. Don't be surprised if the first question asks you about the 1960s and the second question about the 1760s!

Carter's Moderate Liberalism

Policy Orientation in the Carter Administration

Carter sought to conduct the presidency on democratic and moral principles. The former peanut farmer, however, often misread political sentiment on Capitol Hill: the administration typically proposed complex programs but failed to support them through the legislative process.

The Economy

Carter approached economic problems inconsistently. In 1978, he proposed voluntary wage and price guidelines. Although somewhat successful, the guidelines did not apply to oil, housing, and food. Carter then named Paul A. Volcker as chairman of the Federal Reserve Board. Volcker tightened the money supply in order to reduce inflation, but this action caused interest rates to go even higher. High interest rates depressed sales of automobiles and houses, which in turn increased unemployment. By 1980, unemployment stood at 7.5 percent, interest at 20 percent, and inflation at 12 percent.

Domestic Achievements

Carter offered amnesty to Americans who had fled the draft and gone to other countries during the Vietnam War. He established the departments of Energy and Education and placed the civil service on a merit basis. He created a "superfund" for cleanup of chemical waste dumps, established controls over strip mining, and protected 100 million acres of Alaskan wilderness from development.

Affirmative Action

Attempts to provide more equal access to higher education for American minorities led to affirmative action programs for admission to both undergraduate and graduate institutions. In a 1978 Supreme Court decision, *Bakke v. the Regents of the University of California*, the justices ruled that affirmative action programs were constitutional, but strict racial quotas were not.

Carter's Foreign Policy

Human Rights

Carter sought to base foreign policy on human rights but was criticized for inconsistency and lack of attention to American interests.

Panama Canal

Carter negotiated a controversial treaty with Panama, affirmed by the Senate in 1978, that provided for the transfer of ownership of the canal to Panama in 1999 and guaranteed its neutrality.

China

Carter ended official recognition of Taiwan and in 1979 recognized the People's Republic of China. Republicans called the decision a "sellout" of our long-standing allies in Taiwan. Subsequently the People's Republic of China assumed Taiwan's seat on the UN Security Council.

SALT II

In 1979, Carter signed the Strategic Arms Limitation Treaty II with the Soviet Union. The treaty set a ceiling of 2,250 bombers and missiles for each side, and set limits on warheads and new weapons systems. It never reached the Senate floor.

Camp David Accords

In 1978, Carter negotiated the Camp David Accords between Israel and Egypt. Bringing Anwar Sadat, president of Egypt, and Menachem Begin, prime minister of Israel, to Camp David, Maryland, for two weeks in September 1978, Carter sought to end the state of war that existed between the two countries. Israel promised to return occupied land in the Sinai to Egypt in exchange for Egyptian recognition, a process completed in 1982. An agreement to negotiate the Palestinian refugee problem, however, proved ineffective.

Afghanistan

The policy of détente went into decline. Carter criticized Soviet restrictions on political freedom and reluctance to allow dissidents and Jews to emigrate. In December 1979, the Soviet Union invaded Afghanistan. In response, Carter stopped shipments of grain and technology to the Soviets, withdrew his support for SALT II, and barred Americans from competing in the 1980 Moscow Summer Olympics.

The Iranian Crisis

The Iranian Revolution

In 1978, a revolution forced the Shah of Iran to flee the country, replacing him with a religious leader, Ayatollah Ruhollah Khomeini. Because the United States had supported the shah with arms and money, the revolutionaries were strongly anti-American, calling the United States the "Great Satan."

Hostages

After Carter allowed the exiled shah to come to the United States for medical treatment in October 1979, some 400 Iranians broke into the American embassy in Teheran on November 4, taking the occupants captive. They demanded that the shah be returned to Iran for trial and that his wealth be confiscated and given to Iran. Carter rejected these demands; instead, he froze Iranian assets in the United States and established a trade embargo against Iran. He also appealed to the United Nations and the World Court in the Hague. The Iranians eventually freed the African American and women hostages, but kept 52 others.

In April 1980, Carter ordered a rescue attempt by the Army's Delta Force, but it collapsed after several helicopters broke down and another crashed, killing eight men. Secretary of State Cyrus Vance resigned in protest before the raid began, and Carter was widely criticized for its failure.

The Election of 1980

The Democrats

Carter, whose approval rating in public opinion polls had dropped to about 25 percent in 1979, successfully withstood a challenge from Senator Edward M. Kennedy of Massachusetts for the Democratic presidential nomination. But as he faced the 1980 election, the president had been politically weakened.

The Republicans

The Republicans nominated Ronald Reagan of California, who had narrowly lost the 1976 nomination and was the leading spokesman for American conservatism. Reagan chose George Bush, a New Englander transplanted to Texas and former CIA director, as his vice presidential candidate. One of Reagan's opponents, Congressman John Anderson of Illinois, continued his presidential campaign on a third-party ticket.

The Campaign

While Carter defended his record, Reagan heavily favored increased defense spending, but also called for reductions in government spending and taxes. Reagan talked of granting more power to the states. He advocated what were coming to be called traditional values—family, religion, hard work, and patriotism.

Reagan's Victory

Reagan won by a large electoral majority, and the Republicans gained control of the Senate and increased their representation in the House.

(Before taking the quiz noted below, please review the summary timeline for this chapter on the following pages.)

Domestic Prosperity and International Responsibilities (1945–1980)

Historical Timeline (1945–1980)

1946	Churchill gives "Iron Curtain" speech George Kennan proposes containment policy
1947	Truman Doctrine aids nations resisting communism Marshall Plan provides economic aid to Europe House Un-American Activities Committee investigates Hollywood Jackie Robinson breaks color line in baseball Taft-Hartley Act slows growth of labor unions
1948	Soviets block access to West Berlin in Berlin Airlift Alger Hiss case begins Truman signs armed forces desegregation order Israel becomes a nation Truman defeats Dewey in presidential election
1949	NATO formed Soviet Union explodes atomic bomb Mao leads communist takeover in China
1950	Korean War begins U.S. troops invade North Korea Chinese troops enter war Rosenberg spy trial begins McCarthy begins anti-communist campaign U.S. begins hydrogen bomb program
1951	Gen. MacArthur relieved of command in Korea Peace negotiations begin in Panmunjon, Korea
1952	U.S. ends Japan occupation Eisenhower elected president
1953	Korean War ends with truce and demilitarized zone Stalin dies
1954	*Brown v. Topeka Board of Education* Army-McCarthy hearings French surrender at Dien Bien Phu in Vietnam Sen. McCarthy censured by Senate
1955	Martin Luther King, Jr., begins Montgomery Bus Boycott
1956	Suez crisis Soviets crush Hungarian revolt
1957	Soviets launch Sputnik Eisenhower Doctrine commits economic aid to Middle East Little Rock school desegregation crisis
1959	Castro takes over in Cuba Soviet Premier Khrushchev visits U.S.
1960	Kennedy and Nixon participate in first televised presidential debates Greensboro sit-in protests Kennedy defeats Nixon

Historical Timeline (1945–1980)

1961	Bay of Pigs invasion fails Freedom rides Berlin Wall built Peace Corps established Alliance for Progress established
1962	Cuban Missile Crisis Students for a Democratic Society formed
1963	Martin Luther King, Jr., begins Birmingham desegregation efforts University of Alabama admits first black student Civil Rights March on Washington Premier Diem of South Vietnam toppled by U.S.-approved coup President Kennedy assassinated
1964	President Johnson announces war on poverty Freedom summer vote registration campaign in Mississippi Civil Rights Act passed VISTA established Berkeley Free Speech Movement Gulf of Tonkin Resolution passed U.S. begins bombing of North Vietnam Johnson elected president
1965	Medicare funding begins Race riots in Watts Malcolm X assassinated American combat troops sent to Vietnam
1966	National Organization for Women (NOW) formed Stokely Carmichael leads black power movement
1967	Race riots in Detroit and Newark Massive antiwar protest in Washington, D.C. Israel, Arab neighbors fight Six-Day War
1968	Viet Cong launch Tet Offensive Johnson withdraws from presidential race Dr. Martin Luther King, Jr. assassinated Robert Kennedy assassinated Protests at Chicago Democratic Convention Nixon elected president
1969	Woodstock festival Apollo 11 crew lands on moon Stonewall Riots launch gay liberation movement
1970	U.S. invades Cambodia Kent State Massacre
1971	Nixon visits People's Republic of China Détente begins with Soviet Union SALT I Treaty signed with Soviet Union
1972	Watergate break-in occurs at Democratic headquarters Nixon defeats McGovern for presidency Haiphong Harbor in North Vietnam mined by U.S.

Historical Timeline (1945–1980)

1973	U.S., North Vietnam sign Paris Peace Accords *Roe v. Wade* expands abortion rights Yom Kippur War in Israel Vice-President Agnew resigns in disgrace
1974	Impeachment proceedings begin against President Nixon *U.S. v. Richard Nixon* rules that tapes must be turned over Nixon resigns; Vice President Ford succeeds him Ford pardons Nixon
1975	U.S. abandons South Vietnam as it falls to North Vietnam
1978	*Bakke vs. University of California Regents* affirmative action case Camp David Accords between Israel and Egypt
1979	U.S. and China establish diplomatic relations Iran deposes shah Iran militants capture U.S. embassy and take hostages Soviet Union invades Afghanistan Three-Mile Island nuclear accident Sandinistas overthrow Somoza in Nicaragua
1980	U.S. boycotts Moscow Olympics Reagan elected president

Chapter 11

The Rise of Conservativism, Post–Cold War Challenges, and a Changing Population (1980–present)

American Hostage Crisis Ended

After extensive negotiations with Iran, in which Algeria acted as an intermediary, Carter released Iranian assets and the hostages were freed on January 20, 1981—the day of President Ronald Reagan's inaugural. It had been 444 days since the Americans had been taken captive.

The Reagan Presidency: Attacking Big Government

Tax Policy

An ideological though pragmatic conservative, Ronald Reagan acted quickly and forcefully to change the direction of government policy. He placed priority on cutting taxes. His approach was based on "supply-side" economics, the idea that if government left more money in the hands of the people, they would invest rather than spend the excess on consumer goods. The results would be greater production, more jobs, and greater prosperity, and thus more income for the government despite lower tax rates.

Economic Recovery Tax Act

Reagan asked for a 30 percent tax cut, and despite fears of inflation on the part of Congress, in August 1983 obtained a 25 percent cut spread over three years. The percentage was the same for everyone; hence, high-income people received greater savings than middle- and low-income individuals. To encourage investment, capital gains, gift, and inheritance taxes were reduced and business taxes liberalized. Anyone with earned income was also allowed to invest up to $2,000 a year in an Individual Retirement Account (IRA), deferring all taxes on both the principal and its earnings until retirement.

DIDYOUKNOW?

Nintendo first sold its Nintendo Entertainment System (NES) in the fall of 1986. The system came with two controllers and the original Super Mario Brothers game, and was priced at $199—about $400 in today's dollars.

Government Spending

Congress passed the Budget Reconciliation Act in 1981, cutting $39 billion from domestic programs, including education, food stamps, public housing, and the National Endowments for the Arts and Humanities. While cutting domestic programs, Reagan increased the defense budget by $12 billion.

Unions

Reagan earned a reputation as a tough negotiator when he fired 11,000 air traffic controllers in August 1981 following a nationwide strike. Calling the strike illegal—because of a law that banned strikes by government unions—and a "peril to national safety," Reagan demanded that controllers return to work or risk losing their jobs. They refused, he fired them, and their union was decertified. Before 1981, the nation averaged 300 strikes per year. In 2006, there were 30 strikes in the entire nation.

SDI

Reagan concentrated on obtaining funding for the development of a computer-controlled Strategic Defense Initiative (SDI) system, dubbed by the press "Star Wars" after the movie of that name. SDI would destroy incoming enemy missiles from outer space. Skeptical about its technological feasibility and fearful of enormous costs, Congress balked and scaled back the proposal during Reagan's second term.

Increasing Revenue

Because of rising deficits, Reagan and Congress increased taxes in various ways. The 1982 Tax Equity and Fiscal Responsibility Act reversed some concessions made to business in 1981. Social Security benefits became taxable income in 1983. In 1984, the Deficit Reduction Act increased taxes by another $50 billion. But the deficit continued to increase.

Assassination Attempt

John W. Hinckley shot Reagan in the chest on March 30, 1981. The president was wounded, but made a swift recovery. His popularity increased, helping his legislative program.

Women and Minorities

Although Reagan appointed Sandra Day O'Connor to the Supreme Court, his administration gave fewer of its appointments to women and minorities than had the Carter administration. The Reagan administration also opposed "equal pay for equal work" and renewal of the Voting Rights Act of 1965. The Republican Party had dropped support for the Equal Rights Amendment at the 1980 GOP Convention that nominated Reagan as president.

Asserting American Power

Soviet Union

Reagan took a hard line against the Soviet Union, calling it an "evil empire." He placed new cruise missiles in Europe, despite considerable opposition from Europeans.

Election of 1984

The Democrats

In the 1984 presidential campaign, Walter Mondale, a former senator from Minnesota and vice president under Carter, won the Democratic nomination over Senator Gary Hart and Jesse Jackson, an African American civil-rights leader. Mondale chose

Geraldine Ferraro, a three-term congresswoman from New York, as his running mate. Mondale criticized Reagan for his budget deficits, high unemployment and interest rates, and reduction of spending on social services.

The Reagan Victory

The Republicans renominated Ronald Reagan and George Bush. Reagan drew support from groups such as the Moral Majority, founded by fundamentalist evangelist Jerry Falwell. (Evangelicals had become a major political presence, voicing opposition to abortion, advocating an amendment to allow prayer in public schools, and identifying with the cause of Israel and a strong military defense budget.) Reagan's appeal also derived from an in-your-face anti-Soviet stance and decreased inflation, interest rates, and unemployment during his watch. He defeated Mondale handily, gaining nearly 60 percent of the vote by breaking apart the Democratic coalition of industrial workers, farmers, and the poor that had existed since FDR's time. Yet his coattails proved short: the GOP lost two seats in the Senate and gained little in the House.

Second-Term Foreign Concerns

Libya

Reagan challenged Muammar al-Qaddafi, the anti-American leader of Libya, by sending Sixth Fleet ships within the Gulf of Sidra, which Qadhafi claimed. When Libyan gunboats challenged the American ships, American planes destroyed the gunboats and bombed installations on the Libyan shoreline. Soon after, a West German nightclub popular among American servicemen was bombed, killing a soldier and a civilian. Reagan, believing the bombing was ordered directly by Qadhafi, launched an air strike from Great Britain against Libyan bases in April 1986.

Soviet Union

After Mikhail S. Gorbachev became the premier of the Soviet Union in March 1985 and took a more flexible approach toward both domestic and foreign affairs, Reagan softened his anti-Soviet stance. But despite the Soviets' assurances that they would honor the unratified SALT II agreement, Reagan argued that they in fact had not adhered to the pact; as a result, he sought to expand and modernize the American defense system.

Arms Control

Reagan and Gorbachev had difficulty in reaching an agreement on arms limitations at summit talks in 1985 and 1986. Finally, in December 1987, they signed an agreement eliminating medium-range missiles from Europe.

Iran-Contra Affair

Near the end of 1986, a scandal arose involving William Casey, head of the CIA, Lieutenant Colonel Oliver North of the National Security Council, Admiral John Poindexter, national security advisor, and Robert McFarlane, former national security advisor. In 1985 and 1986, they had sold arms to the Iranians in hopes of encouraging them to use their influence in getting American hostages in Lebanon released. The profits from these sales were then diverted to the Nicaraguan contras in an attempt to get around congressional restrictions on funding the contras. The president was forced to appoint a special prosecutor, and Congress held hearings on the affair in May 1987.

Second-Term Domestic Affairs

Tax Reform

The Tax Reform Act of 1986 lowered tax rates, changing the highest rate on personal income from 50 percent to 28 percent and on corporate taxes from 46 percent to 34 percent. At the same time, it removed many tax shelters and tax credits. The law did away with the concept of progressive taxation, the requirement that the percentage of income taxed increased as income increased. Instead, over a two-year period it established two rates, 15 percent on incomes below $17,850 for individuals and $29,750 for families and 28 percent on incomes above these amounts. The tax system would no longer be used as an instrument of social policy.

Economic Patterns

Unemployment declined, reaching 6.6 percent in 1986, while inflation fell as low as 2.2 percent during the first quarter of that year. The stock market was bullish through mid-1987.

Deficits

The federal deficit reached $179 billion in 1985. At about the same time, the United States experienced trade deficits of more than $100 billion annually, partly because management and engineering skills had fallen behind Japan and Germany, and partly because the United States provided an open market to foreign businesses. In the mid-1980s, the United States became a debtor nation for the first time since World War I. Consumer debt also rose from $300 billion in 1980 to $500 billion in 1986.

Black Monday

On October 19, 1987, labeled "Black Monday" on Wall Street, the Dow Jones Industrial Average dropped more than 500 points, or over 20 percent. Between August 25 and October 20, the market lost over a trillion dollars in paper value. Fearing a recession, Congress in November 1987 reduced 1988 taxes by $30 billion.

NASA Tragedy

The explosion of the space shuttle *Challenger* soon after liftoff on January 28, 1986, damaged NASA's credibility and reinforced doubts about the complex technology required to implement the Strategic Defense Initiative. All aboard perished, including a New Hampshire teacher, Christa McAuliffe, who was the first private citizen to go into space. The Rogers Commission investigated the accident and it was determined that faulty O-rings and extreme cold caused the fuel leakage that caused the explosion. Commission member Richard Feynman, a Nobel Prize-winning physicist, criticized the official report, which downplayed the poor safety procedures. The shuttle program was suspended for 31 months following the *Challenger* disaster.

Supreme Court

Reagan reshaped the Court. In 1986, he replaced Chief Justice Warren C. Burger with Associate Justice William H. Rehnquist, probably the most conservative member of the Court. Although failing in his nomination of Robert Bork for associate justice, Reagan successfully appointed other conservatives to the Court: Sandra Day O'Connor, Antonin Scalia, and Anthony Kennedy.

AIDS

In 1981, scientists announced the discovery of acquired immunodeficiency syndrome, or AIDS, which was especially prevalent among—but not confined to—homosexual males and intravenous drug users. Widespread fear and an upsurge in homophobia resulted. The revelation that a Florida dentist, who had died in 1990, had transmitted human immunodeficiency virus, or HIV, to six patients led to calls for mandatory testing of healthcare workers. There were calls as well for fast-tracking drug approvals. In 1998, the federal Centers for Disease Control and Prevention estimated that between 400,000 and 650,000 Americans were HIV-positive, meaning that they had the virus that causes AIDS.

TEST TIP

Be sure to include transition words and phrases in your essays. Words such as *then, next, because, since, in contrast, and as a result* help guide scorers through your argument and make your ideas clearer to the reader.

Election of 1988

The Candidates

After a sex scandal eliminated Senator Gary Hart from the race for the Democratic presidential nomination in the 1988 campaign, Governor Michael Dukakis of Massachusetts emerged as the victor over his major challenger, Jesse Jackson (see sidebar). He chose Senator Lloyd Bentsen of Texas as his vice-presidential running mate. Vice President George Bush, after a slow start in the primaries, won the Republican nomination. He chose Senator Dan Quayle of Indiana as his running mate. Bush easily defeated Dukakis, but the Republicans were unable to make any inroads in Congress.

Bush Abandons Reaganomics

Budget Deficit

Soon after George H. W. Bush took office as president on January 20, 1989, the federal budget deficit for 1990 was estimated at $143 billion. With deficit estimates continuing to grow, Bush held a "budget summit" with congressional leaders in May 1990, and his administration continued talks throughout the summer. In September, the administration and Congress agreed to increase taxes on gasoline, tobacco, and alcohol, establish an excise tax on luxury items, and raise Medicare taxes. Cuts were also to be made in Medicare and other domestic programs. The 1991 deficit was now estimated to be over $290 billion. The following month, Congress approved the plan, hoping to cut a cumulative amount of $500 billion from the deficit over the next five years. In a straight party vote—Republicans voting against and Democrats voting in favor—Congress in December gave the power to decide whether new tax and spending proposals violated the deficit-cutting agreement to the Congressional Budget office. This power had been in the hands of the White House Office of Management and Budget.

Savings and Loan Debacle

With the savings and loan industry in financial trouble in February 1989, largely because of bad real estate loans, Bush proposed to close or sell 350 institutions, to be paid for by the sale of government bonds. In July, he signed a bill that created the Resolution Trust Corporation to oversee the closure and merging of savings and loans, and provided $166 billion over 10 years to cover the bad debts. Estimates of the total cost of the debacle ran to upward of $300 billion.

Scandals in the Financial Markets

Charges of insider trading, stock manipulation, and falsification of records resulted in Drexel Burnham Lambert, a major securities firm, pleading guilty in December 1988 to six violations of federal law. The company filed for bankruptcy and Michael Milken, its "junk bond king" (junk bonds are bonds below an investment grade of BB or Bb, which because of their risk carry a two- to three-point interest advantage), pleaded guilty to conspiracy, among other charges, in 1990. Meanwhile, in July 1989, 46 futures traders at the Chicago Mercantile Exchange were charged with racketeering.

For African Americans in Politics, Progress Comes Slowly but Surely

(U.S. Library of Congress)

Civil-rights leader, Baptist minister, and politician, Jesse Jackson was the first black man to make a serious bid for the U.S. presidency—in the Democratic Party's nomination races in 1983–84 and 1987–88. Before him, Shirley Chisholm, who in 1968 had become the first black woman elected to the U.S. Congress, made a bid for the Democratic nomination for U.S. president in 1972, winning 152 delegates before withdrawing from the race.

After taking up residency in Washington, D.C., Jackson attained elective office when, in 1990, the Washington City Council created two unpaid offices of "statehood senator"—better known as "shadow senator"—to lobby Congress for statehood for the District of Columbia. Fusing the church pulpit with the bully pulpit, he has been effective not just in articulating the needs of blacks, but of the underprivileged class in general.

(Continued on next page)

Economic Slowdown

The gross national product slowed from 4.4 percent in 1988 to 2.9 percent in 1989. Unemployment gradually began to increase, reaching 6.8 percent in March 1991, a three-year high. Every sector of the economy except for medical services and all geographical areas experienced the slowdown. The "Big Three" automakers posted record losses, and Pan American World Airways and Eastern Airlines entered bankruptcy proceedings. In September 1991, the Federal Reserve lowered the interest rate.

Other Domestic Issues Under Bush

Exxon Valdez Accident

After the *Exxon Valdez* spilled more than 240,000 barrels of oil into Alaska's Prince William Sound in March 1989, the federal government ordered Exxon Corporation to develop a clean-up plan, which it carried out until the weather prevented it from continuing in September. The *Valdez* captain, Joseph Hazelwood, was found

DIDYOUKNOW?

The 2010 BP oil spill in the Gulf of Mexico released an estimated 172 million gallons of oil into the Gulf. That's nearly 16 times the 10.8 million gallons spilled in the *Exxon Valdez* accident.

An associate of Rev. Dr. Martin Luther King, Jr., Jackson went on to found Operation PUSH (People United to Save Humanity), a Chicago-based organization that advocated black self-help and gave him a platform for his liberal views. A Jackson-led voter-registration drive was key to the election of Harold Washington as Chicago's first black mayor in April 1983. New York, Los Angeles, Cleveland, Baltimore, Atlanta, and Washington, D.C., also elected black mayors in the last two decades of the twentieth century.

Overall, as the 20th century wound down, more blacks were gaining local office, but seldom were they winning statewide elections. According to the Joint Center for Political and Economic Studies, a Washington, D.C., think tank that researches the political and economic conditions of black Americans, the U.S. had 8,868 black elected officials (including Jackson's own son, Rep. Jesse L. Jackson Jr. of Illinois) in 1998, up 212 from the year before. That number, however, accounted for only 1.7 percent of all officials holding elective office in the U.S. Some states, such as Colorado, Georgia, Illinois, and Ohio, have elected black lieutenant governors and state attorneys general, but in Massachusetts on Jan. 4, 2007, Deval Laurdine Patrick became only the second African American elected governor in the nation's history. The first was Virginia's L. Douglas Wilder, the grandson of slaves, who served one term, from 1989 to 1994. The distinction of being the first black governor belongs to P.B.S. Pinchback, who was acting governor of Louisiana during impeachment proceedings against Henry Clay Warmoth from December 9, 1872, to January 13,1873.

guilty of negligence the following year. Exxon, the state of Alaska, and the U.S. Justice Department reached a settlement in October 1991 requiring Exxon to pay over $1 billion in fines and restitution through 2001.

Pollution

The Clean Air Act, passed in October 1990 and updated the 1970 law, mandated that the level of emissions was to be reduced 50 percent by the year 2000. Cleaner gasolines were to be developed, cities were to reduce ozone (an ingredient in photo-chemical smog), and nitrogen oxide emissions were to be cut by one-third.

Supreme Court Appointments

Bush continued to reshape the Supreme Court in a conservative direction when, upon the retirement of Justice William J. Brennan, he successfully nominated Judge David Souter of the U.S. Court of Appeals in 1989. Two years later, Bush nominated a conservative African American, Judge Clarence Thomas, also of the U.S. Court of Appeals, upon the retirement of Justice Thurgood Marshall. Thomas's nomination stirred up opposition from the NAACP and other liberal groups, which supported affirmative action and abortion rights. Dramatic charges of sexual harassment against Thomas from Anita Hill, a University of Oklahoma law professor, were revealed only days before the nomination was to go to the Senate. The charges provoked a reopening of Judiciary Committee hearings, which were nationally televised. Nonetheless, Thomas narrowly won confirmation in October 1991.

Bush's Activist Foreign Policy

Panama

Since coming to office, the Bush administration had been concerned with Panamanian dictator Manuel Noriega because he allegedly provided an important link in the drug traffic between South America and the United States. After economic sanctions, diplomatic efforts, and an October 1989 coup failed to oust Noriega, Bush ordered 12,000 troops into Panama on December 20. The Americans installed a new government headed by Guillermo Endara, who had earlier apparently won a presidential election that was nullified by Noriega. On January 3, 1990, Noriega surrendered to the Americans and was taken to the United States to stand trial on drug-trafficking charges, a trial that began in September 1991. Found guilty in 1992, he was sentenced to 40 years' imprisonment. Twenty-three United States soldiers and three American civilians were killed in the Panamanian operation. The Panamanians lost nearly 300 soldiers and more than 500 civilians.

China

After the death in April 1989 of reformer Hu Yaobang, formerly general secretary and chairman of the Chinese Communist party, students began pro-democracy marches in Beijing. By the middle of May, more than one million people were gathering in Beijing's Tiananmen Square and elsewhere in China, calling for political reform. Martial law was imposed and in early June the army fired on the demonstrators. Estimates of the death toll in the wake of the nationwide crackdown on demonstrators ranged between 500 and 7,000. In July 1989, U.S. National Security Advisor Brent Scowcroft and Deputy Secretary of State Lawrence Eagleburger secretly met with Chinese leaders. When they again met the Chinese in December and revealed their earlier meeting, the Bush administration faced a storm of criticism for its policy of "constructive engagement" from opponents arguing that sanctions were needed. Although establishing sanctions on China in 1991 on high-technology satellite-part exports, Bush continued to support renewal of China's Most Favored Nation trading status.

Collapse of East European Communism

Bush-Gorbachev Summits

The East German government announced in November 1989 that restrictions on travel to West Germany, including West Berlin, would no longer be enforced. This effectively marked the end of the Berlin Wall, which was torn down in 1990. Amid the collapse of communism in Eastern Europe, Bush met with Mikhail Gorbachev in Malta from December 1 through 3, 1989; the two leaders appeared to agree that the Cold War was over. On May 30 and 31, 1990, Bush and Gorbachev met in Washington to discuss the possible reunification of Germany, and signed a trade treaty between the United States and the Soviet Union. The meeting of the two leaders in Helsinki on September 9 addressed strategies for the developing Persian Gulf crisis. At the meeting of the "Group of 7" nations (Canada, France, Germany, Italy, Japan, the United Kingdom, and the United States) in July 1991, Gorbachev requested economic aid from the West. A short time later, on July 30 and 31, Bush met Gorbachev in Moscow, where they signed the Strategic Arms Reduction Treaty (START), which cut United States and Soviet nuclear arsenals by 30 percent, and pushed for Middle Eastern talks.

Persian Gulf Crisis

July 1990: Saddam Hussein of Iraq charged that Kuwait had conspired with the United States to keep oil prices low and began massing troops at the Iraq-Kuwait border.

August 1990: On August 2, Iraq invaded Kuwait, an act that Bush denounced as "naked aggression." One day later, 100,000 Iraqi soldiers were poised south of Kuwait City, near the Saudi Arabian border. The United States quickly banned most trade with Iraq, froze Iraq and Kuwait's assets in the United States, and sent aircraft carriers to the Persian Gulf. After the UN Security Council condemned the invasion, Bush on August 6 ordered the deployment of air, sea, and land forces to Saudi Arabia, dubbing the operation "Desert Shield." At the end of August there were 100,000 American soldiers in Saudi Arabia.

September 1990: Bush encouraged Egypt to support American policy by forgiving Egypt its debt to the United States. He also obtained pledges of financial support from Saudi Arabia, Kuwait, and Japan, among other nations, to help pay for the operation.

October 1990: On October 29, the Security Council warned Hussein that further actions might be taken if he did not withdraw from Kuwait.

November 1990: In November, Bush ordered that U.S. forces be increased to more than 400,000. On November 29, the United Nations set January 15, 1991, as the deadline for Iraqi withdrawal from Kuwait.

January 1991: On January 9 Iraq's foreign minister, Tariq Aziz, rejected a letter written by Bush to Hussein. Three days later, after an extensive debate, Congress authorized the use of force in the Gulf. On January 17, an international force that included the U.S., Great Britain, France, Italy, Saudi Arabia, and Kuwait launched an air and missile attack on Iraq and occupied Kuwait. The United States called the effort "Operation Desert Storm." Under the overall command of the army's General H. Norman Schwarzkopf, the military effort emphasized high-technology weapons, including F-15E fighter bombers, F-117A stealth fighters, Tomahawk cruise missiles, and Patriot antimissile missiles. Beginning on January 17, Iraq sent SCUD missiles into Israel in an effort to draw that country into the war and hopefully break up the U.S.-Arabian coalition. On January 22 and 23, Hussein's forces set Kuwaiti oil fields on fire and spilled oil into the Gulf.

February 1991: On February 23, the allied ground assault began. Four days later, Bush announced that Kuwait was liberated and ordered offensive operations to cease. The United Nations established the terms for the cease-fire: Iraqi annexation of Kuwait to be rescinded; Iraq to accept liability for damages and return Kuwaiti property; Iraq to end all military actions and identify mines and booby traps; and Iraq to release captives.

April 1991: On April 3, the Security Council approved a resolution to establish a permanent cease-fire; Iraq accepted the UN terms on April 6. The next day the United States began airlifting food to Kurdish refugees on the Iraq-Turkey border who were fleeing the Kurdish rebellion against Hussein, a rebellion that was seemingly encouraged by Bush, but who nonetheless refused to become militarily involved. The United States estimated that 100,000 Iraqis had been killed during the war, while about 300 U.S. and allied troops were killed.

TEST TIP

If you are having a hard time understanding a question, try circling or underlining keywords and ideas from the question stem. Then focus on defining or restating those parts in your own words to help you figure out the purpose of the question.

Toward a Middle East Conference

On February 6, 1991, the United States had set out its postwar goals for the Middle East. These included regional arms control and security arrangements, international aid for reconstruction of Iraq and Kuwait, and resolution of the Israeli-Palestinian conflict. Immediately after cessation of the conflict, Secretary of State James Baker toured the Middle East attempting to promote a conference to address the problems of the region. After several more negotiating sessions, Saudi Arabia, Syria, Jordan, and Lebanon accepted the United States proposal for an Arab-Israeli peace conference by the middle of July; Israel conditionally accepted in early August. Despite the continuing conflict with Iraq, including UN inspections of its nuclear capabilities, and new Israeli settlements in disputed territory which kept the conference agreement tenuous, the nations met in Madrid, Spain, at the end of October. Bilateral talks in early November between Israel and the Arabs concentrated on procedural issues.

Breakup of the Soviet Union

Collapse of Soviet Communism and the End of the Cold War

The Soviet Union began to break up in 1990, when Lithuania declared its independence. In the aftermath of an attempted coup by hard-line Communists later that year, other Soviet republics followed suit. For the United States, the collapse of the U.S.S.R. meant that the Cold War, which had begun in 1945, was finally over. The United States was now the world's only superpower. In September 1991, President Bush announced that the U.S. would carry out the unilateral removal and destruction of ground-based tactical nuclear weapons in Europe and Asia, removal of nuclear-armed Tomahawk cruise missiles from surface ships and submarines, immediate destruction of intercontinental ballistic missiles covered by the START treaty, and an end to the 24-hour alert for strategic bombers, which the United States had maintained for decades. Gorbachev responded the next month by announcing the immediate deactivation of intercontinental ballistic missiles covered by START, removal of all short-range missiles from Soviet ships, submarines, and aircraft, and destruction of all ground-based tactical nuclear weapons. He also said that the Soviet Union would reduce its forces by 700,000 troops, and he placed all long-range nuclear missiles under a single command.

New foreign policy challenges emerged, however. Yugoslavia broke up into several different nations, and the region was plunged into a brutal war. Conflict threatened other parts of the world as well. The disintegration of the Soviet Union meant more nations had nuclear weapons, as several of the former Soviet republics had access to them.

The Election of 1992

In the 1992 campaign for the White House, William Jefferson Clinton, governor of Arkansas, overcame several rivals and won the Democratic presidential nomination, choosing Senator Al Gore of Tennessee as his candidate for vice president. Clinton and Reform Party candidate H. Ross Perot emphasized jobs and the economy, as well as the debt. Bush stressed traditional values and his foreign policy accomplishments. In the general election Clinton won 43 percent of the popular vote and 370 electoral votes, thereby defeating George Bush, who received 38 percent of the vote, and independent candidate Ross Perot, who took 19 percent of the vote, but won no electoral votes.

The Clinton Presidency—A Rocky Start

Upon taking office, Clinton created a storm of protest when he proposed lifting the ban on homosexuals in the military. In July 1993, a compromise "Don't ask, don't tell" policy was struck, requiring gays and lesbians to be discreet about their sexual orientation and not to engage in homosexual acts. On the legislative front, Clinton was strongly rebuffed in a first-term attempt, led by First Lady Hillary Rodham Clinton, to comprehensively reform the nation's healthcare system. In the 1994 mid-term elections, in what Clinton himself considered a repudiation of his administration, the Republicans took both houses of Congress from the Democrats and voted in Newt Gingrich of Georgia as Speaker of the House. Gingrich had helped craft the Republican congressional campaign strategy which he labeled the "Contract with America" to dramatically shrink the federal government and give more power to the states.

Clinton, however, was not without his successes, both on the legislative and diplomatic fronts. He signed a bill establishing a five-day waiting period for handgun purchases, and he signed an anti-crime bill emphasizing community policing. He signed the Family and Medical Leave Act, which required large companies to provide up to 12 weeks' unpaid leave to workers for family and medical emergencies. He also championed welfare reform (a central theme of his campaign), but made it clear that the legislation he signed into law in August 1996 radically overhauling FDR's welfare system disturbed him on two counts—its exclusion of legal immigrants from getting most federal benefits and its deep cut in federal outlays for food stamps; Clinton said these flaws could be repaired with further legislation. In foreign affairs, Clinton signed the North American Free Trade Agreement (NAFTA), which, as of January 1994, lifted most trade barriers with Mexico and Canada. Clinton sought to ease tensions between Israelis and Palestinians, and he helped bring together Itzhak Rabin, prime minister of Israel, and Yasir Arafat, chairman of the Palestine Liberation Organization, for a White House summit. Ultimately, the two Middle East leaders signed a 1994 accord establishing Palestinian self-rule in the Gaza Strip and Jericho. In October 1994, Israel and Jordan signed a treaty to begin the process of establishing full diplomatic relations. Rabin was assassinated a year later by a radical, right-wing Israeli. The Clinton administration also played a key role in hammering out a peace agreement in 1995 in war-torn former Yugoslavia—where armed conflict had broken out in 1991 between Serbs, Croats, Bosnian Muslims, and other factions and groups.

President Clinton plays the saxophone he received as a gift from a beaming Russian President Yeltsin at a dinner party in 1994. (White House photo by Bob McNeely)

Controversy Swirls Around the President

The president came to be dogged by a number of controversies, including his and his wife's role in a complex Arkansas real estate deal called Whitewater, the removal of employees from the White House travel office, the suicide of Deputy White House Counsel Vince Foster, and a sexual harassment suit (later settled out of court) brought against the president by Paula Jones, a former Arkansas state employee. Whitewater spawned the Justice Department's appointment of an independent counsel, Robert B. Fiske, to look into it. Fiske's successor, Kenneth W. Starr, would expand the scope of the investigation. (Congress ultimately soured on the independent counsel law—enacted as a kind of coda to Watergate—and allowed it to expire in mid-1999.)

The Election of 1996

Clinton recaptured the Democratic nomination without a serious challenge in the 1996 campaign, while longtime GOP Senator Robert Dole of Kansas, the Senate majority leader, had to overcome several opponents but orchestrated a harmonious nominating convention with running mate Jack

DID YOU KNOW?

The Internet grew explosively during the mid-1990s. At the end of 1993, Internet service provider AOL (America Online) had just 600,000 subscribers. In less than three years, that number had grown to some 6 million.

Kemp, a former New York congressman and Cabinet member during the Bush administration. In November 1996, with most voters citing a healthy economy and the lack of an enticing alternative in Dole or the Reform Party's Perot, Clinton received 49 percent of the vote (47 million popular votes and 379 electoral votes), becoming the first Democrat to be returned to the White House since FDR, in 1936. Dole won 41 percent (39 million popular votes, 159 electoral votes) and Perot polled eight percent of the total (8 million popular votes). The GOP retained control of both houses of Congress.

Clinton Foreign Policy

During his second term, Clinton faced continued political unrest and civil war in the Balkans. In 1999, the Serbian government attacked ethnic Albanians in Kosovo, a province of Serbia. In response, NATO forces, led by the United States, bombed Serbia. Several weeks of bombing forced Serbian forces to withdraw from Kosovo. Meanwhile, Clinton was instrumental in bringing about a historic peace agreement in Northern Ireland, while the land-for-peace accord he tried to broker between the Palestinians and Israel proved elusive. Clinton also continued to seek a policy of expanding international trade by relaxing or eliminating trade barriers.

Historic Economic Boom Falters

As of February 1, 2000, the U.S. economy had enjoyed its longest stretch of uninterrupted growth in the nation's history. Much of this growth, which had begun in March 1991, was fueled by a new industry, electronic commerce on the Internet. Stock prices generally rose, but share prices for Internet companies rose especially fast, soaring to extraordinary heights. In 2000, investors came to see e-businesses' and high-tech stock prices as unreasonably high. A number of such stocks tumbled, with some losing as much as 90 percent of their value. Soon many formerly high-flying Internet companies were folding and by the close of 2000 the future of the surviving e-businesses, as well as the economy as whole, was uncertain.

Clinton's Impeachment

Clinton was plagued by rumors of sexual impropriety before and throughout his presidency. Special Prosecutor Kenneth Starr obtained the testimony of 23-year-old White House intern Monica Lewinsky about her sexual encounters with Clinton. In December 1998, he became only the second president to be impeached by the House of Representatives. In February 1999, he was tried and acquitted by the Senate on charges that he had lied under oath about the Lewinsky affair.

The Election of 2000

The Democrats nominated Vice President Al Gore for president and Senator Joseph Lieberman for vice president. The Republican Party nominated Texas Governor George W. Bush (son of President George H.W. Bush). After some conflict, the Reform Party nominated Patrick Buchanan. The Green Party ran Ralph Nader. Although Gore received over 500,000 more popular votes than Bush, the Electoral College count was very close, and a number of irregularities in Florida made it difficult to determine the winner. Following several court challenges and a 5-4 Supreme Court decision in *Gore v. Bush* that prevented recounts, Bush was declared the winner.

DIDYOUKNOW?

In a dissenting opinion in the 5-4 *Gore v. Bush,* decision, which essentially awarded the presidency to Bush, Justice John Paul Stevens commented: "One thing ... is certain. Although we may never know with complete certainty the identity of the winner of this year's Presidential election, the identity of the loser is perfectly clear. It is the nation's confidence in the judge as an impartial guardian of the rule of law."

9/11 Terror Attacks Change America

Major symbols of U.S. economic and military might—the World Trade Center in New York and the Pentagon just outside Washington, D.C.—were attacked on September 11, 2001, when hijackers deliberately crashed commercial jetliners into the buildings, toppling the trade center's 110-story twin towers. A third plane crashed near Shanksville, Pennsylvania, during a heroic attempt by some passengers to wrest control from hijackers. Over 3,000 people died in the worst act of terrorism in American history. Saudi exile Osama bin Laden, head of the Al Qaeda organization of militant Muslims, masterminded the attack. Terrorist attacks had continued to be a grim reality overseas through the 1980s and early 1990s, with Americans frequently targeted. Yet such incidents had come to be viewed as something the United States wouldn't have to face on its own soil. Congress quickly passed the PATRIOT Act to provide law enforcement officials with more latitude in pursuing terrorists in the United States (see sidebar "PATRIOT Act: Controversial Response to 9/11 Attacks").

New York's World Trade Center twin towers were destroyed in the Sept. 11, 2001, terror attacks. (Wikimedia Commons)

Afghanistan Invasion

The United States government responded to the 9/11 attacks beginning on October 7 by bombing strategic Taliban centers in Afghanistan, where Al Qaeda operated training bases and Bin Laden was thought to be hiding. The subsequent invasion was swift, and major fighting had ended by the middle of 2002, though U.S. troops remain in Afghanistan today.

The invasion of Afghanistan was the first application of the Bush Doctrine that stated that the U.S. would use pre-emptive strikes against perceived threats to American security.

Iraq

American and international intelligence agencies believed Iraq possessed a number of weapons of mass destruction (WMD). The United Nations Security Council passed Resolution 1441, requiring Iraq to open up to UN weapons inspectors or else face "serious consequences." The U.S. and a number of allies ("the coalition of the willing") invaded Iraq on March 17, 2003, without receiving UN authorization. The invasion lasted only a short time, and the Iraqi government and military collapsed within three weeks. Saddam Hussein was found in a spider-hole and captured on December 13. Evidence of an active weapons of mass destruction program was never found in Iraq. Continued suicide bombings and the number of American and allied nations' casualties led to a steady decline in popular support for the war.

2004 Presidential Election

George Bush was unopposed for renomination by the Republicans in the 2004 election and was opposed in the general election by Democratic Senator John F. Kerry of Massachusetts. Kerry chose Senator John Edwards as his running mate. Kerry supported same-sex civil unions, embryonic stem cell research, and was pro-choice. The Bush campaign effectively targeted Kerry as a "flip-flopper," one who changed positions frequently. Kerry remarked at one point concerning

PATRIOT Act: Controversial Response to 9/11 Attacks

Following the terror attacks on the World Trade Center and the Pentagon on September 11, 2001, both houses of Congress passed and President Bush signed the USA PATRIOT Act, which strengthened the authority of U.S. law enforcement agencies to fight terrorist acts both in the United States and in foreign nations.

The PATRIOT Act has come under criticism by some individuals and groups who believe that portions of it are unnecessary and infringe upon American freedoms, including speech, press, and the right to privacy. The most controversial element is Section 215, which allows government agents to look into phone and Internet records on the basis of "an ongoing investigation concerning international terrorism or clandestine intelligence activities." In addition, this section allows FBI agents to obtain secret warrants from a federal court to review library or bookstore records of an individual connected with an international terrorism or spying investigation. Prior to the PATRIOT Act, such orders were granted only on the grounds of probable cause as detailed in the Fourth Amendment to the United States Constitution.

Public support for the PATRIOT Act, which was quite high in the period immediately after the September 11 attacks, began dropping in 2003. According to the Gallup Poll, in January 2002, 47 percent of Americans wanted the U.S. government to stop terrorism even if it reduced civil liberties. By November 2003, this number had dropped to 31 percent. By 2005, the public was divided almost evenly for and against the PATRIOT Act.

One of the main arguments against the PATRIOT Act is that while significantly expanding federal investigative authority, it did not provide checks and balances protecting civil liberties that were normally included in legislation. The Act did, however, include "sunset," or temporary, provisions that were set to expire on December 31, 2005. After that date, the authority was to remain in effect only for investigations previously begun. The temporary provisions deal with wiretapping in terrorism and computer cases, sharing wiretap and foreign intelligence information, nationwide search warrants for electronic evidence, and several other areas. The PATRIOT Act was reauthorized, however, by two bills in 2005 and 2006.

The PATRIOT Act comprises a controversial aspect of post–9/11 American life, as it created a new crime category of "domestic terrorism." It amended immigration, banking and money laundering, and foreign intelligence laws in its attempt to enhance federal law enforcement capabilities. Hailed by many as an important and necessary reaction to terrorism, the PATRIOT Act also inspired serious concern among others who fear restrictions on civil liberties. The American Civil Liberties Union, for example, filed challenges to a number of PATRIOT Act provisions and ran an ad campaign beginning in August 2004, claiming, "So the government can search your house... My house... Our house... Without notifying us. Treating us all like suspects. It's part of the Patriot Act."

funding for the Iraq war: "I actually voted for the eighty-seven billion—before I voted against it." Bush won 51 percent, while Kerry won 48 percent. The final electoral vote total was 286 for Bush and 251 for Kerry. Republicans also gained strength in both houses of Congress.

Patriot Act Reauthorized

Although many of the law enforcement provisions of the Patriot Act were set to expire at the end of 2005, Congress chose to reauthorize it in 2005 and 2006, despite significant erosion of popular support.

Public Education

One of the Bush administration's major initiatives was the No Child Left Behind Act, which sought to measure and close the gap between rich and poor student performance, provide more funding for low-income schools, and give options to parents with students in low-performing schools. Passed with bipartisan support, it quickly became a target for critics who claimed that its focus on frequent testing and narrow curriculum limited creativity and handcuffed teachers.

Economic Downturn

In December 2007, the United States entered its longest post–World War II recession. The national debt grew significantly during the Bush Administration due to a combination of tax cuts and wars in both Afghanistan and Iraq. In September 2008, the crisis took a serious turn for the worse when the government was forced to takeover Fannie Mae and Freddie Mac, which was followed by the collapse of Wall Street giant Lehman Brothers. Unemployment, which was 4.1% in 2001, had climbed to 7.2% by the end of Bush's presidency. By the end of 2008, the U.S. had lost a total of 2.6 million jobs. Adding to the nation's economic woes was a crisis in the home mortgage industry as the recession led to a massive drop in home values and numerous foreclosures.

Immigration

President Bush urged Congress in 2006 to allow more than 12 million illegal immigrants to work in the United States as temporary guest workers. It is estimated that eight million immigrants came to the United States from 2000 to 2005, with at least half of them entering illegally. Bush also urged Congress to provide additional funds for border security. He supported the Comprehensive Immigration Reform Act of 2007, which proposed a legalization program for illegal immigrants with a path to citizenship, a guest worker program, and a series of border and work site enforcement measures. The bill was defeated in the Senate, mainly due to lack of support from conservative Republicans.

2008 Presidential Election

As the nation struggled with its economic difficulties and the reality of two unpopular wars in Afghanistan and Iraq, the two major political parties sought candidates in the 2008 election who would provide answers to significant problems. The Republicans nominated Senator John McCain, a prisoner of war during the Vietnam War. He, in turn, selected Alaska Governor Sarah Palin as his vice presidential candidate. Palin had little experience on the national stage and no foreign policy background, but she proved to be a strong campaigner. The Democrats nominated Barack Obama, a first-term senator from Illinois. The economy and the war were the top two campaign issues. Obama promised "universal health care, full employment, a green America, and an America respected instead of feared by its enemies," in addition to withdrawing from Iraq. McCain supported the Iraq war. Obama won a decisive victory in the popular vote and the Electoral College.

First Obama Administration, 2009–2013

Withdrawal from Iraq

Implementing a plan to remove all U.S. troops from Iraq was a campaign promise of President Obama, who announced in February 2009 a deadline for the withdrawal of combat troops from Iraq. A transitional force remained until the last U.S. troops left in December 2011.

Closing Guantanamo Bay Prison Camp

Another campaign promise involved the closing of the Guantanamo Bay Prison Camp in Cuba. The prison had been established in 2002 during the Bush Administration and housed a number of prisoners accused of terrorism and war crimes. Obama's order to close the prison camp, which had become controversial for alleged human rights violations, was overturned by a federal judge. Subsequent attempts to close the camp via Congressional legislation also failed. As of March 2014, over 150 prisoners remained in Guantanamo.

Health Care Reform

Providing affordable health care to all Americans, particularly those who were underinsured or uninsured, was a major focus of the first term of the Obama administration. Despite significant opposition from Republicans, Democrats were able to pass the Patient Protection and Affordable Health Care Act, popularly known as Obamacare, in March 2010. It was challenged in the courts, but upheld by the Supreme Court.

The Election of 2008: History is Made

AP/Wide World Photos

Barack Obama

Barack Obama's presidential election victory in November 2008 marked a milestone in the progress of black political officeholders in the United States.

As race was no longer a barrier to voting with the 15th Amendment in 1865, some Reconstruction-era former slaves were elected to office in the South during the period immediately following the Civil War. But the enactment of black codes, grandfather clauses, and literacy tests effectively removed the franchise (or the right to vote) for blacks in Southern states and these black officials were turned out of office. The last black congressman elected in the 19th century was George Henry White of North Carolina, who took office in 1897. By the turn of the century, most Southern blacks had lost the right to vote.

All of the black Reconstruction-era elected officials ran as members of the Republican Party. Virtually all blacks who could vote were registered as Republicans from 1865 until the 1930s. The election of Democrat Franklin Roosevelt in 1932, however, caused a massive switch in allegiance from the Republican to the Democratic Party, as New Deal programs offering economic opportunities and labor protections benefited black voters. In addition, the migration of blacks from the deep South to the North and West which began during World War I accelerated during the 1930s, affecting local politics. By the election of John F. Kennedy in 1960, almost all black voters were Democrats and voting in regions outside of the former Confederacy.

The passage of the Voting Rights Act in 1965, following the voting registration drives by civil rights workers throughout Southern states in the early 1960s, finally provided blacks with unfettered access to the ballot box and, subsequently, black candidates were elected. However, with the Great Migration north and west since the 1940s, no states were comprised of black majority populations. This meant that candidates needed to broaden their appeal to other ethnic groups to become elected. Since 1965, 92 black House of Representative members have been elected to Congress. All but two were Democrats. In addition, three black senators have been elected in modern times: Edward Brooke of Massachusetts and Carol Moseley Braun and Barack Obama, both of Illinois.

Obama's victory over fellow U.S. Senator John McCain in the 2008 presidential election was a milestone in a number of ways. It shattered the record of campaign contributions received by a candidate when his campaign raised over $640 million. The election also brought to the White House the first president born after the birth of the American civil rights movement in the mid-1950s. However, the main message may be what the election says to blacks in America. In a *Time* magazine article written just before the election, *Atlantic Monthly* contributing editor Ta-Nehisi Coates wrote: "Consider this fact: the most famous black man in America isn't dribbling a ball or clutching a microphone. He has no prison record. ... Words like hope, change, and progress might seem like naïve campaign sloganeering in a dark age. But think of the way those words ring for a people whose forebears marched into billy clubs and dogs, whose ancestors fled north by starlight, feeling the moss on the backs of trees."

In the 232-year history of the United States, the presidential election of 2008 was truly a monumental event. A black man had been elected president.

Nobel Peace Prize

The Norwegian-based Nobel Committee awarded President Obama the Nobel Peace Prize in October 2009 for his efforts to support nuclear nonproliferation and promote a new climate of international relations, particularly in the Muslim world.

Arab Spring

Beginning in 2011, a wave of revolutionary demonstrations and protests swept the Arab world, with rulers in four nations (Tunisia, Egypt, Yemen, and Libya) being toppled. Although supportive of the democratic spirit of the protestors, many of whom were young, American officials were also alarmed by the violence and instability caused by the revolts. Dictator Muammar Qaddafi in Libya was overthrown and later killed by Libyans rebels. On September 11, 2012, a heavily armed group of over 100 stormed the American Embassy in Benghazi, killing U.S. Ambassador J. Christopher Stephens and three others.

Death of Osama bin Laden

Following the 9/11 bombings, the Central Intelligence Agency launched one of the largest manhunts in history in an effort to locate, capture, and kill Osama bin Laden. On May 2, 2012, a special operations force of Navy SEALS flew on a secret mission into Pakistan, stormed the Al Qaeda leader's compound, and killed him.

(Before taking the quiz noted below, please review the summary timeline for this chapter on the following pages.)

The Rise of Conservativism, Post-Cold War Challenges, and a Changing Population (1980–present)

Historical Timeline (1980–present)

1981	Iran releases hostages Reagan breaks air traffic controller strike Sandra Day O'Connor named first female Supreme Court justice AIDS epidemic reaches U.S.
1982	241 Marines killed in Lebanon U.S. invades Grenada
1985	Gorbachev takes power in Soviet Union
1986	Iran-Contra affair *Challenger* space shuttle explodes after takeoff
1989	*Exxon Valdez* oil tanker runs aground in Alaska Students begin pro-democracy demonstrations in China Berlin Wall falls
1990	Saddam Hussein of Iraq invades Kuwait
1991	Operation Desert Storm ends Iraq's occupation of Kuwait Soviet Union breaks up as Cold War ends
1992	Los Angeles riots follow Rodney King verdict Clinton elected president
1993	North American Free Trade Agreement approved
1995	U.S., NATO forces enforce peace in Bosnia
1999	Clinton acquitted following House impeachment
2000	George W. Bush defeats Gore in disputed election
2001	Hijackers crash planes into World Trade Center towers and Pentagon U.S. invades Afghanistan to overthrow Taliban government USA PATRIOT Act gives U.S. broad powers to investigate terrorism

Historical Timeline (1980–present)

2004	George W. Bush re-elected president
2006	Congress reauthorizes the USA PATRIOT Act
2008	Barack Obama becomes the first African American to be elected President
2009	Conservatives organize Tea Party protests
2010	"Don't ask, don't tell" armed forces policy concerning homosexuals repealed
2011	Osama bin Laden killed by U.S. forces in Pakistan U.S. troops withdraw from Iraq
2012	Barack Obama defeats Mitt Romney for president

AP U.S. History
Mini-Test 2 (covers chapters 7-11)

This mini-test is also available online at the REA Study Center with the additional benefits of timed testing, automatic scoring, and a detailed topic-level score report (www.rea.com/studycenter).

TIME: 20 minutes
20 multiple-choice questions

Directions: Each of the questions or incomplete statements below is followed by four suggested answers or completions. Select the best answer for each question.

Questions 1–4 are based on the following excerpts:

That on the first day of January, in the year of our Lord one thousand eight hundred and sixty-three, all persons held as slaves within any State or designated part of a State, the people whereof shall then be in rebellion against the United States, shall be then, thenceforward, and forever free; and the Executive Government of the United States, including the military and naval authority thereof, will recognize and maintain the freedom of such persons, and will do no act or acts to repress such persons, or any of them, in any efforts they may make for their actual freedom…

—Abraham Lincoln, Emancipation Proclamation, September 22, 1862

"The Emancipation Proclamation has done more for us here [in London] than all our former victories and all our diplomacy. It is creating an almost convulsive reaction in our favor all over this country. The *London Times* furious and scolds like a drunken drab. Certain it is, however, that public opinion is very deeply stirred here and finds expression in meetings, addresses to President Lincoln, deputations to us, standing committees to agitate the subject and to affect opinion, and all the other symptoms of a great popular movement peculiarly unpleasant to the upper classes here because it rests on the spontaneous action of the laboring classes."

—Henry Adams, writing in London, January 1863

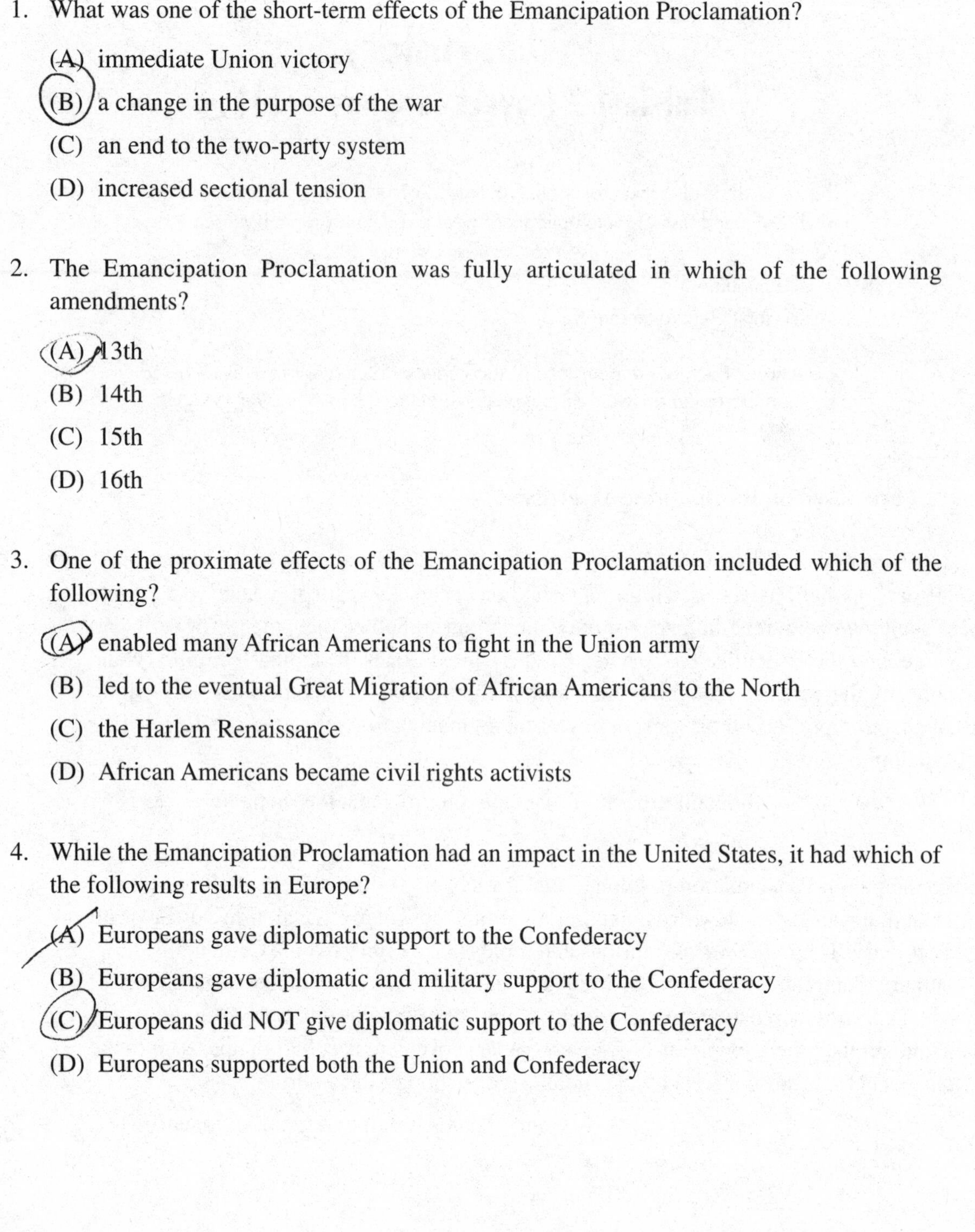

1. What was one of the short-term effects of the Emancipation Proclamation?

(A) immediate Union victory

(B) a change in the purpose of the war

(C) an end to the two-party system

(D) increased sectional tension

2. The Emancipation Proclamation was fully articulated in which of the following amendments?

(A) 13th

(B) 14th

(C) 15th

(D) 16th

3. One of the proximate effects of the Emancipation Proclamation included which of the following?

(A) enabled many African Americans to fight in the Union army

(B) led to the eventual Great Migration of African Americans to the North

(C) the Harlem Renaissance

(D) African Americans became civil rights activists

4. While the Emancipation Proclamation had an impact in the United States, it had which of the following results in Europe?

(A) Europeans gave diplomatic support to the Confederacy

(B) Europeans gave diplomatic and military support to the Confederacy

(C) Europeans did NOT give diplomatic support to the Confederacy

(D) Europeans supported both the Union and Confederacy

Questions 5 and 6 are based on the following cartoon:

— "The New Diplomacy," *Puck*, 1905

5. Which of the following groups would support the foreign policy objective displayed in this cartoon?

   (A) labor unions

   (B) Populists

   (C) Progressive reformers

   (D) advocates of overseas expansion

6. Which of the following presidents would most support the foreign policy stance depicted in this cartoon?

   (A) Ronald Reagan

   (B) George Washington

   (C) Abraham Lincoln

   (D) Franklin Roosevelt

Questions 7 and 8 refer to the following excerpt from a statement of President Harry S. Truman about the decision to drop the atomic bombs:

"I had then set up a committee of top men and had asked them to study with great care the implications the new weapons might have for us. It was their recommendation that the bomb be used against the enemy as soon as it could be done. They recommended further that it should be used without specific warning. On the other hand, the scientific advisors of the committee reported... that no technical demonstration they might propose, such as over a deserted island, would be likely to bring the war to an end. It had to be used against an enemy target. The final decision of where and when to use the atomic bomb was up to me. Let there be no mistake about it. I regarded the bomb as a military weapon and never doubted it should be used."

—Harry S. Truman, 1946

7. One of the short-term effects of this statement was which of the following?

(A) Japanese Americans were interned
(B) the mass mobilization of American society and troops
(C) the United States achieved victory over the Axis powers
(D) an end to the Great Depression

8. Which of the following was a long-term effect of Truman's decision?

(A) The development of the "military-industrial complex"
(B) U.S. isolationism
(C) activists began to call for economic equality
(D) a growing private sector and growth of the suburbs

Questions 9 and 10 refer to the following telegram to German Ambassador to Mexico Heinrich von Eckardt:

"We intend to begin on the first of February unrestricted submarine warfare. We shall endeavor in spite of this to keep the United States of America neutral. In the event of this not succeeding, we make Mexico a proposal or alliance on the following basis: make war together, make peace together, generous financial support and an understanding on our part that Mexico is to re-conquer the lost territory in Texas, New Mexico, and Arizona. Please call the President's attention to the fact that the ruthless employment of our submarines now offers the prospect of compelling England in a few months to make peace."

—Telegram sent by German Foreign Minister Arthur Zimmermann, January 1917

9. This telegram is similar to which of the following events?

   (A) the Philippine insurrection
   (B) the attack on Pearl Harbor
   (C) the Great Migration
   (D) the military engagement in Korea

10. What other factor besides the Zimmermann Telegram led President Woodrow Wilson to ask Congress for a declaration of war against Germany in April 1917?

   (A) the Spanish-American War
   (B) Wilson's use of the American Expeditionary Force
   (C) Wilson's call for the defense of democratic principals
   (D) social tensions created by increased international migration

Questions 11 and 12 refer to this written statement of Gerald R. Ford:

"As President, my primary concern must always be the greatest good of all the people of the United States whose servant I am. As a man, my first consideration is to be true to my own convictions and my own conscience…Now, therefore, I, Gerald R. Ford, President of the United States, pursuant to the pardon power conferred upon me by Article II, Section 2, of the Constitution, have granted and by these presents do grant a full, free, and absolute pardon unto Richard Nixon for all offenses against the United States which he, Richard Nixon, has committed or may have committed or taken part in during the period from January 20, 1969 through August 9, 1974."

—Gerald R. Ford, September 1974

11. One of the effects of President Ford's pardon of Richard Nixon was which of the following?

   (A) Federal programs expanded and economic growth reshaped American society.
   (B) Conservatives promoted their own values and ideology.
   (C) Americans had a sense of economic optimism.
   (D) The American public lost faith, trust, and confidence in the government after public scandals.

12. The cause of the pardon of Richard Nixon by President Ford was which of the following?
    (A) the Vietnam War
    (B) debates over the power of the presidency
    (C) abuses of natural resources
    (D) the increase of federal programs

Questions 13 and 14 refer to the following photograph and excerpt from a Supreme Court decision:

Cotton mill workers, North Carolina, 1908 (Wikimedia Commons)

[Suit was brought] by a father in his own behalf and … his two minor sons, one under the age of fourteen years and the other between the age of fourteen and sixteen years, employees in a cotton mill at Charlotte, North Carolina, to enjoin [stop] the enforcement of the act of Congress intended to prevent interstate commerce in the products of child labor… The controlling question for this decision, is it within the authority of Congress in regulating commerce among the states to prohibit the transportation in interstate commerce of manufactured goods, the product of a factory in which … children under the age of fourteen and sixteen years have been employed or permitted to work more than eight hours in any day, or more than six days in any week?... In our view, the necessary effect of this act is purely a state authority. Thus, the act in a two-fold sense is repugnant to the Constitution.... [I]t not only transcends the authority delegated to Congress over commerce, but also exerts a power as to a purely local matter.

—*Hammer v. Dagenhart, 1918*

13. The long-term cause of the suit filed in the *Hammer* case was which of the following?

(A) large scale industrialization

(B) international migrants who came to the United Sates

(C) the previous decision in *Plessy v. Ferguson*

(D) improved standard of living

14. The decision by the Supreme Court in the *Hammer* case took place during which period?

(A) the Progressive Era

(B) the Great Depression

(C) the canal era

(D) Manifest Destiny

Questions 15 and 16 refer to the following Supreme Court decision:

"A free negro of the African race, whose ancestors were brought to this country and sold as slaves, is not a 'citizen' within the meaning of the Constitution of the United States.

...When the Constitution was adopted, they were not regarded in any of the States as members of the community which constituted the State, and were not numbered among its 'people or citizens.' Consequently, the special rights and immunities guarantied to citizens do not apply to them. And not being 'citizens' within the meaning of the Constitution, they are not entitled to sue in that character in a court of the United States, and the Circuit Court has not jurisdiction in such a suit.

...The Constitution of the United States recognizes slaves as property, and pledges the Federal Government to protect it. And Congress cannot exercise any more authority over property of that description than it may constitutionally exercise over property of any other kind."

—*Dred Scott v. Sandford*, 1857

15. Along with the *Dred Scott* decision, which of the following was an attempt to resolve the issue of slavery in the territories?

    (A) the Mexican-American war

    (B) the Louisiana Purchase

    (C) the Articles of Confederation

    (D) the Kansas-Nebraska Act

16. Which of the following amendments rescinded the first argument made in the excerpt above from the *Dred Scott* decision?

    (A) 13th

    (B) 14th

    (C) 15th

    (D) 17th

Questions 17 and 18 refer to the following selection:

> "When the Eighteenth Amendment was ratified, Prohibition seemed…to have an almost united country behind it. Evasion of the law began immediately, however, and strenuous and sincere opposition to it—especially in the large cities of the North and East—quickly gathered force. The results were the bootlegger, the speakeasy, and a spirit of deliberate revolt which in many communities made drinking "the thing to do." From these facts in turn flowed further results: the increased popularity of distilled as against fermented liquors, the use of the hipflask, the cocktail party, and the general transformation of drinking from a masculine prerogative to one shared by both sexes together."
>
> —Frederick Lewis Allen, *Only Yesterday: An Informal History of the 1920s* (Bonanza Books, 1986)

17. Prohibition was the manifestation of which of the following?

    (A) New Deal legislation

    (B) World War I

    (C) cultural conflicts

    (D) the rise of the Democratic party

18. During the same period, which of the following movements occurred?

(A) the beginning of conservationism with regard to natural resources

(B) the Harlem Renaissance

(C) suburbanization

(D) interventionist foreign policies

Questions 19 and 20 are based on the following excerpt:

"Between the 1929 Crash and 1932, the cruelest year of the Depression, the economy's downward spiral was accelerated by measures which, according to all accepted canons, ought to have brought recovery, and which in practice did the opposite. To protect investments, prices had to be maintained. Sales ebbed, so costs were cut by laying off men. The unemployed could not buy the goods of other industries. Therefore sales dropped further, leading to more layoffs and a general shrinkage of purchasing power, until farmers were pauperized by the poverty of industrial workers, who in turn were pauperized by the poverty of farmers. 'Neither has the money to buy the product of the other,' an Oklahoma witness testified before a congressional subcommittee, explaining the vicious circle: 'Hence we have overproduction and underconsumption at the same time and in the same country.'"

—William Manchester, *The Glory and the Dream* (Little, Brown, 1973)

19. Which of the following was a long-term effect of the problems described by Manchester?

(A) The United States transformed into a limited welfare state.

(B) a further commitment to *laissez-faire* capitalism

(C) the rise of an industrial society

(D) Gays and lesbians began to call for social equality.

20. How did Franklin Roosevelt attempt to alleviate the problems associated with the Depression?

(A) He became more conservative.

(B) He let the state governments deal with unemployment problems.

(C) He focused on immediate relief and not long-term recovery and reform.

(D) He initiated the New Deal to remedy both the causes and the effects of the Great Depression.

Answer Key
Mini-Test 2

1. (B)
2. (A)
3. (A)
4. (C)
5. (D)
6. (A)
7. (C)
8. (A)
9. (B)
10. (C)
11. (D)
12. (B)
13. (A)
14. (A)
15. (D)
16. (B)
17. (C)
18. (B)
19. (A)
20. (D)

Answer Explanations
Mini-Test 2

1. (B)

Lincoln issued the Emancipation Proclamation following the battle of Antietam (or Sharpsburg). While not a clear-cut victory for Union forces, Confederate General Robert E. Lee's hope to control Maryland was thwarted. Antietam was the single bloodiest day of fighting in American history. Prior to the Emancipation Proclamation, the purpose of the war had been to keep the Union together, after the proclamation, it changed to freeing the slaves.

2. (A)

The 13th amendment, ratified in 1865, freed all the slaves in the United States. The 14th and 15th amendments were also passed during reconstruction and declared the freedmen citizens and gave black men the right to vote.

3. (A)

The key with this question is *proximate*, which means nearest. The most near-term effect of the Emancipation Proclamation was the enlistment of black men from the south into the Union army.

4. (C)

The English had been attempting to help the Confederacy with the hopes that a division in the United States would better serve them, but at the same time, they were against the institution of slavery. When Lincoln issued the Emancipation Proclamation, making the war about freeing the slaves, the English (and other European powers) decided to deny support to the Confederacy.

5. (D)

In the late 19th and early 20th century, American foreign policy was imperialist in nature, with Teddy Roosevelt becoming one of the most vocal advocates of overseas expansion. During his presidency, he began building the Panama Canal and issued his Roosevelt Corollary to the Monroe Doctrine, which expanded American economic and military presence in the Caribbean. Roosevelt said "speak softly and carry a big stick" in a speech and this phrase became symbolic of his foreign policy while president.

6. (A)

In the 1980s, President Reagan abandoned *détente* and increased defense spending and military action in order to win the Cold War.

7. (C)

Truman never apologized for his authorization of the use of atomic weapons. He felt the war with Japan justified their use. After the dropping of two atomic weapons, the war with all of the Axis powers was over.

8. (A)

The long-term effect of the development and use of the atomic bomb was the American-Soviet arms race which led to the development of an American nuclear arsenal which became known as the "military industrial complex."

9. (B)

The Zimmermann Telegram played a critical role in bringing the U.S. into World War I. Intercepted and decrypted by British code-crackers, the telegram angered American authorities. This is somewhat similar to the trigger for the United States to enter World War II: the attack on Pearl Harbor.

10. (C)

President Wilson declared that the United States must make the world "safe for democracy." Ironically, Congress passed the Espionage and Sedition Acts during World War I, which were decidedly un-democratic.

11. (D)

In 1974, President Nixon resigned due to the Watergate scandal, which involved high-level presidential aides. This scandal combined with the unsuccessful outcome of the Vietnam War led to a sharp decline of public confidence in elected officials and the government in general.

12. (B)

During the Watergate scandal, President Nixon attempted to exercise executive privilege numerous times while he was being investigated. Persistent questions over the power of the presidency—centering on a growing belief that he had overreached and abused his power—ultimately led to his resignation.

13. (A)

The Industrial Revolution took place during the Gilded Age and was noted for poor working conditions as well as the use of child labor.

14. (A)

By the late 1890s, many reformers began to seek better working conditions and an end to child labor. The period is known as the Progressive Era.

15. (D)

The decision in the *Dred Scott* case was seen as a huge loss by abolitionists and free-soilers as it rendered invalid the attempts of Northerners in Congress to control the spread of slavery. The Kansas-Nebraska Act was an earlier attempt to also settle the issue of the spread of slavery. The act allowed for popular sovereignty in the Kansas and Nebraska territories. In Kansas, the pro-slavery settlers and the abolitionists did not settle their differences peacefully and it became known as "Bleeding Kansas."

16. (B)

The *Dred Scott* decision ruled that slaves were not citizens of the United States. The 14th amendment (ratified in 1868) stipulated that all persons born in the United States are citizens.

17. (C)

The 1920s was a time of immense cultural conflict due to the rapid modernization of cultural values and ideas. The urban versus rural and fundamentalist Christian versus scientific modernism are also symbolic of the cultural conflicts of the 1920s.

18. (B)

As a result of the Great Migration (the movement of African Americans to the North for work during World War I), many African Americans settled in Harlem, which became a beacon of literature, jazz, poetry, and art in the 1920s.

19. (A)

In an effort to combat the effects of the Great Depression, President Roosevelt initiated numerous programs that provided employment and aid to unemployed Americans. This forever changed the social fabric of the United States. Citizens began to look to their government for help during difficult economic times. This led to the development of a social welfare state.

20. (D)

Franklin Roosevelt's New Deal was comprised of programs to give immediate employment relief (the Civilian Conservation Corps), provide recovery (the Agriculture Adjustment Act), and achieve financial reform (the Securities and Exchange Commission).

Practice Exam
Section I

TIME: 55 Minutes
55 Multiple-Choice Questions

Directions: Each of the questions or incomplete statements below is followed by either four suggested answers or completions. Select the one that is best in each case and then fill in the appropriate letter in the corresponding space on the answer sheet.

Section 1, Part A: Multiple-Choice Questions

Questions 1–2 refer to the following excerpt.

"After the defeat of the kaiser in Germany [in World War I], a spirit of optimism and positive expectation swept across Harlem. The Allies won the war for democracy, so now it was time for something to happen in America to change the system of segregation and lynching that was going on. In Europe, the black [African American] troops were welcomed as liberators; so when they came back to America, they were determined to create a situation that would approximate the slogans they had been fighting for. They wanted democracy at home in the United States."

—African American newspaper editor Howard Johnson

1. What was the short-term cause of what Johnson describes in this excerpt?

   (A) The "Great Migration" during World War I

   (B) The anti-imperialist movement

   (C) The Spanish-American War

   (D) The New Deal

2. The situation that Johnson is describing is known as which of the following?

   (A) The Progressive Movement

   (B) Modernism

   (C) The Harlem Renaissance

   (D) Xenophobia

Questions 3–4 refer to the following newspaper article:

"In a government where sectional interests and feelings may come into conflict, the sole security for permanence and peace is to be found in a Constitution whose provisions are inviolable. … Every State, before entering into that compact, stood in a position of independence. Ere yielding that independence, it was only proper that provision should be made to protect the interests of those which would inevitably be the weaker in that confederacy. ... [The framers of the Constitution] acted wisely, and embodied in the Constitution all that the South could ask. But two Constitutional provisions are necessary to secure Southern rights upon this important question, —*the recognition of slavery where the people choose it and the remedy for fugitive slaves.* … We hold that the Constitution of the Union does recognize slavery where it exists. … "

—An Anonymous Georgian, "Plain Words for the North," *American Whig Review*, XII

3. The author of the article could best be characterized as

(A) an abolitionist

(B) an opponent of the fugitive slave law

(C) supporting restrictions on slavery's expansion into Western territories

(D) being opposed to Congress interfering with the institution of slavery

4. Which of the following events prompted this letter?

(A) The outlawing of international slave trade

(B) The Compromise of 1850

(C) The Missouri Compromise

(D) Enlightenment philosophies and ideas that inspired many political thinkers

Practice Exam 1

Answer Sheet
Practice Exam 1

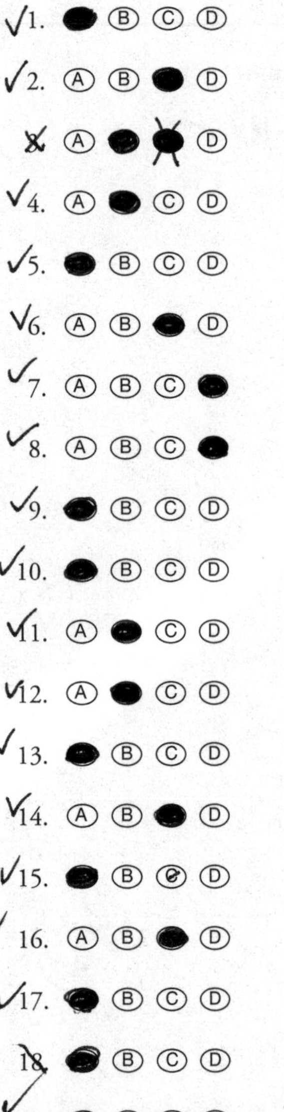

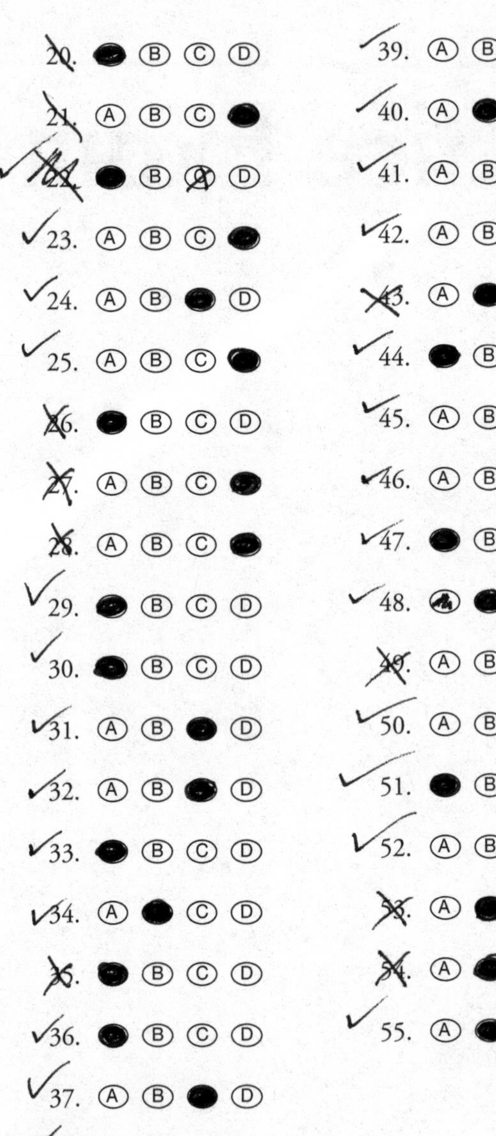

Questions 5–7 refer to the following excerpt.

> "We, men and women who hereby constitute ourselves as the National Organization for Women, believe that the time has come for a new movement toward true equality for all women in America, and toward a fully equal partnership of the sexes as part of the world-wide revolution of human rights now taking place within and beyond our national borders. There is no civil rights movement to speak for women, as there has been for Negroes and other victims of discrimination. The National Organization for Women must therefore begin to speak."
>
> —National Organization for Women (NOW), Statement of Purpose, 1966

5. People who agreed with the statement made in the excerpt would most likely have recommended which of the following?

   (A) A stronger government role in ensuring social justice

   (B) A slowing down of the African American civil rights movement in order to focus on women

   (C) An end to the Great Society programs

   (D) An end to the Cold War

6. The goals of NOW as described in the excerpt have the most in common with women's activism during which of the following earlier periods?

   (A) The Great Depression

   (B) The Gilded Age

   (C) The Second Great Awakening in the first half of the 1800s

   (D) The decades following the American Revolution

7. Many historians consider which of the following to be one of the major causes of the unrest described in the excerpt?

   (A) World War I

   (B) The Progressive Era

   (C) Internal migration

   (D) Middle-class suburbanization

Questions 8–9 refer to the following selection.

"The conditions which surround us best justify our cooperation; we meet in the midst of a nation brought to the verge of moral, political, and material ruin. Corruption dominates the ballot-box, the legislatures, the Congress, and even touches the ermine of the bench. The people are demoralized. … The newspapers are largely subsidized or muzzled, public opinion silenced, business prostrated, homes covered with mortgages, labor impoverished, and the land concentrating in the hands of the capitalists. The urban workmen are denied the right to organize for self-protection. … The national power to create money is appropriated to enrich bondholders; a vast public debt payable in legal-tender currency has been funded into gold bearing bonds, thereby adding millions to the burdens of the people. … Silver, which has been accepted as coin since the dawn of history, has been demonetized to add to the purchasing power of gold by decreasing the value of all forms of property as well as human labor, and the supply of currency is purposely abridged to fatten usurers, bankrupt enterprise, and enslave industry."

—The People's (Populist) Party platform, 1892

8. The authors of this excerpt are primarily made up of which of the following groups?

(A) Bankers

(B) Corporate leaders

(C) Politicians

(D) Farmers

9. Supporters of the above excerpt would most likely desire which of the following?

(A) A stronger role for the federal government in the American economic system

(B) Redesigned financial and management structures such as monopolies

(C) Corporate control of agricultural markets

(D) Tenant farming systems

Questions 10–12 refer to the excerpt below from President Andrew Jackson's veto message on the recharter of the Bank of the United States.

"It is to be regretted that the rich and powerful too often bend the acts of government to their selfish purposes. Distinctions in society will always exist under every just government. … In the full enjoyment of the gifts of Heaven and the fruits of superior industry, economy, and virtue, every man is equally entitled to protection by law; but when the laws undertake to add to these natural and just advantages artificial distinctions, … to make the rich richer and the potent more powerful, the humble members of society—the farmers, mechanics, and laborers—… have a right to complain of the injustice of their Government.

—Andrew Jackson, veto message, July 10, 1832

10. Which of the following would have supported the ideas expressed in this excerpt?

    (A) Farmers with large mortgages

    (B) Manufacturers

    (C) Whig congressmen

    (D) Wealthy merchants

11. This excerpt reflects what shift in American society?

    (A) A decrease in sectional tensions

    (B) A more participatory democracy

    (C) The loss of regional identity

    (D) The Romantic belief in human perfectibility

12. Jackson's themes in the veto message would also have been admired by

    (A) abolitionists in the 1850s

    (B) Populists in the 1890s

    (C) imperialists in the 1890s

    (D) isolationists in the 1930s

Questions 13–15 refer to the selection below.

"Worst of any, however, were the fertilizer men, and those who served in the cooking rooms. These people could not be shown to the visitor—for the odor of a fertilizer man would scare any ordinary visitor at a hundred yards, and as for the other men, who worked in tank rooms full of steam, and in some of which there were open vats near the level of the floor, their peculiar trouble was that they fell into the vats; and when they were fished out, there was never enough of them left to be worth exhibiting—sometimes they would be overlooked for days, till all but the bones of them had gone out to the world as Dunham's Pure Beef Lard!"

—Upton Sinclair, *The Jungle*, 1906

13. Publication of the previous excerpt was instrumental in galvanizing which of the following?

(A) Twentieth-century Progressive reformers

(B) Large corporations that came to dominate the U.S. economy

(C) Populist movements that pushed Franklin Roosevelt toward more extensive reforms

(D) African Americans who were a part of the Great Migration

14. The change in the role of the federal government that this excerpt would help usher in was most similar to which decade?

(A) 1790s

(B) 1870s

(C) 1930s

(D) 1950s

15. Working conditions in American factories was one of the targets of Sinclair's exposé of the meat-packing industry. Which of the following was a cause of the industrial growth in the late 18th and early 19th centuries?

(A) Immigrant labor

(B) Major overhauls of the capitalist system

(C) The elimination of the laissez-faire philosophy

(D) No tariffs

Questions 16–17 refer to the following cartoon published in 1942.

"Waiting for the Signal From Home . . . ,"
Theodore Geisel (Dr. Seuss)
Source: paperlessarchives.com

16. The attitude expressed in this cartoon played a role in which of the following?

    (A) Dropping the atomic bomb

    (B) Declaring war after the attack on Pearl Harbor

    (C) The internment of Japanese

    (D) American neutrality

17. The point of view of this cartoon is indicative of a continuation of which of the following?

    (A) Xenophobia

    (B) Mass mobilization for the war

    (C) Technological and scientific advances

    (D) Social Darwinism

Questions 18–19 are based on the following excerpt from President Reagan's 1981 inaugural address.

> "The economic ills we suffer have come upon us over several decades. … They will go away because we as Americans have the capacity now, as we've had in the past, to do whatever needs to be done to preserve this last and greatest bastion of freedom. … In this present crisis, government is not the solution to our problem; government is the problem. From time to time we've been tempted to believe that society has become too complex to be managed by self-rule, that government by an elite group is superior to government for, by, and of the people…All of us need to be reminded that the Federal Government did not create the States; the States created the Federal Government. Now, so there will be no misunderstanding, it's not my intention to do away with government. It is rather to make it work—work with us, not over us; to stand by our side, not ride on our back. Government can and must provide opportunity, not smother it; foster productivity, not stifle it."
>
> —Ronald Reagan, January 20, 1981

18. President Reagan's philosophy about the role of government was the result of which of the following?

    (A) The growth of evangelical Christian churches increasing their political participation

    (B) The increasing role of the federal government during the 1960s and 1970s

    (C) A reinvigorated anti-communist foreign policy due to the government's failure with containment

    (D) An increasingly homogeneous mass culture

19. Which group of Americans would most likely have supported Reagan's views expressed in the excerpt?

    (A) Critics of the Great Society

    (B) Ardent anti-communists

    (C) Individuals receiving federal welfare funding

    (D) Civil rights leaders

Questions 20–21 are based on the maps below.

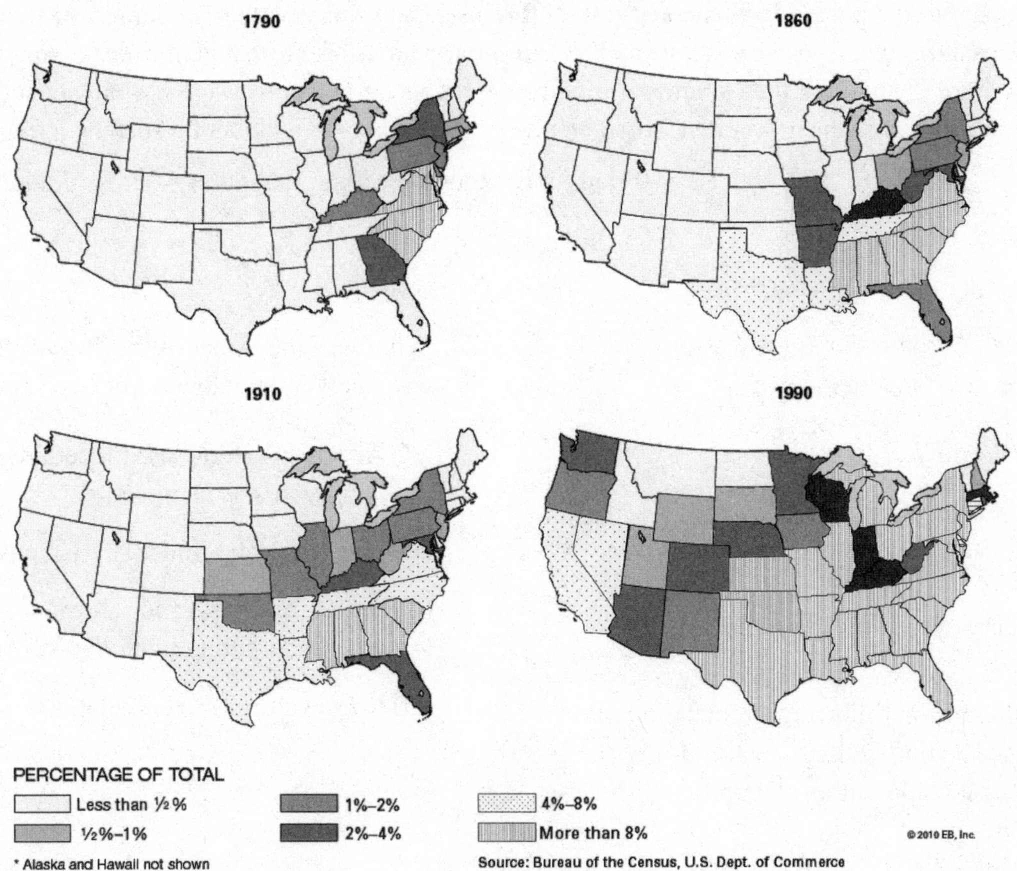

20. Which of the following is a cause for the trend seen between the maps of 1910 and 1990?

    (A) The Civil Rights movement

    (B) The success of Reconstruction

    (C) The Harlem Renaissance

    (D) The Great Migration

21. Which of the following is a cause for the trend seen between the maps of 1790 and 1860?

    (A) The growth of an abolitionist movement in the North

    (B) The Second Great Awakening

    (C) The use of Southern cotton to furnish the raw material for manufacturing in the North

    (D) The Civil War

Questions 22–24 refer to the following excerpt.

"It is to be hoped that the normal balance of executive and legislative authority may be wholly adequate to meet the unprecedented task before us. But it may be that an unprecedented demand and need for undelayed action may call for temporary departure from that normal balance of public procedure...I shall ask the Congress for ... broad executive power to wage a war against the emergency, as great as the power that would be given to me if we were in fact invaded by a foreign foe."

—Franklin D. Roosevelt, First Inaugural Address, March 4, 1933

22. Which of the following situations precipitated the statement above?

(A) World War II

(B) World War I

(C) The Great Depression

(D) The spread of Communism

23. Which of the following groups did *not* allow Frankin D. Roosevelt to fulfill the promise made in this excerpt?

(A) Liberals

(B) Progressives

(C) Local reformers

(D) The Supreme Court

24. What was the effect of the "broad executive" power described in the excerpt?

(A) Africans Americans stopped identifying themselves as Democrats

(B) The economy immediately recovered

(C) Relief, recovery, and reform programs were incorporated into the New Deal

(D) Roosevelt rejected regulation

Questions 25–26 refer to the excerpt below.

"There is no Declaration (Bill) of Rights, and the Laws of the general Government being paramount to the Laws and Constitutions of the several States, the Declarations of rights in the separate States are no Security. …

By declaring all Treaties supreme Laws of the Land, the Executive and the Senate have in many Cases, an exclusive Power of legislation. …

There is no Declaration of any kind for preserving the Liberty of the Press, or the Trial by Jury in Civil Cases; nor against the Danger of standing Armies in time of Peace. …

This government will set out a moderate Aristocracy; it is at present impossible to foresee whether it will, in its operation, produce a Monarchy or a corrupt, tyrannical Aristocracy. It will most probably vibrate some years between the two, and then terminate in the one or the other."

—George Mason, "Objections to This Constitution of Government", 1787

25. According to this excerpt, which of the following does George Mason desire?

(A) The ratification of the Constitution

(B) Revisions of the Articles of Confederation

(C) The creation of political parties

(D) The addition of a Bill of Rights

26. The concerns expressed by Mason will be echoed in the future by which of the following?

(A) Whigs

(B) States' rights activists

(C) Federalists

(D) Supporters of the New Deal

Questions 27–28 refer to the excerpt below.

> "If slavery is right, all words, acts, laws, and constitutions against it, are themselves wrong, and should be silenced, and swept away. If it is right, we cannot justly object to its nationality—its universality; if it is wrong, they cannot justly insist upon its extension—its enlargement. … Wrong as we think slavery is, we can yet afford to let it alone where it is, because that much is due to the necessity arising from its actual presence in the nation; but can we, while our votes will prevent it, allow it to spread into the National Territories, and to overrun us here in these Free States? If our sense of duty forbids this, then let us stand by our duty, fearlessly and effectively. … Let us have faith that right makes might, and in that faith, let us, to the end, dare to do our duty as we understand it."
>
> —Abraham Lincoln, Cooper Union Address, February 1860

27. Which of the following events led to the debate that Lincoln is addressing?

    (A) The Missouri Compromise

    (B) The Mexican-American War

    (C) Innovations in railroads and steam engines

    (D) The Union victory over the Confederacy

28. What was the immediate impact of the ideas expressed by Lincoln?

    (A) The Republican Party was formed.

    (B) The 14th Amendment was passed.

    (C) Lincoln's election led various Southern states to secede from the Union.

    (D) The 13th Amendment was passed.

Questions 29–31 refer to the following excerpt.

"Hawaii is ours; Porto Rico is to be ours; at the prayer of her people Cuba finally will be ours; in the islands of the East, even to the gates of Asia, coaling stations are to be ours at the very least; the flag of a liberal government is to float over the Philippines, and may it be the banner that Taylor unfurled in Texas and Fremont carried to the coast."

—Albert J. Beveridge, The March of the Flag, 1898

29. Which of the following is Beveridge describing?

(A) American imperialism

(B) The Civil War

(C) The American System

(D) Immigration

30. Which of the following led to the U.S. acquisition of the territories mentioned in Beveridge's speech?

(A) The Spanish-American War

(B) World War I

(C) The Mexican-American War

(D) Labor shortages

31. Shortly after the speech by Beveridge, which of the following debates occurred?

(A) Debates over the use of natural resources in factories

(B) Debates over the League of Nations

(C) Debates between imperialists and anti-imperialists

(D) Debates over Mexican immigration

Questions 32–33 refer to the recruitment poster below.

James Montgomery Flagg, "Wake up America!"
Source: American Treasures of the U.S. Library of Congress.

32. This recruitment poster used during World War I is similar to posters that were produced during which of the following decades?

    (A) 1920s

    (B) 1930s

    (C) 1940s

    (D) 1950s

33. In an effort to fulfill the goals expressed in the poster, President Wilson advocated which of the following after World War I?

    (A) The League of Nations

    (B) American isolationism

    (C) High tariffs

    (D) Imperialist ventures

Questions 34–36 refer to the following front page from the *New York Journal*.

$50,000 REWARD.—WHO DESTROYED THE MAINE?—$50,000 REWARD.

EDITION FOR GREATER NEW YORK

NEW YORK JOURNAL

AND ADVERTISER.

DESTRUCTION OF THE WAR SHIP MAINE WAS THE WORK OF AN ENEMY

$50,000!

$50,000 REWARD!
For the Detection of the Perpetrator of the Maine Outrage!

Assistant Secretary Roosevelt Convinced the Explosion of the War Ship Was Not an Accident.

The Journal Offers $50,000 Reward for the Conviction of the Criminals Who Sent 258 American Sailors to Their Death. Naval Officers Unanimous That the Ship Was Destroyed on Purpose.

$50,000!

$50,000 REWARD!
For the Detection of the Perpetrator of the Maine Outrage!

NAVAL OFFICERS THINK THE MAINE WAS DESTROYED BY A SPANISH MINE.

Hidden Mine or a Sunken Torpedo Believed to Have Been the Weapon Used Against the American Man-of-War—Officers and Men Tell Thrilling Stories of Being Blown Into the Air Amid a Mass of Shattered Steel and Exploding Shells—Survivors Brought to Key West Scout the Idea of Accident—Spanish Officials Protest Too Much—Our Cabinet Orders a Searching Inquiry—Journal Sends Divers to Havana to Report Upon the Condition of the Wreck.

Source: *New York Journal*, February 17, 1898.

34. Which of the following occurred as a result of the event described in this newspaper?

    (A) World War I

    (B) The Spanish-American War

    (C) The Mexican-American War

    (D) World War II

35. Which of the following events also led Americans to demand that the United States declare war?

    (A) The restriction of civil liberties during wars

    (B) The success of the American Expeditionary Force

    (C) The military presence in the Caribbean

    (D) The attack on Pearl Harbor

36. Which of the following territories did the United States acquire in the years immediately following the publication of this article?

    (A) The Philippines

    (B) The Mexican Territory

    (C) African colonies

    (D) Vietnam

Questions 37–38 refer to the following sermon by Jonathan Edwards.

> "The God that holds you over the pit of hell, much as one holds a spider, or some loathsome insect over the fire, abhors you, and is dreadfully provoked: his wrath towards you burns like fire; he looks upon you as worthy of nothing else, but to be cast into the fire; he is of purer eyes than to bear to have you in his sight; you are ten thousand times more abominable in his eyes, than the most hateful venomous serpent is in ours. You have offended him infinitely more than ever a stubborn rebel did his prince; and yet it is nothing but his hand that holds you from falling into the fire every moment. … And there is no other reason to be given, why you have not dropped into hell since you arose in the morning, but that God's hand has held you up. Therefore, let everyone that is out of Christ now awake and fly from the wrath to come."
>
> —Jonathan Edwards, "Sinners in the Hands of an Angry God," July 8, 1741

37. Which of the following was a result of this sermon?

    (A) A renewed commitment of Puritans who sought to establish a community of like-minded religious believers

    (B) Greater emphasis on commercial economy in the Atlantic world

    (C) Greater religious independence and an increase in piety among members of Protestant churches.

    (D) Regional distinctiveness among the British colonies diminished

38. The religious movement that occured during the 1740s was most similar to religious developments in which of the following periods?

    (A) 1780s

    (B) 1830s

    (C) 1860s

    (D) 1890s

Questions 39–40 refer to the following excerpt.

"Our religious and political foes are not only within our gates, but are coming by the hundreds of thousands, bringing chaos and ruin of old European and Asiatic countries to un-Americanize and destroy our nation, and make it subserve the purposes of the Pope in his aspirations for world supremacy."

—*The Good Citizen*, Ku Klux Klan, 1924

39. The nativism expressed in the excerpt was most similar to which of the following periods?

(A) 1660–1670

(B) 1780–1790

(C) 1840–1850

(D) 1860s

40. How did the federal government respond to the nativism expressed in this excerpt?

(A) The government encouraged the protection of the civil liberties of immigrants.

(B) The government passed highly restrictive immigration quotas.

(C) There was a call to restrict immigration of the Irish.

(D) The government supported labor and labor strikes.

Questions 41–43 refer to the following excerpt.

"Then—Resolve,—Thet we wunt hev an inch o' slave territory;
That President Polk's holl perceedins air very tory;
Thet the war's a damned war, an' them thet enlist in it
Should hev a cravat with a dreffle tight twist in it;
Thet the war is a war fer the spreadin' o' slavery";

—James Russell Lowell, *The Biglow Papers*, 1846

41. This excerpt refers to which of the following conflicts?

(A) The Spanish-American War

(B) The Missouri Compromise

(C) The Civil War

(D) The Mexican-American War

42. Which of the following philosophies led to the war that Lowell is addressing?

(A) Romantic beliefs in human perfectibility

(B) Rising xenophobia

(C) Manifest Destiny

(D) The American System

43. Which of the following groups in the late 1890s would have held a similar view to Lowell's?

(A) The anti-imperialists

(B) The imperialists

(C) African Americans who migrated north

(D) Interventionists

Questions 44–45 refer to the graph below.

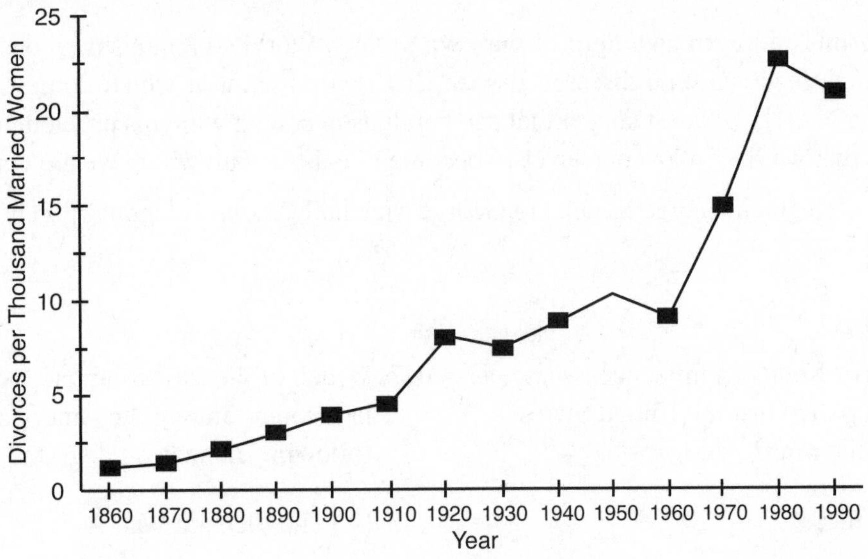

Graph from article entitled "Welfare; History, Results and Reform" by Travis Snyder, 2004.

44. Which of the following was a significant cause of the trend from 1960-1990 shown in the graph?

    (A) The rise of the modern feminist movement

    (B) The distrust in the government's ability to solve social problems

    (C) The growth of a gay and lesbian movement for equality

    (D) The growth of a civil rights movement

45. Beginning in 1980, which of the following was one of the results of the trend shown in the graph?

    (A) A renewed commitment to the Great Society programs

    (B) An increasingly homogeneous mass culture

    (C) A growth of evangelical and fundamentalist Christian churches

    (D) A demand among conservatives for "big government" to help solve social problems

Questions 46–47 refer to the following excerpt.

> "Much depends on health and vigor of our own society. World communism is like [a] malignant parasite which feeds only on diseased tissue. This is [the] point at which domestic and foreign policies meet. … The greatest danger that can befall us in coping with this problem of Soviet communism, is that we shall allow ourselves to become like those with whom we are coping."
>
> —Telegram, George Kennan to George Marshall ["Long Telegram"], February 22, 1946

46. As a result of Kennan's influence, what was the foreign policy that the United States adopted at the time?

    (A) Isolationist

    (B) Imperialism

    (C) Containment

    (D) Decolonization

47. Which of the following had the least popular support among the American public following Kennan's telegram?

    (A) The Vietnam War

    (B) The Korean War

    (C) The war on terrorism

    (D) The 1948 Berlin airlift

Questions 48–50 refer to the following excerpt.

"It is difficult to estimate the influence which this Canal has exerted upon the commerce, growth, and prosperity of the whole country, for it is impossible to imagine what would have been the state of things without it. The increase of the commerce and the growth of the country has been very accurately measured by the growth of the business of the Canal. It has been one great bond of strength, infusing life and vigor into the whole. Commercially and politically, it has secured and maintained to the United States the characteristic of a homogeneous people."

—Senate Executive Documents, 32d Congress, 1st session

48. Which of the following was an effect of the canal described in the excerpt above?

(A) Less of a reliance on agriculture

(B) Production of goods for distant markets

(C) A decrease in African slave labor

(D) A decrease in migration

49. The events described in the excerpt above symbolized which of the following?

(A) The market revolution

(B) The Second Great Awakening

(C) The Missouri Compromise

(D) The Louisiana Purchase

50. Which of the following most directly undermines the assertion that the canal fosters a "homogeneous people"?

(A) There was an increase in American manufactured items.

(B) A global market was created.

(C) The South remained culturally different from other sections of the United States.

(D) Technological innovations were developed in the construction of the canal.

Questions 51–52 refer to the following excerpt.

"The walk-out was a complete surprise to the officials. ... Mr. Pullman had offered to allow the men the privilege of examining the books of the company to verify his statement that the works were running at a loss. ...At that time a ballot was taken which resulted: 42 to 4 in favor of the strike. One department at a time, the men went out so that by 10 o'clock 1500 men were out."

—*Chicago Tribune*, May 12, 1894

51. People who disagreed with the action of the workers described in the *Chicago Tribune* most likely would have supported which of the following ideologies?

(A) Social Darwinism

(B) Manifest Destiny

(C) A limited welfare state

(D) Progressive reforms

52. The excerpt was the result of which of the following trends during the Gilded Age?

(A) A call for a "New South"

(B) The industrial workforce expanding through migration across national borders

(C) Labor and management battling for control over wages and working conditions

(D) Business leaders becoming allies with the government

Questions 53–55 refer to the following excerpt.

"For too many years, black Americans marched and had their heads broken and got shot. They were saying to the country, 'Look, you guys are supposed to be nice guys and we are only going to do what we are supposed to do—why do you beat us up?' … After years of this, we are at almost the same point—because we demonstrated from a position of weakness. We cannot be expected any longer to march and have our heads broken in order to say to whites: come on, you're nice guys. For you are not nice guys. We have found you out."

—Stokely Carmichael, "What We Want," *New York Review of Books*, September 1966

53. Carmichael is expressing frustration over which of the following?

(A) Tensions among civil rights activists over tactical and philosophical issues

(B) White resistance at desegregation

(C) The *Brown v. Board of Education* decision

(D) The Civil Rights Act of 1964

54. Carmichael's anger was primarily directed toward which of the following?

(A) Malcolm X

(B) Advocates of non-violent resistance

(C) Elijah Mohammed

(D) Advocates of the "Back to Africa" movement.

55. Which of the following groups would have been least likely to have supported Carmichael's view?

(A) Liberals

(B) Conservatives ·

(C) Members of the counterculture

(D) Democrats

End of Part A

If you finish before time is called, you may check your work on Part A.

Do not go on to Part B until you are told to do so.

Section 1, Part B: Short-Answer Questions

TIME: 50 Minutes
4 Questions

Directions: Read each question carefully. Use complete sentences; an outline or bulleted list alone is not acceptable.

1. Using your knowledge of United States history, answer parts a and b.

   a) Briefly explain why ONE of the following events best represents the beginning of America as a world power. Provide at least ONE piece of evidence from the period to support your explanation.

   - The rise of America as an industrial power
   - The Spanish-American War
   - World War II

   b) Briefly explain why ONE of the other options is not as persuasive as the one you chose.

Courtesy of the National Archives

2. Use the image above to answer parts a, b, and c.

   a) Briefly explain the point of view expressed through the image about one of the following:

      - The Progressive movement
      - Political participation
      - Civil rights

   b) Briefly explain ONE cause *or* ONE outcome of what you see in the image.

   c) Compare this to another example for a struggle for democratic rights in American history.

"We love to indulge in thoughts of the future extent and power of this Republic—because with its increase is the increase of human happiness and liberty. ... What has miserable, inefficient Mexico—with her superstition, her burlesque upon freedom, her actual tyranny by the few over the many—what has she to do with the great mission of peopling the New World with a noble race? Be it ours, to achieve that mission! Be it ours to roll down all of the upstart leaven of old despotism that comes our way!"

—Walt Whitman, Editorial, *Brooklyn Daily Eagle*, July 7, 1846

"... the Mexican war, a murderous war, a war against the free states, a war against freedom, against the Negro, and against the interests of workingmen of this country, a means of extending that great evil and damned curse, negro slavery. For my part, I would not care if, tomorrow, I should hear of the death of every man who engaged in that bloody war in Mexico, and that every man had met the fate he went there to perpetrate upon unoffending Mexicans."

—Frederick Douglass, *On Mexico,* 1849

"The vistas of all from Jackson to Polk were maritime and they were always anchored to specific waterways along the Pacific Coast. Land was necessary to them merely as a right of way to ocean ports—a barrier to be spanned by improved avenues of commerce."

—Norman Graebner, "The Land-Hunger Thesis Challenged," 1963

3. Using the excerpts above, answer parts a, b, and c.

   a) Briefly explain ONE major difference between Graebner's and Whitman's views on the war with Mexico.

   b) Briefly explain how someone supporting Whitman's view on the war with Mexico could use ONE piece of evidence from the period 1840 to 1865 not directly mentioned in the excerpt.

   c) Briefly explain how someone supporting Douglass's view on the war with Mexico could use ONE piece of evidence from the period 1840 to 1865 not directly mentioned in the excerpt.

4. Answer parts a, b, and c.

   a) A new American culture developed from 1754 to 1800 and from 1800 to 1848. Briefly explain ONE important similarity in the reasons why a new American culture emerged in these two time periods.

   b) Briefly explain ONE similarity in the effects of the new American culture in these two time periods.

   c) Briefly explain ONE difference in the new American culture in these two time periods.

End of Section I

If you finish before time is called, you may check your work on this section.

Do not go on to Section II until you are told to do so.

Section II, Part A: Document-Based Question

Suggested reading period: 15 minutes
Suggested writing period: 40 minutes

Directions: Question 1 is based on the accompanying documents. You are advised to spend 15 minutes reading and planning and 45 minutes writing your answer.

In your response, you should do the following:

- State a relevant thesis that directly addresses all parts of the question.
- Support the thesis or a relevant argument with evidence from all, or all but one, of the documents.
- Incorporate analysis of all, or all but one, of the documents into your argument.
- Focus your analysis of each document on at least one of the following: intended audience, purpose, historical context, and/or point of view.
- Support your argument with analysis of historical examples outside the documents.
- Connect historical phenomena relevant to your argument to broader events or processes.
- Synthesize the elements above into a persuasive essay that extends your argument, connects it to a different historical context, or accounts for contradictory evidence on the topic.

1. Compare and contrast the American views toward immigration between 1882 and 1924. Evaluate how understandings of national identity, at the time, shaped these views.

Document 1

Source: Excerpt from the Chinese Exclusion Act, 1882

"WHEREAS, in the opinion of the Government of the United States the coming of Chinese laborers to this country endangers the good order of certain localities within the territory thereof: Therefore,

Be it enacted, That from and after the expiration of ninety days next after the passage of this act, and until the expiration of ten years next after the passage of this act, the coming of Chinese laborers to the United States be, … suspended; and during such suspension it shall not be lawful for any Chinese laborer to come, or, having so come after the expiration of said ninety days, to remain within the United States."

Document 2

Source: Grover Cleveland Veto Message, March 2, 1897

"It is said, however that the quality of recent immigration is undesirable. The time is quite within recent memory when the same thing was said of immigrants who, with their descendants, are now numbered among our best citizens.

It is proposed by the bill under consideration to meet the alleged difficulties of the situation by establishing an educational test by which the right of a foreigner to make his home with us shall be determined. Its general scheme is to prohibit from admission to our country all immigrants 'physically capable and over 16 years of age who can not read and write the English language ...' its provisions are unnecessarily harsh and oppressive, and … its operation would result in harm to our citizens."

Document 3

Source: Article from the *New York Times*, December 8, 1905

GOMPERS CRIES FOR LESS IMMIGRATION;
STIRS NATIONAL CONFERENCE TO A HOT DEBATE

"I take second place to no man, declared Mr. Gompers. In recognizing the fundamental right of man to move where he pleases on the face of this earth of ours. The question which this conference has to solve, however is not merely academic. It is concrete, practical."

I would be the last man to deny in the abstract that a man has the right to go where he pleases. When by so doing, however, he jeopardizes the rights and well-being of other men, it is an entirely different proposition.

I respectfully dissent from the assertion that the question of immigration is unimportant. I maintain with all the strength of my being that there is no more vital question today before the people of these United States. But to those who labor to live, if they do not live to labor, the immigrant presents a problem that concerns his very being. The Chinaman is a man. I have nothing against the Chinaman as a Chinaman, but there is a great deal of difference between a Chinaman and an American. I am not in favor of excluding the Chinaman from our shores because he is a Chinaman, but because his ideas and his civilization are absolutely opposed to the ideals and civilization of the American people."

Document 4

Source: "Close the Gate," *Literary Digest*, 1919

CLOSE THE GATE.
—Orr in the Chicago *Tribune*.

Document 5

Source: Ku Klux Klan March, Washington, D.C., 1924

Document 6

Source: Speech by Senator Ellison Smith, South Carolina, April 1924 *(Congressional Record,* 68th Congress, 1st Session)

"I think we now have sufficient population in our country for us to shut the door and to breed up a pure, unadulterated American citizenship. I recognize that there is a dangerous lack of distinction between people of a certain nationality and the breed of the dog. Who is an American? Is he an immigrant from Italy? Is he an immigrant from Germany? If you were to go abroad and someone were to meet you and say, 'I met a typical American,' what would flash into your mind as a typical American, the typical representative of that new Nation? Would it be the son of an Italian immigrant, the son of a German immigrant, the son of any of the breeds from the Orient, the son of the denizens of Africa? We must not get our ethnological distinctions mixed up with our anthropological distinctions. It is the breed of the dog in which I am interested."

Document 7

Source: "Looking Backward," Joseph Keppler, 1893

End of Documents for Question 1

Section II, Part B: Long Essay Question

Question 2 or Question 3
Suggested writing period: 35 minutes

Directions: Choose EITHER question 2 or question 3. You are advised to spend 35 minutes writing your answer. Write your responses on the lined pages that follow the questions.

In your response, you should do the following:

- State a relevant thesis that directly addresses all parts of the question.
- Support your argument with evidence, using specific examples.
- Apply historical thinking skills as directed by the question.
- Synthesize the elements above into a persuasive essay that extends your argument, connects it to a different historical context, or connects it to a different category of analysis.

2. Evaluate the extent to which early American foreign policy contributed to maintaining continuity as well as fostering change in the United States from 1790 to 1848.

3. Evaluate the extent to which the expanding role of the federal government contributed to maintaining continuity as well as fostering change in the United States from 1900 to 1980.

When you finish writing, check your work in Section II if time permits.

STOP

END OF EXAM

Answer Key

Section I, Part A

1. (A)	15. (A)	29. (A)	43. (A)
2. (C)	16. (C)	30. (A)	44. (A)
3. (D)	17. (A)	31. (C)	45. (C)
4. (B)	18. (B)	32. (C)	46. (C)
5. (A)	19. (A)	33. (A)	47. (A)
6. (C)	20. (D)	34. (B)	48. (B)
7. (D)	21. (C)	35. (D)	49. (A)
8. (D)	22. (C)	36. (A)	50. (C)
9. (A)	23. (D)	37. (C)	51. (A)
10. (A)	24. (C)	38. (B)	52. (C)
11. (B)	25. (D)	39. (C)	53. (A)
12. (B)	26. (B)	40. (B)	54. (C)
13. (A)	27. (B)	41. (D)	55. (B)
14. (C)	28. (C)	42. (C)	

Detailed Explanations of Answers

1. (A)

The excerpt describes the impact World War I had on African Americans in Harlem, New York. Although most African Americans remained in the South despite legalized segregation and racial violence, some began to move out of the South to pursue new economic opportunities offered by World War I. The "Great Migration" refers to the mass movement of African Americans out of the South and into the North during World War I; most moved to the North for economic reasons.

2. (C)

The excerpt describes the Harlem Renaissance movement. After World War I, there arose in Harlem an outpouring of various cultural expressions, principally by African American artists. These artists, most notably Langston Hughes, used their poetry and art to express the desire for democracy and equality.

3. (D)

The author of this text clearly states that he supports Southern rights to maintain the institution of slavery and that the Constitution supports that position. He also expresses the belief that states have a large degree of independence, which became the rallying cry for the Confederacy during the Civil War—"states' rights." Therefore, the author would be opposed to Congress interfering with the institution of slavery.

4. (B)

The Compromise of 1850 dealt with the issues of a strict fugitive slave law and popular sovereignty for the new territories gained in the Mexican-American War. The Compromise was written by Henry Clay, and the strict fugitive slave law infuriated many Northerners. As a result, the path to disunion intensified. The article states that there is a need to remedy the problem of fugitive slaves and supports the desire for popular sovereignty, which was included in the Compromise of 1850. Since the Whig party was not established until 1834, the outlawing of the international slave trade (1808) and the Missouri Compromise (1820) are incorrect answers. The document is not an example of Enlightenment thought.

5. (A)

After Betty Freidan wrote *The Feminine Mystique* in 1963, she and other women formed NOW (the National Organization for Women) in 1966 in an effort to pressure the federal government to uphold anti-discrimination policies. NOW took an active role in leading the fight to secure passage of the Equal Rights Amendment during the 1970s and early 1980s. Supporters of NOW seek active support from the federal government to enact legislation to protect their rights.

6. (C)

The Second Great Awakening was centered on the belief that humans could be perfected and that the government could assist in ensuring that democratic principles were given to all Americans. This belief resulted in various reform movements that included women's rights. Women activists supported abolition, temperance, and prison reform. Many also supported a growing movement to ensure equal rights for women. In 1848, Elizabeth Cady Stanton and Lucretia Mott organized a convention in Seneca Falls, New York, and demanded the right to vote.

7. (D)

(D) After World War II, most middle-class white women left their factory jobs and became suburban housewives, ushering in the baby boom. The suburbs were known for their conformity to traditional gender roles. When Betty Freidan wrote *The Feminine Mystique*, she uncovered the dissatisfaction that many suburban women felt with just being a wife and mother; it is this dissatisfaction that was a contributing factor to the growth of the modern feminist movement, which the National Organization for Women represents.

8. (D)

The Populist Party was primarily made up of Southern cotton farmers and wheat farmers in the Plains states. The agrarian industry suffered from a dramatic drop in agriculture prices due to the overproduction of crops. They were hostile to banks, railroads, and elites in general.

9. (A)

The Populist Party platform included the desire for the federal government to control the railroads and telephone/telegraph companies, an eight-hour workday for government employees, the monetization of silver, and a government-operated postal savings bank. The Populist Party saw the federal government as the answer to many of their problems and the private sector (banks, railroads, and corporations) as the cause of their problems.

10. (A)

The excerpt by Jackson clearly attacks the wealthy in society; he argues that they benefit from the national bank while the "humble members of society" are taken advantage of. This is indicative of the period of a new mass democracy in which the common man had a voice. The Whig Party, which was largely made up of ex-Federalists, was not founded until 1834 (two years after Jackson's famous Bank veto); after its founding, Whig leaders such as Henry Clay typically promoted the interests of wealthy merchants, bankers, and manufacturers. Therefore, farmers would most support Jackson's veto message.

11. (B)

During the period of Jacksonian democracy (1820–1840), the white man who did not own property was able to gain suffrage. This change dramatically altered the electorate and the causes that politicians championed. As a result of this more participatory democracy, politicians begin challenging the "rich and powerful," as Andrew Jackson does in his veto message.

12. (B)

The Populists also viewed the bankers and corrupt politicians from both the Democrat and Republican parties as primary causes of their economic problems. The Populists saw themselves as that period's "common man."

13. (A)

Progressive reformers responded to economic instability, social inequality, and political corruption by calling for government intervention in the economy, expanded democracy, greater social justice, and conservation of natural resources. Progressive President Theodore Roosevelt championed consumer protection and, after reading Upton Sinclair's publication, he supported the creation of the Meat Inspection Act.

14. (C)

Progressive reformers looked to local, state, and federal governments to address the economic, social, and political problems that plagued society at the beginning of the twentieth century. Likewise, during the Great Depression, Americans turned to the federal government to respond to the economic issues. The liberalism of President Franklin Roosevelt's New Deal program drew on earlier progressive ideas and represented a multifaceted approach to address both the causes and effects of the Great Depression, using government power to provide relief to the poor, stimulate recovery, and reform the American economy. The Progressives and the New Dealers both sought to use the government to fix problems.

15. (A)

The "new immigration" that took place from approximately 1880 to 1920 provided a surplus of cheap labor for the new industrial society and it was this surplus of labor that helped stimulate and sustain the Industrial Revolution. These immigrants primarily came from southern and eastern Europe and migrated to the industrial Northeast and Midwest. A large number of Asian immigrants came to Angel Island (off the coast of San Francisco) and helped build the transcontinental railroad.

16. (C)

After the Japanese bombed Pearl Harbor in December 1941, President Franklin Roosevelt issued an executive order that resulted in the internment of thousands of Japanese Americans who lived on the Pacific coast. The cartoon depicts Japanese in America as loyal to Japan and thus a threat to America. It was this belief—which was never backed up with hard evidence—that led to the internment of Japanese Americans.

17. (A)

The fear of strangers or foreigners (xenophobia) is a recurring theme in American history. During times of war this type of fear is especially heightened and often results in civil liberties being compromised.

18. (B)

The increasing role of the federal government led to an increasing demand for less government, especially among members of the Republican Party. The Great Society social programs and numerous business regulations led to this desire for less government. Public confidence and trust in government also declined in the 1970s, in the wake of economic challenges, political scandals, foreign policy setbacks, and a sense of social and moral decay. The Vietnam War, the Watergate scandal, high unemployment, and high inflation led to an overall distrust of the government.

19. (A)

Reagan is clearly critical of the federal government's ability to solve the nation's problems. Critics of Lyndon Johnson's Great Society programs would be the most likely to agree with Reagan's view that "government is not the solution to our problem; government is the problem." The Great Society programs attempted to utilize the federal government to eliminate poverty and racial injustice. Liberal Democrats, individuals receiving welfare, and civil rights leaders would not have supported

Reagan's view; they believed the federal government was the answer to the nation's problems.

20. (D)

Although many African Americans remained in the South despite racism, many migrated to the North during World War I (1917–1918) to pursue economic opportunities. The map clearly shows a dramatic increase in the number of African Americans in the North after 1910.

21. (C)

The cotton gin, invented in 1793 by Eli Whitney, could quickly and easily separate the cotton fiber from the seeds of the cotton plant. This led to an increase in African American slaves in the Southern states because more slaves were needed to pick the cotton. The raw cotton was sent North to the textile mills where it was manufactured into a finished product.

22. (C)

Following the stock market crash of 1929, the United States fell into the worst economic downturn in American history, known as the Great Depression. Numerous banks closed and the unemployment rate rose as high as 25%. President Herbert Hoover (1929–1932) was blamed and Franklin D. Roosevelt was elected on his promise to solve the nation's economic woes.

23. (D)

The Supreme Court deemed unconstitutional a number of Roosevelt's programs—most importantly, the National Recovery Act (NRA) and the Agricultural Adjustment Act (AAA)—to combat the Great Depression. When this happened, Roosevelt attempted to get Congress to pass a law that would increase the number of Supreme Court justices. This did not work and became known as the Court Packing Plan.

24. (C)

The New Deal was a series of programs that provided immediate relief to the unemployed with a series of work programs and recovery programs (e.g., bank holiday, Agricultural Adjustment Act). It also included long-term recovery programs (e.g., the Federal Deposit Insurance Corporation).

25. (D)

During the process of ratifying the United States Constitution, there were numerous concerns about the lack of a Bill of Rights. The Anti-Federalists feared a strong central government and demanded protection of civil liberties. Mason is demanding the addition of a Bill of Rights to the Constitution. The first ten amendments to the Constitution were added to ensure civil rights were protected.

26. (B)

States' rights activists have also argued that the federal government trampled on the rights of individual states with regard to the issues of the tariff and slavery. The leaders of the South would eventually secede from the Union due in part to their unwavering commitment to states' rights.

27. (B)

The acquisition of new territory in the West and the U.S. victory in the Mexican-American War were accompanied by a heated controversy over allowing or forbidding slavery in the newly-acquired territories. Lincoln is addressing what to do with the new territories gained in the Mexican-American War.

28. (C)

This excerpt deals with the issue of the expansion of slavery. Lincoln argued against the spread of slavery into the newly-acquired United States territories. Lincoln was a member of the Republican Party, which was formed in 1854 by anti-slavery activists. He was viewed as a radical abolitionist by many Southern states due to the ideas he expressed in speeches like this address at the Cooper Union. Because of this, many Southern states seceded after he was elected president in 1860.

29. (A)

In the late 19th century, America began to expand overseas, which led to the acquisition of new territories in the Pacific and the Caribbean. This expansion is known as Imperialism.

30. (A)

In 1898, the United States defeated Spain in the Spanish-American War and, as a result, acquired Guam, Puerto Rico, and the Philippines (Cuba, for the most part, remained sovereign). The people of the Philippines wanted their independence, and thus criticized the United States for being oppressors, much like the Spanish before them. Anti-imperialists were outraged by these territorial acquisitions, arguing that the United States had violated the very spirit of its own Declaration of Independence.

31. (C)

Many Americans (including high-profile figures such as Mark Twain and William Jennings Bryan) felt that America was betraying its republican principles by extending control over areas that did not want America there, specifically, the Philippines. These Americans, known as anti-imperialists, formed the Anti-Imperialist League and argued vehemently against American expansionism. Supporters of imperialism argued that America needed the resources and the military bases that the new territories provided. Imperialists also argued in favor of the "White Man's Burden," which was the belief that America had an obligation to spread civilization around the globe.

32. (C)

World War II also elicited a popular commitment to advancing democratic ideals. The propaganda campaigns for both world wars were very similar.

33. (A)

In the years following World War I, Woodrow Wilson proposed the idea of an international organization (the League of Nations) that would maintain world peace by preventing war through collective security. The image depicts the need for the United States to become involved in World War I in order to save civilization, which was also the goal of the League of Nations.

34. (B)

In 1898, the U.S.S. *Maine* blew up while it was patrolling the coast of Spanish-controlled Cuba. Americans blamed Spain for the explosion and the Spanish-American war then ensued.

35. (D)

The newspaper article detailing how the Spanish blew up the U.S.S. *Maine* served as a catalyst to galvanize American support for a war with Spain. The attack on Pearl Harbor similarly vaulted the United States into a war, World War II.

36. (A)

The American victory in the Spanish-American War led to the U.S. acquisition of island territories and an expanded presence in the Caribbean and Latin America. After Commodore Dewey's defeat of the Spanish navy in the Pacific, the United States acquired the Philippines.

37. (C)

Jonathan Edwards's sermon was a significant part of the First Great Awakening, which was an evangelical movement that swept the American colonies in the 1730s and 1740s. The First Great Awakening challenged established authority and led to greater religious independence along with an increase in personal piety. It added to the spirit of freedom that led to the American Revolution.

38. (B)

The Second Great Awakening was a Protestant revival movement during the early 19th century. It stimulated many reform movements designed to remedy the evils of society and also led to the formation of new religious denominations.

39. (C)

In the 1840s, substantial numbers of new European immigrants (many from Ireland) entered the United States, giving rise to a major, often violent, nativist movement that was strongly anti-Catholic. The Know Nothing Party was formed in an effort to limit new immigrants' cultural influence and political power.

40. (B)

The United States Congress passed the Immigration Act of 1924, which limited the annual number of immigrants who could be admitted from any country to 2% of the number of people from that country who were already living in the United States in 1890. The goal was to restrict Eastern and Southern Europeans from entering the United States.

41. (D)

In 1846, President Polk led the United States to war with Mexico in order to gain the territory in the Southwest portion of the United States. The U.S. victory in the Mexican-American War was accompanied by a heated controversy about allowing or forbidding slavery in newly-acquired territories. In the *Biglow Papers*, James Russell Lowell accused President Polk of starting the war to spread slavery.

42. (C)

The idea of Manifest Destiny, which asserted U.S. power in the Western Hemisphere and supported U.S. expansion westward, was built on a belief in white racial superiority and a sense of American cultural superiority. Manifest Destiny helped shape the era's political debates and contributed to the further demise of the Native American population in the West.

43. (A)

Just as Lowell was against the Mexican-American War and United States expansion, anti-imperialists during the late 19th century also argued against American expansion.

44. (A)

Although the image of the traditional family was still dominant, between 1960 and 1980 there was a drastic increase in the number of divorces. This increase coincides with women entering the workforce and the modern feminist movement. Working women began to be able to support themselves and were not as bound to traditional gender roles, which led to a rise in the number of divorces.

45. (C)

In response to the sexual revolution, AIDS, and a high divorce rate, the religious fundamentalist movement soared during the 1980s. Groups like the Moral Majority and Focus on the Family, along with famous television evangelists like Jerry Falwell and Jim Bakker, became extremely popular during the 1980s.

46. (C)

The United States sought to "contain" Soviet-dominated communism through a variety of measures. Shortly after World War II, President Harry Truman articulated what would become known as the Truman Doctrine, which stipulated that the United States would assist any nation trying to remain free. The United States then assisted Greece and Turkey to ensure they did not fall to communism. The policy of containment included many other measures as well, such as battling communism in Korea and Vietnam.

47. (A)

Although the Korean conflict produced some minor domestic opposition, the Vietnam War saw the rise of sizable, passionate, and sometimes violent antiwar protests that became more numerous as the war escalated. As a result, many Americans began to question the foreign policy of containment.

48. (B)

During the early 1800s, the United States entered the "Canal Era" as a part of the American System. The canal referenced in the document is the Erie Canal, which was completed in 1825 to connect the Great Lakes region in the west to the Hudson River in the east. The canal was primarily used to transport manufactured goods from the East to the West and agricultural goods from the West to the East.

49. (A)

Developments in textile machinery, steam engines, interchangeable parts, canals, railroads, and the telegraph served to expand markets and drive economic changes known as the market revolution. This revolution, combined with the Industrial Revolution, transformed the U.S. in the direction that Alexander Hamilton had once envisioned. As a consequence, Thomas Jefferson's agrarian vision, based on virtuous yeoman farmers, would slowly die off by the late 1800s.

50. (C)

The Senate report claimed that the canal made the United States commercially and politically homogeneous, but the reality was quite different. The stark differences between the American South and North undermined the claim that the United States was homogeneous. The Southern economy was agriculturally based; Southern cotton furnished the raw material for manufacturing in the North. The South relied on slave labor while the North became a manufacturing center.

51. (A)

This excerpt describes a labor strike that would be opposed by most business leaders in the late 19th century. Many industrialists supported the theory of Social Darwinism. Social Darwinism applied the biological concepts of natural selection and survival of the fittest to the economy. Social Darwinists generally argued that the strong should see their wealth increase and the weak should see their wealth decrease. They often supported laissez-faire capitalism and generally did not support the demands of labor.

52. (C)

The Industrial Revolution led to labor and management battling for control over wages and working conditions, with workers organizing local and national unions and/or directly confronting corporate power.

53. (A)

Carmichael is criticizing the efforts of the civil rights activists who were committed to utilizing non-violence in order to secure civil rights. By the late 1960s, a more militant civil rights movement developed, epitomized by the Black Panthers. The Black Panther Party was formed in 1966 and believed that African Americans had a right to defend themselves; the party evolved into a Marxist revolutionary group that advocated the arming of all African Americans. This directly contradicted the non-violent tactics used by Martin Luther King, Jr., who was awarded the Nobel Peace Prize in 1964.

54. (B)

Carmichael criticized Martin Luther King, Jr., and others who advocated a non-violent challenge to segregation and racism. Carmichael's "black power" sentiments gained support during the late 1960s.

55. (B)

By the 1960s, a new wave of conservatism had arisen. Adherents to this political philosophy feared juvenile delinquency, urban unrest, and challenges to the traditional family. As such, they increasingly promoted their own values and ideology. Ronald Reagan rose to national prominence by speaking during the 1964 Republican National Convention; the popularity of his speech among conservatives would eventually help carry him to the White House in 1980.

Section 1, Part B: Short-Answer Questions

Short-Answer Question I

Scoring Guide

0–3 points

a) 1. The response explains why one of the listed events is best. The explanation must employ appropriate understanding of the events.

0–1 point

a) 2. The response provides one piece of evidence from the event to support your explanation.

0–1 point

b) The response explains why one of the other options is not as persuasive. The comparison must employ appropriate historical knowledge.

Notes

Option 1: The rise of America as an industrial power

a) 1. The Industrial Revolution during the Gilded Age brought large-scale production of manufactured goods to a dominant position in the U.S. economy. The rapid industrialization caused businesses and foreign policy-makers to look outside U.S. borders in an effort to gain greater influence and control over raw materials and markets.

2. Evidence may include the consolidation of corporations into trusts that were able to exert immense power over Congress and the courts (John D. Rockefeller/Standard Oil or Andrew Carnegie/Steel). The need for markets and resources led to a foreign policy that emphasized imperialist tendencies, including the desire to control resources and markets in the Pacific, Asia, and Latin America. The Open Door Policy, the annexation of Hawaii, and the Roosevelt Corollary to the Monroe Doctrine may be considered evidence of imperialism.

b) The Industrial Revolution was initially primarily a domestic venture. The British and other European countries were already industrialized and symbolized competition for the United States, not the status of world power. The domestic problems associated with the Industrial Revolution, such as rundown tenement housing, low pay, long hours, and dangerous working conditions, were not dealt with until the Progressive Era.

Option 2: The Spanish-American War

a) 1. The Spanish-American War was the first overseas territorial expansion for the United States. It signaled the beginning of imperialist ventures in the Pacific, Caribbean, and Asia. The United States began to compete with European powers for markets and resources and control of the seas.

2. After the American victory in the Spanish-American War, the United States gained the territories of the Philippines, Puerto Rico, and Guam, as well as a naval base in Cuba. These territories established the United States as an imperial power; shortly thereafter, Theodore Roosevelt began the building of the Panama Canal, which increased American world power.

b) The United States was not the only imperial power. The Berlin Conference of 1884–1885 had already taken place, during which the European powers divided the continent of Africa. The Open Door policy in China did not give exclusive trade rights to the United States but rather allowed it to compete with a number of European powers.

Option 3: World War II

a) 1. By the end of World War II, the United States and the Soviet Union were the two world powers.

2. The United States' entry into World War II and the D-Day invasion of Normandy established the United States as a world power. It then developed and dropped the first atomic bomb in order to end World War II, which cemented its claim as a world power. The Cold War began at the end of World War II and pitted the United States against the Soviet Union. In an effort to remain a world power, the United States began a policy of containment and took part in both the arms and space races.

b) The Soviet Union remained a formidable foe and world power. It also helped end World War II. At the Yalta and Potsdam conferences, the Soviet Union exerted enormous power. It was able to outflank both the British and Americans and take over Eastern Europe after the war.

Short-Answer Question 2

Scoring Guide

0–3 points

a) The response explains one point of view suggested by the image about the Progressive movement, political participation, or civil rights.

0–1 point

b) The response explains one cause or outcome of what is in the image.

0–1 point

c) The response compares the action depicted in the image to another struggle for democratic rights in American history.

Notes

a) Points of view suggested by the image could include the following:

—The Progressive movement sought to bring about social change by calling on the federal government to ensure democracy for all American citizens. The Progressives, as illustrated in the image, actively fought for reforms to make America a safer place to work and live. Not only did they publicly picket, they exposed corruption of local governments and big business.

—Political participation and civil rights are viewed as essential elements to a democratic society. The woman in the image is exposing the hypocrisy of the United States during World War I, in which the United States sought to expand democracy abroad but denied political participation to women at home.

b) Relevant causes or outcomes of what is depicted in the image could include the following:

After the Civil War and the passage of the 15th Amendment, which gave black men the right to vote, women began a suffrage movement in earnest. Susan B. Anthony and Elizabeth Cady Stanton founded the National Suffrage Association in 1869. Women's participation in World War I also galvanized suffragettes to demand the right to vote. The outcome included the passage of the 19th Amendment, which gave women the right to vote in 1920.

c) Examples of various struggles for democratic rights in American history:

- The abolitionist movement to end slavery
- The radical Republicans' desire to pass the 13th, 14th, and 15th Amendments
- The civil rights movement to end segregation (Civil Rights Act of 1964)
- The fight for gay rights (Stonewall riots/marriage equality)
- The fight for labor to ensure basic human rights (AFL/Cesar Chavez)

Short-Answer Question 3

Scoring Guide

0–3 points

a) The response explains one major difference between the two interpretations.

0–1 point

b) The response explains how one appropriate piece of evidence supports Whitman's view.

0–1 point

c) The response explains how one appropriate piece of evidence supports Douglass's view.

Notes

a) Major differences between views could include the following:

—Whitman sees the war with Mexico as a positive good, essential to the development of America and as a way to expand democracy and liberty, which have been critical to American identity since the American Revolution. He also expresses the racism that has often accompanied American expansion as a method to justify the war effort. He does not take into account the Mexican point of view or the irony in taking land by force in the name of expanding a republic.

—Graebner sees the war with Mexico as a continuation of past expansionism in an effort to expand American commerce. He sees expansion as needed in order to have access to the Pacific Ocean. He asserts that the presidents who led expansion did not desire a spread of liberty but rather the growth of American economic power. Polk's compromise with Britain over the Oregon Territory would support this view.

b) Evidence supporting Whitman's view could include the following:

—The idea of Manifest Destiny was articulated in 1845 by John O'Sullivan, who claimed that providence (i.e., God's will) had given the whole continent to the United States in order to expand liberty and the concept of self-government.

—After the war, the land gained from Mexico became U.S. territories or states, thereby becoming a part of the republic of the United States.

—In the period 1840–1865, thousands of Americans moved West, bringing economic prosperity to the region.

c) Evidence supporting Douglass's view could include the following:

—Many abolitionists, such as Henry David Thoreau, saw the war as a way to extend slavery. Some of the land gained in the war was to be reserved for slave-based states according to the Missouri Compromise. President Polk was a Southerner and slave owner.

—After the war, the Compromise of 1850 was made in an effort to appease both the North and the South. California would be a free state, but popular sovereignty would be used to decide the issue of slavery in the Utah and New Mexico territories. Therefore, they could have been new slave states.

—The Republican Party formed in 1854 as a party with the specific goal of stopping the expansion of slavery.

Short-Answer Question 4

Scoring Guide

0–1 point

a) The response briefly explains ONE important similarity in the reasons why a new American culture emerged in these two time periods.

0–1 point

b) The response briefly explains ONE similarity in the effects of the new American culture in these two time periods.

0–1 point

c) The response briefly explains ONE difference in the new American culture in these two time periods.

Notes

a) Reasons that a new American culture emerged in the periods are:

- The increase in the desire and commitment to Republican ideals

  —1754–1800: The desire for representation in Parliament ("No taxation without representation") and later the rule by the consent of the governed, once the United States had become an independent nation.

  —1800–1848: The expansion of the electorate and mass democracy during the Age of Jackson, where the Common Man reigned supreme.

- The increase in westward expansion
- The strengthening of a strong federal government
- The growth of an American economy
- An isolationist foreign policy

b) Similarities in the effects of the new American culture in the periods are:

- The desire for Republican ideals to spread

  —1754–1800: Republican motherhood became a popular concept, the Constitution was ratified, white land-owning men could vote, and political parties developed (Federalists and Democrat-Republicans)

—1800–1848: Seneca Falls occured, white men who did not own land could vote, and political parties developed (Democrats and Whigs)

- The displacement of Native Americans

  —1754–1800: After the Proclamation of 1763, the territory was settled by Americans via the land ordinances; slavery was banned with the Northwest Ordinance

  —1800–1848: The Trail of Tears; slavery was banned in the North with the Missouri Compromise

- The federal government grew in strength

  —1754–1800: The National Bank; Whiskey Rebellion crushed

  —1800–1848: The American System (including the Second National Bank); the Marshall court

c) Ways in which the new American culture was different in the time periods could include the following:

   1754–1800: An elite aristocracy declared independence from Great Britain, wrote and ratified the Constitution, and ran the government. The Bill of Rights was ratified. Although Abigail Adams asked her husband, John Adams, to "Remember the Ladies," there was not a movement to expand democratic rights to women or slaves. The economy was mostly based on agriculture or fishing/timber/trade.

   1800–1848: With the rise of the first mass democracy, Andrew Jackson ushered in the era of the Common Man where the likes of Davy Crockett served in the federal Congress. A wave of reform movements took place in which women began to demand a political voice and abolitionists became fervent. The United States doubled in size with the Louisiana Purchase, and a protective tariff was approved. A textile industry developed in the North.

Section II, Part A: Document-Based Question

Notes for Question 1

Sample Thesis Statements

Possible thesis statements could include the following.

—Arguments about immigration were often framed in terms of who was considered "American" and who was considered a dangerous outsider.

—Contrasting views about immigration were linked to who was being affected by the vast numbers of immigrants.

—Debates over immigration centered on whether or not immigrants would "un-Americanize" America or if they would help America.

—Supporters of immigration restrictions used racist rhetoric to support their views, while opponents of immigration restriction used the history of America to support their views.

—The tendency for Americans to be xenophobic can be linked to American identity, while the openness of Ellis Island and Angel Island are also closely linked to American identity.

Analysis of the Documents

In order to earn full credit for analyzing documents, responses must include at least one of the following for all or all but one of the documents: intended audience, purpose, historical context, author's point of view. Students must also demonstrate that they understand the document and use the information in the document to support the thesis or a relevant argument.

Document 1

Excerpt from the Chinese Exclusion Act, 1882

Components of the document analysis may include the following:

—The document supports immigration restriction based solely on nationality

—Intended audience: Chinese citizens who may want to immigrate to the United States and the American public

—Purpose: To restrict Chinese immigration

—Historical context: This act was passed after thousands of Chinese citizens flooded into the West Coast to build railroads. Racial tensions and employment tensions increased as the Industrial Revolution took place.

—Author's point of view: This is an act passed by Congress and signed by the president and therefore has a tone of legalese in discussing the immigration restriction. The point of view is that this restriction will be a positive good for the laborers of America and lessen their competition for jobs.

Document 2

Grover Cleveland Veto Message, March 2, 1897

Components of document analysis may include the following:

—The document does not support immigrant restrictions.

—Intended audience: The American people and the Congress who passed the Literacy Act.

—Purpose: To convince Americans and Congress that the Literacy Act is un-American and would be destructive to the United States.

—Historical context: From 1880 to 1920, the United States experienced extremely high immigration from non-English-speaking countries (southern and eastern European countries). As these immigrants came in droves, xenophobia was the result and a popular plan to restrict them from coming in was to require a literacy test.

—Author's point of view: Stated by a U.S. president who pointed out that America is a nation of immigrants and that keeping out immigrants could potentially damage the United States in the future. He suggests that they may become some of America's best citizens.

Document 3

Article from the *New York Times,* December 8, 1905

GOMPERS CRIES FOR LESS IMMIGRATION;
STIRS NATIONAL CONFERENCE TO A HOT DEBATE

Components of document analysis may include the following:

—This document supports immigration restriction.

—Intended audience: The American Federation of Labor, other laborers, the United States Congress and the general American public.

—Purpose: To persuade and convince the American public that the Chinese immigrants are so different from Americans that they should be banned from coming to the United States.

—Historical context: Gompers said this after the Chinese Exclusion Act was passed in the 1880s, so his views on the Chinese can cross over to the southern and eastern Europeans who were flooding into the United States. They were also accused of being uncivilized.

—Author's point of view: Stated by a leader of the labor union, the American Federation of Labor, Gompers was most likely speaking on behalf of all laborers. Labor was often threatened by the flood of immigrants and the cheap labor they provided. His point of view was shaped by a sense of economic prosperity for American Labor. He also expresses his xenophobia toward the Chinese by expressing that they are opposed to the American ideals.

Document 4

Political Cartoon: "Close the Gate," *Literary Digest,* 1919

Components of document analysis may include the following:

—This cartoon supports immigration restrictions.

—Intended audience: The readers of the *Literary Digest* and the general United States public.

—Purpose: To warn the readers and the American public that immigrants represent a real danger to the United States; to elicit strict immigration laws.

—Historical context: Many of the immigrants from southern and eastern Europe were accused of being anarchists, most notably Sacco and Vanzetti from Italy. The "undesirables" were from areas of the world that had a history of undemocratic governments. Many Americans feared that they would come to the United States and wreak havoc on the democratic system.

—Author's point of view: The caption of the cartoon reads "Close the Gate"; therefore, the author views immigrants as dangerous and wants Congress to enact strict immigration laws that are targeted for specific groups or nations of people. He is suggesting that all immigrants are entering the United States to bring destruction, not to find a better life.

Document 5

Photograph: Ku Klux Klan March, Washington, D.C., 1924

Components of document analysis may include the following:

—The rise of the Ku Klux Klan represents support of immigration restriction.

—Intended audience: The U.S. federal government (president and Congress), the immigrants, and the general American public.

—Purpose: To demonstrate a unity in preserving the "American" culture.

—Historical context: The Ku Klux Klan (KKK) originally began in the South during Reconstruction as a way to intimidate African Americans. When reconstruction ended, membership in the KKK dwindled. Due to the large numbers of immigrants coming to the United States in the early 20th century, membership in the KKK grew as their message became anti-immigrant. Membership was at an all-time high in the 1920s, and prominent politicians joined. The KKK took specific aim at Catholics and Jewish immigrants.

—Author's point of view: The photographer wanted to show the prominence of the KKK and the expanse of the march. The backdrop of the American capital and the prominence of the American flags are imagery associated with patriotism and love of country.

Document 6

Speech by Senator Ellison Smith, South Carolina, April 1924

Components of document analysis may include the following:

—This document supports immigration restriction.

—Intended audience: The senator's constituents, Congress, and the general American public.

—Purpose: To elicit support for immigration restrictions.

—Historical context: In 1924, Congress enacted an immigration act that limited the annual number of immigrants who could be admitted from any country to two percent of the number of people from that country who were already living in the United States in 1890. The law was aimed at preserving the ideal of American homogeneity.

—Author's point of view: Stated by a U.S. senator who held a leadership position and wanted to increase his support by playing on the racism that existed throughout the country, especially in the South. He clearly uses that racism to suggest that America is changing with the incoming immigrants and he wants to stop that from happening.

Document 7

Cartoon, "Looking Backward," Joseph Keppler, 1893

Components of document analysis may include the following:

—This document would not be supportive of immigration restriction.

—Intended audience: Newspaper readers and the general United States public.

—Purpose: To draw attention to the nation's history and its identity as a nation of immigrants.

—Historical context: This cartoon was drawn after the Chinese Exclusion Act was passed but before other restrictive immigration acts were passed. By the early 1890s, the Industrial Revolution and the jobs associated with it led to a drastic increase in immigrants and also an increase in xenophobia.

—Author's point of view: The title of the cartoon, "Looking Backward," shows that Keppler is pointing out the hypocrisy of the anti-immigrant movement. He is pointing out that every American (except the Native Americans) was an immigrant at one point in time. He is also commenting on the opportunity that the United States offers: the well-dressed, affluent men were once pauper immigrants.

Analysis of Outside Examples to Support Thesis/Argument

Possible examples of information not found in the documents that could be used to support the stated thesis or relevant argument could include the following:

—The Chinese Exclusion Act

—Chinatown/Little Italy

—Angel Island and Ellis Island

—The Gentleman's Agreement

—World War I

—The Russian Revolution

—The Palmer Raids

—Prohibition

—The Immigration Act of 1924

—The idea of open immigration and the meaning of the Statue of Liberty on Ellis Island

—The trial of Sacco and Vanzetti

—The Industrial Revolution and the movement of many Americans from rural areas to big cities

—The American Federation of Labor and Labor Unions

Contextualization

Students must accurately connect their thesis or argument to broader historical events. These events may include the following:

- The Industrial Revolution

  —The movement to cities necessitated the need for large numbers of workers to provide cheap labor, which attracted immigrants and led to hostility and nativism.

—Carnegie Steel, the building of the railroads, and other monopolies may be mentioned as sources of employment for immigrants.

—Life in the cities led to large slum areas developing, which was blamed on immigrants.

- The Russian Revolution in 1919 led to many Americans fearing that communism would come to America with increased immigration.
- World War I led to a general distaste and distrust of anyone who did not speak English.
- Imperialism and Social Darwinism led to increased racism and xenophobia on the American home front.
- The tension of the 1920s between the old and the new fostered the anti-immigration movement.
- The rise of the Mafia in the 1920s and the link of the Mafia to Italian immigration.

Synthesis

Students must extend or modify the analysis in the essay by using dissimilar and/or contradictory evidence from a primary or secondary source, or by connecting to another historical time period or context. Examples could include the following:

—Linking the argument to earlier debates about immigration in the early 1800s that centered on an anti-Irish sentiment.

—Linking the argument to later debates about immigration in the late 1900s and early 2000s that center on the southern American border and Mexican immigration.

Section II, Part B: Long Essay Question

Notes for Question 2

Thesis

Possible thesis statements addressing continuity and change include the following:

- Early American foreign policy continued to be focused on preserving the integrity of the continental United States.
- Early American foreign policy continued to serve the economic self-interests of the United States.
- America continued to steer clear of permanent alliances.
- America continued to expand across the continent and gained land either from purchases or war.
- Early American foreign policy changed from isolationism to Manifest Destiny.
- Foreign policy changed as political parties changed.

Support for Argument

Possible evidence that could be used for an argument stressing continuity over time includes the following:

- In the 1790s, the United States supported an isolationist policy in response to the French Revolution for our own interests; the war of 1812 was primarily fought to defend American self-interests with regard to impressment; the expansion of the United States was also a continuation of expanding American self-interests.
- The Louisiana Purchase, the War of 1812, the Monroe Doctrine, and the Mexican-American War were all primarily focused on foreign policy on the North American continent.
- George Washington's *Farewell Address* warned against permanent alliances and this philosophy continued during this entire time period.
- The United States continued to grow economically due to foreign policy. The Louisiana Purchase gave the United States the Mississippi River; the War of 1812 led to the market revolution; protective tariffs spurred American manufacturing; and the Mexican-American War gave the United States access to the Pacific Ocean.

Support for Argument

Possible evidence that could be used for an argument stressing change over time includes the following:

- Isolation in the 1790s changed by the early 1800s. The United States went to war with Great Britain in 1812 and declared war on Mexico by the 1840s. By the 1840s, the United States was not reacting to the actions of foreign nations but was taking the lead in orchestrating interventionist foreign policy. For example, the War of 1812 was in response to the actions of the British, but the Mexican-American War was a part of an expansionist philosophy of Manifest Destiny. President Polk deliberately provoked the Mexicans in order to declare war.
- The early Federalists/Whigs desired isolation (Washington's Farewell Address, the Hartford Convention), but with the change to Democrats, foreign policy changed to a more expansionist policy.
- In the 1790s, Alexander Hamilton had proposed a protective tariff and it was rejected. The support of protective tariffs changed, and by 1819 America adopted the use of this foreign policy.

Application of Historical Thinking Skills

Essays earn points by using the evidence offered in support of the argument to identify and illustrate continuity and change over time. Examples include:

- As America grew in strength and size, foreign policy changed significantly to become more interventionist.
- America continued to focus on building a reputation in the world as a sovereign nation that would not succumb to European powers. For example, the XYZ affair, the Barbary Pirates, and the Monroe Doctrine.
- As the population of the United States grew (through increased birth rates and immigration), foreign policy continued to demand westward expansion. For example, the Louisiana Purchase, the Indian Removal Act, the acquisition of the Oregon Territory, and the Mexican-American War.
- Economic foreign policy changed over time; in the early 1800s, there was not a protective tariff and, for a brief time, there was the Embargo Act; by the 1820s, the United States adopted economic foreign policies that would benefit New England manufacturers.

Synthesis

Essays can earn the synthesis point by extending or modifying the analysis in the essay, by introducing another category of historical analysis, or by making a connection to another historical period or context. Examples include the following:

- Explain how continuity and change in early American foreign policy impacted domestic policy. For example, the Embargo Act created a boom in American manufacturing and the Mexican-American War led to deep divisions among the American public with regard to whether the new territory should allow slavery or be free.

- Connect the continuity and change in early American foreign policy to foreign policy in later time periods. Discuss the similarities or differences of Manifest Destiny to late 18th and early 19th century imperialism.
- Explain how continuity and change in early American foreign policy proved to provide long-term economic benefits to the United States while at the same time it often came at the expense of others (the Native Americans or Mexicans).
- Connect early American foreign policy to a broader context. For example, the French Revolution, the war between France and Britain, and the conflict between Mexico and Texas.

Notes for Question 3

Thesis

Possible thesis statements addressing continuity and change could include the following:

- The role of the federal government continued to expand from the Progressive era, the New Deal, and the Great Society, while those who benefited from this expanded role changed over time.
- The federal government continued to become more powerful as state governments waned in power, while the social issues that the federal government took control of changed over time.
- The American people continued to look to the federal government to solve social and economic problems that the United States faced, while the political parties that supported a larger role of the federal government changed.

Support for Argument

Possible evidence that could be used for an argument stressing continuity over time includes the following:

- The federal government took on the role of addressing the social problems associated with the problems created during the Gilded Age. Examples could include but are not limited to these: the Meat Inspection Act, the Pure Food and Drug Act, the Clayton Antitrust Act, women's suffrage, and improved working conditions and safety standards after the Triangle Shirtwaist Factory Fire.
- The federal government took on the role of helping fight the Great Depression in the 1930s. Examples could include, but are not limited to these: the Works Progress Administration, the Tennessee Valley Authority, the Civilian Conservation Corps, the Federal Deposit Insurance Corporation, the Social Security Act, and the Agricultural Adjustment Act.
- The federal government took on the role of helping in the civil rights movement and aiding the poor in the 1960s. Examples could include, but are not limited to: the Civil Rights Act of 1964, the Voting Rights Act of 1965, the Civil Rights Act of 1968, the War on Poverty, the Food Stamp Act of 1964, Head Start, Medicaid, and Medicare.

Support for Argument

Possible evidence that could be used for an argument stressing change over time includes the following:

- Progressive-era reforms were aimed at regulation of big business and expanding democracy rather than directly aiding specific individuals.
- New Deal reforms were aimed at direct aid to individuals. The federal government took on the role of "priming the pump" by creating jobs for individuals through various programs.
- Great Society reforms were aimed at helping specific minority groups, like African Americans and the poor in the Appalachian Mountains region.
- In the 1970s, the Environmental Protection Agency and Affirmative Action programs were examples of continuities in the growth of the federal government.

Application of Historical Thinking Skills

Essays earn points by using the evidence offered in support of their argument to identify and illustrate continuity and change over time. Examples include, but are not limited to, the following:

- The inequality that was exacerbated with the Industrial Revolution, the Great Depression, and the prosperity of the 1950s led to an increased demand for government intervention. The role of the federal government has continued to expand.
- Americans began to look to the federal government to solve social problems.
- The shift from regulating business or consumer protection of the Progressive era changed significantly by the end of the period to helping the disadvantaged through affirmative action programs.

Synthesis

Essays can earn the synthesis point by extending or modifying the analysis in the essay, by introducing another category of historical analysis, or by making a connection to another historical period or context. Examples include the following:

- Explaining how continuity and change in the role of the federal government ended the previous laissez-faire approach to economic and social problems and introduced a demand that the government take the lead in solving problems.
- Connecting the role of the federal government to different periods—for example, the Affordable Care Act, prescription pill coverage, and government bailouts of large companies that took place in period 9.
- Connect the expansion of the federal government to the rise of the conservative movement in the 1980s and the Tea Party in the 2010s.

Practice Exam 2

Available at the REA Study Center *(www.rea.com/studycenter)*

This practice exam is available at the REA Study Center. Although AP exams are administered in paper-and-pencil format, we recommend that you take this online practice exam for the benefits of:

- Instant scoring
- Enforced time conditions
- Detailed score report of your strengths and weaknesses

Appendices

- Appendix A: America's Major Wars
- Appendix B: Key Presidential Elections
- Appendix C: Important International Treaties
- Appendix D: Key Characters in American History

Appendix A: America's Major Wars

In George Washington's 1797 Farewell Address, he warned against "entangling alliances" that might draw the United States into wars, particularly with European powers, in addition to encouraging American citizens to take full advantage of their isolated position in the world. Since then, however, both declared and undeclared wars have been an important part of American history. Below is a brief summary of America's major wars, noting the main causes, the treaties that settled them, their results, and the number of casualties during the conflicts.

French and Indian War (1755–1763)

Causes: Known as the Seven-Years War in Europe, this conflict broke out following competition between French and British fur-trading outposts and settlements in the Ohio River Valley. Indian tribes allied themselves with either European power. While not strictly an American war, a number of American colonists fought for the British.

Treaty: The Treaty of Paris was signed on February 10, 1763.

Results: France lost all of its North American possessions to the British. Great Britain assumed responsibility for virtually all of the territory between the Appalachian Mountains and the Mississippi River, a huge tract of land. It then looked to the American colonies to help pay for both the war and the cost of maintaining the British troops that remained in the colonies. This new imperial taxation policy, which now included raising revenue in addition to regulating trade, led to resentment among the colonists, particularly merchants and residents of urban areas. Groups began forming throughout the colonies to resist the taxation, eventually leading to the American Revolution.

American Revolution (1775–1783)

Causes: The discontent of the American colonies that developed following the new imperial policies, which began in 1763 and had both economic and ideological sources. New taxes on a variety of goods led to some violent responses, such as the burning of the British customs schooner *Gaspée* in 1772 and the Boston Tea Party in 1773. The ideological argument for independence developed partly due to the writings of English philosopher John Locke, who argued that in any society people are endowed with certain natural rights to "life, liberty, and property." Locke also argued that engaging in revolution when rights are abused is not just a right, it is a responsibility and that governments derived their power from the consent of the governed. Scottish philosopher David Hume emphasized the importance of human reason as a source for society's proper organization. Thomas Jefferson's phrase, "we hold these truths to be self-evident," in the Declaration of Independence displays Hume's influence.

Treaty: The Treaty of Paris was signed September 3, 1783.

Results: While the fighting of the American Revolution ended with the British surrender at Yorktown in 1781, independence was not officially recognized until the 1783 Treaty. The United States was acknowledged as an independent nation with territory extending from the Mississippi River on the west, the Great Lakes on the north, and Florida on the south.

American casualties: Approximately 50,000 dead and wounded.

War of 1812 (1812–1815)

Causes: Just three decades after the close of the American Revolution, British and American forces once again engaged in land and naval battles. The impressment of American sailors on British ships, a desire for Canadian lands, and British aid to Indian tribes led a group of War Hawks in Congress to encourage President Madison to declare war on Great Britain, which he did in 1812.

Treaty: Treaty of Ghent signed December 24, 1814.

Results: The U.S. and Great Britain returned to a *status quo antebellum* (situation prior to the war) following the fighting with none of the major issues resolved. One of the major impacts of the war in the U.S. was the development of a national consciousness. The period following the war is known as the Era of Good Feelings, as the nation focused on internal developments, expansion, and economic growth.

American casualties: Approximately 20,000 dead and wounded.

Mexican-American War (1846–1848)

Causes: A desire for lands in what is now the American Southwest and for Mexico led to an offer to purchase territory followed by hostilities in Texas and California.

Treaty: Treaty of Guadalupe Hidalgo signed February 2, 1848.

Results: The U.S. agreed to pay $15 million for half of Mexico's northern territory. Mexico also gave up all claims to Texas and recognized the Rio Grande as America's southern boundary. The Mexican-American War increased tension between pro- and anti-slavery forces as the question of the presence of slavery in the newly-acquired territories predominated in Congress.

American casualties: Approximately 17,000 dead and wounded.

Civil War (1861–1865)

Causes: Southern resistance to growing Northern influence in Congress led to the secession of nine Southern states following the November 1860 election of Abraham Lincoln to the presidency. States' rights on the part of the South and the desire to preserve the Union on the part of the North were the initial stated causes, though the issue of slavery was never far from people's minds. With the issuance of the Emancipation Proclamation in 1863, President Lincoln clearly identified slavery as the cause of the fighting.

Treaty: Confederate General Robert E. Lee surrendered to Union General Ulysses S. Grant on April 9, 1865. Lee received very generous terms from Grant who allowed the enlisted men to return home and the officers to retain their guns and their horses.

Results: Slavery, which was officially ended with the passage of the 13th Amendment in February 1865, now was actually abolished throughout the South. The South enters a long period of political Reconstruction as the U.S. becomes one nation.

Total casualties (North and South): Approximately 1.5 million killed and wounded.

Spanish-American War (1898)

Causes: A number of alleged Spanish colonial administration atrocities in Cuban concentration camps, along with an explosion on the *U.S.S. Maine* in Havana Harbor led to President William McKinley's declaration of war.

Treaty: Treaty of Paris signed December 10, 1898.

Results: Spain gave up control of Cuba, Puerto Rico, Guam and the Philippine Islands. The U.S. paid Spain $20 million for the Philippines. This marked the end of the Spanish presence in the Western Hemisphere and the South Pacific. It also marked the ascendance of the U.S. as a world power.

American casualties: Approximately 4,000 killed and wounded.

World War I (1914–1918)

Causes: A conflict that involved most of Europe began with the assassination of Archduke Ferdinand of Austria-Hungary in 1914. The U.S. joined the war in 1917 following the German resumption of unrestricted submarine warfare and the discovery of the Zimmermann Telegram, which promised German assistance to Mexico in recovering lost territory in exchange for Mexico forming a military alliance with Germany.

Treaty: Surrender of German troops took place on November 11, 1918. Treaty of Versailles signed June 28, 1919.

Results: The map of Europe and the Middle East was redrawn by the participants at Versailles. Germany was forced to give up its colonies, pay reparations to the victors, and accept sole responsibility for the war. The U.S. became a creditor nation as a result of loans issued during World War I.

American casualties: Approximately 320,000 killed and wounded.

World War II (1939–1945)

Causes: World War II began in September 1939 with Germany's invasion of Poland, followed by it conquering most of Europe in the subsequent two years. The U.S. joined the conflict following a surprise attack by Japan on Pearl Harbor on December 7, 1941, and an invasion of the Philippines.

Treaties: German General Alfred Jodl signed an unconditional surrender on May 7, 1945. No formal peace treaty with Germany was signed. Japanese officials signed an unconditional surrender on September 2, 1945.

Results: Germany and Japan were occupied by victorious forces. The United Nations was established in 1945. The Nuremberg Tribunals and Tokyo War Crimes Trials tried German and Japanese military and political officials of war crimes and helped define crimes against humanity.

American casualties: Approximately 1 million killed and wounded.

Korean War (1950–1953)

Causes: The division of Korea into two nations (communist North Korea and non-communist South Korea) following World War II with neither nation recognizing the other as legitimate led to tensions in the region. An invasion by North Korean troops of most of the South in 1950 was followed by a United Nations force (95% American) sent to South Korea.

Treaty: An armistice between United Nations and North Korean officials was signed on July 27, 1953, creating a Korean Demilitarized Zone. No peace treaty was ever signed.

Results: The division of the Korean peninsula into two nations was made permanent. Korea remained an area of dispute and conflict throughout the Cold War. Hostilities continue through the present day.

American casualties: Approximately 125,000 killed and wounded.

Vietnam War (1961–1975)

Causes: As in Korea, Vietnam was split into the communist North and non-communist South following World War II. French troops left Vietnam in 1954 after the battle of Dienbienphu. The U.S. sent military advisors to support the non-communist South and, with the growing Viet Cong influence in the South, began a massive commitment of troops, ships, and air power following the 1964 Tonkin Gulf Resolution.

Treaty: The Paris Peace Accords were signed on January 27, 1973, though they were not approved by the U.S. Senate.

Results: A ceasefire took place and all of Vietnam came under the control of the North, led by Ho Chi Minh. The last U.S. troops left Vietnam on April 29, 1975.

American casualties: Approximately 200,000 killed and wounded.

First Persian Gulf War—Operation Desert Storm (1991)

Causes: An Iraqi invasion of Kuwait led to a coalition of nations organizing land and air attacks on Iraqi forces.

Treaty: A ceasefire between coalition and Iraqi forces was established in February 1991.

Results: The Iraqi military withdrew from Kuwait and a no-fly zone was created over Iraq.

American casualties: Approximately 1,100 killed and wounded.

Afghanistan War—Operation Enduring Freedom (2001–)

Causes: The Taliban government's support and protection of Al-Qaeda cells launching the 9/11 attacks in 2001 led to U.S. attacks on the Taliban government, which was overthrown.

Results: Taliban political rule was ended and NATO forces (mainly from the U.S.) supported Afghan political and economic reforms.

American casualties: 20,000 killed and wounded.

Second Persian Gulf War—Operation Iraqi Freedom (2003–2011)

Causes: The rumor of weapons of mass destruction (WMD) controlled by Iraqi dictator Saddam Hussein prompted an invasion by American and British forces. No such weapons were ever discovered.

Treaty: A Status of Force Agreement was signed in 2008 agreeing that all U.S. military personnel would leave Iraq by the end of 2011.

Results: Saddam Hussein was captured and executed and his Ba'ath Party dissolved. Democratic elections chose a new Iraqi government in 2005.

American casualties: Approximately 36,000 killed and wounded.

Appendix B: Key Presidential Elections

Every four years American voters select the next president. At least they do so indirectly, as the Electoral College actually makes the choice and its members are not required to follow the choice of the voters. In addition to that oddity, the individual who receives the most votes is not guaranteed the White House, once again because of the Electoral College procedures, in this case the winner-take-all nature of Electoral College voting as it works for most states. Five presidents (John Quincy Adams in 1824, Rutherford Hayes in 1876, Benjamin Harrison in 1888, George W. Bush in 2000, and Donald J. Trump in 2016) were awarded the presidency despite receiving fewer popular votes than their opponent.

Sometimes presidential elections are uneventful. For example, incumbents nearly always win. At other times, they are controversial. Since 1824, active campaigning has been a feature of most elections, though in 1860 Abraham Lincoln won the presidency as a Republican without doing any personal campaigning. The seventeen elections below were significant in some way. The winner is listed first, followed by his major rival(s).

1796: John Adams (Federalist) vs. Thomas Jefferson (Democrat-Republican)

Many expected George Washington to seek a third term. When he did not, Adams, the incumbent Vice President, faced Jefferson, the Secretary of State. Democrat-Republicans accused the Federalists of wanting to establish a monarchy, while Federalists identified the violence of the French Revolution with the Democrat-Republicans. Because the current practice of a president and vice president running mate had not yet been established, Jefferson became Adams' vice president in what turned out to be an awkward pairing.

1800: Thomas Jefferson (Democrat-Republican) vs. John Adams (Federalist)

Jefferson actually tied for the presidency in the Electoral College with his vice-presidential candidate, Aaron Burr, and the election had to be decided in the House of Representatives. The 12th Amendment prevented this from occurring in the future. The key issues were new taxes imposed because of the quasi-war with France, and the Alien and Sedition Acts, though Adams' unpopularity probably doomed him to defeat as well.

1824: John Q. Adams (Democrat-Republican) vs. Andrew Jackson (Democrat-Republican)

In what became known as the Corrupt Bargain Election, Adams won the presidency in the House of Representatives, as no candidate received a majority of the electoral votes cast. Jackson, who finished first in the popular voting, was viewed as the candidate of the common man but was passed over by the House in favor of Adams, who chose Henry Clay, Jackson's bitter political enemy, as his Secretary of State. This election marked the end of the caucus system, in which members of Congress selected party candidates, and the beginning of active campaigning, with songs promoting candidates gaining popularity and newspapers endorsing candidates.

1828: Andrew Jackson (Democrat) vs. John Q. Adams (National Republican)

Following his painful defeat in 1824, Jackson waged an aggressive campaign against Adams, whose supporters responded with charges of bigamy against Jackson's wife and pointed to Jackson's fondness for dueling as unbecoming to a president. Jackson was able to win the support of Western farmers and Eastern workers. Jackson's victory is often seen as the beginning of the modern two-party system as well as the beginning of mudslinging campaigns.

1860: Abraham Lincoln (Republican) vs. Stephen Douglas (Democrat)

As the nation moved toward divisions resulting in the Civil War, Lincoln was elected president as the Democrats split into Northern and Southern factions. Republican opposition to the expansion of slavery into the Western territories infuriated pro-slavery Democrats and Lincoln's name did not even appear on a number of Southern states' ballots. Douglas and John Breckenridge were both nominated as Democratic candidates, with John Bell of Kentucky representing a compromise Union faction. Lincoln easily won the electoral vote, though he polled less than 40% of the popular votes cast. Following his election, South Carolina led ten other Southern states in seceding from the Union and forming the Confederate States of America.

1876: Rutherford Hayes (Republican) vs. Samuel Tilden (Democrat)

Electoral irregularities in several Southern states led to disputed Electoral College results and the formation of an Electoral Commission with representatives from both parties. Although Tilden had won the popular vote, Hayes was awarded the presidency in the unwritten and informal Compromise of 1877. Federal troops were removed from the South and economic assistance was promised for the South. In exchange, Hayes became president.

1896: William McKinley (Republican) vs. William J. Bryan (Democrat-Populist)

The 1890s witnessed the worst economic crisis up to that point in American history, with a depression marked by high unemployment, violent labor strikes, and low prices. William Jennings Bryan waged a vigorous campaign focused on economic issues, chiefly the free coinage of silver. Bryan ran strongest in the South and rural Midwest and presented his campaign as one of working men and small farmers against wealthy merchants and bankers. McKinley's supporters were a coalition of skilled workers, businessmen, and prosperous farmers. This coalition favored tight control of the money supply and high protective tariffs.

1912: Woodrow Wilson (Democrat) vs. Theodore Roosevelt (Progressive), William H. Taft (Republican)

Incumbent Taft was Roosevelt's hand-picked successor, but when Taft did not live up to Roosevelt's Progressive ideals, some Republicans formed the Progressive (or Bull Moose) Party with Roosevelt as their candidate. The two candidates split the Republican vote and Democratic Party nominee Wilson won easily. This was the first time a third-party candidate had played a major role in a presidential race as Socialist Eugene Debs polled over 900,000 votes. The 1912 election effectively had four Progressive candidates seeking the White House.

1932: Franklin Roosevelt (Democrat) vs. Herbert Hoover (Republican)

Hoover had the misfortune to be president when the 1929 Stock Market Crash occurred and most of his one term coincided with the worst economic depression in U.S. history. Hoover brought a serious, conservative approach to dealing with the problems of the Great Depression. Roosevelt presented a starkly different approach, the New Deal, which proposed massive government programs of relief, recovery, and reform.

1948: Harry Truman (Democrat) vs. Thomas Dewey (Republican)

Truman took office in 1945 following Franklin Roosevelt's death. He had little international experience and was thought to be a sure loser to Dewey, a longtime Republican governor. Both polls and newspapers predicted a Dewey victory, but Truman won the 1948 election with a margin of more than 100 electoral votes.

1960: John Kennedy (Democrat) vs. Richard Nixon (Republican)

Incumbent Vice President Richard Nixon had more legislative and foreign affairs experience than his opponent, Senator John F. Kennedy of Massachusetts. Kennedy's Roman Catholic faith was also seen as an impediment to his candidacy. A series of televised debates may have swung the election to Kennedy, who won by a margin of less than 120,000 votes nationwide.

1968: Richard Nixon (Republican) vs. Hubert Humphrey (Democrat)

President Lyndon Johnson announced in March 1968 that he would not be a candidate in the November elections. Tension over an increasingly unpopular Vietnam War led many Democrats to support antiwar candidate Senator Robert Kennedy, but he was assassinated during the primaries. Incumbent Hubert Humphrey faced Nixon in a race that also included George Wallace, former segregationist Alabama governor.

1980: Ronald Reagan (Republican) vs. Jimmy Carter (Democrat)

Carter had a disappointing single term following his 1976 victory over Gerald Ford. The Iranian hostage situation, raging inflation, and the energy crisis plagued his administration. California Governor Ronald Reagan easily won the Republican nomination and defeated Carter by 440 electoral votes. Reagan advocated deep government spending cuts and a supply-side approach to economic issues.

2000: George W. Bush (Republican) vs. Al Gore (Democrat)

Al Gore, the incumbent Vice President to Bill Clinton, who was only the second president to face an impeachment trial, won the popular vote by over 500,000 votes. The Electoral College vote was much tighter, however, and some disputed ballots in Florida prevented a clear victory for either candidate. In a 5-4 Supreme Court decision (*Gore v. Bush*), the Florida ballots were not recounted and Bush was declared the winner.

2008: Barack Obama (Democrat) vs. John McCain (Republican)

Obama, a first-term senator with virtually no foreign affairs experience, strongly opposed the Iraq War while U.S. Navy veteran and former prisoner-of-war McCain advocated a strong military role for the U.S. A steep downturn in the economy in the fall of 2008 proved harmful to McCain's candidacy and Obama became America's first African-American president.

2016: Donald J. Trump (Republican) vs. Hillary Clinton (Democrat)

This was Democrat Hillary Clinton's second run for the presidency, having lost her party's nomination to Barack Obama in 2008. The former first lady, U.S. senator, and secretary of state became the first woman to be nominated for president by a major party. Following a bitterly fought campaign, Republican (and onetime Democrat) Donald J. Trump, a real estate developer and political novice, was elected the 45th U.S. president. Trump's election was widely viewed as a repudiation of the establishment. The election of 2016 marked the fifth time in American history that a candidate had ascended to the presidency with fewer popular votes than his opponent.

Appendix C: Important International Treaties

In his Farewell Address, President George Washington warned Americans about engaging in foreign political disputes, particularly with European nations. Thomas Jefferson extended this idea in his inaugural address, stating that the U.S. should have "friendship with all nations, entangling alliances with none." Since then, the U.S. has entered into a number of treaty agreements with other nations. Article II of the Constitution states that the president shall have "power, by and with the advice and consent of the Senate, to make treaties."

Below is a list of the major international treaties of the United States.

1778 – Treaty of Alliance (France). Following the American victory in the Battle of Saratoga during the American Revolution, France agreed to send men, war materiel, and money to the newly-formed United States. This assistance proved vital for the American cause and contributed to the final victory at Yorktown.

1783 – Treaty of Paris (Great Britain). Once the fighting during the American Revolution had ceased, the Continental Congress sent John Adams, John Jay, and Benjamin Franklin to negotiate a permanent settlement. The British recognized the U.S. as an independent nation with a western border established along the Mississippi River. The British agreed to evacuate their troops from forts on U.S. territory and the Continental Army was disbanded.

1795 – Jay's Treaty (Great Britain). The British agreed to remove troops still stationed on American soil and to pay for damages for American ships that the Royal Navy had illegally seized in the years following the American Revolution. In exchange, the U.S. agreed to pay outstanding debts to British creditors.

1795 – Pinckney's Treaty (Spain). This agreement gave the U.S. access to the Mississippi River port of New Orleans in an exchange for promises of nonaggression in the West. The ability to use the entire Mississippi River system for trade was important to settlers throughout the Ohio and Mississippi River valleys.

1803 – Louisiana Purchase (France). When Thomas Jefferson, a strict constructionist, purchased the Louisiana Territory from France, he was violating his philosophical principles, but seizing an incredible opportunity for the U.S. Federalists strongly opposed the purchase as they foresaw its benefits for the Democrat-Republican Party. The purchase price was $15 million, about four cents per acre.

1814 – Treaty of Ghent (Great Britain). The U.S. experienced limited success in the War of 1812, as the U.S. Navy consisted of just a few gunboats and the army was quite small. The treaty affirmed that neither side had gained nor lost any territory and there was no mention of impressment or the seizure of American ships. Days after the treaty was signed, Andrew Jackson scored a huge victory over the British at New Orleans.

1817 – Rush–Bagot Treaty (Great Britain). The United States and Great Britain agreed to demilitarize the Great Lakes, establishing one of the longest demilitarized borders in the world.

1819 – Adams–Onís Treaty (Spain). The purchase of Florida was approved and a boundary dispute in Texas was settled. It came at a time of growing tension between the U.S. and Spain and was hailed in the U.S. as a victory for American diplomats.

1842 – Webster–Ashburton Treaty (Great Britain). – The treaty settled the boundary disputes between the U.S. and Great Britain over the ore-rich Great Lakes region and stipulated that both nations would jointly occupy the Oregon Territory.

1846 – Oregon Treaty (Great Britain). President James Polk pressured Great Britain to relinquish Oregon and even threatened war, but eventually signed the compromise treaty to split Oregon at the 49th parallel. The British took British Columbia while the U.S. took all the territory that eventually became Washington, Oregon, Idaho, and sections of Montana.

1848 – Treaty of Guadalupe Hidalgo (Mexico). The Mexican-American War was settled with this treaty, in which California and most of New Mexico, Arizona, Nevada, Colorado, and Wyoming were ceded to the U.S. Mexico abandoned its claims to Texas as the Rio Grande River was established as the border between Texas and Mexico. The U.S. agreed to pay Mexico $15 million for all of the land it acquired.

1868 – Burlingame Treaty (China). China was granted most-favored-nation status by the U.S. and friendly relations were established between the two countries. In addition, a promise of non-discrimination and religious freedom was extended to Chinese working in the U.S. The construction of the transcontinental railroad necessitated a huge labor force and this treaty encouraged immigration, but not naturalization.

1898 – Treaty of Paris (Spain). This ended the Spanish-American War and marked the end of the Spanish empire in both the South Pacific and in the Americas. Spain surrendered control of Cuba, the Philippines, Puerto Rico, and Guam to the U.S.

1901 – Hay–Pauncefote Treaty (Great Britain). The treaty nullified the 1858 Clayton–Bulwer Treaty and allowed the U.S. to build a canal through Panama. When Colombia refused to sell land for the canal in Panama, President Theodore Roosevelt struck a deal with Panamanian rebels to guarantee their independence in exchange for the canal zone.

1919 – Treaty of Versailles (many nations—not ratified by the U.S.). President Wilson joined representatives of Italy, France, and Great Britain in signing the treaty that formed the League of Nations and forced Germany to accept full responsibility for World War I, pay $33 billion in war reparations to the victorious nations, give up some of its territory, and abandon its overseas colonies. After a bitter fight, the Senate refused to ratify the treaty and the U.S. never joined the League of Nations.

1922 – Washington Naval Treaty (France, Great Britain, Italy, and Japan). This treaty restricted the size of the navies of the five nations and limited the size of guns on ships. This marked a halt in the construction of battleships, though several nations converted them into aircraft carriers. A supplementary provision to restrict submarine warfare and ban chemical warfare was rejected by France.

1928 – Kellogg–Briand Pact (62 nations). Sponsored by the U.S. and France, this agreement called for "the renunciation of war as an instrument of national policy" and promised not to use war to settle "disputes or conflicts of whatever nature or of whatever origin they may be, which may arise among them." It passed overwhelmingly in the U.S. Senate.

1941 – Atlantic Charter (Great Britain). British Prime Minister Winston Churchill and President Franklin Roosevelt met off the coast of Newfoundland and signed an agreement concerning the goals of the Allies for the post World War II world. While not an official treaty, it demonstrated the U.S. commitment to the Allies before the U.S. officially entered the war.

1949 – North Atlantic Treaty or Treaty of Washington (12 nations). This established the NATO mutual defense organization in light of a perceived Soviet threat in Europe. The self-defense clause was never invoked during the Cold War, but was invoked following the 9/11 terrorist attacks in 2001.

1972 – SALT I—Strategic Arms Limitation Talks Agreement (Soviet Union). This pact froze the number of strategic ballistic missile launchers and allowed for the addition of new launchers only after older intercontinental ballistic missile launchers were destroyed. A subsequent agreement (SALT II) was not ratified by the U.S. Senate.

1973 – Paris Peace Accords (North Vietnam). U.S. military involvement in the Vietnam War ended with the signing of this agreement, which also enforced a temporary ceasefire between North and South Vietnamese forces. A unification of Vietnam was to be "carried out step-by-step through peaceful means." The U.S. Senate refused to ratify the agreement.

1994 – North American Free Trade Agreement (NAFTA) (Mexico, Canada). This treaty sought to eliminate trade and investment barriers among the three nations and established the largest free trade bloc in the world. Some observers have asserted that the agreement has jeopardized the viability of Mexican farms, particularly corn farms, and threatened Mexico's agricultural self-sufficiency.

Appendix D: Key Characters in American History

Period 1: 1491–1607

Atahualpa An Inca emperor who was briefly used by the Spaniards to control his people until the Spanish executed him in 1533, thus effectively ending the Inca empire.

Jacques Cartier An early French explorer of the New World; Cartier's three voyages into Canada helped establish France's claims in the early 1500s.

Samuel de Champlain The colony of New France in present-day eastern Canada was established by Champlain in 1608.

Hernando Cortés A conquistador who brought considerable treasure back to Spain; Cortés conquered the Aztec capital at Tenochtitlán (Mexico City) in 1521.

Christopher Columbus Sailing for Spain, Italian explorer Columbus is credited with discovering the New World in 1492 when he landed at San Salvador in the Caribbean.

Hernando de Soto A Spanish explorer, de Soto led a group through the American southeast in the mid-1500s.

Moctezuma An Aztec ruler in power when the first contact with Europeans took place in Mexico; Moctezuma was killed by Spanish forces in 1520.

Francisco Pizarro A Spanish explorer and conquistador, Pizarro conquered the Incas in the 1520s and claimed all of the land from Peru to Panama for Spain.

Sir Walter Raleigh Queen Elizabeth granted Raleigh a royal charter in 1587 to establish the Roanoke colony in Virginia. It disappeared within a few years.

Amerigo Vespucci An Italian explorer who wrote about his New World adventures and was rewarded by having both North and South America named after him by a German mapmaker.

Period 2: 1607–1754

Nathaniel Bacon A landowner and farmer, Bacon assembled a small armed force and attacked Native American tribes in Virginia. This developed into Bacon's Rebellion and was the earliest colonial rebellion.

Jonathan Edwards An 18th century theologian, Edwards was one of the most effective preachers of the Great Awakening. His "Sinners in the Hands of an Angry God" is one of America's most famous sermons.

Anne Hutchinson A Puritan living in Massachusetts Bay Colony, Hutchinson was expelled from the colony in 1535 for criticizing the Puritan leadership.

John Locke A 17th century Enlightenment philosopher, Locke theorized that citizens enter into a contract with their rulers to guarantee protection of their rights and retained the right to revolt if rights were not provided. His theories helped shape the thinking of some of the leaders of the American Revolution, particularly Thomas Jefferson.

Popé An Indian religious leader in what is now New Mexico, Popé led the 1680 Pueblo Revolt against Spanish rule. The Pueblos killed 300 Spaniards and expelled colonists from New Mexico for twelve years until a military force was able to retake control in 1692.

John Rolfe A Jamestown colonist, Rolfe saved the early Virginia colony at Jamestown by discovering a strain of tobacco that was very profitable. This led England to establish future colonies in America. Rolfe married Pocahontas and promoted peaceful relations with Native Americans.

John Smith A mercenary who wrote fanciful tales of his many adventures, Smith took control of the Jamestown colony during its early days and rescued it from starvation and Indian attacks.

Roger Williams Forced to leave Massachusetts Bay for his unconventional religious beliefs, Williams founded Rhode Island on the basis of toleration and respect for Indian land ownership. He was an early proponent of the separation of church and state.

George Whitefield Perhaps the most famous Great Awakening preacher, Whitefield traveled throughout the colonies, which resulted in many religious conversions and an increased emphasis on personal piety.

John Winthrop Governor of the Massachusetts Bay Colony, Puritan Winthrop penned the "City Upon a Hill" speech that defined the Puritan goals of a theocratic society.

Period 3: 1754–1800

John Adams Adams earned his first fame by defending the British soldiers accused of murder in the Boston Massacre. He served as a delegate to both Continental Congresses and as a diplomat in both Paris and London. As first vice president and second president of the U.S., Adams proved to be an ineffective leader and lost the election of 1800 to Thomas Jefferson after serving just one term, though he did prevent a naval war with France.

Samuel Adams Bostonian Adams organized the first Committee of Correspondence during the American Revolution and was a strong advocate for the patriot cause.

Benjamin Franklin A multitalented inventor, diplomat, and philosopher, Franklin was a member of both the Constitutional Convention and the Second Continental Congress, which drafted the Declaration of Independence. His diplomatic efforts in France during the American Revolution were critical to obtaining French assistance.

George III Ruler of Great Britain during the last half of the 18th century, King George became a symbol of British tyranny to American patriots, such as Thomas Jefferson and Thomas Paine.

George Grenville British prime minister at the close of the French and Indian War, Grenville instituted the new imperial policy of taxation that stirred colonial dissent in the years leading up to the American Revolution. He enforced the Navigation Acts and urged Parliament to pass the Stamp, Sugar, Currency and Quartering Acts in the 1760s.

Alexander Hamilton Hamilton strongly supported the adoption of the Constitution and co-wrote *The Federalist Papers* to promote its ratification. He later served as the first Secretary of the Treasury and instituted a number of programs to establish the financial security of the new nation. A bitter enemy of Thomas Jefferson, Hamilton led the Federalist Party until his death in a duel with Aaron Burr.

Thomas Jefferson A young Virginia planter and lawyer when he drafted the Declaration of Independence, Jefferson served as an early ambassador to France, the first Secretary of State, and the third president of the U.S. He was the leader of the Democrat-Republican Party and a strict constructionist who opposed the concentration of power in the national government. One of his main accomplishments was the purchase of Louisiana from France.

James Madison Sometimes referred to as the "father of the Constitution," Madison played an important role in building support for its ratification in his essays in *The Federalist Papers*. He wrote the Bill of Rights and became a leader of the new Democrat-Republican Party. He and Thomas Jefferson drafted the Kentucky and Virginia Resolutions in response to the Federalist Alien and Sedition Acts and served as fourth president of the U.S.

Thomas Paine Exiled from England, Paine wrote the influential pamphlet "Common Sense," which articulated the reasons for American independence. His writings were circulated widely through the colonies during the American Revolution.

Pontiac An Ottawa chieftain, Pontiac united a number of tribes following the French and Indian War in attacks on colonists in the Ohio River Valley.

Daniel Shays A farmer in western Massachusetts, Shays became an unlikely leader of a group of 1500 disgruntled farmers who revolted against the Massachusetts government in 1786. His revolt led many leaders to call for a reform of the Articles of Confederation and the establishment of a more powerful central government.

George Washington While a young lieutenant in the French and Indian War, Washington was captured and released by the French. He earned a military reputation that led him to be made commander of American forces during the American Revolution. He effectively led the Continental Army, avoided major defeats and cooperated with French naval and land forces to win the decisive battle at Yorktown. Washington presided over the Constitutional Convention and served as the first president of the United States.

Period 4: 1800–1848

John C. Calhoun Calhoun was the leading advocate of the states' rights position of Southern politicians during the first half of the 19th century. As Andrew Jackson's first vice president, he led the campaign to nullify the hated 1828 Tariff of Abominations and wrote *The South Carolina Exposition* urging active defiance of the federal government.

Henry Clay A proponent of the American System of internal improvements, a national bank, and protective tariffs, Clay became the leader of the anti-Jackson Whig Party. He authored the Missouri Compromise and was a strong advocate of the Compromise of 1850. Though defeated in all three attempts to become president, Clay is viewed by many as one of America's greatest statesmen.

Charles G. Finney The leading preacher of the Second Great Awakening, Finney spoke to huge revival meetings in camp meetings. He also spoke strongly against slavery and for an increased role for women in the leadership of churches.

Andrew Jackson A war hero from Indian battles and the War of 1812, Jackson lost the presidential election of 1824 to John Quincy Adams despite winning the most popular votes. Following his victory in the 1828 presidential election, Jackson became a hero for the common man and an activist president, attacking anyone who opposed him. The South Carolina nullification crisis, the War over the Bank of the U.S., and the expulsion of Indians from the American southeast were major events during his presidency.

Horace Mann As secretary of the Massachusetts Board of Education, Mann pushed for compulsory public education. He stressed the value of a secular curriculum, higher teacher standards, and increased pay for teachers.

John Marshall Chief Justice of the Supreme Court, Marshall established the principle of judicial review in his *Marbury v. Madison* opinion. His decisions consistently strengthened both the independence of the Supreme Court and the power of the national government during his career from 1801 to 1835.

James K. Polk A relatively unknown politician before his election to the presidency in 1844, Polk secured territory in the northwest with the Oregon Treaty and led the U.S. to enter the Mexican-American War in an effort to take territory from Mexico.

Joseph Smith Founder of the Mormon Church in upstate New York, Smith and his followers moved to Missouri and then Illinois, where he was killed by an anti-Mormon mob. His successor, Brigham Young, led the Mormons to Utah.

Elizabeth Cady Stanton A prominent early American feminist, Stanton demanded equality for women. She was one of the organizers of the 1848 Seneca Falls Convention and drafted the Declaration of Sentiments.

Tecumseh Along with his brother The Prophet, Tecumseh organized a number of Indian tribes in the Mississippi and Ohio River Valleys into the Northwest Confederacy in an attempt to halt the increasing settlement by Americans. He was defeated at the 1811 Battle of Tippecanoe by General William Henry Harrison who had been authorized by Congress to destroy the Confederacy.

Period 5: 1844–1877

John Brown Brown was a radical abolitionist who led a murderous raid against pro-slavery settlers in Kansas and then planned an ill-fated raid on a federal arsenal in Harper's Ferry, Virginia, in 1859 in an attempt to start a slave uprising. He was executed, but became a symbol to abolitionists for his commitment to the cause of ending slavery.

Dorothea Dix A tireless worker who, on behalf of the mentally ill and insane, traveled thousands of miles throughout the U.S. to urge humane treatment for those in jails and mental hospitals. Congress voted to fund mental hospitals, but President Franklin Pierce vetoed the bill.

Stephen Douglas Douglas was the leading Democratic politician of the 1850s and the author of the Kansas-Nebraska Act, which applied the principle of popular sovereignty to the problem of slavery in the Western territories. He participated with Abraham Lincoln in the famous 1858 Lincoln-Douglas debates during the Illinois senatorial campaign during which he developed the Freeport Doctrine. Douglas was one of two Democratic presidential candidates in 1860.

Frederick Douglass A former slave and abolitionist activist, Douglass travelled throughout the North writing and speaking against slavery. His autobiographical *Narrative of the Life of Frederick Douglass, an American Slave*, effectively combatted the contention of slavery advocates that blacks lacked the intellectual capacity to function in white society.

William Lloyd Garrison The publisher of *The Liberator* and a strong advocate for the immediate abolition of slavery, Garrison earned the hatred of many Southerners for his radical views. In the first issue of *The Liberator*, he wrote on the issue of the abolition of slavery: "I am in earnest — I will not equivocate — I will not excuse — I will not retreat a single inch — AND I WILL BE HEARD."

Jefferson Davis When Mississippi seceded from the Union, Davis left the U.S. Senate and was elected president of the Confederate States of America. He attempted to lead the South but was plagued by economic woes and the lack of enforcement powers. Following the end of the Civil War, he was imprisoned for two years.

Andrew Johnson Johnson was a Tennessee Democratic senator who was added to the Republican ticket as vice president in 1864. He was ill-suited for the presidency, which he assumed following Lincoln's assassination. He constantly feuded with the Radical Republicans about the course of Reconstruction. He was impeached by the House of Representatives, but the Senate trial fell one vote short of removing him from office.

Abraham Lincoln A lawyer and one-term congressman from Illinois, Lincoln developed a national reputation during the Lincoln-Douglas debates in which he argued forcefully against the expansion of slavery into the Western territories. He was elected president as a Republican in 1860, causing the South to secede. He fought at first to keep the South in the Union and later to end slavery, but was killed by an assassin days after the Confederate army surrendered in 1865.

George McClellan One of the many generals Lincoln appointed to command Union armies, McClellan scored an important though inconclusive victory at Antietam that gave Lincoln the opportunity to issue the Emancipation Proclamation. After being relieved of command by Lincoln, McClellan ran for president in 1864 as a Peace Democrat.

Dred Scott When Scott, a slave to a Missouri doctor, moved with his master to the North during the 1830s, he contended that he should be declared a free man and sued for his freedom. Chief Justice Roger Taney and the Supreme Court ruled against him in a crucial 1857 decision that stated that constitutional protections did not apply to blacks and that Congress had no right to restrict slavery in the territories.

Harriet Beecher Stowe As author of *Uncle Tom's Cabin*, one of the most widely read books in American history, Stowe became an important voice in the abolitionist movement. When presented to Abraham Lincoln, he supposedly remarked, "So this is the little woman who wrote the book that started this great war."

Period 6: 1865–1898

Jane Addams A leader in the settlement house movement Addams founded Hull House in Chicago in 1889 to assist immigrants in adjusting to American life and obtaining job skills. The settlement house movement spread to several cities and was an early source of urban reform efforts.

William Jennings Bryan Bryan delivered perhaps the most famous American political campaign oratory in the 1896 presidential election with his "Cross of Gold" speech. As a candidate of both the Populist and Democratic parties, Bryan spoke out against the eastern moneyed establishment and in support of the unlimited coinage of silver to support western farmers and miners. His famous speech ended, "Do not crucify mankind upon a cross of gold." Bryan went on to become Woodrow Wilson's Secretary of State and opposed Clarence Darrow in the 1925 Scopes Monkey Trial.

Andrew Carnegie Using the vertical integration system to control the manufacturing and sale of steel products, Scottish immigrant Carnegie controlled much of the steel industry in the U.S. He used violence to put down the Homestead Strike against steel workers in 1892 and following the sale of his company to J.P. Morgan, he spent the rest of his life giving away his fortune. He wrote *The Gospel of Wealth* to explain the obligation the wealthy have to use philanthrophy to help others.

Eugene Debs Co-founder of the Socialist Party, Debs organized the Pullman Strike in Chicago in 1894. He ran for president in 1912, was imprisoned for violating the Sedition Act during World War I by speaking out against the draft, and ran again from his jail cell in 1920, polling almost one million votes.

Thomas Edison One of the world's most prolific inventors, Edison developed the electric light, the stock ticker, many different types of batteries, and the motion picture camera in his laboratory in Menlo Park, New Jersey.

Henry George In his book *Progress and Poverty*, George advocated that all taxation should be based on land value and argued strongly against both tariffs and the uneven distribution of wealth that existed in the U.S.

Samuel Gompers A Jewish immigrant from England and a cigar maker by trade, Gompers formed the American Federation of Labor in 1886 to represent skilled workers. He fought for higher wages, shorter hours, and better working conditions. When asked by a journalist what he wanted, Gompers responded, "More."

John D. Rockefeller Rockefeller used the horizontal integration system to control the oil industry in the U.S. during the final third of the 19th century. He formed the Standard Oil Company in 1867 and ruthlessly forced out his competitors on the way to monopolizing the industry.

Frederick Jackson Turner An American historian who wrote the influential essay "The Significance of the Frontier in American History" in 1891, Turner argued that Western migration and settlement had a profound effect on American social, political, and economic development.

Booker T. Washington A former slave, Washington was president of the historically black Tuskegee Institute. He favored gradualism as the best approach for blacks to obtain political and social equality and recommended developing job skills rather than higher education to obtain economic equality. He was strongly opposed by some other black leaders, including W.E.B. DuBois.

William Tweed Informally known as Boss Tweed, this Democratic mayor of New York City controlled the Tammany Hall political machine, controlling politics and much of the economic life of New York with bribes and jobs in exchange for votes. He was imprisoned for corruption, but bribed his jailer and escaped. The Tweed Ring was an example of the widespread graft and corruption in city politics in much of the East.

Period 7: 1890–1945

Emilio Aguinaldo Filipino leader who opposed Spain and later the U.S. to try to gain the independence of the Philippines. U.S. troops who remained in the Philippine Islands following the conclusion of the Spanish-American War became his target. Aguinaldo led Filipino forces in guerrilla fighting against the U.S. but was captured and forced to take an oath of allegiance to the U.S.

W.E.B. DuBois A co-founder of the NAACP (National Association for the Advancement of Colored People), DuBois called for immediate political and social equality for blacks. His views conflicted strongly with Booker T. Washington, who advocated a gradual approach based on economic advancement.

Henry Ford Ford invented the Model T automobile and revolutionized the assembly-line process, reducing the cost of cars while raising the pay of workers. Ford produced the first cars that middle-class Americans could afford, transforming the transportation landscape in the U.S.

Marcus Garvey Born in Jamaica and an influential civil rights leader in the 1920s, Garvey encouraged blacks to take pride in their cultural achievements and sponsored a back to Africa movement that attracted a large number of followers. Some black leaders, such as W.E.B. DuBois, strongly opposed Garvey's separatist approach.

Herbert Hoover Following a career as an engineer and successful head of the Food Administration during World War I, Hoover was elected president as a Republican in 1928. The Stock Market Crash and the Great Depression proved to be significant challenges for Hoover, who called on Americans to not panic and opposed massive government intervention to deal with the economic catastrophe. Hoover was defeated by Franklin Roosevelt in the 1932 election.

Huey Long A senator from Louisiana, Long criticized Franklin Roosevelt for not taking stronger governmental action to assist those suffering economically and organized Share the Wealth clubs across the U.S. with the motto "Every Man a King." Long favored imposing high taxes on the rich and distributing wealth more evenly. His popularity altered the course of the New Deal, but he was assassinated in 1935, soon after announcing his candidacy for the presidency.

William McKinley A Republican governor from Ohio, McKinley won the presidency in 1896 and 1900, defeating William Jennings Bryan both times. He supported the gold standard and opposed free silver, while supporting high tariffs. In 1898, he asked Congress to declare war on Spain, convinced that God had called him to take action. McKinley was assassinated in September 1901, six months into his second term.

Robert Oppenheimer The director of the Manhattan Project, Oppenheimer assembled a team of scientists to develop the atomic bomb during World War II.

Alice Paul A suffragist who helped organize the fight to pass the 19th Amendment to give women the right to vote in national elections, Paul was the activist leader of the National Women's Party.

Gifford Pinchot Acting as head of the U.S. Forest Service during the Taft administration, Pinchot opposed Secretary of the Interior Richard Ballinger's proposal to sell publicly-owned lands. Taft fired Pinchot, disappointing the Progressive members of the Republican Party.

Franklin Roosevelt A cousin of Theodore Roosevelt, Roosevelt served as Democratic governor of New York before defeating Herbert Hoover in the 1932 presidential election. Roosevelt proposed a New Deal program to counter the effects of the Great Depression. Several of his programs were ruled unconstitutional and the nation did not recover from the Depression until the start of World War II. Roosevelt was elected to the presidency three more times and declared war on Japan and then Germany in 1941 following the Pearl Harbor attack. He did not live to see the successful conclusion of World War II and died in office in 1945.

Theodore Roosevelt Roosevelt took office as president following the assassination of William McKinley. He was an active Progressive, pushing reforms in many areas of American life, including enforcing antitrust legislation. He also gained control of the Panama Canal Zone and authorized construction of the canal. After leaving office in 1909, he became disappointed with the policies of his successor, William Howard Taft, and led a new group, the Progressive (or Bull Moose) Party in the 1912 presidential election. His entry split the Republican votes and Democrat Woodrow Wilson was elected president.

Margaret Sanger As founder of the American Birth Control League (renamed Planned Parenthood), Sanger was a Progressive reformer who sought to provide family planning information and birth control to poor urban women. She opened the first birth control clinic in the U.S. in 1916.

John T. Scopes A Tennessee school teacher who challenged a state anti-evolution law, Scopes became the centerpiece of a modernist vs. fundamentalist trial in 1925 that pitted famed defense lawyer Clarence Darrow against former presidential candidate William Jennings Bryan. Scopes was found guilty and given a small fine, but most considered the trial a setback for the fundamentalist cause.

Upton Sinclair One of the most influential muckrakers, Sinclair wrote *The Jungle*, exposing unhealthy conditions in the meat-packing industry. Sinclair's exposé led to the passage of the Pure Food and Drug Act in 1906.

Woodrow Wilson As president from 1913–1921, Wilson attempted to maintain U.S. neutrality as World War I broke out. German submarine attacks and the interception of a telegram from Germany to

Mexico led Wilson to ask Congress for a war declaration in 1917. Following the war, Wilson led the U.S. delegation to the Versailles Peace Conference where he proposed plans for postwar peace, including the League of Nations. To his great disappointment, the U.S. Senate refused to approve the treaty and the U.S. did not join the League.

Period 8: 1945–1980

Cesar Chavez Co-founder of the United Farm Workers, Chavez successfully organized migrant farm workers, winning concessions from growers in a number of states while utilizing non-violent tactics.

Dwight Eisenhower Eisenhower was selected by the Allied leaders to direct the European campaign against Germany in World War II. He was later the first supreme commander of NATO forces and U.S. army chief of staff before being elected president in 1952. As Cold War tensions increased, he advocated the buildup of nuclear weapons rather than land forces to counter the Soviet threat. He quietly opposed the McCarthyism campaign and sent federal troops to help integrate a school in Little Rock, Arkansas, in 1957.

Betty Friedan Her publication of *The Feminine Mystique* in 1963 helped launch the modern feminist movement. She founded and was the first president of the National Organization for Women.

Lyndon B. Johnson Vice president under John F. Kennedy, Johnson assumed the presidency in November 1963 after Kennedy was assassinated. Johnson pushed several important civil rights bills through Congress and declared a war on poverty with his ambitious Great Society programs. He also presided over the buildup of American troops in the Vietnam War and was blamed for the quagmire there. Johnson announced in March 1968 that he would not seek a second term as president and ordered a halt to the bombing of North Vietnam.

Joseph McCarthy McCarthy used his position on a Senate committee to launch a reckless campaign of accusation and innuendo in an attempt to expose communist infiltration into the American government. During the Army-McCarthy hearings, his techniques were broadcast on television and he lost support both in the Senate and in the public. McCarthy was censured by the Senate in 1954 for his actions.

George Marshall A general during World War II, as Truman's Secretary of State Marshall oversaw the implementation of the Marshall Plan, which provided massive economic aid to western Europe in the postwar period.

John F. Kennedy Defeating Richard Nixon in the 1960 presidential campaign, Kennedy brought a sense of optimism and youthful exuberance to his brief administration, which was cut short by his assassination in November 1963. He accomplished little on domestic issues, but boldly stood up to the Soviet leadership during the Cuban Missile Crisis and in a famous visit to Berlin.

Martin Luther King, Jr. America's leading civil rights leader, King used his effective oratorical skills and nonviolent protest tactics to reshape attitudes and laws. His first civil rights campaign was a bus boycott in Montgomery, Alabama. King led a series of fights against segregation and injustice through the 1950s and 1960s and was awarded the Nobel Peace Prize in 1964 before he was assassinated in 1968.

Richard Nixon A former vice president under Dwight Eisenhower, Nixon won the 1968 presidential race over Hubert Humphrey and George Wallace. He reduced the presence of American ground troops in Vietnam through Vietnamization while at the same time increasing the bombing of North Vietnam and Cambodia. His diplomatic efforts included visiting China and negotiating with the Soviet Union to defuse Cold War tensions. A series of illegal break-ins and coverups during the Watergate crisis led to a Senate investigation and Nixon's eventual resignation in the midst of rising calls for an impeachment trial.

Rosa Parks Parks was arrested in 1954 for refusing to give up her seat on a segregated bus. The resulting protest boycott helped change laws and launched the modern civil rights movement.

Earl Warren As chief justice of the Supreme Court, Warren issued one of the most important opinions in court history in the *Brown v. Topeka Board of Education* case in 1954. The Warren Court ruled that the separate but equal doctrine that had been in place in the U.S. since the 1896 *Plessy v. Ferguson* decision was unconstitutional and that schools needed to be desegregated "with all deliberate speed."

Malcolm X A former prison inmate, Malcolm became a leading black-power advocate during the 1960s as a member of the Black Muslims. In his later years, he left the organization. He was assassinated in 1965. Critics felt he advocated violence against whites, while supporters felt he was a strong advocate for the rights of blacks.

Period 9: 1980–present

Osama bin Laden The head of the extremist Wahhabi Muslim Al Qaeda organization, bin Laden ordered the 9/11 attacks on the Pentagon and World Trade Center as well as other terrorist bombings. Hunted for years by the CIA and military, bin Laden was found hiding in Pakistan and killed by a team of Navy SEALs in May 2011.

George H.W. Bush A former ambassador to China and CIA director, Bush was Ronald Reagan's vice president from 1981-1989 and won the 1988 presidential election. During his administration the Soviet Union collapsed and the Berlin Wall fell. Bush struggled with domestic economy issues and famously broke a pledge of "no new taxes" which alienated many conservative Republicans. Bush was defeated in the 1992 presidential election by Bill Clinton.

George W. Bush Bush defeated Al Gore in the controversial 2000 presidential election, which was settled by the *Gore v. Bush* Supreme Court decision. His foreign policy agenda was driven by events in the Middle East, particularly the 9/11 attacks in 2001. His War on Terror included military incursions into both Iraq and Afghanistan which proved costly in money and lives. In domestic policy, Bush approved large tax cuts, the No Child Left Behind bill, and Medicare prescription drug benefits for seniors.

Bill Clinton A former Arkansas governor, Clinton served as president from 1993 to 2001, instituting welfare reform and obtaining congressional approval of the North American Free Trade Agreement. He was unable to implement health care reform, however, and his terms in office were marked by controversy and alleged misconduct. He was impeached for obstruction of justice and perjury, both related to his sexual relationship with White House intern Monica Lewinsky. The Senate acquitted him of all charges in 1998.

Bill Gates As chairman and CEO of Microsoft, Gates created the world's largest computer software company. In developing a form of BASIC and then Windows software, Gates and his partners developed both operating systems and applications in use by most computers around the world.

Saddam Hussein The dictator of Iraq from 1979 until his death in 2006, Saddam led an invasion of Kuwait that led to the first Gulf War. He carried out ruthless campaigns against Shi'ite and Kurdish opponents and was accused of assembling weapons of mass destruction by the U.S., Great Britain, and other nations, which invaded Iraq in 2003 in an effort to depose him. He was captured, tried, and executed.

Steve Jobs Jobs is sometimes referred to as the "father of the digital revolution" for his creative impact on the computer industry. As CEO of Apple Inc., Jobs introduced a number of innovative hardware and software products, including the Macintosh computer, the Laserwriter printer, the iPod, iPhone, and iPad and the immensely successfully iTunes and App Store.

Barack Obama Obama, a Democrat, was a community organizer and law school professor before being elected to the Illinois state senate and then the U.S. Senate. He won the 2008 presidential election on a campaign promise to end the Iraq War. He was awarded the Nobel Peace Prize in 2009. His most significant domestic policy accomplishment was the passage of the Affordable Care Act, which provided health insurance to many uninsured citizens. The capture and killing of Osama Bin Laden was the most notable foreign policy accomplishment of his first term.

Ronald Reagan A former actor, Reagan was elected twice as governor of California and then twice as president in 1980 and 1984. He brought a fiscally conservative supply-side approach to federal economic policy, including cutting taxes, deregulating industries, and reducing government spending. He took a strong Cold War stance against the Soviet Union early in his administration, but later met with Soviet General Secretary Mikhail Gorbachev and agreed to reductions of nuclear arsenals. The collapse of the Soviet Union and the fall of the Berlin Wall occurred soon after Reagan's leaving office.

Glossary

9/11 Attacks Series of attacks by radical Islamic group al-Qaeda that took place on September 11, 2001; resulted in the destruction of New York City's World Trade Center, significant damage to the Pentagon, and thousands of civilian casualties.

Abolitionist movement Anti-slavery movement that grew greatly from 1830 until the Civil War; some abolitionists supported the immediate and complete emancipation, while others promoted working through Congress; major movement leaders included William Lloyd Garrison and Frederick Douglass.

Act of Religious Toleration Law guaranteeing political rights to all Christians, both Catholic and Protestant, in the proprietary colony of Maryland; signed by proprietor George Calvert in 1649.

Adams-Onis Treaty Treaty between the United States and Spain ratified in 1819; granted the United States control of Florida and extended the Mexican border to the Pacific in exchange for U.S. assumption of $5 million in Spanish debts to U.S. merchants.

Agricultural Adjustment Act Legislation passed in 1933 to support farm-product prices; gave farmers a subsidy to reduce production; found unconstitutional in 1936 over a tax issue.

Agricultural Marketing Act Legislation passed in 1929 that created a Federal Farm Board to support agricultural commodity prices.

AIDS Sexually transmitted disease that damages the function of the immune system; first arose as a major killer of homosexual men and drug users in the early 1980s before spreading to the general population.

Alien and Sedition Acts Controversial legislation passed by the Federalists in 1798; Alien Act made it more difficult for immigrants to obtain U.S. citizenship; Sedition Act granted Adams administration more power to censor newspapers that criticized the government.

Alliance for Progress Kennedy initiative that worked to provide aid to Latin America.

American Federation of Labor (AFL) Major national labor union combining the strength of several smaller craft unions; used strikes and collective bargaining to achieve labor goals, but remained unaffiliated with radical movements.

American Indian Movement (AIM) Civil rights group that strove to achieve greater rights for Native Americans; founded in 1968.

American System Political program promoted by Henry Clay that proposed high tariffs on imports to generate revenue to pay for internal improvements; foundation of Clay's unsuccessful 1824 bid for the presidency.

Anaconda Plan Union plan engineered by General Winfield Scott in the early portion of the Civil War; relied on a combination of a naval blockade and Union control of the Mississippi River to split the South and squeeze out its incoming resources.

anarchist Radical who supports the end of all government.

Anasazi Pre-Columbian civilization in the Southwest; built cliff dwellings called pueblos and extensive systems of roads and irrigation canals; declined in the fourteenth century.

Annapolis Convention Convention held in September 1786 intended to discuss problems relating to interstate commerce; attended by delegates from only five states; major effect was decision to hold Philadelphia convention in 1787 to revise the Articles of Confederation.

annexation Process of formally adding territory to a city, state, or nation.

Anti-Federalists Group in support of limited national government and central authority, preferring to reserve powers for the states; generally favored revision of the Constitution to protect state and individual power before ratification; included Samuel Adams and John Hancock.

Appomattox Courthouse Site of the final major battle of the Civil War and Confederate General Robert E. Lee's surrender to Union General Ulysses S. Grant on April 9, 1865.

Articles of Confederation First governing document of the United States; allowed for a Congress with one house and extremely limited national powers; reserved nearly all powers, including the powers to impose taxes, raise armies, and regulate trade, to the states; resulting government was too weak to adequately govern the new United States.

assembly line Manufacturing process innovated by automobile manufacturer Henry Ford in the early twentieth century; employed unskilled workers to perform repetitive, standardized tasks; greatly increased industrial productivity while cutting production costs.

Atlantic Charter Statement issued by FDR and British prime minister Winston Churchill calling for a post–World War II world based on national self-determination and FDR's Four Freedoms.

automobile Form of transportation that became widespread during the 1920s; contributed to growth of the U.S. highway and paved road system, along with a dramatic change in U.S. lifestyles; major twentieth-century industrial employer and source of innovation.

Aztecs Large and highly developed pre-Columbian civilization centered in Tenochtitlán in what is now Mexico; ruled by a strong king; elite classes of priests, tax collectors, and warriors along with merchants; conquered in 1519 by Hernán Cortés.

Bacon's Rebellion Revolt led by Nathaniel Bacon in 1676; Bacon worked to oppose Virginia Royal Governor Sir William Berkeley, ultimately beginning a rebellion after a disagreement over Native American policy; Bacon's supporters burned Jamestown and briefly controlled much of Virginia, but Bacon's death at the height of the rebellion ended the conflict.

Bank of the United States First founded at the suggestion of Alexander Hamilton in 1791, this national bank managed national debt, currency, and tried to prevent private state-level banks from issuing too much credit; always highly contested by small-government supporters; lost its charter between 1811 and 1816; essentially killed by Jackson in 1832 when he removed all federal money from its coffers.

bank run Withdrawal of substantial amounts of money by the depositors of a bank; major cause of bank failures during the early years of the Great Depression.

Barbary War First major U.S. overseas conflict; took place from 1801 to 1805, during which time U.S. naval forces battled ships in the Mediterranean attempting to take tribute from Western shipping vessels; ended inconclusively.

Battle of Midway Battle of World War II between the United States and Japan that involved a great deal of air and naval fighting; turning point in the Pacific Theatre in favor of the United States.

Battle of the Bulge Major German effort during World War II to push Allied forces away from German territory; ultimately unsuccessful.

Bay of Pigs Cold War conflict between the United States and Cuba that saw U.S. forces invade the island to attempt to overthrow communist leader Fidel Castro; ended disastrously for the United States and heightened tensions between the nations.

Beats Group of young writers and intellectuals of the 1950s who resisted traditional values and supported a more hedonistic lifestyle; major works included Jack Kerouac's *On the Road* and Allen Ginsburg's controversial poem *Howl.*

Bering Strait Narrow body of water separating Siberia and Alaska; formerly the site of a land bridge over which immigrants came to the Americas from Asia approximately 15,000 to 30,000 years ago.

Berlin airlift Provision of supplies to Berlin in 1949 after the city was blockaded by the Soviets; one of the opening acts of the Cold War.

Berlin Wall Wall physically dividing Soviet-controlled Communist East Berlin and democratic West Berlin; built in 1961 almost overnight; torn down amid German reunification efforts in 1989.

Bill of Rights Series of first ten amendments added to the U.S. Constitution to protect individual liberties and states' rights.

Black Codes Series of Southern laws restricting the rights and freedoms of African Americans.

Black Monday Stock market crash on October 19, 1987; fueled worries of a recession and led to a large tax cut.

Black Panthers Militant African-American group that worked for Black Power; originated in Oakland, California.

Bleeding Kansas Tense and often violent situation in Kansas between pro-slavery and anti-slavery elements in the mid-1850s as two rival governments in Kansas competed for dominance.

Bonus Army Group of World War I veterans who marched to Washington, D.C., in 1932 to call for the early payment of a promised government bonus for their war service; clashes between bonus marchers and police led Hoover to order the U.S. Army to forcibly remove the marchers and their families from the shantytown they had built in the capital.

border ruffians Group of pro-slavery Missourians who entered Kansas to vote in that territory's referendum on slavery; helped install a pro-slavery government in Kansas.

Boston Massacre Conflict between British soldiers and Boston colonists in 1770 that resulted in the deaths of five colonists; used to foment discontent among American colonists.

Breed's Hill Site near Bunker Hill at which a major conflict of the American Revolution took place in June 1775; resulted in significant British casualties but little change in position for either side.

Brown v. Board of Education of Topeka Landmark Supreme Court decision issued in 1954 that outlawed segregation in public schools.

Bull Moose Party (Progressive Party) Popular nickname for the short-lived Progressive Party that formed to support the candidacy of Theodore Roosevelt in 1912; the entry of the Bull Moose candidate helped split the vote, leading to the election of Woodrow Wilson.

Bull Run Site of two major battles of the Civil War; first battle showed Southern strength at the outset of the war; second battle propelled the South on an ultimately unsuccessful invasion of the North.

Cabinet Group of appointed presidential advisers first gathered during the Washington administration; Washington's cabinet included Thomas Jefferson as Secretary of State, Alexander Hamilton as Secretary of the Treasury, Henry Knox as Secretary of War, and Edmund Randolph as Attorney General.

Cahokia Largest pre-Columbian Native American settlement in the Mississippi Valley; population as high as 40,000 in the thirteenth century; contained large earthen mounds used for religious purposes; declined in fourteenth century.

Camp David Accords Series of diplomatic agreements negotiated between Egypt and Israel under the guidance of U.S. President Jimmy Carter in 1978; generally considered Carter's greatest foreign policy achievement.

captains of industry/robber barons Terms used alternately to praise and attack highly wealthy industrial leaders of the Gilded Age such as Andrew Carnegie and John D. Rockefeller.

carpetbagger Southern derogatory term describing Northerners who came to the South to conduct business.

cash crop Agricultural product grown primarily for sale at a profit; basis of the Southern economy from the time of colonization until the late nineteenth century; included tobacco, cotton, rice, indigo, and other crops.

Civil Rights Act of 1957 Legislation that created a Civil Rights Commission and a Civil Rights Division of the Justice Department to work to protect voting rights for African Americans.

Civil Rights Act of 1964 Federal legislation that barred racial discrimination by employers and unions, created the Equal Employment Opportunity Commission, and ended voting restrictions on African Americans.

Civil Works Administration New Deal agency that employed millions of unemployed people in temporary positions and paid them out of federal funds; operated only from November 1933 to April 1934.

Civilian Conservation Corps (CCC) New Deal program that employed young men on various conservation projects; provided housing in a work camp and payments to families in return for their efforts.

Clayton Antitrust Act Legislation passed in 1914 that strengthened the anti-trust protections of the Sherman Anti-Trust Act; considered a key part of Wilson's New Freedom program.

Coercive Acts Series of four British laws passed in 1774; closed the port of Boston in response to the Boston Tea Party; decreased the power of the Massachusetts legislature while increasing the power of the colony's royal governor; allowed royal officials in Massachusetts to seek trial elsewhere; strengthened the Quartering Act by allowing royal forces in Massachusetts to board anywhere; grouped with the Quebec Act as the Intolerable Acts.

colonization Establishment of settlements by an external group or power; in North America, largely undertaken by the Spanish, English, and French beginning in the sixteenth century.

Columbian Exchange Transfer of people, animals, crops, and diseases between Europe and the New World during the 1500s.

Committee on Public Information U.S. government organization created in 1917 that engaged in a massive propaganda campaign to generate support for the war effort; led by journalist George Creel.

committees of correspondence Groups formed by colonial legislatures in order to communicate with one another over grievances resulting from British actions.

Common Sense Pamphlet published by colonist Thomas Paine in early 1776, calling for a declaration of colonial independence from Great Britain.

Compromise of 1850 Series of legislative efforts proposed by Henry Clay to ease sectional tensions over slavery; major provisions included the admission of California as a free state, the use of popular sovereignty in other territories acquired from Mexico, and the enacting of a strict Fugitive Slave Law.

Compromise of 1877 Informal compromise granting Republican candidate Rutherford B. Hayes the necessary contested Electoral College votes to become president and ending the federal military presence in the South; considered the end of Reconstruction.

Confederate States of America Nation formed by the states that had seceded from the Union; led by President Jefferson Davis, who had relatively weak powers; capital at Richmond, Virginia.

Congressional Reconstruction Stringent plan for Reconstruction that aimed to forcibly require the South to accept significant changes and federal authority; included Military Reconstruction.

conquistadores Spanish adventurer and conquerors in the New World during the sixteenth century; explored Caribbean islands, Mesoamerica, and parts of North America; included Balboa, Cortés, Cabeza de Vaca, Coronado, and others; also called conquistadors.

conservation Efforts to preserve and promote environmental protection and natural, wild areas; first became a national priority under Theodore Roosevelt, who supported such actions as the creation of the national park system.

Constitution Plan for the U.S. government; based on the principles of popular sovereignty, separation of powers, and federalism; ratified in 1789.

consumer economy Economic system driven primarily by consumer spending, and thus reliant on levels of consumption for its growth or recession.

containment U.S. foreign policy begun in the early Cold War era that sought to limit the influence of communism by preventing its spread; based on the domino theory, which stated that if one nation fell to communism in a region, others would follow like dominoes falling in a line.

Cotton Kingdom Term applied to describe the Southern regions where cotton production provided the driving economic force; encouraged the perpetuation of the institution of slavery.

Counterculture Social movement of the 1960s led primarily by young people that rejected traditional social and economic values.

court-packing plan Proposal by FDR to reshape the Supreme Court by allowing the president to add new members to the court if aging justices refused to retire; driven by Supreme Court rulings overturning some New Deal programs; failed to attract congressional support or public opinion; ultimately never enacted.

craft union Labor union that seeks to unite workers in a particular line of work or craft, such as a carpenters' union.

Cuban Missile Crisis Period of extreme concern over the threat of nuclear war between the United States and the Soviet Union that took place in October 1962, after U.S. planes discovered evidence of missile sites being built in Cuba; ended with the withdrawal of Soviet missiles from Cuba and U.S. missiles from Turkey.

cult of domesticity Social idea that defined women's roles during the first half of the nineteenth century, particularly in the North; emphasized the role of women as mothers.

Dawes Act Legislation passed in 1887 that aimed to assimilate Native Americans into mainstream U.S. culture by encouraging them to purchase tribal lands from the government; remaining lands were opened to white settlement, decreasing both overall Native American autonomy and territory.

Dawes Plan Begun in 1924, a system of loans aimed at reducing World War I-era war debts and reparations in Europe; under the plan, U.S. banks loaned money to Germany, Germany paid war reparations to Allied European nations, and Allied European nations repaid loans to U.S. banks.

D-Day invasion Successful U.S.-led invasion of a series of beaches in Normandy, France, in June 1944; gave Allied forces a base from which to regain France from Germany.

Declaration of Independence Formal statement of colonial independence from Great Britain, written in 1776; primarily composed by Thomas Jefferson; drew on contemporary political ideas of natural rights.

Declaration of Sentiments and Resolutions Formal statement issued at the Seneca Falls Convention in 1848, proposing major goals for women's rights; considered the founding document of the feminist movement; modeled in part on the Declaration of Independence.

Declaratory Act British law passed in 1766 claiming British authority to impose taxes and make laws for the American colonies regardless of those colonies' lack of parliamentary representation.

deficit financing Government practice of spending more money on programs than it has in tax income and other revenues.

Democratic Republican Party Political party that emerged around 1828 to support the presidential candidacy of Andrew Jackson; forerunner of the modern Democratic Party.

détente Initiative under the Nixon administration to ease Cold War relations with the Soviet Union.

Dollar Diplomacy Foreign policy, promulgated mostly under President William Howard Taft, that aimed to support U.S. interests abroad and encourage greater political, economic, and social stability through economic motivation.

Dominion of New England Unified English government over New England, New York, and New Jersey attempted between 1686 and 1689; suppressed colonial self-government and Puritanism; led by highly unpopular royal governor Sir Edmond Andros; collapsed shortly after the Glorious Revolution with colonies returning to their original forms.

draft riots Popular uprisings protesting the use of conscription during the Civil War; largest and best-known draft riots took place in New York City in 1863.

Dred Scott v. Sandford Landmark Supreme Court decision that declared African Americans were not U.S. citizens, and thus entitled to no protections under the law.

Eastern Woodland Indians Pre-Columbian Native Americans living east of the Mississippi River; lived mostly in small, family-based clans led by elders; peoples spoke Algonquian, Iroquoian, and Muskhogean languages.

Eisenhower Doctrine Foreign policy statement under President Dwight D. Eisenhower supporting the use of U.S. military force against communist influence in the Middle East.

Election of 1860 Presidential election that resulted in the victory of Republican candidate Abraham Lincoln; seen by many Southerners as proof that the North planned to end slavery; touched off the secession crisis that began the Civil War.

Election of 2000 Presidential election that resulted in the eventual victory of Republican candidate George W. Bush in the Electoral College despite a popular vote win by Democratic challenger Al Gore; marred by allegations of voting irregularities in Florida, where a vote recount was ended by a Supreme Court decision.

Electoral College Elective body formally responsible for selecting the president; state delegates determined by number of Senators plus number of Representatives.

Emancipation Proclamation Statement issued by Abraham Lincoln formally freeing all enslaved persons in rebelling states as of January 1, 1863; helped shift the focus of the war to a moral one supporting the end of slavery.

Embargo of 1807 Disastrous shipping embargo initiated by Jefferson in an attempt to ensure U.S. neutrality in the conflict between Great Britain and France; barred U.S. ships from traveling to foreign ports; resulted in a severe economic depression, especially in the Northeast; later replaced by the Non-Intercourse Act barring trade only with Great Britain and France.

Enlightenment European philosophical movement that emphasized the use of reason in all matters; major proponents included John Locke, whose political arguments in support of natural laws and consent of the governed greatly contributed to colonial American revolutionary thought.

Espionage Act of 1917 Legislation criminalizing the making of false statements that helped the enemy, encouraged military insubordination, or tried to interfere with military recruitment or conscription; also permitted the removal of printed materials encouraging treason or rebelling from the mail system; curtailed civil liberties.

Essex Junto Group of New England Federalists who unsuccessfully tried to form a secessionist movement in the region in 1804.

European Theatre Area of European operations by the U.S. military during World War II; included major efforts in France, Italy, and Germany.

Fair Deal Domestic agenda promulgated by President Harry S. Truman; gained little support in Congress, but raised the minimum wage and expanded old-age benefits.

Fair Labor Standards Act Legislation passed in 1938 that first created the federal minimum wage.

Family and Medical Leave Act (FMLA) Legislation passed under President Bill Clinton that guaranteed a period of unpaid leave to employees facing family or medical emergencies; a signature Clinton domestic achievement.

Federal Reserve system Financial system created by the Federal Reserve Act of 1913; provides for a system of regional reserve banks overseen by a Federal Reserve Board.

Federalist Papers Series of essays explaining and supporting the newly written Constitution; written by Alexander Hamilton, James Madison, and John Jay; remain in use to explain the intentions of the authors of the U.S. Constitution.

Federalists Group in support of a stronger national government and greater central authority; generally favored ratification of the Constitution as it was originally written; included Alexander Hamilton, James Madison, and John Jay.

Federalists (political party) One of the nation's first two political parties; supported a looser interpretation of the rights given to the federal government by the Constitution; generally supported federal superiority over the states; led by Alexander Hamilton.

Fifteenth Amendment Amendment officially preventing states from restricting the right to vote based on race or previous status as a slave.

First Continental Congress Meeting of colonial leaders that took place in Philadelphia in September 1774 to discuss colonial response to the Coercive Acts; resulted in declarations against the Intolerable Acts and efforts to strengthen colonial militia.

First New Deal Legislation enacted as part of FDR's New Deal program between 1933 and 1935; included efforts to restore confidence in the bank system, encourage employment, and support business.

flapper Young woman of the 1920s who challenged existing social roles by wearing short dresses, getting a short hair cut, smoking, drinking, and engaging in other independent, hedonistic activities; although only a tiny portion of U.S. women, flappers symbolized greater independence for women in general.

Food Administration Federal agency created in 1917 to oversee food production and rationing to ensure adequate supplies for the military abroad; instituted programs such as "Wheatless Mondays" and "Meatless Tuesdays" to encourage food conservation; headed by Herbert Hoover.

Fort Sumter Site of the first shots fired in the Civil War on April 12, 1861, near Charleston, South Carolina.

forty-niners Gold seekers drawn to California during the Gold Rush of 1849; arrival helped California achieve sufficient population to apply for statehood.

Four Freedoms Freedoms endorsed by FDR in his 1940 inaugural address; included freedom of religion, freedom of speech, freedom from want, and freedom from fear.

Fourteen Points Wilson's plan for peace following the end of World War I; called for such measures as open peace treaties, free trade, freedom of the seas, self-determination, and the creation of the League of Nations.

Fourteenth Amendment Amendment officially establishing birthright citizenship in the United States and guaranteeing equal protection under the law.

Free Soil Party Political party dedicated to preventing the expansion of slavery into newly acquired U.S. territories; active but never politically dominant during the late 1840s and early 1850s.

free state A state that did not permit slavery.

Freedmen's Bureau Federal bureau created in 1865 to help freed slaves find shelter, food, work, and educational opportunities; worked generally to help rebuild the South and protect the interests of African Americans.

Freedom Riders Group of both black and white civil rights activists who rode buses across the South to protest segregation in 1961.

Freeport Doctrine Political philosophy that the people of a territory could choose to prevent slavery from existing in their territory by refusing to pass any of the laws typically used to protect slavery; stated by Stephen A. Douglas during the Lincoln-Douglas debates.

French and Indian War North American conflict, begun in 1754, between the British and French along with their respective Native American allies; occurred largely over control of the Ohio Valley and other western lands; considered part of the European Seven Years' War begun in 1756; ended in 1763 by the Treaty of Paris, which gave France's North American lands to the British.

Fuel Administration Federal agency created in 1917 to oversee energy production and consumption to ensure adequate supplies for the war effort; largely encouraged the conservation of coal; led by Harry A. Garfield.

Fugitive Slave Law Legislation that allowed African Americans in the North to be captured and sent to slaveholders in the South, when identified by slave catchers as runaways, without allowing the accused a trial or the opportunity to prove his or her free status; passed as a result of the Compromise of 1850.

Fundamental Orders of Connecticut First written constitution in the Americas; created a representative form of government; signed in 1639.

Gadsden Purchase Strip of land in what is now southern New Mexico and Arizona that was purchased from Mexico in 1863; initially intended as the southern route of a proposed transcontinental railroad.

gag rule Rule pushed through the House of Representatives by Southern members in 1836 that banned any discussion of slavery in the House; ended in 1844.

***Gaspee* Affair** Incident in Rhode Island in which a group of colonists disguised as Native Americans seized and destroyed a British ship seeking customs violators and smugglers; led to the formation of colonial committees of correspondence.

general strike Work stoppage involving all the unions in a particular city or industry; best-known is the failed Seattle general strike of 1919.

Geneva Accords Agreement signed in 1954 dividing North and South Vietnam along the 17th parallel and calling for free South Vietnamese elections; set the stage for the Vietnam War.

Gibbons v. Ogden Landmark Supreme Court decision that affirmed federal authority to regulate interstate commerce; helped strengthen federal authority.

Glorious Revolution English political revolution in 1688 that removed the Catholic James II from the throne and installed the Protestant rulers William and Mary.

glyph Character used in the Mayan writing system to represent a concept or sound.

Good Neighbor Policy Foreign policy under FDR that aimed to improve relations with Latin American nations.

Great Awakening Period of religious revivalism in the colonies between the 1720s and the 1740s; led by outspoken preachers such as George Whitfield, who called for a stronger personal connection with faith in order to achieve salvation; encouraged the growth of colonial colleges to train ministers and the willingness to reject claims by those in power.

Great Compromise Plan for government combining features of the Virginia Plan and New Jersey Plan; divided federal authority among an executive branch and a Congress with two houses; representation in the Senate shared equally among states; representation in the House of Representative based on population.

Great Society Johnson administration social programs that worked to improve conditions for the impoverished, elderly, and others; primarily focused on reducing poverty.

greenbacks Union-issued paper currency that was not backed by gold or other resources; used during the Civil War.

Gulf of Tonkin Resolution Resolution approved by Congress in 1964 that permitted the president to take any force necessary to retaliate to attack on U.S. forces; provided the legal basis for the escalation of the Vietnam War; later repealed.

habeas corpus Legal procedure stating that imprisoned persons cannot be held indefinitely without being charged with a crime or tried in court; suspended during the Civil War.

Harlem Renaissance Flowering of African-American arts, literature, music, and thought in the Harlem neighborhood of New York City in the 1920s.

Hartford Convention Meeting of New England Federalists in late 1814; group issued statements against War of 1812 and suggesting nullification and even secession as possibilities for New England; U.S. victory in Battle of New Orleans soon after greatly damaged the party's reputation, and it soon faded away.

Hawley-Smoot Tariff Tariff passed in 1930 that raised import taxes on agricultural and manufactured products; failed to support the U.S. economy and may have contributed to the spread of the Great Depression internationally.

Hiroshima and Nagasaki Japanese cities on which U.S. forces dropped atomic bombs during World War II, effectively ending the war but causing immense civilian devastation.

Homestead Act Legislation passed in 1862 that granted settlers 160 acres of free land under the condition that they remain and farm the land for at least five years; greatly encouraged the settlement of the West.

Hooverville Informal name for any shantytown that sprung up during the early years of the Great Depression; referenced what struggling people saw as the woefully inadequate efforts of President Herbert Hoover to provide economic relief.

House of Burgesses First representative assembly in the Americas; established in Virginia in 1619.

Hudson River School Artistic movement focused on landscape painting showing the natural world and Native Americans; major artists included George Catlin and John James Audubon.

Hundred Days First legislative session of the FDR administration during which a great deal of New Deal legislation was enacted; term has been applied to the opening era of many presidents' tenures since the 1930s.

Impeachment of Clinton Series of trials held in Congress in late 1998 and early 1999 accusing President Clinton of committing perjury in regard to inquiries about an alleged affair with a White House intern; led to impeachment by the House but acquittal by the Senate.

implied powers Those powers indirectly granted to the government under the U.S. Constitution because they were not specifically denied to the government.

Inca Largest and wealthiest pre-Columbian American empire centered at capital city of Cuzco in what is now Peru; developed extensive agriculture, irrigation, and road systems; conquered in 1532 by Francisco Pizarro.

indentured servitude System of labor under which an individual contracted to work for another person for a period of time, often several years, in exchange for passage to the Americas; such servants often labored on large farms under extremely harsh conditions; more common in the Southern colonies; decline of this system contributed to rise of slavery.

Indian Removal Act of 1830 Federal law providing federal enforcement of the forcible removal of all Native Americans to west of the Mississippi River; despite the decision in *Worcester v. Georgia* preventing its implementation against the Cherokee, Jackson ordered the law's execution, resulting in the infamous Trail of Tears.

industrial union Labor union that seeks to unite workers in a particular industry regardless of specific job, such as an auto workers' union.

interchangeable parts Technological innovation designed by Eli Whitney that standardized manufactured parts, allowing many items to be made more quickly and cheaply; one of the foundations of industrialization.

Interstate Commerce Act Legislation passed in 1887 to provide greater federal oversight of potentially corrupt and abusive railroad shipping and pricing practices.

Iran Hostage Crisis Crisis that spanned late 1979 to early 1981, in which a group of Iranians captured and held a large group of Americans at the U.S. Embassy in Teheran; Carter's attempts to secure the hostages' release failed repeatedly, but the group was eventually freed on the day Ronald Reagan assumed the presidency.

Iran-Contra Scandal Scandal over the illicit sale of U.S. weapons to the Iranians and funneling of arms profits to the Nicaraguan *contras*; investigated by Congress in 1987; implicated members of the Reagan administration.

Iron Curtain Metaphor used by British Prime Minister Winston Churchill to describe the separation between the democratic West and the Soviet Eastern Bloc following World War II.

Iroquois A group of Eastern Woodlands Native Americans speaking Iroquoian languages who lived between the Hudson River and the Great Lakes region; comprised the Seneca, Cayuga, Oneida, Onondaga, and Mohawk peoples; also known as the Five Nations of the Iroquois.

island hopping Strategy used by General Douglas MacArthur in the Pacific Theatre of World War II; relied on taking or neutralizing one Japanese stronghold and then moving on to another, and another.

isolationism Foreign policy of remaining uninvolved in world affairs, particularly global conflicts; supported in the United States before both the First and Second World Wars.

Jamestown First permanent English settlement in North America; located in Virginia; founded by the Virginia Company in 1607 for the purpose of exploiting the area's natural resources to generate a profit.

Jay's Treaty Treaty between the United States and Great Britain, signed in 1794, that attempted to ease trade and conflicts at sea over impressment between the two nations; named for U.S. negotiator John Jay.

Jim Crow laws Southern laws restricting the rights of African Americans and typically enforcing segregation.

John Brown's Raid Raid by abolitionist John Brown and a group of followers on the federal arsenal at Harpers Ferry, Virginia, in order to seize weapons to give to slaves to incite a slave revolt; led to Brown's conviction and execution for treason, but made him a martyr in the eyes of many Northerners.

Johnson's Reconstruction Moderate plan for Reconstruction that closely mirrored Lincoln's earlier plan, with the requirement that states ratify the Thirteenth Amendment ending slavery and suggesting that freed slaves be given the vote.

joint-stock company Colonial-era company that raised money by selling shares of stock; several helped colonize North America, including the Virginia Company, the Massachusetts Bay Company, and the Dutch West India Company.

Judiciary Act of 1789 Established the Supreme Court, a series of district courts, and three courts of appeal; granted the Supreme Court power to determine constitutionality of state laws.

Judiciary Act of 1801 Legislation passed by the Federalists near the close of John Adams's term that permitted the Federalists to appoint several supporters to judicial office, including U.S. Supreme Court Chief Justice John Marshall.

Kansas-Nebraska Act Legislation that organized a section of territory in the Midwest as the states of Kansas and Nebraska; repealed the Missouri Compromise's provision barring slavery north of Missouri's southern border and instituted popular sovereignty in its place.

Kellogg-Briand Pact Treaty signed by most major nations in 1928 renouncing war and outlawing aggression against other foreign powers; lacked any plan of enforcement.

Kent State Massacre Anti-Vietnam War protest by students at Kent State University in Ohio that resulted in the deaths of four students after National Guard members opened fire on the crowd.

Kentucky and Virginia Resolutions State-level reactions to the Alien and Sedition Acts written by Thomas Jefferson and James Madison; declared that states had the authority to nullify federal laws that they believed to be unconstitutional.

Knights of Labor Major labor union that permitted membership by immigrants, African Americans, and women as well as native-born white workers; grew to number over 1 million, but declined after the bloody Haymarket Riot in 1886.

Know-Nothing Party Political party that emerged in response to heavy immigration in the 1840s and early 1850s; dedicated to nativist policies opposing immigrants and Catholics.

Korean War War between United Nations and U.S. forces and communist Chinese and North Korean troops during 1950 and 1951; ended with an armistice that returned the North/South Korean border near the 38th parallel.

Korematsu v. United States Landmark Supreme Court decision that supported the federal government's policy of internment of Japanese Americans during World War II.

Ku Klux Klan White supremacy organization first formed during Reconstruction that sought to terrorize African Americans and others; experienced significant revival during the 1920s.

labor unions Organized groups of workers who strove together for better working conditions, pay, or other workplace goals; often achieved goals through strikes or collective bargaining; emerged during the era of industrialization.

Land Ordinances of 1784 and 1785 Pair of laws establishing a system of territorial government and township surveying in the West.

League of Nations International body charged with maintaining peaceful relations among nations; suggested by Wilson in his Fourteen Points; despite heavy support by Wilson, the United States never joined the body, and it ultimately failed.

Lend-Lease Act Legislation passed in 1941 that allowed the United States to sell and provide allied nations with war materials without a "cash and carry" payment requirement.

Lewis and Clark Expedition Exploration commissioned by Jefferson to investigate the new Louisiana Territory and seek the Northwest Passage; found headwaters of the Missouri and mapped a great deal of previously unexplored North American land.

Lexington and Concord Sites of the first conflict on the American Revolution; shots fired between British regular troops and colonial militia; resulted in great damages to the British forces involved.

limitation of powers Political restrictions placed by the U.S. Constitution to prevent any one level from becoming too powerful; includes division of powers between federal and state governments under the federal system.

Lincoln-Douglas Debates Series of debates between Stephen A. Douglas and Abraham Lincoln during the 1858 U.S. Senate campaign; helped solidify Republican arguments against slavery and made Lincoln a national figure.

Lincoln's Reconstruction Moderate plan for returning those states that had seceded to the Union; allowed states to rejoin the Union after 10 percent of the population swore loyalty to the Union and accepted the end of slavery; prevented former rebel officers and high-ranking officials from returning to power.

Little Rock Nine Group of African-American students who were the first to integrate a Little Rock, Arkansas, high school; required the presence of the National Guard to enforce.

Lost Generation Literary group of the 1920s that railed against the perceived hypocrisy and materialism of U.S. society; major writers included Ernest Hemingway, Sinclair Lewis, and F. Scott Fitzgerald.

Louisiana Purchase Massive land purchase made in 1803; Jefferson sought to purchase New Orleans through an agent, but instead Napoleon offered to sell the United States all of French Louisiana; resulting land more than doubled the size of U.S. territory; purchase showed power of federal government.

Lusitania British passenger liner sunk in 1915, resulting in the deaths of nearly 1,200 people including 128 Americans; contributed greatly to pro-Allied sentiment in the early days of World War I.

maize Crop grown in Mesoamerica that is the ancestor of modern corn.

Manhattan Project Secret research project conducted during World War II era; led to the development of the atomic bomb; led by J. Robert Oppenheimer.

Manifest Destiny Belief that it was the God-given destiny and duty of Americans to expand to the Pacific Ocean; greatly influenced expansion efforts during the mid- to late nineteenth century.

Marbury v. Madison Landmark Supreme Court decision that cemented the Supreme Court's power of judicial review.

March on Washington Major civil rights rally in Washington, D.C., in 1963; brought together some 200,000 to protest in favor of a civil rights bill; site of Dr. Martin Luther King Jr.'s famous "I Have a Dream" speech.

margin Amount borrowed from a broker to finance the purchase of stock and then used as collateral against that loan; practiced during the 1920s; one of the reasons for the stock market crash of 1929.

Marshall Plan Economic program designed by George C. Marshall that provided some $12 billion in aid to rebuild post–World War II Europe.

matrilineal System of inheritance under which goods and property rights transfer from mother to daughter.

Maya Pre-Columbian civilization centered in Central America and the Yucatán; developed sophisticated systems of writing, mathematics, and agriculture as well as an accurate calendar; began to decline around 800.

Mayflower Compact Document written and signed by Pilgrim leaders aboard the ship *Mayflower* in 1620; created a government based on the consent of the governed.

McCulloch v. Maryland Landmark Supreme Court decision that declared states had no authority to interfere in federal business and supported an interpretation of the Constitution with "implied powers"; strengthened federal authority.

mechanization Process of employing standardized mechanical processes to do work previously done by humans; mechanical inventions such as the sewing machine and reaper helped speed industrialization in the North before the Civil War.

mercantilism Economic theory that underlaid British policy during the colonial era; believed in government control of the economy in order to support political authority; encouraged the establishment of colonies that could provide raw materials to the mother country and serve as markets for that country's exports; focused on achieving a favorable trade balance for colonizing power.

Mexican War War between the United States and Mexico that began in 1846 after years of growing tensions over the admission of Texas as a state and other territorial disputes; ended by the Treaty of Guadalupe-Hidalgo in 1848, which granted the United States a great deal of land in the West known as the Mexican Cession for $15 million, and U.S. assumption of $3.25 million in Mexican debts to U.S. citizens.

Military Reconstruction Act Legislation dividing the South, except Tennessee, into five military districts overseen by strong military governors.

missionaries Priests and other religious persons who travel to a place to convert that place's inhabitants to their own religion.

Missouri Compromise Congressional compromise reached in 1820 that admitted Missouri as a slave state and Maine as a free state, to maintain the balance of free and slave representation in the Senate; barred the expansion of slavery in the rest of Louisiana Territory north of the southern border of Missouri; engineered by House Speaker Henry Clay.

Monroe Doctrine Policy instituted by President James Monroe in 1823; stated the United States considered the Western Hemisphere no longer available for European colonization.

Moral Diplomacy Foreign policy, promulgated mostly under President Woodrow Wilson, that aimed to encourage the growth of democratic capitalist governments around the world by offering U.S. support only to democratic capitalist governments.

Moral Majority Conservative Christian group under leader Jerry Falwell that began to exercise greater political influence during the 1980s; promoted conservative social values and a strong national defense.

Mormons Religious group founded by Joseph Smith in 1830; forced to leave New York, first for the Midwest and later for the area around the Great Salt Lake that is now Utah, because of popular objections to their practice of polygamous marriage.

Morrill Land Grant Act Legislation passed in 1862 that granted large tracts of federal lands to states for the construction of agricultural and technical colleges; encouraged the creation of several major state universities.

muckrakers Investigative journalists and authors who worked to encourage Progressive reforms through their stories; included Lincoln Steffens, Ida Tarbell, and Upton Sinclair.

NAFTA (North American Free Trade Agreement) Treaty among the United States, Canada, and Mexico, signed in 1994, that eliminated most trade barriers; critics argue that the treaty has damaged U.S. industry and factory workers.

Natchez Warlike pre-Columbian people of the Mississippi Valley who endured for a time past contact with Europeans; class-based society ruled by leader called the Great Sun; organized into confederacies of farming villages.

National Association for the Advancement of Colored People (NAACP) Civil rights organization founded in 1909 to work for improved civil rights for ethnic minorities; early efforts included the promotion of anti-lynching legislation.

National Industrial Recovery Act New Deal legislation that worked to stabilize the economy by providing federal guidelines for wages, prices, production levels, and quotas; granted workers the right to unionize; enforced by National Recovery Administration; eventually found unconstitutional.

National Origins Act Legislation passed in 1924 that set strict immigration quotas favoring Northern and Western Europeans and greatly limiting or eliminating immigration for other groups, particularly Southern and Eastern Europeans and Asians; remained in effect until the mid-1960s.

nationalism Feeling of great pride in the characteristics and achievements of one's own nation; may be expressed through cultural, social, or political means.

nativism Belief that American-born U.S. citizens were superior to immigrants; generally anti-immigrant and anti-Catholic.

natural rights Enlightenment-era series of human and political rights considered vital and unbreakable; also known as inalienable rights.

naval blockade Act of using ships to prevent supplies and trade vessels from reaching their intended ports.

Navigation Acts Series of four laws passed between 1651 and 1673 that required colonial goods to be shipped only on English or American ships; required certain "enumerated" goods to be shipped to only England or English-controlled colonies; required practically all colonial imports to first enter an English port.

Neutrality Acts Series of legislation in the mid- to late 1930s, asserting U.S. neutrality in the growing conflict in Europe; permitted Britain to buy war goods on a "cash and carry" basis.

New Deal coalition New coalition of Democratic voters including Southerners, farmers, union workers, and African Americans that emerged during the FDR administration.

New Federalism Political agenda under the Nixon administration that aimed to increase state-level authority; a contrast to the escalation of federal authority under Kennedy and Johnson.

New France Territory controlled by France in parts of what is now Canada and the United States between the early sixteenth century and the end of the French and Indian War; sparsely populated; mostly centered on the fur trade.

New Freedom Program of legislation pursued under the Wilson administration; included major efforts in banking reform, tariff reduction, and anti-trust legislation.

New Jersey Plan Plan for government proposed by William Paterson; called for a Congress with one house; equal representation among all states.

New Spain Territory controlled by Spain in the Americas from the early sixteenth century into the early nineteenth century; economy characterized first by large-scale agriculture on *encomiendas* and later *haciendas,* both known for their harsh working conditions; highly segmented social system populated by a mix of Spaniards, African slaves, and Native Americans.

nonviolent protest Form of protest involving the use of peaceful methods such as boycotts and sit-ins to effect social change; primary method employed by civil rights protestors of the 1950s and early 1960s.

North African Theatre Area of North African operations by the U.S. military during World War II; included a notable effort to defeat German General Erwin Rommel's Afrika Korps at the Battle of Kassarine Pass.

North Atlantic Treaty Organization (NATO) Treaty signed by numerous Western European and North American powers providing for mutual self-defense in the event of foreign aggression.

Northwest Ordinance of 1787 Law granting western settlers a bill of rights and barring slavery north of the Ohio River.

Northwest Passage Water route through or around North America to Asia; explorers unsuccessfully searched for this route from the fifteenth century into the nineteenth century.

Nullification Crises Set of two political crises, first in 1828 and later in 1832, over federal tariffs; during each crisis, Southern interests threatened to refuse to collect federal tariffs within their states, claiming states had the right to nullify certain federal laws; Jackson used force to collect taxes during the Second Nullification Crisis, but agreed to a gradual reduction of tariffs.

Oklahoma City bombing Bombing of an Oklahoma City federal building in 1995 that resulted in 168 deaths; deadliest act of domestic terrorism in U.S. history.

oligopoly Business structure under which a few large corporations dominate a particular industry.

open shop Unionized workplace allowing nonunion workers.

Oregon Treaty Treaty between the United States and Great Britain ratified in 1846 that set the U.S.-Canada border at the 49th parallel.

Pacific Theatre Area of Asian and Pacific island operations by the U.S. military during World War II; included the Battle of Midway.

Palmer Raids Series of raids in late 1919 and early 1920 that resulted in the arrests of thousands of purported communists and illegal aliens; discredited when only a small number of the arrests were found to be justified, contributing to the end of the first Red Scare.

Panama Canal Canal built across the Isthmus of Panama to link the Atlantic and Pacific Oceans; first initiated by the French, the project later came under the control of the United States, which then administered the canal until the late twentieth century.

pan-Americanism U.S. foreign relations stance begun in the Gilded Age that worked to achieve peaceful conflict resolution and support a shared customs union among nations in the Americas.

Panic of 1857 Brief but intense economic depression that resulted from problems with overspeculation, banking, and capital availability.

Peace Corps Kennedy initiative that sent young volunteer workers to engage in various service projects in the developing world.

Pearl Harbor Site of a U.S. naval base in Hawaii; surprise Japanese attack on Pearl Harbor on December 7, 1941, brought the United States into World War II.

Pendleton Act Legislation passed in 1883 aimed at reforming the federal civil service system by instituting a series of open, competitive examinations to fill civil service jobs.

Peninsula Campaign Union plan engineered by General George B. McClellan in 1862 that saw slow Union advancement through Virginia toward Richmond; ultimately resulted in a Union retreat to Washington, D.C.

Pentagon Papers Classified Defense Department documents leaked to the press and published in 1971 that revealed government efforts to misinform the U.S. public about the Vietnam War.

Persian Gulf Conflict War between the United States and Iraq in 1991 over the Iraqi invasion of Kuwait; ended in U.S. victory after less than two months, but left a great deal of instability in the region.

Pilgrims Group of English religious dissidents who immigrated to America aboard the *Mayflower;* wrote the *Mayflower Compact;* founded Plymouth Colony in 1620.

Pinckney Treaty Treaty between the United States and Spain, signed in 1796, that granted the United States commercial access to the Mississippi River, allowed U.S. right of deposit at the port of New Orleans, and set the northern boundary of Florida at the 31st parallel; named for U.S. negotiator Thomas Pinckney.

plantation Large farms dedicated to growing cash crops in the American South; relied heavily on enslaved labor; dominated Southern economy from colonial times until the Civil War era, but made up only a small minority of Southern farms.

Platt Amendment Legislative amendment passed in 1901 that granted the United States considerable control over Cuba; required Cuba to allow U.S. forces to maintain a military base at Guantanamo Bay.

pocket veto Form of indirect presidential veto by which the president simply fails to sign a bill into law in a 10-day period after its period during which Congress has adjourned.

political machine Informal political organization dominated by a specific political party that controlled a certain city or region and rewarded party loyalists with government jobs or contracts.

popular sovereignty Political process by which government reflects the will of the people; often used to describe the process by which voters decided whether a state would allow or bar slavery in the years just preceding the Civil War.

Populist Party Political party that gained strength in the early 1890s; founded as a coalition of farmers, urban workers, and the middle class; supported reforms including the coinage of silver, labor reform, and the direct election of senators; declined after the 1896 presidential election.

Potsdam Conference Meeting of Truman, Stalin, and British prime minister Clement Atlee that resulted in agreements on war crimes tribunals and plans to demilitarize and reorganize Nazi Germany.

price discrimination Practice of charging less in some areas than in others in order to undercut competition; barred under the Clayton Antitrust Act of 1914.

Proclamation of 1763 British declaration formally barring American settlement west of the Appalachians; issued in the wake of the French and Indian War to help ease tensions with Native Americans; angered colonists, who wished to build settlements and establish trade in the West.

Proclamation of Neutrality Statement issued by Washington in 1792 formally asserting U.S. neutrality in the war between France and other European powers; broken by Citizen Genet, who tried to generate popular support for the French cause.

progressive reforms Wide-reaching series of reforms calling for changes in such fields as politics, labor, monopolies, and racial and gender equality; resulted in the direct election of senators, the creation of new forms of city government, child labor laws, conservation policies, anti-trust actions, and other reforms.

Progressives Loose coalition of reform-minded individuals who worked to effect change during the early twentieth century; included members of all social classes and both major political parties.

Prohibition Ban on the manufacture and sale of alcohol in the United States instituted by the Eighteenth Amendment in 1918; enforced only weakly; led to the rise of organized crime in major cities such as New York and Chicago; repealed by the Twenty-third Amendment in 1933.

Prohibitory Act British declaration in 1775 that the colonies were in rebellion and no longer enjoyed the protection of the king.

proprietary colony English colony under the direct control of a proprietor or group of proprietors.

Pueblo Pre-Columbian peoples in the Southwest named for their distinctive cliff dwelling; influenced by the building styles and religious practices of the Anasazi; developed drought-resistant crops.

Pullman Strike Major labor strike in 1894 by the American Railway Union under the leadership of activist Eugene V. Debs; ended after federal troops violently broke up the strike.

Puritans Group of English religious dissidents who had experienced great conflict with the English king; formed a joint-stock company called the Massachusetts Bay Company in 1629; established Massachusetts Bay Colony under the authority of John Winthrop in 1630.

Quakers Religious sect with beliefs in direct connections with God, pacifism, and the unimportance of human institutions; became the core settlers of the Pennsylvania colony, founded on principles of religious freedom, in the late seventeenth century.

Quartering Act British law passed in 1765 that required American colonists to pay for a standing British army of up to 10,000 troops.

Quasi-War Undeclared naval war between the United States and France that took place during 1798 and 1799; erupted as a result of the XYZ Affair; all trade ended between the United States and France, and U.S. captains were permitted to attack and take French ships; ended after the ascension of Napoleon.

Quebec Act British law passed in 1774 that expanded the colony of Quebec to the Ohio River, established Roman Catholicism as that colony's official religion, and set up a representative government in Quebec; angered colonists because it hampered colonial hopes of expansion west; grouped with the Coercive Acts as the Intolerance Acts.

Radical Republicans Political faction composed of fervently anti-slavery Republicans; significant force in Congress during the Civil War and Reconstruction.

radio Primary form of mass communication and entertainment in the United States from the 1920s to the birth of television in the 1950s; helped create a U.S. mass culture.

Realism Literary movement of the Gilded Age that explored social problems, urban landscapes, and other real-life problems; major writers included Mark Twain, Henry James, and William Dean Howell.

Reconstruction Finance Corporation Congressional corporation authorized to provide up to $2 billion in loans to support railroads and financial institutions; helped prevent the failure of firms but did not provide immediate relief to average citizens.

Red Scare (1919) Period of intense fear and concern that swept the United States in 1919 about the influence of communists, radicals, and those perceived to support those causes, such as immigrants and labor union members.

Red Scare (late 1940s–early 1950s) Period of intense fear and concern that swept the United States in the late 1940a and early 1950s about the influence of communists; saw numerous people investigated as potential communists by the House Committee on Un-American Activities and rabid anti-communist Senator Joseph McCarthy.

reparations Payments made by one power to recompense another power for costs incurred because of a war; typically made from a losing aggressive force to a winning defensive forces.

Republican Party (1850s–present) Political party that emerged to replace the Whigs in the 1850s; opposed the expansion of slavery; forerunner of the modern Republican Party.

Republican Party (18th–19th century political party) One of the nation's first two political parties; supported a strict interpretation of the rights given to the federal government by the Constitution; generally supported state superiority over the federal government; led by Thomas Jefferson; unrelated to modern Republican Party.

reservations Areas of land set aside by the federal government for the resettlement of Native American tribes.

return to normalcy Campaign promise made by successful Republican presidential candidate Warren G. Harding during the election of 1920; implied a return to traditional values and ideas after the period of wartime upheaval and ensuing economic worries.

Revenue Act of 1918 Legislation passed in 1918 that raised direct federal incomes tax on personal incomes to support the war effort.

Revenue Act of 1942 Legislation expanding the direct income tax to affect most Americans and creating the payroll deduction system for income taxes.

Romanticism Artistic and literary movement of the antebellum era that focused on emotions over reason, self-improvement, and a belief in human goodness; major U.S. writers included Walt Whitman, Henry Wadsworth Longfellow, Herman Melville, and Edgar Allan Poe.

Roosevelt Corollary Expansion of the Monroe Doctrine in 1904 that asserted the right of the United States to intervene in the affairs of Latin American nations to prevent European powers from using military force to collect debts.

royal colony English colony under the direct control of the English crown or its official; came to include the majority of the thirteen colonies as the crown assumed control of them from joint-stock companies or proprietors.

Russian Revolution Overthrow of the czarist Russian government and institution of a communist government led by the Bolsheviks in 1919; led to Russia's withdrawal from World War I in Europe and heightened concerns over communism in the United States.

Sacco and Vanzetti Two Italian immigrant anarchists tried and convicted for murder in a highly publicized 1921 trial; although executed in 1927, debate over their possible innocence and mistrial continued for decades. A 1977 gubernatorial proclamation said they had been treated unjustly.

Saratoga Site of an important colonial victory in 1777 that convinced the French to offer open support to the rebelling colonists; considered the turning point of the American Revolution.

Saturday Night Massacre Controversial Nixon order for the attorney general to fire a special prosecutor looking into the Watergate scandal; the attorney general's resignation and subsequent execution of the presidential order generated much controversy.

Savings and Loan Crisis Financial crisis in 1989 brought about by the making of numerous bad real estate loans by savings and loan institutions; led to hundreds of bank closures and cost the economy an estimated $300 billion.

scalawag Southern derogatory term describing Southerners who worked to help Reconstruction efforts.

scientific management Principle of business and industrial management, set forth by Frederick W. Taylor, that instituted specific times required for the completion of various workplace tasks; helped increased industrial efficiency during the 1920s.

Scopes Trial Trial held in 1925 over the ability of science teachers to teach the then-controversial theory of evolution rather than the religious theory of creation; galvanized national attention and displayed the changing morals and beliefs of the era.

secession Act of formally removing a political unit from participation in a larger unit; used by Southern states, beginning with South Carolina, that wished to detach from the Union, sparking the Civil War.

Second Continental Congress Meeting of colonial leaders that began in Philadelphia in May 1775, to discuss possible actions against the British; despite disagreement among leaders over the advisability of warring with Britain and the Olive Branch Petition to King George III in an effort to avoid war, it resulted in increased preparations by colonial militias for war.

Second Great Awakening Revival of religious feeling that began in 1801; encouraged beliefs in personal salvation, direct connection to God, and individual religiosity; embraced by women and African Americans; encouraged the growth of later reform movements.

Second New Deal Legislation enacted as part of FDR's New Deal program from 1935 onward; included the Social Security Act, the Wagner Act, and others.

sectional tensions Term used to describe the disagreements and conflicts between the North and the South before the Civil War; primarily stemmed from the economic, political, and social differences stemming from Southern reliance on slavery.

Sedition Act of 1918 Legislation criminalizing and criticizing the government, the U.S. flag, or military uniform, regardless of the outcome of this criticism; curtailed civil liberties; famously led to the imprisonment of Socialist leader Eugene V. Debs for making an anti-war speech.

Selective Service Act Legislation passed in May 1917, allowing for a wide-scale federal draft into the U.S. armed forces.

separation of powers Political system dividing governmental authority among various branches; in the United States, three branches work to together in a series of "checks and balances" under separation of powers.

settlement house Reform institutions that worked to provide support and services to immigrant communities; typically founded in large, urban immigrant neighborhoods; most famous was Jane Addams' Hull House in Chicago.

Share Our Wealth society Society created by Huey Long that called for redistribution of wealth through confiscation and heavy taxation; fizzled after Long's assassination in 1935.

Shays' Rebellion Farmers' revolt led by Daniel Shays in western Massachusetts; caused by economic problems and high taxes resulting from war debts; rebels temporarily closed court to prevent seizure of land and sentencing of debtors to prison; resulted in widespread concern and illustrated the failings of the Articles of Confederation.

Sherman Anti-Trust Act Legislation passed in 1890 that subjected corporate monopolies to federal prosecution if they worked to restrict trade and competition.

Sherman's March Campaign led by General George T. Sherman that caused significant devastation through much of the South, including the sacking and burning of Atlanta and Savannah.

slave state State that permitted slavery.

slave uprisings Revolts by enslaved people against white owners or white society in general; rarely succeeded by any measure, but caused a great deal of fear among whites in the South; best-known slave uprisings include those of Gabriel Prosser in 1800, Denmark Vesey in 1822, and Nat Turner in 1831.

Social Darwinism Theory proclaiming that success in life was based on survival of the fittest; used to justify the unequal distribution of wealth resulting from capitalism and rapid industrial development during the Gilded Age.

Social Gospel Reform movement based in Christianity that encouraged sweeping reform efforts in the late nineteenth and early twentieth centuries; included settlement houses, improved health services, and improved schools, along with other reform areas.

Social Security Act Legislation passed in 1935 that created government old-age pensions, unemployment insurance, and support for the disabled; funded by federal payroll taxes.

Solid South Term describing the consistent support of the South as a Democratic voting bloc from the end of Reconstruction until the Civil Rights era.

Sons of Liberty Group of American colonists who formed in the wake of the passage of the Stamp Act to work against what they saw as unfair British taxation on the colonists, who were unrepresented in Parliament; formed by Massachusetts colonist Samuel Adams.

Spanish American War War between the United States and Spain that took place in 1898, primarily in Cuba and the Philippines; ended by the Treaty of Paris of 1898, which granted the United States Guam and Puerto Rico, and gave up Spanish claims over Cuba and the Philippines; helped begin U.S. imperialism.

spoils system System of rewarding party supporters with government civil service jobs; largely ended by the Pendleton Act.

stagflation Combination of stagnant growth and high inflation that negatively affected the U.S. economy during much of the 1970s.

Stamp Act British law passed in 1765 that levied the first direct tax on the American colonists; imposed taxes on printed goods such as newspapers; greatly angered colonists, who saw the taxes as unfair due to their lack of representation in Parliament; led to the meeting of the colonial Stamp Act Congress, at which representatives from several colonies met to discuss their grievances; later repealed.

Statute of Religious Freedom Document guaranteeing freedom of religion and establishing separation of church and state in Virginia; written by Thomas Jefferson; served as basis for the freedom of religion clause of the First Amendment.

steamboat Transportation innovation of the early nineteenth century; used steam to power engines on large ships; eased trade and long-distance travel, particularly along new canals.

Stonewall Riots Violent demonstrations in New York City in 1969 that began after a police raid on a bar popular with homosexuals; considered the starting point of the U.S. gay rights movement.

Strategic Defense Initiative (SDI) system Computer-controlled missile defense system proposed by President Reagan to protect against Soviet missiles; derisively termed "Star Wars." Strategic Arms Limitation Treaty (SALT) Treaty between the United States and the Soviet Union, signed in 1972, that reduced the number of antiballistic missiles controlled by each power.

Strategic Arms Limitation Treaty (SALT) II Treaty between the United States and the Soviet Union in 1979 that limited armaments and weapons systems; failed to be ratified by Congress.

Student Nonviolent Coordinating Committee (SNCC) Civil rights group formed in the early 1960s that worked to end segregation and attain African American voting rights through sit-ins and other peaceful protests.

Students for a Democratic Society (SDS) Left-wing student activist group founded in 1960; aimed to encourage participatory democracy and social change among young people.

Suez Canal crisis International crisis stemming from Egyptian nationalization of the Suez Canal and Egypt's opening of diplomatic relations with communist powers; involved a brief period of military action by the Egyptians, Israelis, British, and French.

Sugar Act British law passed in 1764 that imposed higher taxes on imported goods in the colonies; aimed at raising revenue; enforced in admiralty court, which was not subject to due process or trial by jury; also known as the Revenue Act.

Sun Belt Region of the United States spanning the South and West; experienced significant population growth after World War II.

supply-side economics Economic system promoted under Ronald Reagan that favored low taxes and less government spending; sometimes termed "Reaganomics." Taft-Hartley Act Legislation passed in

1947 that limited many of the pro-union provisions of the Wagner Act; protected the right of workers to unionize, but outlawed the closed shop, required waiting periods for strikes, and enacted other pro-management measures.

Tea Act British law passed in 1773 that allowed direct importation of tea to the colonies by the British East India Company, resulting in lower tea taxes and prices; aimed at forcing Americans to recognize the right of Britain to tax their goods; resulted in colonial resistance to the importation of the tea and, ultimately, the Boston Tea Party.

Teapot Dome Scandal Scandal that took place during the Harding administration in which the Secretary of the Interior accepted bribes from the oil industry in exchange for leasing them oil fields at Teapot Dome, Wyoming.

Teheran Conference Meeting of FDR, Churchill, and Stalin in 1943 to discuss Soviet commitment to aiding the Allied efforts and to make war strategies.

temperance Moderation or abstinence in the use of alcohol; major reform movement during the nineteenth and early twentieth centuries.

Tennessee Valley Authority New Deal–era public corporation that built numerous dams along the Tennessee River and engaged in other natural resources efforts.

Tet Offensive Major Vietcong attack on U.S. and South Vietnamese holdings in South Vietnam in early 1968; named for the Vietnamese New Year (Tet); contributed to the turn of U.S. public opinion against the war.

Texan Revolution Begun in 1836 by white Texans who wished to form their own nation outside of Mexican rule; resulted in the creation of the short-lived Republic of Texas.

Thirteenth Amendment Amendment officially abolishing slavery.

Three-Fifths Compromise Constitutional provision providing for the counting of each enslaved person as three-fifths of a free person for purposes of direct taxation and congressional representation.

Townshend Acts Series of laws passed in 1766 that imposed taxes on goods imported to the American colonies; provided for trial in the admiralty courts in the case of offenses, the imposition of writs of assistance, and payment of customs officials from fines collected over violations; later repealed.

Transcendentalism Mid-nineteenth-century movement based in Massachusetts that aimed to go beyond traditional intellectual boundaries to achieve a higher state of thought and connection with God; major proponents included Ralph Waldo Emerson and Henry David Thoreau.

Treaty of Greenville Treaty between the United States and Ohio-area Native Americans, signed in 1794; forced the region's Native Americans to move elsewhere.

Treaty of Paris of 1783 Treaty between Great Britain and America ending the American Revolution; granted independence to the new United States; established the new nation's western boundary at the Mississippi River and southern boundary at the northern border with Florida; the British granted Florida to Spain; allowed private British lenders to collect colonial debts; encouraged the return of confiscated property to British loyalists in the United States.

Tripartite Pact Agreement forming an alliance of Germany, Italy, and Japan as the Axis Powers; signed in September 1940.

Truman Doctrine Foreign policy statement under President Harry S. Truman that the United States should support all free peoples who resisted communist domination.

Tuskegee Institute Educational institution founded by African American leader Booker T. Washington in Tuskegee, Alabama; worked to educate African Americans.

Uncle Tom's Cabin Anti-slavery novel written by Harriet Beecher Stowe in response to the Fugitive Slave Law; increased anti-slavery feeling in the North.

underconsumption State of economic imbalance in which workers produce more goods than consumers purchase.

Underground Railroad Network crossing the United States through which escaping slaves could find shelter or assistance as they tried to reach freedom and safety; best-known "conductor" was Harriet Tubman.

United Farm Workers Union of Mexican American farm laborers organized by Cesar Chavez in 1962; led major national grape boycott to call attention to problems associated with migrant labor system.

unlimited submarine warfare Policy of attacking all ships, regardless of their involvement in World War I, in a large portion of the Atlantic Ocean; a major point of contention between the then-neutral United States and belligerent Germany; contributed greatly to U.S. entry into the war.

urbanization Transfer of population from rural areas to cities; led to the growth of major industrial hubs with associated problems such as crime, disease, sanitation, overcrowding, and the growth of political machines.

USA PATRIOT Act Legislation passed in response to the 9/11 terrorist attacks that greatly increased the powers of the federal law enforcement agencies to conduct intelligence operations and fight suspected terrorist activities; generated controversy over potential civil liberties infringements.

Utopians Movement aimed at creating a perfect world away from the increasingly impersonal industrial world; members typically lived in simple, self-sufficient communes; major communes included Brook Farm, New Harmony, Nashoba, Oneida Community, and Amana; Shakers are perhaps the best-known utopian group.

Versailles Treaty (1919) Treaty ending World War I; mostly shaped by the United States, Great Britain, France, and Italy; despite Wilson's objections, placed heavy reparations and blame on Germany for World War I; failings contributed to the rise of nationalism and, later, World War II in Europe.

Vietnam War Conflict between the United States and democratic South Vietnam and communist North Vietnam; U.S. involvement escalated from military advising and support in the 1950s to full-scale combat in the mid-1960s; unpopular with large segments of the U.S. public, particularly the counterculture movement; U.S. involvement ended under Nixon.

Vietnamization Strategy used under the Nixon administration to shift the bulk of fighting the Vietnam War from U.S. troops to South Vietnamese forces.

Virginia Plan Plan for government proposed by Edmund Randolph in 1787; called for a Congress with two houses; representation based on population.

Volstead Act Legislation passed in 1919 that allowed for federal enforcement of Prohibition through the treasury department.

Voting Rights Act of 1965 Federal legislation that allowed the attorney general to select federal officials to register voters and oversee election practices; primarily aimed at ensuring voting rights for African Americans in the South.

Wade-Davis Bill Legislation passed by radical congressional Republicans in 1865, requiring a majority of Southerners who had been registered voters in 1860 to swear a strong oath that they had never been disloyal to the Union; rejected through a pocket veto.

Wagner Act Legislation passed in 1935 to guarantee the right to unionize, prohibit unfair labor practices, and encourage better labor-management relations through the National Labor Relations Board.

War Industries Board Federal agency created in 1917 to oversee business matters such as raw material use, production, prices, and labor relations to the benefit of fighting World War I; led by Wall Street broker Bernard M. Baruch.

War Labor Board Federal agency created in 1918 to prevent labor strikes and work stoppages in wartime industries; encouraged higher wages, shorter working hours, and the growth of union membership.

War of 1812 Conflict between the United States and Great Britain over the British practice of impressment and other perceived violations of U.S. rights; saw the new capital of Washington, D.C., burned by the British; inspired the writing of the "Star-Spangled Banner"; ended by the Treaty of Ghent in 1814, two weeks before the final battle of the war took place under General Andrew Jackson at New Orleans.

War Powers Act Legislation passed in 1973 that required congressional approval for any commitment of U.S. combat troops for longer than 90 days.

War Production Board Federal agency created in 1942 to manage the use of raw materials during World War II.

Warren Court Supreme Court of the 1950s and 1960s under Chief Justice Earl Warren; supported an interpretation of the Constitution that saw increased rights for ethnic minorities, women, accused criminals, and others.

Warsaw Pact Treaty signed by the Soviet Union and numerous other communist nations providing for mutual self-defense in response to the creation of NATO.

Washington Naval Conference Major international conference held in 1921 that resulted in treaties calling for naval arms reduction, affirming the sovereignty of China, and barring most aggression in the Pacific.

Watergate Scandal Presidential scandal that began with a break-in at Democratic national headquarters in 1972; in time, President Nixon and other administration figures were accused of a massive cover-up, leading Nixon to resign in 1974 before facing certain impeachment proceedings; contributed to a general decline in public trust of the federal government.

Whig Party Political party that emerged in the early 1830s to oppose actions taken by Andrew Jackson; declined after the election of 1852.

Whiskey Rebellion Popular uprising that took place in Pennsylvania in 1794; began as a response to excise taxes on whiskey imposed under Hamilton's new economic program; ended when Washington sent a large federal militia to deter the angry farmers from interfering with tax collectors.

White House tapes Series of recordings made in the Oval Office that Congress repeatedly tried to subpoena as part of the Watergate investigation; Nixon's refusals on the basis of executive privilege led to a Supreme Court decision against him.

Whitewater Affair Scandal during the Clinton administration over the propriety of the Clintons' involvement in certain real estate transactions in Arkansas; led to a congressional investigation and the appointment of an independent prosecutor.

Wilmot Proviso Legislation proposed during the Mexican American War barring slavery in any territory acquired by the United States from Mexico; failed to pass Congress, but further riled sectional tensions.

woman suffrage Right to vote for women; after decades of activism, granted by the ratification of the Nineteenth Amendment in 1920.

Women's Liberation Movement Social movement of the 1960s and 1970s that supported new roles and rights for women, such as equal pay and access to abortions; supported the ultimately unsuccessful Equal Rights Amendment (ERA) that would have guaranteed equality between men and women in the U.S. Constitution.

Works Progress Administration (WPA) New Deal program that employed people on relief in construction and arts jobs; led to the creation of a great deal of infrastructure, public buildings, and murals, among other works.

Writs of Assistance Series of search warrants used by British colonial officials to inspect American merchants' goods with the purpose of stopping colonial evasion of British trade restrictions; angered colonists, who believed the Writs intruded upon their natural rights.

XYZ Affair Scandal of 1798 resulting from French efforts to obtain bribes from a U.S. delegation to Paris seeking to end French interference with U.S. shipping; resulted in popular feeling against France; the name refers to the three unnamed French officials who attempted to obtain bribes, codenamed "X," "Y," and "Z." Yalta Conference Meeting of FDR, Churchill, and Stalin in 1945 to make plans for the postwar world; called for free elections in liberated Europe and the creation of a United Nations.

yellow journalism Form of popular journalism based on sometimes exaggerated stories that appealed to emotion; force for reform during the late nineteenth and early twentieth centuries.

yeoman farmers Class of white, independent small farmers in the South before the Civil War; made up the largest part of the region's population; owned few, if any, slaves; typically grew corn rather than cotton.

Yorktown Site of the decisive battle of the American Revolution that resulted in the surrender of British General Charles Cornwallis to American General George Washington on October 17, 1781.

Zimmermann Telegram Secret communication between Germany and Mexico in which Germany offered Mexico the return of its previous lands in Texas, Arizona, and New Mexico if Mexico fought alongside Germany against the United States in the event of war; intercepted by the British and given to U.S. authorities in early 1917; release to the press greatly stirred U.S. public opinion in favor of war.

Index

A

C

D

E

H

I

J

K

L

M

Q

R

S

T

U

V

W

X

Y

Z

NOTES